CRAPPIE
WISDOM

An In-Fisherman
Handbook of Strategies

CRAPPIE
WISDOM
An In-Fisherman
Handbook of Strategies

Doug Stange
Gary Korsgaden
Dan Sura
Steve McCadams
Rich Zaleski
Dave Csanda
Bob Ripley
Al Lindner
Ron Lindner

Published by
Al Lindner's Outdoors, Inc.

The In-Fisherman®
"Handbook of Strategies" Book Series

One of the

(F) Fish + (L) Location + (P) Presentation = (S) Success℠

Educational Services

Book Compiled by Bob Ripley and Dan Sura
Cover Art by Larry Tople
Artwork by Dan Vickerman
Typesetting by Bang Printing
Litho Prep by Quality Graphics
Printing by Bang Printing
Copyright 1985 by Al Lindner
All rights reserved
Published by Al Lindner's Outdoors, Inc.
P.O. Box 999, Brainerd, Minnesota 56401
Printed in the United States of America

ISBN 0-929384-51-2

First Edition, 1985
Second Printing, 1987
Third Printing, 1987
Fourth Printing, 1988
Fifth Printing, 1989
Sixth Printing, 1990
Seventh Printing, 1992
Eighth Printing, 1994

Library of Congress Catalogue
Card Number 85-081299

ACKNOWLEDGEMENT

Countless individuals are directly or indirectly responsible for assembling all the priceless information in a book as complete as this one. Because fishing is an ancient art which draws on experimental tradition, we are indebted to those many men and women who have fished, studied, and triumphed with the authors, thus adding to the wealth of crappie wisdom.

In particular, we want to thank people like Dan Gapen and the legendary Joe Ehrhardt for their invaluable input. A special thanks goes to the inimitable Bill Binkelman for developing the background theory which the Calendar Periods are based upon. Of course, pros like Bill Dance, Gary Roach, Doug Hannon, Horace Carter, Larry Dahlberg and Tom Neustrom all deserve a note of thanks for their contributions. We are also grateful to Professor Jeff Gunderson, Sea Grant Fisheries agent—University of Minnesota, for his fish cleaning and keeping tips. We also offer a special *IN-FISHERMAN* "hats off" to fisheries biologists Mike Colvin, Missouri, and Bill McLemore, Kentucky, for their invaluable assistance with very pertinent scientific studies. In addition, the fisheries departments of California, Nebraska, Oklahoma, Iowa, Wisconsin, Indiana, Michigan, Maryland, Arizona, Ohio, Kentucky, Missouri, Georgia, Arkansas, Montana, Minnesota, Texas and Mississippi all supplied bits and pieces of information which helped solve the crappie puzzle.

No book of this type would be complete without the numerous photos and illustrations which add to the book's enjoyment and educational value. Therefore we are especially grateful to our technicians: Jim Lindner for his striking photography and Dan Vickerman for his detailed illustrations.

This short list could certainly be expanded, but suffice to say that this book could never have been written by just the nine major authors. Each author has shared in major breakthroughs on crappie location and presentation in different waters. Their combined on-the-water experience, both individually and with crappie anglers all over North America, enables them to pass on to you their many secrets, tips and tricks in this original edition of *Crappie Wisdom: A Handbook of Strategies*.

TABLE OF CONTENTS

ACKNOWLEDGEMENTS

INTRODUCTION

I CRAPPIE KNOWLEDGE

II CRAPPIE LOCATION AND PRESENTATION

III CRAPPIE EXTRAS

INTRODUCTION

The crappie has been called *everyone's fish*. Indeed, it is exactly that: A fish anyone can fish for—a bank fisherman with a cane pole or an angler outfitted with a $25,000, ultra-deluxe bass boat.

Yes, the rainbow trout may be more beautiful; the musky larger and more savage; and the bass surely more acrobatic. Yet, in every pond, pit, river, reservoir and lake where it swims, the crappie wins the popularity contest hands down.

From the timber-filled, sprawling impoundments of Texas to the stark, sharp, rocky banks of the northern border, crappie cultists are legion. They tie their boats to shallow brush, anchor in deep water or line banks awaiting a "school of slabs."

Why all this attention and devotion? Well, for anyone who has thrilled to the satisfaction of "getting into them," the answer is simple. They are just plain fun, and what more can any angler ask?

Yes, big crappies are fun to catch. They also are no slouch when it comes to fighting, especially on light tackle. And, of course, their reputation as table-fare is also legend. Yes, anytime you have a fish that is accommodating on the hook, fights well, and also tastes good, you have all the ingredients for wide-spread, indeed, universal popularity.

Yet, in spite of this widespread interest, popular acclaim and angling attention, the crappie is not well understood by anglers. Indeed, in some waters and during some seasons, its activities are still a mystery.

However, a number of major advancements in crappie fishing have occurred in the last few decades. The use of depth finders, graphs, and new fishing systems have all helped put together the pieces of the crappie puzzle.

Crappie fishing is more than just "minnow soaking," tiny-jig pitching or structure fishing. For example, we know that predictable crappie movements occur in lakes. We've determined that crappies may use timber as cover in some reservoirs, yet avoid such cover areas in others. We are now aware of a complex predator/prey relationship that affects not only the health of a crappie fishery, but also fish location and how fish react in a particular body of water. We have cracked their seasonal code: how crappies will most likely respond in spring, summer, fall and winter. We also definitely know how and why they react differently in lakes, rivers, pits or reservoirs.

All of these new facets and dimensions—indeed, formerly missing dimensions—are part of this fascinating book titled *CRAPPIE WISDOM*.

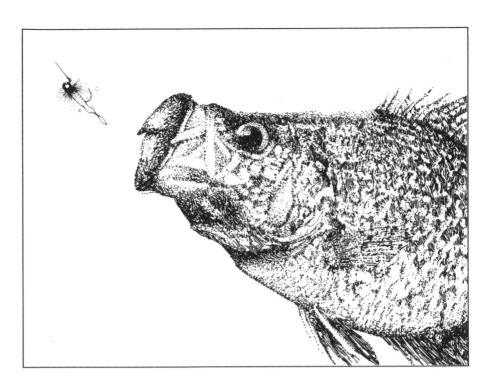

Chapter 1

CRAPPIE

The Calico Scrapper

How do you spell fun? For many anglers all across North America, it's C-R-A-P-P-I-E. Catching a bunch of good eating, slab-sized crappies is a fantastic way to spend a day. Crappies bite well and put up a respectable fight. That's fun! Crappie fishing is also a great way to introduce kids to fishing. Crappies are biters, and if you can find 'em, you can generally catch a mess of 'em.

Each year, young and old alike take buckets of crappies through the ice in winter and in the shallows during spring. And even though summer crappies may be a bit of a mystery to some folks, they are still catchable once their habits are understood.

Add all this to the fact that crappies can be caught by using a wide variety of simple techniques, on everything from a cane pole to a boron rod, and you have the makings of a great time. You'll also fill the freezer. So, whether you soak minnows from the bank or cast ultralight jigs from the deck of an ultra-sophisticated bass boat, you can get in on the action. The essence of crappie fishing is understanding crappie habits. That's what this book is all about: catching crappies all season long on any body of water.

The crappie is a fairly adaptable critter, as evidenced by its widely diverse geographic distribution and the numerous aquatic environments it inhabits. Crappies provide angling thrills to folks throughout the United States and southern Canada. Lakes, rivers, reservoirs, ponds, pits and canals are all "home" to the crappie. But, as happens so many times with other species, there are first-rate and there are fourth-rate crappie waters. What factor or combination of factors makes some bodies of water prolific producers of slab crappies, while other waters only produce so-so fishing, and still others host merely paper-thin, featherweight fish? Good question, and a tough one to answer.

Let's begin our study of this fascinating fish by reviewing a few crappie facts. Like all fish, the crappie is at one time both predator and prey. Simply stated, all fish are predators. While the "predator" crappie is munching on zooplankton, insects or small minnows, the "prey" crappie may be munched on by a still larger predator like a pike or bass. Big fish eat smaller fish, and so on; it's the food chain game of who eats whom. In general, if the amount of varied prey is sufficient to support predators, the potential exists for slab crappies.

The crappie's normal feeding method is not really an "attack." Usually, they simply "suck in" their prey from underneath, then close their mouth and swallow. Crappies aren't blessed with the strong jaws of bass or the teeth of pike, and this limits the type of prey they can successfully take.

The feeding apparatus of a crappie resembles a funnel. Pull a crappie's lips open sometime and note the "intake tube." This funnel-type feeding apparatus limits the size prey a crappie can consume. Food items must be small enough to be sucked in whole and not needed to be rearranged before swallowing. Also note that most of the mouth is a paper-thin membrane.

Ron Lindner's "environmental door" concept helps explain this complex environmental relationship. In order to sustain life, crappies and all fish need certain conditions from birth to death. The entire life process is like a series of doors along the fish's path of life. First, the various doors must be present; second, the fish must be able to move through them. The first door could be spawning habitat; a second, nursery areas for young fish; and a third, living areas for adult fish. Available prey, water quality, competing species and fishing pressure (in some cases) all have a bearing on whether the doors ultimately open, how far they open, or whether they open at all.

All of these factors, plus others, affect the crappie's ability to survive and grow in any body of water. Various fisheries studies indicate that the life span and growth rates of crappies vary widely from one water to another. For example, in some waters few crappies live longer than 3 years, yet in others many typically live 8 years or more. Growth-wise, a 4-year-old crappie can be only 7 inches long in one lake and more than 12 inches long in another. Biologists are trying to solve this mystery and isolate the factors which affect longevity and growth.

Crappies will adjust to a body of water as best they can, using the available environmental options. These options vary, depending on the body of water. Lakes, rivers and reservoirs are all different and offer varying environments. Yet, by simply "reading" the water and applying a little basic information on the crappie's lifestyle, you can locate prime areas in each body of water you fish. It all boils down to understanding how a body of water functions and what predator/prey relationships exist.

CRAPPIE CHARACTERISTICS

The crappie's body construction is an exercise in moderation. Its flat, relatively compact body allows it to make quick, responsive turns and function in and around weeds and brush. Its moderately sleek, head-to-tail construction allows successful, but limited use of open water.

Much like bass, crappies appear to be ambush predators only when at rest and in a negative or neutral feeding mood. When actively feeding, however, there is no doubt that crappies are hunters.

SUSPENSION TENDENCIES

On many waters, suspension is a way of life for crappies. In other words, they often suspend at various depth levels in lakes and reservoirs. While it's impossible to make hard-and-fast rules about how crappies suspend, there are some general tendencies.

In many lakes, crappies suspend in order to take advantage of the drifting masses of zooplankton (microscopic animals) and minnows that are their common prey. Similarly, crappies often suspend in reservoirs and feed on zooplankton and young shad that inhabit open-water areas. Many times, the depth at which zooplankton suspend is controlled by light intensity and defensive movements. Some zooplankton like Daphnia (water fleas) often migrate vertically in response to changing light levels. Daphnia rise when it's dark and descend when it's light. Others like Copepods depend on darting, evasive ac-

Crappie Angler of 1900's

tion to escape predators. Crappies make major locational changes during the day in response to zooplankton movement. Thus, they follow their food on a daily as well as seasonal basis.

Generally speaking, crappies will roam until they encounter a suitable prey. If there are no zooplankton (or other prey) on a structural element, crappies will generally move through the area. However, in areas where concentrations of prey are high, crappies will remain until the food is grazed down and then they'll move on.

The "hunt" usually takes them to where zooplankton or minnows—probably their preferred forage—are. That's usually "confined open water" or cover such as brush or weeds. Resting crappies may suspend in confined open water or near obvious cover. The point is, crappies are opportunists. Their tendency to suspend, and their body construction, allow them to function in cover or confined open water.

CONFINED OPEN WATER

What about "confined open water?" While crappies often suspend, they are not a true, open-water fish. True open water involves large expanses of water where fish relate to light penetration, water stratification, forage, and occasionally the bottom. True open-water fish are powerfully built and streamlined, can easily travel distances, and are able to quickly charge into free-roaming schools of bait. Chinook salmon and stripers are examples of true, open-water fish.

Crappie and Confined Open Water

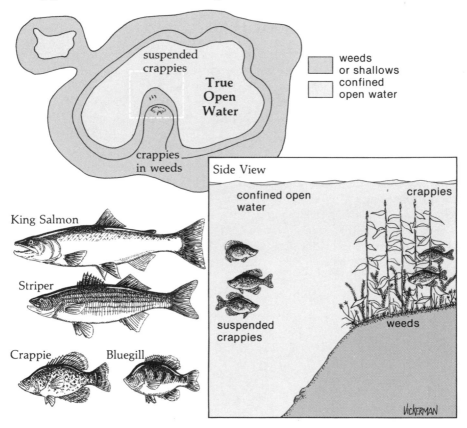

Open water is divided into two categories: "confined" and "true" open water. True open water involves large expanses of water, and fish inhabiting such areas have streamlined shapes and powerful muscles to function in this environment. Striped bass and chinook salmon are examples of true, open-water fish.

Crappies are not true, open-water fish, even though they love to suspend. The crappie's flattened body and moderately sleek, head-to-tail construction enables successful use of cover such as weeds and timber, and "confined" open water. Bluegills often suspend and use confined open water, too, but are even better shaped for using cover.

Confined open water is open water on a much smaller scale. Confined open water is open water relatively close to, or surrounded by cover such as timber, brush, weedlines, the bottom or the surface. Crappies are opportunists that function well in cover, or confined open water. Thus, they have their own particular niche.

On the other hand, "confined" open water is open water on a smaller scale. Confined open water is always *near* definite structural conditions. For example, in large bays, there's often confined open water in the center, but the bottom, surface, shoreline or weedline are still relatively nearby.

In main-lake areas, open water extends off weedlines, timberlines or points; but at some spot, all association with the weedline, timberline or point is lost. At that location, we enter true open water. But the water *relatively close to* a weedline, timberline, point or large inside turn in the drop-off is "confined" open water.

Crappies often use confined open water but rarely use true open water. Obviously, there are exceptions.

A FEW OTHER CHARACTERISTICS

Crappies are light-sensitive fish, and in clear bodies of water they often bite best during twilight hours, after dark, or in deeper water during midday.

In lakes with a bit of water color, crappies often bite consistently in shallower water right through midday. However, even on these lakes, look for twilight activity; changing levels of light intensity often trigger crappie activity. Our experience is that night bites are not consistent on dark-water lakes. But you may disagree.

Remember that crappies feed *up* better than *down*. In other words, they see forage and baits better parallel with or, better yet, *above* eye level. Take a look at where and how the eyeballs in ol' paper lips are positioned—pretty well up and forward on the face. Actually, most predators have their eyes set topside and forward. The result is a *tendency* to feed up. However, the crappie is one of the most notorious up-feeders we know of. Keep this in mind when you're presenting baits.

Trigger Zone

Side View

Top View

Up and At 'em

Most predators have their eyes set topside and forward, resulting in a tendency to feed up. But the crappie is one of the most notorious up-feeders we know of. Try to position baits parallel to, or slightly above crappie eye level for best results.

MIGRATION

Crappies are the gypsies of the freshwater world. Roaming like nomads in search of food, a school of crappies will usually locate near a food source of some kind. While crappies are generally not considered long distance migrators, in some rivers and riverine (fast flow-through) impoundments they might move seasonally to locate suitable habitat or prey. A study on Wheeler Reservoir, a TVA impoundment, showed that tagged white crappies migrated 80 miles upstream and 8 miles downstream. Even though this example may be extreme, it indicates that crappies will migrate long distances in some waters. It's not their normal behavior, however.

On many slower flowing rivers and streams, crappies may move several miles upstream in spring and stage in the tailwaters below dams. Anglers in the know can easily catch a bunch of crappies in adjacent slack water areas or eddies. Further, on other rivers during low-water years in fall and winter, crappies typically migrate to locate areas of deeper water. In general, deeper pools, slower flowing side channels, flood-plain lakes and connected lakes are all potential holding areas. These spots can be tough to find, but they will hold numbers of crappies.

SCHOOLING BEHAVIOR

A crappie is a crappie, but there are two distinct crappie species—white and black. In addition, in waters where both species are present, hybrids sometimes occur.

While the behavior of the crappie cousins may be somewhat different, a tendency to school is common. Crappies are extremely gregarious critters. In general though, white crappies do not school as tightly as black crappies. While the schooling tendency can mean super fishing for anglers, it can also spell doom for crappies.

By their basic nature, crappies are fairly aggressive fish; in fact, they are the smallmouth bass of the panfish world. Crappies are definitely *biters*, and when this is combined with their schooling behavior, the results can be a feast-*then*-famine situation on some waters. Believe it or not, the adult crappie population on some bodies of water can be quite fragile and over-harvesting can lead to a lake with few, good-sized fish. No, the lake isn't fished out, but it is *fished down* and may not produce any number of big crappies for several years. We found out the hard way.

A couple of years ago, big crappies (honest pounders) were plentiful in one of our favorite central Minnesota lakes. Lake "X" provided a quality environment for crappies. It is a 250-acre, fertile lake with fairly clear water, healthy weedgrowth on the flats (reeds and cabbage), hard bottom and plenty of confined open-water areas. Northern pike control the deep weedlines while largemouth bass rule the flats as the top predators in the lake. Crappies, meanwhile, school in the confined-open-water areas adjacent to the weedline. In summer they suspend just off the weed edge. In winter, the fish school heavily in the deeper areas.

During winter two years ago, the word leaked out that the big crappies were "on a bite" in Lake X. A dozen or so local ice fishermen hit the lake and pounded the crappies. Nearly everyone was taking a bunch of good-sized crappies every time out. Eventually the word got out and the steady fishing pressure and removal of fish took its toll. The average size decreased and the larger, older fish were scarce as hens' teeth. In two years the lake was fished down to a point where you'd be hard-pressed to catch a couple big crappies. While the lake still has a viable crappie population, it'll be several years before any number of big fish return.

Remember, fishing pressure can make a difference on some waters. So, catch a lot of fish, keep some to eat and release the rest. We're not advocating a wholesale catch and release practice for crappies, but rather a selective-harvest approach. In a nutshell: Take what you can eat and don't waste the resource.

THE SMALL-CRAPPIE SYNDROME

The national average crappie is about 8 to 10 inches long, weighs 1/2 to 3/4 of a pound and is 3 years old. Obviously, average size varies depending on the fish's environment. While eating-sized fish comprise the daily catch of most folks, in some areas, giant slab crappies can be taken. Prime northern waters can yield 2-pound-plus fish, while 3-pound-plus crappies are caught each year in southern lakes and reservoirs. However, under marginal conditions, stunted, paper-thin crappies die of old age—the small-crappie syndrome.

While many factors affect the crappie growth rate, one of the most important is the abundance and quality of food. In order for crappies to develop and grow, they must have suitable prey at each stage of their life.

Typically, young crappies prey heavily on plankton and insects; however, adult fish feed on small baitfish, when they're available. In fact, in many waters, baitfish comprise the majority of the adult crappie's diet. Apparently, a high-protein, minnow diet is essential for growing slab crappies. Prime, northern, black-crappie waters have healthy baitfish populations for prey, while in southern waters, white crappies prey heavily on newly hatched gizzard or young threadfin shad. The result can be big crappies and lots of them.

The "small-crappie syndrome" is a challenge facing many biologists. Why are many waters teeming with pint-sized crappies? Too many fish (crowding), limited habitat, lack of quality food, and overharvesting have all been suggested as probable causes.

Feast your eyes on these slab-sized black crappies. Veteran anglers Gary Roach and Ron Schara teamed up to catch these often overlooked Canadian crappies. Their secret: Rock piles and Fuzz-E-Grub jigs.

Currently, some states use panfish management programs to control crappie populations, prevent stunting, and provide a better quality fishery. Introducing slot-size limits on predators like largemouth bass and transplanting or thinning out stunted panfish are typical procedures. In addition, progressive-minded fisheries people are experimenting with prey management. The small-crappie syndrome is the bane of anglers in some waters, yet the reasons for this problem are not fully understood.

Mike Colvin, a fisheries research biologist from Missouri, has compiled a large amount of data from ongoing reservoir research projects. He coupled the data with his research studies and concluded that on the reservoirs studied, most of the crappies were small because they were young, not stunted. Most of the fish were growing well but hadn't lived long enough to get big. Tagging studies on Missouri reservoirs have revealed that anglers harvest about 60% of the adult crappie population. In addition, some fish die from natural causes, and as a result, less than 10% of the crappies ever live to be 4 years old. So, few crappies over 10 inches long are harvested. No wonder there are few big fish.

Crappie overharvest was not considered possible until recently; however, it is a reality. The management plan for the study-lake was to reduce the bag limit and implement a 10-inch-minimum size limit on selected waters. As a result, the average size has increased to about 11 inches. Catch and release of small crappies will yield big fish on some reservoirs. The end result is to provide a balanced fishery with good numbers of eating-sized crappies.

On some waters, crappies often experience dramatic population fluctuations. They can be extremely abundant for several years; then their numbers suddenly drop, although the average fish may run larger than normal. What happens? No one knows for certain. There are many theories, but not much concrete evidence.

One possible theory seems logical and explains the fluctuating nature of some crappie populations. After a highly successful hatch, the surviving crappies become the dominant-year-class. During successive years, hordes of dominant-year-class crappies swallow up swarms of their own fry and seal the doom of the other year-classes for several years.

Finally, after the adult, dominant-year-class begins to thin out or die off, the population stabilizes as younger fish are recruited into the population. Eventually, a healthy population of fish with several year-classes represented is present. However, after another super successful, crappie hatch, the cycle will start over again. It makes sense, but may be too simplistic to explain all crappie population variations.

Fisheries biologists don't have the answer. However, they are investigating the phenomenon. Research studies aimed at pinpointing the factors involved in the variation of survival rates of newly hatched crappie fry are currently being conducted. The end result is to manage the crappie population and minimize boom-or-bust fisheries.

SUMMARY

Obviously, consistent crappie fishing is more challenging than most folks realize. Spring fishing usually isn't too tough, but it can be difficult to catch big, suspended slabs in the middle of summer. Consistently successful fishing takes a combined knowledge of crappies and their habits, plus a definite ability to work them effectively. Above all, it takes patience. Yet patience is aptly compensated for when you locate fish and are able to pull them up as fast as you drop in a line.

You are especially rewarded when you find crappies in a unique area or situation that few anglers know about but which you figured out and experimented with yourself. The information contained in this book will put you into the elite class of successful anglers who are able to do just that.

Chapter 2

THE CRAPPIE'S PROFILE

Even though the crappie is one of, if not the *most* popular panfish in this country, the crappie's life style in some waters is still a bit of a mystery. To date, only a handful of biologists have conducted any extensive, ongoing crappie research. However, by combining the data from scientific studies with practical, on-the-water experience and observation, we know enough to be able to sketch the crappie's life story in many waters. Before you can catch white or black crappies consistently, it is essential to have a fundamental understanding of what makes them tick.

White and black crappies are members of the sunfish family (Centrarchidae) which also includes largemouth and smallmouth bass, bluegills, pumpkinseeds, rock bass, and others. These fish characteristically have wide, laterally flattened bodies that resemble the shape of a spade. Centrarchids have spines in their dorsal and anal fins. The pelvic fins in crappies are located beneath the pectoral fins and the anal fin is about the size of the dorsal fin. Large eyes are another characteristic of the sunfish family, and this trademark is particularly obvious in crappies.

White and black crappies are the only members of the genus Pomoxis. While there are many physical similarities between them, there are also noticeable differences. Interestingly, in waters where their range overlaps, the two species intermingle and hybridization occurs. These hybrids can confuse the issue, because they typically display traits from both parents.

WHO'S WHO CRAPPIE IDENTIFICATION

What's the difference between black and white crappies, and why is it important to anglers? Well, knowing which crappie species is present or dominant in a body of water can give a clue to understanding the overall water environment. Changes in the distribution and abundance of both species may serve as "biological indicators" of lake productivity and water quality. In addition, fish location and presentation options may be affected.

WHITE CRAPPIE

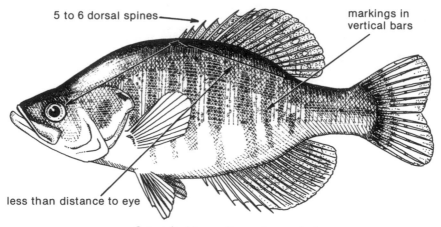

5 to 6 dorsal spines

markings in vertical bars

less than distance to eye

Scientific Name: Pomoxis annularis
World Record - 5 lbs. 3 oz.
Alias: silver crappie, white perch, pole crappie, white, and many others

While both species resemble each other in body shape and overall appearance, there are some fairly significant, visible differences. Generally, both fish have a golden to olive-green or brownish-green back with many bluish-green and silvery reflections, irregular dark mottling on their silvery sides and a white belly.

Here are some clues to help you tell them apart. Usually, the white crappie has a lighter overall appearance and seems to be slightly more elongated than the black. The white is normally paler in color, and the bluish-black blotches on its sides tend to be arranged in 5 to 10, dark, vertical bars. In contrast, the black crappie has a darker, heavily speckled, more mottled appearance.

A word of warning: The characteristic markings are not a foolproof guide to black and white crappie identification, because the markings of both species intensify during spawning. During the Spawn Period, the male, black crappie normally appears heavily mottled, with dark, purplish-black blotches over most of its body. Meanwhile, the male white crappie's markings visibly darken around the head, breast and back. These colorations are produced by hormones and are lost soon after spawning occurs. In waters that contain both white and black crappies, identification can be difficult.

So who's who? At times it is difficult to tell. Further, there is a tendency for crappies from clear waters to have more prominent markings than fish from dark, murky waters. Remember, depending on the Calendar Period and the body of water a fish lives in, identification by color can often be tricky. So, don't rely on color alone to distinguish between black and white crappies.

A glance at the accompanying crappie illustrations shows that the mouths of both species of crappies are large and moderately inclined. A line drawn at a right angle to the corner of the mouth will intersect the dorsal fin of the black

BLACK CRAPPIE

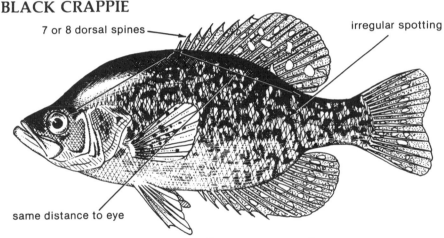

7 or 8 dorsal spines

irregular spotting

same distance to eye

Scientific Name: Pomoxis nigromaculatus

World Record - 6 lbs.

Alias: calico or strawberry bass, speckled crappie, crappie, and numerous others

crappie but will fall in front of the dorsal fin of the white crappie. This difference can be used as a secondary identifying characteristic. The crappie's mouth is made up of soft tissue and, as many anglers have discovered, it tears easily. Among the crappie's numerous aliases is "papermouth," and it sure fits.

Here are a few additional clues to help you draw the line between black and white crappies. The dorsal fin is shorter in the white than in the black crappie and is a reliable distinguishing characteristic. Usually, the white crappie has only 5 or 6 spines in the dorsal fin, while the black crappie has 7 or 8.

Another peculiarity is the distance from the dorsal fin to the eye. In the white crappie, the distance from the front of the dorsal fin to the eye is distinctly longer than the length of the dorsal fin. In contrast, this distance and the length of the dorsal fin are about equal in the black crappie.

DISTRIBUTION

Originally, crappies were native only to the area from southern Canada and the Great Lakes to Florida, and from Nebraska to the Gulf coast. However, since the turn of the century man has introduced both species into suitable waters throughout North America. Apparently, they are quite adaptable. Crappies have found a niche in numerous waters and have often flourished. Through stocking programs, both state and federal agencies have greatly expanded the crappie's range. Additionally, fish rescue operations and reservoir construction have extended the crappie's distribution. Today, their range includes the lower 48 states, southern Canada and northern Mexico.

The black crappie was originally found from the Canadian border, through the Mississippi River watersheds and along the Atlantic coast to Florida. The white crappie was native to the mid-states and south to the Gulf coast. When you look at the crappie distribution map, you'll understand why crappies are such popular fish. Except for lakes and rivers in the high elevations of the Rocky Mountains where crappies are absent, the crappie is an all-American fish.

Combined Range of Black and White Crappies

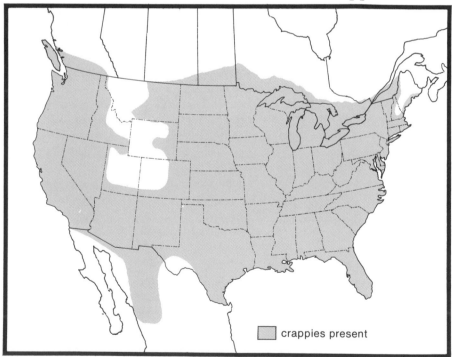

crappies present

White and black crappies thrive in many ponds, pits, lakes, rivers, bayous and reservoirs. Yet, even though their ranges overlap considerably, the white crappie is usually more abundant in the turbid, warmer waters of southern reservoirs, while the black crappie is normally more common in the natural lakes of Florida and the North.

Obviously, a host of factors affect how a particular fish adapts to its environment, and certainly there is no simple answer as to how they accomplish it. In a nutshell, environmental conditions that favor one species may limit another.

For example, black crappies inhabit the cooler, clear-water, natural lakes of the northern United States and southern Canada. You'd be hard pressed to find any number of white crappies in these waters. Apparently, the environmental conditions that the lakes in this area provide are suitable for black crappie survival and growth. However, this same environment is inhospitable to white crappies, and they are seldom present. On the other hand, the black crappie plays second fiddle to the white crappie in many, murky, warm-water reservoirs of the South. Here the white crappie is king and the black crappie scratches out an existence.

The accompanying map shows the combined range of the black and white crappie without detailing their individual distribution. Here are a couple of interesting facts concerning the occurrence of white and black crappies:

(1) The white crappie isn't present in Florida. The white crappie is normally considered to have the more southern range of the two species and is more tolerant of turbid waters. However, the black crappie dominates in Florida's natural lakes and rivers.

(2) The reservoirs of the central United States are primarily the "white crappie's domain." In fact, studies show that on some large reservoirs, white crappies comprise 90% or more of the crappie population.

(3) Black crappies are far more common in tidal rivers and brackish waters along the East and Gulf coasts. Apparently, the black crappie can tolerate brackish water better than the white crappie. Many times, these brackish-water fish are overlooked by anglers. For instance, crappies inhabit virtually all the fresh and brackish, headwaters of Chesapeake Bay's tributary systems. Yet, even though it's within reach of millions, few anglers utilize this fishery.

(4) Rivers, pits and ponds are scattered throughout the country from Maine to Montana, and all of these waters can provide crappie fisheries. For reasons no one can explain, black crappies inhabit some waters, white crappies, others, and they reside together in many more. Which of these waters develop a quality fishery is dependent on many factors like crappie abundance, available prey, competing species, water quality and others. In rivers, the older, more fertile ones with an extended flood plain are best. For example, the Mississippi, Missouri, Columbia, and Ohio rivers all provide excellent crappie fishing opportunities in waters adjacent to the mainstream and in backwater areas.

(5) Pits and ponds are common in many areas of the country and can offer topnotch, largemouth bass and crappie fishing. Depending on the environment that each provides, these smaller waters can be a feast or famine affair. Overcrowding and a limited food supply in some will yield only small, thin crappies, while others with a balanced fish population and plenty of food can produce some real tackle busters. In fact, several state record crappies have been taken from ponds.

Contrary to common belief, crappies and other fish don't appear to prefer any particular set of environmental conditions. They simply *adapt* to whatever conditions a lake, river or reservoir provides. Some species of fish are more adaptable than others to various environments and can tolerate marginal conditions better. Normally, these fish will prosper. Many factors are involved, like habitat, predator/prey relationships, water clarity, competition, feeding efficiency, and others. Therefore, depending on the environment in any given body of water, it could contain black crappies, white crappies or both, plus hybrids.

In general then, black crappies are more abundant in cool, clear, deep, natural lakes and reservoirs. But, they may also be found in Florida waters with temperatures as high as 80°F. Typically, these natural lakes contain marl, sand or gravel bottoms with some vegetation present.

On the other hand, white crappies are far more common in the warm, murky, shallow lakes and impoundments of the South. Depending on location, these waters can provide a variety of aquatic environmental conditions. Standing timber, brush, areas of both hard and soft bottom, vegetation and stained-to-dark water are common features.

Regardless of which crappie species inhabits the waters you fish, an understanding of crappie behavior plus a few presentation options will put plenty of fish on your stringer.

REPRODUCTION

Male and female crappies are sexually mature and begin spawning when they're 2 to 3 years old and 6 to 9 inches in length. But, in waters where crappie growth rates are fast, fish may mature in one year. Age is more important than size, because a stunted fish may spawn when it's only 4 inches long, but 3 years old. One researcher reports that larger fish appear to spawn deeper and earlier in the year than smaller fish. By spawning early, these larger fish face less competition for prime spawning sites from other crappies and largemouth bass.

Crappies are spring spawners through most of their range. The bulk of their spawning activity usually occurs from March through May. However, studies indicate that in some areas in the South, spawning activities may begin as early as mid-February, and in the North as late as mid-July.

Under normal weather conditions, the bulk of the crappie spawning activity will occur when the water temperature ranges from about 60°F to 68°F. However, some spawning activities have been observed at temperatures as low as 50°F and as high as 80°F. These varying spawning temperatures depend on seasonal weather trends which affect how rapidly the water warms. Water clarity also plays a part, because shallow, turbid waters typically warm faster than deep, clear waters. For example, when most fish in a shallow, dark-water reservoir may have finished spawning, in a nearby, deep, clear-water reservoir or lake, the bulk of the crappies may be just beginning to spawn. Interestingly, the angle of the sun's rays and length of daylight also seem to have an influence on triggering crappie spawning activities.

Studies note that crappies often spawn deeper than other panfish. This habit enables them to survive in carp- and gar-infested waters because most of their nests are outside the activity areas of rough fish. While crappies typically spawn in water from 2 to 10 feet deep, fish nests have been spotted in water less than 12 inches deep to more than 20 feet deep.

Biologists have linked crappie spawning depth in reservoirs to water clarity and have come up with this rule of thumb: The clearer the water, the deeper they spawn. This fact is important because water clarity varies from one body of water to another and even within the same waters. For example, a dark-water reservoir may have crappies spawning at 1 to 3 feet deep, while in a clear-water reservoir, crappies may spawn 10 feet deep or more. Obviously, water clarity will affect crappie location and is one of the most important pieces of the crappie puzzle.

Observations indicate that during the early Pre-spawn Period, crappies will congregate in areas adjacent to actual spawning grounds. As the water warms to the mid-50°F's, the males move into shallow water and scout the area for the best nesting sites. At this time, males will assume their darker spawning colors. After establishing a territory, each male sweeps out a shallow, bowl-shaped nest about 6 to 10 inches in diameter. Nest building takes about 2 days to complete. Meanwhile, the females are located nearby, awaiting the onset of spawning.

Crappie Spawning Depth

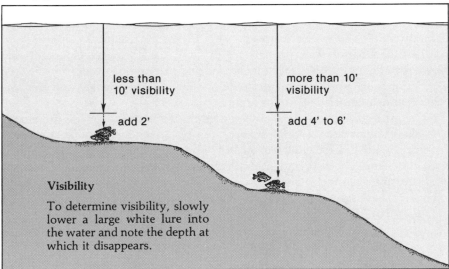

less than
10' visibility

more than 10'
visibility

add 2'

add 4' to 6'

Visibility

To determine visibility, slowly lower a large white lure into the water and note the depth at which it disappears.

While reservoir crappies have been observed spawning in water ranging in depth from 1 to 24 feet, water clarity controls the depth at which crappies spawn. If visibility is less than 10 feet, add 2 feet to the maximum depth you can see in order to estimate the spawning depth. If visibility is over 10 feet, add 4 to 6 feet to approximate the spawning depth.

Knowing this likely depth can help you find potential, crappie spawning areas on reservoirs. This method may not work in natural lakes where crappies often spawn in shallow, weed or reed cover. Still, it's a good tip to keep in mind.

Missouri Department of Conservation research data

Depending on the available habitat, nests can be found on a wide variety of bottom materials, such as gravel, sand, rubble, marl, muck, clay, or a combination of these materials. Usually, nests are located in the backs of protected bays and coves, near submerged vegetation, brush or stumps. In waters where prime spawning habitat is at a premium or where competition for spawning sites is high, crappies may spawn on rocks or fallen trees along steep banks.

Yearly fluctuations in water levels are common on some rivers and reservoirs, and as water levels change, crappies will seek out the best available habitat. What's best this year may be high and dry next year. In addition, unstable weather and receding water levels can cause crappies to abandon their nests.

After the nest is completed and the water temperature remains suitable, the female moves into the spawning area and is recruited by a male. The female deposits her eggs which are fertilized by the male, and then she leaves. Crappies usually spawn in colonies which contain 3 to 50 nests and females may spawn with more than one male. Hybrids are fairly common since white and black crappies often intermingle.

The number of eggs that a female produces varies with the size of the fish. Females weighing around 8 ounces may contain 20,000 to 60,000 eggs, while larger fish may produce 150,000 or more eggs. Even though crappies are believed to be very prolific, a Missouri study points out that females may only deposit 20 to 30 percent of their eggs.

Under suitable conditions, incubation of the eggs usually lasts 3 to 5 days. Stable weather and water temperatures in the 70°F's are ideal conditions. In contrast, incubation can last up to 15 days under marginal conditions. However, egg mortality is high and studies indicate over 50% mortality when incubation is extended. During this time, the male guards the nest and prevents other fish from entering the nest area.

After the eggs hatch, the fry are guarded by the male for several more days until the fry are mature enough to move out of the nesting area. There is only limited scientific data available on distribution patterns of young crappies after they leave the nest and scatter. Evidence suggests that young crappies often inhabit open-water areas.

Eggs   Fry

Biologists believe that fluctuations in year-class strength are a result of poor survival of the young crappies (less than 1/2-inch long) shortly after they desert the nest. Unfortunately, the cause(s) of this poor survival rate is not known at this time. But, the result can be a feast or famine crappie fishery that is common in some waters.

Biologists are studying this phenomenon and have come up with several theories. Predation by bass or dominant-year-class crappies is one explanation. Another theory is that the overcrowding of crappies may prevent egg formation. Still others suggest predator/prey relationships, water quality or temperature as causes.

AGE

Crappies are generally considered to be short-lived fish; however, their longevity (life span) is similar to other members of the sunfish family. On many waters, crappies typically live 3 to 6 years, with individuals in some waters reaching 8 years or more. The oldest reported crappie was an ancient, 13-year-old fish. In comparison, other sunfish like bluegills and pumpkinseeds normally live from 4 to 8 years. Largemouth bass, another relative, typically live from 6 to 10 years in many waters, with some fish reaching 12 to 15 years of age. Thus, even though they don't appear to live a long time, crappies have a "normal" life span on many waters when compared with other family members.

Age vs. Growth Rates of Crappies from Selected Waters

Species	Water	Length (Inches) At End of Each Year								
		1	2	3	4	5	6	7	8	9
White	Lake Moultrie, South Carolina	2.2	8.2	11.3	13.4	14.6	15.0	14.9		
White	Kentucky Lake, Kentucky	4.6	7.9	10.4	11.9	12.8				
White	Missouri, (State Average)	2.7	5.7	8.1	9.6	11.0	11.5			
White	Lake Decatur, Illinois		7.3	9.1	10.5	10.6	12.2	12.3		
White	Oklahoma, (State Average)	2.9	5.9	7.8	9.8	11.9	13.2	14.2	15.0	
White	Mississippi River, Minnesota	2.6	6.0	9.1	10.8	11.7				
Black	Norris Reservoir, Tennessee	5.0	10.9	12.2						
Black	Clear Lake, Iowa	2.3	5.1	7.2	8.6	10.5	11.6	11.9		
Black	Lake Moultrie, South Carolina	2.3	6.3	10.6	12.4	13.2	14.0	15.0	15.0	
Black	Lake George, Florida	4.4	8.1	9.9	11.5	12.5	12.1			
Black	Lake Havasu, California	2.9	6.7	8.6	9.9	10.7				
Black	Lake Harris, Florida	1.9	4.2	6.6	8.5	9.8	11.2	12.2	13.0	13.8
Black	Wisconsin (Southern)	4.3	7.0	8.3	9.8	10.1	10.1	11.0	11.2	12.3

The accompanying chart shows the yearly growth (in inches) of white and black crappies in selected lakes, rivers and reservoirs. Note that crappies in southern waters generally grow faster than those in northern waters. In addition, black crappies in northern, natural lakes normally live longer than white crappies in southern reservoirs. Typically, 6-plus-year-old white crappies and 8-plus-year-old black crappies are considered ancient. While some fish live longer, they're relatively rare in most waters.

Overall, the black crappie is generally considered to have a longer life span than the white crappie. However, the longevity of both species is highly variable and is regulated by many factors. In the end, the environment a crappie lives in determines how long it lives.

For example, a study in Lake of the Ozarks Reservoir, MO, found few white crappies more than 3 years old. Additionally, an Oklahoma study concluded that over 95% of the crappie population was less than 5 years old. These findings seem to indicate a short life span. Yet by comparison, in Minnesota and Florida some black crappies live from 8 to 10 years. Apparently, a short life span may be characteristic of crappie populations in some waters, while crappies may live twice as long in others. While biologists don't have absolute, concrete answers to this puzzle, some believe that high adult mortality may be due to stress (physiological burnout) during hot summer months, disease or overharvesting. Current research studies are aimed toward answering the interesting question of why relatively few crappies live longer than 3 or 4 years in some waters.

GROWTH

The small-crappie syndrome has plagued anglers for years. Why do some waters produce only small, stunted fish while others grow 2-pound slabs? Once again, there is no single, clear-cut answer.

The rate at which crappies grow is directly linked to several environmental factors. Habitat, turbidity and temperature of the water, amount and type of available food, geographical location, competition for food and living space, plus other factors, all play a role. Growth rates for crappies can vary greatly in different waters and can even vary from year to year in the same body of water.

Crappie growth may be fast or slow in all parts of the range but, in general, growth is faster in the South than in the North. For example, a 3-year-old white crappie in a southern reservoir might be 10 inches long; whereas a 3-year-old black crappie in a northern, natural lake would be about 7 inches long. In addition, in waters where both exist, one species will usually dominate. Depending on the environment, the odds could tip in favor of either the white or black.

It's a balancing-act game, with each fish situated at opposite ends of an environmental see-saw. Water clarity, prey, competition, temperature, habitat, plus a host of other factors, all determine which direction the environment shifts and, ultimately, which species of crappie will dominate. These same conditions also determine the abundance, growth rate, and size of the fish.

DIET

Crappies are predators and are neither general nor specific in their feeding habits. They are mainly sight feeders as their large eyes might suggest. At times, crappies are opportunistic feeders and may take advantage of an aquatic insect hatch. At other times, they may feed almost entirely on small fish. Actually, crappies are intermediate, semi-selective feeders. They may consume a wide range of food items in some waters or be selective and feed on only a few items in others. It all depends on what's available.

The amounts and types of food items eaten also vary with the time of the year, crappie size, and the availability of prey. Both white and black crappies eat zooplankton, crustaceans, aquatic insects and fish. Zooplankton is the major food of most young crappies. As they grow, small larvae and adult, aquatic insects become very important foods. Ultimately, small fish become the most important food item of adult crappies in most waters.

Seasonally, the adult crappie's diet may vary to take advantage of the most abundant food items. A typical pattern for adult crappies features plankton and aquatic insects as the dietary mainstay during spring and early summer.

Typical Aquatic Food Chain

"The Game of Who Eats Whom"

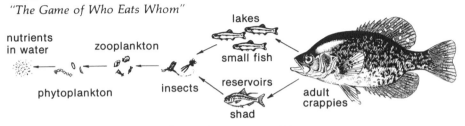

What Crappies Eat

Shad	Zooplankton
Aquatic Insects	Minnows
Sunfish	Carp
Catfish	Black Bass
Striped Bass	Drum
Bluegills	Crappies
Crustaceans	

Size is of the essence, and small is best. Normally, adult crappies eat young-of-the-year fish, if available. However, their diet can vary from one body of water to another, and even seasonally on the same body of water.

As summer progresses, young-of-the-year fish become available and are used as forage. In fall, fish are the primary food in most waters. During winter, food items vary depending on location of the water. While fish and insects may be important items in the South, zooplankton, miscellaneous aquatic insects and minnows (if available) are common forage in the North.

In waters containing both black and white crappies, their diet, growth rate and survival may vary dramatically. A recent study indicates that adult black crappies are less adapted than white crappies to capturing preyfish in turbid waters. Blacks apparently don't feed efficiently in warmer, turbid waters, and simply expend too much energy in search of prey. Thus, adult black crappies may be forced to continue feeding on plankton and insects, while their cousins—white crappies—are able to switch forage types and dine on small fish. Thus, in dark waters containing mixed populations, whites usually have the edge, because they're able to utilize the forage base more efficiently.

Once crappies reach about 6 inches in length, they're not highly adapted to feeding on small plankton because the larger spaces between their gill rakers prevent the retention of tiny food items. Consequently, blacks can get caught in an "energy trap" if they cannot effectively switch to a fish diet. In some turbid waters, blacks remain plankton feeders and literally "burn out" trying to feed. Therefore, white crappies dominate. Here, 3-year-old white crappies might be 9 inches long while black crappies might be only 6 inches long. It's simply survival of the fittest.

Here are several zooplankton that panfish commonly feed on. Copepods sense predators and make darting, evasive maneuvers to avoid panfish. Daphnia exhibit a constant bobbing or fluttering movement, but offer no evasive actions. However, they have the ability to migrate vertically in the water to coincide with the low-light levels which makes them difficult to see.

 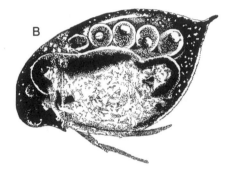

(A) Here are two types of copepods. The one on the left is a calanoid copepod; on the right is a cyclopoid copepod. They reach sizes of about 1/10 of an inch.

(B) The common water flea or Daphnia is about the size of a pinhead.

On the other hand, given a cooler, clearer-water environment, blacks often prosper. Here, they can compete for available food and space on an equal (or better than equal) basis with white crappies. There are also numerous "in between" waters with both species present, and when the environment favors one species or the other, that species will generally dominate.

AVAILABILITY OF PREY

Apparently, for a lake or reservoir to support a healthy, stable, crappie population, it must provide a suitable prey during the critical transition period when crappies switch to a fish diet. Basically, crappies are flesh eaters (carnivores), and small fish are important food items. In fact, in some reservoirs, studies show that, seasonally, young gizzard and threadfin shad comprise a majority of the crappie's diet. Crappies will gorge themselves on plentiful, high-protein shad, if available.

Prey size also seems to be very important. Crappies generally utilize smaller, young-of-the-year shad in the 1- to 3-inch range. Once shad grow over 4 inches in length, crappies are unable to use them as a food source; they're simply too large to eat. But, by dining on younger shad, crappies are able to grow rapidly to world-class size.

Young threadfin and newly hatched gizzard shad are the keys to good crappie growth in many impoundments. The presence (or lack) of young shad in some reservoirs seems to be related to the growth and overall condition of the crappie population. In some cases, the white crappie's diet is composed of 45 to 90 percent shad.

Threadfin shad have multiple spawns—spring and fall—on some waters. This yields an abundance of high-protein forage for the crappies and can result in numbers of slab-sized fish.

In reservoirs where shad aren't a primary prey, crappies will feed upon the fry of largemouth bass, white bass, perch or sunfish. They also eat insects, crustaceans, mollusks, and various minnows. However, while crappies can "hack" this diet, they generally don't flourish on it.

A similar transition to a fish diet takes place in natural lakes. However, since shad may not be available, largemouth bass fry, perch, bluegills and miscellaneous minnows take the place of shad in the crappie's diet.

Jim and Al Lindner combined to catch a bunch of early-spring, pre-spawn crappies. These fish were caught from a shallow bay of a natural lake on ultralight tackle, 4-pound-test line and 1/16-oz. jigs.

Age in Relation to Length

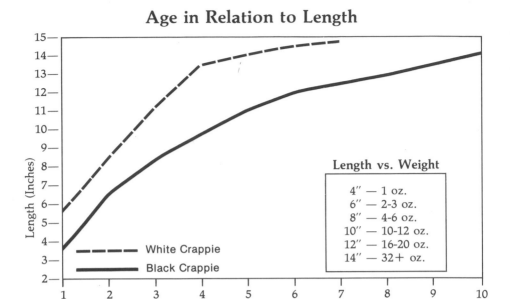

Length (Inches) — Age (Years)

Length vs. Weight

4" — 1 oz.
6" — 2-3 oz.
8" — 4-6 oz.
10" — 10-12 oz.
12" — 16-20 oz.
14" — 32+ oz.

White Crappie
Black Crappie

This graph illustrates the approximate length for different year classes of white and black crappies. Growth rates vary considerably between waters, yet the values reflect typical growth in some better lakes and reservoirs. In general, male and female crappies grow at similar rates, although hybrids are fast growing and predominantly males.

Weight-wise, the black crappie is heavier for its length than the white crappie. Yet, the white crappie grows faster in many waters. Depending on diet and many other factors, the weight of crappies can also vary from the approximate values. All in all, crappie longevity and weight is tied to the local environment. With optimum conditions, a crappie will double its weight as it grows from 8 to 10 inches and nearly double again when it reaches 12 inches. Slab, 2-pound crappies are usually 14 to 16 inches long and 5 to 8 years old—honest-to-goodness trophies.

In small lakes and reservoirs, pits and ponds, the crappie's growth rate depends on the amount of available prey and other factors. In many waters, crappies are stunted because too many fish must compete for a limited prey resource. With limited prey, growth is slow and the maximum size of adult fish may be only 4 to 6 inches. On the other hand, small waters with a balanced fishery can grow slab-sized crappies. Competition for food and living space is less, and the fish may grow and thrive if conditions permit.

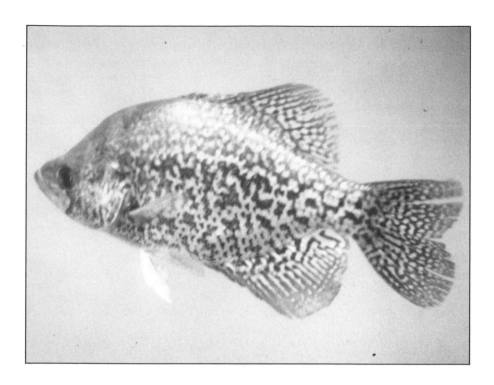

Chapter 3

INTRODUCTION TO THE CALENDAR PERIODS

To catch crappies 365 days a year requires an indepth knowledge of crappie behavior on a yearly, seasonal and daily basis. This may sound difficult, but it's easier than you might think. The foundation of successful crappie fishing is built upon understanding the crappies' way of life and how they adapt all season long to their changing aquatic environment.

Our normal system of measuring time is the Gregorian calendar, which contains 365 days and 12 months. It's the calendar hanging on your wall and built into the LCD watch on your wrist. Actually, it's a good, accurate system for recording daily, monthly and yearly periods; however, the calendar is *fixed* and doesn't take into account the whims of nature that affect the biological community.

The *IN-FISHERMAN* Calendar, on the other hand, divides the year into 10 periods of fish response. These seasonal periods replace the standard days, weeks and months of the normal calendar. Because the *IN-FISHERMAN* Calendar Periods are at the mercy of Mother Nature, they do not last a certain number of days, nor do they occur on specific dates each year. Since the Calendar Periods depend on climate and water conditions, they will vary in length from year to year depending on weather trends. And, if you want crappies tugging on your line, you must recognize the Calendar Periods and predict the crappies' response.

Calendar Periods which might last a few days one year could last a month the next year. For example, last year in "Secret Lake" the crappies may have completed spawning during the first week of May, while this year, due to a late spring, the crappie spawning period in Secret Lake might run from Memorial Day until mid-June. Obviously, the timing of the Calendar Periods fluctuates.

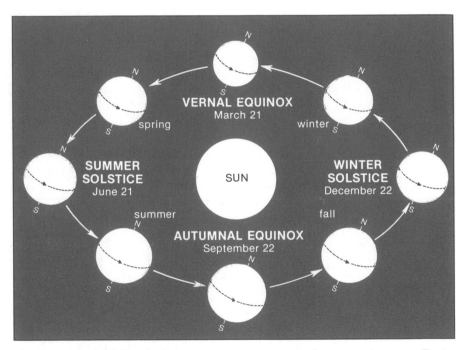

Spring, summer, fall and winter are common events in the temperate zones. During these separate and distinct seasons the pendulum swings noticeably between periods of lightness and darkness. We can easily recognize seasonal patterns in nature.

On land, seasonal changes are quite evident, but under the water it's difficult to see nature's forces at work. Consequently, aquatic seasonal cycles are a confusing mystery to some people. However, it is in this mysterious and constantly changing environment that fish live, so to catch crappies with consistency, you must be in touch with their aquatic environment.

Crappie behavior is not haphazard. A host of factors affect fish, and there are sound reasons for each and every activity. In order to survive, fish simply adapt to conditions. Studies show that the photoperiod (length of daylight) regulates the tempo of the environment, from microorganisms to top-of-the-line predators. Seasonally, these light levels change as the earth rotates around the sun. The intensity and duration of light in its yearly cycle can regulate migrations, spawning, and feeding, and may trigger other activities.

Additionally, a Calendar Period might occur months earlier in one region of North America than in another. For instance, in areas of Canada, the Summer Calendar Period might arrive in July and only last a few weeks. Meanwhile, in Florida, the Summer Period may arrive in May and last for 5 months or more. This difference in timing is caused by the change in the angle of the sun to the earth's surface as you proceed from the equator northward. The more direct angle of the sun in the South provides an overall warmer environment.

There is a south-to-north progression (Florida to Tennessee to Minnesota) in the onset of the Calendar Periods since southern states begin warming earlier in the year than northern ones. In fact, spring usually arrives about one week later for every 100 miles you proceed north. Conversely, fall arrives earlier in the northern states and progresses southward.

Some of the *IN-FISHERMAN* Calendar Periods relate primarily to the crappie's biological demands, such as reproduction. These include the Pre-spawn, Spawn and Post-spawn Periods. Other periods like the various Summer, Fall (Cold Water), and Winter (Coldest Water) Periods relate more to water temperature and seasonal environmental conditions.

Thus, Calendar Periods are not simply the seasonal conditions of a body of water. A lake, river or reservoir may be in a seasonal time frame (spring, summer, fall or winter), but the *crappies' response* to that environment determines their Calendar Period. In any given body of water, different species of fish, as well as different groups of the same species, can be in different Calendar Periods at the same time. Since not all crappies spawn simultaneously, groups of Pre-spawn, Spawn and Post-spawn fish can be present at the same time, and the location and attitude of each group will be different. There are subtle, but significant, changes in behavior that affect the "catchability" of crappies during each Calendar Period.

You might assume that the best time to fish would be during a Calendar Period when the water temperature is at an optimum for crappie metabolism, causing them to feed the most. But, it doesn't always work that way. The available food supply, timing of feeding movements, and overall population levels and competition, all play an important role in angling success. We considered these factors when we developed the *IN-FISHERMAN* Calendar Periods.

Once you learn to "read the signs," you'll have little difficulty identifying one period from another and determining when various species are in different Calendar Periods. The difference between the unsuccessful angler and the truly successful one often boils down to the ability to recognize seasonal movements and the crappies' response patterns. If you know the Calendar Periods from A to Z, you'll be several boat lengths ahead of the crowd and on your way to more and bigger crappies.

In the final analysis, the only way to understand how different Calendar Periods function in a particular body of water is to spend enough time on the water identifying these patterns. Comparing notes with other anglers will help you get a grasp on crappie behavior during the Calendar Periods. Keeping a daily log of weather and water conditions, as well as fish feeding patterns, will also help. A review of last year's fishing log often provides an insight into seasonal fishing patterns you may not have noticed before. In this way, you can learn both the seasonal circumstances that trigger fish response, and the locational patterns that result from them.

As we examine the Calendar Periods in depth, we'll include clues on crappie location and behavior that'll help you understand the ins and outs of crappie activity on any body of water.

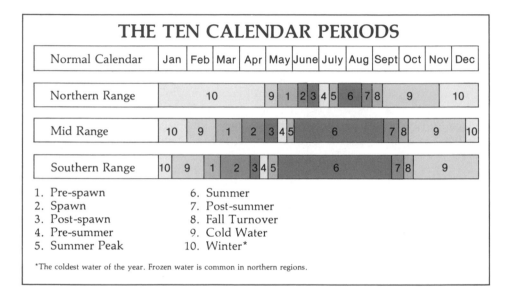

THE TEN CALENDAR PERIODS

Normal Calendar	Jan	Feb	Mar	Apr	May	June	July	Aug	Sept	Oct	Nov	Dec
Northern Range	10				9	1	2 3 4 5	6	7 8	9		10
Mid Range	10	9	1	2	3 4 5	6			7 8	9		10
Southern Range	10	9	1	2	3 4 5	6			7 8	9		

1. Pre-spawn
2. Spawn
3. Post-spawn
4. Pre-summer
5. Summer Peak
6. Summer
7. Post-summer
8. Fall Turnover
9. Cold Water
10. Winter*

*The coldest water of the year. Frozen water is common in northern regions.

The key to understanding the 10 Calendar Periods of fish response is to realize that the periods can (and do) vary in length from year to year, and in some waters they may overlap from time to time. Obviously, unusually warm or cool weather will affect the length of the periods. They can vary as much as 4 weeks from one year to the next. Remember, the periods are not based on the Gregorian calendar, so they do not occur on specific dates each year. Instead, the Calendar Periods are based on nature's clock.

In addition, the Calendar Periods vary by regions of the country. Being in a warm climate, the rivers, lakes and reservoirs of the South experience an extended Summer Period and brief Cold Water and Winter Periods. In contrast, the lakes along the U.S./Canadian border normally have extended Cold Water and Winter Periods and a brief Summer Period. So, crappies in Florida or Texas could be in the Spawning Period while those in northern Minnesota are still "iced up" in the Winter Period.

Bodies of water located between these two extremes experience Calendar Periods that lie somewhere in between these examples, with the overall length of the periods adjusted accordingly. For example, fish in the TVA reservoirs of Kentucky/Tennessee experience intermediate Calendar Period lengths when compared with fish in northern and southern waters.

The IN-FISHERMAN Calendar Period guide can be used to determine what crappies will be doing on a season-long basis. The normal calendar is included as an approximate reference point. Using this information, you can create a "Crappie Calendar" for your locality.

CALENDAR PERIOD REGIONAL TIMETABLE

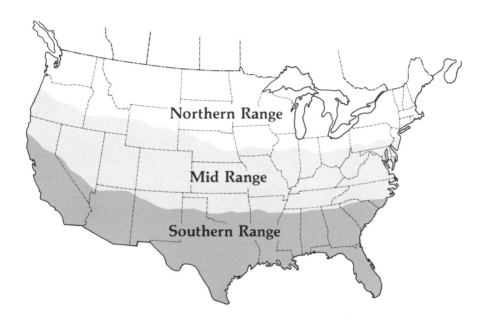

The timing of the crappie's Spawn Period illustrates the region-by-region progression of the Calendar Periods. Region (latitude), water temperature, weather trends, length of daylight, and inter- and intra-species competition for habitat are just a few of the factors which influence the exact timing of the spawn. Remember, not all crappies spawn at the same time even in the same body of water. While the bulk of the adult fish on a given lake may spawn during a few days of ideal conditions, there will still be some early- and some late-spawning fish.

Regionally, the onset of crappie spawning may begin in early March in the South or as late as mid-July in southern Canada. The following chart lists typical spawning months for crappies in representative areas:

TYPICAL SPAWNING MONTHS

AREA	MONTH(S)
Florida	March-April
Alabama	March-April
Texas/Oklahoma	March-May
Kentucky/Tennessee	April-May
Missouri/Illinois/Iowa	April-June
Ohio	April-July
Oregon	March-June
Minnesota/Wisconsin	May-July
Ontario	June-August

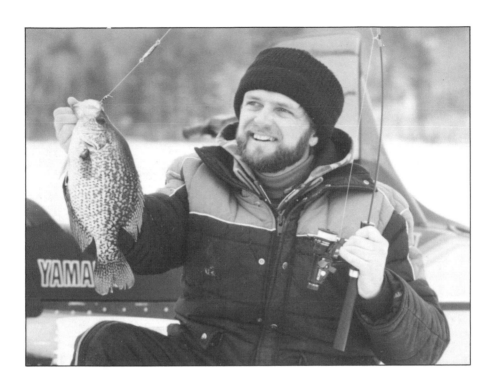

Chapter 4

THE CALENDAR PERIODS

Crappies Throughout The Seasons

To catch crappies consistently, you must understand their fascinating life-style throughout the changing seasons. Crappies follow the rhythm of nature with their own distinct patterns of behavior. As the water warms from spring into summer, crappies respond to the increasing pace of life with more movement and aggressiveness. Then, as the water cools from fall into winter, the tempo of life gradually slows and crappies become more sedentary and selective. Good crappie anglers understand these seasonal tendencies and adjust their tactics to keep in step with nature's changing tune.

This chapter describes the fundamental principles of crappie location and behavior during each of the *IN-FISHERMAN* Calendar Periods. Once we lay the foundation, we'll take a more detailed look in the following chapters, at each Calendar Period. Let's begin our adventure as winter gives way to early spring.

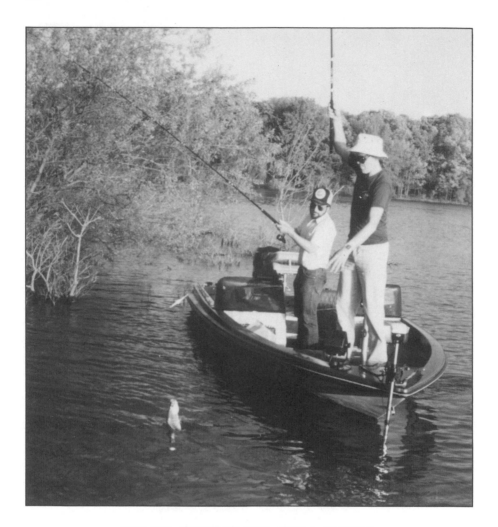

THE SPRING SEASON
Which includes: Spring Cold Water, Pre-spawn,
Spawn, and Post-spawn Periods

THE COLD WATER PERIOD (SPRING)

A Time of Preparation
Surface Water Temperature Range: Mid 30°F to 50°F
General Fish Mood: Neutral

The Spring Cold Water Period is a time of preparation—a prelude to the crappie's annual spawning ritual. It is also a period of transition from the lethargy of winter to the cool-water environment of spring.

In northern lakes, the Spring Cold Water Period begins just after ice-out with water temperatures in the low 30°F. In more southerly waters, it may commence with water temperatures in the low 40°F, depending on how low the water temperature dropped over the winter. In either case, it arrives as winter grudgingly releases its icy grip and the water begins to warm.

In northern natural lakes, crappies generally suspend along or somewhere adjacent to the deep weedline/first drop-off area at ice-out. In small lakes and ponds, it's not uncommon for them to be smack-dab in the center of the deepest hole in the lake from 5 to 20 feet below the surface. Reservoir fish display a similar tendency, although the fish usually tend to be more object-oriented, relating to deep treelines, channel edges, etc., rather than suspending away from cover.

Stable, warm weather—particularly calm, sunny days—will start drawing some crappies into the shallows almost immediately, if sheltered areas exist. These occur in the form of channels, bays, cuts, harbors, backwaters, etc. In essence, they are areas of shallow water that are exposed to the sun and protected from the wind. The best ones generally lie on the northern shores of lakes or impoundments since these areas receive the best sun exposure and have the most shelter from harsh north winds.

Many anglers think these initial, shallow-water forays are pre-spawn movements. They're not. Actually, they're associated with food. Crappies follow minnows into the warming shallows as the tiny baitfish seek the microscopic plankton that are beginning to bloom there.

The best shallow crappie areas usually have some form of cover to attract and hold fish in the general area. In natural lakes, cover generally occurs in the form of reeds, dock pilings, brush, and remnant shallow weeds from the previous year. In rivers and reservoirs, flooded brush, stumps, fallen trees and fish attractors do the trick.

Early, shallow crappie movements occur at the mercy of Mother Nature. Stable weather draws the fish in, and cold-front conditions drive them back out again. Thus, depending on the conditions, you may find the bulk of the crappies in a bay or cove area to be: (1) shallow (ideal conditions); (2) along the first drop-off outside a shallow, protected cut (intermediate conditions); (3) suspended outside the drop-off (frontal conditions). However, just knowing that they'll be somewhere in the vicinity of shallow bays, backwaters or cuts gives you a starting place to begin your search.

In general, lakes or reservoirs with shallow bays or cuts will see shallow crappie movements just after ice-out or just as the water begins to warm. However, when bodies of water lack such protected areas, it may take several additional weeks for the wind-exposed shallows to warm sufficiently to attract fish. In such lakes, the bulk of the fish usually remain suspended along the first drop-off/channel edge until the shallows warm up enough to attract them.

As the water continues to warm up toward 50°F, the environment grows more stable. The bulk of the crappies will generally be somewhere in the area from the extreme shallows out to the first drop-off, although they will begin shifting their activity toward areas where they will eventually spawn. These may or may not be the same areas they used earlier, depending on the available bottom content and cover. It all depends on what options the body of water offers.

THE PRE-SPAWN PERIOD
A Time of Anticipation
Surface Water Temperature Range: 50°F to 63°F
General Fish Mood: Neutral to Positive

At this stage, crappie activity begins centering around spawning areas. In reservoirs and rivers, these generally occur (1) where the bottom is sufficiently soft—generally sand/marl, but not mucky—for crappies to sweep out a nest; (2) near some form of cover; (3) at the appropriate depth. This combination of factors varies from lake to lake, but there are several guidelines you can use to locate fish.

In general, bay, backwater or cove areas with cover (timber, stumps, brush piles, etc.) will attract most of the fish, rather than main-lake shorelines. However, the fish will really key in on the sections of these general areas with cover at the proper depth. This depth varies with water clarity, but is generally *slightly below* the depth of maximum sunlight penetration. Crappies may even forego areas with decent bottom and cover if they're too shallow, and may elect to spawn around deeper fish attractors or on horizontal branches of flooded timber if it lies in their favored depth range. This is particularly true if the fish face severe competition for spawning areas with largemouth bass.

In any case, pre-spawn crappies will congregate around these areas as the water rises above 50°F. Males are the first fish to enter the spawning areas and remain there. Females may mill in and out, or stay a bit deeper, right up until the actual time of spawning. This is particularly true in natural lakes where crappies spawn around reed or weed cover in the shallows. This form of natural cover tends to draw pre-spawn fish shallower than they might move on reservoirs with the same water clarity.

Early pre-spawn males will move directly into generalized areas of cover. When they first move in, they'll mill about and display an overall spooky attitude. However, the longer they remain in the shallows, the more aggressive and territorial they become. Hormonal changes begin to trigger a darker color change in the males. In clear-water natural lakes, you can often spot them as dark spots inside the tangled masses of reed clumps.

The more the water warms, the more fearless the fish become. They are quite easy to catch with a variety of bobber presentations—particularly once they select their spawning site and begin sweeping out a nest. Eventually, a male will seek out or attract a female and spawning will occur.

The actual spawning act may only take a couple of hours. However, spawning usually requires several days and is resumed as more eggs and milt ripen in the fish. Most females deposit their eggs within a day or two unless the process is interrupted by unstable weather.

In general, all the crappies in a body of water do not spawn at exactly the same time, since all areas of a lake do not warm up at the same pace. Thus, you can expect the shallowest, most protected areas to see spawning use first, while it takes a bit longer for deeper or more exposed areas to warm enough for spawning to commence.

THE SPAWN PERIOD

A Time of Tension
Surface Water Temperature Range: 64°F to 72 + °F
General Fish Mood: Negative

This is a brief and variable period usually lasting from one to three days for female crappies and a little longer for males. Fish may spawn earlier or later, but most of the eggs will usually be deposited somewhere within this temperature range. Fish which spawn extremely deep (20 feet in clear reservoirs) may appear to spawn later, but when you consider how long it takes the water temperature at the spawning depth to warm to the proper level, the general rule applies.

While a fish that has not spawned yet is still technically in its Pre-spawn Period, in reality, the closer it comes to spawning, the less likely it is to strike a bait or exhibit other pre-spawn traits. While feeding activity is practically non-existent during spawning, some fish may make reflex strikes at intruders into the nest area. Since crappies tend to spawn in loose groups, some fish in an area may be spawning while others are in a pre-spawn or post-spawn attitude.

In smaller bodies of water, most crappie spawning will occur over a span of a couple weeks. In larger reservoirs, however, all areas do not warm up simultaneously. Therefore, in some areas, the fish may have finished spawning, while in others they are in the process or are preparing to do so. In the event that spawning areas are limited, the fish may make use of them in "waves," with fish staging outside the spawning areas until nesting sites are available.

Eventually, the bulk of the spawning activity in an area will occur, and the females will begin filtering out of the shallows. The males remain behind, fanning the nest to oxygenate the eggs and guarding the nests from hungry predators.

THE POST-SPAWN PERIOD

A Time of Recuperation
Surface Water Temperature Range: Mid-70°F
General Fish Mood: Negative to Neutral

Post-spawn is a somewhat mysterious period, largely because of the lack of concentrated female crappies. We can generalize and assume that the water temperature will usually be in the 70°F, but water temperature is not the only factor influencing fish behavior. Since it is a recuperation period, time is also of the essence. Depending on the body of water and local weather conditions, it may take a couple weeks for the crappies to recuperate from the rigors of spawning.

The location and behavior of male and female crappies is quite different during this period. After spawning, the male protects the nest against predators and fans the nest to provide oxygen, remove waste and prevent siltation. The eggs generally take about a week to hatch, although the male usually remains and guards the fry until they disperse from the nest.

During this time, male crappies are extremely vulnerable to fishing pressure. It can be like "shooting fish in a barrel" once you locate them. However, we suggest that you do not remove the fish, or better yet, do not fish for males on the nest. Removing the male crappie from the nest simply allows the eggs to be eaten by predators like bluegills. We suggest fishing for other species, or searching for female crappies outside the spawning area.

After leaving the nest, females will filter out across the adjacent area. Small groups of fish may linger around shallow cover like fish attractors or weed clumps; in general, however, they'll slowly move toward the nearest drop-off or developing weedline area.

Drop-off fish do not school tightly at this time, although there may be a large aggregation of fish in general areas. These deeper fish may suspend anywhere from 5 to 15 feet beneath the surface and slowly roam about in search of food. While they may be adjacent to a channel edge or weedline area, they are more likely to be scattered across a wide band from just inside to just outside it.

These loose groups of crappies typically roam slowly back and forth along channel edges and drop-offs, perhaps stopping occasionally at a distinct feature like a weed clump, underwater point, or channel bend.

Eventually the male fish will leave the nest and join the females, forming larger and more distinct schools. Depending on conditions, Post-spawn slowly blends into the Pre-summer Period.

In general, once you no longer see fish on the nest, the Post-spawn Period has ended.

THE SUMMER SEASON
Which includes: Pre-summer, Summer Peak,
Summer, and Post-summer Periods

THE PRE-SUMMER PERIOD
A Time of Transition
Surface Water Temperature Range: Mid-70°F
General Fish Mood: Neutral to Positive

While Post-spawn is considered a resting stage when crappies scatter and feed sporadically, a change in behavior is imminent. The crappies require nourishment, and the resumption of more regular feeding patterns indicates the beginning of Pre-summer. This usually happens once the water temperature reaches the mid-70°F.

Pre-summer is a time of emerging weedgrowth and developing food chain. The environment begins springing to life with insect hatches, clouds of newly hatched fry, and activity of all kinds. Feeding opportunities and patterns develop at a variety of depths, and some crappies may be caught on flats, along drop-offs, or suspended.

In general, however, crappies will continually shift deeper during this stage. They'll filter out across shallow flats, and perhaps use timber or weed clumps on the deeper edges. They'll roam channel edges in reservoirs or weedlines in natural lakes, and leave the backwaters in rivers for areas with a bit more current flow. Still, the variety of feeding opportunities (insects, larvae, minnows, fry) lends itself to fish feeding fairly actively all day long in a variety of areas.

Slowly, and perhaps imperceptibly, crappies begin zeroing in on the habitat they'll occupy during the upcoming Summer Period. In natural lakes and ponds, points and turns in the deep weed edge draw more and more fish. In reservoirs, deeper, timbered channel edges toward the mouths of the coves collect schools of crappies. The extreme shallows may become nearly devoid of crappies, while the drop-offs and confined open water outside them begin to host most of the fish.

Pre-summer is a time of transition when a body of water transforms from the cooler-water environment of spring to the warmer-water environment of summer. Crappies begin to regroup, and classic patterns begin to emerge.

THE SUMMER PEAK PERIOD

A Time of Fulfillment

Surface Water Temperature Range: Mid to Upper 70°F
General Fish Mood: Neutral to Positive

As early summer progresses, the Pre-summer Period develops into the Summer Peak. Basically, it's the time when summer patterns kick into high gear and schools of fish set up on classic summer spots. At this time, it is impossible to not feel nature's increased rhythm; nature is alive, conscious and moving.

Most of a lake's ecosystem reaches its maximum development during this cycle. All of the cool- and warm-water species will have spawned. The transformation from a cool to a warm environment is complete. Insect hatches explode, and rooted weedgrowth matures. In natural lakes, distinct weedlines develop, and crappies roam their edges like race cars circling a track. In reservoirs, crappies gorge themselves on shad along the edges of creek and river channels. Crappies congregate in heavy schools, and the action can be fast and furious. It's a great time to be on the water.

Basically, then, a combination of environmental factors stimulates Summer Peak activity: (1) The fish are hungry, aggressive and catchable; (2) Heavy schooling creates competitive group activity and fast-action fishing; and (3) The lake is alive and brimming with food. It is truly a time of fulfillment.

THE SUMMER PERIOD
A Time of Plenty
Surface Water Temperature Range: Maximum Temperature of the Year
General Fish Mood: Neutral to Positive

Summer arrives and with it come hordes of mosquitos and water skiers. But to anglers, summer brings the "dog days"—scorching sun and high humidity. "Dog days" is a misnomer that implies lethargy, but this is an illusion. More than at any time of year, nature is in full gear converting the sun's energy to living matter.

Abundant prey is available in the form of fry, fingerlings and insects. Lakes blossom with food, and fish often become more selective in their choice of meals. Controlling factors like thermoclines, sunlight, increased metabolism and competing species all demand order. Nature responds by regulating feeding times.

Crappies become a mystery to many folks at this time, largely because people are still seeking to catch them in the shallows. But the fish have moved. Their love of deeper cover and confined open water takes them far out of the realm of shallow-water anglers.

Summer crappies roam the edges of cover, generally somewhere in the 12- to 22-foot range; the clearer the water, the deeper they'll usually be. Active fish may be right on the edges of cover or penetrate slightly into it, while inactive or resting fish often suspend a distance outside.

This general rule applies equally well to natural lakes, strip pits, ponds and impoundments; only the types of cover vary. In natural lakes, the best summer areas are deep cabbage or coontail weed edges—particularly the points and turns in those edges—and rock piles that rise slightly above the level of deepest sunlight penetration. Here, the underwater weed forest or moss-covered rocks attract and hold the baitfish that crappies thrive on.

In most reservoirs, flooded timber, deep stumps, and manmade fish attractors take the place of natural weed cover. But the same principles apply. Crappies use the best "wood" along the edges of creek and river channels, and select a prime depth range based on water clarity. Active fish are in and around the cover, while fish suspended outside are usually either moving or not aggressively feeding.

Suspension is common—particularly during the daylight hours. During summer, crappies often shift the majority of their feeding activity on clear-water lakes toward the twilight and night hours. Fishing the edges of cover during the hours before and after dawn and dusk often brings the best summertime catches. However, some dark-water lakes and reservoirs may have crappies feeding during the bright light of midday.

In general then, summer crappie activity occurs deeper than in spring, although the fish still remain above the thermocline if one exists. They roam the confined open water zone near cover and relate to it at a suitable depth based on water clarity, although prime conditions like twilight or cloudy weather may draw them a bit shallower. Where cover is abundant, crappies have many options and you must search for them. Where cover is scarce, as in many highland reservoirs, even a single flooded tree can attract and hold fish.

Basically, summer is a time of plenty—plenty of food, plenty of cover, and plenty of distractions in terms of boat traffic, sunlight penetration, cold fronts and the like. This completes the warming trend for the year.

THE POST-SUMMER PERIOD

A Time of Impending Change

Water Temperature Range: The Water Begins Cooling
Rapidly From its Highest Temperature Range
General Fish Mood: Neutral to Positive

Post-summer, in effect, is a reversal of the Pre-summer process. It occurs at the tail end of summer when a body of water begins changing back from a warmer to a cooler environment. Hot days with dead-calm periods, followed by cool nights, are typical. The days grow shorter, sending a signal to the eco-system that things are slowing down.

Most of the food in any lake, river or reservoir has already been produced for the year, and the time of plenty slowly gives way to diminished food supplies. Weeds thin out, insect hatches dwindle, and river-water levels are generally low, often forcing the fish into deep holes or river bends.

Crappies generally respond to the changing environment by holding tighter to cover and showing less of a tendency to suspend. You might fish your way along a weedline or timberline and never spot a suspended fish with your depth finder, and yet catch a nice bunch of crappies by casting a jig up into the flooded trees or weeds. Thus, you must "fish 'em" to find 'em, rather than being able to locate them visually with your depth finder.

This tendency can work in your favor, however, by concentrating on the crappies on the deep edges of cover. This places them in easy-to-locate areas and makes them easier to catch all day long. Once you find them, you can usually catch a bunch of fish from a small area, and not have to worry about following a suspended, moving school.

Post-summer is a time of impending change when the aquatic environment begins winding down from the hectic pace and warm water of summer.

THE FALL SEASON

Which includes: Turnover and Fall Cold Water Periods

THE TURNOVER PERIOD

A Time of Turmoil

Water Temperature Range: Variable
General Fish Mood: Very Negative

As a time of turmoil, the Turnover Period is relative. First, all bodies of water do not thermocline during summer, so they do not "turn over" as such. Most rivers are a case in point. Lakes and reservoirs, too, may or may not stratify. Usually, shallow bodies of water—which the wind periodically stirs

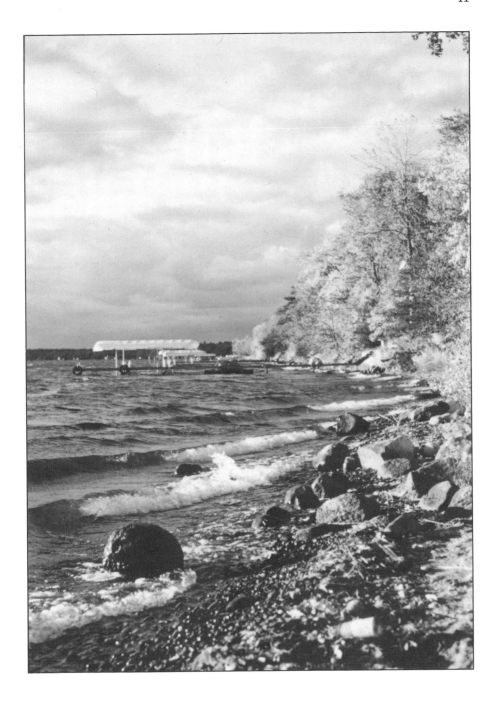

up—or ones with a lot of current flowing through them, are fairly immune to the stratifying process. Consequently, the fish in these waters are not subjected to as much stress as fish in waters where the transition from a warm- to a cold-water environment is an explosive event. Nonetheless, the change from a warmer- to a cooler- to a colder-water environment demands some adjustment.

The most classic (drastic) turnover situation occurs in bodies of water which set up (stratify) in distinct temperature layers during the summer. Since cold water is heavier than warm water, the warmer water stays on top and the colder water sinks and builds up on the bottom; in between lies the narrow band of rapid temperature change from warm to cold called the thermocline.

In these waters, a thermocline condition usually remains in effect throughout the tail end of the Post-summer Period. As the sun grows less direct, seasonal, hard driving, cold winds and rain begin chilling the surface temperature of the water very quickly. As the heavier (colder) water begins sinking, it comes in contact with the warmer water below. This action forces the lighter, yet warmer, deeper water back to the surface. Eventually, the narrow thermocline layer ruptures, and a mixing or "turning over" process takes place. As the wind beats the water, the mixing action continues until it thoroughly homogenizes the water to a point where the whole body of water is the same temperature. This process also reoxygenates the deep water.

Turnover usually occurs after several days to a week of the first late-summer cold snap characterized by a succession of dark, cold, wind-driven, rainy days. This is a signal that the Cold Water Period is about to arrive. At times, you can actually smell the stagnant bottom water as it rises to the surface. You might even see dead weeds, decomposed fish and other bottom debris floating on the surface or washed ashore.

The actual turnover process itself takes place once the thermocline layer ruptures. But the turmoil that takes place usually adversely affects the fish for a period of time before and after this event actually occurs. In general, once the water temperature drops to about 55°F and the water clears perceptibly, cold water fishing patterns emerge.

Fishing during the Turnover Period on bodies of water that actually thermocline is tough, to say the least. However, since all bodies of water do not turn over at the same time, it is usually best to switch to waters which have already turned over--or bodies of water which have not yet begun to—or to waters which don't thermocline.

Exactly what happens to fish, and crappies in particular, during turnover, has yet to be documented. In fact, anglers are some of the best sources of information about this turbulent time. Fish are stressed during unstable conditions, so the best fishing usually occurs in areas where the turnover effect is minimized. Shallow waters are usually best, or perhaps, the shallowest areas of a lake which are least affected by the main-lake turnover.

If you're forced to fish a lake under these conditions, seek out the best available shallow-water cover. While you probably won't get into numbers of fish, a few stragglers could save the day from being a complete waste. Areas with weeds or wood are good choices.

The Turnover Period is a time of turmoil when fish activity grinds to a halt, although action will pick up as conditions gradually stabilize.

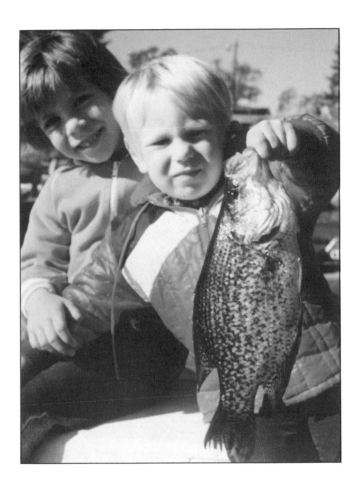

THE COLD WATER PERIOD (FALL)

A Time of Stability

Surface Water Temperature Range: 55°F and Below,
Down Near the Lowest Temperature of the Year
General Fish Mood: Neutral

This period spans the entire time frame from the end of Turnover to freeze-up, or down to almost the coldest water of the year on bodies of water that don't freeze. It is a gradual slowing down and stabilization of the entire eco-system. The water temperature descends to nearly its lowest level of the year, and the crappie's metabolism slows in response to the cooling water.

The combination of falling water temperature and diminishing light levels appears to stimulate crappies to shift into deeper water. In many cases, the turnover has literally opened the door to deeper, formerly unusable areas which were below the thermocline during summer. Now, some of this deep, reoxygenated water becomes usable.

Early on, fall crappies may still relate to the deep edges of healthy weed beds in natural lakes. In fact, they remain in such areas if the weeds remain healthy or if there is a lack of suitable structural elements in deeper water. However, once the weeds begin to die or competition for space with other larger predators becomes too tough, the crappies will leave. In some cases, they begin suspending in confined open water again on a regular basis.

If deeper, rocky points or sunken islands are available, however, these become extremely attractive to crappies. On meso lakes, humps in the 20- to 30-foot range may draw schools of fish as fall progresses.

Reservoir crappies begin schooling very heavily in deep (15- to 30-foot) creek channel bends with cover (wood). In flatland impoundments, the best areas generally lie at the mouth of coves as fish shift away from the current of the main lake. In highland impoundments which generally lack cover, even a single tree on a steep point may attract fish.

On large rivers, crappies leave the current areas in favor of deep (5- to 15-foot) backwaters or connected natural lakes. Apparently, the fish don't want to fight current in the cold water, so they stack up in slack-water areas. Huge schools of fish are possible by late fall. In small rivers without deep back-waters, however, the fish may be forced into deeper, main-river holes, pools and channel bends as the water level drops.

In all cases, crappies usually show less tendency to suspend near the surface. They may suspend, but it'll usually be within 5 or 10 feet of the bottom. Crappies often lie right on the bottom, in fact, and are very hard to distinguish on your depth finder, unless they become active and start swimming around, slightly above the bottom.

The Cold Water Period is a time of stability. While everything may move at a slower pace, it is nevertheless prime time for crappie angling. Heavy schooling concentrates fish in distinct areas, and once you locate them, you can have a field day. Slow, careful, bottom-oriented presentations are generally best to tempt the fish into biting.

THE WINTER SEASON
Which includes: The Winter Period

THE WINTER PERIOD
A Time of Tranquility
Surface Water Temperature Range: When a Body of Water is at its
Coldest for an Extended Period of Time
General Fish Mood: Neutral

This time frame spans the longest period of the coldest water of the year. Ice is common in the crappie's northern range; in fact, ice may cover the waters for up to 5 months or more in some areas. In more southerly waters, ice cover may occur only briefly in coves or wind-protected bays, while the main lake doesn't freeze. In other waters, the temperature may not even drop below 40°F, depending on geological location. In any case, the Winter Period encom-

In the North, winter offers both cold weather and hot crappie action. Here, Don Pursch, Camp Fish Senior Instructor, hefts a real braggin'-sized crappie. The magic lure? A tiny ice-fishing lure fished about 4 inches below a small Kastmaster spoon.

passes the longest period of the coldest water of the year.

Crappies continue to feed regularly all through the Winter Period, and in the North they can provide some of the best opportunities for ice fishing. In the South, open-water angling can be equally as good, although far fewer anglers pursue them at this time of year. Apparently, trying to fish a 1/16-ounce jig, 20 feet deep, from a boat, in the face of winter wind/rain/snow/sleet is too much of a challenge (grief!) for most folks. However, fishing from a toasty-warm fish house lying on top of a stable ice platform opens up numerous possibilities for crappie success.

In general, crappies relate to the same types of areas they used during the Fall Cold Water Period. The deep edges of cover (weeds or timber), channel edges, rocky humps, etc., all produce fish. The best areas usually lie in less than 30 feet of water and seldom as much as 40. In very small lakes, ponds, or small bays, the fish may actually move out right over the basin in the center of the deepest hole.

Similar to the Cold Water Period (Fall), most early and midwinter crappie activity will occur near the bottom. The fish may suspend within the first 5, 10 or 15 feet from the bottom, but are still somewhat bottom-related. Later in the period, as the ice cover thins or the water begins to warm, the crappies may show a tendency to suspend nearer the surface.

In all but lakes, rivers and reservoirs with the darkest water, the best winter crappie activity seems to occur around the low-light periods of dawn and dusk, or at night. Anglers night fishing from fish houses note that fish are attracted to the lighted area beneath their holes, just as night reservoir anglers see crappies drawn to the glow of the lanterns they lower below bridges. All in all, night fishing can be surprisingly productive during the winter months.

Crappies are extremely concentrated and catchable at this time *if* you fish very slowly with small lures and/or live baits, presented at their precise depth level. It may take a bit of experimentation, but it can pay dividends of big crappies and lots of 'em, when you hit the right combination.

Now let's take an indepth look at the various bodies of water that crappies live in. The following chapters on crappie waters will familiarize you with the details of lakes, rivers and reservoirs. Then, in later chapters you'll learn how to catch crappies all season long.

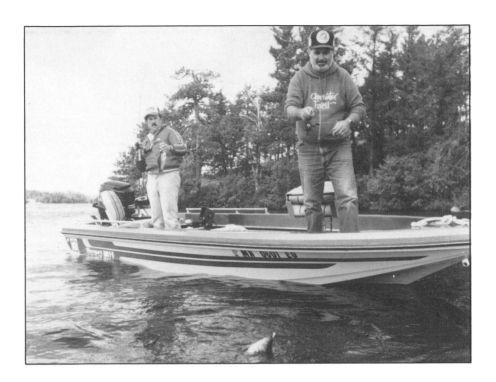

Chapter 5

INTRODUCTION TO CRAPPIE WATERS

In order to fully understand crappie behavior and location in any body of water, you must first determine the type of lake, river or reservoir you are fishing. The *IN-FISHERMAN* has classified each. The following chapters describe the classification procedure and identify those waters which can support viable crappie populations. We'll examine, in depth, the prime types of lakes, rivers and reservoirs that house crappies, and we'll explain how to identify each of them. The classification system is easy to understand and is an efficient method for analyzing waters. It's a building block in our educational process.

To begin with, it is important to understand how to categorize various bodies of water. We do this because different types of waters provide different kinds of fish habitat. Since fish location and behavior can vary between different kinds of bodies of water, you must have some idea of what options the fish have, in order to catch them consistently.

Natural lakes, for example, can be broken into "age stages" that begin at the youngest stage (primarily cold-water environments), advance to the middle-aged stage (primarily cool-water environments), and finally proceed to the oldest stage (primarily warm-water environments). In between these major categories lie numerous waters in transitional stages as well. These environmental shifts affect the entire fish community, and understanding them is vital to your fishing success.

Forces That Cause Lakes To Age

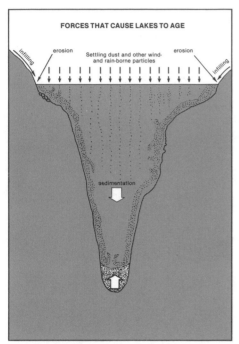

A number of natural forces combine to "age" a lake. Two are gravity and the weathering process. As a result, you have the following: 1. INFILLING—higher surrounding terrain tends to fill in lower terrain; 2. EROSION—large material is broken down into smaller material; 3. SETTLING—rain and wind-borne particles settle to fill in areas; and 4. SEDIMENTATION—material accumulates at the bottom of bodies of water.

Yes, there are many different lake types, and each category often has a distinct bearing on crappie population, location and behavior. This aging process is also true for rivers and reservoirs since they take on the characteristics of the surrounding terrain. In short, all waters are not alike, and you must approach them in the proper fashion in order to score consistently.

UNDERSTANDING WATER CLARITY

Water is the common ingredient in all lakes, rivers and reservoirs. Yet, even water characteristics can vary. Think of it: Some waters are visibly clearer than others. Water clarity is a very important factor in understanding any aquatic environment. Many times it is a key to fish location and influences your choice of presentation.

Let's take a closer look at water clarity, how to determine it, and how it affects fish behavior. As a matter of fact, water clarity has several major effects on crappie location, behavior and feeding strategies.

Take your generic lake—a hole filled with water. Now add fish, weeds, plankton, siltation, and run-off from the surrounding land. You no longer have clean, clear water, but some stained, off-colored variations. Even the clearest lakes, rivers and reservoirs aren't completely clear. Add even a few impurities, and the water is bound to pick up some color which affects the clarity.

How clear is clear? Well, you have very clear, clear, medium-clear, sort-of-clear—it's pretty tough to come up with an exact way to break it down. But you really don't have to. For all intent and purposes, fish response will be basically the same in any of these conditions providing the water is clear enough for the fish to see fairly well. How clear is that? Well, if you want a yardstick to work by, lower a white lure, like a jig, into the water on a sunny day, and if you can still see it at a depth of 6 feet or more, figure the lake to be clear.

When a white lure disappears between about 2 and 6 feet, consider that to be stained; by stained water, we mean discolored. The fish can still see fairly well, and weeds can still grow, but not like in clear water. Even though fish do not have clear vision, they make up for it through their sense of hearing.

See the difference? Clear-water fish can do one heck of a job on sight alone, but when they inhabit stained water, vision begins to lose its primary importance. Stained-water fish rely more on a mixture of sight and hearing (sound/vibration) to locate their prey.

The Three Basic Degrees of Water Color

Clear Water	Stained Water	Dark Water
lure disappears at 6 ft. plus	lure disappears at 2-6 ft.	lure disappears at 0-2 ft.

Lower a white lure into the water. Note the depth at which it disappears. This gives you a general idea as to fish behavior and the relative importance of sight vs. sound/vibration.

Let's carry it a step further. Put your white lure into the water, and if it vanishes in less than 2 feet, it's dark water. How'd you like to be down there trying to find your way around? It's pretty tough to see anything.

In dark water, vibration becomes extremely important. Fish can't see what's out there, but they can sense vibration and sound through their lateral line and inner ear. You can't count on fish to see much unless they are really close. But if you put some kind of noisemaker down there, chances are they can find it easier.

To help you visualize clear, stained and dark water designations, simply think of each in terms of weather conditions. Consider this analogy: Clear water would be similar to a bright, sunny day when visibility for you may be miles. A hazy or light-to-medium fog condition would approximate stained water, where your visibility may vary from a few hundred yards to a couple hundred feet. Dense fog would be comparable to dark water where visibility can be limited to several yards. Since visibility is restricted, sight becomes of secondary importance. For example, fog horns warn mariners of unseen dangers.

It's much the same for fish that inhabit the diverse waters of lakes, rivers and reservoirs. In essence, visibility is limited by decreasing water clarity, and fish must use other senses to locate food as the water becomes darker.

FISH BEHAVIOR

Most clear-water fish tend to feed at low-light hours like dawn and dusk, or during darker, overcast days. They can often be at a variety of depths, and can see your offering. Dark-water fish, conversely, often feed during the brightest hours. In fact, many dark waters experience "hot," midday bites under sunny skies. These fish are often restricted to shallow locations, and a little sound/vibration in your lure will help them find it.

Now, if clear-water fish are generally sight oriented and dark-water fish are vibration conscious, what about stained-water fish? Well, since that's an in between condition, you get in between reactions. The feeding times tend to be more spread out, fish can be on several patterns in different locations, and both sight and sound/vibration play an important part in lure selection. Slightly stained water makes "sight" lures like tiny jigs the higher percentage baits, whereas a darker stain reduces visibility and means you should use an action lure of some kind. It's an environmental balancing act, and water color is a key ingredient.

Besides affecting crappie behavior, water clarity will influence your presentation options. In clear-water conditions, you may have to use 2- or 4-pound test line for crappies; in dark water, you can often move to 12- or 20-pound

Clear Water	Dark Water
Fish can see well	Fish can't see much at all
Fish rely heavily on sight	Fish rely heavily on sound/vibration
Good light penetration	Poor light penetration
Oxygen is deeper	Low oxygen in depths
Weeds grow deeper	Weeds restricted to shallows
Fish can be found deeper	Fish often restricted to shallows
Fish feed more toward morning and evening, or at night	Fish feed more toward midday
Fish are more active on cloudy days	Fish are more active on sunny days
Heavy schooling	Fish tend to be scattered
Fish roam	Fish are object-oriented
Fish chase lures	Fish don't chase lures
Fish are spooky	Fish are less spooky
Water warms or cools slowly	Water warms or cools quickly

STAINED-WATER FISH FALL
SOMEWHERE IN BETWEEN

test line. By making these adjustments your catch rate will be greatly increased. Water clarity dictates these differences.

Clear-water fish rely heavily on sight and are generally less restricted in behavior due to their more varied environment. Dark-water fish rely heavily on sound and often live in a far more restricted environment, with fewer options. Stained-water fish are nearest the balancing point. Depending on the degree of water color, their behavior can swing either way.

Clear-water fish rely heavily on sight and can see well. The rule-of-thumb when fishing it is light line and small lures. Even if you look closely you'll barely see the 2-pound test line, split shot and tiny jig.

PERMANENT VS. TEMPORARY WATER CLARITY

So far, we've discussed clear-, stained- and dark-water conditions. They're more or less "permanent" or "typical" conditions caused by the local environment (surrounding soil, run-off, wind erosion, etc.). But what happens when it rains unusually long or hard, or when a heavy wind tears up a shoreline and washes all sorts of foreign material into a lake? Or how about when an algae bloom temporarily fills the water with suspended particles? Shouldn't that have a categorization all its own?

Normally clear water becomes dirty or turbid when rain or wind introduces outside substances into the lake. This is especially common in rivers and reservoirs. It might be a temporary condition, which changes the environment or a portion of the environment for a period of time. In this instance, normally clear water *temporarily* behaves like stained water, and the fish must respond by relying more on their ability to detect sound/vibration. Similarly, normally stained water temporarily takes on the characteristics of dark water under these conditions. Sight is reduced, and fish must rely more heavily on sound than they normally would. In order to catch fish, you'd use the same tactics that you'd normally rely on when fishing lakes with characteristically dark or turbid waters.

Permanent Conditions	Temporary Conditions
Clear	Normal
Stained	Dirty
Dark	Muddy

SUMMARY

As you can probably begin to see, many factors come into play when you evaluate the different environments that fish live in. The better you understand the options that fish have, the more effective you'll be at catching them. Water clarity is one such critical factor affecting these options. Be sure to keep it in mind as the following chapters describe the different classifications of lakes, rivers and reservoirs. Once you get a "feel" for them, you'll be able to predict crappie location and behavior wherever you travel.

Chapter 6

NATURAL LAKES

Every body of water has its own unique personality, a personality characterized primarily by its overall physical make-up. No two lakes are exactly alike. The lake's predator/prey relationships, amounts and types of aquatic vegetation, and numerous other structural considerations determine its classification. Very broadly, lakes are classified into three geological age groups: oligotrophic (young), mesotrophic (middle-aged), and eutrophic (old).

No matter where your favorite lake is situated, that body of water is constantly *changing*. In some remote areas, the change can be so slight that it passes unnoticed and might take a century or more to show a visible change. In other waters, this change might occur in 10, 5, or even fewer years.

This is the natural aging process (eutrophication) that all lakes pass through. In essence, according to water quality standards, a lake is getting older not so much in time as in *condition*. The initial stages of change may take thousands of years, but the final ones may happen quickly—especially with the addition of manmade causes. Throughout this process, the total environment of a lake—its structural condition, food chains, vegetation levels and dominant fish species—changes considerably. Man-caused eutrophication (aging) is due to expanding human population and, consequently, waste product disposal.

These changes in lakes have occurred so quickly that man has accomplished in a generation what nature would have taken hundreds or even thousands of years to do.

So, we classify natural lakes according to their environmental condition, not their chronological age. A lake is basically either young, middle-aged or old. Since some lakes are in between these broad types and almost defy classification, our classifications should not be taken as absolute. Instead, each category is meant to be a convenient point of reference—a definition we can start to learn from.

As lakes "age," their character changes. Generally speaking, geologically "young" lakes are deep and clear; older lakes are shallow and murky.

The natural order is such that on one end of the aging scale we find young lakes (oxygen-rich, deep water) which can support fish like lake trout and whitefish. At the other end, we find old lakes (weed-choked, oxygen-poor water) which can only support fish such as carp and bullheads.

A lake trout cannot live in a shallow, murky, weedy, low-oxygen, warm-water lake of the midwestern prairies; and carp have a tough time making it in the rocky, cold-water, weedless environment of a Canadian shield lake. Between these two extremes fall lakes of all types—each more or less hospitable to certain species of fish. We categorize natural lakes in the following nine phases.

THE AGING PROCESS

THE STABLE, YOUNG, INFERTILE,
COLD-WATER ENVIRONMENT PHASES
1. Early stage oligotrophic
2. Mid-stage oligotrophic

THE TRANSITION FROM COLD- TO
COOL-WATER ENVIRONMENT PHASES
3. Late stage oligotrophic
4. Early stage mesotrophic

THE STABLE, MIDDLE-AGED, MODERATELY FERTILE,
COOL-WATER ENVIRONMENT PHASE
5. Mid-stage mesotrophic

THE TRANSITION FROM COOL- TO
WARM-WATER ENVIRONMENT PHASES
6. Late stage mesotrophic
7. Early stage eutrophic

THE STABLE, OLD, FERTILE,
WARM-WATER ENVIRONMENT PHASE
8. Mid-stage eutrophic

THE TRANSITION FROM WARM- TO
VERY WARM-WATER ENVIRONMENT PHASE
9. Late stage eutrophic

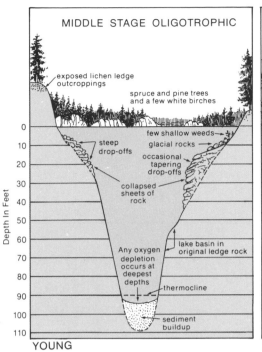

MIDDLE STAGE OLIGOTROPHIC

exposed lichen ledge outcroppings

spruce and pine trees and a few white birches

few shallow weeds

steep drop-offs

glacial rocks

occasional tapering drop-offs

collapsed sheets of rock

Depth In Feet
0
10
20
30
40
50
60
70
80
90
100
110

Any oxygen depletion occurs at deepest depths

lake basin in original ledge rock

thermocline

sediment buildup

YOUNG

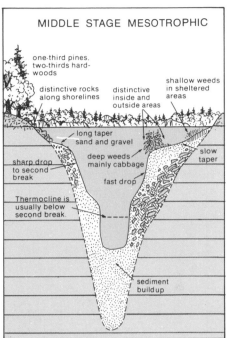

MIDDLE STAGE MESOTROPHIC

one-third pines, two-thirds hard- woods

distinctive rocks along shoreline

distinctive inside and outside areas

shallow weeds in sheltered areas

long taper sand and gravel

sharp drop to second break

deep weeds mainly cabbage

slow taper

fast drop

Thermocline is usually below second break.

sediment buildup

MIDDLE-AGED

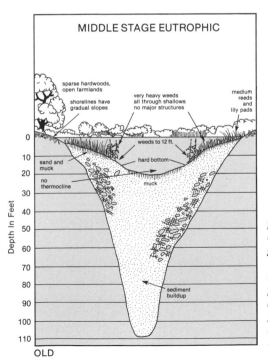

MIDDLE STAGE EUTROPHIC

sparse hardwoods, open farmlands

shorelines have gradual slopes

very heavy weeds all through shallows no major structures

medium reeds and lily pads

weeds to 12 ft.

sand and muck

hard bottom

no thermocline

muck

Depth In Feet
0
10
20
30
40
50
60
70
80
90
100
110

sediment buildup

OLD

The aging process depicted in the accompanying illustrations shows the basic changes of the lake basin, depths and weed-growth.

When you analyze a particular lake, remember that these categories are simply points of reference to work from. However, as you become familiar with the system, you will be able to more easily recognize a lake as being early stage eutrophic—instead of late stage mesotrophic, etc.

The youngest type of lakes—oligotrophic—typically have rock basins and are found almost exclusively in the upper portions of the North American continent. They usually have steep, sharp drop-offs, few weeds, pine-studded shorelines and a fish population composed chiefly of cold-water fish like lake trout and members of the whitefish family. The nutrient level of the water is usually low and oxygen is available in deep water at all times. Thus, the lake is termed infertile. Normally, "oli" lakes support low gamefish populations; a few pounds of gamefish per acre is common.

As this type of lake ages, the shorelines become less gorge-like and the drop-offs less abrupt and steep. Big boulders turn to smaller rock, and more sand and gravel becomes apparent. Weedgrowth develops. The trees that bound the lake also tend to change. Since the surrounding terrain changes, the water quality takes on a new character (more nutrients). These are the first signs of the transitory process between the oligotrophic and mesotrophic categories.

DISTRIBUTION OF LAKE TYPES

Mostly Oligotrophic

Mostly Mesotrophic

Mostly Eutrophic

Little by little, the lake changes and eventually develops characteristics typical of a middle-aged (mesotrophic) lake. When a lake reaches its mid-mesotrophic stage, much of the exposed rock, except right along the shoreline, is gone. Sand and some gravel now prevail in the lake's basin. The shoreline tapers become more gradual, more weeds appear in the shallows, and the trees that surround the lake begin changing from evergreens to hardwoods. A distinct thermocline and oxycline usually form. The lake is moderately fertile and is capable of producing many pounds of gamefish per acre.

By the time the next transition (mesotrophic to eutrophic) stage occurs, a lake, by geological aging standards, is getting old. First, it is becoming shallower. Sand begins turning to muck or clay in certain sections, and the erosion process results in less extensive shoreline tapers than in the mid-meso classification. Secondary drop-offs in deep water are obliterated or less defined.

Marshy areas usually dot certain adjacent sections. Hardwood trees and flat shorelines, rather than steep cliffs or high hills, rim the lakeshore. The lake is changing from a cool- to a warm-water environment.

When a lake shifts into its mid-eutrophic stage, it becomes a true warm-water environment. In its oligotrophic stage this body of water was a cold-water environment; in its "meso" stage, a cool-water environment; and now in its eutrophic stage, a warm-water environment.

By geological standards, this lake is now quite old. It has become very shallow, and the erosion process is near completion. Farmlands usually surround these waters. Thermoclines generally don't develop or last a long time. Shallow weedgrowth is thick, and sandy areas become quite soft. Water color becomes darker, so weeds only grow in shallow water, and the shoreline just sort of blends into the basin of the lake. Such lakes are often called "dishpan lakes" due to their overall depth and shape. Typically, these old lakes are very fertile and have high fish populations, although a significant percentage may be rough fish.

In a nutshell, this is the aging process all natural lakes go through. Study the accompanying drawings carefully, so you understand the different types of natural lakes. Most importantly, as you learn to recognize lake types, you'll learn what to expect in terms of crappie size and probable population density.

NATURAL LAKE TYPES								
OLIGOTROPHIC			MESOTROPHIC			EUTROPHIC		
EARLY	MIDDLE	LATE	EARLY	MIDDLE	LATE	EARLY	MIDDLE	LATE
CONDITIONS OF ENVIRONMENT								
COLD WATER		TRANSITION STAGES		COOL WATER	TRANSITION STAGES		WARM WATER	
LAKE TROUT								GAR BOWFIN BULLHEAD
				WALLEYE				
						LARGEMOUTH BASS		
					CRAPPIE			

The accompanying chart shows which species of fish will probably be present as a natural lake ages. Oligotrophic lakes are the youngest and eutrophic lakes the oldest, geologically. In between these two extremes lie mesotrophic lakes.

Crappies appear in late "oli" lakes. In fact, there are many lakes in southern Ontario that have viable populations of good-sized crappies. However, the prime, crappie waters for slab-sized fish are mid- to late-"meso" lakes which offer "confined open-water" environments.

By the time a lake reaches the mid-eutrophic stage, crappie populations may be high, but the average size fish is usually small. Apparently, inter- and intra-species competition for food and habitat takes its toll.

rocks and brush

SHALLOW WATER

reeds

pondweeds (cabbage)

mixture sand, gravel and rock

sand and sandgrass

shallow sandgrass and sparse weeds

sand

Typical Spawning Area

The cross-section on these two pages shows the various structural elements that could be found in many—but not all—natural lakes. The depths are relative. The edge of the weedline, for example, could occur at 8 feet or 18 feet, depending on water clarity. Some lakes might have extensive weedgrowth on the flats, and others very little. Reeds might be present or not. Some lakes have only one breakline or drop-off; others may have two. The shallow water, food shelf might be extensive or very short. There might be exposed rock or a limestone ridge, or there might be none. It all depends on the LAKE CLASSIFICATION TYPE.

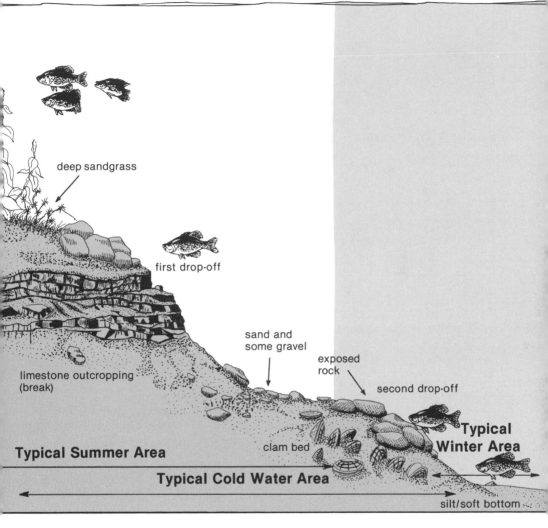

DROP-OFF AREA

BASIN

CONFINED OPEN-WATER ZONE

deep sandgrass

first drop-off

sand and some gravel

exposed rock

second drop-off

limestone outcropping (break)

Typical Winter Area

clam bed

Typical Summer Area

Typical Cold Water Area

silt/soft bottom

Nevertheless, the terminology holds. The shoreline is always the shoreline. The edge of the weeds is always a point of reference. Familiarize yourself with these terms. They will be used constantly.

Crappies use various portions of a natural lake on a seasonal basis. Note that during summer the crappies make heavy use of the confined, open-water area and often suspend within this zone at various depths. The key to catching summer crappies is usually finding schools of suspended crappies just outside structural elements and presenting a lure at the proper depth to entice a strike.

Many natural lakes produce jumbo crappies. This young fella caught this 1-3/4-pound fish from a deep reed bed in spring. Note the dark spawning color pattern of this male fish.

In the final analysis, this will help you fish smarter—not harder!

As a lake ages, the distribution of the various gamefish species also changes. "Oli" lakes chiefly support cold-water fish species like trout and whitefish. However, as the lake becomes more fertile and moves toward the mesotrophic stage, the cold-water fish begin to disappear. Walleyes often become the dominant species while crappies and bass begin to establish populations. The combination of weedgrowth, prey species and structural elements in these middle-aged lakes make them very conducive to supporting a variety of cool- and warm-water fish.

In fertile lakes, plants will root and form shallow weedbeds. Most oligotrophic lakes, however, do not have the proper conditions for such weedbeds. Instead, the plant life is free-floating and suspends at levels where species such as whitefish can graze on them and still remain within range of the trout. In these lakes, plant life is more abundant in deeper water than in the shallows.

In eutrophic (very fertile) lakes, shallow, rooted plant life provides both food and cover for all fish. Walleyes, crappies and other "semi open-water" fish begin to disappear, and the species associated with weeds, such as bluegills and largemouths, become dominant. The plant and animal life that sustained an open-water fishery in a mesotrophic lake diminishes sharply. This change continues until the lake ultimately degenerates to a point where only rough fish can survive.

Besides a lake's classification (which may not always fit into a neat little pigeonhole), another key element to understanding crappies is the available structural conditions. Some of the key items are: bottom configuration, bottom content, vegetation and water characteristics. In other words, what's the shape of the lake and how deep is it? What's the bottom composition—sand, gravel, rock or muck? What types of weeds are present and how deep is the weedline? What is the water clarity? Does the lake thermocline? All these features are important and play a significant role in determining where the crappies can be.

Youngsters and crappies go together like peanut butter and jelly. Several kids caught this nice mess of fish from shore. They used a simple cane pole, small bobber and minnow to get'em.

Obviously, no two lakes are the same; however, the structural conditions on many are similar. This similarity allows the *comparison* of lakes and aids in generalizing crappie location within a lake. Review the elements of structure and familiarize yourself with the terminology, because a thorough understanding of the principles will help you visualize what's beneath the surface of a lake.

Our information on crappie behavior, coupled with an understanding of a lake's structural conditions, are two of the key ingredients for success.

SUMMARY

Many lakes contain crappies, yet very few of them have the capacity to produce honest, 2-pound-plus fish. So, if you're after big slabs, be certain to select a lake that contains the size fish you're looking for.

Large, deep, clear lakes with plenty of open water generally grow the largest crappies. Crappies, by their basic nature, are a fish that often suspends in open water adjacent to some form of cover, and these lakes usually give the fish plenty of prime habitat. Therefore, when you're looking for crappies, figure on the best trophy lakes to be at least 500 acres or more in size.

Based on our *IN-FISHERMAN lake classification system, such lakes are* termed mesotrophic, or middle-aged. They're not only large, but are generally quite fertile as well. These lakes support an abundance of baitfish, insects and other aquatic life that crappies feed on. And, their varied structural make-up—scattered rock piles, sunken islands, weed-rimmed drop-offs, etc.—provides prime environments for both predator and prey. All in all, middle-aged lakes offer the best combination of elements for producing trophy crappies.

If you examine smaller, shallower (older) bodies of water, trophy crappies become noticeably rare. After all, such lakes generally have a restricted, open-water environment. Weeds are more prevalent, often choking the shallows. The entire life cycle of the crappies might, therefore, take place *within* the weedgrowth. Since crappies are not particularly suited to that type of environment, their growth predictably suffers. Such lakes are generally more conducive to largemouth bass or bluegills, and the crappies in these waters seldom approach trophy size.

In summary, this information, coupled with a few simple questions to the proper individuals (fisheries personnel, other anglers or bait shop owners), is the basis for evaluating a lake's potential. Of course, there's no better way to check out a lake than to fish it; however, this is a good procedure for narrowing down several possible lakes to a couple logical choices.

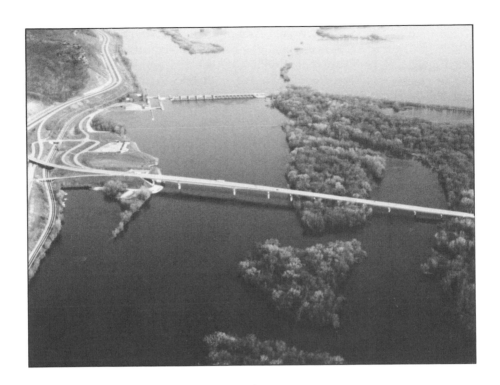

Chapter 7

RIVERS

Rivers come in many shapes, lengths and widths, and provide habitat for numerous species of fish. There are clear mountain rivers, silt-laden agricultural rivers, brackish tidal rivers, stained swamp rivers and many more. All are different in character and, therefore, provide varying aquatic environments for fish. While many rivers can support crappies, some rivers provide a better environment than others. In fact, different stretches of the same river can have contrasting personalities and, consequently, different fish species.

Similar to lakes and reservoirs, rivers age geologically. *Young, middle-aged* and *old* are terms used to describe a river's age. For example, a young, clear, cold-water river plunges downhill, flowing over and cutting through solid rock; here, trout and grayling could thrive. As a river matures, it becomes increasingly fertile, flows more slowly and begins to meander. In this mature section, the cool-water environment favors species of fish like walleyes and smallmouth bass. Finally, in old age, a river winds through a flood plain where the warm-water environment supports largemouth bass, catfish and rough fish. Each aging stage tends to favor specific species of cold-, cool- or warm-water fish.

Where do crappies fit in? Actually, crappies could exist in isolated stretches of most rivers that provide minimal environmental requirements. Yet, while they could "hack it" in a marginal situation, they'll rarely flourish. Oddswise, middle-aged and old rivers (or stretches) provide large areas of suitable crappie habitat with abundant prey. Depending on location, such rivers can be either slightly cool- or warm-water environments. Typically, these rivers offer a diversity of habitat that supports healthy fish populations.

Middle-aged and old rivers are slow-flowing, shallow rivers with broadened flood plains. The wide flood plains can create huge, complex, backwater areas with abundant crappie habitat. Flooded backwaters, oxbow lakes, and connecting lakes can be excellent crappie areas. Flooded brush, stumps and timber are common crappie attractors in river backwaters.

This is a hypothetical section of the Upper Mississippi River showing typical habitat areas. High and low water dictates the movement of fish from backwaters to the main channel. Side channels have reduced current while attached lakes provide very little current.

In addition, a maze of channels often provides a connection to other prime spots. Since backwaters can be a mile or more from the main channel, they don't function like a river. Current flow is usually negligible, and flooding is often controlled by a dam. Actually, these backwaters function more like a reservoir than a river. In fact, many are reservoirs and should be approached as such.

In summary, the combination of moderately high fertility, abundant prey and ideal habitat create a crappie paradise. Backwaters of the Mississippi, Ohio, Tennessee and St. Lawrence Rivers are all prime examples of river areas that offer hot, crappie action—both in numbers and size.

Oxbow and Flood Plain Lakes

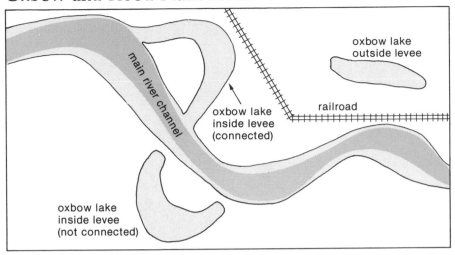

In the lower sections of the Mississippi River, oxbow lakes are very important crappie waters. Some oxbows are connected to the main river; some are not. A few lie outside the levee system while others lie inside the levees included in the flood plain. Oxbows connected to the river channel and lying within the levee systems normally provide the best crappie fishing.

RIVER CLASSIFICATION

Since there are variations in the aging progression along the sections of a stream, as well as some overlap between the abundance and presence of the cold-, cool- and warm-water fish species, the only way to view a stream is by stretches. In this sense, a particular stretch can be young, old, or somewhere in between in terms of geological makeup.

For instance, a stream might be quite shallow, have a slow taper for several miles, and possess a number of backwater areas with soft bottom and aquatic weedgrowth. Here, crappies and largemouth bass might find adequate habitat. But all of a sudden, this same stream might break into a sharp gradient as it shoots through a rocky, cliff-like area, creating a rapids and finally pouring into a boulder-based pool. This younger stretch, although further downstream, could house smallmouth bass and possibly stocked rainbow trout.

Different stretches of the same stream can have different personalities and different fish species. Rarely is a stream the same from beginning to end, because few regions are geographically consistent.

Because of these limitless variations, we devised the following method of classifying streams. With these categories, we can identify and recognize most river stretches found in North America. Of course, there will be exceptions; those parts in transition between types are much like a natural lake that has eutrophic bays while the main body of the lake is mesotrophic in character.

These classes are best viewed as guidelines to better understanding the rivers you fish and the quantity and types of predominant fish you can expect to find in them.

Distribution of Species by River Age Category

RIVER (STRETCH) TYPES						
VERY YOUNG	YOUNG	ADULT	MATURE	MIDDLE-AGED	OLD	VERY OLD
CONDITIONS OF ENVIRONMENT						
BEST SUITED FOR COLD-WATER SPECIES	TRANSITION STAGES	BEST SUITED FOR COOL WATER SPECIES		TRANSITION STAGES	BEST SUITED FOR WARM-WATER SPECIES	

VARIOUS TROUT ▪▪▪▪▪▪▪▪

WALLEYE ▪▪▪▪▪▪▪

SAUGER ▪▪▪▪▪▪▪

CRAPPIES ▪▪▪▪

SMALLMOUTH BASS ▪▪▪▪▪▪

LARGEMOUTH BASS ▪▪▪

Key: ▬▬▬▬▬▬ strongest populations
▬ ▬ ▬ ▬ ▬ weaker populations

This chart shows the species present in each river category. Notice how a particular fish's numbers peak and then gradually fade out as the river evolves. Note that each aging stage tends to favor certain varieties of cold-, cool-, or warm-water species.

Young, picturesque trout streams found in the mountains are usually unpolluted and unaffected by the hands of man. Despite their beauty, these streams are quite infertile since they run over rock beds and gain few nutrients from the land. For this reason, very young and young streams cannot support large fish populations. This relatively sterile environment limits them to a few types of fish.

Cold-water species such as trout disappear in the adult stage. In these sections with less gradient and a warm climate, the water flows slower and warms to a higher temperature where trout cannot survive. The environment now favors cool-water fish like smallmouth bass. In the mature stage, other cool-water fish like walleyes, saugers, northern pike and muskies enter the picture. Then, as a river gets older, the cool-water species begin to fade. Warm-water fish like largemouth bass and catfish become dominant, and rough fish like carp become common.

1. VERY YOUNG	—Brook trout and/or grayling
2. YOUNG	—Stocked trout and pike
3. ADULT	—Appearance of cool-water fish
4. MATURE	—Good populations of smallmouths and some crappies
5. MIDDLE-AGED	—Crappies, walleyes and saugers
6. OLD	—Crappies and largemouth bass
7. VERY OLD	—Mostly rough fish and a few crappies
8. TIDAL	—Backwaters of the ocean. Sometimes crappies.

Within this context, we can isolate stretches which best support crappies. These conditions usually occur in river stretches we term Mature, Middle-Aged, and to some degree, Old.

The accompanying charts describe the generalized makeup of the key river types.

	MATURE	MIDDLE-AGED	OLD
SHAPE OF CROSS-SECTION	Flood Plain	Broadened Flood Plain · Channel Bottom is Completely Smooth · Sand and Gravel Deposits	Natural Levees · Bluffs may Form · Sand and Mud Deposits
SOURCE AND GEOGRAPHICAL DRAINAGE AREA	This stretch may either emerge from or cut through a pastoral landscape, usually composed of sandstone and other soil types. The drainage area can include farmland as well as major urban and industrial areas, which can have a major impact on pollution levels. The number of tributaries start to decrease at this stage.	This stage often has a farmland origin. The drainage area is very large and fertile due to adjacent agricultural areas. Tributaries consist mainly of adult rivers.	Of pastoral origin and with a very large drainage area, siltation is common and considerable and must be controlled by dredging. A very broad, expansive flood plain has developed along with natural levees. This bottom-land is highly prized farm acreage. There are a very few tributaries.
WATER CLARITY	The water will be semi-clear to semi-murky. During high water periods, it will be very turbid, especially around agricultural areas, usually taking four to five days to clear up after a rain. Slower-running water will make the temperature higher. Aging will accelerate because of agricultural and industrial pollutants.	The water is murky to quite turbid most of the time due to the suspended mineral and soil particles and increased organic nutrients. Turbidity is a constant factor because of the large size of the watershed, a situation that makes angling difficult. Where this river broadens into a large lake, settling will occur and water quality will temporarily improve.	There is constant turbidity. Quality improves slightly where tributaries enter.
PROBABLE SPECIES PRESENT	Walleyes, sauger, some smallmouths, northern pike, muskies, catfish, white bass, sturgeon, a few largemouths, perch, crappies, carp, suckers, buffalo, and rock bass.	Northerns, saugers, walleyes, some smallmouths, crappies, a few muskies, silver bass, good largemouths and catfish.	Largemouths, catfish, crappies, some northern pike if the temperature remains low. The water temperature will determine available species.

	MATURE	MIDDLE-AGED	OLD
TYPICAL ILLUSTRATIONS	These stretches can be found in major drainage areas in any part of the country. For example, large stretches of the Mississippi and the lower Allegheny River in Pennsylvania.	The St. Lawrence River bordering the U.S. and Canada has middle-aged stretches, as does the Detroit River, and, of course, a good part of the Mississippi and Ohio Rivers.	Large rivers like the lower stretches of the Mississippi, the Ohio, and the Arkansas Rivers are examples.
KEY I.D. FEATURE	The ability to produce quantities of preferred game species such as walleyes, small-mouths, sauger, crappies, and northern pike. Deep pools provide refuge, and back-waters with cover (hooded brush) provide crappie spawning grounds. A mature stream can produce good populations of several kinds of gamefish; sandy, rock sections with fast water will hold smallmouths while the deeper, slower sections or pools will contain walleyes.	The presence of naturally reproducing walleyes and saugers mixed with fair levels of largemouth bass, plus some crappies, smallmouths, and northern pike. There is a diversity of habitat for just about any kind of fish. This is the last stage for quantities of naturally reproducing cool-water fish like smallmouths. Crappies become more abundant.	The absence of cool-water fish, especially the disappearance of natural walleyes. Oxbows are present.
GRADIENT AND DEPTH	Gradient: 1.5- to 2-foot drop per mile. Depth: Depth will vary. Some stretches will be four to five feet deep, while deeper holes can be fifteen to twenty feet. There is a lot of eight- to ten-foot water.	Gradient: One- to 1.5-foot drop per mile. Depth: Depth will vary from shallow, one foot deep, weedy backwater pockets to forty-foot pools. Runs to twelve feet are common. Under dams, gouges of fifty feet can occur.	Gradient: very slow, one to .5 foot drop per mile. Depth: depths can be quite substantial, running to twenty feet or more. Sixty-foot holes are not uncommon. Depth is a function of the amount of siltation and dredging activity. Most of these rivers are dredged. Gamefish location is often limited to banks and backwater areas.

	MATURE	MIDDLE-AGED	OLD
GEOGRAPHICAL MAKE-UP AND BOTTOM CONTENT	The main channel is composed mostly of sand. Siltation is now a significant factor; wing dams are sometimes constructed to control this. There are some rock outcroppings. Aquatic growth is common, along with a higher nutrient level.	Flows mostly through soft sedimentary rock and sandy subsoils. Sand is the dominant riverbed material. Time and erosion have pulverized the rocks and gravel. There will be a few rock outcrops along the banks of the river. This stage will exhibit well developed flood plains; flooding is common.	The stream bed flows over gravel and sandy areas (its own deposits). A hardwood forest occupies the flood plain. Sand mixed with mud forms the bottom. Rock and gravel are rare.
COMMON TRAITS	Rapids nonexistent; at best, a few shallow "riffles" will occur. Mature rivers can and do overflow their banks. They will begin to meander and develop flood plains. On this river stage, dams actually create miniature impoundments. Although they are called "pools," they function much like reservoirs. At certain times of the year, usually spring or fall, several species could be stacked up against the dam! The stream is an *IN-FISHERMAN* paradise and is the first stage that produces multiple quantities of preferred gamefish.	This stretch usually flows by river towns and metropolitan areas where pollution can be a severe problem. It is at this stage that a river really starts to show the buildup of nutrients, erosion, and pollution. Except for trout and salmon, just about any type of fish can survive. This stream will offer the most pounds of gamefish per acre, if it is unpolluted. Flood plains can create backwater sloughs or flat, high, fertile fields. A dredged, midship channel is usually maintained for barges, and dams with locks are common.	This stretch has often been straightened, leaving oxbow lakes connected or not connected to the main channel. Some oxbows are located within levees, while others lie outside. Flood plains create backwater sloughs and side channels.

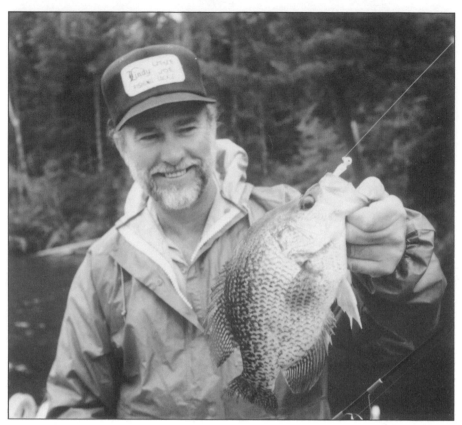

Do rivers contain crappies? You betcha, and here's the proof. Flooded backwater areas provide prime crappie habitat in many rivers.

Chapter 8

RESERVOIRS

What are some of the best crappie waters for both size and numbers of fish? Reservoirs! Yes, many impoundments provide world-class, crappie fishing action on a year-'round basis. The crappie is the undisputed king of many reservoirs.

Most anglers have heard of the fantastic crappie fishery on some southern impoundments. Many reservoirs offer mind-boggling fishing action for eatin'-sized and trophy crappies, all season long. In fact, their reputation for producing crappies is almost legendary. Each year, folks catch millions of tasty, 1/2- to 1-pound fish from reservoirs in many diverse areas of North America. Some impoundments also turn out a fair share of 2-, 3-, and occasionally even 4-pound-plus fish! And, the current world record white crappie which weighed 5 lbs. 3 oz. was caught from Enid Dam Reservoir, Mississippi, in 1957.

Obviously, the reservoir environment provides that special combination of ingredients which produces crappies, and lots of them. Let's take a closer look at reservoirs and pinpoint common denominators that may affect the growth and survival of crappies in impoundments.

A reservoir is an impounded body of water that is held back by a dam. The artificially impounded water floods the natural landscape such as marshes, plains, hills, mountains, plateaus or canyons. This provides a clue to reservoir classification.

The geographic area a reservoir is situated in has a direct bearing on the resulting fishery. In general, reservoirs in the North provide a cooler-water environment than those in the South. Yet, crappies exist in each area. For instance, a Wisconsin, lowland reservoir (flowage) can offer some good walleye fishing plus overlooked crappie angling. Similarly, a lowland impoundment in Florida may provide fishing for both lunker bass and slab crappies.

Taking a cross-section of North America, you'd see that some areas might be low and sort of swampy or marshy, or rather flat like an old flood-plain region. In other places, the terrain is hilly. Still others have mountains and highland ridges rising up to form foothills. These are usually low mountain ranges like the Boston or Ouachita ranges in Arkansas, the Appalachian chain in the East, the Cumberland highlands of Kentucky and Tennessee, or the low coastal ranges of the West Coast.

These changes in terrain provide a clear-cut basis to classify waters, since reservoirs lying within each of these landforms all have the same basic configuration. In other words, they have a similar cross-section and shape. For example, all canyon reservoirs are long and snake-like with towering, sharp, nearly vertical walls. On the other hand, waters impounded in flood plains tend to be wide with expanses of shallow flats.

KEYS TO IMPOUNDMENT CLASSIFICATION

The *IN-FISHERMAN*, impoundment classification system identifies six

Reservoirs constructed in similar landforms—even if they're in different parts of the country—are enough alike that we can fit them, for identification purposes, into six basic groups. These groups are: canyon, highland, plateau, hill-land, flatland, and wetland/lowland.

broad categories: canyon, plateau, highland, hill-land, flatland, and low-land/wetland. These classes are based on regional and geological aspects of North America's various landforms. Very simply, natural and manmade characteristics place an impoundment into one class or another. We'll discuss mainly reservoirs of more than 1000 acres, because many smaller ones defy orderly classification.

The basic shape of an impoundment is the major factor in determining its overall classification. By simply studying a topographical map of an impoundment, you'll be able to fit it into its broad classification slot. While there are some discrepancies, most times the classification is correct.

The broad classification of a reservoir's individual personality is also important. This personality is unique and depends on local factors such as bottom content, water characteristics, vegetation types, availability of prey, and fish species present. All of these may vary with the location of the impoundment.

A few of the most important facets of a reservoir's personality are: (1) annual water level fluctuation, (2) water clarity, (3) fertility, (4) temperature, and (5) effects of wind. All of these affect the personality of a reservoir which directly affects the resulting crappie fishery. By understanding both the reservoir's classification *and* its personality, you'll gain insight into the location and behavior of crappies.

PRIME RESERVOIRS

Prime crappie reservoirs usually fall into the flatland or hill-land classification. Barkley Lake, KY/TN; and Santee-Cooper, SC; are classic flatland examples and display the following features: stained water; shad forage; minimal water level fluctuations; shallow cuts and coves containing weeds, brush or timber; and a large, moderately shallow, main-lake area. In other words, they have lots of good, crappie habitat. Obviously, there are many other features to consider, and many other reservoirs have crappies in both size and numbers. However, flatland impoundments seem to be ideal and often provide the magic combination of ingredients to grow big crappies.

Hill-land reservoirs can also provide an excellent crappie environment—especially the upstream sections which are similar to a flatland reservoir. Toledo Bend on the Texas/Louisiana border is a prime example. Highland or plateau reservoirs can also offer a quality fishery in sections of the impoundment that contain hill-land/flatland characteristics. However, the greater depth and scarcity of cover in these reservoirs often preclude their being prime crappie waters.

Canyon reservoirs are normally a tough environment for panfish; however, a limited fishery may exist in some. Lowland/wetland impoundments, meanwhile, can offer good fishing, depending on the region and available habitat. In general, the crappies run small if the reservoir is weed-choked. If there are open-water areas and a modest amount of cover, the fish can grow to decent size.

TYPICAL IMPOUNDMENT FEATURES

The accompanying illustrations show various impoundment features. There are so many regional variations, that we were forced to adopt or coin words or phrases to describe them. For example, we dropped the word "bay" and became more specific by using the terms "cove" or "cut." The accompanying example is not meant to depict any specific type of impoundment. It is simply a composite. Note that it is divided into three sections.

secondary feeder creek

back end of cove

wash or gully

ditch

COVE

mouth of cove

INLET AREA

FLAT

headwaters or source

UPSTREAM THIRD

MID-LAKE THIRD

CUT
(cove not fed by creek, ditch, etc.)

bluff bank

straight run

FLOW

outside bend

inside bend

tongue

outside bend

inside bend

FLOW

RIVER OR CREEK CHANNEL BED

This illustration shows the difference between an inside and outside bend. The outside bend of a river or creek is "washed" the hardest by the water flow. Tongue areas are especially attractive. Remember, obstructions such as a fallen tree can slow the flow and provide cover.

primary
feeder
creek

RIVER ARM

large tributary

creek channel

creek
point

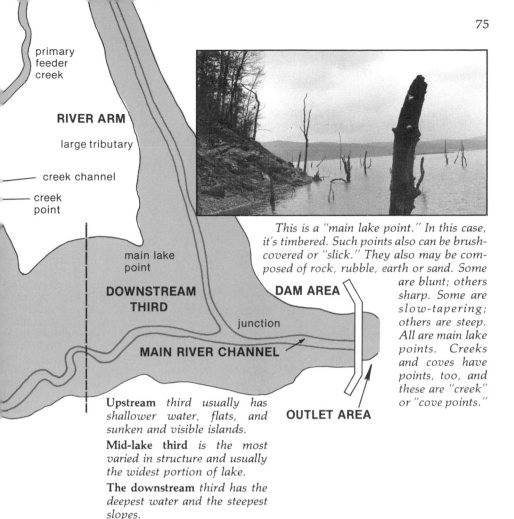

main lake
point

**DOWNSTREAM
THIRD**

DAM AREA

junction

MAIN RIVER CHANNEL

OUTLET AREA

This is a "main lake point." In this case, it's timbered. Such points also can be brush-covered or "slick." They also may be composed of rock, rubble, earth or sand. Some are blunt; others sharp. Some are slow-tapering; others are steep. All are main lake points. Creeks and coves have points, too, and these are "creek" or "cove points."

Upstream *third usually has shallower water, flats, and sunken and visible islands.*

Mid-lake *third is the most varied in structure and usually the widest portion of lake.*

The downstream *third has the deepest water and the steepest slopes.*

bluff
bank

River and creek channels with the proper depth are the "main highways" in a reservoir. Bends, the degree of bank slope, the make-up of the bank top, the amount of timber or brush at the top of the banks, and obstructions in the channel itself, all affect the exact location of fish.

steep
bank

top of channel bank

top lip of
channel bank

bottom may continue
to slope or break

← outside channel bank

← sloping bank

← inside channel
bank

river or creek bed

CANYON IMPOUNDMENT

Examples: Lake Powell, UT; Lake Havasu, AZ/CA; Lake Mead, NV/AZ; Flaming Gorge, WY/UT.

Some very long
tributary arms

River channel
may run near
shore

Water at inlet begins to get
deep quickly and remains deep.

Note: Practically no flats or humps
in water shallow enough to make
any difference.

Points along shore are
very apparent

Back ends of some coves
may be very narrow, steep
and have many feeders

Back ends of coves
usually pointed

Some very long
tributary arms

Back ends of some
long coves or arms can be
plateau in character

Two or three creeks
in backs of coves
are common

150-600 feet
deep

A

B

TOP VIEW

CROSS-SECTIONS

300 feet

dish-shaped
channel

may be small step in canyon wall

A

215 feet

steps may occur on
one side

one side slopes

channel is small cut

overhangs occur in some areas

one side vertical

B

PLATEAU IMPOUNDMENT

Examples: Lake Meredith, TX; Roosevelt, AZ; Clear, CA; Ft. Peck, MT; Garrison, ND; Banks, WA.

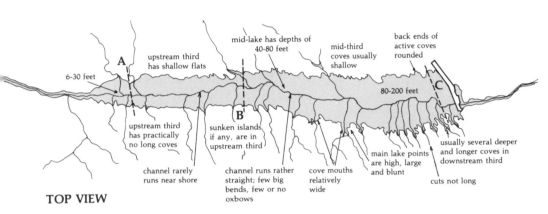

upstream third has shallow flats

mid-lake has depths of 40-80 feet

mid-third coves usually shallow

back ends of active coves rounded

6-30 feet

A

80-200 feet

C

B

upstream third has practically no long coves

sunken islands if any, are in upstream third

usually several deeper and longer coves in downstream third

channel rarely runs near shore

channel runs rather straight; few big bends, few or no oxbows

cove mouths relatively wide

main lake points are high, large and blunt

cuts not long

TOP VIEW

CROSS-SECTIONS

some bluffs present

shoreline flat or tapers before rising to bluffs

A   6-10 feet   dish- or V-shaped channel

50-60 feet   channel is dish-shaped

step, then a taper to basin

B

big, high bluffs

one side slopes more

flat bottom channel

bottom usually clean

basin may be steplike   80-200 feet

C

HIGHLAND IMPOUNDMENT

Examples: Bull Shoals, AR/MO; Dale Hollow, TN; Broken Bow, OK; Sidley Lanier, GA; Don Pedro, CA; Hopatcong, NJ; Amistad, TX.

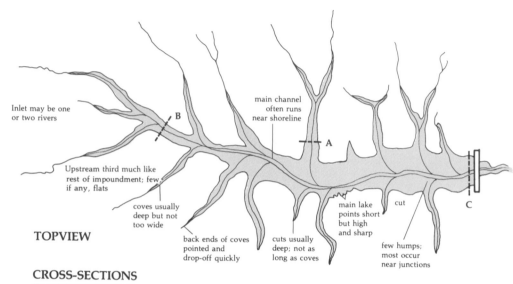

Inlet may be one or two rivers

Upstream third much like rest of impoundment; few if any, flats

coves usually deep but not too wide

main channel often runs near shoreline

back ends of coves pointed and drop-off quickly

cuts usually deep; not as long as coves

main lake points short but high and sharp

cut

main lake points short but high and sharp

few humps; most occur near junctions

TOPVIEW

CROSS-SECTIONS

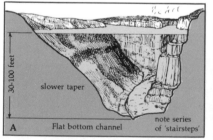

30-100 feet

slower taper

Flat bottom channel

note series of 'stairsteps'

A

30-60 feet

steep slope

flat channel

Bank not as steep as those on main lake

nearly vertical wall

B

very steep

may be 'stairsteps'

flat bottom channel

50-200 feet

C

HILL-LAND IMPOUNDMENT

*Examples: Lake Shelbyville, IL; Toledo Bend, TX; Felsenthal, AR; D'Arbonne, LA;
Kinzua Reservoir, PA; Council Grove Reservoir, KS.*

TOP VIEW

back ends of coves
not rounded nor sharp;
moderate depth

main river seldom
near shore

some flats

cuts short
compared to
creek coves

A

B

inlet area not
extremely wide

moderately
wide cove
mouths

extensive small humps

main lake not
very wide

C

points more pronounced
than flatland but not
sharp like highland;

CROSS-SECTIONS

moderate
drop-off

slope to basin
is moderate

6-12 feet

flats

A

no humps

flat creek bed

one side may
be very steep

slower taper

30-60 feet

B

small dish shaped bed

one side steeper
than other

45-175 feet

sometimes flat

C

slight roll at bank top, but no hump

dish-shaped river bed

FLATLAND IMPOUNDMENT

Examples: Kentucky Lake, KY/TN; Santee Cooper, SC; Ross Barnett, MS; Greenwood, NJ/NY; Carlyle, IL; Lake Seminole, FL/GA; Castle Rock, WI.

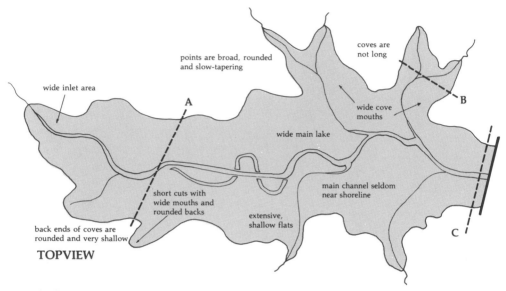

coves are not long

points are broad, rounded and slow-tapering

wide inlet area

A

B

wide cove mouths

wide main lake

short cuts with wide mouths and rounded backs

main channel seldom near shoreline

extensive, shallow flats

back ends of coves are rounded and very shallow

C

TOPVIEW

CROSS-SECTIONS

A

levee

6-12 feet

farmland

slow tapering drop

small v-shaped creek bed

B

12-15 feet

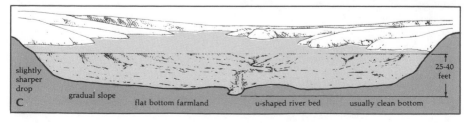

slightly sharper drop

gradual slope

flat bottom farmland

u-shaped river bed

usually clean bottom

C

25-40 feet

LOWLAND/WETLAND IMPOUNDMENT

Examples: Chippewa Flowage, WI; Bond Falls, MI; Black Bayou, LA; Taylor Creek, FL.

TOP VIEW

area near dam usually narrow

bays short and wide

few small cuts

50% marsh or bog

main river channel seldom near shore line

adjoining marsh

large flats

main body of lake wide numerous islands

old pond

channel bends are often gradual

many small islands

feeder creek almost undistinguishable

main lake points broad, big and rounded

coves usually wide

often indistinct, marshy shorelines

points often have some hard bottom

perhaps floating bogs

bays shallow

river channel almost undistinguishable

little rock piles main attraction

wide inlet area

fed by small rivers or creeks

indistinct channel at upper end

CROSS-SECTIONS

5-10 feet

channel silted in

A

flats may have timber or stumps

slow taper

10-15 feet

channel bank rolls

u-shaped creek bed

B

wide, soft-bottomed flats

18-35 feet

narrow, u-shaped creek bed

C

COMPARATIVE IMPOUNDMENT CHARACTERISTICS

Impoundment Classification	Crappie Forage	Depth	Main River Channel Characteristics	Feeders
Flatland	Shad, minnows	20-40' at dam 6-12' upstream	Seldom near shoreline, meanders, grealy altered, straightened with levees, dikes. Trees and brush along banks. Oxbows where channel has been straightened.	Creeks or ditches usually less than 20' wide. 1-6' deep, V-shaped bed.
Hill-Land	Shad, minnows	45-175' or more depending on region	Near center of reservoir. Natural state, usually quite straight. River bed is usually rounded.	Most have a distinct channel with sloping banks, brush and/or tree-lined.
Highland	Shad, minnows	60-200' or more depending on size.	Often runs near shoreline. Natural state has many junctions of creeks and river channels that are mostly too deep for bass use. Flat channel with steep walls.	Some are "dry-wet" (carry water only after heavy rains), rock bottoms
Plateau	Shad, minnows	50-200' depending on location	Runs through center of reservoir, quite straight, usually not deep with flat beds. Banks are generally clean, some brush may be found. Downstream ⅓ is generally too deep for bass use.	Little gullies or washouts from flash floods. Main feeders have high walls. Feeders most prevalent on downstream third. Short and wide at mouth.
Canyon	Shad, minnows	500-600' downstream; a few feet to 40 or 50 ft. at the inlet	May run near shore. Less distinct downstream. Very distinct, dish-shaped gorge upstream. Usually is too deep to be used by bass.	Very long creeks and small rivers. Can be 40-60 mi. long, and are shaped like main channel.
Wetland/ Lowland	Wide variety; depends on region.	Depends on region	The diversity of lowland impoundments makes them difficult to categorize.	

Cuts and Coves	Points	Shoreline	Bottom Content	Brush, Timber or Vegetation	Common Man-made Features
Coves are short, shallow with a small feeder creek running through, and have wide mouths. Short cuts with wide mouths and rounded backs. May contain weeds, brush & timber.	Broad, rounded, slow tapering. Some with brush; usually lack timber.	Mainly long, slow tapers. Steeper bluff banks on rare occasions.	Black soil, mud flats, some hard clay.	Standing timber in main lake is common—mainly cypress and willow. Brush in backs of coves. "Moss" is main vegetation.	Dam, roadbeds, causeways, ponds, levees, building foundations, rip-rap, cemeteries.
Coves are deep downstream, and may have large timber stands. Upstream much like flatland coves. Short cuts.	Rounded, usually with standing or cut timber. Some rare cases have boulders.	Slopes quickly to 7-12 ft. of water, then gradually to main river channel.	Sand, clay, loam, some mud flats, extensive small humps.	Brush and timber in coves, "moss" on shallow flats in main lakes. Has most weed growth of any reservoir type in the South.	Dam, rip-rap, high lines and pipe lines, fence rows, rock piles, road beds, cemeteries, drainage ditches, railroad beds, building foundations, marinas.
Coves are deep but not wide, and can be very long. Brush and timber common, sharp rocky points, some steep walls, some flatter, shallower. Deep cuts, not as long as coves.	Short, but very sharp and steep. Some slick; some with trees or brush. Mostly rocky.	Varies from heavily-timbered, moderate slope to cliffs. "Stair-step" ledges in some cases.	Sand, clay, rock, shale, limestone.	Timber is mainly hardwoods or pines and cedar. Brush varies regionally. Moss or weeds not common.	Same as hill-land except causeways, bridges, and rip-rap are not as common.
Coves have flat basins, short, usually wide in relation to length. Some brush may be present. Shorelines are steep in deep coves, flat in shallow coves. Short cuts with high sloping walls in downstream ⅓. Not as prevalent upstream.	Vary depending on region from very sharp to rounded.	Steep bluffs downstream; gradual slope upstream.	Varies from rocky to sandy, to silt depending on region. Usually clean. Upstream ⅓ has shallow flats.	Quite limited. Some in backs of coves. Some vegetation in upstream third.	Dam, roadbeds, marinas, spillways, others as mentioned above not common because of low populations.
Almost all coves are creek or river-fed. Some "dry-wet" with wide mouths can be very long. Some with 2 or 3 creeks.	Very distinct along sheer walls of reservoir and downstream portions of cove. Most composed of jagged rock. Can rise 1200 feet above water and drop 300 feet below water.	Sheer cliffs with mainly, some broken rock, slightly sloping solid rock faces or "mesas."	Mainly rock, some sand and gravel in backs of coves.	Some sage brush or other scrub vegetation found occasionally. Cottonwood trees and some highland cedar at extreme backs of coves.	Very few, some marinas, dams.

TVA'S FISH ATTRACTOR PROGRAM

Natural vegetation is sparse or almost totally lacking in many TVA reservoirs. This lack of vegetative "cover" for fish, together with other factors, results in the dispersion of fish populations. Recent experimentation with manmade "cover" in the form of artificial fish attractors has proven effective in concentrating fish in the area for food and shelter, and as a location for increased angling success.

A population study conducted on Barkley Lake indicated that brush fish attractors harbored 19 times the weight of crappies found in open-water areas without attractors, as well as 13 times more largemouth bass.

In joint effort, TVA and Mississippi, Alabama, and Tennessee State Fisheries biologists began attractor installation in Tennessee Valley reservoirs in 1977, and to date have put over 12,000 individual structures in 18 reservoirs.

Fish attractors are especially helpful to anglers unfamiliar with reservoir topography and conditions, and to those who don't have sophisticated gear for locating natural concentrations of fish. Fish attractors can increase catch rate and angler satisfaction, and achieve a better balance of sport fish harvest with the individual reservoir's ability to produce fish.

FISHING ON ATTRACTOR SITES

Fish attractors are piles of brush anchored to the bottom of the lake. Anglers can locate them by using a weighted line or a depth recorder. The following suggestions should help you catch fish that take cover in attractors:

1. To avoid getting hung, use wire hooks which will bend and pop free with a strong tug.
2. When fishing directly over attractors, put your anchors on either side of the brush pile to avoid scaring the fish. Slowly lower your bait or lure until you feel resistance, and then stop. (Count the turns of the reel so you can return to the same depth.) Hold a live bait steady in one place, or move a lure up and down. Both can be fished above attractors with a float.
3. If you are casting, stay to one side of the attractors and work your lure over the top or through the brush pile.
4. Trollers do well around attractors in coves, and around elongated deep-water sites. Troll parallel to strung-out brush piles, around the end, and down the other side.

Deep-water attractors are of two types and are marked by white buoys with a design depicting a fish. A single buoy indicates the center of a one-half-acre brush pile. Two buoys indicate either end of a long brush pile.

Cove attractors start in shallow water and generally extend in a straight line into deep water. Each site contains about ten brush piles. At the heads of coves, a white, 6-foot pole or a tree painted white to a height of 6 feet marks where attractors are located.

RESERVOIR TYPES					
CANYON	PLATEAU	HIGHLAND	HILL-LAND	FLATLAND	WETLAND
CONDITIONS OF ENVIRONMENT					
COLD	COOL			COOL AND WARM	

TROUT

WALLEYE—(NORTH)

LARGEMOUTH BASS—(SOUTH)

CRAPPIE

SMALLMOUTH BASS

Key:

——————— strongest populations

‑ ‑ ‑ ‑ ‑ ‑ ‑ weaker populations

Due to the wide geographic distribution of reservoirs, it is difficult to generalize about which species of fish may be present. For example, a shallow, wetland impoundment in the northern U.S. may contain walleyes and only a few largemouth bass. Yet a similarly shaped reservoir in the deep South may contain big bass and no walleyes! Obviously, geographic area plays a big part in determining the resulting fishery. In general, northern reservoirs provide a cooler environment than those located in the South, and the local environment may favor one species over another despite similar structural shape.

As far as crappies go, black crappies are typically more prevalent in northern impoundments, and whites tend to dominate in southern waters. Central-latitude lakes (Kentucky, Ohio, etc.) often have mixed populations, with the edge going to whichever species is most suited to the local environment.

Crappies tend to do best in a reservoir that provides a confined, open-water environment. There is both adequate cover (flooded trees, brush, etc.) present, and enough open water for suspended- or deep-water use. Thus, the best crappie impoundments tend to be moderately deep with a healthy amount of cover; hill-land and flatland reservoirs are classic examples.

Good crappie impoundments are seldom extremely shallow and choked with cover, as is the case with some wetland impoundments, nor are they deep or nearly devoid of cover, like most plateau and canyon waters. Some highland reservoirs, however, may host good crappie fisheries if they provide an adequate amount of submerged cover and suitable spawning areas. If not, crappies may be present, but not in significant numbers. It all depends on what's available.

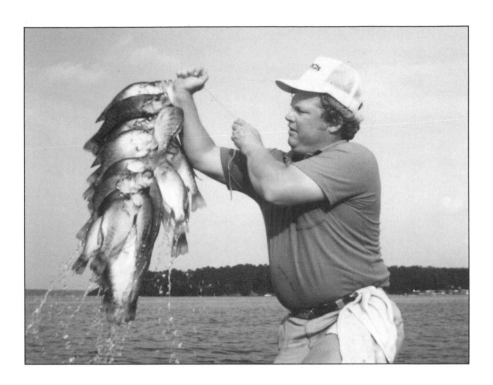

Chapter 9

SPRING

Cool-Water Crappies

When spring approaches, a lake comes to life. In northern natural lakes, for example, as the ice thins, the water warms and increased sunlight penetration sets off a new cycle of weedgrowth. This new weedgrowth produces more oxygen, raising the oxygen level in the water.

Other forms of life too small to be seen by the naked eye also begin to flourish. As various forms of plankton bloom, minnows feast on the newly found food, and crappies eventually follow suit. Even as the ice is retreating from the shorelines, crappies can be in the midst of a feeding binge that continues until long after the ice has left the lake.

This late-winter/early-spring feeding spree generally occurs first in small, shallow eutrophic lakes, because these lakes warm up very quickly. It's not unusual to find crappies in the shallow bays and channels of these lakes just several days after ice-out. Thus, these smaller lakes normally furnish the first open-water crappie fishing of the year, although you will seldom catch many trophies. The average fish size tends to be small since the crappies in smaller eutrophic lakes seldom achieve the large average size of their counterparts in larger, deeper mesotrophic waters.

About the time you're catching crappies in smaller lakes, larger natural lakes in the area will start becoming ice-free. After another week or so, the big lakes will finally have open water, and you can start thinking about slab crappies from these waters. Crappie location at ice-out in larger mesotrophic lakes, however, can be quite different from their location in small eutrophic lakes, depending on the available habitat. You'll have to make locational adjustments in order to contact fish.

Many mesotrophic lakes are so large and deep that they warm much slower than smaller eutrophic ones. It may take several additional weeks for a big lake to warm enough to draw baitfish and crappies into the shallows—particularly if there are no shallow bays or channels that warm up quickly. Until

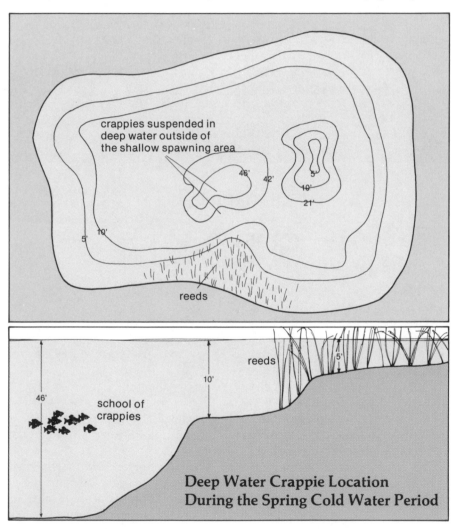

It's common to find schools of crappies suspended outside their spawning grounds in early spring. Later, as the water warms, they make a full-fledged pre-spawn movement into the shallows. You can get in on the action early, though, by locating them even before they move into the spawning areas.

then, the crappies remain suspended over deep water. Look for them outside of weedy flats, above sunken islands or near creek mouths.

A depth sounder or graph is an invaluable tool for locating these suspended fish. Slowly crisscross deeper areas adjacent to the shallows. Once you've located fish, it'll take actual fishing to determine whether the fish you see are crappies or baitfish.

When the ice goes out, crappie feeding periods may occur only during morning and late evening. But, as the days grow longer and the water warms, crappies will feed for longer periods of time until they seem to be feeding almost constantly. Remember, a fish's metabolism is regulated in part by the water temperature; as the water warms, the fish become more aggressive.

Eventually the water warms enough so both the baitfish and crappies enter the shallow water. The first places you'll find them are the same types of areas they use in smaller lakes—shallow weeds, back bays, channels, etc.—wherever the water is warmer than in the surrounding area.

There's one important point to remember about these ice-out, shallow-water movements. They are *not* spawning movements. Spawning usually occurs much later—at least a month after the ice goes out. Instead, these early spring cold-water movements are associated strictly with food. Crappies merely follow their food as it enters the shallow, warmer water. They will feed heavily in order to build up reserve energy for the rigors of the upcoming spawn.

Shallow, cold-water movements occur at the mercy of the weather. A stretch of warm, sunny days will draw fish into the shallows. A prolonged cold snap, however, will drive them out completely, and you'll find them suspended, once again, over deep water. Be aware that fish location can shift as the weather changes.

PRE-SPAWN LOCATIONAL ELEMENTS ON NATURAL LAKES

As the water continues to warm, crappies shift into a pre-spawn attitude. This generally occurs when the water temperature in shallow, protected areas of the lake reaches the mid 50°Fs. The key to locating crappies at this time is to find areas of shallow water that have the proper bottom content for spawning and are warmer than the rest of the lake.

Crappies generally spawn on a bottom that consists of either soft sand, sandy loam, or marl. This semi-soft bottom allows them to fan out a circular nest in which to lay their eggs. Hard sand or gravel may be too firm for nest construction, whereas soft muck is too loose to retain the nest's shape and is very difficult for the fish to keep clean. Given a choice, crappies will choose the bottom type that best suits their needs.

On mesotrophic lakes, the areas crappies use for spawning generally have a sandy bottom. These lakes, however, usually have large expanses of sand in the shallows, so sand by itself is not the only drawing point. Cover also becomes an important factor.

In mesotrophic lakes, spawning crappies often choose reeds as a favorite form of shallow-water cover. Reeds provide a network of obstructions that hide crappies from larger predators and protect the nest from egg-stealing in-

Typical Shallow Spawning Bay

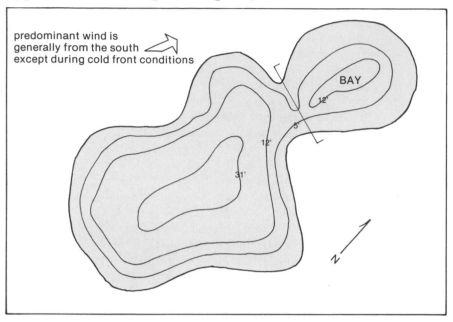

predominant wind is generally from the south except during cold front conditions

BAY

Shallow bays located at the north end of a lake are typically the first areas to warm in early spring. They receive the most sun exposure, and also collect warm surface waters blown in by southerly winds. Then, too, they are shielded from harsh northerly winds during frontal conditions. Such bays generally draw the first, shallow-spawning movements of spring crappies.

truders. Since meso lakes typically produce the largest crappies, you'll find that reed beds generally offer the best chance for catching trophy crappies during the spring season.

Reeds draw pre-spawn/spawn crappies in meso lakes, but where do the crappies spawn in eutrophic lakes? After all, eutrophic lakes generally have a softer bottom content and reeds are noticeably absent. In this case, crappies generally spawn around stumps or weed clumps in areas where the bottom content is conducive to spawning—the best available combination of cover and suitable bottom condition.

In eutrophic lakes, crappies often spawn in the same areas as largemouth bass. Bass are generally the predominant gamefish in eutrophic lakes and the crappies play "second fiddle" to the more aggressive largemouth. With an increase in panfish numbers and a decrease in open-water areas on these smaller lakes, the crappies are forced to "make do" in an environment they're not particularly suited to. They can hack this environment, but their numbers and size usually suffer.

The spawning areas for both crappies and bass in eutrophic lakes are typically back bays and channels where the bottom is sandy loam. Here, a thin build-up of decayed organic matter usually covers the bottom. The fish are able to sweep this away, down to a sandy base, forming a shallow, bowl-shaped nest.

When largemouths and crappies compete for the same spawning areas, largemouths generally spawn before crappies at a water temperature in the low to mid 60°Fs. About the time that largemouths have finished spawning, crappies move into the same areas to spawn. In fact, it's not unusual to see crappies and late-spawning bass in the same general area. This staggered use of limited habitat is nature's way of making the best use of available spawning habitat.

SPECIFIC CRAPPIE LOCATION DURING THE PRE-SPAWN PERIOD

We've established that crappies prefer to spawn on a sandy type soil in the vicinity of some form of shallow cover. The final locational aspect we need to consider is water temperature. Once this is determined, pre-spawn crappies are easily located.

Crappies have an innate ability to locate and eventually spawn in shallow areas that are warmer than the surrounding water. Whether they seek the warmer water or just accidentally find it and remain there is open to debate. Nevertheless, once you locate warmer areas having the proper cover and bottom content, you'll find fish.

Typical warmer areas are small bays and channels that are located along the north shore of the lake. These areas receive the full warming effect of the sun; those along the southern shore are usually shaded since the sun is low in the southern sky at this time of year.

Furthermore, predominantly warm, southerly winds blow the warmer surface waters toward the northern shore, warming the water further still. And in the event of a cold front, the northern shoreline protects the shallows from cold, harsh, northerly winds. Thus, shallow, protected areas at the north end of the lake are generally your best bet for the earliest pre-spawn movement of crappies.

Sunlight plays an even larger part in the spawning cycle than simply warming the water. The sunlit areas support an abundance of small minnows and plankton, providing newly-hatched crappies with the food source they require. By comparison, shaded areas are cold and sterile and contain far fewer fish—adults as well as young.

Wind is another factor to contend with. The better spring crappie areas are usually fairly calm and are protected from excessive wind or wave action. High winds can force crappies out of their spawning areas and out to the deeper adjacent drop-offs. Once the weather stabilizes, the fish usually move back into the shallows. However, a long period of high winds with cool temperatures will delay and sometimes even prevent spawning. That's one reason why shallow, protected bays are good at this time of the year. They not only warm fast and hold their temperature, but the lack of high winds striking the bay allows the warm water to remain in the bay instead of being washed out and replaced by the cooler water of the main lake.

Another favorable aspect of bay areas is that the water is usually slightly darker than in the main part of the lake. Why? Many bays are heavily choked with weeds during the summer months. During winter these weeds die and fall to the bottom and decay. Small floating particles from these weeds can color or stain the water. These particles absorb the sun's energy, warming the water more rapidly than clearer, main-lake water. Cloudy water also holds its temperature longer when the weather begins to cool.

Main-lake, shoreline weed areas can also attract fish, but it's usually only during ideal spawning times—a hot sun with warm, calm days or merely a slight breeze. Play the percentages by fishing areas that are protected from wind, because you're much more likely to find crappies here than in wind-swept areas.

Creek outlets are also excellent crappie areas in spring, especially if there's cover nearby. Creek outlets act as funnels (somewhat like the drain in your bathtub) to draw off the warmer surface water. As the warm surface water is pulled toward the creek, the area adjacent to the creek mouth becomes much warmer than the main lake, creating an ideal spring spot for crappies. Such areas remain good until the temperature of both the run-off water and the lake equalizes.

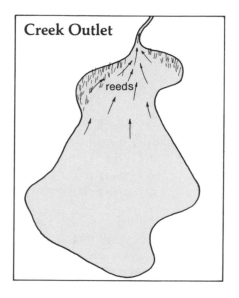

The pulling action of a creek outlet draws warm surface waters to the area as it drains the lake. It's another good place to look for crappies in the spring.

If cover is nearby creek inlets are also very good areas. Since creeks pour warm, spring, run-off water into the main lake, it always pays to check them out. These areas, however, only remain good as long as the run-off water temperature exceeds that of the main lake.

One last valuable point to remember about both inlets and outlets is the huge buildup of small insects, zooplankton and young baitfish for crappies to feed on. These always attract fish early in the year.

CRAPPIE PRESENTATION

Let's begin our look at crappie presentation with crappies that are still suspended in deep water—prior to their shallow pre-spawn movement. Although suspended crappies are often difficult to locate during most of the year, they're usually fairly easy to find prior to spawning time. Why? Because you know the general vicinity of the lake they'll be in. Even if they're still suspended, they're usually close to the shallow areas where they'll spawn. This narrows down your locational options to a relatively small portion of the lake.

As soon as the ice leaves the lake, scan the shallows with polarized sunglasses to determine potential crappie-spawning areas. While you're doing this you should be able to spot any crappies that have penetrated the shallows. If you fail to spot a concentration of crappies, proceed to the first deep-water area adjacent to shallow bays or potential spawning sites and look for any crappies suspended nearby.

As we said before, the depth finder or graph is a valuable tool for spotting these fish. A systematic scan of the area will tell you the location of fish. You'll spot a wide band of fish signals up well off the bottom, which indicates suspended fish.

Begin fishing by drifting or slowly trolling across the area where you've spotted fish. Turn the power up on your depth finder; this helps you spot fish easier. Crappies appear as flashes on the dial, and stray fish may range out as far as fifty feet from the main school. You want to fish the main concentration of crappies, so try to position yourself near the biggest concentration of flashes.

Perhaps the best way to catch suspended crappies is with a tiny jig/minnow combination. Hook a small fathead minnow on the back of a 1/16-ounce crappie jig and cast it out across the crappie school. Light spinning tackle and

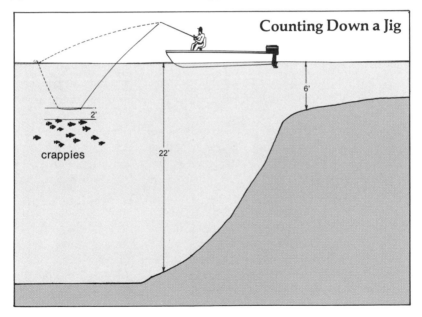

One of the best ways to catch deep-water crappies is to count a jig down to their level and then retrieve it through or slightly above the school. If they're active, they'll keep coming up to a jig cast above them. By doing this, you catch a lot of fish without spooking the school below.

If the crappies are relatively inactive, though, you've got to put the jig right in the midst of them. Then you risk spooking them. But the trick of keeping the jig above them should be kept in mind for prime conditions.

4-pound-test line enable you to do this with ease. Allow the jig to sink until it reaches a depth at, or slightly above, the level of the crappies. Then gradually swim the jig through this depth level by slowly reeling it in.

The best jigs to use in this deeper, cold water are usually tiny marabou jigs. A very slow drop rate and minimum action is perfect for crappies.

Each jig has a drop speed that is characteristic of its design. By counting "one thousand, two thousand, three thousand, etc." you'll know how far the jig has sunk. When it reaches the level where your depth finder indicates the crappies are, begin your retrieve.

It's generally best to keep the jig just above the level of the crappies, rather than below them. Crappies show a definite tendency to move up for food instead of down for it. By keeping the jig above them, you're making it an easy meal.

If you start catching crappies directly beneath the boat, you don't need to cast for them. Simply lower the jig to their level and hold it there. This is easily achieved by placing a rubber band around the spool of your spinning reel once the jig has reached the proper depth. This prevents excess line from running out. Each time you lower the jig it returns to the proper depth and stays there.

You can experiment with a slow pumping action but, in general, you don't want to add extra action to the jig by moving the rod tip. Keep the jig's movement slow and steady.

Crappies prefer this type of lure movement, particularly in cold water. They're not about to chase a meal, but they will strike a lure that is presented directly in front of them.

Suspended crappies are generally most active during the low-light periods of morning and evening. That's not to say you can't catch them during the day, however. It's just a little harder to trigger them. When you do hook a fish, let it fight momentarily in the vicinity of the school. This generally triggers their competitive urge and you may trick a number of fish into becoming active and hitting your jig.

As the weather and water grow steadily warmer, crappies progressively shift more toward the shallows. You can follow them on a daily basis and catch them long before shallow-water anglers make contact. You'll also know approximately when they're ready to move up into the shallows, so you'll be able to take advantage of it.

Just prior to their movement into the shallows, crappies remain directly outside the spawning areas, generally along a deep weedline or drop-off. They'll use this "pivot point" area for several days, and then finally move up into the shallows. Cold weather, however, often chases them right back out again. This is sort of a balancing act, with fish location and behavior depending on the weather. The weedline drop-off (pivot point) will almost always attract and hold some fish as they move in or out of the shallows. It's especially good to know these holding areas if bad weather strikes and the fish are forced out of the shallows.

The jig presentation discussed earlier is excellent for catching crappies in this holding area. You can simplify it even further by placing a bobber on the line. This keeps the jig at exactly the proper depth. The bobber is only effective, however, if the fish are within 8 feet of the surface. In deeper water, a bobber

Spring and fast crappie action go hand in hand. Dave Csanda hoists an honest 2-pound black crappie taken from a deep reed clump.

Pattern Progression In Spring

Crappie Location in a 5 Pattern Lake — Shortly After Ice-out — 450 acres

rock · reeds · mixed pond weeds and coontail — weedgrowth to 8-10'

*Note: This is not meant to depict exact location. For example, crappies in the pivot area aren't necessarily suspended off the drop-off, but may be up on the flat at times.

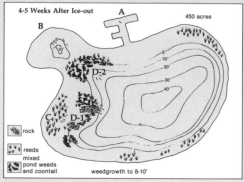

4-5 Weeks After Ice-out — 450 acres

rock · reeds · mixed pond weeds and coontail — weedgrowth to 8-10'

1-1/2 Weeks After Ice-out — 450 acres

rock · reeds · mixed pond weeds and coontail — weedgrowth to 8-10'

Crappie Location Based on Available Shallow Patterns — 450 acres

rock · reeds · mixed pond weeds and coontail — weedgrowth to 8-10'

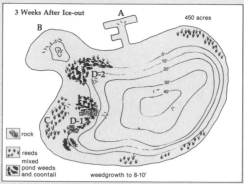

3 Weeks After Ice-out — 450 acres

rock · reeds · mixed pond weeds and coontail — weedgrowth to 8-10'

5 Pattern Lake

| | Shallow Patterns | | | Deep Patterns | |
	Canals	Bays	Reeds	Pivot Point (drop-off)	Open Water
Week 1	yes	no	no	yes	yes
Week 2	yes	yes/no	no	yes	yes
Week 3	yes	yes	yes/no	yes	yes/no
Week 4	yes/no	yes	yes	yes/no	no
Week 5	yes/no	yes	yes	yes/no	no

At ice-out, expect crappies schooled mainly along drop-offs or in open water. If canals are available (AREA A), expect some pivot-point (drop-off) crappies to move to canals, and some open-water fish to move to the pivot point. Later, if bays (AREA B) are also available, expect more pivot-point crappies to move to them, and still more open-water crappies to move to the pivot-point. Still later, if reed beds are available (C), expect most of the remaining pivot-point and open-water crappies to move into them. Finally, deep reed humps (D-1, D-2) will draw fish. This progression may take 3 to 5 weeks, as shown in the 5 PATTERN LAKE example.

If shallow-water options aren't available, crappies hold longer in the two deep-water patterns. For example, note that the 4 PATTERN LAKE has no canals and sees little or no shallow-water crappie activity the first two weeks after ice-out. The 3 PATTERN

LAKE *has even fewer options; with no canals or shallow bays to warm up early, the crappies remain in deep-water areas for a much longer time. It may take three weeks for the shallow, reed areas to warm up enough to attract fish.*

In short, fish relate to the available habitat. However, once you understand their options, you can catch them consistently.

4 Pattern Lake
(no canals)

| | Shallow Patterns | | | Deep Patterns | |
	Canals	Bays	Reeds	Pivot Point (drop-off)	Open Water
Week 1	no	no	no	yes	yes
Week 2	no	yes/no	no	yes	yes
Week 3	no	yes	yes/no	yes	yes
Week 4	no	yes	yes	yes	no
Week 5	no	yes	yes	yes/no	no

3 Pattern Lake
(no canals or bays)

| | Shallow Patterns | | | Deep Patterns | |
	Canals	Bays	Reeds	Pivot Point (drop-off)	Open Water
Week 1	no	no	no	yes	yes
Week 2	no	no	no	yes	yes
Week 3	no	no	yes/no	yes	yes
Week 4	no	no	yes	yes	yes/no
Week 5	no	no	yes	yes	no

Fewer shallow water patterns mean crappies spend more time in deep water.

arrangement becomes unwieldy and you're better off casting a jig and letting it sink to their level.

Once the crappies leave the holding area and penetrate the shallows, you're in for some of the most exciting fishing of the year. Shallow crappies are generally easy to locate, but if you expect to catch fish, you still must match your presentation to the areas being fished. The easiest way to do this is to tailor your approach to the type of cover the fish are using. Here's how to catch shallow-water crappies using the tips and techniques described in Chapter 14.

Crappies in meso lakes usually spawn in the reeds. At this time of year you'll find that the ice has bent or broken many reeds. Mixed among these are the straighter stalks of reeds which are beginning to grow. This jumble of reeds provides cover and indicates a prime crappie spawning area.

A bobber and jig set-up is the best way to fish reed clumps. Place the bobber approximately 2 feet above the jig. You seldom need to add a minnow to the jig, because pre-spawn crappies in these areas are generally quite active and will readily strike a plain jig.

We prefer to use a long 9- or 10-foot rod when fishing reeds. The long length serves a dual purpose. First, it allows for easy casting of the light jig/bobber combination. A nice, slow, even arm motion is all it takes to lob the jig out. It should enter the water with minimum splash to prevent spooking the fish.

Second, and very important, the long rod will give you increased leverage

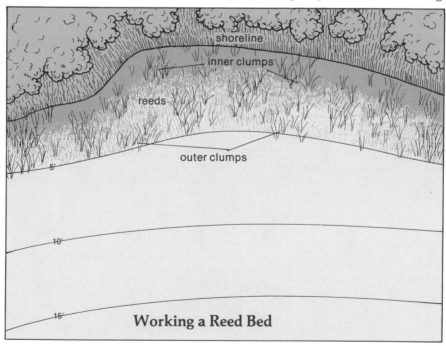

Working a Reed Bed

It's usually best to work the outer reed clumps first, and then move into the reed bed. This allows you to catch the outer fish first and then go after the ones inside. If you just shoot right inside, you run the risk of spooking many of the crappies. Work the edges first.

on the fish. You'll be able to lift even the largest crappies to the surface and drag them across the tops of the broken reeds. Shorter rods don't allow you to do this; they force you to fight the fish down in the reeds. With light, 4- or 6-pound-test line you'll break the fish off repeatedly unless you bring them to the surface.

The first reed clumps that crappies use are generally located on the outside, deeper edge of the reeds. Many anglers fish only these outer areas, because they occasionally catch fish there. These outer spots are excellent areas during the early pre-spawn, but later most of the crappies generally penetrate the main body of the reeds. They'll spread out and relate to the thickest reed clumps, and it's not unusual to catch several fish from a single heavy clump.

The best way to catch these fish is to cast the jig and bobber to the windward side of visible reed clumps. Allow the wind to drift the lure into the clumps. It doesn't take long to learn if the fish are present.

In order to take maximum advantage of an area, first work the outer reed clumps. After they've been fished thoroughly, proceed into the reeds and work the inner clumps. This is better than blasting your way right into the reeds and spooking the fish. Use your electric motor to slowly and effectively work the area, and you'll catch plenty of crappies.

Stumps provide a somewhat different situation and need to be approached in a slightly different manner. Many stumps hold one or two fish, but you'll seldom see a large concentration of crappies in one spot. This tends to make

Crappies Relating to Stumps

Crappies often relate very closely to stumps in early spring. It's common to find small groups of fish down among the washed-out roots. They're not too anxious to leave the protection of the roots, and usually you're forced to fish them very slowly and carefully in order to entice a strike.

them spooky and more reluctant to feed. Stump crappies don't exhibit the tight schooling behavior and competitive urge that reed crappies do, so you're generally forced to fish stump areas more slowly and carefully in order to catch fish.

Since stump crappies are often spooky it pays to approach stumps with the sun in your face to prevent throwing your shadow across the water. You can use the same jig and bobber set-up as in reeds, but fish slower. Cast three feet upwind of a stump and let the wind drift the jig past one side of the stump. Then cast again and let the jig drift by the other side. Stump crappies seem more prone to contemplate your offering, so it pays to fish your way very slowly and quietly through the area.

COMPARING SPRING CRAPPIE LOCATION ON LAKES, RIVERS AND RESERVOIRS

While we've keyed on natural lakes thus far, pre-spawn crappie behavior is strikingly similar in reservoirs, as well. As the water warms, crappies will begin shifting into shallow cuts and coves in search of warmer water.

Since fluctuating water levels often prevent or hinder substantial weed-growth from developing in impoundments, you can expect crappies to relate heavily to "wood"; stumps, timber, brush, fish attractors, etc., are all potential areas if they lie at the proper depth. Chapter 13, "Reservoirs," describes this aspect of spring crappie movement in detail.

River crappies generally move into shallow backwater (non-current) areas in spring. Their behavior is almost a carbon copy of that displayed by crappies in impoundments. As the other areas warm, they become productive, too.

Once you understand the available habitat, crappie behavior becomes predictable. For example, in the accompanying illustration, crappies are moving toward shallow, protected areas in spring. In the natural lake, they use canals; then bays; then shoreline reed beds; and finally, main-lake reed clumps. As each area warms, it begins to attract fish.

Note the parallels in the other examples. In the shallow reservoir cove, the crappies first use shallow, protected cuts; then cover in the general end of the cove; then shoreline "wood;" and finally, deeper brushy humps in the main cove. In the oxbow lake connected to a river, the fish first use shallow back-

Spring Crappie Areas

Back bays and shallow coves with sheltered cover typically provide the best pre-spawn/spawn crappie areas. Oxbow lakes or flooded river backwaters are classic examples. Crappies will hold along the edges of deep weeds or timber prior to spawning, and then move into the shallows to feed or seek nesting sites.

Large reservoirs and natural lakes usually have main-lake crappie spawning, too. All of the fish don't head for the bays or coves. Shallow, brushy humps in reservoirs, or main-lake reed beds in natural lakes, often host a portion of the spawn—particularly for the big fish. Since the water in the main lake typically warms more slowly than in back bays or coves, the best activity there typically occurs a week or two after the shallows start poppin'.

NATURAL LAKES

In spring, natural-lake anglers often rely on three, shallow-crappie locational patterns: canals (AREA A), bays (AREA B), and main-lake reed beds (AREA C).

Canals warm quickly, and crappies may begin to use them shortly after ice-out. The best canals are wind-protected, have some water color, only one inlet as opposed to flow-through canals with two or more, and secondary arms. Good canals also offer cover, often in the form of boat hoists or docks.

A week or so after crappies begin to use canals, they may enter shallow bays. The

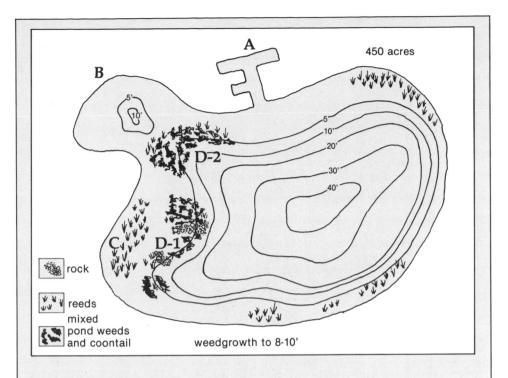

450 acres

weedgrowth to 8-10'

rock

reeds

mixed pond weeds and coontail

AREA	CONDITION		
A	canals, shallow cuts, or connected waters	C	main-lake, shoreline-oriented cover
B	back ends of bays, coves, or backwaters	D	shallow, main-lake hump with cover

best bays warm quickly and offer cover. A good bay usually also has a deeper hole in it. Holes offer refuge to shallow crappies when cold-front conditions strike.

Eventually, crappies begin to frequent main-lake reed beds. The best reed beds are usually the largest beds offering the most cover. Reed-bed activity usually begins 2 to 3 weeks after canal activity, and a week or so after activity in bays. To find crappies in reed beds, use your electric motor to quietly slide through the reeds and look for them.

A fourth, largely ignored pattern occurs in AREAS D-1 and D-2. Deep, 3- to 5-foot reed beds often host a portion of the crappie spawn—particularly for big fish. These are the last spawning areas to warm up and see the last spawning activity. They're often tough to fish due to their exposure to the wind, however.

RESERVOIRS

Here's a typical, shallow-spawning cove in a reservoir. The spring-crappie areas may look different than those in a natural lake, but the principles are the same. Once you get the hang of it, you'll notice many similarities in how crappies adapt to available habitat.

AREA A is a shallow, protected, brushy cut, off the back end of the cove. It's probably the first area to warm and attract spring crappies. AREA B is the brushy end of the cove itself. The brush-lined shorelines are the next areas to attract shallow fish.

AREAS C-1 and C-2 are similar to B, but are more main-lake oriented. They'll attract fish, but usually later than A or B due to the deeper, cooler, slower-warming water at the mouth of the cove.

AREA D is a shallow, brushy hump along the main river channel. It's a big-fish spot. It's also the last spawning area to warm, and will see the last flush of spawning fish.

During cold fronts, crappies may pull off the flats, shorelines and humps and head

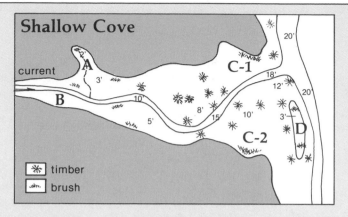

toward deeper water. Deep trees along the channel edge, the bottoms of the outside channel bends, and deep water adjacent to the hump (D) could all draw fish during frontal conditions. The more severe the front, the farther toward the main lake fish will retreat.

RIVERS

Rivers aren't all current areas. There are backwaters, bays, cuts, etc. where crappies can get out of the current and spawn in slack water. Small, brushy backwaters or connected lakes like AREA A often see the first spring crappie use. Large areas like the oxbow lake shown here warm up slower. (The old river channel runs through the oxbow. When the river shifted course, the oxbow became a slack-water area connected to the river.)

AREAS B-1 and B-2 are brush-filled cuts or small bays in the back end of the oxbow. Great spots! C-1 is a brush point on an island. It's deeper, more exposed to the wind, and will attract crappies a bit later than AREA B.

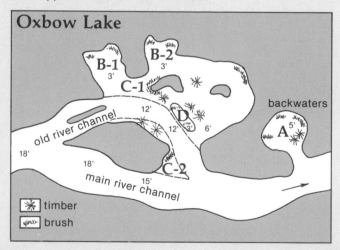

AREA C-2 is similar to C-1, except that it's more exposed to the river current. It's a late-spawning spot, but is a good choice if backwaters are absent or they lack suitable bottom content and/or cover. AREA D, meanwhile, is a shallow, brushy hump near the old river channel. It's also more exposed to the elements, and is a "late" spot.

During cold front conditions, crappies will pull out of the shallow cover and gather in deep timber, or lie in the bottom of the old river channel. Some fish may even school up at the intersection of the oxbow and the river if an eddy (calm water area) forms at C-2.

waters; then cuts in the oxbow itself; then shoreline brush near an island; and finally, a deeper, brushy hump. In each case, the pattern repeats itself. The environments may be a bit different, but the general principles still apply.

THE SPAWN

As we've seen, crappies follow a predictable pre-spawn progression, using each available area as the water warms to the proper temperature (the low 50°Fs). As you might expect, they follow a similar progression at spawning time. As each area begins warming into the low 60°Fs, the crappies in that area will begin displaying spawning-related behavior.

There are several tip-offs to this transition other than water temperature. For example, note the appearance and mood of the fish. When crappies first penetrate the shallows, they are typically very light in color and spooky. However, the longer they are in the shallows, the more they change. Males begin displaying a darker color, triggered by hormonal changes, and become increasingly territorial and aggressive. Rather than just using a reed bed or brush pile, for example, they'll stake out a particular reed clump or brush pile, begin sweeping out a nest and defending it against intruders. They often become so fearless that they're extremely easy to approach and catch.

Bingo, another crappie bites the dust! Reservoir expert Steve McCadams and Dan Sura team up to spank Kentucky Lake crappies. Their ammo? Light spinning tackle with a small jig tipped with a minnow fished around stake beds.

Crappie Spawning Depth

Water clarity has a distinct bearing on how deep crappies spawn. However, since water clarity varies from lake to lake and can even change from year to year on the same body of water, we must establish how fish react to water clarity before we can zero in on spring crappies.

In general, clear bodies of water permit deep sunlight penetration into the water; dark bodies of water, in contrast, have poor sunlight penetration. Stained waters fall somewhere in between.

In each case, the visibility is a good general indicator of fish behavior. You can estimate visibility by noting how deep you can see the bottom or how deep you can see a large, white lure lowered into the water on a calm, sunny afternoon. (Biologists use a white object called a Secchi disk as a standard measure of light penetration. In essence, it measures how deep sunlight can penetrate the water and reflect back up to the surface.)

In most reservoirs, crappies apparently prefer to nest slightly below this level if favorable conditions exist there. In general, if visibility is less than 10 feet, the level 2 feet below this depth is a typical nesting depth. If the visibility is greater than 10 feet, the depth range 4 to 6 feet below this level is a common nesting area.

Apparently, the amount of light available at that depth is favorable for egg development, and the crappies do no need to move shallower to spawn successfully unless the combination of conditions there are more attractive.

THE PROPER COMBINATION

Crappie spawning depth does not depend on visibility alone; it actually varies according to the combination of how clear the water is; the bottom content; the depth, type and amount of cover available; competing predators; etc. For instance, in clear-water mesotrophic lakes, crappies often spawn in the deepest (4 to 6 feet), thickest reed clumps even though the water is clear enough to permit successful spawning much deeper. Apparently, the combination of depth, thick weed cover for protection, and suitable bottom content is so favorable that the crappies prefer to spawn at this depth level. While some fish may spawn shallower or deeper, you can expect the bulk of the population to use approximately the same depth.

Contrast this condition with a stained-to-dark-water reservoir. In this case, crappies generally relate to the best available cover at the "proper depth level." The proper depth level, however, can vary from year to year due to changes in water clarity. Variations in spring snowmelt and/or rainfall can create big differences in water clarity from year to year. Faced with these conditions, crappies adjust their spawning depth to match the prevailing conditions.

By comparison, natural-lake crappies generally experience far less severe changes in water clarity. Thus, you can expect most fish to spawn at approximately the same depth, in and around the same types of natural weed cover, every year.

Clear-water reservoirs, meanwhile, often permit crappies to spawn quite deep—20 feet is not unusual in the clear water of Table Rock Lake, Missouri, for example. The fish often spawn on minor ledges or on whatever timber is available in the proper depth range. Without the presence of natural weed cover (as in natural lakes) to draw them shallow, crappies react by choosing the best combination of elements at a favorable depth level.

Deep-crappie-spawning behavior in highland reservoirs is probably also due in part to competition with largemouth bass for limited spawning areas. Under such conditions, crappies often spawn deeper and later than largemouths. However, when you consider that the water at the 15- or 20-foot level takes longer to warm up than it does in the shallows, crappies may actually be spawning under the same temperature conditions as the bass; it simply occurs at a later time.

In general, then, water clarity provides a good guideline to begin your search for spring crappies. However, you must still locate the best combination of elements available to the fish for consistent springtime success.

MESOTROPHIC NATURAL LAKES

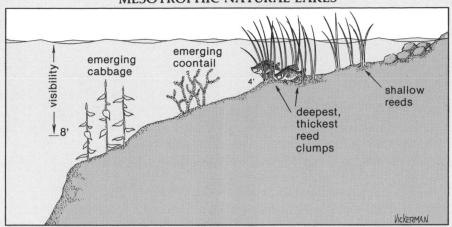

Crappies often spawn in deep reed clumps even though the water is clear enough that they could spawn deeper. Apparently, the combination of thick cover and proper bottom content is attractive enough to draw them moderately shallow.

STAINED-TO-DARK-WATER RESERVOIRS, RIVER BACKWATERS OR STRIP PITS

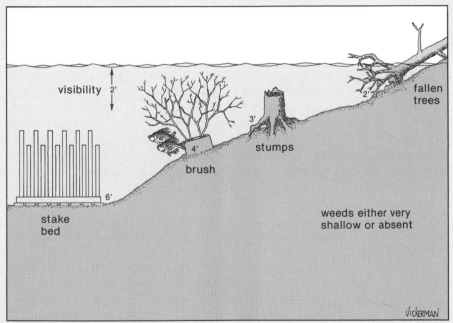

Crappies choose spawning depths depending on water clarity: In dirty-water years, they'll spawn shallow; in clearer-water years, they'll spawn deeper. In any case, they'll relate to the best available cover in the proper depth range. General rule: If the visibility is less than 10 feet, crappies often spawn about 2 feet deeper than you can see on a calm, sunny afternoon.

CLEAR-WATER RESERVOIRS OR STRIP PITS

visibility 12'

general
scarcity
of cover

17'

timber

VICKERMAN

Crappies relate to the visibility, and cover if it's available. General rule: If visibility is greater than 10 feet, fish usually spawn about 4 to 6 feet deeper than the depth you can see on a calm, sunny afternoon.

At some point, females will begin joining males in the nest, and actual spawning will occur. Females will mill in and out of the area, although the males will stick stubbornly to their nesting sites.

The entire spawning cycle may take several weeks. At any particular time you might encounter pre-spawn, spawn or post-spawn crappies, depending on which spot you're in and how much the water has warmed. Eventually, only males will remain in the shallows, guarding the nests against attack from predatory panfish, while the females begin drifting out toward deeper water. While they're technically post-spawn fish, the crappies are still in the immediate general vicinity of their spawning sites.

Crappies can be extremely easy to catch while on the nest, which often creates a problem of overharvest. In waters with poor crappie populations and/or limited spawning areas, the fish can be devastated by intense fishing pressure. On the other hand, some huge reservoirs with excellent crappie populations are able to withstand the heavy spring harvest. It all depends on what is available.

We strongly encourage you to practice catch and release during the spring spawning phase (pre-spawn/spawn/post-spawn) unless the crappie population is exceptionally good. In that case, take a few fish to eat and perhaps a trophy for the wall. But, *don't* load up the freezer. In most waters, we'd recommend not taking fish off the beds at all—particularly post-spawn males. Letting them protect the developing eggs will help ensure a crappie fishery for the future. In this event, we recommend fishing other areas or other lakes where the fish have not yet spawned or have finished spawning and left the spawning area completely.

POST-SPAWN LOCATION

Once spawning is completed, the search for post-spawn crappies begins. This isn't as difficult as you might believe, because the males remain fairly aggressive, and after only a few days of rest the females return to normal status.

The obvious place to begin searching for post-spawn crappies is just outside their spawning areas. Crappies don't instantly move to their summer areas once spawning is completed. You're dealing with an in-between stage, and the way crappies react depends upon what's available to them. Let's look at a few

Figure 1
Typical Crappie Lake

inlet

fast drop-off
outside reeds

2000 acres

gradual
slope
outside
reeds

bay

N

shallow
sunken
island

58'

outlet

reeds

scattered
weed clumps

examples. Once again, we'll key on natural lakes for our examples. A detailed explanation of reservoir, post-spawn crappie movement is described in Chapter 13.

BAY MOUTHS

Post-spawn crappies leave the confines of shallow spawning bays and congregate at the bottlenecks or just off the entrance to the bay areas. Such areas typically have a short, shallow flat just outside the bay that drops off into deeper water, perhaps down to the main basin of the lake (*FIGURE 2*).

The first area sought by post-spawn crappies is some form of weedgrowth on the deeper portion of the flat or along the drop-off. However, weedgrowth is often poorly developed at this time and usually occurs only in clumps rather than extensive beds. Faced with this condition, crappies might spread out across a wide area, relating to the available clumps.

At this time of the year, some bay mouths have little or no weedgrowth present, so crappies have no choice but to suspend. They'll school up along the drop-off just outside the bay. Early in the Post-spawn Period you can expect to find crappies immediately outside the bay mouth. Later, as the lake warms and

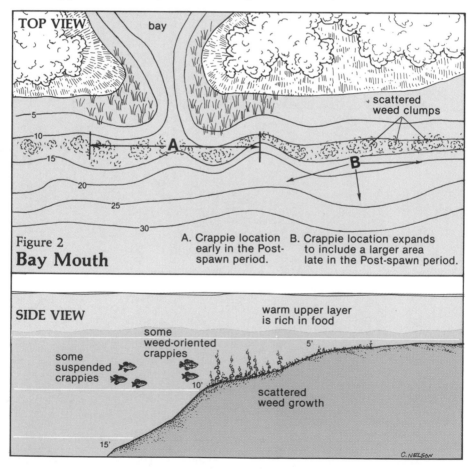

TOP VIEW   bay

scattered
weed clumps

5
10
15
A
B
20
25
30

Figure 2

Bay Mouth

A. Crappie location early in the Post-spawn period.

B. Crappie location expands to include a larger area late in the Post-spawn period.

SIDE VIEW

warm upper layer
is rich in food

some
weed-oriented
crappies

some
suspended
crappies

5'

10'

scattered
weed growth

15'

C. NELSON

weedgrowth develops, they'll roam wider areas along the drop-off. Finally, when summer arrives and the weeds reach their full growth, the crappies might range far and wide and use a variety of places. But directly after the spawn, expect to find them just outside the bay.

The depth at which crappies suspend depends mainly on water color. The clearer the water, the deeper they'll move. In dark water they might be only a couple feet from the surface, whereas in clear water, crappies might be 6 to 10 or more feet down.

Another reason crappies remain near the surface is that the warm layer of surface water is rich in food. Small insects and minnows, particularly the small shiners that are often the crappies' main forage, inhabit this shallow zone. The crappies, understandably, remain very near to or in this feeding zone.

Since shallow bays are generally the warmest water available at this time of year, they generally host the best available food supply. The food chain here gets a head start on the rest of the lake. Wind currents will blow plankton, insects and minnows out of the bay, right to the waiting crappies. Therefore, any time you have a bottleneck situation, chances are you'll find a concentration of crappies. Remember, crappies will never be far from their food.

CREEK INLETS AND OUTLETS

Creek mouths function much the same as bays, but have the added influence of current. The water flow means inlets and outlets are a perfect place to find food drifting by, making them particularly good attractors. Let's look at each.

Creek inlets generally find crappies spawning on either side of the current flow (*FIGURE 3*). Then as they leave the shallows, the fish once again set up on one or both sides of the current. They'll either relate to the best weedgrowth

Figure 3
Crappie Location:
Creek Inlets

Figure 4
**Crappie Location:
Creek Outlets**

that adjoins the current flow, or simply suspend out in front of the main flow. If the force of the current is strong, they'll remain far out off the drop-off. However, if the current is mild, they'll be tight to the drop-off. Whichever the case, the creek is the main source of their food supply and they won't be far from it.

The main difference in an outlet area is that the current is less well defined and the crappies are more free to roam. They could be found along the drop-off on either side of the outlet (*FIGURE 4*). In years of low food supply, they'll roam longer distances from the spawning area. In years with good hatches of insects or minnows, however, the crappies can remain in the general outlet area for a long time, until the main lake weeds begin to flourish.

SHORELINES

Reed-studded shorelines attract spawning crappies, so again it's logical to assume that post-spawn crappies will lurk somewhere nearby. Exactly how they relate to the area, once again depends on what's available. Let's examine two extreme cases.

The first area is a gradually sloping shoreline with a weedy flat between the reeds and the drop-off (*FIGURE 5*). The basic shallow layout of this area means that the water will warm up on top of the flat, weeds will grow fairly early, and there should be plenty of food. In particular, baitfish will work all along this shallow growth, making it a prime area for post-spawn crappies.

Crappies will hang off the deep edge of these flats during the day. If healthy weedgrowth exists, they'll hug the edge. However, since weeds are seldom well developed at this time, it's more likely that the crappies will suspend out, off the drop-off. They'll remain over deep water during the day and make brief feeding forays toward the food-laden flats during the morning and evening twilight hours.

Figure 5
Crappie Location: Gradual Shorelines

morning and
evening location

daytime
location

reeds

scattered
weeds

15'

reeds

B

A

suspended fish probably
at B due to nearness
of deep water to shallows

5

10

15

20

weed oriented fish
probably at A if
weed growth is
sufficient to attract
them

Figure 6
Crappie Location: Steep Shorelines

warm surface water
morning and
evening location

daytime
location

fish
suspended

5

reeds

15

reeds

A

B

10

20

30

40

A. morning & evening
location (feeding zone)

B. daytime location—
suspended

C.NELSON

Take a close look at the structural layout of the area. There's generally a sharp drop-off along some portion of it—usually to one or both sides. The proximity of the deep water to the flat makes *AREA B* the prime spot for crappies to suspend.

The second type of shoreline has little or no flat at all (*FIGURE 6*). The shore simply drops off quickly into deep water. This situation furnishes crappies an ideal spawning location without their having to venture a long distance into the shallows.

In these instances, crappies are more likely to roam up and down the entire drop-off. There's nothing to hold them in one specific spot. Baitfish roam the area outside the reeds, and once again the crappies move in to feed during the low-light periods of morning and evening.

The last areas to warm and the final place the crappies will spawn are reed-studded sunken islands out in the main lake (*FIGURE 7*). Locating post-spawn crappies in these areas is much more difficult because of the vast amount of open water for the fish to suspend in. And since these areas are slow to warm

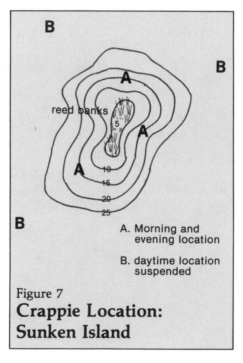

A. Morning and
   evening location

B. daytime location
   suspended

Figure 7
**Crappie Location:
Sunken Island**

up, the food supply is generally limited in spring. Consequently, the crappies are forced into longer forays when searching for food, and they might roam a few hundred yards out over deep water. This often makes locating them quite difficult.

Fortunately, the usable water is limited to the warmer, upper 10 feet or so, because that's where the baitfish will be. This fact helps you limit your search as far as depth goes, but you still have to cover a lot of water.

The most important factor in locating these open-water fish is prevailing winds. For example, a few days of strong winds from one direction will push suspended algae and plankton clouds (food for the baitfish) up against a shoreline. The baitfish, and consequently the crappies, will pile in along that shore to feed.

It's important to remember that the crappie is actually a confined open-water fish. It's not unusual for crappies to move long distances in the course of a few days as they follow their food. And these movements don't have to be in relation to any form of cover. Also, this roaming behavior points out a difference between shore-related crappies that spawn in shallow bays, shorelines, or creek mouths, as opposed to open-water fish that spawn on shallow, main-lake sunken islands.

Here's another interesting aspect of crappie behavior that occurs later in summer. In the course of their post-spawn roaming, fish often run across open-water rockpiles. Some of these rockpiles become prime attractors later, during the Summer Period. The best ones usually top off within 6 to 12 feet of the surface, where sunlight penetration striking the rocks produces a mossy growth that attracts minnows.

Don't expect to find crappies on these rockpiles too early in the season, though. Mid-lake post-spawners are far more likely to roam. The only time they use the rockpiles early in the season is in years of limited food supply.

In conclusion, there are several key features to look for when searching for post-spawn crappies. They shouldn't be too hard to find, because there are fairly obvious structural elements in a good crappie lake. Generally, concentrate your fishing in the warm surface layer of water within these areas. Crappies feed quite aggressively, even during their Post-spawn Period, so they are a fine, early season choice—especially at a time when other gamefish can be very difficult to catch.

The crappie's wide-ranging tendencies make it very difficult to stay on them. However, intense pressure during the vulnerable spawning cycle can take its toll. Once depleted, it takes a long time for the fish to refill a void left by over-harvest. Always exercise a conservation-minded approach when fish come in shallow to spawn.

PRESENTATION

Presentation techniques for post-spawn crappies are basically the same as summer and fall tactics. In most cases, you'll be after suspended fish. Small jigs or jig and bobber combinations are the best choice.

The exact approach depends on conditions and how the crappies relate to a particular area. As we've already seen, different kinds of areas, types of weed-growth, etc., result in a different fish response. For instance, fish holding along weed edges can be easily caught by casting or bobber fishing. Open-water crappies, however, require covering a lot of water to locate them, so a trolling approach is usually more effective. Trolling lets you cover a wide area quickly and efficiently. You must attack each area in the most effective manner, depending on what you're faced with.

No matter which type of area you're in, however, one invaluable tool is your depth finder. It's very effective for spotting suspended fish. Once you spot the crappies and determine how they're relating to the available habitat, you can then determine your best approach, and 60% of the battle is already won.

Start your search near a bay mouth such as we described in *FIGURE 2*. Slowly motor back and forth across the drop-off where fish might suspend, and watch for suspended fish!

If there's some weedgrowth present, begin fishing there. Pick out the deeper stands of weeds, perhaps in 8 or 10 feet of water. Place a small 1/16-ounce jig about 5 feet below a thin, pencil-type bobber. Tip your jig with a tiny shiner minnow or, if you can't get small shiners, use a 2-inch fathead.

You can cast this combination, but you're usually better off slowly trolling it with your electric motor. Cast out perhaps 30 feet and begin a slow, S-shaped, trolling pass in and out of the weed edge. If crappies are in the weeds, they're usually scattered. That's what makes this trolling approach so effective. You cover a lot of water.

If the crappies aren't right in front of the bay, proceed up or down the drop-off area. Remember, they show a tendency to roam, and you might have to cover a wide area to find them.

Your next choice is between an open shoreline area or a creek mouth. Choose whichever you think has the warmest water. Let's say there's a shore-line area on the north shore that gets good sun exposure and has developed some good weedgrowth. Once again, begin working the weed edge in front of the reed bed. Troll in and out of weeds, keeping an eye out for suspended fish.

If the weedgrowth is poor, don't be afraid to troll out over deep water. Chances are the crappies are suspended. Again, pay careful attention to areas with a sharper drop-off. That's the choice location for suspended fish.

Position the boat just outside the drop-off and try casting a jig up over the weed edge and then swimming it back out to the boat, or cast all around the boat. You never know just where they'll be. Once you locate suspended fish, they're usually concentrated. Stay on them and experiment until you hit the right color pattern, depth and retrieve speed; chances are you'll catch a bunch.

If the shoreline has no weedy flat—just a steep drop like in FIGURE 6—it's a good bet that the fish will be schooled and suspended near the reeds. Try moving all along this area. Cast the jig and minnow combination to the reeds and swim it back.

Another deadly lure combo is a small floating jig with a split shot, 24 to 36 inches ahead of it. Hook a minnow and cast it like a regular jig. The drop speed is incredibly slow, even slower than a 1/16-ounce jig, so it works well on finicky fish.

After checking out the shoreline areas, take a look at the creek mouths. Again, the basic procedure is the same. Just remember that if the current is fairly strong, the crappies won't be right in it. They'll relate to the available weed cover on either side of the flow, or suspend off the drop-off where the current is weak enough to be comfortable.

Finally, check out the sunken islands. Use a silent electric motor/bobber trolling technique to cover the weed edge, the drop-off, and the immediately adjacent deeper water.

Chapter 10

SUMMER

Warm-Water Crappies

Since summer is often the most difficult time to locate crappies, especially slabs, many anglers give up after the fish leave their easy-to-find spawning grounds. Crappies make a locational shift as spring progresses and warmer weather arrives; they begin to seek deeper water during the day. Unlike bass, crappies don't prefer shallow weedbeds, lily pads or grassy areas. Instead, they prefer confined open water or deep cover like brush piles, rock piles, deep weedbeds, or wherever schools of baitfish are found. First, we'll look at summer crappie behavior in natural lakes, and then we'll examine their reactions in reservoirs.

In northern mid-mesotrophic and some early eutrophic lakes that house slabs, the two major types of structure crappies relate to are rocks and weeds. Rock piles, without a doubt, are the best trophy spots. Small rock piles are especially good, since they confine the crappies to a much smaller area than a large weedbed. On many lakes, the rocks and weeds will be adjacent to each other, creating particularly attractive crappie sites.

ROCK PILES

The best rock piles peak about 1 to 5 feet above the level of maximum light penetration. The level of effective light penetration usually corresponds with weedline depth. So, the better rock piles will top off slightly shallower than the weedline. These rock piles may drop off into depths of anywhere from 25 to 60 feet, depending on the lake.

During summer, sunlight encourages the growth of a light, green moss on the rocks. This moss, in turn, attracts small minnows, bullheads and other forage that feed on aquatic insects and other organisms attracted by the moss. Summer crappies usually feed at such sites from predawn through the mid-morning hours.

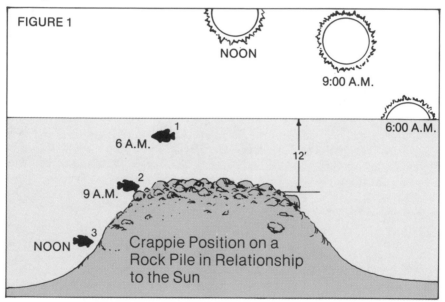

FIGURE 1

NOON

9:00 A.M.

6:00 A.M.

6 A.M.

9 A.M.

NOON

12'

Crappie Position on a Rock Pile in Relationship to the Sun

Let's go through a typical morning crappie movement on a rock pile as shown in *FIGURE #1*. Assume it's been three days since the last cold front. The sun is shining and there are a few, fluffy white cumulus clouds in the sky. In other words, the weather has been stable.

From predawn until about 5 A.M. or 6 A.M. the fish will be positioned over the rock pile as in *POSITION #1*. They may even suspend up to the surface. The crappies tend to be rather loosely grouped at this time of day, since they aren't affected as much by sunlight during these early morning hours.

As the sun rises (between 6 A.M. and 10 A.M.) the crappies will seek the shaded side (usually the west side) of the rock pile (*POSITION #2*). The fish will move to the first drop-off and group closer together. This position is generally about 2 to 4 feet above the depth of maximum light penetration. During the mid-morning hours, the fish are still relatively unaffected by the light and will continue to feed near the bottom.

As the sun's rays gradually become more direct, the crappies will congregate tight against the shady side of the drop-off *(POSITION #3)* and drop to a deeper level as midday approaches. The big crappies—lazy fish by nature—feed at their leisure on minnows that swim past the sharp breakline.

The outside or deep edges of the cabbage weeds on the drop-offs are also excellent crappie spots on these lakes. If rock piles are absent, the deeper cabbage beds will be the preferred midsummer location. The larger weedbeds—usually found on the edge of a shallow, sandy flat that tapers slowly from the shore—will inevitably hold the most crappies.

It is often difficult to find crappies along these big weedbeds, because there is just too much cover. Generally, they'll be located along the drop-off, but you'll still have to look for some irregularity (points or pockets) in the weeds that will attract and hold fish. The thicker cabbage patches are often key sites, since they provide more cover and usually more forage. There may be some weeds all along the entire shoreline drop-off, but they'll often grow thicker in certain places.

Small, isolated cabbage beds on drop-offs can also draw crappies. However, because of their small size they will not hold numbers of fish, but may concentrate a few, easily accessible fish.

Rock piles adjacent to weedbeds are often more attractive than a weedbed alone. The rocks may begin at the edge of the weeds (or even shallower) and extend down to 25 or 30 feet. Where the weeds end and the rocks begin is generally the best place to start. A bottom-bouncing jig or a finely tuned depth finder is the best way to find these rocky sites.

Once you locate a rock pile, scout around until you learn its shape. Then you'll know where to work the area and what part of the structure might hold fish. In fact, this is a good practice with any key spot such as an underwater rock pile or a large weedbed.

Sunken islands with weeds are also prime crappie locations, especially when rocks are present. Depending on the time of day, large groups of fish may work all sides of such an area, shading themselves from the sun. In the morning, the west side would shield them. Around noon, the only place to go would be deeper. Toward evening, the crappies may be up on the east side of the island.

Sunken islands vary considerably in size, shape and weed content. We've found the best ones have at least a hard, sandy bottom—and preferably rock or gravel. Sunken islands with muck bottoms do not seem to be as productive, probably because mucky bottoms do not support cabbage weeds.

Curly cabbage is the weed type most commonly used by crappies. However, coontail is also good. In fact, it often grows to a greater depth than cabbage. Since coontail is thick and spongy, the fish often lie buried in the weeds. Deep coontail serves as a prime holding spot for straggler crappies after a cold front has passed.

CRAPPIE POSITION IN RELATION TO THE WEEDS

Let's look at a typical, shoreline, weedy drop-off. A weedy, sunken island would also produce the same reaction in crappies. *FIGURE #2* shows crappies

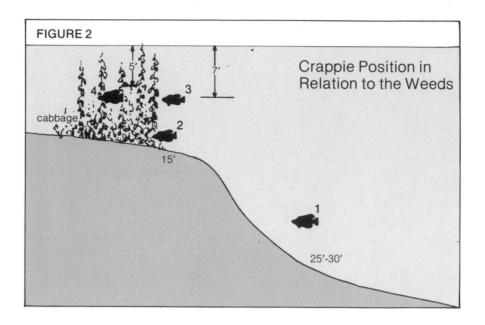

FIGURE 2

Crappie Position in Relation to the Weeds

cabbage

at four different sites in relation to a weedline.

POSITION #1 finds the fish suspended anywhere from 5 to 15 feet off the bottom in 25 to 30 feet of water. Crappies will often suspend off a lip like this during the middle of the day under direct sun. This position is also used during cold-front conditions when the fish have a neutral or negative feeding attitude.

POSITION #2 shows the crappies at the base of the weeds. They will often take this position when feeding. Under favorable conditions the entire school may locate at this point, especially in the late afternoon as the sun becomes less direct and the fish no longer need depth for cover.

Schools of crappies feeding along the edge of the weeds often move horizontally along the weedline and suspend about 5 to 8 feet below the surface *(See POSITION #3)*. This usually will take place in the evening near sunset. Under ideal conditions, you'll see fish "popping" and feeding on the surface as far as 100 feet out from the edge of the weeds. They may cover a considerable distance in their search for food, traveling about 5 feet below the surface.

Under ideal conditions, crappies may move into the weedbed itself *(POSITION #4)*. You may locate some stray fish in the weeds under normal warming trends, but only after several days of warm, stable weather may you find any number of fish moving into the weeds. When they enter the weeds, they tend to be anywhere from near the surface, to about 5 feet down.

To further illustrate crappie location, let's zero in on a specific area in a mid-meso lake that contains several of the areas we've talked about. *FIGURE #3* shows a section of weedline. There are several holding areas that we will need to locate, identify and check.

AREA A, a rock pile sitting on the weedline, is the type of spot that will be a fish magnet for many types of fish throughout the season. It is a prime crappie spot, one that deserves concentrated effort.

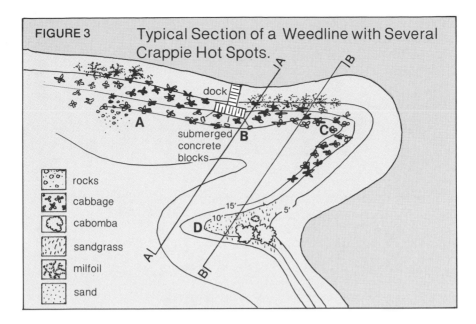

FIGURE 3 — Typical Section of a Weedline with Several Crappie Hot Spots.

A dock extends out to the edge of the weeds at *AREA B*. This particular dock happens to be a floating dock with its deep end anchored by three large concrete blocks. The fish relate to these blocks. Large numbers of crappies could even mill around this spot long after the dock has been removed.

AREA C is a sharp inside turn in the weedline. At this point, a school of fish moving parallel to the weedline would be forced to do one of several things: Either they could take the turn and follow the weedline out to the weed-covered point, or they could stop and pause at the inside turn. If they stop, they could spread out into shallower water to feed. If they turn and follow the breakline, they would soon show up at the end of the point *(AREA D)*.

FIGURE 4
Cross Section A

18'

clean
sand

milfoil

1

2

Cross Section B

scattered
patches of
cabomba   sandgrass

8'

The *CROSS-SECTIONS A* and *B* in *FIGURE #4* show the bottom contours found along this stretch, as well as the breaklines formed by weedlines and bottom content. Generally, a school of crappies moving along the shoreline stretch will be found at the edge of the weedline—5 to 8 feet below the surface *(POSITION #1)*. On bright days, you'll find them deeper, at *POSITION #2*, over the edge of the firm bottom, very close to the base of the weeds. The weedgrowth along the shoreline drop-off is primarily a mixture of coontail in the shallows and cabbage in deeper water.

On the weedy point, at *POSITION #3* in *CROSS SECTION B*, the weeds are mostly sandgrass with a few scattered patches of coontail. If the crappies are actively feeding, they'll usually spread out on top and suspend about a foot or two above the sandgrass. They rarely move shallower than 6 feet. When they are less aggressive, they hold on the very end of the bar above the clean sand bottom, and hang about 15 feet under the surface.

The same pattern will hold true at the inside turn *(AREA C in FIGURE #3)*. When they are feeding heavily, they often move into the weedgrowth, or just over it. When they have a neutral attitude, they tend to remain outside the vegetation and suspend at about 15 feet, even though that's closer to bottom here than on the end of the point.

In fact, there often seems to be a "key" depth on various lakes at which crappies hold or move along weedlines. But, they will leave this depth when they're actively feeding in or around cover. The key depth varies from lake to lake, depending on conditions. By keeping an eye on the depth finder while moving around the lake (especially when you're in crappie areas), you'll often see suspended fish. Don't waste time trying to catch fish every time your depth finder shows some but, you will notice that the bulk of the fish are in a band

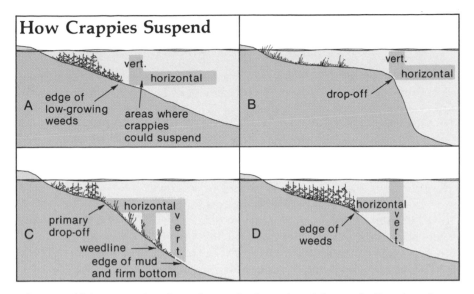

How Crappies Suspend

In natural lakes, crappies often relate to the deep edge of the weeds. But, they also use the edge of the drop-off, and even the breakline formed where hard bottom meets the muck bottom of the lake's deep-water basin.

Obviously, a sensitive depth sounder is an invaluable aid in locating suspended crappies, measuring their depth and how they're relating to a breakline. Knowing the relationship between a breakline and the path that a school of crappies is traveling is a must if you expect to stay in contact with moving fish.

POSITION A shows the fish in a fairly typical late summer position, assuming that they are in a lake in which there are some deep growing, low-lying weeds, preferably sandgrass. In a lake where this type of condition is common, the crappies might position themselves in this area frequently throughout the course of the season, although it seems to be much more prevalent at the tail end of summer and into the Post-summer Period.

POSITION B illustrates the common position of suspended crappies in lakes where the weedgrowth does not extend all the way to the drop-off. Depending on the type and location of their prime forage, crappies will usually relate to the drop-off either horizontally or vertically.

A similar situation is often found in extremely clear lakes, where the weedgrowth often grows well past the drop-off. This is shown in POSITION C. Note that there is a larger area for the fish to relate to, and finding them is that much more difficult. In a situation like this, they could suspend either vertically or horizontally from the edge of the drop-off or weedline, or relate to both breaklines simultaneously.

POSITION D shows two positions. It shows the fish suspended horizontally from the deep edge of the weedgrowth, and also suspended vertically from the breakline formed where soft and hard bottom meet at the edge of the basin area. Fish relating to the deep edge of the weeds could be just about any distance horizontally off the weedline. But, if they are at the approximate depth of the deep edge of the weeds, it's a good bet that they are relating to that edge and will follow its contours.

of a few feet. When you start looking for crappies, start at that depth range.

Be opportunistic and pinpoint the fish in areas where they are most likely active. For the most part, this means fishing schools which are either "holding" at one of the areas we've mentioned and/or have moved "over the cover" and are actively feeding. On the section of lake shown in FIGURE #3, A, B, C & D are such areas.

FISHING THE AREA

Let's assume that during the course of the morning you've noticed suspended fish just outside the weedline at 12 feet. After lunch, you decide to give the crappies a go, so where do you start?

First, locate irregularities along the weedline. Then move the boat along the weedline, using an electric motor, while tossing a jig and "swimming" it back. At this point, watch the depth finder to search for some unusual bottom feature. Before long, you may locate a rock pile. Fish this spot from the bottom up to about 7 feet, using both casting and vertical fishing methods, and allow about ten minutes for some sign of activity.

If you don't make fish contact, move to the next spot, "fishing through" the intermediate area by casting jigs and watching the depth finder for additional areas. Once you reach the dock, just repeat the procedure you used at the rock pile. This process should be continued all along the weedline.

Crappies located between "hot spots" should be treated as a moving school. If you find them at the rock pile, on the other hand, assume that they are holding there. When dealing with a moving school, it's important to determine the direction they're traveling. Drop a marker when contact is made and then fish 30 or 40 yards past the marker in one direction. If no contact is made within 15 minutes or so, quickly check the marked spot again to see if the crappies might be holding at some overlooked feature. If the fish are no longer there, it would be safe to assume that they are moving in the opposite direction. Move down the breakline in that direction, fifty yards or so, casting ahead of the boat, and you'll make contact again.

Generally, moving fish are slightly more active and more prone to take a lure, but holding fish are easier to present a lure to. Each situation has its advantages and disadvantages, but crappies can be caught in either case. However, you must have an idea of what you're dealing with if you expect to score heavily.

During summer, active crappies seem to spend a majority of their time moving parallel to some type of weedline. Therefore, location becomes the key. Once the fish are located, presentation is generally not too difficult.

PLAYING THE WIND

Another key to crappie location is the velocity and direction of the wind. Small minnows which are crappie prey, feed primarily on free-floating microorganisms and plankton. The plankton, which the minnows follow, is moved by wind-formed currents. Often, crappie fishing will be excellent on the side of the lake receiving the wind and poor on the protected shore. Apparently, there is a plankton buildup along the windward shore that triggers feeding activity.

Do the crappies follow the minnows around the lake? Probably not. Rather, the crappies in the wind-blown areas become active, triggered by the influx of an abundance of prey, while the crappies on the opposite shore turn off when their food supply temporarily disappears.

PRESENTATION

One of the major thrills of catching big slab crappies is landing them on light tackle. Because crappie lures are small, light tackle is necessary to work the lures effectively. Not only are you looking for fish that are larger than the typical panfish, but you're going to have a lot of fun catching them, as well.

No doubt jigs account for more crappie catches than all other methods combined. Jigs in the 1/16- to 1/8-ounce range are generally the most effective. They are small enough to appeal to crappies and heavy enough for easy casting or backtrolling.

By experimenting with sizes and styles of jigheads along with varieties of body dressing, you can achieve any type of action that the crappies may desire. One important fact to remember is that lures in the 1½- to 2½-inch range are generally the most effective. Don't overdo the action. Keep it slow and simple.

It generally pays to tip a crappie jig with a small minnow. Actively feeding fish may strike a plain jig, but neutral-attitude fish usually must be tempted. A 1½- to 2-inch fathead minnow, hooked upward through the jaw and out the top of the skull, is perfect. Small shiners are also good, although they require more careful handling than the durable fatheads. A small strip of pork rind or a 2-inch Twister-type tail is also a good substitute if bait is not available. In addition, you can add a scent product if it gives you confidence. However, experience has shown that scent products are more effective in cold water.

TACKLE

Specialized tackle will help you present these small lures properly. Although you can get by with standard spinning equipment, a long, sensitive, ultralight rod will make crappie fishing much easier.

Light lures require long rods for casting. It's similar to casting a split-shot/nightcrawler combination for walleyes. You need an extra long rod to swing the bait out on a cast, rather than casting with a quick snap of the wrist, which usually rips the bait off the hook.

A good crappie rod is long, flexible and light enough to handle 2- to 4-pound-test line. It allows you to fight crappies without putting undue pressure on the line. Let the rod absorb the strain, not the line. And, since a crappie's mouth structure is quite delicate, it's best to use a soft rod that will absorb shock and prevent tearing the hook from the fish's mouth.

A quality, ultralight spinning reel is also recommended. The larger, standard-size reels are too bulky to efficiently handle 2- to 4-pound-test line.

CATCHING CRAPPIES NEAR THE BOTTOM

The most efficient way of working crappie jigs in deep water is to slowly backtroll. This is extremely effective when the fish are near the bottom, such as at the base of a weedline or on the edge of a rock pile. The jig is constantly in productive water, as compared to casting, where the jig is in the fish zone for a relatively small amount of time.

The key to backtrolling 1/16- to 1/8-ounce jigs successfully is to move the boat very slowly. The best way to accomplish this is to drift and occasionally use an electric motor to keep the boat in proper position. Moving slowly lets you use a short line and fish vertically while keeping the jig in contact with the bottom. You also retain maximum lure control and are in an excellent position to feel a strike.

Crappies often hit the jig very lightly, so you must pay careful attention to any change in the feel of the jig. In fact, it pays to watch the line where it enters the water. Your only indication of a strike may be a slight twitch in the line when the crappie sucks in the jig; you may not even feel it. We strongly suggest that you rest your index finger on the line in order to enhance your sense of feel.

Working the jig with a slow, lift/drop action is very effective. Simply raise and lower the rod tip about a foot. This approach will maintain frequent contact with the bottom but reduce the tendency to get snagged. Try pausing occasionally, or even giving the jig a slight jerk once in awhile. It may trigger an inactive fish into striking. In general, though, keep the action to a minimum for crappies. Even a slow drag across the bottom can produce, providing the area is relatively snag free.

For example, to work a deep rock pile, slowly backtroll a jig around the top lip, and then progressively work your way down the shaded side in depth increments of two feet or so. Make a pass at 18 feet, then 20, then 22, etc. It's a very effective, thorough way to check an area. Backtrolling the base of a weedline or the adjacent drop-off would be much the same. We prefer not to anchor in these areas, because that will usually spook the school.

LIVE BAIT RIGS

Another excellent way to take crappies that are near the bottom is with a live-bait rig with a very light slip sinker (preferably 1/8-ounce) or a slip shot. The rigs can be backtrolled or drifted along the weedline or the edge of a rock pile and are an effective way to present a small minnow in deeper water.

Again, the best choice is a 1½- to 2-inch fathead minnow. Shiners will work, but they tend to swim higher, while fatheads will try to duck down into the rocks and moss. This attempt to hide seems to trigger neutral crappies.

A long leader (4 to 6 feet) is preferable, especially if the fish are several feet above bottom. In this case, use shiners, and let them swim up to the crappies. Otherwise, stick to fatheads.

Pay careful attention to how crappies hit the minnow. If they run after a strike, it's an indication of a competitive, aggressive, feeding fish. In this case, switch to jigs which will allow you to fish faster. If the crappie doesn't run, it could indicate two things: You've either hit a straggler, or the school is inactive and not feeding; subsequent casts will determine this.

If there are more fish present, try removing the swivel from the live-bait rig, which will allow the slip sinker to slide down to the minnow. You can then jig the minnow, achieve a little more action, and perhaps trigger a few more fish. Should the fish turn on and start feeding, switch to a jig and minnow combination.

SUSPENDED FISH

These are the ones you spot on your depth finder—the times when you're running across the lake, and suddenly your depth finder lights up like a Christmas tree. You have a huge school of fish from 12 to 17 feet suspended over 30 feet of water. How do you handle it?

First, remember that fish suspended near a weedbed or rock pile will tend to be much more catchable than fish that are seemingly unrelated to anything. Why? Because fish that are near their food source are usually there for a reason. They are going to feed or have fed recently. Those that have little inclination to feed can be suspended anywhere. Percentage-wise, stick with those that are near a food source.

You can catch these fish by placing a jig and minnow at the proper depth. Either lower a jig and hold it there, or suspend it with a bobber.

To keep a jig at the right depth without a bobber, place a rubber band around your reel spool when you've let out the proper amount of line. After you catch a fish, let the line out again and the rubber band will stop it at the proper depth.

When vertically jigging, always set your depth so the tip of the rod is only a few inches from the surface of the water when the lure is at its lowest point in your jigging motion. This allows you to keep the line out of the wind, results in better feel, and gives you maximum rod sweep when setting the hook. Also, if you place the line over your index finger as if you were backtrolling (but with the bail closed), you'll be able to feel the light peck of a crappie when it inhales the jig.

The most efficient way to present a lure to deep-water, suspended crappies is to fish vertically. But most lures are very difficult to work in this manner. With this thought in mind, who does more vertical fishing than an ice fisherman? Ice-fishing tackle provides one of the best vertical-fishing lures, the jigging Rapala. This lure hangs horizontal when stationary and swims around in circles when moved. Crappies prefer the two smallest (3 and 5 cm) sizes. Jigging Rapalas work best with either a very slow, rhythmic pumping action (1 to 2 feet) or by holding them still as possible while you drift.

Deep-water bobber techniques require a slip bobber. Place the bobber stop on your line at the proper depth, and you can backtroll, drift or even cast. The bait automatically returns to the proper depth. You'll have the same degree of control as with the rubber band/spool combination.

CRAPPIES NEAR THE SURFACE

Most of the time, crappies near the surface are adjacent to a weedbed or brush pile. Such shallow depths (1 to 6 feet) allow you to cast as well as backtroll or drift. In fact, casting is the better technique, since it places the lures out and away from the boat which prevents spooking shallow fish.

The best way to check a weedbed is by swimming a jig over the tops of the weeds. Simply cast a jig over the weeds; let it sink to the approximate depth of the top of the weeds, and slowly reel in the line. Trial and error will determine how long to let the jig sink and how fast to reel in to get the right combination.

Crappies suspended just outside the weeds can also be fished by swimming a jig. Of course, you'll have to get the proper depth. And remember, the larger crappies are usually slightly deeper than the smaller ones. If you're catching small crappies, let your jig sink a little deeper. If the small crappies hit your jig before it sinks far enough, try casting past the school and retrieving a little deeper so the bigger fish will have an opportunity to hit it.

Use your electric motor and move down a weedline, casting ahead with the jig. Meanwhile, a second person can simultaneously backtroll a jig on the bottom. In this way you'll cover all depths. It's a very quick and efficient way to cover water and locate fish.

A bobber works well for fishing crappies near the surface. It's better when the fish are actually inside the weeds, since it's hard to swim the jig through heavy weeds by casting. When the fish are just beneath the surface (1 to 4 feet), you can get by with a standard bobber. If they're deeper, you'll need a slip bobber to cast effectively. In either case, rig the jig/minnow, or a minnow hooked beneath the dorsal fin with a number 6 or 8 hook, at the proper depth below the bobber.

When working these shallow crappies, remember to keep a low profile. If you stand up in the boat, you may spook the whole school. But if you stay low, you can work right on top of them.

INSECT-FEEDING CRAPPIES

When the crappies are feeding on insects, use a tiny jig (1/32 or 1/64 ounce). Obviously, this small size makes casting, trolling, and general handling very difficult. Fortunately, crappies feed on emerging insects just as the insects emerge from the bottom, or just as they rise to the surface.

Trim down a 1/16-ounce marabou jig so the chenille-wrapped jig has only a quarter-inch of marabou extending past the hook shank. The real key, however, is to tie a 2-foot section of floating fly line one foot above the jig. Splice this onto your main line. The secret is that the fly line acts as a super sensitive float. Work the lure with a series of slow twitches, never allowing the jig to sink more than a couple feet. The action is almost unreal, and produces slab crappies.

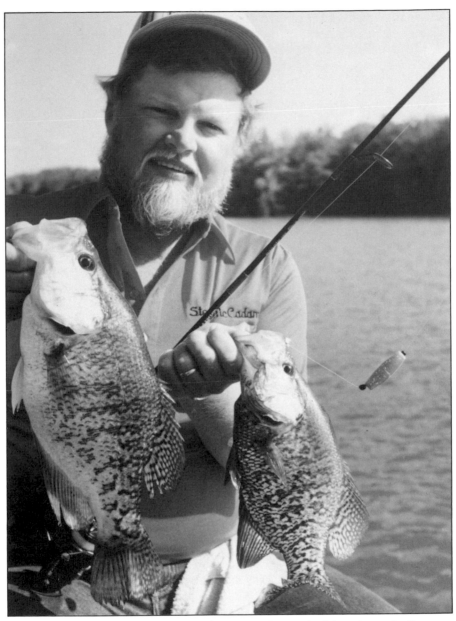

A tiny 1/64-ounce jig fished 2 feet below the surface tricked these insect-feeding crappies. Don't underestimate the value of small jigs when fishing crappies—they're dynamite.

When crappies feed on insects near the surface, you can often spot these smaller insects on the surface. This is common in late afternoon or early evening during the summer period. The best way to take these fish is to use a small bobber and suspend a tiny 1/64-ounce jig, 12 to 24 inches below the surface, or use the tip shown in the accompanying illustration—using a piece of floating fly line. Move the jig in short, slow movements (a few inches at a time), and allow long pauses between movements.

The opposite situation would occur when crappies are feeding on emerging insects near the bottom. This commonly occurs several days after a severe cold front. It's not an easy time to fish for crappies, because they appear to be adversely affected by cold fronts. But, there are some things you can do.

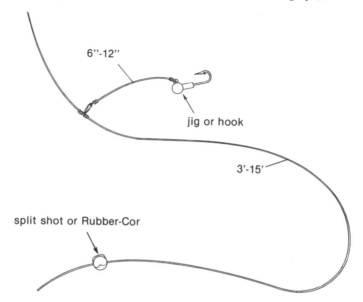

We've had considerable success with a light tackle variation of the tightline rig for backtrolling for suspended fish in summer. A single No. 8 hook or a 1/16-ounce jighead is tied on a short dropper at least three and sometimes as much as 15 feet from the end of the line. A big split shot is lightly crimped to the line beyond the dropper. The split shot (or a Rubber-Cor sinker) can be moved up or down the line to control the distance that bait is presented off bottom. When using this rig, the bait is lip-hooked, as opposed to the typical method of hooking minnows behind the dorsal fin.

This set-up allows you to keep your bait a specific distance above bottom, and the tight line maintained by the heavy split shot tremendously increases your sense of feel. It works well with just a plain crappie jig as well. Using this type of set-up allows you to backtroll slowly for suspended fish in open water and provides precise control over (and direct contact with) your lure or bait at all times. No other backtrolling presentation for suspended fish provides this.

Your hooking ratio will skyrocket with this type of backtrolling set-up as opposed to a slip-sinker jig with a long snell and floating jig.

A cold-front dropper rig can be used to present a 1/64-ounce jig or a dull-colored trout nymph near the bottom. Tie the jig to a 3- to 6-inch dropper line about 18 inches above the end of the main line, and then place a #5 split shot on the end of the main line. It's sort of an ultralight version of the Wolf River Walleye Rig!

To retain maximum feel of the dropper rig, keep the line as vertical as possible, directly below the boat. Because of its light weight, drift or backtroll the rig very slowly, keeping the split shot in contact with the bottom. The split shot not only allows precise depth control with a tiny jig, but in the event of a hang-up, a firm pull on the line will release it, and all you've lost is a split shot.

Chapter 11

FALL

Cold-Water Crappies

As summer winds down, autumn arrives bringing shorter days and cooler temperatures. Autumn includes two Calendar Periods: the Turnover Period and the Cold Water Period. In response to seasonal environmental changes, crappies make adjustments in their behavior.

The most drastic fall turnover situation occurs in bodies of water which stratify in distinct temperature layers during the summer. Since cold water is heavier than warm water, the warmer water stays on top and the colder water sinks and builds up on the bottom; in between lies a narrow band of rapid temperature change from warm to cold water called the thermocline.

In these waters, the thermocline condition usually remains in effect throughout most of the summer. But during the tail end of summer the angle of the sun to the earth becomes less direct, and the environment begins to cool. Additionally, seasonal, hard-driving, cold winds and rain begin rapidly chilling the surface temperature of the water. As the heavier (colder) surface water begins sinking, it comes in contact with the warmer water below. This action forces the lighter, yet warmer, deeper water back to the surface. Eventually, the thermocline layer ruptures, and a mixing or "turning over" process takes place. As the wind whips the water, the mixing action continues until it thoroughly homogenizes the water to a point where the whole body of water is the same temperature. This process also reoxygenates the deep water.

The actual turnover process itself takes place once the thermocline layer ruptures. But the turmoil (side effects) that results usually adversely affects the fish for a period of time before and after this event actually occurs. Fishing doesn't pick up again until conditions stabilize. In general, once the water temperature drops to about 55°F and the water clears perceptibly, cold-water fishing patterns emerge.

As a time of turmoil, the Turnover Period is relative. First, all bodies of water do not thermocline during summer, so many do not "turn over" as such. Most rivers are a case in point. Lakes and reservoirs, too, may or may not stratify. Usually, shallow bodies of water—which the wind periodically stirs up—or waters with a lot of current flowing through them, do not stratify. Consequently, the fish in these waters are not subjected to as much stress as fish in waters where the transition from a warm- to a cold-water environment is a traumatic event. Nonetheless, the change from a warmer- to a cooler- to a colder-water environment demands some adjustment by both fish *and* fisherman.

In any case, fishing during the Turnover Period on bodies of water that actually thermocline is tough, to say the least. However, since all bodies of water do not turn over at the same time, it is usually best to avoid fishing this condition by switching to: (1) waters which have already turned over, (2) bodies of water which have not yet begun to turn over, or (3) waters which don't thermocline at all—such as rivers or large, shallow, windswept lakes.

The entire time span from the end of the turnover to freeze-up (on bodies of water that freeze over) is termed the Cold Water Period. This period is characterized by a gradual slowing down of a fish's metabolism and stabilization process of the entire ecosystem.

As the days grow steadily shorter, weedgrowth, insect hatches and plankton blooms diminish. In addition the chemical characteristics of the water can vary considerably with the changing season, and this has multiple effects on plant and fish life.

Let's take a close look at cold-water crappie location and presentation on mesotrophic lakes, Canadian shield lakes, and reservoirs.

MESOTROPHIC LAKES

As summer wanes and September arrives, the weather generally takes a turn for the worse. The wind switches to the north, delivering a week or so of icy blasts, heralding the end of summer and the arrival of the fall turnover. The sudden drop in temperature and strong winds churn the lakes into a state of turmoil, mixing the water and breaking up the summer thermocline. The locational patterns of the fish are disrupted, and feeding activity comes to a virtual halt. It's a tough time for both fish and fisherman!

After a week or ten days of this confusion, conditions generally stabilize. Fall has arrived. The weather takes on a more predictable pattern, although the general trend moves toward an increasingly cooler environment. The thermocline is gone, so both the temperature and oxygen content of the lake are virtually constant from top to bottom. This reopens a wide range of deep lake zones for fish use.

Under these conditions, smallmouths, walleyes and northerns generally begin to move deeper. Largemouths begin deserting the extreme shallows and pile up on the weedlines and weedy flats. Everything seems to be moving deeper. Everything, that is, except crappies!

Cold-Water Crappie Location

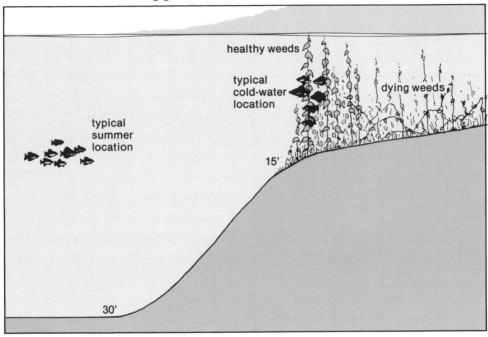

Note the difference in fall crappie location as opposed to their usual summer pattern. During the summer, crappies spend a large part of the day suspended in open water outside the weeds. In early fall, however, they'll usually be right up against the weeds, or even a bit inside of them. A quick check of the weedline should tell you if there's any fish using the area.

Strangely enough, at this time, crappies may move *toward* the shallows rather than away from them! *Toward* them, but not *into* them. It's an important point that requires explanation.

Early fall crappies generally remain in the same areas they inhabited before the fall turnover; however, now they'll move in much *closer to cover*. Rather than suspending 100 feet away from a deep weedline as in midsummer, they'll generally be right next to or even a few feet inside it. Similarly, instead of suspending well off the side of a rock pile or weedy sunken island, they'll remain very near the edge.

Fall crappies converge into smaller, more well defined areas than they did in summer. This naturally makes them a bit harder to locate than summer fish. Simply cruising along the deep weedline is no guarantee that you'll spot the fish on your depth finder. You'll probably have to fish weed edges or the rims of weedy sunken islands in order to locate crappies. Once you find them, however, their compact schooling tendency leads to fast action and lots of fish.

Fall crappies can continue to display this weedline-oriented behavior as long as the deep weeds remain green and healthy. How long does this last? Well, a lake's shallowest weeds characteristically begin dying early in the fall, giving off offensive hydrogen sulfide gas. This drives bass, bluegills and other fish out to the weedline. Yet, the deepest growing weeds generally remain healthy far into the Fall Cold Water Period and are a major attraction for various species of fish. As long as the weeds remain healthy, they may attract and hold fish.

Since the deepest-growing weeds generally remain the healthiest in late fall, it stands to reason that lakes with very deep weedgrowth should have the best weedline concentrations of crappies late in the fall season. Experience bears this out.

Smaller and/or dark-water lakes with shallower weedlines (8 to 10 feet) cool off faster and are less able to support healthy weedgrowth as fall progresses. Conversely, big, deep, clear mesotrophic lakes—the ones that usually grow trophy crappies—generally have deeper weedlines (typically 14 to 18 feet) that

Gary Korsgaden displays a 3-lb.-class crappie. Monster crappies are Gary's specialty; he has contributed much to our knowledge of these elusive fish.

remain quite healthy until the lakes begin to freeze. Therefore, it's easy to see that large lakes not only give you the best shot at trophy crappies, but also have the best concentrations of late fall weedline fish, as well.

LATE FALL LOCATION

A time comes when even the deepest weeds begin dying off and become poor fish habitat. This occurs first in shallow lakes and eventually in deep, clear ones. Since the weeds are no longer suitable to the fish, something has to give.

It does. Once the deep weeds die, both the baitfish and the crappies leave the area. At this point, crappies may revert to their characteristic behavior and suspend again if there are no suitable deep-water structural elements available for their use. They'll move out over the deeper water in the lake, suspending near a food source at whatever depth is most comfortable to them.

Once you find them, crappies are still very catchable at this time, but rather than being on an edge (a weedline or a rock pile), the crappies could now be out in the middle of nowhere. It's back to the hunting approach of summer to locate crappies.

The best way to locate crappies under these conditions is to look just outside the areas which they used in early fall. Begin searching the adjacent deep water. Slowly cruise back and forth, watching your depth finder. Look for the telltale flashes that signal suspended fish. It may take awhile, but once you locate crappies, you can catch a bunch.

ROCK PILES

A far easier condition to fish occurs when deep crappies congregate in the vicinity of deep structural elements. Deep rock piles are perhaps the most consistent, fall-crappie producers, yet they're usually the most ignored areas. That's because most anglers simply don't understand how crappies live. Many people think that crappies live in the weeds—which is quite the opposite of what actually occurs. Open-water rock piles attract crappies—often the largest ones in the lake.

Any time a rock pile is shallow enough to receive some degree of sunlight, moss (algae) will grow on the rocks. This kicks off a food chain of tiny organisms which serves as food for small minnows. And where there are tiny minnows, chances are that crappies are nearby. Inactive crappies suspend off the sides of such areas and move in to feed on the minnows.

Rock piles remain productive through the entire fall season, as opposed to weed areas which lose their attractiveness as the weeds die out. In fact, rock piles seem to get better as fall progresses, because as healthy weeds become more scarce, crappies shift location and many of these displaced fish relocate on rock piles. Late fall often finds massive concentrations of crappies in such spots, where they'll remain until just before the lake freezes. Then the crappies often move to open water to suspend for the winter.

In a nutshell then, crappies may relate to deep, healthy weedgrowth or rock piles during much of the early Fall Cold Water Period. As the weeds die, the fish shift toward other healthy weeds or onto the rocks. Or, in lakes with poor weedgrowth, crappies may shift deeper directly after the turnover. Finally, just before freeze-up, crappies often move out and suspend over the deepest water in the lake. That's where you'll find them during most of the winter.

SUNLIGHT AND FISH POSITION

Crappies are by nature low-light feeders, so most anglers experience their best success during the morning and evening hours. It's at these times that summer crappies are nearest the weedlines and in an aggressive feeding mood. Many anglers think crappies live in the weeds, because that's the only place they catch them.

The few crappie anglers probing the lakes in fall usually experience improved fishing, because crappies remain near the weedline area and are accessible. In addition, the sun is lower in the sky, the days are shorter, and the crappies are more prone to feeding all day long, instead of just during morning and evening. All in all, conditions are ripe for consistent action.

Cloudy weather really triggers some superb crappie fishing. Photosynthesis slows down during cloudy weather, so the amount of oxygen produced by the weeds is reduced. Consequently, baitfish move outside the weed edge and become easy prey. Feeding occurs all day long, so conditions are perhaps best for taking fall crappies. Contrast this situation with deep-water, fall small-mouth activity, which is usually best on sunny days! Knowing how different species behave lets you adjust your approach to take advantage of weather conditions.

EQUIPMENT

Catching fall crappies seldom requires more than a few, simple, jigging techniques; a handful of small jigs; a few bobbers; and a bucketful of small minnows. There's no need to invest in fancy equipment, because when it comes to crappies, the more simple your approach, the better.

JIGS

The most productive crappie jigs are in the 1/32- to 1/8-ounce range. These lightweight jigs sink slowly and provide excellent depth control, which is essential when you're fishing for suspended fish. You can easily keep the smaller jigs at the crappies' level; heavier jigs tend to sink too fast. Crappies also prefer smaller jigs which match the small-sized food they generally feed on. If you place a larger, bulkier 1/4-ounce jig right on their noses, chances are they'll simply ignore it. It's simply too big.

Gary Korsgaden feels that the best, all-around, crappie jigs are 1/16- and 1/8-ounce marabou jigs. The slow-breathing action of the marabou is very enticing, even when the jig is motionless. He prefers to thin out the jig by shortening and pulling out about half the marabou. This cuts the bulk to a minimum. This may seem picky, but in the long run it makes a difference.

Is marabou the only jig style to use? Not necessarily. If the crappies are slightly into the weeds, the marabou feathers may pick up stringy moss and

The accompanying photo shows several of the more popular crappie jigs. First, (upper left) is a 1/16-ounce Bass Buster marabou. It's an excellent choice for most conditions.

In the center is a Lindy Fuzz-E-Grub and at the upper right is one of Gapen's Ugly Bugs. They're also good in most instances—especially in areas where moss tends to cling to a marabou jig.

At the lower left is Northland's Whistler jig. The tiny propeller makes it sink very slowly and helps it remain at a constant depth level when retrieved.

Finally, at the lower right is Grassl's Flu-Flu jig. It's only 1/32 ounce, but will catch fish under conditions when they ignore larger sized jigs.

Experience shows that light-colored jigs outproduce darker shades many times over when it comes to crappies. Crappies feed chiefly on small minnows, which are usually light or silvery in color. White, yellow or chartreuse jigs match this natural food best and are your top, color choices for crappies.

completely lose their attractiveness. You'd be better off with a rubber-bodied jig, because it will come through the weeds clean and is much more effective in this instance. It all boils down to matching your jig to conditions.

Finally, when using a jig and bobber approach, a 1/32-ounce Grassl's Flu-Flu jig or similar jig works very well. It's very light, tiny, and may be difficult to cast unless you have the extra weight of a bobber to help cast it. But for a bobber approach, ultra-small jigs are excellent.

BOBBERS

There are several bobber styles to choose from, and naturally each has its strong point. Let's examine each of them.

A long, thin, quill-type bobber has the least water resistance and is a natural choice for finicky crappies. It works best in and around reeds for spawning crappies or when crappies are near the surface. It's an excellent choice, when there isn't too much wind. If the wind kicks up, though, these lightweight bobbers become very difficult to cast.

Here are three types of bobbers that fit the bill for crappies. The quill type (left) has little water resistance and has the least spooking effect. The Adjust-A-Bubble (center) can be partially filled with water, giving you some added weight to make casting easier. At the right is the slip-bobber arrangement that allows you to fish at any depth. The small bobber stop placed on the line keeps your lure at the proper depth.

For windy conditions, a plastic bubble like the Adjust-A-Bubble is dynamite. You can partially fill it with water, giving it added weight for casting into the wind. Its unique, thread-on, twist-tighten feature doesn't damage your line like most bobbers do. This is a real plus, because when you're fishing 4-pound-test line to begin with, there's no room for error. A damaged line doesn't last long.

Finally, when the fish are deeper than 4 feet, you'll probably need a slip bobber. A slip bobber and a bobber stop will let you fish the jig at any depth. It works as well in 6 feet as it does in 20, so you can fish wherever the fish are.

TACKLE

The light line and tiny lures used for crappie fishing should be teamed with quality spinning gear. Although you can use standard spinning tackle, serious crappie addicts prefer to specialize a bit. A premium, ultralight spinning outfit is perfect for casting or trolling tiny jigs. However, a long, 8-foot fly-rod blank might serve your purpose better for casting small, lightweight bobbers. The extra length lets you lob the bobber out, instead of casting with a quick wrist snap. A spinning rod made from such a fly-rod blank is not a very versatile piece of equipment, but it really fits the bill for this approach. If you really get into fishing crappies, consider buying or making one.

PRESENTATION

The best way to choose a jigging technique is to match each approach to the type of cover and fish's position. That's exactly what you do when you're on the water. Let's take a look at each of them and examine the strong points of each.

WORKING THE WEEDLINE

Let's say you suspect that fall crappies are relating to a particular point or bar formation. The best way to check for the presence of crappies is to fish the weedline. Remember, late-summer or early-fall crappies are often so tight to the weedline that you can't count on spotting them with your depth finder. They'll blend in with the weeds. Therefore, you'll need to manually fish the area to see if they're present.

Begin at one end of the area and position the boat just outside the weedline. One person should cast a small jig into the weeds and then slowly swim it back to the boat. Adjust your retrieve speed so that the jig occasionally touches the weeds without fouling too often. The other person should cast parallel to the

Typical Early Fall Crappie Locations in a Meso Lake

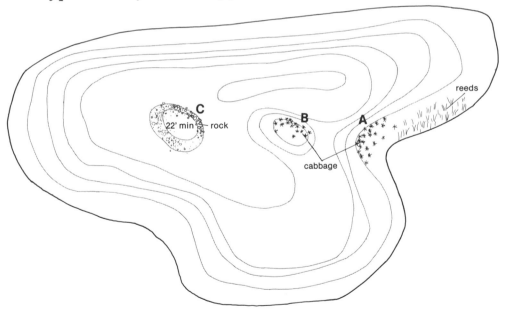

A quick look at this lake map section gives you a pretty good idea where to begin looking for fall crappies. The major attractions would be the weedy point, weedy sunken island, and the rocky hump.

Since crappies suspend and have an affinity for deep, open water, you'd generally find them on the sides of these areas that have the fastest drop to deep water. Fall fish would typically be along the healthiest weedgrowth on the fast-dropping sides of the shoreline point (A) or the sunken island (B), or on the sharp, rocky deep drop-off (C) on the sunken island.

Small jigs are deadly on big crappies. This slab white crappie was caught by vertically fishing a 1/8-ounce jig tipped with a small minnow along the outside bend of a reservoir creek channel.

weed edge, letting the jig sink part way to the bottom, and then swimming it back to the boat. How far the jig should be allowed to sink can only be determined by trial and error. Be sure to count the jig down so you'll know its depth. Crappies may be a few feet beneath the surface, or 6 to 12 feet down. It all depends on water color, cloud cover, etc. You never know for sure until you check it out.

Boat control is very important. Either drift or use an electric motor to carefully and systematically work the entire weed edge. Chances are you'll encounter a thick patch of healthy weedgrowth or a particularly sharp section of the drop-off that concentrates the crappies in a small area. Then the fun begins.

If the crappies are somewhat active, they'll hit the jig as it sinks or swims by. If they're not particularly aggressive, you may have to use a slower presentation. Get the bobbers out and suspend tiny jigs right at or just above the crappies' eye level. Once you trigger a few fish, the rest may become excited enough to improve their feeding mood. Then you can go back to swimming a jig. It's quicker, easier, and you may catch a bunch of fish in a hurry.

Weedy sunken islands are worked in the same fashion. Here, though, you may be able to use a short cut for locating fish. Crappies will generally be along the sharpest-dropping side of the sunken island. Concentrate your fishing along the side that has the fastest drop to deep water.

FISHING ROCK PILES

In fall, rock-pile crappies are perhaps the deepest crappies that you'll encounter. Again, they can be very close to or right up tight to the rocks. This makes backtrolling a small jig a perfect approach.

Backtroll an 1/8-ounce jig very slowly across the rocks. Since the jig is quite small, you have to move very slowly to remain in contact with the bottom. An electric motor lets you move slowly and remain directly above the fish without spooking them.

Jigging a Rock Pile

active crappie position

15'

evening position

neutral to inactive crappie position

daytime or unstable weather position

VICKERMAN

Big fall crappies frequently relate to deep-water rock piles. They'll suspend off the edges during the day and move up onto the hump to feed on small minnows during the evening hours. Backtrolling a small jig is one of the top ways to catch them.

If there are no fish present on top of the rock pile, progressively work deeper down the sides. When a fish hits, hover there with the electric motor. Don't drop anchor. The fish are spooky and the drop of an anchor will spook them. By carefully hovering above them, you can catch a lot of fish before they eventually spook.

SUSPENDED FISH

As we've said, at some point in late fall, crappies will leave the cover they've been using and suspend over deep water. There are a couple ways to deal with this situation.

The first thought, naturally, is to use the sink and swim technique with a jig. It's effective until the water gets really cold. Then it may simply be too fast a presentation for the fish to respond to. Try switching to a stationary-slip-bobber approach. Let the jig hang motionless, giving the fish a chance to respond.

Let's assume that it's very late in the year, and you have to crack a bit of ice to get your boat in. The crappies are there, but they really don't seem to respond to the jigging approach. What next?

Drop a small ice fly down to the fish. That's right, a tiny ice-fishing lure. Sounds crazy, but it works! Use the standard, small jigging stick that winter anglers use. Drop the lure through the school at 6-inch intervals. Big crappies are quite susceptible to this approach, particularly at sunset. It's a little trick that may really pay off. So, if you find fish during the day but they won't hit, come back as the sun starts to set. That's prime time for big slabs.

CANADIAN LAKES

Many of the rocky, Canadian shield lakes in western Ontario lack the massive, 100-foot-plus depths of deep, clear, trout waters. Instead, 25 to 40 feet is more common, with water clarity ranging from stained to medium-clear. Given enough shallow, reed-filled spawning grounds and plenty of small baitfish, these lakes produce huge crappies in unbelievable numbers.

The cooler nights of August signal a changing environment. As the water temperature slowly drops to the low 60°F's, crappies begin schooling very tightly, suspending 10 to 20 feet down over deeper water.

After the fall turnover—usually completed once the water temperature reaches 55°F—crappies drop even deeper. With plenty of oxygen in the depths, and a fairly consistent water temperature from top to bottom, there are no barriers to deep-water movement. Both crappies and the small baitfish they prey upon continue shifting deeper, to 25, 30, 35 feet or more by late fall. As the crappies continue grouping into huge "mega-schools"—hundreds of fish—they become extremely vulnerable, once you find them. Here are a few keys to locating fall crappies.

GENERAL CRAPPIE LOCATION

Cooling water temperatures slow crappie metabolism, reducing the distances that fall crappies travel. They move slowly within a general area, foraging for food. But they won't range too far. They usually remain somewhere in the general vicinity.

As with many species of fish, fall location centers around quick access to deep water—in other words, sharp drop-offs rather than gradual-tapering flats. The sharp-dropping sides of shoreline points, the steep edges of deep (20-foot) rock humps, etc., are key areas to begin your search. Areas like these

Typical Good Crappie Bay on a Rocky Canadian Shield Lake

The accompanying map depicts a good crappie bay on a rocky Canadian lake. Note the maximum depth of about 40 feet. If it were deeper, the amount of usable area would be decreased, and the bay would probably host far fewer crappies.

AREA A depicts a saddle area between two islands. AREA B is a similar saddle between a rocky hump and a shoreline point. Crappies would tend to lie in the saddle area during the day and move toward the drop-offs in the evening. AREA C shows a school of crappies that have done just this. Note that the fast taper of the shore gives the school quick access to deep water.

AREA D shows a school of fish suspended over the deep flat, halfway in relation to the drop-off. AREA E, meanwhile, has two groups of fish suspended in relation to, basically, nothing. Yes, D and E are very frustrating to anglers who want to nail down a rhyme and reason for every bit of fish behavior. In this case, it's easier to accept the fact that some of the fish might be very far away from a structural element, and not give yourself a headache trying to figure out why. It's much easier to concentrate on more predictable fish like those in AREAS A, B and C!

Detail of Area A

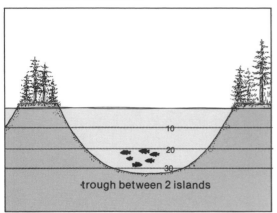

10
20
30
trough between 2 islands

Detail of Area B

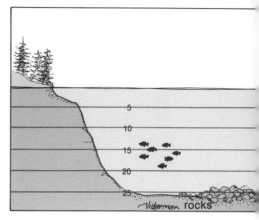

5
10
15
20
25
rocks

within bays or in the shallow (20 to 40 feet) portions of the main lake are your focal points for late-summer/fall crappies.

A key feeding area for active fish is at the base of a drop-off where it stops dropping and meets the lake's softer basin. A school of crappies using a sunken hump, for example, might slowly circle the base of the hump, searching for minnows. They'll follow this deep-water transition (edge) between the hard hump and the soft basin, like a road map. This is a particularly good early-morning/late-evening pattern.

Are crappies always on these edges? No, which brings up the interesting phenomenon of suspended fish. As we've said, crappies can be somewhere in the general vicinity of these areas. That often means off to the sides, somewhere out over the lake's soft basin.

If that sounds intimidating—like you have to cover hundreds of acres of open water to find them—don't panic. They're usually somewhere near distinct structural elements. Thus, the deep flat adjacent to (within 100 to 200 feet) a deep point, hump, etc. is a likely fish attractor. The saddle area between two islands or between the top of the shoreline point and an adjacent sunken island, for example, are key spots.

In the past, we've termed these areas confined open water, and it's a good concept. It's the open water near structural elements rather than out in the wide-open lake. If you keep this in mind, it takes the mystery out of searching for open-water crappies.

You can eventually contact these fish by drifting small lures across the adjacent, open water and waiting for a bite. However, when searching for suspended fish, it's much more effective to use a depth finder, graph or LCR to scout the areas adjacent to points and humps. Crappies show up as light flashes on the depth finder. Sometimes they're near bottom, and sometimes they're 5, 10, or 15 feet above it. Your depth finder not only tells you where they are, but how deep to fish your lures. You can't beat that!

Circle the Wagons!

That's what wagon trains used to do when surrounded by hostile Indians. In this case, it's a school of "hostile" crappies slowly circling a good feeding area. The area has several good humps and points with a 35-foot hole between them.

A crappie school might slowly circle this area, foraging for minnows, contacting each feeding spot every hour or so. If you're anchored on the point, you might pop a few fish every once in a while, and then deadsville. However, if you can predict their movement, jump ahead, and be ready for their arrival. You can catch 'em consistently!

As a general rule, in early evening, fish tend to be nearer the drop-offs, and both morning and evening fish are fairly tight to bottom. On darker, cloudier days, they tend to hug tighter to the bottom for longer periods of the day. The fish tend to move less than they do on sunny days and are definitely a little finicky about what they'll strike.

On sunny mornings and evenings or during most days, crappies tend to rise off the bottom. They'll suspend 5 to 15 feet off the bottom over 25 to 40 feet of water, becoming extremely active and catchable.

This midday, sun-related activity is probably due to the stained or tea-colored water common to these lakes. The sun makes it easier for crappies to spot their food and may also slightly warm the water. The increased light penetration produces a greater amount of zooplankton activity and resulting minnow activity. Even this tiny increase in sunlight is sufficient to trigger the growth of microscopic organisms and, therefore, kick off the food chain.

By late afternoon or early evening, many crappies tend to move to the drop-offs surrounding points and rock piles. The action can be fast and furious for 1-1/2 hours, or so, before sunset.

Thus, a typical Canadian fall-crappie day would go something like this. You might catch several early-morning crappies by swimming a small jig across the bottom in 28 feet of water and never see a suspended fish on your depth finder. Yet, as the hours pass the school might begin rising. By 11:00 A.M. the majority of the fish might suspend in 12 to 18 feet of water and be extremely active and aggressive. They could remain that way most of the day. By evening, however, many of the fish would probably begin moving tight to nearby points and drop-offs. As you can see, your presentation approach should be modified during the day.

PRESENTATION

Your first step should be to find a good lake map (if available) and to pick out bays off (or sections of) the main lake with 20- to 40-foot maximum depths. Begin your morning fishing by scouting for fish with your depth finder

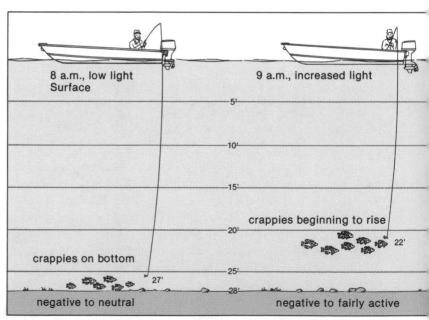

The accompanying illustration shows how crappie position and activity typically changes throughout the course of a day. In early morning, they're tight to the bottom and inactive. As the day wears on, they eventually rise to an active position.

The suspended, active position is also more common on sunny, rather than cloudy

and drifting the areas adjacent to sharp-dropping points or sunken islands. One angler should keep his jig right on the bottom, the other a few feet off bottom. If there are no results, keep lifting your lures up a few feet on each drift until you begin catching fish or spot fish on the depth finder.

Toss out a floating marker to mark the general area; it'll keep you on fish and help you plan your drift patterns. Concentrate your efforts at that depth until you stop catching fish. Then it's time to experiment with depth again or move to a different spot.

For best results, keep your equipment light. Anytime you're after panfish, a good ultralight spinning outfit is usually your best bet. If that doesn't fit your budget, you can get by with a regular, medium-action spinning rod like you'd use for walleyes. Just be sure the rod has a soft, sensitive tip. This allows you to lift up slightly and watch the rod tip to sense if a finicky fish has sucked in your jig, instead of having to pull up too hard and spook the fish. While 4-pound-test line is adequate for most conditions, you can go up to 6-pound test for snag-infested conditions, although it makes presenting a tiny jig in deep water much more difficult. If you're a sport and don't mind losing a few fish, you can even experiment with 2-pound-test line.

Without a doubt, there's no better lure to fish for suspended crappies than a tiny jig. Day in and day out, a 1/16- or 1/8-ounce, white or chartreuse jig is hard to beat. Other colors—usually light to imitate light colored minnows—will produce, but these two are superb.

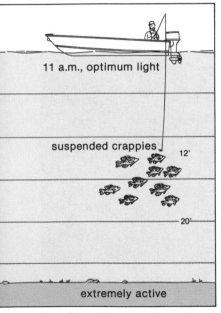

days. Tom Neustrom has noticed a correlation between it and the barometric pressure. Rising or fairly high barometers of 29.60- to 30.00-plus (typical of sunny days) generally show suspended fish. Lower readings of 29.2 to 29.6 generally indicate darker days and fish located more on the bottom.

Small marabou, chenille-body/marabou-tail, or plastic-body/marabou-tail jigs are all dynamite. They have a natural-breathing action at rest and entice even fussy fish. Tip them with a small, 1-1/2-inch crappie minnow (if available) by inserting the hook up through the minnow's bottom jaw and out the top of its head.

If live minnows aren't available, fish the jigs plain—or use dead minnows. You can't transport live minnows across the Canadian border from the U.S., so pack dead minnows in a bag of ice (no water) if you can't buy live ones locally. They'll stay fresh and usable for days.

You can even add a sliver of throat skin cut from a crappie. It's a little trick that pays big dividends. At times, adding a drop of a scent product may produce even better results—especially when minnows aren't available. (In some areas of Canada, live bait is difficult to obtain or even illegal.)

As an alternate approach, try drifting a floating-jighead/sliding-sinker, minnow rig. Keep the snell short (2 feet or less) and use a sinker just heavy enough to scrape along the bottom on the drift. It's deadly for fish on or just off the bottom. Whatever the case, simplicity is the key. Whether it's a small jig or just a plain hook, always tie directly to your line. Adding snaps and swivels will hamper the natural action of these tiny lures.

FISHING THE JIG

Jig presentation varies, depending on the activity and position of a crappie school, and also weather conditions. For example, let's say it's very calm and

Small and simple is the rule for crappies. Any attempt to exaggerate lure size or movement is usually counterproductive. A small assortment of 1/16- and 1/8-ounce, light-colored jigs usually does the trick.

Top row, left to right: A Cordell Doll Fly marabou jig and a Lindy Fuzz-E-Grub (plastic-body/marabou-tail).

Bottom row: Blakemore Road Runners with (1) a chenille-body/marabou-tail and (2) a plastic Twister tail, and a Windels Rabbit Hair jig.

you've used your depth finder to locate a school of suspended crappies. Under these conditions, it's very easy to hover directly above the fish and vertically jig your lure right through the school. If there's a gentle wind, simply drift. If it's calm, you can fish a 1/16-ounce jig very effectively; there's no need to go to a bulkier, 1/8-ounce jig like you need to maintain "feel" in windy conditions.

With 4-pound-test line, the jig will sink approximately 1 to 2 feet per second, depending on the body style. Open your bail and let the jig sink to the approximate depth of the fish; watch the line for the telltale twitch of a fish hitting the sinking line.

Once your jig reaches the proper depth level, close the bail and place your index finger on the line to help detect soft strikes. Lift your rod tip 2 or 3 feet, hold it there for a few seconds, and then slowly drop it again. Pause between lifts for a count of about five, and watch that rod tip. Crappies generally hit a stationary or falling jig best. Since their eyes face upward, crappies feed most effectively in that direction. But, it's not a vicious strike! Instead, it's more of a subtle twitch—a slight pressure you detect by gently lifting the rod tip.

When you hook a fish, make sure your partner casts or drops a jig in the vicinity of the hooked fish. Often, several fish will be excited by the hooked crappie and follow it. You can catch another fish by simultaneously reeling a jig past them. In fact, if you can, try to keep a hooked fish struggling, say halfway to the boat, until your partner hooks one. Then reel yours in. It'll keep 'em in a frenzy. Take turns!

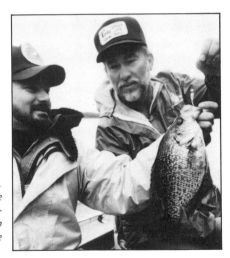

Pausing before you set the hook, especially on cloudy/windy days when the fish are fussy and you have a hard time feeling a strike, is very essential. A soft, rod tip is critical in these conditions to help sense the strike.

If you can, work above or right at the top of a crappie school. Keep drawing the fish up rather than dragging hooked fish up through the entire school. That might spook 'em eventually. By using this trick, we've caught many slab crappies off a deep rock pile before spooking them.

Another variation to fishing suspended crappies is a swing and drop method. It works well in areas with a large concentration of fish that are not tightly schooled. Cast the jig out 10 to 15 yards. Close the bail and place your index finger on the line. The jig will swing and drop back below the boat in an arc, while covering a range of depths. You can even just cast out, let the jig sink to the proper depth, and slowly reel in.

This method is particularly deadly with an action jig like a Twister Tail or a spinner jig like a Blakemore Road Runner. Watch your rod tip and line closely, because crappies will follow, suck in the line, keep swimming, and create slack that's very difficult to detect. Pay attention!

FLATLAND RESERVOIRS

Flatland reservoirs are some of the finest, multi-species fisheries in North America. Depending on the region, they may 'host bass, crappies, saugers, walleyes, catfish, and even a big musky or two.

An important key to fishing flatland reservoirs is realizing their commonly stained or off-colored water tends to keep fish shallow much of the year. Granted, the water is usually clearer in the main reservoir, and it's possible to catch fish deeper there. However, creek arms, where a major segment of the fish are located, are usually darker than the main lake. The crappie populations found there tend to remain shallow. To be more specific, for most of the season the crappies in creek arms may be spread out on shallow, massive flats, often relating to flooded cover like brush piles, stump beds and fallen trees. Such is the case on good, multi-species, flatland reservoirs like Kentucky or Barkley Lakes in Kentucky and Tennessee.

THE FALL DRAWDOWN

About October, the Corps of Engineers commonly finishes dropping the lake level of these reservoir types about 2 to 6 feet to winter pool. This strategy builds a "cushion" so heavy spring run-off won't overrun the capacity of the reservoir and helps minimize ice damage to shorelines on lakes that freeze. If you think this fall drawdown has a big effect on the lake, just think what it does to the fish!

The fall drawdown effectively "pulls the plug" on many shallow, summer-fishing spots. As the water drops, those beautiful, 2- to 6-foot-deep brush, stump and fallen tree areas on the flats begin drying up, or at least become too shallow for fish to use consistently. The fish have no choice but to vacate these areas for deeper water.

As the water recedes, it literally sucks the fish off the flats, concentrating them in specific kinds of deeper spots.

FALL CRAPPIES

During spring and summer, a portion of the crappie population often uses similar (but deeper) areas as largemouth bass. After the fall drawdown, they tend to prefer a different kind of area than bass. Rather than moving to steep shoreline points, crappies generally move to deep outside bends in the creek channel, usually somewhere in the 10- to 20-foot range. In moderately stained water, 10 feet is sufficiently deep. However, since the water color tends to clear somewhat in fall, 15 to 20 feet is more typical.

Typical Cove in a Flatland Reservoir

MAIN RESERVOIR

A

6'

8'

3'

4'

12

14

6'

4'

B

10'

16'

fallen tree

brush

stumps

boulders

11'

23'

14'

10'

18'

C

inside
bend

10'

10'

20'

8'

outside
bend

25'

12'

D

The accompanying map shows a good, year-'round crappie area on a flatland reservoir. AREA A is a typical, shallow, spring-crappie spawning spot. After spawning, crappies will usually filter out of these shallow areas. Some fish will scatter into available cover on the adjacent flats in AREA B. Generally, the more cover on the flat, the more fish it will attract and hold. Other fish will move to the main-channel area of the reservoir; AREA D is a typical crappie main-lake summer haunt. In fall, crappies will move from the main-lake areas back toward the bays and will pile up in the outside edges of creek-channel bends (AREA C). Meanwhile, crappies that inhabited the flats in AREA B during the summer will also move into AREA C after the fall drawdown.

As crappies move off the brush piles and flats, they'll follow the creek channel out to a creek bend at a "comfortable" depth level. While this occurs, they are often joined by crappies from the main lake that are making a "reverse" fall movement back toward the mouths of the creek arms. As the fish pile into creek-bend areas, huge fall schools begin to form.

Cover in the form of brush or sunken trees is a definite plus, although this condition is not common unless some enterprising angler sinks his own fish attractor in deep water. Many of the best, creek-bend areas, therefore, can be almost devoid of wood. Crappies, however, are effective open-water predators and do just fine without it.

Large schools of crappies will gather in the slightly deeper, outside edges of the channel bends, and you can spot them on your depth finder. They'll appear as multiple flashes, generally within the first 4 feet or so of bottom. Once you've cruised the channel, scouted a few creek bends and spotted signs of fish near the bottom, you're all set for some fast and easy fishing.

PRESENTATION

Many, reservoir, crappie anglers rely on heavy line, large hooks and heavy sinkers to drop a minnow (hooked through the back) into brush piles. While a case can be made for such a heavy-duty approach when the fish are down inside massive brush piles, don't make the mistake of thinking you need such heavy tackle for deep, open-water fish in the channel bends. An ultralight

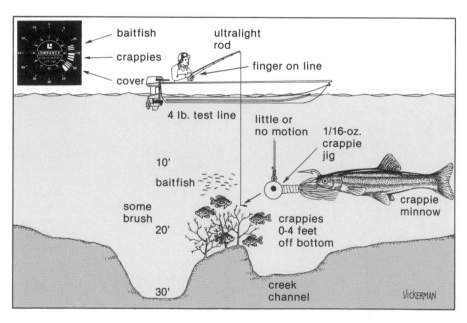

Slow and simple is the rule for deep crappies. Hover right over the fish and let out just enough line to hit bottom. When the line goes slack, engage the reel and place your finger on the line. It'll help you detect "soft" strikes. For crappies, use minimum motion in your presentation. The best jigging motion is often no motion at all—just hold the jig still. Since crappies often suspend, try to spot 'em on the depth finder and hold the jig at their depth level. It's deadly.

spinning outfit with 4-pound-test line gets your bait down deeper, easier, and the fish put up one whale of a fight to boot!

Tiny crappie jigs in the 1/16- to 1/8-ounce range are deadly for these conditions. One favorite is the pink and white Lindy Fuzz-E-Grub—a real killer in both clear and stained water. However, pink, white, yellow and chartreuse are all superb color choices. Small marabou- and chenille-bodied jigs are productive, too.

Feast your eyes on these monster fall black crappies. How big are they. Believe it or not the three largest fish weighed in at nearly 11 pounds! The fish were caught from a northeastern, natural lake on a 1/8-ounce chartreuse Charlie Brewer Crappie Slider.

Southern anglers seem to fish a jig or a minnow but seldom fish the two together—a common "Yankee" technique. Simply insert the hook beneath the minnow's lower jaw, poking it out the top of the head. Tipping a jig with a minnow is deadly on cold-water crappies.

Lower your jig to the bottom; close the bail on the reel; pick up the line with your index finger, and simply hold it there. After a few seconds, lift the jig up 6 inches to a foot. Again hold it steady. Don't jig it up and down. Crappies prefer a steady lure rather than a wildly hopping one. Use your electric motor to slowly cruise along the channel basin, sometimes holding it 1, 2 or 3 feet off the bottom—particularly if you spot fish suspended above the bottom.

Strikes are light, so pay attention to any little twitch or change in the feel of the jig. Stick 'em hard and then enjoy the fight of a big crappie bulldogging around 15 or 18 feet down. It takes a long time to get 'em up from that depth, especially on ultralight tackle.

Throw out a floating marker; get your jig back down; and do it again. Redrift and work the school over and over. A good channel bend can attract hundreds of crappies by fall and perhaps even thousands by mid-winter. Talk about the mother lode: all the fish you could ever want and probably few, if any, anglers fishing them this late in the year. The term "like shooting fish in a barrel" is appropriate!

The fall drawdown on flatland reservoirs is not a calamity! In fact, it's an eagerly awaited event for those in-the-know. The reduced water level concentrates fish in easily identified spots, and you can get on them if you know what to look for.

Frankly, we're astonished by the lack of anglers on many mid-South impoundments in November and December. The fishing's just getting good. Don't pass up this incredible opportunity to enjoy fall crappies.

Chapter 12

WINTER

Coldest-Water Crappies

Because of the crappie's wide range, winter creates two extremely contrasting fishing situations: ice fishing in the North and open-water angling in the South. For both areas, this time frame encompasses the coldest water temperatures of the year.

Even during this Coldest Water Period, crappies feed actively and are very catchable. In fact, some real trophies are caught during early winter in northern lakes and southern impoundments. December may be the month for trophy fish throughout the South.

FIRST ICE

Crappies are light sensitive, and in clear bodies of water they often bite best during twilight hours, after dark, or in deeper water during midday; ice fishing is no exception, although you can experience good, daytime angling, too. During first-ice, you can almost always catch some midday crappies in clear-water lakes from cover such as weeds or timber. And, of course, the heavy ice and snow cover of late season cuts light penetration and may intensify midday feeding.

In lakes with a bit of color, crappies often bite consistently in shallower water right through midday. However, even on these lakes, look for twilight activity. Changing light intensity at dusk and dawn often triggers crappie and other gamefish activity.

Most consistent fishing patterns key around the location of forage. Zooplankton and minnow concentrations often mean crappie concentrations. To illustrate this concept, let's examine one area that usually concentrates zooplankton and draws minnows during first-ice.

When any relatively large, shallow bay or creek arm freezes, a good portion of the baitfish present will be sucked out toward the main body of water. We're not exactly sure why this happens, but we have seen the phenomenon enough to be sure it occurs. When conditions stabilize, the baitfish may move back into the bay or creek arm.

After the baitfish make a mass exodus from a shallow bay or creek arm, they hold for a time in the first main-lake or reservoir cover they encounter. Cover might be either weeds, timber or brush on an adjacent main-lake or reservoir flat; weeds or timberlines near the edges of the flat; the deeper-water drop-off area, etc. When the bait moves out, the crappies move in—not into the shallow bay or creek arm but into areas *adjacent to* the mouth of the bay or creek arm. Crappies head 'em off at the pass, and the collision of bait and crappies can produce some of the finest crappie fishing of the year.

By now you should have a clear picture of a general type of area to look for. Let's get more specific. As you might expect, large bays or creek arms generally offer more potential than small bays or creek arms, because large areas generally attract more bait. However, whatever size the bay or creek arm is, it must be shallow enough so that freeze-up (or very cold weather prior to freeze-up) causes bait to migrate from the shallower areas.

A bay or creek arm with a deep hole or channel may upset this pattern, because the bait may not move all the way out. Still, the flat or drop-off at the mouth of the bay or creek arm would be worth checking. In the case of a creek arm, check the flat or drop-off next to the channel. A better option in this instance is fishing either the hole in the bay, or the fringe of the creek channel. If these areas attract and concentrate forage, they likely will also hold crappies.

The more the mouth of a bay or creek arm narrows down, bait and crappies are more likely to be channeled into a specific area. Obviously, this is an advantage. A wide bay or creek-arm mouth can be a problem, because bait can leave the area anywhere. The crappies will also spread out. Excellent fishing usually results when conditions funnel baitfish, and subsequently predators, into a confined area. Such perfect conditions frequently exist in lakes, but only seldom in reservoirs.

As bait vacates a bay or creek arm, it contacts the flat immediately outside the area. Some flats are better than others. First, a good flat should have cover like remaining stands of leafy pondweed, or timber, or both. A flat without cover will not hold fish very long.

The flat should also be deep enough to contrast with the depth inside the bay or creek arm. In other words, for a flat outside a bay or creek arm to hold fish for long, it should be at least as deep as the bay or creek arm it is adjacent to.

"Bait Out/Crappies In"

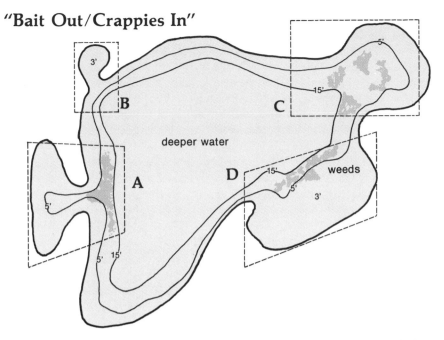

The "bait out/crappies in" pattern is based on the movement of bait out of relatively shallow bays into main-lake areas, where they are intercepted by crappies. Although we observe this happening at first ice, it probably occurs before then. In other words, hardy, late-season boat anglers can also key on this pattern.

The best crappie fishing usually occurs outside large, relatively shallow bays with narrow, main-lake openings. The narrow, main-lake opening should lead to a fairly deep, and moderately sized flat, with cover extending all the way to the drop-off. None of the areas on our test lake exhibits perfect conditions, but they all may still attract crappies. Let's look at each area.

AREA A—A relatively shallow bay with a narrow opening to a cover-filled, main-lake flat. Everything you're looking for except a distinct area on the flat or drop-off to concentrate fish. One of the best (perhaps the best) first-ice areas on the lake.

AREA B—The bay is too small to hold much bait, and the flat is too small to hold many crappies for long, but any crappies attracted to bait moving out of this bay will be in the clearly defined area of the inside turn just outside the bay. If this inside turn was at the mouth of AREA A, you'd have a tremendous spot!

AREA C—The opening at the mouth of the bay is too large, and the flat outside the bay is too large, to really concentrate fish, but there will be crappies here. The drop-off is a big plus in this area. The 15-foot water juts into the bay and creates a clearly defined holding area.

AREA D—There'll be plenty of bait and crappies, but everything will be spread out, making fishing more difficult.

If we had to choose between the four areas, we'd fish AREA A first, followed by AREA C. Actually, we'd probably check AREA B quickly before moving to AREA C. AREAS C and D would probably offer the most sustained crappie activity over the entire winter season, but that, too, is another story.

The same principles apply to reservoir creek arms, as well.

Of course, it's better if the main lake or reservoir flat is deeper. In a lake, a good situation would occur where a 7- to 15-foot-deep flat adjoins a bay with depths from 3 to 5 feet. A good creek arm situation would have 7- to 15-feet-deep water on the flat and creek channel adjacent to the creek arm. Inside the creek arm, the flats would run 3 to 5 feet deep, and the channel no deeper than 7 or 8 feet. These, however, are optimum conditions.

Obviously, these examples are relative to the type of water you're fishing. For example, the bays on shallow eutrophic lakes are seldom as deep as those in deep, clear mesotrophic lakes. The same would be true if you were comparing this pattern on hill-land and flatland reservoirs. The key is *contrast in depth* from the interior of the bay or creek arm to adjacent structural elements outside.

Does the size of the main-lake or reservoir flat make a difference? Yes, it does. But it's not as simple as "large-flat-lotsa-fish/small-flat-few-fish." Actually, a small flat adjoining a big bay can host a dynamite fishery. After all, once the bait leaves the bay and the crappies move in, there are not many locational choices for crappies, or anglers. You'll know where the fish should be and that can mean great fishing.

Small flats don't hold many fish for long. Expect good fishing to be short lived. The opposite can be true of big flats. Big flats (with cover, of course) adjacent to large bays or creek arms may hold many fish for a long time, but the crappies may be spread out.

DROP-OFFS

If a flat holds crappies, the drop-off will *definitely* hold them. But even when flats hold few fish, drop-offs may still hold crappies. Expect the most consistent crappie activity to take place in: (1) the confined open water just outside the drop-off, (2) on the drop-off itself, or (3) on the first part of the flat

Many reservoirs don't freeze over but still experience a Winter Calendar Period comparable to lakes which freeze up. Remember, this period features the coldest water of the year. At this time, the most effective presentation is usually an ultra-slow and simple one similar to ice-fishing techniques. Here's a slab 2-pound crappie caught from a deep, timbered point on a small jig fished nearly motionless near the bottom.

immediately adjacent to the drop-off.

The drop-off area must be distinct, although it does not need to fall into the deepest water in a body of water. A distinct drop-off has either a quick depth change or an abrupt halt to cover. Thus, a drop-off created by a flat that slowly tapers to 7 feet and then suddenly drops into 18 feet of water will often hold fish. Usually, however, this condition offers short-lived fishing, just as a small flat does.

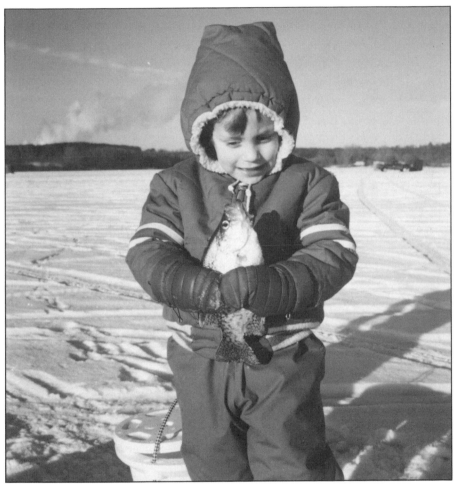

"Hey, Mom and Dad, look what I caught!" Modern, warm, winter clothing has made ice fishing an angling adventure for the entire family.

FLATS AND DROP-OFFS

The best type of drop-off has a depth change and cover that extends all the way to the drop-off. A timber-covered flat adjacent to a drop-off into the main reservoir is a good example. In a lake, weedgrowth should extend all the way to the drop-off.

Good Time Flats and Drop-offs

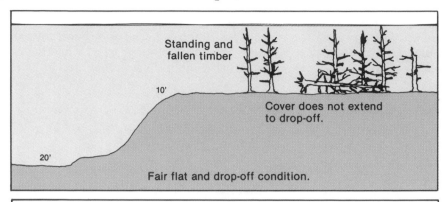

Standing and fallen timber

10'

Cover does not extend to drop-off.

20'

Fair flat and drop-off condition.

Cover extends to drop-off.

10'

20'

The best flat and drop-off condition.

Fair flat and drop-off condition.

The best flat and drop-off condition.

10'

timber

The point concentrates fish.

5'

5'

Weeds extend to drop-off.

inside turn in drop-off

15'

20'

The best flat and drop-off condition.

The best flats outside relatively large, shallow bays offer plenty of cover extending all the way to the drop-off. The best drop-offs have points or inside turns to help concentrate fish.

One final thought before proceeding: The mouths of canals, necked-down areas between different locations on a body of water, or even small feeder creeks may also attract bait and crappies. These situations are different, yet akin to the pattern we're keying on.

LIGHT INTENSITY AND CRAPPIES

Some lakes develop distinct patterns at certain times. While we can't tell you ahead of time exactly *when* crappies will bite in the bodies of water you fish, we can talk about *tendencies*.

There are four major fishing zones: (1) the flat, (2) the small slice of flat immediately adjacent to the drop-off, (3) the drop-off, and (4) confined open water near the drop-off. On all bodies of water, crappie activity is possible in all four areas during the twilight periods of morning and evening. Changing light intensity often triggers crappies just as it does walleyes.

In dingy waters, crappie activity usually occurs during the day. Where? Any of the four areas may hold fish if the prerequisites are present. However, in dingy water, the confined-open-water zone is the most marginal pattern. In dingy lakes, crappies tend to relate to something definite. We have not done well fishing at night in these waters, but we admit that our night fishing has been limited.

In clear water, look for daytime activity on the flat only if there is good cover. Even then, expect the fishing to be sporadic because the fish are likely to be scattered. A better chance for schooling-fish is possible on the drop-off or the flat area immediately adjacent to the drop-off. Confined open water will usually hold many fish. Expect intense night feeding to take place on the drop-off and the flat. Nighttime activity may occur in confined open water but is more common later in the season.

Crappie activity often occurs at evening twilight, then shuts off abruptly, and begins again in a hour or two. Crappies have a vision advantage over minnow prey during the twilight hours. They also have an advantage after dark—when their eyes have readjusted. In our experience, things usually slow down for a short time just after dark.

LATE SEASON LOCATION

By late season, many—probably most—crappies and plenty of baitfish have been sucked into deep water. The reason may be no more complex than that the water is comparatively warm and stable there. Water is most dense at about 39 °F, so the temperature in deep water is probably around 39 °F. Water just below the ice is near 32 °F. The temperature rises toward 39 °F as you proceed toward the bottom.

There are some crappies on shallow bars, and some move shallow from deeper water. But, the percentages are for finding the most crappies by using three types of areas: (1) the deep-water edges of prominent structural elements such as bars, points, sunken islands, or shoreline inside-turns; (2) the confined open water off these edges; and (3) the true open water of deeper-water holes in (A) shallower bays, and (B) small, shallow, dishpan-type lakes.

Structural elements in deep lakes include, for the most part, prominent points or inside-turn areas. Keep the "U-factor" in mind. A U-shaped turn in the drop-off can represent either a big inside turn or the opposite—a point. Look for U-factor spots to find crappies.

Look for U-factor spots on a grand, not a small scale. It's the general area off

Crappie Location in Deep Lakes and Bays

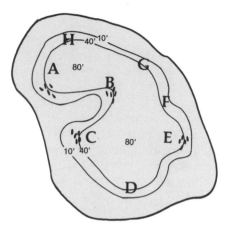

Take a big "U-turn" when you're looking for crappies in a deep lake or bay. A right-side-up "U" represents a big inside turn, and a turned-over "U", a point. Look for U-turns.

In our Deep Lake, spots A thru H are all U-turn areas. Spots A, B and C are the most distinct and, therefore, the most significant areas, but the others may also attract crappies at times. Crappies may indeed be roaming over the deepest-water sections of the lake, but your chance for finding them are better in U-turn areas.

Yes, yes. Most crappies are deep, but some will be using the shallows in spots like A, B and C.

Crappie Location in Shallow Lakes and Bays

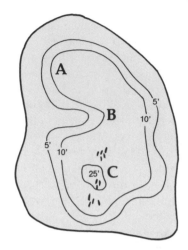

Crappie location can be much different in shallow, dishpan-type lakes or bays. While crappies may use points and inside turns such as A and B, they are more likely to relate to the deep water surrounding deeper lake holes. In shallow lakes and bays, it's not uncommon for crappies to completely ignore points and inside turns.

the tip of a major point that's important. Small projections (points) off a major point are fairly insignificant. Likewise, small "U" spots (inside turns) on prominent bars are also insignificant to general crappie location. Large U-factor spots tend to gather crappies relating to confined open water, so a huge inside turn, formed where the base of a major point turns, is a good crappie spot. Crappies often use confined open water, but only occasionally use true open water. However, late winter is one yearly period when they do.

In large lake or bay areas, look for crappies to suspend off but near obvious points or inside turns. However, in smaller bays that have enough deep water (25 to 45 feet deep) to hold crappies, conditions are slightly different. More of the crappies may relate to the deepest water area in the lake or bay area, to the obvious disregard of shoreline points and inside turns. The same may hold true in smaller, dishpan-type lakes up to about 400 acres in size.

When crappies first start to appear in deeper water, there's a tendency for deep suspension. In a 40-foot hole, it's common to find crappies at the bottom

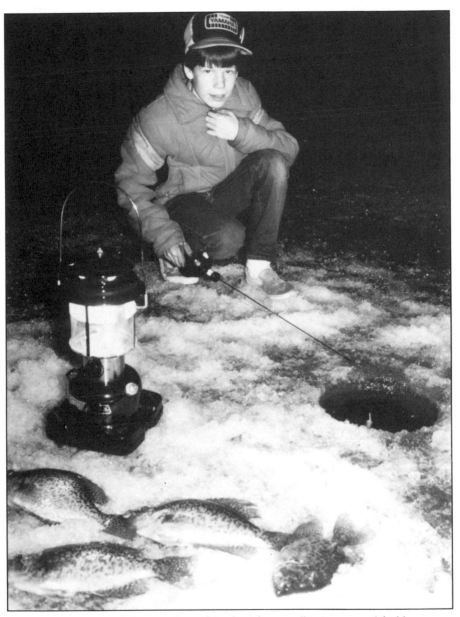

A light-action, ice-fishing rod combined with a small minnow and bobber means crappie fun. This young fella has found a hot hole.

or at least suspended within 1 to 10 feet off bottom. It's uncommon for them to suspend halfway down from the surface.

By late season, crappies tend to suspend at many different depths. Yet the best chance to find them on any given night is still 1 to 10 feet off bottom.

Here are good tips for locating crappies: Look (1) in or near a deep hole in a smaller lake or a bay, or (2) in the confined open water off a large main-lake or bay point, or an inside turn. When they are schooled deep, they usually spread out horizontally. Taking a few crappies at 4 feet above the bottom often means most of the fish will be caught there.

When schools suspend higher, they tend to spread out both horizontally and vertically. Larger-size, deep-water crappies are only occasionally tightly schooled. Large, loose schools are more common and, at other times, many small schools seem to take the place of large schools.

Crappies in deeper holes in small, dishpan-type lakes or in bays off a large lake are not always over the deepest water. Simply picture a school or schools somewhere in the lake near the deepest hole. Schools roam but tend to stay in

Suspension Tendencies

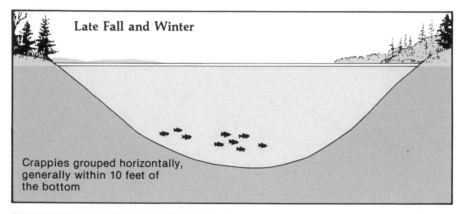

Late Fall and Winter

Crappies grouped horizontally, generally within 10 feet of the bottom

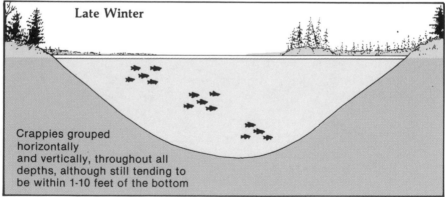

Late Winter

Crappies grouped horizontally and vertically, throughout all depths, although still tending to be within 1-10 feet of the bottom

Crappies begin to use deeper lake areas during late fall or early winter. Although it's impossible to make hard/fast rules about how crappies suspend when they're in deeper water, here are two general tendencies.

When crappies first begin to use deep water, look for them to suspend horizontally, and near the bottom. As a rule, through most of winter, we find crappies within 10 feet of the bottom.

As ice-out approaches, this may change. Crappies may still be found near the

this lake or bay region. Schools sort of "drift", rarely making drastic locational changes, although they may drift several hundred yards or more from one day to the next. But again, drifting will probably take place near or around the deeper water in the open-water portion of the smaller lake or bay.

That's general location. Specific location is a matter of looking with a depth finder and fishing in the general areas where crappie schools are working. At times, crappies tend to stay over harder-bottom areas off points or inside turns. Usually, however, you'll see nothing particularly different about an area, but the fish will tell you *that's the spot* by consistently being there.

bottom, but there is a tendency for them to suspend both horizontally and vertically. This suspension is often from the bottom into the upper half of the depths, although the percentage is still for fish to be within 10 feet of the bottom.

Where crappies suspend in deep water often differs from one type of lake to another. In deep lakes and bays, look for crappies off points and inside-turn areas. In shallow, dishpan-type lakes and bays, look for them near deeper holes, often to the obvious disregard of points and inside-turn areas.

It's best to attach hooks and lures to 4- or 6-pound-test line when you're fishing for crappies, but that doesn't mean you have to fill an entire reel spool with it. In fact, that's counterproductive, because monofilament is hard to handle if you're hand-lining crappies.

Dacron's the answer. Fill your reel with 27- or 36-pound dacron and you have a line that's easy to handle and see. It'll mean more fish, because you can get back down faster. Attach your 4- or 6-pound-test line to a loop or swivel on the end of the dacron.

This shot also shows one of the 39-inch, graphite, H.T. Enterprise rods (a GJL-31) that we prefer for crappie fishing when we fish outside. A buoy-type bobber is also pictured.

In case you're new to the ice-fishing scene, the plastic reel is a line storage device and isn't used to reel crappies up and down. That's too slow. After setting the hook with the rod, hand-over-hand 'em in.

ICE-FISHING EQUIPMENT

There are many varieties of ice-fishing rods on the market; obviously, it's best to have a rod that's strong enough to whip good fish yet is light and sensitive. Sticks (rods) with pegs for hand-wrapping line work well in many instances. However, we prefer a reel so it's easy to store line and to fish in both deep and shallow water.

For panfish, the reel should be light. Choose one with a reliable drag system because a 2-pound crappie can put quite a strain on light line.

Light line? For crappies, 2- or 4-pound test is usually sufficient, unless you're fishing in timber. Six-pound-test line is adequate in most cover situations.

LURES AND BAITS

The standard rig and bait for catching crappies through the ice is a small minnow on a size 6, 8, or 10 hook held at an appropriate depth by a small split shot. Often as not, this arrangement is suspended below a bobber. This ap-

It's hard to beat the standard minnow-on-a-small-hook rig held in place by a split shot and bobber, but there are other options that work better on occasion. Starting in the upper left hand corner and moving clockwise, other crappie ice-fishing lures include: our "search lure" (a Kastmaster plus a suspended leadhead jig); two lead-wire-wrapped hooks; a small leadhead jig; two daphnia-imitating concoctions from H.T. Enterprises; a Swedish Pimple; a jigging Rapala; and, in the center, two teardrops. Grubs or bits of fish flesh are usually added for triggering power, although minnows also work great on the search lure, teardrops or the small leadhead jig. You may need to add a split shot for extra weight when using a minnow (hook it under the dorsal fin) on a teardrop.

proach to triggering winter crappies is the standard that other methods are judged by. However, this doesn't mean other methods won't work better at times.

A versatile angler pursuing crappies through the ice should also carry an assortment of teardrops or ice flies, jigging lures that swim when jigged, and jigging lures that flash (to attract fish) when vertically raised and dropped. All of these lure options have their moments. As a matter of fact, these options outproduce the standard minnow-on-a-small-hook rig on many occasions.

Crappies, even the large ones, often feed on tiny creatures (zooplankton) no bigger than a pinhead. Small, plain (no hair or other dressing) teardrops, ice flies, weighted wire hooks, and small leadhead jigs dressed with grubs probably all do a good job of imitating zooplankton.

Leadhead jigs are one of your best options when searching for fish. A jig dressed with a grub or two is easy to move from hole to hole without fuss; there's no hooking and unhooking minnows or sticking your hand in the bait bucket (we invariably forget a small minnow net). Once you find fish, you can continue to fish the jig and grub, switch to a teardrop and minnow, work a plain minnow, or try another jigging lure.

A SEARCH LURE

Some lures attract fish, some trigger fish, and some do both in certain instances. We'd like to highlight an effective compromise lure. The lure is good

---

Lures/Rigs

SEARCH LURE

To make a search lure, remove the treble hook from an Acme Kastmaster. Add a drop-line of about 2-1/2 inches, and hang a small leadhead jig, teardrop or plain hook on the dropper. The flash attracts fish, and the small lure or hook dressed with grubs, fish flesh or a minnow triggers them when they're drawn close. This lure can be fished effectively in deep (down to 60 feet) or shallow water.

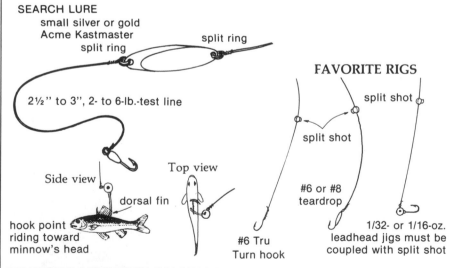

SEARCH LURE
small silver or gold Acme Kastmaster
split ring
split ring

2½" to 3", 2- to 6-lb.-test line

Side view
Top view
dorsal fin

hook point riding toward minnow's head

#6 Tru Turn hook

FAVORITE RIGS

split shot

split shot

#6 or #8 teardrop

1/32- or 1/16-oz. leadhead jigs must be coupled with split shot

HOOKING MINNOWS ON LEADHEAD JIGS

Most anglers assume that minnows can only be hooked through the lips when they're used on leadhead jigs. And, as an alternative, some anglers also hook a jig under a minnow's dorsal fin, perpendicular to the backbone.

We believe that hooking a minnow under the dorsal fin parallel to the backbone results in more consistent hooking. Make sure that the hook point rides toward the minnow's head. Teardrops can be used the same way.

when you're on fish, but it is especially effective as a "search lure" when you're probing for fish.

The search lure is a small Acme Kastmaster with the treble hook removed. Tie a small piece of light line on the bottom split ring. Add either a small 1/32- or 1/64-ounce, plain leadhead jig or a small teardrop to the end of this line. The bait should hang below the Kastmaster about 2-1/2 to 3 inches. If the line is too long, it'll tangle when you jig the lure. If it's shorter, you'll lose some of the lure's triggering power. Add a grub, minnow, fish meat, or a fish eye to the jig or teardrop.

This lure gets deep fast and can be effectively fished at any depth. It also has flash, thereby extra attracting power, and offers a small morsel as a triggering device once fish have been attracted. Again, once you find fish, you might consider switching to another lure with more triggering power.

JIGGING OPTIONS

The type of ice-fishing lure and the jigging motion you should use may depend on the type of zooplankton that panfish are feeding on. Two typical zooplankton options are daphnia and copepods. Daphnia bob and flutter but rarely move horizontally unless they're swept by current. Copepods, on the other hand, make quick darting movements and usually remain in the upper-water layer. Daphnia imitations usually work well at all times, while copepod imitations usually work best during midday.

Because daphnia exhibit an almost constant fluttering motion that rarely

You should have a variety of different lures like spoons and jigs—some with long-shank hooks (for adding larger grubs) and others with short-shanks hooks. Stick with 3 basic color approaches: (1) subdued colors such as black or purple, (2) bright colors such as fluorescent orange or chartreuse, or (3) subtle colors such as white or yellow. Colors are probably more important for attraction than for close-up triggering effect. Note the small size of the lures and bobber.

moves them horizontally, a slow or rapid jiggling motion (the bait vibrating vertically about 1/16 to 1/8 inch) is a proper presentation with a teardrop and grub. To imitate copepods, your jigging approach should be more aggressive.

Most ice-fishing presentations should be a mixture of: (1) *attraction jigging* to get the fish's attention, and (2) *enticement jigging* to get fish to strike. Thus, make larger, intermittent jigging movements to draw attention to the presence of your bait. But, frequent pauses are also necessary in order to detect panfish bites. Thus, the basic jigging motion becomes jiggle-jiggle-jiggle (1/16- to 1/8-inch moves), pause, jiggle-jiggle-jiggle, pause, hop-hop (1-foot moves). Repeat the procedure.

Obviously, you should experiment by deviating from this basic pattern. Especially, try lengthening the pause. You're rarely able to hold a bait perfectly still, and on some days such slight movement may be the trigger. A small bobber allows you to suspend a bait nearly motionless. Studies show that panfish seldom take dead daphnia, so baits should rarely be still all the time.

THE HOOK SET

Some anglers are puzzled by when to set the hook. Should you let a crappie take the bobber under 6 inches, a foot, or 2 feet?

Often, when a crappie inhales an entire minnow, the bobber will distinctly "pop" up or down an inch or two. If you see this "pop," and your bobber doesn't return to its exact former position, set the hook.

Crappies that swim up to take a bait often make the bobber float up as if there were no weight on it. Set the hook. And, crappies that hit a bait and immediately move off (the bobber moves down) with it, usually have it, too. Set the hook.

A hook set should be a firm, steady lift and not a jerk; a crappie has a tender mouth. We try to make the initial hook set using the flex in a light rod to be sure the hook doesn't tear out. If you're not using a spinning rod and reel combo, the set is followed by immediately hand-over-handing the fish up firmly and quickly. Don't allow any slack line or the fish is likely to come off on the way up.

FLORIDA LAKES

Now it's time to look for some winter open water, and that leads us to the speckled perch (black crappies) of Florida. W. Horace Carter has fine tuned a system that takes black crappies year 'round on Florida's natural, shallow lakes. This entails trolling a neutrally buoyant lure in the deepest areas of the lake. In most Florida lakes, the deepest water is often only 10 to 16 feet deep.

The neutral-buoyant approach consists of the following: a 12- or 14-foot cane pole or telescopic crappie rod; 8- or 10-pound-test monofilament line a foot or two longer than the pole or rod; a 2- to 2-1/2-inch-long, oblong-shaped styrofoam or cork bobber; a Garland Mini Jig or Hal Fly jig; two or three medium-size split shot, about 8 inches apart, the last one about 8 inches above the jig; and one or two minnows tipped on the jig.

With Carter's system, the fastest action comes by trolling across the deepest areas of the lake about a foot off the bottom. When motionless, the lure will

Typical Florida Lake

This is a typical Florida lake that normally contains a mixture of freshwater species. Usually largemouth bass, crappies and other panfishes are present. Hydrilla and hyacinth may be present along with lily pads and some reeds.

The two main areas for open-water trolling are: AREA A is usually most productive during spring and summer. AREA B is trolled during late fall and winter. Troll with the wind in both areas.

Carter uses 1-1/2-inch minnows tipped on a Hals Flies. Smaller minnows produce more fish and two can be used under tough conditions. Hook the first one through the eyes and the second one in the dorsal fin. It looks like a tiny windmill propelled through the water.

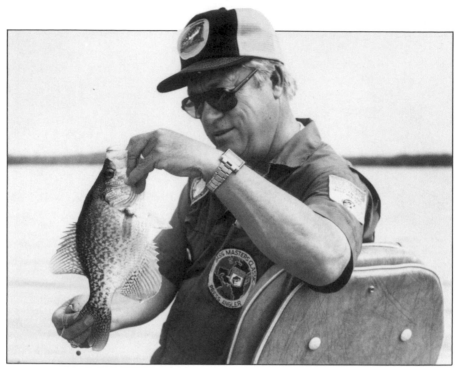

W. Horace Carter hits the Florida black crappies year-'round by trolling the open water.

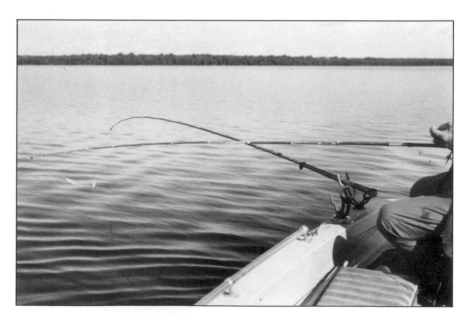

Rod holders keep the poles parallel to the water. Notice the bobber just breaking the water at a 60-degree angle.

sink to the bottom, but trolling will incline your line at about a 60-degree angle and hold the jig up off the bottom. The poles or rods are held in holders perpendicular to the boat and parallel to the water. The best pole position is off the sides of the bow and stern.

Using the pole holders is necessary, because the fish are hooked when they hit. The bobber rides in the water and a hit can be seen immediately. Also, the pole or rod tip will hit the water, giving you another clue.

Look for the open-water stretches of the lake and troll with the wind. Best action occurs during early morning hours and again at evening. An electric, bow-mounted motor helps control the boat and keeps your trolling rate exact.

RIVERS

River crappies often display distinct movement away from strong current areas in late fall/early winter. The types of slack-water areas available determine exactly how crappies respond to the cooling environment.

For example, small, shallow rivers typically have few, if any, deep backwater areas for crappies to use during fall or winter; the only non-current areas adjacent to the river might be only a few feet deep, choked with weeds or brush, or prone to freezing solid. Faced with such conditions, crappies may have no choice but to retreat to deeper holes and channel bends where the current is reduced or minimal. It's the only type of area that offers security in the form of depth, reduced current and sufficient depth under the ice.

Late-Fall/Early-Winter River Crappie Hot Spots

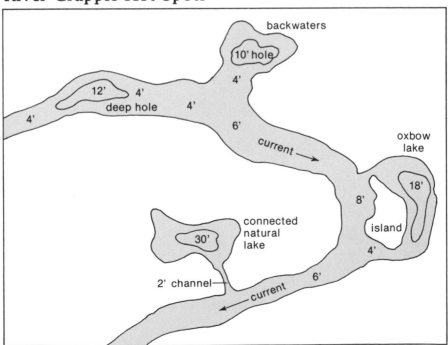

Larger rivers, however, usually offer a wide variety of locational options. They often feature deep backwater areas or connected oxbow lakes anywhere from 6 to 20 feet deep. Crappies may even have direct access to adjacent natural lakes connected to the river by creeks or channels; in each case, crappies may leave the river in favor of deeper, non-current areas of 10, 20, 30 feet or more.

In short, crappie location depends on what's available for fish use. However, anytime there are non-current or minimal-flow areas adjacent to a river which are deep enough so they don't freeze solid, chances are they'll attract crappies during fall and winter.

Faced with such conditions, simply approach them like you'd approach a natural lake. If there is open water, drift the deeper holes or backwater areas and drag a jig and minnow along or near the bottom. If the backwaters freeze, use the same types of ice-fishing techniques we described. There's really no mystery to catching the fish once you understand where they are and how they react to the seasonal conditions.

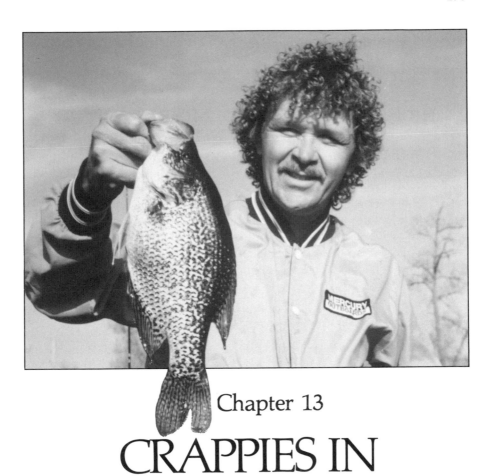

Chapter 13

CRAPPIES IN RESERVOIRS

From the Rockies to the Blue Ridge Mountains and on both sides of the Mason-Dixon Line, sprawl large reservoirs that satisfy man's demand for energy, flood control, or a dependable water supply. One by-product of these impoundments is a fantastic crappie fishery. A little versatility and a bit of crappie savvy will yield consistent stringers of "slabs" all season long from these big waters. This chapter will familiarize you with crappie behavior in several types of reservoirs.

Every impoundment has a unique personality, and no two are exactly alike. However, there are common features which are shared by most. What does a large lake in Kentucky have in common with a Wisconsin, South Carolina or California impoundment? For starters, there are submerged creek channels, cuts and coves, secondary bays, islands, and a main river channel. The anatomy of reservoirs is further broken down into both visible (above water) and submerged structural elements like brush or flooded timber. In addition, there's usually a direction of water flow with a prevailing current. A quick review of Chapter 8 (Reservoirs) will give you a detailed description of impoundment characteristics.

Highland, hill-land and flatland reservoirs usually provide the best crappie fishing, so we'll key on them. Let's begin with the highland category.

HIGHLAND/HILL-LAND IMPOUNDMENTS

Typical characteristics of highland impoundments generally include clear water, hard bottom, and steep, rocky shorelines that drop quickly into deep water. Other common features are narrow and even non-existent flats between the base of the shoreline drop and the edge of the river channel, and a relative lack of cover. Highland reservoirs, because of their clear water and low surface-acreage to volume ratio, also tend to be cooler than hill-land or flatland types. Which of these features makes the highland type impoundment a seemingly more hospitable environment for black crappies than whites is up for question. In all likelihood, a combination of several of these features is important.

UNITED STATES RESERVOIRS*

RANK	STATE	NUMBER OF RESERVOIRS	TOTAL AREA IN ACRES	RANK	STATE	NUMBER OF RESERVOIRS	TOTAL AREA IN ACRES
1	Texas	193	1,547,000	28	Nevada	10	108,000
2	Oklahoma	57	590,000	29	Colorado	52	101,000
3	Tennessee	31	475,000	30	Virginia	16	97,000
4	N. Dakota	11	469,000	31	Ohio	41	92,000
5	S. Dakota	15	454,000	32	Michigan	42	84,000
6	Alabama	35	432,000	33	Nebraska	19	82,000
7	Montana	44	424,000	34	Pennsylvania	31	77,000
8	California	143	370,000	35	New Mexico	16	66,000
9	S. Carolina	16	356,000	36	Iowa	8	51,000
10	Washington	43	351,000	37	Minnesota	11	49,000
11	Arkansas	58	338,000	38	Indiana	20	43,000
12	Georgia	27	262,000	39	Florida	8	43,000
13	Idaho	42	248,000	40	Massachusetts	5	32,000
14	Louisiana	34	245,000	41	New Hampshire	18	30,000
15	Utah	19	222,000	42	Connecticut	12	16,000
16	Kentucky	19	202,000	43	Maryland	8	16,000
17	Oregon	51	196,000	44	New Jersey	11	14,000
18	Wisconsin	71	182,000	45	West Virginia	7	11,000
19	Maine	21	180,000	46	Vermont	9	8,000
20	Missouri	25	178,000	47	Alaska	2	4,000
21	N. Carolina	37	169,000	48	Rhode Island	2	4,000
22	Kansas	29	148,000	49	Delaware	0	0
23	New York	51	131,000	50	Hawaii	0	0
24	Mississippi	15	131,000		Interstate	1,520	9,693,000
25	Wyoming	25	128,000		Duplications	−40	
26	Illinois	38	121,000				
27	Arizona	22	116,000			1,480	

*Reservoirs greater than 500 acres at average pool levels, ranked by total area at mean annual pool levels. Interstate reservoir areas are apportioned to the respective states. (As of January 1, 1976.) Source: *National Reservoir Research*

Impoundments which harbor strong populations of white crappies are typically flatland to hill-land in their overall characteristics. Black crappies are frequently common in reservoirs that range more toward highland characteristics, even though they also do well in certain hill-land impoundments.

Black crappies seem somewhat more adaptable than whites. When the two species coexist in a body of water, it's almost always in an impoundment that's more suited to the needs of white crappies rather than black crappies. Therefore, where they coexist, the whites usually dominate. Yet impoundments which are extremely well suited to blacks usually have no white crappie population at all. Since white crappies tend to dominate shallower, more turbid reservoirs, and blacks thrive in deep, clear reservoirs, it makes sense to plan your fishing accordingly. Fish for whites in dirty-water impoundments and for blacks in clear-water reservoirs.

While the techniques used to catch black and white crappies are almost interchangeable, the environmental conditions present in their prime reservoir types vary. This creates subtle differences in each species' seasonal movements and habits. Simply put: *Habitat affects habits!* The behavioral patterns of black crappies in deeper, clear-water impoundments are markedly different than those exhibited by white crappies in shallower, turbid environments. Black crappies in highland-type impoundments display similar behavioral tendencies to those they exhibit in mesotrophic natural lakes, with the exception that weeds aren't usually a key factor in reservoirs. While weeds aren't common in most highland impoundments, when weeds are present, crappies may use the confined open water zone adjacent to them.

One of the major differences in behavior between the two species of crappies is centered around spawning activities. It's not so much a difference in spawning activity as it is a condition dictated by the environment in which each lives. Most white crappie spawning takes place in bays, while most black crappie spawning, at least in highland impoundments, often takes place along main-lake shorelines.

In many highland impoundments which are "home" to viable populations of black crappies, "prime" spawning areas are at a minimum. Most sunfish species like largemouth bass and crappies nest in relatively shallow water on moderately firm bottom. Given the opportunity, they'll also spawn in areas protected from heavy current and main-lake wind and wave action. Because the ideal spawning temperature and habitat requirements of largemouth bass and crappies are similar, competition for spawning sites can take place.

When a shortage of prime spawning spots occurs, the largemouth population in many highland impoundments typically "owns" the prime area for an extended period of time. In these impoundments, more than in most environments, largemouth bass tend to spawn in "waves". Rather than a massive spawning movement occurring when the water temperature reaches the high 60°F's or low 70°F's, spawning often starts in approximately 63°F water in early May and continues into the mid-70°F's—well into summer.

Many highland impoundments can support more bass than there is habitat for all the bass to spawn in at one specific time. In addition, highland reservoirs warm more slowly than shallow, turbid waters, and this also tends to extend the spawn. Consequently, the crappies don't get a chance to use those same bays for spawning! In competition for territory between largemouths and crappies, the largemouths are likely to win most of the time. The end result is that most of the crappie spawn takes place in "unusual" habitat along main-lake shorelines.

The Crappie Shuffle

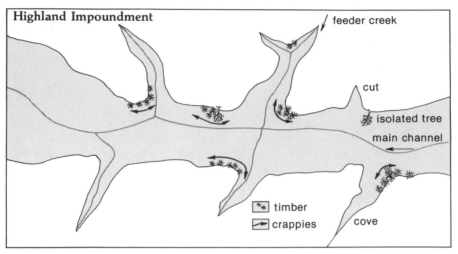

Highland Impoundment

feeder creek

cut

isolated tree

main channel

timber

crappies

cove

In many highland and some hill-land reservoirs, crappies use the main lake area extensively, all season long. Many times, competition with largemouth bass for spawning sites pushes the crappies out of any shallower bays and coves and into the main lake. During spring, crappies may spawn in fallen trees, on broken rocks or in flooded bushes along shorelines in the main lake and major feeder-creek arms.

In summer, the crappies usually suspend near the fast-dropping shoreline in the main-lake area. Typically, they'll suspend in water from 15 to 40 feet deep—the "crappie zone" in these waters. Fallen or standing timber will provide a holding spot for crappies.

During early fall, crappies may move shallow. Then, in late fall, they'll drop into deep cover. Depending on the environment, timber along the creek channel, a deep ridge or a rocky stair-stepping ledge may hold fish.

The key to locating crappies is finding the multi-seasonal habitat areas in the main lake and larger creek arms. Crappies will shuffle along horizontally and vertically in these areas seeking habitat and food.

What about black crappies in canyon and plateau reservoirs? In general, they're not the best crappie environments because of their extreme depth and lack of cover. However, some creek arms may provide environmental conditions similar enough to a highland impoundment to support crappies. The key to fishing canyon or plateau reservoirs is to consider each creek arm as a localized crappie area, and approach it just the way you'd fish a highland impoundment. Look for fish suspending near the shoreline. Any submerged trees could be superb crappie hot spots.

With the abundance of rock along these typically steep shoreline slopes, there doesn't appear to be much spawning habitat for crappies. Yet many highland impoundments host thriving black crappie populations. So how do they adapt to this seemingly inhospitable environment? Find a lake with a good crappie population, and fish it during the prime spawning period (water temperature 62 °F to 66 °F) and you'll have a hard time finding a crappie on a "bed." However, try looking in fallen trees along the steep rocky banks and inundated brush along the shorelines, and you'll find crappies.

Yup! They're spawning *on* the cover. Instead of creating a recognizable "bed," crappies often drop their gelatinous eggs on whatever cover exists to keep them elevated off the bottom. In fact, some crappies will spawn in the shallowest branches of fallen trees that are hanging over 35 feet of water!

"TREED" CRAPPIES

In many reservoirs, the forest of flooded timber can be mind-boggling. Where do you start? Which trees are best? While we can't detail every situation, we can give you a couple guidelines for identifying which trees are potential crappie hotspots. Depending on the local environment, the areas with productive standing timber can vary. River and creek channels, ridges, humps, depressions and other terrain changes are all possible locations for standing timber. Seasonally, crappies will utilize different areas of the reservoir, and timber can provide a "holding" spot for the fish.

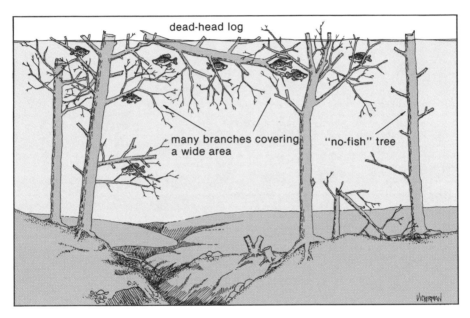

The most productive "crappie trees" supply plenty of cover. They provide an "umbrella effect" with many branches of all sizes poking in all directions. Find a couple of these adjacent to each other and you've found a crappie paradise.

Normally, the most productive trees have a maze of branches that provides cover. The best trees have many large and small branches covering a wide area and depth range. Normally, bigger is better. In addition, any floating, deadhead logs that get wedged into the branches are frosting on the cake.

In reservoirs with fast-dropping, main-lake areas, fallen timber can provide cover. Crappies may use the shallower branches to spawn on in spring and then move out and relate to the branches in deeper water during summer. While crappies will often suspend away from cover, when contact is made, many will hold around the branches of a fallen tree. If cover is sparse, even a

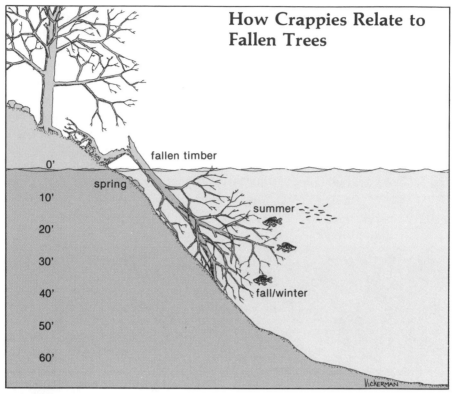

How Crappies Relate to Fallen Trees

fallen timber

0'

spring

10'

summer

20'

30'

40' fall/winter

50'

60'

VICKERMAN

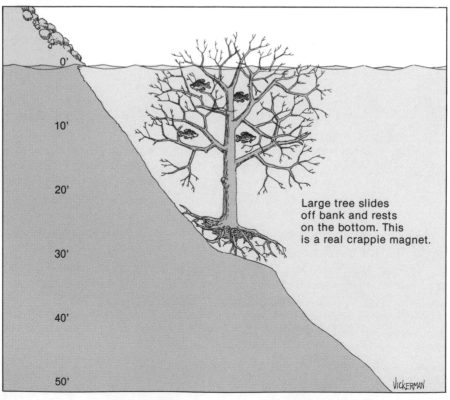

0'

10'

20'

Large tree slides
off bank and rests
on the bottom. This
is a real crappie magnet.

30'

40'

50'

VICKERMAN

single tree will hold fish. This condition often occurs on highland, hill-land and some canyon reservoirs.

All this isn't to say that blacks in highland impoundments *never* spawn in protected shallow bays, or that whites in flatland impoundments *never* spawn in main-lake areas among the branches of brush or timber. Certainly there are impoundments in which those options may be the rule; but the tendencies outlined here are more typical, and help to illustrate how the available habitat can affect crappies' habits.

End result? Fishing during the Pre-spawn Period can be a totally different ballgame for blacks in highland impoundments than it is for whites in flatland impoundments. Keep in mind that this difference will also dictate (or at least influence) the location of crappies during all Calendar Periods. Blacks in a highland-type impoundment move into shallow "backwater areas" early in the season to feed. However, they often must move out of those areas and back to main-lake shorelines before spawning. Not so with whites, because they can remain in shallow, protected areas until spawning time. Also, blacks in a highland reservoir usually spawn in the area of their summer habitat, so there's no true Post-spawn dispersal.

SUMMER

In summer, the behavior of black and white crappies in reservoirs isn't too dissimilar. However, the differences in the physical characteristics of the typical black crappie impoundment and the typical white crappie impoundment tend to create the *appearance* of substantial behavioral differences.

Traditionally, most anglers consider crappies to be cover-oriented fish. That's actually misleading because both species of crappies spend *most* of their time suspended in confined open water. In natural lakes, highland reservoirs, and even tidal rivers, summertime crappies spend a majority of the time suspended. On Kentucky and Barkley Lakes, KY/TN, many locals believe that white crappies seldom suspend. During the summer, crappies are caught almost exclusively from brush and timber along the channel drop-offs. Of course, that's where most of the crappie anglers ply their trade. However, crappies frequently suspend—and they are catchable.

On a recent trip to Kentucky Lake, KY, we found crappies suspended at an outside turn in the main river channel. We caught a mess of slab whites by swimming a 1/16-ounce jig approximately 12 to 15 feet down over 25 feet of water. Yes, the fish were suspended but still catchable.

Over three days, we were able to find that same school of whites every day, always in the 12- to 15-foot-depth range. They spent most of their time over 20 to 25 feet of water on top of the flat, but each day at around noon, they'd move out over the creek bed. We won't begin to try to figure out why.

The behavior of these crappies was similar to that exhibited by summertime blacks in many waters. For example, in many northern, natural lakes, crappies typically spend 90% of their time suspended 12 to 20 feet down, and they rarely venture over water more than 40 feet deep. In highland reservoirs, the amount of water between 15 and 40 feet is normally a relatively narrow band around the perimeter of the main lake. Only in coves and creek arms do you

Rule of Thumb: The "12 to 22" Crappie Zone

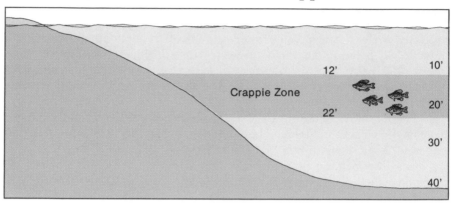

During the Summer Calendar Period, the best crappie fishing is usually in the 12- to 22-foot range. Yes, there are many exceptions, but the "crappie zone" is a good place to start your fishing on many waters.

find any considerable expanse of water in this depth range.

So blacks *seem* to be more shoreline related because they don't normally roam over extremely deep water. Even though they're suspended, crappies are usually within 100 feet or so of shore. However, in shallower hill-land and flatland impoundments, crappies have *much more water* within the 15-to 40-foot-depth range, and will roam over more wide-open spaces.

There are few generalities that apply to any fishing situation. Here's one as close as you'll ever find to an axiom: The best daytime crappie fishing during the Summer Calendar Period is *usually* within 5 feet of the 17-foot depth! That's 12 to 22 feet deep.

Certainly the rule can't be applied to bodies of water in which there is little or no water of that depth. With few notable exceptions, lakes and impoundments that *don't* offer deep water aren't the *best* places to fish for crappies. Florida's natural lakes are the most notable exception to this. Typically, very shallow impoundments and eutrophic lakes in many areas of the country can hold tremendous numbers of crappies, but they're often small and paper thin, averaging a few ounces in weight and topping out at well under a pound.

In a quality crappie lake, there's plenty of open water adjacent to cover. There's also an abundance of open-water preyfish. For best crappie growth, it's important that a year-'round supply of forage fish exists in the 1- to 3-inch range. In some natural lakes in the North, the baitfish requirement is filled by landlocked alewife populations; throughout the South and in most flatland and hill-land reservoirs, it's threadfin shad. A variety of minnow species, including common shiners, spot-tail shiners and dace fill the bill elsewhere.

These prey species are plankton feeders. In most lakes, the heaviest plankton layer during the summer (when the water is stratified) is located from the surface down to approximately half the distance of the deepest level of light penetration. Plankton feeders tend to congregate just *under* the heaviest layer of plankton, and crappies will concentrate below these plankton feeders.

Wind is an important factor in open-water crappie fishing. A steady breeze out of the same direction over a period of several days will "push" plankton clouds, and the fishing will usually be better on the downwind areas. A heavy blow, however, churns the water and disperses the plankton, which tends to break up the schools of baitfish. The end result is poor, open-water, crappie fishing. Immediately following a severe windstorm, most crappies will be caught in and around cover, yet usually within the same depth range that they had been using.

In summary, depending on wind, water clarity, density of the plankton and species of prey following the plankton, crappies will be found between 12 to 22

Impoundment A is a flatland reservoir which is a classic white crappie environment. Here the "crappie zone" is extended because of the amount of shallower water and the normally dark water color. Crappie movement can be in any direction.

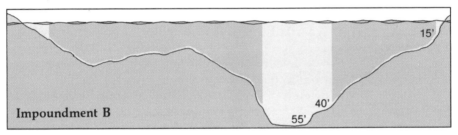

Impoundment B is a hill-land impoundment typical of those where white crappies flourish. The shaded zone represents the area 15-40 feet deep—the crappie zone. Note that the water is slightly deeper and clearer than the average flatland impoundment.

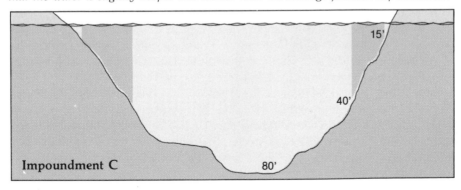

Impoundment C, a clear-water highland impoundment, is often dominated by black crappies. Notice that there is less area of 15-40 foot water. Crappies exhibiting typical behavior here would appear to be shoreline oriented because the crappie zone is much narrower. Cover is usually scarce, and even a lone tree within this zone may attract fish.

feet down most of the time. Remember, the rule of 17 includes the 12- to 22-foot depth range.

The most common exception to the 12- to 22-foot-depth-range guideline occurs just before dusk on calm, midsummer days. At this time (twilight), many light-sensitive organisms migrate toward the surface. In response to this movement, plankton-feeding baitfish and crappies may follow.

This is also a peak period of insect hatches. Areas of organic bottom are especially conducive to this, but during certain hatches, gravel bottom areas are also very productive. Just by being aware that late afternoon hatches are always a possibility during the summer should make you aware of the potential. Under these conditions, keep your eyes open for surface-feeding crappies.

Even the most minnow-oriented crappies will take advantage of this "bonus" food source. We're not really sure why, but crappies will almost always take the emerging insects at or just under the surface, even though the bugs may be coming up quite a distance from the bottom. The result is that the crappies will remain near the surface and can provide some mighty fine fishing.

If crappies spend so much of their time suspended, how did they ever develop such a strong "cover-oriented" reputation? The answer lies as much in traditional fishing techniques as it does in crappie behavior. While suspended *away* from cover, a school of crappies is seldom stationary. However, a school of suspended, moving crappies may pause when they make contact with some type of cover. When you find a school of crappies suspended away from cover, staying on them can be a chore. But when you find crappies suspended around a standing tree or mingled among the branches of a fallen tree that's hanging out over deep water, odds are they'll hold there for awhile.

In addition, any "stragglers" seem to hang around cover at the depth range that most crappies are using. Find crappies moving and you're usually lucky to catch more than a few before losing contact; find 'em at a tree and you'll likely catch a dozen or more before they move on. Why? Well, you have a specific area (tree) that will hold fish, instead of trying to cast to a moving school that you don't really comprehend the boundaries of!

On a highland impoundment, the movement of the crappies tends to roughly follow the bank. Remember, they seem to stay in that 15- to 40-foot-deep band of water. On a flatland impoundment, however, movement can be in any direction, and it's much more difficult to maintain contact with a moving school. Thus, given existing fishing methods, percentages dictate that most crappie fishing should be done at the "breaks" that hold a school of crappies temporarily during their wandering. This is true to a degree on all types of water, but on flatland reservoirs, fishing "cover" is usually the name of the game. It's either this or adopt new techniques that allow you to maintain contact with a moving school and more precisely control the depth of presentations in open water.

The growing popularity of chart recorders will have considerable influence on this factor. With a graph, it's much easier to visualize the actual location of the school and estimate its boundaries. With a school of suspended crappies moving across an open flat, if you can graph 'em two or three times as they move, dropping a marker buoy each time, you can fairly accurately predict their path, making it much easier to stay in contact with them. Certain adaptations of backtrolling techniques may also come into play as a means to maintain contact with a suspended school of open-water crappies.

The summer movement patterns also hold into the Turnover Period in most reservoirs, as long as the lake remains stratified and plankton "clouds" remain surface oriented—not necessarily *near* the surface, but some distance away from the surface. Even though adult crappies in the best impoundments rarely rely on plankton as a direct food source, it remains the key to locations of open-water, prey species which crappies relate to.

Black or white? Two species of crappies are common in some reservoirs. Note the characteristic color variations between white (left) and black (right) crappies.

After the fall turnover, in most reservoirs both species of crappies exhibit behavioral traits more in keeping with their "cover oriented" reputation. As the water temperature drops from the 50°F's and into the 40°F's, impoundment crappies spend less time roaming over open water. In highland reservoirs, crappies appear to migrate toward any cover in or adjacent to the deepest available water. In a highland reservoir, one or two good fallen trees reaching into 45 or 50 feet of water along a bluff bank may draw large schools of black crappies by the time the water temperature is about 45°F.

Whether you call it an aggregation or a "mega-school," it's a huge quantity of crappies in a confined area, and it's a fishing goldmine. Actually, it's the best crappie fishing of the year. Similar behavior exists on typical white crappie reservoirs, but the aggregation isn't usually as strong because prime cover isn't nearly so scarce in most waters.

While the 15- to 20-foot-depth range in highland impoundments remains productive, everything from the top edges of cover down to the bottom (yes, even 50 feet or more) becomes potential crappie-holding water. There are so many crappies jammed into such a limited area, especially on deep, relatively cover free impoundments, that crappies have to stack over a wider vertical range.

FLATLAND IMPOUNDMENTS

Although many deeper, highland or hill-land reservoirs generally contain clear water, popular flatland impoundments have shallow basins with large bays and numerous feeder creeks where stained or dark water is common. In flatland impoundments, the average depth of the coves might only range from 5 to 10 feet. The lake probably has deeper channels, but the calling card seems to be plenty of *cover* at all depths.

Crappies thrive in such environments, and dingy water allows them to stay relatively shallow (less than 20 feet). The abundant cover provides excellent habitat, and a slight current flow creates a flushing effect which ensures good water quality. Reservoir crappies do best when their food supply (usually shad) is plentiful. Shad numbers often suffer when the water becomes polluted, but when the shad population is healthy, crappies thrive.

Impoundments more conducive to white crappies usually offer many acceptable spawning areas. Most importantly, the largemouth spawn is more compacted, timewise, than on highland impoundments. There are far fewer "early" spawners, because there's enough suitable spawning environment to serve most of the bass population in a shorter span of time. Also, there are plenty of suitable spawning sites for bass and crappies when co-use enters the picture.

After spawning, the crappies' requirements are no longer fulfilled by shoreline habitat. In flatland impoundments, warming surface temperatures combined with a slightly lower lake elevation (after spring run-off) move the fish to a different depth zone. The key here is "move"; the crappies are moving to their summer areas.

Threadfin shad is often a reservoir's most abundant crappie forage, and schools of this baitfish retreat to deeper areas also. These areas are located away from the shoreline. The prime areas are flats and submerged creek channels in secondary bays and coves. The fish are on a "stair-stepping," post-spawn pattern, moving toward deeper water in the main lake areas.

In short, as the summer sun heats the backwaters of shallow, secondary, coves and bays, and drawdowns begin to make shoreline habitat too shallow

Spring vs. Summer Areas

Crappies usually do not live in one bay or cove all year long. Seasonally, their habitat requirements change and so does their location. AREA A is a secondary cove attached to a main cove and is a prime spring area. However, during summer a majority of the crappies will move to main-lake AREA B.

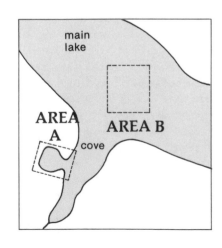

to hold fish, a deep-water pattern emerges. The crappies slowly filter out of the shallows and stack up in deeper areas. Most large, flatland reservoirs start annual drawdown in early to midsummer in anticipation of fall rain. This lowering of the water pulls crappies away from shorelines and out to drop-offs and sandbars adjacent to deep, river channels.

Summer crappies may suspend or school around areas of submerged cover like timber, stump rows or brush, which lie on or near the edge of the creek channel. For example, the top of a bar might be 8 feet deep and then abruptly break to a depth of 25 feet with cover scattered along the break. The key area is on the edge, in between the two extremes. Crappies like this environment because they have easy access to both deep and shallow water. It's a perfect area to intercept roving schools of shad.

At this time, small, underwater points or lips on such bars or humps are key crappie spots. Quite often, crappies reside on the down-current side—par-

DETAIL OF AREA A
Secondary Cove or Bay Attached to a Main Cove

Spring and early summer find crappies moving in and out of shallow, secondary spawning coves that are attached to larger, main coves or to the main lake itself. While the fish tend to follow flooded creek channels, shallow channels are often silted in and are very indistinct. Thus, you can't rule out the possibility of crappies crossing large flats, either. Therefore, your first choice is to look for flooded cover along channel edges and bends. If that option fails, look for flooded brush or manmade fish attractors up on the shallow flats. Even a small, 4' x 4' fish attractor can hold 15 to 20 nice crappies for awhile as the fish cross large flats.

DETAIL OF AREA B
Open-Water, Main-Lake Crappie Areas

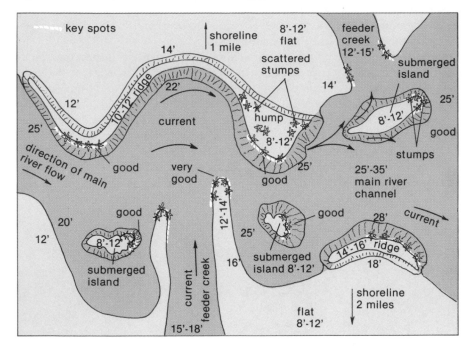

Summer and fall crappies tend to relate more to cover along deep channel edges. On large reservoirs, such spots are often located a mile or more from shore, and depth finders are invaluable for finding them. Pay careful attention to channel bends, humps, and the intersections of two creek or river channels. The best areas usually have some sort of wood cover present.

ticularly at times when the lake level is dropping and the current is at maximum flow. Crappies are basically lazy. They'll lie motionless in the eddy that forms here and let the current bring food to them.

Early summer finds crappies holding near mainstream bars. Not only are shad present, but crappies sometimes supplement their menu by feeding on mayfly larvae. As this early stage of the mayfly emerges from the mud in a wiggly, aquatic procession, crappies gorge themselves on nature's buffet.

This period can sometimes be difficult for crappie anglers because the abundance of food means stiff competition. However, keying in on mainstream points where the current has washed in mayfly larvae can put you on schools of feeding crappies.

Lake elevations are important to crappie movement. Rising water can scatter fish as they attempt to move toward the newly flooded, virgin territory. Just the opposite situation exists when a dropping water level pulls water from bays and creeks. In this instance, the fish often seek deeper water.

Experience has shown that water level changes of 2 to 3 inches affect fish

Seasonal Water Level in Secondary Coves

location. A daily monitoring of the pool elevation will give you a valuable clue to probable crappie location. In addition, the speed of the crappies' response to the changing water level is directly linked to the rate of increase or decrease in pool elevation. For example, if the fish were holding at 15 feet on a ledge and the lake level started dropping, on the next day's outing you would likely find crappies 17 to 20 feet deep.

A stable lake elevation is good, but a rise or fall in water level can actually help you establish a pattern. You can capitalize on the crappie's habits and key in on areas which draw crappies during a change in elevation.

Most big flatland impoundments have sufficient cover in deeper water where wind and ice erosion cannot reach. Although some siltation takes place, deep cover is usually present. A real change, however, occurs in the shallows where annual drawdown exposes shoreline areas. It is here that natural cover disappears over the years due to the forces of nature. Ice erosion, flooding and wind all contribute to loss of shallow habitat.

In contrast to the spring, post-spawn patterns of flatland reservoir crappie dispersal, fall movement takes place back *toward* the secondary channels and humps near the main stream. The fish slowly migrate back into the mouths of coves and bays as the water cools and fall arrives. Why in the world do flatland reservoir crappies move back in fall toward the mouths of the coves?

First, once the fall drawdown of 3 to 5 feet (typical of flatland reservoirs) is complete, the strongest current will be along the main river channel. Cold-water (fall and winter) crappies don't like to fight current, and they'll move toward the mouths of secondary coves. They'll still use relatively deep water (8 to 20 feet), but will move out of the main current.

Second, the cooling process of fall reoxygenates all the water in the lake. Due to the dark water, lack of weedgrowth and/or wind exposure, some shallow coves experience severe summer oxygen depletion in water deeper than 6 or 8 feet. The crappies may literally be chased out of the shallow coves in summer into deeper-water, main-lake areas, even though largemouth bass may remain in the shallow, 1- to 6-foot, flooded cover in the backs of coves. Now, however, they're able to return.

And third, late summer/early fall often finds a *second spawning* of threadfin shad taking place in the secondary coves on these impoundments. Studies show that threadfin shad may experience two spawning peaks on some southern waters—spring and fall. This phenomenon creates a bounty of small baitfish at a time of year when the spring hatch of threadfin and gizzard shad are growing too large for crappies to eat. This abundant, shad forage draws

Crappie-Go-Round

Flatland-reservoir crappies display a predictable cycle of movement throughout the year. The accompanying map shows a portion of Kentucky Lake along the Kentucky/Tennessee border and describes this movement in detail.

The spring spawning season finds large numbers of crappies in the mid- to back-sections of shallow, secondary coves. After they spawn, the fish begin slowly dropping back toward the main lake. Steve McCadams calls it a "stair-stepping" effect. They don't race to deeper water; rather, they gradually migrate toward their summer habitat. During this movement, the fish will be spread out, although natural and manmade cover will hold fish. All of the fish do not do the same thing at the same time, but the bulk of the fish in that portion of the lake will be relating to the general areas indicated here.

Summer crappies relate primarily to the drop-offs along deep creek channels and the main river channel, so you should concentrate your efforts in the main portion of the lake. Then, as the water cools in early fall, the crappies begin moving back toward the large coves again. There is a definite, threadfin shad movement back toward the coves at this time of year, and the crappies follow close behind.

Fall and winter finds huge schools of crappies gathering along channel edges in the center to outer portions of the coves. They don't move as far back into the coves as they did in spring, largely because the drawdown has typically lowered the lake level 3 to 5 feet.

Crappies will relate to cover along the edges of the channel, and to the deep, bottom portions of channel bends and intersections that contain wood for cover.

Get the picture? Following the seasonal cycle of crappie movement on a mid-South, flatland reservoir will keep you on the majority of the fish population. Then it's simply a matter of trying several techniques until you locate and catch fish.

crappies back toward the cove mouths, although the crappies probably won't penetrate all the way to the shallow, back ends.

Fall crappies will continue to mass in these cove-mouth areas. As the water continues to cool (late fall), a collision of hungry predators and easily available prey begins and lasts well into the winter months.

Crappies in most lowland impoundments will behave similar to those in flatland impoundments. However, the species of crappies present should tip you off to some subtleties in their seasonal movements.

The presence of white crappies indicates a warmer environment and the likely presence of a shad food source. Given this environment, you can probably expect the same, classic movement patterns described for flatland reservoirs: namely, seasonal use of all parts of the reservoir and long-distance crappie movement. However, since most reservoirs are constructed by flooding natural swamps, you'll find a lack of natural cover in the deeper areas of the impoundment, and crappies will tend to roam a great deal.

The strong presence of black crappies in a lowland or even flatland impoundment indicates a cooler-water environment which probably lies in the northern half of the United States. In such impoundments, shad are probably minimal or absent, and the crappies will rely more on minnows, insects and small fish for food. Such shallow impoundments will generally have stained-to-dark water, although they seldom warm up to the same extent as the South's famous crappie impoundments. If the water is clear enough, significant weedgrowth may develop since this type of reservoir usually experiences minimal water fluctuation.

Given these conditions, black crappies are much more likely to relate to cover in the bays or shallower parts of the reservoir for a *longer* portion of the season; there's no major incentive or poor environmental conditions to *drive* them toward the deeper areas. Thus, shallow (6 to 10 foot), flooded brush and trees, or the deep edges of weedgrowth are good crappie attractors for much of the year, and you should concentrate your efforts in and around these areas.

Once the fish drop deeper in these impoundments—usually in fall—they'll relate to bends in the river channel or to deep holes. These areas are often silted in and may be only slightly deeper than the surrounding territory. Yet crappies will locate these subtle areas and stack into them. Find such an area with a bit of flooded cover and you have a real crappie magnet.

Interesting, isn't it? Subtle differences in the environment often trigger differences in crappie behavior. Yet when you're able to analyze the conditions, you can often predict the behavior of the fish.

COVER

Although crappies suspended in open water can be taken, this situation is normally less effective than working cover. It's not that you can't catch them; it's just more difficult. In summer, some crappies will suspend in the main river channel! When open-water contact is made, it's usually an indication that crappies are on the move and you may have found them in transit. They are in between stops, and this pattern isn't likely to last. While you may catch some suspended fish, it's tough to stay on fish in a huge body of water.

The most catchable reservoir crappies are often cover oriented. The fish like to hide in cover and let prey come to them. Cover comes in many forms. It may be a weedbed adjacent to deep water or it can be other natural cover like fallen trees. Flooded trees, old stumps, rock piles, and riprap areas are other examples.

Other natural features worth noting are submerged creek channels and sand bars where some natural cover might have been left when the lake was flooded. Deep depressions, humps, ridges or other bottom elevation changes can all draw crappies.

Key areas are points falling off into mainstream or deep bays, as are islands near the mainstream. Down-current sections of submerged islands surrounded by deep water are also prime areas. These are natural crappie spots. They are even better when covered or dotted with debris like brush or original fence rows where trees were cut during the lake building process. In general, on huge impoundments, topographic maps will help you find structure like submerged brush tops and stump rows. Check with local marinas or lake officials to obtain a map before you even launch your boat. Pay attention to the elevation markings and key in on extreme depth changes. Doing your homework will help you locate and visualize bottom contours when you're on the water and will result in more fish.

MANMADE FISH ATTRACTORS

Creating "homemade" crappie spots, where legal, has been the bread and butter of professional guides for years. These are especially effective in older reservoirs where much of the natural cover has disappeared after decades of wind, rain, siltation, and ice erosion. This is particularly true in shallow areas

In reservoirs where shallow-water cover is sparse, artificial fish attractors are the answer. Manmade attractors are easy to build and they will draw lots of crappies.

that dry up during the drawdown. The idea also works well in newly formed lakes where little or no cover exists.

Manmade fish attractors give fish a place to hide; they're a refuge—cover. Some anglers call them crappie "beds or hides." Other popular terms are "mats or huts." They all have the same goal: bringing the fish and the fishermen together. These brush piles attract and concentrate fish. In addition, fish attractors can become mini ecosystems providing crappies with feeding stations.

Many state and federal wildlife agencies are implementing programs of building and marking public fish attractors. Check with local reservoir authorities for maps showing the specific locations of such structures.

Building fish attractors sweetens the "crappie pie." Your effort gives existing fish populations a place to reside and also provides potential spawning habitat. In flatland reservoirs, crappies usually lay their eggs on the roots of bushes and trees. In addition, weedbeds or rock piles may also serve the purpose. However, in some older, flatland reservoirs, shallow-water cover is at a premium and crappies will use the manmade structures to spawn on.

Some of the most popular synthetic attractors are sunken treetops, tires wired together, and wooden "stake" beds built on shipping pallets or driven into the mud. The structures are simple, but effective. The main ingredients are time and labor.

How do you construct them, and where do you put 'em? Trees like willow, birch, ash, and cedar are popular woods. Leftover Christmas trees are good, too. Size can vary, but usually, trees in the 10- to 15-foot range are large enough to hold fish and small enough to transport.

Sometimes, several small trees or bushes can be wired together to form a crappie bed. Use copper wire and a concrete block or rocks as a weight to hold your structures on bottom. Also, standing trees upright in buckets filled with concrete is good for deeper areas, because the trees provide cover and appear to be growing on the lake's bottom.

Wooden stake beds are also super fish attractors. A series of wooden sticks or slabs can either be driven into the shallow mud, or nailed to shipping pallets for sinking in deeper water. The wooden stakes usually run 3 to 5 feet long and are 1 to 3 inches wide.

To place the beds in shallow water, use hip boots or chest waders. Drive the sticks into soft mud or gravel bottoms with a heavy pipe or small sledgehammer. Many anglers choose to build such structures during late fall and winter seasons when reservoir water levels are at their minimum elevation. When spring and summer arrive, the structures—then several feet deeper—hold fish until fall.

For sinking homemade beds in deeper water (12 to 15 feet), you'll need to wire concrete blocks to the wooden pallets after you've nailed 10 to 15 sticks to the studs of the pallet. For shallow stake beds, construct about a 4- to 8-foot square and use as many as 50 stakes. Since deeper structures are usually about 4 feet square, you'll likely have to drop a couple in one spot to create the desired bed size.

Many state agencies use old tires with holes punched in them to facilitate sinking. The tires can be wired to form a teepee image. Brush can also be added to the tires before sinking them to increase their attractiveness. These types

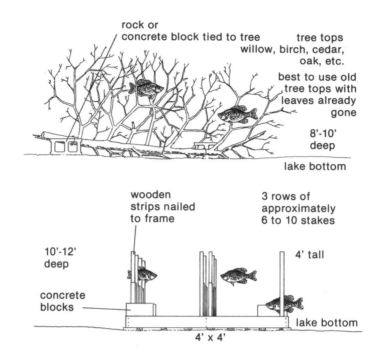

rock or
concrete block tied to tree

tree tops
willow, birch, cedar,
oak, etc.

best to use old
tree tops with
leaves already
gone

8'-10'
deep

lake bottom

wooden
strips nailed
to frame

3 rows of
approximately
6 to 10 stakes

10'-12'
deep

4' tall

concrete
blocks

lake bottom

4' x 4'

Crappie Attractor Food Web

solar
energy

zooplankton

phytoplankton

minnows
small fish
shad

crappies

VICKERMAN

Besides providing cover, crappie attractors are prime habitat for plant and animal communities that live in and around them. Small fish will eat these organisms and crappies will feed on the small fish, minnows, and shad. This is a classic example of a predator/prey relationship.

of beds are quickly and easily put in place, and tires last forever. However, most anglers prefer just plain brush top and stake beds. Although fish seem to hold better in brush cover, tires will still improve a potential spot. In case you're wondering, crappies haven't shown a preference for either bias ply or radial tires.

In summary, the total surface area of your homemade structure will, to a degree, determine how effective it is. More surface area means more nutrients which will draw more fish. That's why brush is better than a single log—more surface area.

On some reservoirs, fish attractors function mainly as cover; however, in others, attractors can be crappie feeding and holding stations. This is especially true in clear-water reservoirs that contain a minimum amount of cover and prey. To be most effective, at least part of the crappie attractor should be placed above the depth of maximum sunlight penetration. The more surface area exposed to the effects of solar energy, the more "food" the attractor can produce. Here, plants (algae) will grow and attract minnows which feed upon the microscopic organisms that live on the structure. Eventually, crappies will locate and use this food source. Remember, while crappie attractors will draw some fish on any body of water, they are ideal in waters (or areas) with limited cover and baitfish. In many impoundments with a plentiful, suspended, shad-forage base, attractors probably serve more as temporary holding stations that crappies wander into in search of shad than as feeding stations. In summary, on many waters, crappies and attractors go hand-in-hand with on-the-water success.

Now, the question of where to place your cover comes up. Place the structures of your choice on the top of a ledge, along the break, and also on the deep side of the bar or ledge. Let the fish decide which depth best suits their needs. Just be sure to place them deep enough so they're not a hazard to navigation at low water. In addition, this also prevents other anglers from spotting your honey holes when the water level drops!

Place your structures in several different locations and depths with different wind directions in mind. Ask yourself where a likely spot with a strong west wind would be. East? North? South? By building a few structures in every situation, you'll be able to launch your boat and string some slabs when the rest of your buddies are back at the boat dock whining and waiting for the wind to subside.

Also note that changing lake levels can trigger seasonal and even daily locational changes. Deeper structures will hold fish when the lake is falling, and the shallow ones will produce best during rising water. During stable water conditions, you might find a few fish at several different depths.

How soon after you place structures on a spot will they yield fish? Sometimes crappies will invade the beds overnight, while others require a few weeks to draw fish. Usually, a structure improves with age.

Older structures allow algae to form. Various types of aquatic plankton utilize the growth, and shad often are attracted by this mini-ecosystem. Guess who follows the shad to these structures? You guessed it! Mr. & Mrs. Crappie are close behind. So the older beds are likely to hold more fish because they offer quality crappie habitat—cover and food.

Depending on the location and size of your structure, a dab of additional cover every 2 or 3 years might be necessary. Limbs break off and siltation occurs. You'll be able to determine the extent of deterioration by feeling the cover below with a "tightline" rig.

TIPS ON FISHING RESERVOIRS

The best lake with "prime structure" will show you no fish if your techniques are wrong. It also holds true that the best bait catches no fish unless it's presented properly. So, to prevent the "no fish" blues, learn to match your tactics to the conditions you're faced with.

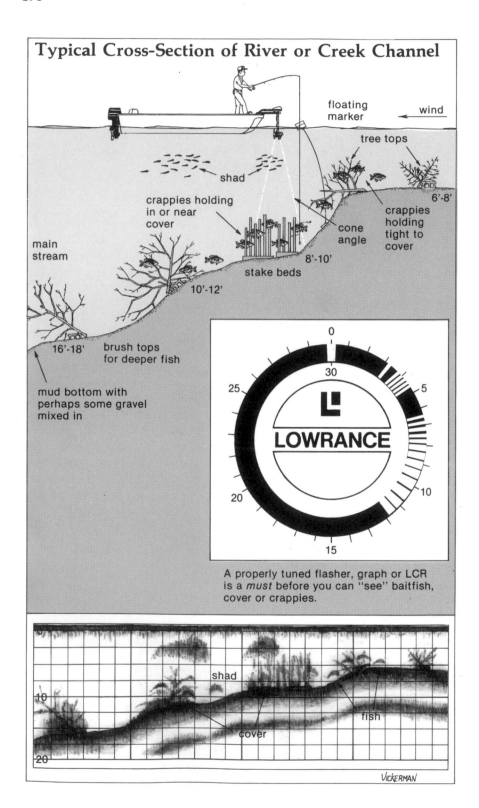

Typical Cross-Section of River or Creek Channel

floating marker

wind

tree tops

shad

crappies holding in or near cover

cone angle

crappies holding tight to cover

6'-8'

main stream

stake beds

8'-10'

10'-12'

16'-18' brush tops for deeper fish

mud bottom with perhaps some gravel mixed in

0

30

25

5

LOWRANCE

20

10

15

A properly tuned flasher, graph or LCR is a *must* before you can "see" baitfish, cover or crappies.

shad

fish

cover

VICKERMAN

On some reservoirs, prime crappie cover is visible. Fallen or standing timber and bushes are examples. However, in deep or dark water, submerged cover can be hard to locate. Just how do you find sunken cover?

Your best bet is to use your depth finder and tightline rig to locate cover. Watch your fish locator signals closely, and simultaneously feel for the cover. Once your bell sinker strikes wood, toss out a marker, back off within casting range and start fishing. In addition, your fish locator will also show the presence of baitfish and suspended crappies. Here are a few tips to help you plan your strategy.

The anticipation of seeing a bobber disappear with a slab crappie tugging on the other end is a lot of fun. At times, bobber fishing can be your best presentation option. Always carry a selection of styles. Bobber fishing allows you to fish over, around and through cover with minimum hang-ups. It's just the ticket for non-aggressive crappies holding tight to cover or for suspended fish.

In spring and fall, when crappies migrate from the deeper, open-water, river bars into shallower secondary creeks, look for them near cover. Crappies may relate to fallen trees in highland reservoirs, standing timber in hill-land impoundments, and manmade fish attractors in flatland reservoirs. When fishing cover, the situation may dictate positioning the boat several feet away from a structure and casting to it. Use a floating buoy marker to pinpoint the cover you want to fish. Presentation options include: (1) using a slip-float, casting bobber, and (2) counting your lure or minnow down into the strike zone.

Pitch a slip-bobber rig baited with a minnow over the cover. See what happens. If you get an instant strike, the fish are probably active and you can cast a jig to them. This is typical on cloudy days. When they're not active, though, they'll hold down and into cover (typical on sunny days), and you must extract them with the bobber rig.

If the crappies are active, simply cast a 1/16-ounce jig or jig & minnow combination across or alongside the cover. Let it sink to different levels on different casts, and slowly retrieve it. Count the jig down so you know the level you're working at, and experiment with retrieves to determine the most productive depth and speed. Bump the wood! Sure, you'll snag and lose jigs occasionally, but you won't catch fish if you're too timid to cast into cover. Continue this approach until the action slows.

Before you leave, drift or use an electric motor to position yourself directly over the cover. Drop your tightline rig directly into it and dig out an additional fish or two. If you snag up, a strong pull will straighten out the light-wire, Aberdeen hook. Bait up and repeat the process.

The old reliable, cane pole/bobber style of fishing for crappies can also be used here. A pole rigged with heavy braided nylon and fished with a slip float and a minnow or jig, is popular. A short, monofilament leader may be used to attach the hook (via a barrel swivel) to the heavy braided line. Hoisting the fish from heavy cover is important, and this simple and easy method works fine.

If you don't have a flasher or graph to help you locate crappie cover, slow trolling is a sure-fire way to find fish. Spider (tightline) rigs allow you to set out several poles at different depths. Then slowly troll or drift across flats or creeks. Scattered crappies are taken this way quite effectively. Consider anchoring your boat over likely spots, but be cautious when you position your anchor so you don't spook the fish.

ROAMING THE RESERVOIRS

Large, sprawling reservoirs appear awesome to many anglers. How do you locate the productive spots with miles of open water staring you in the face? Ask any reservoir angler worth his grits and he'll tell you to get a good topographical map. A map will give you an overview of the reservoir. Channels, creeks, bays and coves plus depth contours are all easy to spot. Many times, detailed maps of the larger creek arms are available at marinas. Be sure to take time to study the map and the map's key because it'll help you locate potential fishing areas. In addition, you'll be gadding about the reservoir like an old-timer in no time.

General areas can be marked at home and checked out once you're on the water. Just apply the location strategies presented in this chapter and you'll be well on your way to becoming a crappie pro on any reservoir.

This braggin'-sized bunch of white crappies was taken from Kentucky Lake, KY/TN. These slab crappies were caught while fishing a small jig tipped with a minnow around manmade fish attractors (stake beds).

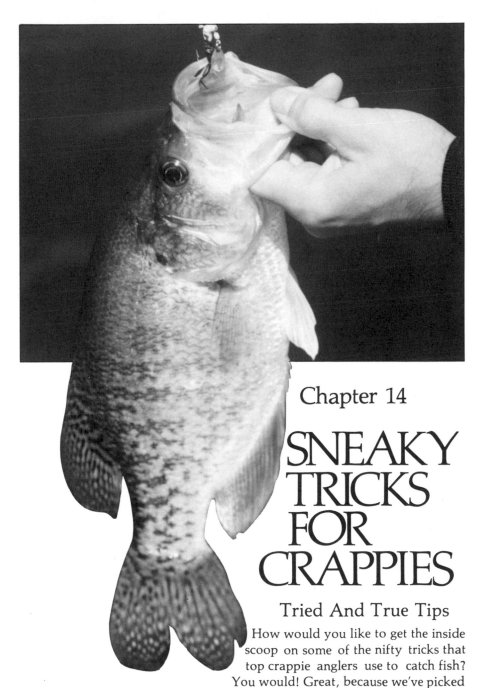

Chapter 14

SNEAKY TRICKS FOR CRAPPIES

Tried And True Tips

How would you like to get the inside scoop on some of the nifty tricks that top crappie anglers use to catch fish? You would! Great, because we've picked the brains of several crappie experts and have assembled a number of hot tips to help you catch more and bigger crappies. These are tips that elite, crappie anglers use day in and day out to locate and catch fish.

Many times it's the little things that make a big difference in fishing. It's the subtle differences in equipment, location or presentation that really pay off. There are tips to help you trigger reluctant, non-aggressive fish; other techniques to use when they're biting ten-on-a-hook; plus inside information on location; and tips to help you catch more fish all season long.

The following information is a potpourri of little-known, productive secrets which you can add to your crappie fishing repertoire. Most of the tips and techniques can be applied to lakes, rivers and reservoirs. So, regardless of where you fish there will be many you can use. In essence, crappie fishing is simply matching your tactics to conditions.

TACKLE

Selecting the proper rod and reel combo or crappie pole is important because a balanced outfit will maximize the effectiveness of your presentation. While almost any outfit will work, it's normally a good/better/best situation as far as crappie tackle goes. You can catch fish by using casting or spinning equipment, a fly rod outfit or a trusty cane pole. Be certain that the type of paraphernalia you choose allows you to use a presentation to match the conditions.

To sharpen your ability to feel the bottom or a bite, choose a casting or spinning rod with a sensitive tip. Then spool the reel with quality monofilament line. Use heavy line (10- to 30-pound test) and casting tackle for bouncing through heavy cover in dark water. For fishing sparse cover or clear water—the extreme opposite condition—use lighter, 2- to 4-pound-test line and spinning gear.

Another option is a 9- to 10-foot, graphite, fly rod (#5 weight). Spool the reel with 4- to 8-pound-test mono instead of fly line. A small jig on this set-up can be worked vertically in and around cover at all depths with maximum sensitivity and minimum hang-ups. A scrappy crappie is the ultimate challenge on this outfit—fun!

A jig worked with a fly rod can be an effective way to catch crappies at all depths.

Ultralight and light spinning tackle are very important in overall crappie presentation. Lighter tackle is a rule of thumb if the water is clear. A 5- to 6-foot, light-action, spinning rod with an open-bail, spinning reel spooled with

Super crappie tackle!

4- or 6-pound-test mono is ideal. Today's emphasis on super-light, leadhead jigs further complements the use of such tackle. The light jigs can be cast either around or over cover, or vertically fished through it.

Casting crappie jigs with weights of 1/16 or 1/32 ounce is best done on 2- or 4-pound line. The wind can play a role in the *feel* of your jig, and tiny split shots or a heavier jighead may be needed to get the lure down to the fish. When working the thick stuff, be prepared to cut and retie often. Decorating the snags with several dozen colorful jigs is common on some waters.

CRAPPIE POLE

Millions of crappie anglers catch tons of crappies using a simple, 10- to 12-foot pole. An inexpensive cane pole works fine, but technology has developed sophisticated, ultra-sensitive, fiberglass and graphite, crappie poles.

For landing big crappies, the most popular pole is a 10- to 12-foot, fiberglass

line to
rig

sensitive tip
section

small hole
drilled in pole
for line feed

line runs
through inside
of pole

line keeper
(no reel)

10- to 12-foot pole

powerful butt section

Sensitivity is the key! Develop your sense of feel to aid in detecting the type of bottom, cover and the subtle bite of a crappie.

or graphite model with a sensitive tip and a strong butt section. The pole telescopes and is hollow on the inside where the line is threaded through and out the tip.

A line keeper is attached near the butt end of the pole where a tiny hole lets the line come up to the keeper. Depth can be regulated easily, because the line feeds (unwraps) off the keeper in one-foot increments. Some poles use a reel fixed to the butt end while others expose the line through eyelets on the rod. They all work, but with the line on the inside of the pole, there seem to be less tangles and more sensitivity.

The heavy-line, tightline, crappie rig is, of course, most effective in dark or stained water. However, by scaling down on the line size (10-pound vs. 30-pound test), the rig can be quite effective in clear water, too.

2 + 2 = CRAPPIES

Always cover water efficiently as you search for crappies. In the shallows, that can mean using a 2-rod/2-bobber approach.

Say you're fishing the shoreline of a bay, or using waders and a float tube (or a boat). You need to cover the shallowest water around the perimeter of the bay as well as the slightly deeper water offshore.

Rig a long, 6-1/2- to 7-1/2-foot, ultralight or light-action rod with 4-pound-test line. Slip a casting bubble such as the A-Just-A-Bubble onto your line. Slide it up to the desired depth and twist the top to hold it in place. Now tie a small, leadhead jig on the end of your line below the bobber. By adding a bit of water (weight) to the casting bubble you can cast this rig a mile. It's perfect for fishing the shallows.

This casting-bubble system fishes most efficiently with 1 to 2-1/2 feet of line

A-Just-A-Bubble Rig   Slip Bobber Rig

bead

1 to 2½ feet

option: place sinkers at 6" intervals to reduce bow in line while retrieving

2 to 5 feet

split shot

12" to 18"

hook

VICKERMAN

hanging below the bobber. The more line dangling below the bobber, the more difficult it becomes to cast.

The other rod can be a short or long, ultralight, rigged with 4-pound-test line. Add a slip bobber to this rig and it becomes your "little-bit-deeper" rod. You'll lose some casting distance, but that's OK because little-bit-deeper crappies aren't quite so spooky.

You'll usually fish this combo in water from 2 to 5 feet deep, although you can fish it deeper or shallower by simply adjusting the bobber stop. Ready? Then step into your float tube and wade in. Pop a few casts out to the deeper water in front of you. Retrieve the bobber a foot before stopping it to let the jig glide back below it.

Now cover the shallow water parallel to shore. Lay your "short" rod across your tube or prop it in a rod holder and fire a cast out with the long rod. Sure, send the bobber out 60 feet. It's amazing how easily a long, light rod casts a casting bubble on 4-pound-test line.

Use this system anytime crappies are relatively shallow. When they drop into slightly deeper water, switch the slip bobber to the long rod and go without a bobber on the shorter rod. The longer rod with a slip bobber will allow you to probe the deeper areas more efficiently. In addition, the shorter, ultralight rod can be used to pitch either a small, subtle jig or an action jig along the deeper edges of a weed- or brushline. By using the countdown technique to control the depth of the lure, a jig can be fished above, through or parallel to cover or a drop-off.

MINNOWS, JIGS AND BOBBERS

Crappies are among the least confusing of all species from a presentation point of view. Since most crappies worth catching are basically minnow- or fish-feeders, most of their feeding is done at mid-depth ranges, among schools of baitfish. Therefore, the range of potentially productive presentations is rather limited.

Normally, live-bait anglers can limit themselves to the most predominant open-water baitfish in any given body of water. Preferred bait size is almost always between 1-1/2 and 3 inches.

Sure, there are exceptions. A few crappies are caught on nightcrawlers. Also, during certain specific periods when crappies are feeding on emerging nymphs or insects, baitfish can go untouched. But for pure productivity, you're still better off with the most common baitfish within the preferred size range in the lake.

Minnow type and size are important factors in crappie fishing. Day in and day out, minnows in 1- to 2-inch lengths seem to produce best with both bobber- and jig-fishing presentations. Remember, match the minnow size to the size of the hook you're using; *don't* impale a small bait on a large hook. Simple and natural is usually best when dealing with crappies.

What are crappie minnows? Well, depending on where and when you buy them, crappie minnows are usually a real hodgepodge of different types. Shiners, fatheads, dace, chubs and shad are all typical varieties that show up in your minnow bucket. In addition, usually a few less desirable minnows like sticklebacks, suckers and carp have a habit of appearing, too; these are *not* preferred types. Know your minnow types and use the best local bait available; it pays!

Normally, you'll catch more fish on fresh, lively bait than on half-dead or unhealthy minnows. Therefore, take special care of your bait; baitfish must be kept cool and well oxygenated. In addition, don't overcrowd minnows. As a rule of thumb, 2 or 3 dozen minnows per gallon of water is about right. A few dozen, lively minnows are a lot better than a ton of dead, smelly bait.

Hooking the minnow is simply a matter of common sense based on the presentation. For example, when you're stationary-bobber-fishing, hook the minnow lightly in the back just behind the dorsal fin, taking care not to break the spine. When trolling, hook the minnow through the lips from the bottom upward so it trails naturally as it's moved along. When jigging, hook the minnow upward through the lower jaw and out the skull, or hook it through the eyes. Hooking the minnow properly will ensure a natural-appearing bait and will make catching crappies much easier.

Hooking minnows properly is important. Although we don't have research evidence, it appears that crappies often take their baitfish sideways or tail first. So, when you're bobber fishing, hook the bait just behind the dorsal fin and above the backbone. A minnow hooked in this manner will stay alive and move around actively. This movement is important in luring the crappie to take the bait.

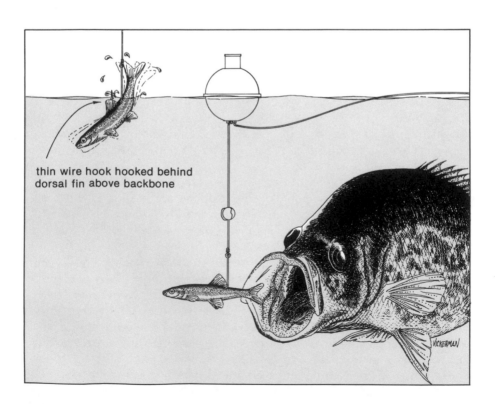

thin wire hook hooked behind
dorsal fin above backbone

In early spring when crappies are bedding in very shallow water, use this method: With the minnow just several inches under the bobber, slowly move the boat (or wade) along the shore, continually dropping the bait into likely spots. The trick is the presentation of the minnow. Reach out with your pole and slowly drop the minnow until it is partially under the surface. It will wiggle frantically, trying to get into the water. Hold it this way for several seconds before dropping it all the way in. Nearby crappies will have a tough time resisting.

Here are a couple tips to use when casting a crappie jig or jig/minnow combo. The drop rate of some jigs can be controlled by trimming the hair or feathers. In addition, tipping the jig with a minnow will add buoyancy. By experimenting with sizes and styles of jigheads, along with varieties of body dressing (plastic, feathers or hair), you can achieve nearly any drop-speed and/or action the fish desire.

Color? Crappie jigs are available in a zillion colors, but a couple basic colors will usually suffice. In clear water, white, yellow, pink and chartreuse seem to work best. However, black, purple and light fluorescent colors can produce in dark-water conditions. In stained water, trial and error will be necessary to determine a color preference. The pinky jig (pink jighead with white hair or feathers) is normally a good choice in clear water, while a pink jighead with yellow hair or feathers is a good pick for stained or dark water. While our general tendency is to try light-colored jigs first, recent experiments with the Color-C-Lector have shown that darker lures are productive at times. Thus, the rule is, *experiment!*

A last minute tip: Try a small loop knot when trolling or casting tiny crappie jigs. The loop gives the jig better action.

Finally, check lighter lines regularly for wear by passing the line over your lips. This technique is more discriminating than eyeball or finger checks and should be used routinely—especially when fishing around cover.

JIGS

Miniature-size plugs; small, straight-shafted spinners; and a variety of other artificials will all take crappies, but jigs are the most productive artificial lures. As with live bait, keep the size small. In fact, for all practical purposes, you can eliminate almost anything over 2 inches long.

SUBTLE JIGS

Subtle jigs also work well in the same areas as action jigs. They simply have less action and are better choices when the fish are less aggressive. Their true strength, however, is that they are deadly when retrieved with minimum movement or even held at rest! Bucktail jigs are buoyant (slow drop speed) and have very subtle action. Marabou "breathes" in a tantalizing fashion even when the jig is motionless. Plastic bodies only transmit the subtle motion *you* place on them. Plastic-body/marabou-tail combinations display the best aspects of both.

In general, most jigs are designed to be fished without a minnow and are somewhat bulky. When you tip a jig with a minnow, it's usually best to thin out the jig by trimming down or pulling out some of the dressing. This reduces the bulk of the combination so it's more appealing to crappies.

Subtle Jigs

Column 1: Knight Tiny Tube, Gopher Mushroom Head, Jack's jighead; Column 2: chenille/marabou jig, Lindy Fuzz-E-Grub, Windels Rabbit Hair Jig.

ACTION JIGS

Action jigs have spinners, wiggling tails, etc., and work better in motion than at rest. They're great for swimming retrieves or when active crappies hit a jig as it falls to the bottom. Action jigs work best for mid-depth retrieves, such as along the edge of brush or a weedline. They are excellent choices before crappies move in shallow (before pre-spawn) or after they leave the shallows (after post-spawn).

Action Jigs

Clockwise from upper left: Northland Whistler, Blakemore Road Runner, Mister Twister Teeny, Bass Buster Chumm'n Minnow.

JIG FISHING TIPS

Here are a couple tricks that'll increase your jig-fishing catch. When fish are aggressive, use an action jig like a Bass Buster Beetle Spin, Blakemore Road Runner or Northland Whistler Jig. For casting a light jig, 4- to 6-pound-test line on an ultralight to light action, 5- or 6-foot rod is preferred. Position the knot on the front of the eye of the jig; it's perfect for swimming retrieves.

note→

However, a slightly different approach works better when subtle jigs like a Knight Tiny Tube, Lindy Fuzz-E-Grub, marabou/hair jig or plain jighead are fished either vertically or below a float. Simply position the knot in the center or slightly back of the jig's eyelet. This allows the jig to remain in a horizontal position and not just hang at an odd angle.

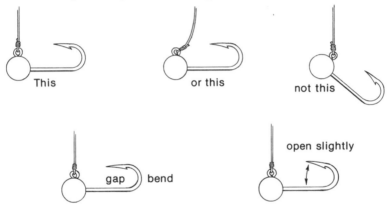

This   or this   not this

gap) bend   open slightly

Remember to re-adjust the knot after catching a fish. An additional tip that will help you hook more crappies is to open the bend of the hook slightly to increase the gap and increase hooking ability.

CRAPPIE JIG BRUSHGUARD/WEEDGUARD

No doubt about it, fishing for crappies in many waters means fishing cover. Whether you fish standing timber in a reservoir, flooded brush in an oxbow lake or heavy reeds in a natural lake, snags and crappie fishing go hand-in-hand. Here's a neat little trick that some good ol' southern boys have used to minimize jig loss. However, the tip can be used anywhere.

Place a small rubber band or dental elastic over the jighead and hook. Put the rubber band over the hook barb and then carefully pull it over the eyelet of the jig. Bingo—a simple yet effective guard.

rubber band

WHY KNOT?

Tying a strong knot is a *must*. Because many crappie presentations require the use of 2-, 4- or 6-pound-test line, knot strength is critical. So, take the time to learn how to tie knots properly and avoid the frustration of losing a slab crappie because the knot failed. Remember, your line is only as strong as the weakest link—the knot. Many anglers are tying knots that can reduce the breaking strength of a line by more than 50%. It's easy to understand why lots of big fish are lost on light lines.

Before each fishing trip, spool up with fresh, premium line; *don't* use the bargain basement stuff. A strong knot tied with quality monofilament line will hold the biggest crappie that swims. The accompanying illustrations describe a few knots that'll help you catch more crappies.

TRILENE KNOT

This knot retains up to 90% of the original line strength. Use it for tying hooks and artificial lures to monofilament line.

Trilene Knot

1. Run end of line through eye of hook or lure and double back through the eye a second time.

2. Loop around standing part of line 5 or 6 times.

3. Thread tag end back between the eye and the coils as shown.

4. Pull up tight and trim tag end.

LOOP KNOT

This knot only has 60 to 70 percent of the line strength, but is a good knot to use when you're casting tiny, 1/64- or 1/32-oz. jigs. The loop knot gives small jigs unrestricted action. However, remember to re-tie often.

Loop Knot

(1) Make an overhand knot. Then (2) pass the free end through the eye of the lure and back through the overhand knot. (3) Snug up the knot by pulling on the free end and standing line. Then tie another overhand knot around the standing line. (4) Snug up the second overhand knot and pull on the standing line to slide the two knots together. (5) Continue pulling until the two knots join. Then trim.

BOBBER RIGS

Bobber rigs fit the bill for shallow-water, cover-oriented fish, or for fish suspended in or near deep cover. They work equally well with jigs, jig/minnow combos, or the old split-shot/hook/minnow standby.

Long, thin, lightweight, "quill" bobbers are excellent for shallow, calm conditions. They enter the water with a light splash rather than a hard "plop." They're sensitive and betray even the lightest crappie hit. A *slight* twitch will rock the bobber and make your jig dance. Their only weakness is that they're difficult to cast in windy conditions.

Plastic floats like the A-Just-A-Bubble serve several functions. First, you can add water inside them, giving you the weight to cast a light jig in windy conditions. Second, the thread-through, twist grip holds the bobber in place without damaging your line and makes it easy to adjust the depth of your bait. About the only drawback is that its heavier weight makes a splash when it enters the water. Use it under windy conditions, but stick to the quill-type bobber when it's calm.

Slip bobbers work at any depth and are easy to cast even when fishing deep water. It's hard to cast a normal bobber rig that's set deeper than 4 feet. Slip bobbers are simple to use; just slide the bobber stop up or down your line and you can fish from 2 to 20 feet deep—or more!

Bobbers work best with subtle jigs. In fact, since the bobber adds casting weight, you can drop down to tiny 1/16-, 1/32-, or even 1/64-ounce jigs. They are deadly on shallow crappies in brush or reeds. Add a small, lip-hooked, crappie minnow to the jig if the fish are reluctant to hit a plain jig. Give the jig a little dab of a scent-attractor product if it gives you more confidence.

From left to right: Columns 1 and 2: pencil/quill-type bobbers; Column 3: standard round bobber; A-Just-A-Bubble, slip bobber with stop and bead, #8 hooks and split shot; Column 4: "pinky" jig, Binkelman jighead, Lindy floss-bodied jig, Windels marabou jig.

FIXED VS. SLIP BOBBERS

What are the differences between bobbers? Are they important? Yes! While there are many bobbers on the market, they can be divided into two general categories—fixed and slip styles. Fixed floats are clipped, pegged or twisted onto the line, allowing you to fish at a specific depth. Normally, a fixed float is used in shallow water that's 1 to 4 feet deep. This style of float allows the bait to remain at the pre-set depth during a retrieve. A slip bobber, on the other hand, slides on the line until it hits the bobber stop. Therefore, you can fish much deeper without causing any casting problems. A slip bobber also allows you to fish at a controlled depth. However, during a retrieve, the bait has a tendency to rise toward the surface because line is being pulled through the bobber. So, retrieve very slowly to minimize this yo-yo effect.

RETRIEVES

Crappie presentations should be slow moving most of the time. That calls for the correct tackle combinations. Light, 1/16- to 1/8-ounce leadhead jigs, fished on 4-pound-test line and a lightweight rod, make casting easy and allow

Three Typical Retrieves

10:30
9:30

Lift-drop Swimming

12:00
11:00
10:00
9:00

**Lift-drop Swimming
(finger on line)**

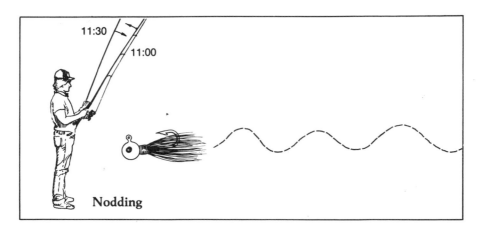

Nodding

Two types of lift-drop swimming retrieves are made in different ways but provide the same, basic, jig movement. Try this when it's calm out and you can watch your line for hits. Cast out, raise your rod tip to about 10:30, and count the jig down to the desired depth: "One thousand, two thousand, etc." Let the jig ride down on a tight line for a bit before slowly reeling down to about 9:30, and then lift back to 10:30. The jig will ride, rise and fall in an enticing manner. Expect most hits to occur as the jig falls.

When it's windy and you're having trouble watching your line, use your finger to detect hits. Cast out and bring your rod tip to 9:00 as you count the jig down. Engage the reel and place your trigger finger on the line. As the jig falls, it's getting closer to you. Let the jig fall as you hold at 9:00. Bring the rod tip to 10:00 and let the jig fall. Do the same at 11:00 and 12:00. Then quickly reel back to 9:00 and start over.

A nodding retrieve is made with the rod tip high. Cast out and count the jig down as you raise the rod tip to 11:00. Your wrist moves the rod tip only from 11:00 to 11:30. Raise the rod tip slowly to 11:30 and then reel back to 11:00.

the proper drop speed as a jig moves and falls during a retrieve.

Slow and simple is the way to go. Most of the time, either a slow, horizontal, swimming motion or a near-motionless presentation is most effective. That's why vertical fishing is so productive whenever you have crappies "nailed down" in heavy cover. You can set the depth of your lure and then try to hold it there. Of course, this becomes impossible when crappies are "on the move" as they typically are when suspended. Either some type of backtrolling (usually with an electric motor) or a cast and slow, steady, retrieve-type technique works best then.

In general, lures should be fished slowly because crappies seem much more willing to hit presentations moving steadily and horizontally than lures that are moving either erratically or up and down.

OPEN-WATER ACTION

Drifting, backtrolling or front trolling are efficient ways to search for crappies. Once you've found them, you have several options. If it's windy, the fish are usually deep or scattered, so it may be a good idea to continue to drift or troll. If the fish are pinpointed and deep, you may wish to anchor over them and fish vertically. When fish are found schooled relatively shallow, it's a good idea to mark the fish and pull back off them; then cast to the school.

Mark the school's location, back off and cast into it using ultralight, spinning gear and small jigs.

FLOATING MARKER BUOYS

Floating markers can be used to locate open-water areas. They're perfect for marking a place where you spotted fish on your locator, graph or LCR, or they can be tossed overboard to mark the spot where a crappie was caught. In addition, they are handy for staking out fish attractors, humps, submerged islands, creek channels, submerged timber, weedlines, drop-offs, ledges and other underwater structures.

Markers allow you to target a specific area and enable you to fish more productively. Because your bait will be in potential crappie water a high percentage of the time, you'll catch more fish, and that's the name of the game.

There are several different styles, shapes, colors and sizes of marker buoys on the market. Which is best? It depends. Most markers are constructed of polyethylene and are either flat or barbell in shape. They come with 50 to 75 feet of nylon cord that wraps around the marker for storage and a heavy lead weight to securely anchor the marker on the bottom. The best flat and low-profile, barbell markers contain balanced ballast weights inside to prevent them from unwinding in current or wind. These low-profile markers offer good visibility if you're close by, yet are difficult for other anglers to spot from a distance.

An innovative company has designed an illuminated marker buoy for night fishing. The unit is powered by a AA battery and burns up to 10 hours. This unit is perfect for night-fishing addicts.

A new, high-visibility, upright, floating buoy is also available. Unlike the low-profile types, this marker has a 7-inch high, cylindrical top with a one-inch strip of reflective tape for added visibility. Like the other markers, this buoy is self-contained. This vertical-style marker will provide high visibility under most conditions—even at a distance—and the reflective tape makes it easier to find at night.

Most markers are either bright yellow or orange and are easy to spot. White, a favorite color for homemade, styrofoam markers is very difficult to locate under bright conditions. If you plan on using a homemade marker, paint it a fluorescent color, and regulate the length of the cord to match the depth of the water. Typically, these homespun markers unwind easily and may keep you off the fish.

In summary, floating marker buoys are a must. Don't leave the dock without them.

DRIFT, DABBLE OR DRAG?

Cover and wind determine your best crappie approach. Here are three examples requiring slightly different approaches.

DRAG: This approach works well with sparse cover and little or no wind. Simply cast a quill-type, bobber/jig combination past the cover (reed clump, flooded brush, stump, etc.) and slowly reel it up to the cover. Pause. Let it sit for 8 to 10 seconds and then give it a *slight* twitch. Repeat the process. Work your jig along the very edge of the cover.

A quill-type bobber is a key part of this presentation. The quill bobber is heavy enough to cast easily, yet it lands with a soft "plop" that won't spook shallow fish. Because the bobber is set at a fixed position on the line, the bait remains at a specific depth during the retrieve (drag).

DRIFT: Drifting works well in sparse cover, although you can rapidly (perhaps too rapidly!) drift a jig and bobber past thick cover, too. Cast slightly upward from the cover and let the bobber drift up the edge. Once it reaches the edge, hold it in place; twitch it, and then let it sit.

No bites? Point your rod tip to the right or left and *steer* the bobber around the edge of the cover. Once it clears the edge, release some line and let it drift by.

This approach works *around* single cover items like a brush pile or *through* sparse areas of cover like thin reed clumps. With repeated casts and a little steering, you can maneuver a bobber rig through a wide area of cover without repositioning the boat.

This type of bobber is perfect for casting in wind. Add water to the float to give you enough weight to cast. In addition, because the bobber is firmly attached to the line, the bait stays at the proper depth during the drift.

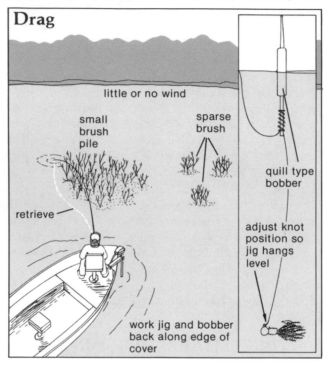

Drag

little or no wind

small brush pile

sparse brush

retrieve

quill type bobber

adjust knot position so jig hangs level

work jig and bobber back along edge of cover

DABBLE: Thick cover requires a dabbling approach. Unless the crappies are very active, they won't come out to the edge. A bobber/jig combo that drags or drifts past the edge won't entice them. Roll up your sleeves and go in after 'em.

A simple cane pole or a 10- to 14-foot, telescoping rod works great under these conditions. Position the boat 6 to 10 feet from the cover; reach out with the rod tip and "flip" the tiny jig into the cover. Ever-so-slowly lower it through the cover, pausing occasionally. Give the jig a slight "wiggle," and pause again.

Don't be in too much of a hurry. Tease the fish. When a fish inhales the jig, don't *jerk*. Simply lift up in a steady, sweeping motion. The flex of the long rod will lift the fish up through cover to the surface. Once the fish is up, drag it slightly away from the cover. When it's in the open, *then* fight it. Don't go toe-in-toe *in* cover, or *you'll lose*.

Think you'll spook 'em? When fish first move into the shallows in spring, they'll be very spooky. After they're in the shallows awhile, they become more fearless. Once fish start to display their dark spawning colors, you can usually approach them quite easily.

This approach works best with light wind conditions when you can hold the

Cast bobber slightly upwind of first reed clump and let it drift to the edge. Steer it left by pointing your rod tip left. Little by little, let out more line. With enough line out and by swinging the rod left to ROD POSITION 2, the bobber will drift to CLUMP 2. Similarly, more line and bringing the rod back to ROD POSITION 3 will drift the bobber to CLUMP 3.

boat in place with an electric motor. It is very difficult to fish heavy cover with a strong wind, however, unless you anchor in exactly the right position on the upwind side of the cover.

In some reservoirs, oxbow lakes and river backwaters, stumps and brush attract crappies. Carefully dabble the bait into the cover, working around a stump's root system. Don't forget to probe for crappies *inside* large, hollow, rotted logs. In some waters, this "stump knocking" technique is deadly.

LEVERAGE: If you can, use the end of a branch or a broken reed as a *lever*. Flip your line over the top, near the tip. The lure will drop straight down from there. This is better than casting horizontally *into* heavy cover, because you'll probably snag up if you do. Fish the jig slowly up and down with frequent pauses. When a fish bites, lift it up and over the cover. You can fish light cover like reeds with 6-pound-test line; whereas heavy brush might require 10- to 30-pound test to muscle the fish out.

UP AND IN

When fishing in cover (reed clumps or brush), the "up and in" technique is the best method for quickly getting a fish out of cover and into the boat. The long crappie pole gives you the leverage necessary to put pressure on the fish without breaking the line. In addition, it absorbs the shock when a slab crappie makes a mad dash for freedom. Crappies have a fragile, "paper thin" mouth, so don't horse 'em or you'll probably tear the hook out—goodbye fish.

A jig worked with a fly rod or long, limber crappie pole is an effective and fun way to catch crappies. This outfit provides maximum "feel" and the softest bite can easily be detected.

When a crappie bites, *don't* rear back and sock-it-to-'em with both hands to set the hook. Usually, all that's necessary is a quick, gentle, upward motion of the pole; the small, sharp hook will easily penetrate the crappie's mouth. In cover, lift the fish up and out of the reeds or brush and swing it gently into the boat. It's much more effective than trying to pull a crappie *through* cover, which often results in a broken line and a lost fish. Remember, "up and in!"

When conditions permit, a fish can also be lifted out of cover, then pulled across the surface on its side to the boat. This technique is great for getting slab crappies up and away from heavy cover bordered by an open area. Also, don't forget a landing net because giant, 2-pound-plus crappies may require a net to get them into the boat. Remember, always carry a net whenever you're on slab-crappie waters; it'll save you the frustration of losing a large crappie at the boat.

COVER, DEPTH AND BOTTOM CONTENT

Pre-spawn crappies will seek out the best available combination of depth, cover and bottom content. Depth and cover can be fairly obvious and easy to locate. Simply use your eyes in clear water. Polarized sunglasses will help you spot bottom conditions; if it's not too windy, the polarized lenses cut the glare

Heavy, deeper (4-5 feet) reeds are some of the best, big-crappie spawning areas on natural lakes. The prime spots have thick, bent or broken reeds in conjunction with a bottom darker than the surrounding area.

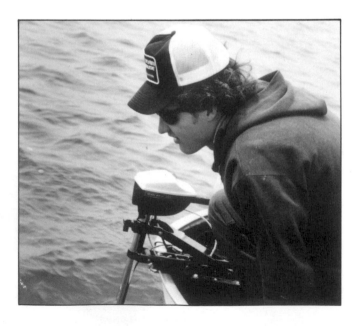

Polarized sunglasses cut glare and enable you to pick out prime, pre-spawn/spawn crappie areas. If the water is fairly clear, you can pick out the best spots and sometimes even see the fish!

This is what reeds look like when you approach them with the sun in your face. The back, shaded sides of the reeds stand out in vivid contrast, betraying the heaviest clumps. It's much easier to fish clumps from this direction. In general, pre-spawn/spawn, natural-lake crappies—particularly the big slabs—will select the deepest, heaviest reed clumps with the proper bottom content. Heavy clumps in 4 to 5 feet of water are more likely to hold larger fish than those in 2 feet.

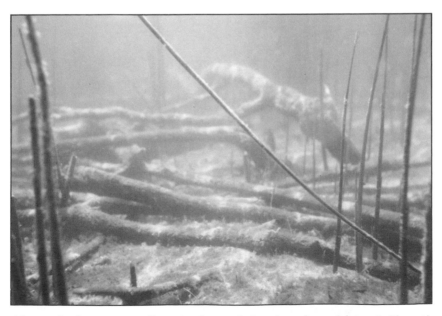

Always check out areas adjacent to beaver lodges for submerged wood. Many times the slightly deep water and sunken branches will draw early season crappies. This type of cover is ideal crappie habitat.

and enable you to see bottom. Pick out the darker areas in conjunction with cover at a likely depth (usually 2 to 5 feet). Under ideal conditions (clear water, sunny skies, no wind) you'll often spot the crappies, too! In dark or stained waters, fish will often spawn at the depth of maximum light penetration.

CRAPPIE RIG

First used in the large lakes of Kentucky and Tennessee, the dingy waters of Lake Barkley and Kentucky Lake gave the crappie rig its fame. Professional guides use it during every season of the year for consistent catches of slab crappies. The crappie rig allows you to present baits at two different depths at the same time. Remember, depth control is crucial in crappie fishing. Deeper-water (12 to 20 feet) anglers favor a vertical, "tightline" technique. This "spreader" rig consists of two hooks with a bell sinker on the bottom.

The crappie rig is designed to be used both with live minnows and with artificial jigs. Shiner minnows are the most common bait, but your favorite marabou or hollow-bodied jig can easily be substituted.

By bouncing bottom with this double-hook rig you can let the sinker be your eyes to the bottom. Any contact with brush, stake beds, etc., is telegraphed to you via the line and pole. Although two fish may be taken at one time, the real purpose of the double hook rig is to present the bait at two different depths. Whether the crappies are holding tight to cover or slightly suspended, you'll have both depths covered.

These slab black and white crappies were "tightlined" from cover located at the edge of a creek channel. Do you recognize the white crappie on the left?

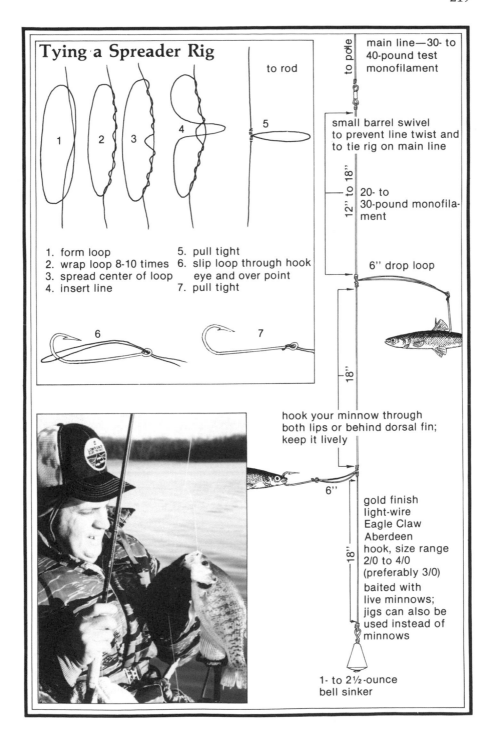

Tying a Spreader Rig

to rod

1
2
3
4
5

1. form loop
2. wrap loop 8-10 times
3. spread center of loop
4. insert line
5. pull tight
6. slip loop through hook eye and over point
7. pull tight

6

7

to pole

main line—30- to 40-pound test monofilament

small barrel swivel to prevent line twist and to tie rig on main line

12" to 18"

20- to 30-pound monofilament

6" drop loop

18"

hook your minnow through both lips or behind dorsal fin; keep it lively

6"

gold finish light-wire Eagle Claw Aberdeen hook, size range 2/0 to 4/0 (preferably 3/0) baited with live minnows; jigs can also be used instead of minnows

18"

1- to 2½-ounce bell sinker

The entire, double-hook rig is tied from one piece of monofilament. The drops are "double loops" where a hook can slide on by putting the line through the hook's eye. Hooks can be changed without cutting the line.

MOON CLOCK

Does lunar influence play a key role in lunker fish activity and catchability? Well, we've got a hot news flash for you! We've compiled evidence which indicates that the moon has a profound effect on fishing—both on a daily and a monthly basis!

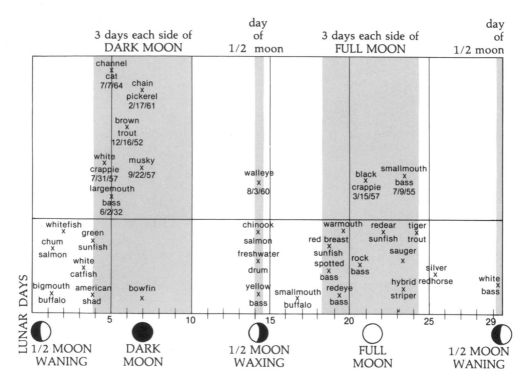

Selected world-record, gamefish catches.(Note: Since all records are not included in this group, it is intended only to represent individual records and not to show a complete picture.)

New world records during 1970-1979.

Important Periods During The Lunar Month

Having reached firm conclusions about the importance of monthly periods surrounding the dark and full moon, we became curious about the success other anglers had during these periods. Because no one apparently kept records as elaborate as Doug Hannon's, we could only go to the 1979 (the year we compiled the information) International Game Fish Association record book and check record fish against the part of the lunar month they were caught. What we found was amazing! The three days on each side of the dark and full moons plus the day of each half-moon, represented about 54% of the month, yet held 73% of the world records caught from 1970-1979! More dramatically, 24% of the month around the full moon held 41% of the world records taken during this period!

Next, we turned to world records for popular gamefish established outside the 1970-1979 period. The white and black crappie, channel catfish, chain pickerel, brown trout, musky, smallmouth and largemouth bass records were all caught within a three-day period either side of the dark or full moon. Clearly, these periods are significant for large fish.

The moon exerts an intense gravitational influence on the earth and this, in turn, seems to affect animal (fish) behavior. Doug Hannon, a true fishing scholar, recognized the significance of the moon's influence. In a manner that anyone can understand, he condensed data and detailed how this information can be related to fishing.

Basically, Hannon identified daily periods of lunar influence—"excellent" and "good" activity periods that coincide with moon-up and moon-down. Major (excellent) periods are triggered by the moon's being directly above or below a particular area of the earth at a given time. Minor (good) periods occur exactly halfway between the major periods.

The real breakthrough, however, is yet to be revealed and may change your fishing habits forever. Are you ready? OK. Fish are also influenced by the moon on a monthly basis. Hannon identified a 3- to 4-day period before and after the new (dark) and full moon, plus the day of the half moon, that has particular significance for trophy fish. An astounding 73% of the world-record fish caught during the years 1970-1979 fell within these time frames.

VEST POCKET GUIDE TO CRAPPIES

Season	Fish Location	Presentation
Spring: March, April, May, June	3' to 15' Near: Shallow Bays Feeder Creeks Creek Channels Brush Piles, Stumps & Trees Protected Weed Shorelines	Jig & Minnow Bobber Rigs Spinners Live Bait: Leeches, Worms, Mayfly Nymphs
Summer: July, August, September	3' to 20' Near: Pockets in Shallow Weeds and Reeds Brush Piles, Stumps & Trees Weedy Bays Deep Edges of Weeds and Timber Weeds and Timber— Both On and Off Bottom	Jig & Plastic Grub Bobber Rigs Spinners Small Crankbaits Live Bait: Minnows, Leeches, Worms, Crickets, Grasshoppers
Fall/Winter: October, November, December, January, February	8' to 30' Near: Sharp Weedline Drop-Offs Deep Rock Piles Deep Channel Edges Deep Creek Channel Bends Deep Brush Piles and Timber	Jig & Minnow Bobber Rigs Live Bait Rigs Live Bait: Minnows, Leeches Mousies, Meal-worms, Waxworms

We've researched reams of data and it all boils down to this: Lunar influence will affect your fishing.

Weather and other environmental factors are bound to affect lunar periods.

It's obvious that unstable weather can cancel the positive effects of the moon. On the other hand, if you combine stable weather conditions with lunar influence and intelligent fishing, the results will amaze you. We're talkin' big crappies and lots of 'em!

A simple assortment of crappie tackle will cover nearly any situation, wherever you fish. Just match your choice to the conditions.

When crappies are aggressive, use an action jig to complement their positive mood. Spinner/jig combos like (COLUMN 1) Bass Buster's Chumm'n Minnow and Beetle Spin, a Whizker Spin, or (COLUMN 2) Northland Whistler or Blakemore Roadrunner are excellent swimming/fluttering lures.

When crappies are less aggressive, you must "subtle-up" your presentation with less flash/vibration, or reduce the jig's movement. Any of the 1/32- to 1/16-ounce jigs shown here will do the trick. Pictured are (COLUMN 2, bottom): a Gopher Mushroom Head Jig, and Earl's Swimming Minnow, (COLUMN 3) shows a Lindy Fuzz-E-Grub, Charlie's Brewer Slider, Windels Crappie Jig, Garland Jig, and a Jack's Jighead (add a minnow).

The ultimate in subtlety is a bobber/jig approach. All of the bobbers shown here let you easily adjust the depth your jig hangs at; set it so it suspends just above the top of a brushpile or stake bed.

Also pictured are several #3/0 Eagle Claw Aberdeen hooks and a few split shot for making a tightline rig. Yes, the hooks are large, but they won't spook fish as long as the water is stained to dark. A strong pull with 20- to 30-pound-test line will straighten 'em out if they get snagged, and you'll get your rig back.

The general tendency of crappie behavior is a gradual, shallow-to-deep-water movement as the season progresses. In spring, crappies typically invade the edges of shallower areas for spawning. After spawning the crappies filter out into adjacent flats. During summer, crappies will suspend in confined open water, grazing on zooplankton, insects and minnows. In early fall, crappies may once again invade the shallower flats, but as winter approaches they drop into deep water.

Even though this pattern seems rather simple, it is important to understand that crappie habitat requirements change seasonally and so does crappie location. You won't catch crappies consistently by beating the shoreline all season long.

Keep in mind that water clarity also plays a major role in crappie movement, because it will often influence the depth of the fish. For example, in dark-water lakes, crappies may spawn in 18 inches of water, while in clear-water lakes the fish may spawn 10 or more feet deep. Remember, habitat affects habits.

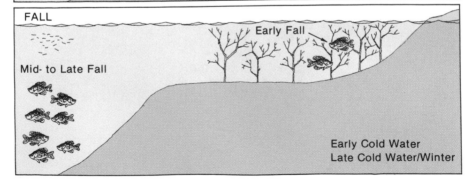

PRESENTATION TIPS

Clear Water	Stained Water	Dark Water
• Light line preferred (2-, 4-, 6-lb. test)	• In-between condition	• Heavier line acceptable (12-, 17-, 20-lb.-plus test)
• Small artificial lures	• Fish have mixed reactions based on amount of stain in water	• Bright fluorescent colors (chartreuse)
• Subtle colors (white, yellow, black)	• Trial and error is the key to proper presentation	• Short casts
• Swimming retrieves		• Maximum sound/ vibration in presentation
• Long casts	• In general, lean toward dark-water approach	• Bright-light conditions favorable
• Minimize sound/ vibration in presentation		• Small jigs productive (1/32-, 1/16-, 1/8-oz.)
• Low-light conditions favorable		• Live bait effective
• Small jigs best (1/64-, 1/32-, (1/16-oz.)		
• Live bait very effective		

Crappie terminal tackle is simple but important. Normally, an ultralight or light-action spinning rod and open-bail reel combo is preferred. However, a cane pole or a crappie stick is the standby of many crappie anglers. Grab a few jigs, hooks, sinkers and bobbers and you're all set.

Chapter 15

NIGHT-BITE CRAPPIES

"How'd ya do?"

"Got 15 nice crappies; all of 'em are between 1 and 2 pounds."

"Really! When?"

"Last night around midnight."

"What! You've gotta be kiddin'—at night?"

"You betcha! Bit like crazy."

"Huh! Ya know, I got skunked yesterday afternoon. There must be somethin' to that night-fishing business. Maybe I'll try it."

If you want to catch numbers of slab crappies plus beat the scorching summer heat, other anglers, or water skiers, then try nighttime crappie fishing. Fishing for crappies at night is an effective way to deal with clear-water lakes and reservoirs that house spooky, hard-to-catch crappies. Under the cloak of darkness even the wiliest fish become catchable.

While many anglers only fish at night in summer, crappies can be caught during other seasons as well. For example, during early winter many of the largest crappies of the year are caught in southern reservoirs by night anglers. This approach has often proven to be the answer to the real trophy fish. Likewise, anglers in the North ice fish for crappies at night during winter with excellent success.

Several, fisheries research studies support the fact that crappies are diurnal (dusk-to-dawn) feeders on many lakes, rivers and reservoirs. Generally, if the water is clear to slightly stained, adult crappies will usually be more active during low-light periods. Such periods include heavily overcast days plus the twilight hours of dusk and dawn. A creel census in Lake Havasu, CA/AZ (an ultra-clear reservoir) revealed that the night-angler catch was 16 times greater than the daytime harvest. While crappies may feed all day long on some waters, the heaviest feeding usually occurs at dusk and dawn.

In addition, there appears to be a general movement of fish into shallower water during low-light periods. On some waters, crappies may move to the edges of shallow-water cover like weeds, brush or trees. On other waters, suspended fish may simply migrate toward the surface to feed.

During summer, zooplankton, aquatic insects and small minnows may congregate near the surface and provide a real smorgasbord for night-feeding crappies. In fact, on a warm, calm summer night, crappies will be feeding just under the surface. Many times their backs will break the surface, and alert anglers can easily spot this activity. This situation is perfect for a fly fisherman.

In contrast, in many dark-water lakes and reservoirs, crappies may feed all day long. This is a common situation on many southern reeservoirs that contain white crappies. However, even on these waters, slab crappies can be a duck-soup proposition at night. Here's how to get your share of nighttime crappies.

The secret to successful night fishing is *organization*. Keep things simple. If you're fishing from a boat, make sure that it is orderly and bring a minimum amount of tackle. Nothing will spook fish quicker than banging around in a boat.

Here's a tip that'll help you keep quiet and catch more fish: Place a piece of indoor-outdoor carpeting on the floor of the boat (especially in aluminum boats). The carpet will significantly cut down the noise level. Shuffling feet, rattling tackle boxes and banging anchors will all spook the fish. In addition, the carpet will provide a nonslip surface.

Tackle should be simple. A 10' to 16', cane or fiberglass/graphite, crappie pole is best. This presentation is effective because there are no backlashes or line snarls to worry about. No muss, no fuss, just more fishing time.

Of course, you can use spinning tackle, as well. Normally, a 6- to 7-foot, light-action spinning rod and open-bail spinning reel spooled with 6- to 10-pound line is adequate for most situations. However, heavier line will be necessary when fishing around heavy cover. If you have problems tying knots and seeing the line at night, try this trick. Get a portable, ultraviolet (black) light and spool your reels with fluorescent line. When the light is activated the line will literally glow in the dark, so tying knots and removing tangles from line will be much easier.

When night fishing it's normally best to have a couple rods rigged and ready

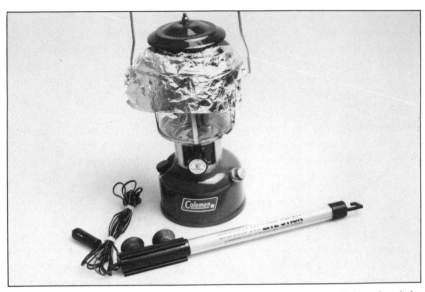

A gas lantern or battery powered lamp hung over the water will draw baitfish and crappies. Note the reflective shield made from aluminum foil that directs the light down into the water.

to use. Rig one with a slip-bobber rig and minnow and the other with a crappie jig or small spinner. Start fishing by using the bobber rig and minnow, and when the action gets hot just toss the jig out and haul 'em in.

Nighttime crappies and a food source go hand-in-hand. Here's how to create a crappie, fast-food restaurant that'll bring the fish to you. At night, a strong light will attract light-seeking organisms. Zooplankton, terrestrial and aquatic insects, minnows and small fish are all attracted to the light. Once these critters are swarming around, it's just a matter of time until the crappies stop by for a snack.

Here's a floating, battery-powered crappie light that's just the ticket for attracting fish. However, make sure that lights are legal for night fishing in your state before using one.

There are many lights available that you can use to attract crappies. Some anglers simply hang a gas lantern over the water from a pole or tree limb, while others prefer the battery-powered, floating crappie lights that shine into the water. In addition, mercury-vapor lights located on marina docks, parks, boat houses, streets or bridges will also attract fish. Be sure to check your state and local regulations for restrictions on portable lights before using one.

The best crappie bite generally takes place at dusk and may last a couple hours. However, all-night crappie bites are common on many clear waters. Typically, the most productive fishing occurs during the dark of the moon. Pick the three days before and after the dark of the moon for peak action—especially on slab crappies.

PRIME FISHING SPOTS

- Tip and sides of long, tapering main-lake points or bars
- Sunken islands with cover
- Underwater, hard-bottomed humps
- Drop-off near mouth of bay or cove
- Drop-off area of creek channel
- Tree or brushline
- Flooded timber or brush
- Manmade attractors (mats, marinas, piers, etc.)
- Junction of two creek channels
- Bridges and causeways

Look for fish in the confined open water adjacent to these areas. If you have a flasher or graph, watch carefully for suspended crappies and note their

Lighted bobbers and highly reflective fluorescent bobbers are both top-notch choices for your night fishing bag of tricks.

depth. When casting, count your lure down so you will know the approximate depth you're fishing. By carefully fishing from top to bottom in this manner, you'll thoroughly cover the water. When fish contact is made you'll know the depth the crappies are at.

When you approach a potential fishing area, cut the big motor and quietly approach with an electric motor, or drift into the spot. Sneaking into an area will allow you to catch fish a lot faster than if you come crashing in. Once you've located a good spot, put your crappie light out and start fishing.

Shore fishing for crappies at night can be a super, family, fishing adventure. Pack up the kids, find a marina, fishing dock or bridge illuminated with a bright light, and you're all set. The light will allow you to keep an eye on the kids, plus it'll draw food for the crappies.

When fishing around piers and bridges, fish as close to the support pilings as possible. Bump the wood and work the lure at different depths to locate fish. If possible, fish around and under the dock or pier. Where it's legal, a crappie attractor (brush pile, etc.) can be placed off the end of the dock—a sure-fire trick. Attractors greatly enhance the areas around floating docks (common on reservoirs) where there is good, overhead cover but few submerged objects to concentrate fish.

In general, bridges and causeways in shallow coves are superb, springtime areas since they form bottlenecks which fish must pass through on their way in and out of spawning areas. Bridges out in the deeper main body of a reservoir tend to attract more fish during summer, fall and winter.

SAFETY

Keep the fun in fishing by practicing a few, simple guidelines that'll ensure a safe trip. If you're fishing from a boat, make certain that the navigation lights operate properly and that all required safety devices are on board. It's always a good idea to have along a horn or whistle, compass and several extra flares. Know the water where you plan to fish. Don't go exploring at night into unknown areas. A little common sense will keep you from getting lost or running into something.

Always wear a Coast Guard-approved life jacket when fishing at night. In fact, a couple strips of reflective tape on the front and back of the vest and on the boat will make you much easier to see by other boaters.

Since it probably will be cool at night, a light nylon windbreaker and a thermos of your favorite warm beverage are both handy items.

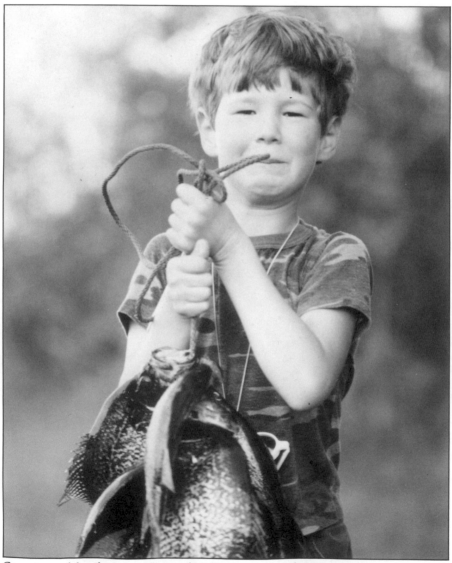

Crappies and family fishing fun go hand-in-hand. Atta boy!

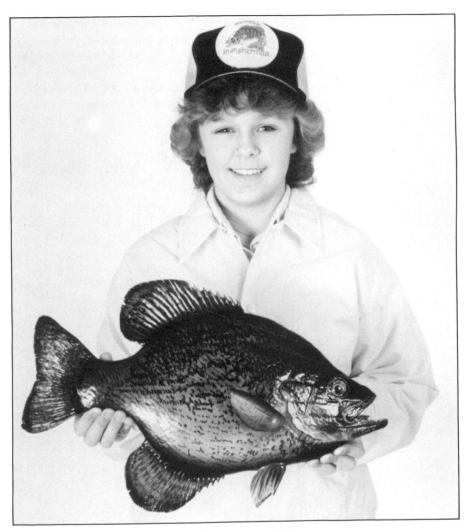

Chapter 16

U.S. CRAPPIE RECORDS

When it comes to state records, crappies may be the most interesting of all freshwater fish species. Why? Well, even as this book is being written, records are being broken. For example, during 1985, Tennessee established a new black crappie record.

Here's an interesting bit of trivia. Approximately 24 state records for black and white crappies were set between 1980-1985. Four state record crappies were caught in 1984. Apparently, there are lots of trophy crappies swimming around today.

Actually, a 2-pound crappie is a huge fish, and a 3- or 4-pounder is mind-boggling. But fish in the 4- to 5-pound range are trophies in every sense of the word. They rank right up there in stature with other, more publicized game-fish like bass, muskies and walleyes.

Here's a summary of the types of waters which record crappies were pulled from: 8 from rivers, 49 from lakes & reservoirs, and 15 from ponds & pits. Check out the record fish in your state. Then, using the information, tips and techniques in this book, grab a rod and get in on the action.

U.S. Crappie Records

STATE	WEIGHT lbs.	oz.	WATERS	YEAR
Alabama				
Black	4	4	Paint Creek	1984
White	4	8	Guntersville Reservoir	1974
Alaska	No Record			
Arizona				
Black	4	10	San Carlos Lake	1959
White	3	5	Lake Pleasant	1982
Arkansas				
Black	4	9	Oladale Lake	1976
White	4	3	Reservoir	1975
California				
Black	4	1	New Hogan Lake	1975
White	4	8	Clear Lake	1971
Colorado				
Black	3	0	CF & I Reservoir #3	1980
White	4	3¾	Northglenn Lake	1975
Connecticut				
Black	4	0	Pataganset Lake	1974
Delaware				
Black	4	9	Noxontown Pond	1976
Florida				
Black	3	12	Newnans Lake	1964
Georgia				
Black	4	4	Acree's Lake	1971
White	5	0	Private Pond	1984
Hawaii	No Record			
Idaho				
Black	2	8	Shepherd Lake	1954
Illinois				
Black	4	8	Rend Lake	1976
White	4	7	Farm Pond	1973
Indiana				
Black	4	9	Big Chapman Lake	1978
Iowa				
Black	4	9	Green Castle Lake	1981

Kansas				
Black	4	10	Woodson County State Lake	1957
White	4	¼	Farm Pond	1964
Kentucky				
Unknown	4	3	Lake Pewee	1969
Louisiana				
Black	6	0	Seaplane Canal Westwego	1969
Maine	No Record			
Maryland				
Black	3	14	Depot Pond	1977
White	2	9	Tuckahoe River	1979
Massachusetts				
Black	4	10	Jakes Pond	1980
White	3	0	Quabbin Reservoir	1977
Michigan				
Black	4	2	Lincoln Lake	1947
White	2	10	Kent Lake	1977
Minnesota				
Black	5	0	Vermilion River	1940
White	2	12	Coon Lake	1982
Mississippi				
Black	2	10	Ross Barnett Reservoir	1984
White	5	3	Enid Reservoir	1957
Missouri				
Black	4	8	Farm Pond	1967
White	4	5	Missouri River	1981
Montana				
Black	3	2	Tongue River Reservoir	1973
White	2	2	Tongue River Reservoir	1978
Nebraska				
Black	4	2	Red Willow Reservoir	1981
White	4	1	Red Willow Reservoir	1980
Nevada				
Black	3	2	Lake Mead	1976
White	2	8	Lahontan Reservoir	1968
New Hampshire				
Black	2	7½	Balch Pond	1983
New Jersey				
Black	3	8	Farm Pond	1980
White	2	8	Woodstown Lake	1984
New Mexico				
Black	4	9	Black River	1983
New York				
Black	3	1	Indian Lake	1977
North Carolina				
Black	4	15	Asheboro City Lake #4	1980

North Dakota				
Black	3	1	Nelson Lake	1981
Ohio				
Black	4	8	Private Lake	1981
White	3	10	Sandy Lake	1981
Oklahoma				
Black	4	10	Ottawa County Pond	1974
White	4	13	Tillman County Pond	1967
Oregon				
Black	4	0	Lost River	1973
White	4	12	Gerber Reservoir	1967
Pennsylvania				
White	3	6	Delaware River	1983
Rhode Island				
Black	3	0	Watchaug Pond	1976
South Carolina				
Black	5	0	Lake Moultrie	1957
White	5	1	Lake Murray	1949
South Dakota				
Black	3	4	South Buffalo Lake	1976
White	3	9	Hughes County Farm Pond	1974
Tennessee				
Black	4	4	Brown's Creek Lake	1985
White	5	1	Garner Brown's Pond	1968
Texas				
White	4	9	Navarro Mills Lake	1968
Utah				
Black	2	11	Lake Powell	1982
Vermont				
Black	1	13	Charcoal Creek	1976
Virginia	No Record		(Records will begin July 1, 1985)	
Washington				
Black	4	8	Lake Washington	1956
West Virginia				
Unknown	4	0	Meathouse Fork	1971
Wisconsin				
Black	3	5	Lake Wingra	1981
White	4	8	Gile Flowage	1967
Wyoming				
Black	2	3	Crook County	1983

Chapter 17

CARE AND KEEPING OF THE CATCH

A Little-Known Art

Care and keeping of the catch is a little-known art that few anglers understand. Take pride in mastering it. But why master keeping-the-catch in this age of catch and release fishing?

There's more to fishing than pre-trip anticipation, on-the-spot fish location and presentation, and catching and releasing fish. For most folks, fishing still means keeping some of the catch. A fishing trip doesn't end until the fish have been cleaned and eaten. Those who enjoy cleaning and cooking their catch, double their fishing fun.

It's a crime what some folks do to the fish they eat. Dragged, tossed, bumped, bruised; left to hang on a stringer in lukewarm water after dying; ground into a soiled, oily, boat floor; filleted with a dirty knife run through festering intestinal tracts; gilled and gutted too late, if at all; improperly cooled, if indeed cooled at all; and then mercifully frozen, but unmercifully frozen improperly.

We have met the enemy and it is us. But we can change. Here's how.

Before you leave home, decide if you're going to keep or release the fish. Being prepared in advance ensures a greater survival rate for released fish and better tasting fish for the table.

Make the decision to keep or release fish when they're caught, and bop the "keepers" on the head (kill them) and put them on ice. This prevents them from jumping around and becoming bruised. Fish flesh is extremely delicate and very perishable—treat it gently with TLC.

Bacterial growth and enzyme action are two primary enemies of fresh fish. In order to keep fish fit for the table, anglers must fight these two enemies from the moment a fish is caught until it is cooked.

It's vital to keep fish as cool (preferably cold) as possible. Fish may be iced whole, but the highest quality fish results when the gills and entrails are removed.

Blood remaining in the flesh produces rancidness in frozen fish and increases their deterioration in cold but not frozen storage. Fish should be bled before they're iced, if they aren't gutted and gilled. With the fish lying flat, cut the blood vessels in the tail with an incision to the bone, or simply clip off the tail with a snippers. Another method is to insert a knife into the chest cavity slightly back of the point where it meets the gills. Move the knife around to ensure cutting blood vessels.

USING ICE

Crushed ice is best for icing fish because it packs closer and cools them faster than blocks or cubes. Place ice inside the body cavity and around a fish so that blood, slime and digestive juices drain to the bottom of your ice chest. Never let a fish soak in water, even cold water, for long. Fish can generally be kept in crushed ice for about 3 days without significantly affecting table quality.

If you want to cool your fish quickly (the quicker the better) or aren't able to freeze or cook your catch for several days, super-chill them. Super-chilled fish can be held for up to 7 days without losing much eating quality.

TO SUPER-CHILL

1. Line the bottom of an insulated ice chest with several inches of ice. Leave the bottom drain open.
2. In another container, make a salt/ice mixture, using a 1:20 ratio of coarse, ice cream salt to crushed ice. About one pound of salt to 20 pounds of ice is a good start for most coolers.
3. Arrange the fish in layers in the ice chest, making sure there's plenty of salted ice between each fish.
4. Before chilling fillets or steaks, wrap them in plastic wrap.

When you are ice fishing, there is no shortage of ice to chill fish. The problem is preventing fish from freezing. Freezing and refreezing them greatly reduces their table quality. If fish do freeze, leave them frozen, wrap them, and place them in the freezer. Then dress fish before they're completely thawed.

A stream angler who doesn't have ice should wait until the last several hours of the trip to keep fish. Place them in an aerated creel lined with a layer of wet

Super Chilly!

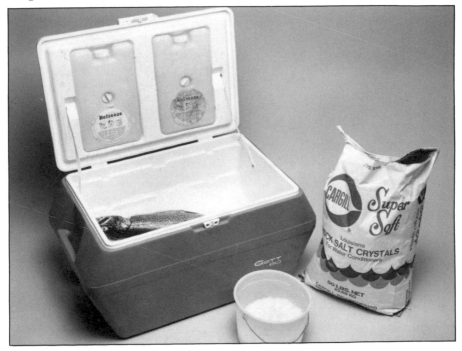

If you're going to keep fish, carry a fish club to dispatch fish with a blow to the back of the head. You need a knife to gut and gill and bleed fish immediately, and a towel is handy to wipe fish with after you've rinsed them. Transfer them to a bed of crushed ice, immediately.

Super-chilling lowers the temperature surrounding fish to about 28°F and allows properly cleaned fish to keep for up to 7 days. Add 1 part of rock salt to 20 parts of crushed ice to make a salt/ice mixture. Make a 3-inch bed of salted ice on the bottom of the cooler and add the fish. Open the drain. Wrap fillets with cling wrap to protect them and to leave space between fish. Add salted ice as needed to keep fish cold.

moss to hold moisture. Evaporation cools the gutted fish.

If fish must be held for more than a few hours, clean, wash and wipe the body cavity dry. Then sprinkle the fish with table salt. Keep them in a cool, slightly moist, shaded container like an aerated creel. Fish will keep up to 24 hours like this. It's a good way to bring fish out of remote areas.

AT THE CLEANING TABLE

At the cleaning table, or wherever you clean your catch, sanitation is critical. Also be sure to have ice available to keep fish that have already been chilled and to cool fish that are still alive when they reach the cleaning table.

Let's say you will be filleting your catch. At the cleaning table you should have:

1. Cleaning utensils including fillet knives and sharpening tools.
2. A bowl of cold water (add ice cubes) to soak fillets in for a short time to

remove blood and bacteria.

3. Several clean towels for wiping slime from fish and keeping the fillet board clean. Another towel to pat fillets dry with after they have soaked for a bit, if they are to be stored without freezing. (A solution of one teaspoon of vinegar to 3 quarts of water helps to cut fish slime.)

4. Packaging material for freezing fish or keeping them in the refrigerator, until they're eaten.

Let's proceed:

1. If the fish are alive, dispatch them with a sharp blow to the head. Bleed them.

2. Remove the fillets, being careful not to rupture the digestive tract with your knife.

3. Pop the fillet into cold water to help remove blood, bacteria and enzymes. Don't let them soak too long. Rinse them with cold, clean water.

4. Discard the carcass; wipe the board and your knife clean, and start another fish. Replace the water in the bowl when it begins to thicken from fish juices.

At the Cleaning Table

PHOTO 1

At the cleaning table you need a cleaning board, a fish dispatcher (club), knives and sharpening tools, clean towels and a bowl of cold water (PHOTO 1). Add ice cubes to the water to chill it. A 1/2 teaspoon of salt (to help neutralize acids and draw out blood) is fine to use with lean fish like walleyes or crappies but may increase rancidity in fatty fish like lake trout or salmon.

Kill the fish by hitting it behind the head with your fish dispatcher. Bleed the fish (PHOTO 2). As you remove the fillets, be careful not to cut into the intestinal tract. Keep everything including your knife clean (PHOTO 3). Remove bacteria from the fillets by soaking them in cold water for a bit.

PACKAGING FOR THE REFRIGERATOR

Placing fish in ice keeps them at 32°F rather than 40°F, which is the approximate temperature of most refrigerators. This allows them to be kept in the refrigerator for several days before they are eaten. Periodically drain the melt water.

Another method also maintains fish quality, although at a slightly reduced level. You can store fish for several days in the refrigerator by starting with clean fillets and keeping them slightly moist but absolutely not wet. Throwing fish into a plastic bag and allowing them to lie in fish juices encourages bacterial growth and deterioration. It's one of the fastest ways to reduce fantastic, firm, fresh fish to smelly mush.

Pat the fillets dry after they've soaked and been rinsed in water. Even though you've patted them dry, they will still be slightly moist. Take a clean, dry dish towel and sprinkle drops of water on it so it's barely moist but not wet. Line the bottom of a bowl or pan with the towel and spread your fillets on it. Cover the bowl with a tight-fitting plastic wrap. The towel soaks up any excess moisture from the fish, yet the fillets don't dry out.

Use the same procedure with whole fish (pan dressed) or steaks.

Packaging for the Refrigerator

PHOTO 1

Method 1—Fill a bowl half full with ice and place the fish on the ice. Cover the fish with more ice and the bowl with cling wrap. Periodically drain the melt water. Fish stored at almost 32°F keep longer than fish stored at 40°F, the temperature of most refrigerators (PHOTO 1).

Method 2—Remove the fillets and pat them dry with a towel. Sprinkle water droplets onto a clean, dry towel so it's damp but not wet. Line a bowl with it and place the fillets on the towel (PHOTO 2). Use cling wrap to seal the bowl. The fish will keep for up to 3 days.

FREEZING FISH

Freezing, the method most often used for long-term fish storage, can keep fish in quality condition for months. Unfortunately, few anglers freeze fish properly. Mistakes usually fall into one, or all, of three categories: (1) using the wrong type of protective packaging, (2) not considering that some fish species can be frozen for a longer time than others, and (3) keeping fish at the wrong storage temperature.

Most fish deteriorate during freezer storage through either (1) dehydration, or (2) oxidation. Freezer burn is an advanced stage of dehydration caused by using porous packaging material that allows water vapor to be sucked from the fish.

Oxidation also results from improper packaging, either by using porous packaging material or not removing the air from the package. The polyunsaturated fats and oils in fish turn rancid when they are in contact with oxygen for long periods of time.

PACKAGING MATERIALS

Proper packaging materials must provide effective oxygen and water vapor barriers. The materials should also cling to fish to prevent air pockets that keep fish in contact with oxygen.

Surprise! Polyethylene bags such as bread bags fail on both counts and are not suitable for storing fish. Waxed paper and cellophane are also poor freezer wraps.

Aluminum foil and polyvinylidene chloride wraps, called cling wraps (like Saran Wrap), provide good barriers to both oxygen and water vapor. It also clings to the fillets which prevents air pockets. However, aluminum foil punctures easily. While it is a good initial wrap, it doesn't serve well as an only or final wrap.

Freezer bags made of polyester also provide good barriers to oxygen and water vapor. Polyester bags include most heavy bags marketed as "freezer" bags. To force the air out of these bags before freezing, submerge the bag in water. Seal the bag or even add a small amount of water to the bag to help force the air out.

Freezer wrapping paper is a fair oxygen and water vapor barrier that serves best as an outer wrap over an inner wrap such as cling wrap or aluminum foil. It's easy to mark the type of catch, the freezing date, and other pertinent information on freezer wrap.

Good Freezing Approaches

PHOTO 1

One of the best ways to freeze fish is tightly wrapped in cling wrap or aluminum foil. A secondary wrapping in freezer wrapping paper is advisable (PHOTO 1). Write the contents and the date it was frozen on the package.

This is the best method for storing fatty fish like lake trout, whitefish, salmon and trout, but it works for all fish.

Another method is to put fish into a polyester freezer bag and submerge the bag in a sink full of water to squeeze out the air (PHOTO 2). Seal the bag, or even add a small amount of water to the bag to help force the air out.

FREEZING IN WATER

Commercial freezers often glaze fish with a coating of ice. Glazing isn't practical for you because it takes an inordinate amount of time and an extremely low freezer temperature.

There are several good techniques for freezing fish in water, however. Fish can be tightly packed into plastic containers such as Tupperware and covered with water. The fish must be covered, but too much water draws nutrients from them and causes them to freeze slowly. The pressure from too much ice crushes fish and makes it mushy, too. Add a little more water to each container after freezing, to cover any fish portions that protrude from the ice.

FINAL FREEZING TIPS

- Divide your fish into family-size servings.
- The faster fish freezes, the better. Place packages in the coldest part of your freezer, usually near the bottom. Don't overload your freezer, and keep it at 0°F, if possible.
- Thawing fish at room temperature may let some parts of fish spoil. Thaw them in the refrigerator, and expect it to take 24 hours for a 1-pound

package. For faster thawing, hold the fish in cold water until it's thawed. Be sure to keep it in the vapor-proof wrapping while it's thawing.

- Refrozen fish are safe to eat but usually taste terrible.
- Properly frozen crappies will keep for 8 to 12 months.

BON APPETIT!

Follow these tips and the fish you keep will taste better than they ever have, whether you eat them immediately or 3 days or 3 months later.

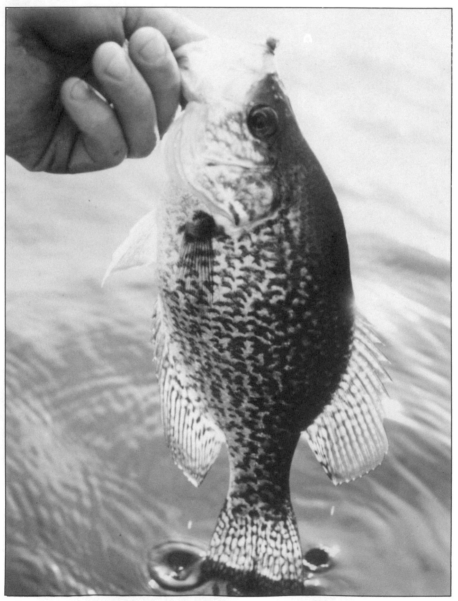

Another scrappy crappie for the frying pan.

CONCLUSION

This is the fifth book in the *IN-FISHERMAN* Masterpiece Series. *CRAPPIE WISDOM: A Handbook of Strategies* takes an indepth look at crappies and how they operate in many waters. Understanding the how's and why's of fish behavior will help you catch more crappies regardless of where you live and fish.

While this book is comprehensive it is not "complete," because as further research is conducted, more nuances of the crappie's personality and lifestyle will be discovered. However, the information contained in this book is an up-to-the-minute compendium of the most productive, crappie fishing methods—they're dynamite.

In addition to this book, we encourage you to read the other books in our *IN-FISHERMAN* Masterpiece Series: *WALLEYE WISDOM: A Handbook of Strategies; BASS: A Handbook of Strategies; PIKE: A Handbook of Strategies*, and *SMALLMOUTH BASS: A Handbook of Strategies.*

Because of the vast scope of each volume, no one man has enough knowledge to tackle such an undertaking. Instead, we took another avenue; each book is written by a collective group of top anglers. Each of these writer's background, experience and expertise qualifies him as a true expert. And they tell all; they hold nothing back.

If you are truly interested in becoming a top-flight angler, we urge you to subscribe to our *IN-FISHERMAN* Magazine, the foundation of this knowledge. We offer a brochure free of charge which lists the books and magazines we publish. Simply write to *IN-FISHERMAN*, Box 999, Brainerd, MN 56401, and ask for the free brochure.

In closing, the staff wishes you tight lines and good fishing. Remember, catch a lot of fish; keep a few to eat and release the rest.

the In-Fisherman GLOSSARY

ADAPTATION: The process of adjusting to or fitting into a particular set of environmental circumstances.

AGGREGATION: A group of gamefish or preyfish holding in an area, but not necessarily moving together in a school. See *school*.

ALGAE: Simple, one-cell plants usually having the ability to photosynthesize sunlight into energy.

ALLEY: Parallel openings between patches of emergent weeds (usually bulrushes), or between emergent weeds and shoreline.

APPETITE MOODS: The three basic attitudes of fish toward feeding. See *positive, neutral and negative feeding moods*.

BACKTROLLING: A system of boat control involving moving a boat slowly in reverse while using lure or bait presentations (casting or trolling).

BACKWATERS: Normally, a shallow-water area off a river.

BASIC NATURE: A species' inherent makeup or tendencies which determine its niche or place in an environment.

BASIC NEEDS: The three basic survival requirements of any fish species: *reproduction, suitable habitat,* and *food*. A favorable environment fulfills these needs.

BASIN ZONE: A lake zone. The area lying below the deep-water zone, beginning where hard bottom ends and soft bottom begins. This zone includes the deepest water areas.

BIOLOGY: The study of living things.

BITING: The feeding action of a hungry fish. See *striking*.

BOAT CONTROL: Boat use to aid bait or lure presentation. See *backtrolling, controlled drifting, front trolling, speedtrolling*.

BOTTOM-BUMPER: A lure or rig which strikes the bottom (i.e. jig).

BOTTOM CONFIGURATION: A locational factor; the relative make-up (shape, size, depth, humps, etc.) of an area of the bottom.

BOTTOM CONTENT: Bottom types in a body of water (rock, sand, gravel, silt, muck, submerged cribs, brush and/or trees, etc.).

BREAK: Any variation in otherwise constant portions of the environment.

BREAKLINE: That point in a body of water where there is a definite change in depth—either shallower or deeper—or a change in a weedline or brushline; a change in bottom composition; where two layers of water meet and differ in temperature, density, oxygen and/or turbidity; the limit of effective light penetration, etc.

BREAKLINE, SECONDARY: A second or auxiliary point of change. For example, a second definite increase in depth after the first drop-off.

BRUSHLINE: The inside or outside edge of a line of brush.

CABBAGE: Any of the pondweeds (*Potamogeton*) usually attractive to gamefish.

CALENDAR, *IN-FISHERMAN:* A calendar based on ten identifiable periods of activity for various species of gamefish. These ten periods constitute a *fish cycle.*

CALENDAR PERIOD: Any of the ten periods of fish activity in the *IN-FISHERMAN* Calendar.

CLEAN BOTTOM: The bottom (usually hard bottom) of a body of water that is free of debris, etc.

CLIMATE: Average weather conditions for a region.

COLD FRONT: The line of impact where cold air forces warm air upward. As a cold front moves, cold air beneath piles up as it is slowed down by contact with the ground. This pile of cold air forces warm air up very rapidly, often causing storms. See *post-front.*

COLD-WATER PERIOD: A period of the fish cycle which occurs twice—in early spring between the Frozen Water and Pre-spawn Periods and in late fall between the Turnover and Frozen Water Periods. Usually applied to the fall season.

COMPETITIVE SPECIES: A *social condition* involving the relationship of species within a body of water, particularly in regard to available food and spawning areas.

CONFINED OPEN WATER: An area of open water adjacent to a structural element, as opposed to an expansive area which is far away from it.

CONTROLLED DRIFT: A system of *boat control* using an outboard, electric trolling motor or oars to keep a boat drifting along a specific course.

COSMIC CLOCK: The sun's effect on water and local weather factors, such as barometric pressure, wind, cloud cover, seasonal change, etc.

COVE: A flooded creek arm in a reservoir.

CRANKBAIT: A lipped, diving plug.

CUT: A small reservoir bay without an active, inflowing creek.

DEEP-WATER ZONE: A lake zone. Hard bottom lying below the first major drop-off and below the open-water zone. It ends where soft bottom begins.

DEPTH CONTROL: One of two primary factors involved in successful bait or lure presentation. Keeping a lure or bait at a desired depth level.

DISSOLVED OXYGEN: Oxygen chemically bound into water by forces such as wind and plants. It is utilized by fish.

DROP-OFF: A point of definite increase in depth.

ECOLOGY: The study of the relationship between organisms and their environment.

ECOSYSTEM: A system formed by the interaction of a community of organisms and their environment.

ELECTROPHORESIS: A chemical-testing process that can determine the genetic make-up of fish.

EPILIMNION: The warmer layer of water above the *thermocline.*

EROSION: The process by which the surface of the earth is continually worn away. The elements most responsible for erosion are rivers, streams, wind, waves and glaciers.

EUTROPHIC: A *lake classification* or lake type characterized by high levels of nutrients in proportion to total volume of water.

FANCAST: A series of systematic casts to cover an area.

FISH ATTRACTOR: Manmade brush pile, stake bed, mat or crib designed to provide cover and attract fish.

FISH CONTACT: Locating fish, usually by catching them. Includes visual observation.

FISH CYCLE: All ten Calendar Periods. See *Calendar, IN-FISHERMAN.*

FISHING PRESSURE: The number of anglers using a body of water, and/or how sophisticated their approach is.

FLAT: An area characterized by little or no change in depth.

FOOD CHAIN: A step-by-step feeding relationship in a community. Food chains originate with the sun's energy and each link in the chain represents energy transfer. All of the food chains in a community constitute a food web.

FOOD-PRODUCING AREA: Portions of a body of water with the characteristics necessary to stimulate food chain production; usually the littoral or shoreline-connected (shallow) areas, because they receive sunlight which fuels plant photosynthesis which in turn stimulates each successive step in the food chain.

FRONT TROLLING: A system of *boat control* with the boat moving forward.

GEOLOGY: The science dealing with the earth's physical history.

HABITAT: The place where a plant or animal species lives.

HARD BOTTOM: Firm-bottom areas (sand, clay, rock, gravel, etc.).

HIGH-PROTEIN FORAGE: High-fat-content, soft-rayed, forage species such as ciscoes and whitefish.

HOLDING STATION: Any specific position regardless of depth where fish spend much of their time.

HYPOED LAKE: A body of water stocked with a species of fish to bolster the natural fishery.

HYPOLIMNION: The colder layer of water below the *thermocline.*

IMPOUNDMENT: A confined area where water accumulates, usually the result of damming a river. See *reservoir.*

INFILLING: The process by which higher surrounding terrain tends to fill in lower terrain.

INSIDE EDGE (OF WEEDS): A line of weeds between the shoreline and the weedline, or the shallow edge of a particular weed type. See *outside edge* (of weeds).

LAKE CLASSIFICATION: Broad categories of lake types: oligotrophic (infertile), mesotrophic (fertile), eutrophic (very fertile).

LAKE-MODIFICATION FORCES: Forces such as ice, wave and wind erosion, etc., which can change the characteristics of a body of water.

LAKE TYPE: A group of bodies of water with characteristics similar enough to one another so they can be viewed from an angling standpoint in much the same manner. See *lake classifications*.

LAKE ZONES: Four designated *IN-FISHERMAN* water zones: *shallow water, open water, deep water and basin zones*.

LIMNOLOGY: The study of the biological, chemical, geographical and physical features of bodies of water.

LITTORAL ZONE: Shallow-water zone.

LOCAL WEATHER FACTORS: Prevailing weather conditions affecting the day-to-day locational patterns of a fish species.

LOCATIONAL PATTERN: Where, why and how a species positions itself to take advantage of its surroundings.

LOOSE-ACTION PLUG: A lure with wide, distinct, side-to-side movements.

MARL: Deposits of sand, clay and silt with a high concentration of shells (calcium carbonate).

MESOTROPHIC: *Lake classification* used to describe fertile bodies of water between late-stage *oligotrophic* and early-stage *eutrophic* classifications.

MIGRATION: The movement of fish from one area to another. Migrations generally occur on a seasonal basis, from one set of distinct environmental conditions to another, such as from winter habitat toward spawning areas. They should not be confused with *movements*.

MORAINE: A mass of rocks, sand, etc., deposited by a glacier.

MOVEMENT: The locational shift of fish from one area to another, generally on a daily or even hourly basis. Also can refer to fish changing from a neutral to a positive feeding mood, with fish shifting only a few feet from a resting to an advantageous feeding position. A *directional* movement is usually made at a fast rate of speed and from one specific area to another. A *random* movement is slow, milling activity within a specific area.

NEGATIVE FEEDING MOOD: An *appetite mood* in which the biting attitude of fish is negative. Fish also are said to be inactive.

NEUTRAL FEEDING MOOD: An *appetite mood*. An attitude of fish which are not actively feeding but could be tempted by a refined presentation. See *striking*.

NICHE: A particular role and physical surroundings which an organism assumes within an ecosystem, based on that species' characteristics and depending on competing species.

NURSERY AREA: Areas where fish species are reared to the fingerling stage.

OLIGOTROPHIC: *Lake classification* used to describe bodies of water characterized by a low amount of nutrients in proportion to the total volume of water. Infertile.

OPEN-WATER ZONE: A lake zone. The upper water layer from the outside edge of the first major drop-off down to the deep-water zone.

OUTSIDE EDGE (OF WEEDS): The *weedline*. The outside edge of a line of weeds.

OXBOW: A lake formed by a change in the course of a river channel; a section of river channel cut off from the main river by a change in the river's path.

PATTERN: Any consistently reoccurring locational/presentational situation.

PHOTOSYNTHESIS: The process by which chlorophyll cells in green plants use the sun's energy to manufacture a simple sugar from water and carbon dioxide. Oxygen is a by-product of this process.

PIT: Flooded, manmade water that is a by-product of excavation—usually mining.

POND: Small artificial or natural body of water. Area, depth, and water quality are factors in the resulting fishery.

POPULATION DENSITY: The number of individuals occupying a certain area. For example, the number of bass per acre.

POSITIVE FEEDING MOOD: An *appetite mood*. The attitude of actively feeding fish.

POST-FRONT: That period after a weather front. Usually used in reference to a cold front when the atmosphere becomes clear and bright, accompanied by strong winds and a significant temperature drop.

POST-SPAWN PERIOD: The period immediately following spawning.

POST-SUMMER PERIOD: A period of the fish cycle following the Summer Period. It can mean a week or more of terrific fishing.

PRECAMBRIAN SHIELD: The Canadian Shield. A geological, rock formation covering much of eastern and central Canada and some of the north central U.S.A.

PREDATOR/PREY RELATIONSHIP: An inter-relationship between a species and an accessible and suitable forage.

PREFERRED FOOD: Food or forage best suited to a species' basic needs.

PRE-SPAWN PERIOD: The period of the fish cycle immediately before spawning when fish position themselves near their spawning grounds.

PRE-SUMMER PERIOD: The period of the fish cycle immediately following post-spawn. Fish mood is often positive, but they establish a wide variety of patterns.

REEDS: Bulrushes or rushes.

RESERVOIR: Impoundment. A place where water is collected and stored.

RIG: A fishing boat; the hook, snell and other terminal tackle for live bait fishing; assembling tackle.

RIVER (OR CREEK) CHANNEL: The original river or creek bed which was flooded when a reservoir was formed.

RIVERINE: Refers to a river-like environment.

SADDLE: A site where a structural element narrows before widening again, or deepens before shallowing again.

SCHOOL (OF FISH): A number of fish of the same or similar species grouped together and moving as a unit to benefit from the defensive and/or feeding advantages associated with coordinated activity.

SECONDARY COVE: A small, shallow cove connected to a larger cove.

SHALLOW-WATER ZONE: A *lake zone*. The area out to the first major drop-off.

SHIELD WATER: Body of water located on the Precambrian or Canadian Shield. Specifically, a body of water in an area where the nutrient-producing rock and sediment layers in the basin and surrounding terrain were eroded away by glaciers.

SLICK: A sand or clay bar, point or drop-off devoid of weeds, brush, rock or boulders, etc. A section of calm, surface water in a river.

SOFT BOTTOM: Bottoms (silt, mud, muck, marl, etc.) which are not hard.

SOCIAL CONDITION: One of three elements helping to determine a species' locational pattern. It includes population density, food availability, competitive species, and how these interrelate.

SNAKETROLLING: A system of *boat control* in which a lure or bait is trolled in a weaving manner to cover a wide area and a range of depth levels.

SPAWN PERIOD: A brief period of the fish cycle when a species reproduces. This period is directly linked to seasonal progression and suitable temperatures.

SPECIES: Closely related organisms which produce offspring when they mate.

SPEED CONTROL: One of the two primary factors in bait or lure presentation. The other is depth.

SPEEDTROLLING: A system of *boat control* in which a lure is trolled behind a fast-moving boat.

SPOOKING: Frightening or "turning off" one or more fish.

STRAGGLERS: Fish lingering apart from others of their species after a movement.

STRIKING: An involuntary reflex action prompted by a bait or lure. Fish are made to bite. See *biting*.

STRUCTURAL CONDITION: One of three elements which determine a species' locational patterns. Structure includes bottom configuration, bottom content, water characteristics, vegetation types and water exchange rate.

STRUCTURAL ELEMENT: Almost any natural or manmade, physical feature in a body of water. See *bottom configuration*.

SUMMER PERIOD: A period in the fish cycle when fish generally hold to patterns established during the last part of the Summer Peak Period.

SUMMER PEAK PERIOD: A short period in the fish cycle after the Presummer Period when fish are grouped in advantageous feeding areas. A prelude to the Summer Period.

SUSPENDED FISH: Fish in open water which are hovering considerably above the bottom.

TAPER: An area that slopes toward deeper water.

THERMOCLINE: The center area of temperature stratification in a body of water. Specifically, the division between the epilimnion and hypolimnion. Temperature changes very quickly.

TIGHT-ACTION PLUG: A lure with short, distinct, side-to-side movements.

TOPWATER PLUG: A floating lure designed for use on the surface of the water.

TOTAL ENVIRONMENT: Both the body of water a species lives in, and any outside stimuli influencing it.

TRANSITION (BOTTOM): The point where one type of bottom material changes to another.

TRIGGER: Lure or bait characteristics (action, color, size, shape, scent, sound, vibration, texture) designed to stimulate positive responses from fish by appealing to the sensory organs of a species.

TURNOVER PERIOD: A very brief period in the fish cycle when some lakes or reservoirs are in turmoil. A mixing or "turning over" of the water takes place as cold water on the surface settles and warmer water from below rises. This turnover reoxygenates and homogenizes lakes that have thermoclined (layered according to water temperature) in summer.

TVA: Tennessee Valley Authority.

TWO-STORY LAKE: A body of water where warm water species inhabit the upper portion and cold water species inhabit the deeper portion.

WATER CHARACTERISTICS: The characteristics of a body of water, usually referred to in terms of mineral content (soft, few minerals; medium, some minerals; hard, many minerals). The mineral content determines fertility.

WATER COLOR: The clarity of a body of water. There are three basic degrees of water clarity: clear (6-foot-plus visibility), stained (2- to 6-foot visibility), and dark (less than 2-foot visibility).

WATER EXCHANGE RATE: The rate at which water enters or leaves a body of water.

WINTER PERIOD: A period of the fish cycle when a body of water is mostly or completely covered by ice. In southern waters which rarely freeze, the sustained period of coldest water.

WORKING METHOD: The aspect of presentation consisting of triggers, controls, gear selection and technique.

Also by Diane Johnson

Persian Nights

Persian Nights

DIANE JOHNSON

ALFRED A. KNOPF   *New York*   *1987*

Copyright © 1987 by Diane Johnson

All rights reserved under International and Pan-American Copyright Conventions. Published in the United States by Alfred A. Knopf, Inc., New York, and simultaneously in Canada by Random House of Canada Limited, Toronto. Distributed by Random House, Inc., New York.

Library of Congress Cataloging-in-Publication Data

Johnson, Diane.   Persian nights.

    I. Title.
PS3560.03746P4   1987   813'.54   86-46009
ISBN 0-394-55804-9

Manufactured in the United States of America

FIRST EDITION

88738

For Alice Adams and Barbara Epstein

A Moment's Halt—a momentary taste
Of BEING from the Well amid the Waste—
And Lo!—the phantom Caravan has reach'd
The NOTHING it set out from—Oh, make haste!

EDWARD FITZGERALD,

The Rubaiyat of Omar Khayyam

My lately acquired and rather artificial liking
for uprootings and travel fits in happily
with the peaceful fatalism natural to the
bourgeoise that I am.

COLETTE, *The Vagabond*

Acknowledgments

My great thanks to those who have helped me with this—to Robert Gottlieb, whose suggestion began it; to Dr. Hibbard Williams, whom I consulted about the Shah; to Dr. John Murray; to Terry and Iraj Alborzian for their help verifying the Iranian details, and Dorothy Ladd for her help with the manuscript.

Quotations are from the Koran, the poetry of Matthew Arnold, and the *Rubaiyat of Omar Khayyam* translated by Edward FitzGerald.

Persian Nights

Chapter One
THE ARRIVAL

Wake! For the Sun, who scatter'd into flight
The Stars before him from the Field of Night
Drives Night along with them from Heav'n, and strikes
The Sultan's Turret with a Shaft of Light

"They're talking about you," said Abbas Mowlavi, noticing Chloe Fowler's glance behind him along the road, where the shrouded women peered at her, the whites of their eyes gleaming balefully out of the shadows of their veils. The veiled figures seemed to Chloe menacing, like the silhouettes of vultures, and there was menace in the unfamiliar cadence of the murmuring voices.

"What do they say?"

"They are saying only that it is interesting that the American woman has arrived alone." He had been surprised himself to find, at the airport, only Mrs. Fowler, not Dr. Fowler too.

"My husband . . . in a few days," murmured Chloe, pulling at her collar. "An emergency—he . . ." She was conscious of her bare arms.

"They admire your pretty dress," said Abbas. "They admire your shoes. I'm sorry for this delay about the key. You must be tired."

"A little," Chloe said, her head swimming with tiredness, for she had come from San Francisco, through New York, on to London, on to Tehran, with no sleep and inconvenient delays on the planes. A fragrance of night-blooming plants rose around them in the dusk. The women swayed in their black shrouds as if to move, but did not move. Cleaning women, kitchen women from Azami Hospital, tired after the day.

Chloe was hungry and wished that Dr. Mowlavi would suggest dinner. He, however, was thinking she would be too delicately jangled by travel to eat, would want to rest. Her wrists were delicate. She and Abbas were standing on the steps of a two-story house made of cement blocks, Villa Two. Her hair was the expensive red-gold you saw here only among women who had gone to school in France—the Empress and her friends, for instance—and on the American wives. Mrs. Fowler's hair did not look dyed, but you couldn't tell in the dusk. He could not tell the color of her eyes, for she still wore, in the dusk, her sunglasses. The women behind him had the opinion, which he didn't translate, that her hair was the hair of a slut.

The house, Villa Two, was ugly. Through the window Chloe could see the hall, lit by a bare bulb on a cord, like a cell, suggesting torture, walls of cement like a dungeon. She had been reading about Iranian torture. Her apartment presumably would be up the stairs and cozier. Someone had been sent for the key.

"It's the eve of a holiday here. That's why people have gone away. Tomorrow you have to stay outdoors all day." He smiled, embarrassed by all this waiting. He was handsome in the style of Greeks and Italians, not a style Chloe liked, gold chains, unbuttoned shirt, hairy chest.

An emaciated old man with sideways eyes brought the key and scuttled away without helping with Chloe's bags. These Abbas gathered up, opening the door with his shoulder so Chloe could go in first. He did not immediately understand her recoil, hand to mouth and shocked look around at him. By the time he had stepped in and smelled it too she had regained her composed manner. It was the urine of cats. He did not see how cats could get in here, but the smell was in the hall rug, putrid stench of cat piss. The help was careless here, he muttered; Hossein had left a window open somewhere. He told Chloe Fowler to go quickly up the stairs.

The strong smell jolted Chloe like smelling salts out of her fatigue, into a shocked awareness of her situation, and of how unwise it had been, how simply silly, to have come on alone, and of how she must go back immediately, tomorrow, regardless. Starved and frightened, she felt she must go back. Abbas opened the apartment door with the second key. He was used to the place; it was where American visitors always stayed, and he didn't really see it any more, though he saw the way her eyes widened. She was tired, he was sure, he said. He showed her where the kitchen was and left her, would see her tomorrow.

The door shut after Abbas Mowlavi but even so the stench from the hall enveloped her. As she looked around in the twilight, the details of the room collected themselves repellently, reminding her of pictures she had seen of mental institutions—bare brown linoleum floor, a thick-armed chair of oak too heavy to pick up and fling at an attendant, its seat covered in green and yellow plaid, two army cots covered with bleak khaki blankets, a dresser and table of Hollywood blond. On the wall a poster of Isfahan showed a beautiful mosque covered in cerulean tiles, as beautiful as she had imagined. In her dreams of Persia she had imagined brasses and rich cushions, intricate tracery screens. Here were heavy metal-rimmed windows, which cranked open stiffly. She struggled with the crank. She was baffled. Famous visiting surgeons were usually housed in luxury—that was her husband Jeffrey, of course, not Chloe, but she was accustomed to the perquisites of his life.

She was shocked that they would treat him so, and then, in spite of her exhaustion, she was embarrassed by her easy American expectation of comfort; wasn't this a developing nation, weren't they here to help? Ostensibly. Her own reasons were more complex and she hadn't examined them in detail. She opened her suitcase. She wished for some dinner. She put her underwear in the top drawer, emotions of indignation and humility contending. It occurred to her that if the bathroom was clean she would be all right, almost happy. If it was not clean she would clean it, like a good American sport. She made her way to look. It did not seem clean, it did not seem dirty, but the bulb was dim, and she didn't want to look closely enough to know for sure. She felt a swoon of sleepiness.

Out the window, through the shabby trees, the lights of other windows. In some lighted room nearby would be Hugh Monroe, with whom she had half begun a love affair. But he wouldn't have expected them tonight. Their meeting tomorrow would be casual, a handshake, overseen by the innocent company of their Iranian hosts and American colleagues. So nice to see you again. Her pleasure in imagining herself in Hugh's arms almost took the chill off this terrible room. They had not seen each other for several months, and she hoped he would feel that the temporary absence of Jeffrey was a piece of good luck instead of, for instance, a responsibility, for Chloe had observed before that men behave differently to a woman when they are not protected from her by her husband.

She falls asleep stupefied under the thin blankets on the rickety camp bed, and then awakens in darkness, not knowing how much later, to sounds so hideous and uncanny that they had leaked into her dreams as a harrowing nightmare of humans being torn to shreds—sinners rent by demons—and her husband Jeffrey's voice saying, gleefully, "You're crazy to go there, a woman alone," although he had said nothing of the kind, and had, in fact, insisted supportively. The shrieks, howls, cries persist, actual, under her window. Animals in their anguish sounding human. Where is she? She breaks into a sweat of panic, entangled by one foot in a torn sheet. She twists, stifles a scream, thinking of shackles and torture. Awake, she untangles her foot; the ideas of Islamic demons quiet, her shudders quiet.

She hates to put her foot on the cement floor—new ideas, of terrible gyms, basements, hookworm, but she creeps over to the window. Moonlit white shapes rush in the shrubbery, baying, snarling wantonly, chasing and tearing. Dogs, it seemed, or it could be wolves—she is near-sighted—but she had never heard of wolves in Iran. She believes in a rational explanation for everything, and so tries to think now of a rational explanation for a pack of wolves under her window. Fearfully, she gets her distance glasses from her purse and peers through them at the dogs, or maybe they are jackals. They are horrible, scrawny and fanged, with tattered fur and broken tails.

Now she is chilly, despite the warm breeze, a scent on it of the pleasant, night-blooming flower. She lies down again on the cot and tries to remember her dream, tries to reassure herself that the human cries had not been real cries of someone, perhaps, attacked by savage dogs, a fate whose horror was not to be compared to the trivial inconvenience of her own situation. Yet her mind keeps drifting to her situation, to its implausibility. On the way here she had kept emphasizing to herself its reasonableness, but now she cannot escape a true view of it as rather reckless. The jackals have moved away. Faint baying farther off.

"Why don't you go on?" Jeffrey had said, and she, foolishly as she now believed, had agreed, arguing vaguely that she felt an obligation to the museum, which had given her a small but important grant, to go through with the project. I feel an obligation to other women, she had also said. Women who got grants and then didn't follow through because their husbands changed their plans or the kids got measles—she didn't approve of them, considered that they gave womankind a bad name and prevented others from getting grants and jobs. Luckily none of her children had come down with anything to complicate this already complicated departure. If they had, she might have stayed home. Then too there was the matter of Hugh Monroe.

Astonishing how any implausible course of action begins to seem plausible the minute you begin it, write the first letter, mail the first application, stop off one noon for the visas, each step connected reasonably and at no far distance from the last,

7

the reach or sweep of the whole invisible around the bend. Here she was but not, strangely, Jeffrey. She gets up again, finds her sweater in her suitcase, and goes in to clean the bathroom.

Chapter Two
BROKEN DREAMS

Then she slept again. When she next woke up, it seemed late in the morning—bright sun struggled in at the dirty glass and someone pounded on the door, communicating panic and ideas of fire. When she realized there was no fire, she leapt up, ashamed to be sleeping so late, whatever time it was. It could be Hugh at the door. She called out and sped around finding her robe and patting her tangled hair in the bathroom mirror.

It was a stranger at the door, an Iranian man, portly and dark, his chin thuggishly blue but his smile attractive and his round balding forehead open and nice. He wore a light suit. She couldn't tell the meaning of his smile, but her disappointment that he wasn't Hugh must have shown on her face, for the smile shrank.

"Mrs. Fowler? I am Dr. Asghari, Mohammed Asghari. I have met your husband once, at the meetings in Boston. I understand he is not here yet?"

"Not yet," admitted Chloe.

"I hope everything is all right here? Your journey was safely performed?"

"Thank you, yes," said Chloe, seeing that he was not the right person to grab and drag in and berate about her living quarters. But you would think he could smell the cat smell. He had, himself, a pleasant, old-fashioned odor of bay rum.

"Today is the last day of Now-Ruz," said Dr. Asghari, "a

holiday where we must not stay indoors, it is bad luck. We stay outdoors until nightfall, and then when we go back in, the house is invested with good luck."

"I'm sorry," said Chloe. "I just woke up. I was awakened in the night, and tired after the trip, and—what time is it?"

"Seven o'clock. I am just on my way to the clinic, but I stopped to invite you to our house—a picnic in our garden, more properly, where you will meet others, and meet my wife, also, who wants to make you welcome."

"That's very kind." Could he smell nothing? Peering past her into the room, he did not seem any more surprised than the man last night had been at the ugly furniture, the odor, the bleakness of the atmosphere.

"Is there anything we can do to help you settle in?"

"I think I should buy some coffee and things," Chloe said, now conscious once more of being hungry. "Will the shops be open?"

Closed, he was afraid, on the holiday, but here were the directions to his house. He thrust a piece of paper toward her, nodded, and took his leave.

Chloe shut the door after him and turned to the room. It was as ugly as it had seemed the night before in the dim light, offensive furniture upholstered in green plaid, and mismatched chairs of molded plywood. But it was clean enough, and large enough. She could buy things to beautify it, wonderful Persian vases, brass lamps. This thought lifted her resilient spirits. Meantime she would be pleased to stay outdoors all day. The yellow-tiled bathroom, now shining clean, was actually quite all right.

It was only now that she remembered that the kitchen was not in here, in the apartment itself, but in the hall, where it was intended to be shared by other residents of Villa Two. Her hopes rose that she might find something left in there to eat. Keeping her door carefully ajar, she crept out into the reeking hallway and into the kitchen, a filthy room covered with crumbs and heaped with unwashed dishes, though the complete absence of any food made this puzzling. Stuck to the walls with Scotch tape were various messages and bits of kitchen lore, in English, exasperated in tone: "Washer works on 3 only. Keep cold water tap closed almost all the way or else. Doesn't spin dry. Good luck." There was something reassuring about the good American fellow feeling that had motivated these admonitions, but they might have left something to eat. But there was nothing whatever edible except some lumpy sugar in the sugar bowl. Chloe sucked on it and went back to her room.

She set her watch to five after seven. What time did the bad luck start? Perhaps it had started already and this was it. Or perhaps it only affected you if you were Iranian. She began to unpack. One dress in yellow cotton was not too wrinkled, so she put it on and went outside.

In the morning sunlight, Azami Compound appeared much as it had been described to Jeffrey and her by one or two of Jeffrey's colleagues—a large walled assemblage of hospital buildings and dwellings where nurses and doctors lived, many of them foreigners invited by the medical school to lecture and advise for a few weeks or months. The Iranian doctors, mostly Western-trained, were conscious of needing help with their project to establish a first-rate medical school in Shiraz, and they had no problem recruiting, by the promise of air fare and quarters to stay in, a number of leading doctors, usually American or English, from among the ones at any given time who were restless, divorcing, eager for a vacation, or wishing to see the remarkable ruins at Persepolis. It was therefore dependable that there would be, in Shiraz, at any one time, a contingent of well-known doctors who would already have met on the circuit of international meetings they all attended or conducted, and Chloe could feel perfectly at home as the wife of Jeffrey Fowler, professor of surgery and member in good standing of this medical jet set.

Her building, Villa Two, stood just inside the high walls of the compound, so she had seen nothing of the grounds the night before beyond what lay between her window and the wall. Now she saw that behind and beyond Villa Two were other residences and outbuildings, and, in front, the large gates through which they had driven last night, now shut fast, though a small door at the side of the gates was open, and people were passing through and walking along the road. She sat on the broad cement steps of Villa Two to watch them.

An impression she had had in the dusk last night of exotic foliage and strange blooms was now corrected—here were bougainvillaea, geraniums, and clumps of iris, and she found it disappointing that they were flowers she could grow perfectly well in California. The grass of the lawn was coarse and grew in clumps, and the corner of the yard where the dogs had been last night was now strewn with rubble and bones. But a light, fresh wind supported her spirits, and the sun was delightfully warm for so early in the morning, warming the pink stucco wall of her new home. Among familiar sounds of birds and insects were other sounds, strange enough to reassure her that she was abroad and far away; her ear could find deep voices calling in an unfamiliar language outside the walls, a bell somewhere. Even the sound of the automobiles was not American-sounding. She could hear that the cars did not proceed along as they did at home but made a racket of untuned engines, of heavy feet on accelerators, slipping clutches, horns, horns, horns. This reassured her. She wanted strangeness, a feeling of being far from home.

The people walking slowly along the road in front of Villa Two seemed scarcely to glance at her, though it was hard to tell about eyes behind veils. She thought the women were pretty in their wrappings, most in black, but some in floating pastel nylon, as if they were twisted up in parachutes, carrying purses. She wondered if she might without incurring bad luck go inside and get her half-written letters to her children.

She had begun letters already, during the four-hour wait at Heathrow. She and Jeffrey had fallen into silence, the long flight from California behind them, in which they had already conducted the conversation of a busy couple in forced companionship, reviewing the household matters they had had no time for, and managing, in the interest of the long journey still ahead of them, to avoid recriminations and criticism on a variety of touchy subjects—things undone, details of child rearing, delayed decisions about the plumbing. Chloe did not say, though she had often thought, that if only Jeffrey would take the children out on some sort of expedition on Saturday afternoons, she could use the time to do some of the things that needed doing around the house. Jeffrey did not say, as he so often did, that if she were more punctilious about certain housekeeping things then the atmosphere would be generally more harmonious and he'd feel like doing more around the house. Maybe they should go ahead with a new sprinkler system, though in principle Chloe, home in the mornings, could take care of the sprinkling. Sara would finish the school year at her present, even though not wonderful, school. A few other things settled, a few deferred again. Second thoughts—maybe instead of the sprinkler system, the priority thing was the roof.

Their lassitude, the drinks on the plane, rendered the waiting nearly bearable. They settled to their books.

Chloe was reading, with horrified fascination, a book about the torture of Iranian political dissidents. It was luridly well-written. The author was a poet. It described people being hung upside down until they were paralyzed. Then there were the usual things—fingernails, electric shocks to the genitals. They had a machine on which the victim, strapped as to a stake, was rotated like a chicken on a spit, being flogged the while. If you were a doctor you were morally neutral, you could go to a country like this because the poor people needed medicine under any regime. But if you were a wife were you more, or less, morally neutral? Would the Iranian authorities search her bags and take this book away from her at the airport?

The harrowing allegations and descriptions renewed her excitement at the prospect of their trip. Chloe put the book down and asked Jeffrey for change to buy a magazine. She noticed for the first time how the place reeked of tobacco.

"You forget how the English smoke," Chloe said. "It's disgusting."

"They don't believe it causes cancer. That seems to be an American belief."

Chloe bought a *Country Life,* an *International Herald Tribune* for Jeffrey, and twenty postcards, and took them back to their post. She had just settled her feet comfortably on the cigarette-strewn table and written the words "Dearest Sara and Max," when a voice spoke loudly into the smoky air of the transit lounge: "Dr. Fowler, Dr. Jeffrey Fowler, please contact the TWA representative, desk eight."

She and Jeffrey stared at each other. Perhaps they'd left something on the plane? They looked at their carry-ons, their coats. "Oh, God, the children," cried Chloe. Before they even got there.

Jeffrey was on his feet, alert and frightened equally of coming bad news and the possibility of an anxiety fit from Chloe, who was inclined to them when away from her children, in proportion to the extent she expected to enjoy herself. Enjoying herself, she suffered from insomnia and could be rather bad company, writhing and tossing with maternal guilt and now, as it was to be an unprecedented four weeks before their children joined them, she would have to be trebly reassured. He insisted that she sit there with their stuff while he answered the page, and she, subdued by her apprehensions, obeyed him. She tried to look again at the pages of *Country Life.* It was full of images of ideal domesticity, thatched cottages, flowers, cows in pens. "Here we are in England," she wrote on the card. It showed a guard in a busby.

As he came into view, Jeffrey waved his hands in a calming way, to cut short at a distance any fears of the worst. The worst had not happened, said the referee's gesture, "safe," of his hands. At the same time, his face was grim and glaring, wearing an expression usually directed at her, of irritation and outrage at something she'd done, or, more usually, hadn't done, so that now she thought she must not have done something. But what?

"That dumb bastard," Jeffrey was saying, shaking his head. "I've been telling him all along, the son of a bitch."

"What? Who?" cried Chloe.

"It's bad-news Henry. He's had an accident in his fucking hang glider."

Chloe relaxed. Only Henry. Henry was Jeffrey's colleague, and of course they were very fond of him. He and Jeffrey collaborated on research, applied for grants together, and shared a private practice.

"Dead?" she asked.

"The extent of his injuries still unknown. Serious injuries. He's in a coma and he can't move."

Normal pity began to stir in Chloe. "Poor Henry, how awful."

"I've told him a million times," said Jeffrey. No doubt he had too, thought Chloe, for Jeffrey never failed to tell people when they were behaving stupidly or dangerously. Poor Henry.

"Will he live?" asked Chloe. Jeffrey shrugged. The details, in their transmission from one TWA desk to another, had become abridged, obscured.

They sat, murmuring sympathy, dismay. Then Jeffrey seemed to be saying he would have to return. Go back to California. She hadn't grasped that implication. Turn around and go back to California. Their patients, their research, all left in Henry's capable hands, which could no longer move. Chloe saw the logic but was dumbstruck all the same. Their pounds of luggage checked through to Shiraz, Iran, all those hours behind them on the plane, the farewells, her mother installed with the children, the satisfaction of everybody—it had appeared—to see them go.

"Until we find out what's what," said Jeffrey.

"Oh," was all Chloe could say, "I can't bear it. What could you do for Henry, anyway?"

"Of course *you* don't need to come back," Jeffrey said, astonishingly. She would later try to remember the exact expression of his face. "In fact, you shouldn't. It's expensive, the kids'll just get upset all over again. You should go on."

"The kids weren't at all upset," snapped Chloe. "They thought it was nice we were going. Of course they didn't really understand how long we'd be gone." Her guilty panic rose. The children were to join them when their school was out. Even so, she had not been apart from them for such a long time as this.

"It makes perfect sense. You can just go on as planned, they're expecting us, the place'll be ready, there'll be someone to meet us, Farmani or Asghari—no problem. I'll find out what's going on, do what needs to be done, and join you as soon as I can."

Like going back, going on seemed a terrible idea. It was like being stuck in a hole in a fence. Venturing into an unknown Middle Eastern country, a woman alone? "It'll be all right," Jeffrey pointed out. "The Rothblatts will be there—you know them—and Hugh Monroe, and many other Americans."

"What'll the kids think, if you come back and I don't?" Chloe objected. The children had been brave, had even feigned indifference at having to stay behind with a rotation of grandmothers until their school was out, when they would travel with Chloe's mother to join their parents for an educational trip to Tehran and the Caspian. As she said this, she acknowledged to herself that in some ways it would be a relief to know that the responsible Jeff would be home to oversee things, even if only for a week or two longer. She'd been uncomfortable with the arrangements, agreeing on the one hand that it would be good for her and Jeff to get away together for a while, afraid on the other that their mothers would not really be equal to the difficulties of two lively children for such a long time.

Also, though she hated to admit it, she was afraid of going to such a place by herself. She knew, in the name of independence, female liberation, confidence, this fear must be mastered. And there was the final, secret reason, that it was slightly too propitious, being alone in the same distant city with Hugh

Monroe. This was the kind of gift of fate only the unwary would accept without inspecting the underside; Chloe was a little in love with Hugh Monroe.

"I can't possibly go by myself," she said firmly.

"Chloe! That's more than a thousand dollars down the drain. Be sensible."

Jeffrey was persuasive. "We can't afford for us both to go back, and there's no point in it either." Nervously she allowed herself to be packed along to the Air Iran boarding lounge by a grim Jeffrey, whose real emotions were not clear to her. Maybe he was just being nice.

"Are you *sure* you don't want me to come?" she kept saying, always expecting to surprise a glint of relief at the offer, but receiving no clue at all to his feelings if they were different from those he was expressing. It really appeared that Jeffrey believed it was more sensible for him to go back to San Francisco, her to go on to Iran, probably for the exact reasons stated: expense, disruption. The Tehran plane was loading.

"I'll be there soon," he said, kissing her. "A week, two at most. The prognosis of these things is usually evident in a few days. It's just a question of doing whatever has to be done in the office and lab." There was something in Jeffrey, she reminded herself, that loved a heroic role.

On the plane she had been reassured, for it was full of women traveling alone or with clusters of children and packages. Some were fashionably dressed in Western clothes and carried snakeskin purses from Mapin & Webb; others concealed themselves in the black veils of the Middle East. The recirculating air of the plane wafted odors of musky oils and strange perfumes.

Chapter Three
NOW-RUZ

Now the New Year reviving old Desires,
The thoughtful Soul to Solitude retires.

Chloe was a housewife, conscious of being unfashionable in this, but active and happy at home, only occasionally discontented, fond of sewing and of her children, fond of solitude yet gregarious, and perhaps too confident of her own powers of rational discrimination. She was, she was apt to say, the most unliberated woman she knew, but this statement was a form of vanity; it was simply that she was out of step with the discontents other women she knew seemed to be experiencing. Also, she usually did just what she wanted. The child of unreproachful parents, she had seldom believed that her actions would affect others.

Fortunately, her activities were largely harmless—affairs of the heart, reading, and an array of somewhat Victorian handiworks; she was, as far as she knew, the last woman her age alive in the world who could tat. She did not feel constrained by either rules or fashions—did not feel, for example, on the one hand that it was necessary to be faithful to your husband, or on the other that if you were not you had to get divorced. Though she felt sympathy for the plights and despair of others, she had no real feeling for the restlessness and anxiety of many of her women friends, as they arrived in their mid-thirties and looked around for lifework, meaning financial independence or emotional lives of revived fascination. She was more interested in abstractions—in political writing or art history—and this last occupied what time she spent outside her home. At present she was a docent at the San Francisco Art Museum and gave lectures on Chinese porcelain from Sung to Ming, a subject she had worked up with the museum staff.

Her friends were apt to find her too opinionated and her views eccentric, but to look at she was soft and pretty, not at all like someone with views. She continued to smile her bright, pretty smile even while she was saying something combative or horrible, a habit carried over from her days as a little child beauty. But she was not, luckily, a monster of self-satisfaction because she didn't think about herself much, though she tried, when she did remember, to work against her own faults, some of which she knew to be laziness, timidity, and absent-mindedness, by keeping busy, daring to do things that scared her, and writing things down. But mostly she drifted along, happily enough, interested in the world around her and in the world inside the large stack of books on her night stand. Men usually liked her, because she was small, pretty, and intelligent, but some did not like in a woman her slightly preoccupied air of self-sufficiency.

"I know what it is about you," a psychiatrist, a colleague of Jeffrey's, had told her at a party. "Free libido."

"That sounds too promiscuous," she objected.

"A kind of unchanneled life force. I'm speaking as a Jungian. I guess I mean that something about you suggests that you aren't really taken." He had smiled hopefully.

"Oh—I suppose I haven't found my métier," Chloe had conceded, smiling into his eyes, changing the subject in the way she had learned was reliable. "What about you?" Excited by her refusal to discuss herself, he had called her for weeks, truly not what she had intended.

And now here she was in Iran, very jet-lagged. As she rested and wrote, the morning seemed to pass quickly. She wrote the children a proper letter, describing the airplane flight, and also two postcards apiece, ahead; one, which showed Anne Hathaway's cottage, on which she described Now-Ruz, and a picture of Buckingham Palace, on which she simply said how much she missed them. She wondered about the mail.

She realized she had dozed a little in the sun. And she found she had a companion. Under the bushes at the corner of the yard, where the dogs had gathered last night, amid the litter of bones she could see a small creature, a puppy—rather an ordinary-looking one with short beige coat and cute little face—probably hidden there by his mother and forbidden to go out, for he remained crouched under the foliage when he had seen Chloe. Perhaps she had frightened him by stretching out her hand. She smiled at him, and watched him from time to time, and saw his bright little eyes watching her back with, she thought, some rapport.

Then she was startled to see, a little distance from this bush, an old man lying full-length under another clump of bushes! She thought it was the old man who had brought the key, now lying on his face, with his arms over his head. He lay so still she became afraid to look, had heard that in some countries people die outside in the open air and their dead bodies are collected from time to time by carts.

He still had not moved when, at eleven, skirting what could be his corpse, she prepared to go along to Dr. Asghari's picnic. Following the directions sketched on the paper, she followed the road in front of her villa, Villa Two, past a big house on the left. If this were a military enclosure, that would be the general's house, and the rest would be the houses of majors and top sergeants—smaller cement-block houses with bikes and trikes in the carports, and everywhere lovely vines entwining eaves and walls, and here or there somebody with a talent for gardening had embellished his paradise with roses or peonies.

She tried to take everything in. She felt a kind of rapture to see that no matter where you were in the world, you were there, same style of clouds up above, same ants and pebbles underfoot, and you didn't feel odd. There must be ants in China. It was said there were no flies there. There were flies here. How pleasant just to wander along a strange road in a strange land, smiling back at the people sitting in their yards smiling at her.

A dozen or so people stood on the lawn of the Asgharis'

bungalow or on the long cement porch. They were not all, to Chloe's rapid glance, Iranian—one woman with a mouse-brown permanent, a couple who from some quality of pinkness about them might be either British or American. A young American woman doctor, Dr. Fay. The Iranians had long sideburns, and the handsome, square-jawed look of the lovers and warriors painted on Persian tiles. No sign of Hugh Monroe.

The mouse-brown curls proved to be her hostess, Heidi Asghari, an Englishwoman, who greeted Chloe warmly and drew her into groups of people who smiled and shook her hand. Chloe was charmed by the beauty of their dark eyes, fine aquiline features. The men had high domed foreheads and curly hair. One woman had a name like moonlight—Noosheen. Chloe made an effort to remember the difficult and unfamiliar names— Pari, Ravi. Of the faces she recognized only Mohammed Asghari, whom she had met that morning, and Abbas, whose last name began with M, the man from last night.

Abbas had been helping Heidi Asghari carry a cooler of soft drinks to the porch and was thinking, for the hundred-thousandth time, that it does not hurt to die from drowning, and then, because he could not help it, the reverie went on, what about the minutes before you die, what about the fear, sinking through the slimy water, knowing, resisting, hoping, struggling. He was thinking of his dead wife, who had been alive at the time of Now-Ruz last year, and now was dead, trying to save their baby from drowning. She would have been thinking of the baby, he could not imagine that she would have had other thoughts, although they say it is given to you to have a million thoughts all at once, of your whole life, and in that case, as the brown waters took her over, had she thought of him? Or of what? Why did he care especially today? His thoughts were interrupted by seeing Heidi greet Mrs. Fowler, the new American wife who had come in advance of her husband. She was explaining about how she came to be alone.

Chloe found that her situation sounded plausible to the others: Dr. Fowler, unfortunately delayed in America, would

arrive as soon as possible; in the meantime, bound by the circumstances of her grant from the San Francisco Art Museum
and the university at Shiraz, Chloe herself had thought it best
to come on schedule. She and Jeffrey had thought it best that
she come on schedule. Her journey had been uneventful. Her
quarters were satisfactory.

Here, though, Chloe found she could not be persuasive. Her
quarters were certainly not satisfactory but horrible, and these
people, who lived in the pretty bungalows amid hibiscuses,
were probably not aware of the state the place had fallen into,
and would know whom to call to fix things, and would not wish,
so evidently kind were they, that she or anyone be uncomfortable. She awaited a chance to mention her plight, perhaps to
the Englishwoman, Heidi Asghari.

Pretty Noosheen—Mrs. Ardeshir—was sympathetic, but
not much help, when Chloe had an opportunity to confide in
her about the state of Villa Two. "I know it is not very nice,"
she said. "We, the wives, put those posters in there, and some
cushions, to make it better, but it is true, it is still not nice,
especially coming from America." She loved America, she said.
The Ardeshirs had lived in Cleveland for nearly two years, and
she would have been willing to discuss Cleveland at length.

"It is much more beautiful here," Chloe said firmly. "I
have never seen such roses."

How kind they all are, how welcoming. Perhaps they are always delighted at newcomers. Do they feel confined within the
walls of the Azami Compound? But on this lawn, under these
trees, one does not feel enclosed but delightfully breeze-blown,
outdoors, free. Far away from America. Chloe helps Heidi and
the other women lay the cloths on the long picnic tables,
weighting the corners with apples and cans of Pepsi, and, im-
probably, a bowl of goldfish. Chloe feels a moment of disappointment to see that they would have hot dogs and potato
chips. You might be in America, this might be the Fourth of

July, except for the addition of candles and a mirror. "It's a tradition," Heidi explains.

They sit on aluminum lawn chairs with plastic webbing, familiar. In the garden familiar flowers bloom but are called differently, strangely. "Here is the Jesus flower, and the Moses," say the Iranians.

She must visit Isfahan, they say. Heidi promises to take her to the bazaar. She and Dr. Fowler must take a few days to visit Persepolis, city of ancient Persia, and in a few weeks they can view the migration of the nomadic tribesmen with their flocks to the mountains to the north from the lower pastures near Abadan, where they had spent the winter. In a manner wonderfully kind, Dr. Ardeshir, the elderly husband of the pretty Noosheen, lays out a conscientious sightseeing program for them—the pink couple, the Hendersons and Junie Fay and Chloe, and Dr. Fowler when he arrives, for they promise not to keep their foreign benefactors at work every moment in the hospital or lecture room. "We are pleased to have visitors and wish them to see everything of the wonders here. The tomb of Cyrus! The footsteps of Alexander the Great!"

"Yes, I've been reading my Persian history," the conscientious Chloe assures him.

Hot dogs, potato salad, a plate of salami, hard-boiled eggs, yogurt. Chloe looks in vain for something Iranian, though the salad of rice and chick-peas has a distant savor of mint. Starved as she is, she tries to eat in a ladylike way and not wolf everything down in the manner of a starving person. She forces herself to eat calmly. Dr. Asghari brings wine, and begins to pour. She watches anxiously when it appears that he will skip the ladies, or pour them only tiny drinks. She notices that Noosheen puts her hand over her glass. Chloe does not.

"Iranian wine is not bad, you'll find. Our vineyards are young, planted only in the last decade—a project encouraged by the Shah, but the wine will become, I think, an important agriculture for Iran. An export."

"Was there no wine before?" Chloe asks. "The ancients must have had wine—I'm thinking of Omar."

Dr. Ardeshir intones a line in Persian. " 'A Jug of Wine, a Loaf of Bread—and Thou.' But you of course have a very fine translation of this poem, 'The Rubaiyat.' "

"Yes, one poem everyone knows."

"In Persia we revere poets."

Chloe sighs. Would they notice if she were to ask, very casually, did they know Hugh Monroe, was he here? Would that be thought odd?

"You must visit the beautiful tombs of the poets of Shiraz. This is a place eminently poetic," says Dr. Ardeshir.

Perhaps Hugh is at some other Now-Ruz gathering, even nearby, or with other Americans, sightseeing on this day off, or perhaps he is at the hospital seeing to patients while the Iranian doctors celebrate the holiday. Endure the holiday. The afternoon wears on. People had set up on their lawns like refugees to wait out the day.

"Abbas Mowlavi is so brave," whispers Heidi to Chloe as the ladies clear away the plates. "It must be so hard for him. This time last year he had a wife, a child, and then the tragedy. Just a few months ago, but he goes on. They drowned, a freakish thing. How could one go on?"

The dessert is a sumptuous plate of melon and grapes. When the places have been cleared and paper plates burnt in the barbecue, Mohammed Asghari brings cards and poker chips and the company sits around the picnic tables to play a game which someone explains to Chloe. They empty their pockets of money.

"You will need some money, Mrs. Fowler," Abbas Mowlavi tells her, and puts a stack of coins in front of her. "I'll stake you." Everyone pushes money around the table and laughs. They count in a strange way. "Panj," "heft," Chloe's turns pass safely when she makes simple choices, her stack of coins dwindles and grows. They almost fail to notice dusk, but at last someone does, with a cry, and everyone rises to take the picnic things indoors. The men carry the chairs and fold away the umbrellas. Chloe gives Abbas his money back. He counts it and returns a handful of coins to her.

"I could not consent to profit from your luck," he says, smiling.

"Dr. Monroe," Chloe suddenly says to the company, her cheeks warming. "We have a friend, Hugh Monroe, who we thought might be here now."

A silence. Abbas Mowlavi glanced at Mohammed Asghari. "We expected him before this," Mohammed said.

Dr. Asghari raised his brows. "I have heard something only last night, that Dr. Monroe is detained in Tehran."

"Detained?" cried Chloe, in spite of her wish to seem indifferent.

"By the authorities."

"Arrested?" Heidi Asghari asked.

"No, no, something about his visa."

"That could take weeks. I hope he's at the Hilton at least," said Heidi.

"We are not exactly sure where he is," said Mohammed.

Chapter Four
NEW FRIENDS

The dogs came in the night again, but now, her second night in Iran, they didn't terrify her for more than an instant. She lay awake, wondering what time it was in California, that she should feel so wide awake now, but she did not let the instant of terror spread and spill over into night fears about whether the children were all right, or whether Hugh Monroe was in trouble in

Tehran, or about why she was here, a million miles from where she should be, in a grim room, on a rickety cot. Though the possibilities for a sleepless night were rich, she did not give in to them, and went to sleep again.

Now, in the morning, she had many things to occupy her. She would have to go to the bank, buy food, clean the hallways and kitchen, throw out the urine-stained rugs, and repair the torn screen where the cats were getting in. Heidi Asghari had kindly offered to show her where the shops and bank were, and she arrived as planned at ten. Noosheen Ardeshir was with her. Chloe was reassured to have been found by two such agreeable women already. She resolved in future to be more attentive to the wives of foreign doctors who came to San Francisco.

The city of Shiraz, which lay outside the walls of the Azami Compound, consisted of old walled houses glimpsed across green courtyards, modern apartment buildings and new villas built of cement blocks. Everything had a leached and dusty aspect, but though the flowers struggled to bloom in the desert air, they bloomed. Water had been brought, she was told, in sophisticated viaducts by the ancient Persians.

People hurried along the street, intent and Western-looking, the men in dark suits or trousers and loose shirts, the women in print dresses that might have come from Penney's or Sears. Many were veiled, but many were not, or wore their hair tucked up in sheer nylon scarves, olive cheeks bright with rouge. Some women wore gypsy clothes of wild colors, with many beads and petticoats, and had hard, sunburnt faces. These were the tribal women who lived in the desert to the south and kept goats and camels and made rugs.

Chloe liked the undulation of the Persian lettering on the signs, like melted letters or dream words. Sometimes words were written in English as well as Farsi. The bank was called Bank Melli Iran. Here she cashed some traveler's checks, just as easily as you might cash them in London. From the wall of the bank, the visage of the Shah stared down, much as the

Queen smiles down in London. "In America no one smiles down on you," Chloe observed.

"Oh yes, the President often does," Noosheen objected. Chloe had never noticed that. "And George Washington often does."

With each reassuring sign that it was well within her power to conduct a regular, comfortable life here, and with each new charming and exotic sight, Chloe's spirits rose. There was a little supermarket, full of recognizable products by Procter & Gamble or Nestlé, and with other products of mysterious allure. She bought a beautiful tin of tea with golden camels on it, and a bottle of skin cream, which showed a ravishing woman hidden behind her veil, promising some Cleopatran secret.

They were riding in Heidi's small car, in which she fearlessly barged in among other cars, taxis, donkey carts, horses, camels, people walking in the street. Chloe was too fascinated to be fearful. Horns blew all around, it appeared from mere exuberance, at the challenges to manhood that, as the driver of a motor vehicle, one constantly met. Horns sounded forth from rushing taxis, from encumbered cars, drivers especially maddened by being stuck behind animal carts, from innumerable buses in faded colors, which hurtled from block to block, stopping with screeches, passengers swaying unperturbed. The drivers of animal carts most stirred Chloe's heart, so disappointed did they look, so affronted by unkind destiny, their little sons tucked up beside them, aware, by the look of their wide, disappointed eyes, of the humiliation of their fathers, a sorrow that would be theirs too if no miracle intervened to put them in charge, in due time, of a motor vehicle.

Heidi drove her on a quick tour of the principal sights of Shiraz—the university, the bazaar, the tombs of Hafez and Sa'adi, mosques, a fortress—so that Chloe would know how to find them and look at them properly at her leisure. They saw the beautiful rose garden at the summer villa of the Shah, and a bit of the ancient viaduct.

"The water is safe to drink," Heidi, noticing Chloe's interest in the water system, assured her.

"There is the building where I study," Noosheen said as they passed the university. "That is where you will be also. I began my studies in Cleveland, but I continue them here. English literature."

"That's wonderful," Chloe said.

Noosheen continued, "And in fact I have cherished a wish to ask you something—but I am almost embarrassed."

"Of course, anything," Chloe said.

"I told Noosheen you certainly wouldn't mind," Heidi said.

"It's about my senior thesis. It's not exactly what I chose, but anyway it's my subject, and I find it is really difficult. If I could just talk to you about it."

"*I'm* completely hopeless at literature," Heidi said. "I was a nurse."

"But what's the subject?" Chloe asked.

"Well, I'm studying Matthew Arnold's masterpiece 'Empedocles on Etna,' and his other poetry as well, of course, but I am writing about 'Empedocles,' and Heidi said you wouldn't mind talking to me about it, or perhaps when I begin to write you might read what I have written, to tell me if it's too stupid or if I missed the point. If we could just have some little chats about Matthew Arnold, that would help me so much."

Chloe, feeling fraudulent, agreed. But she cautioned that she had read very little Victorian poetry. At first "Empedocles" struck her as a strange subject for a young Iranian wife, but upon reflection she saw that for Noosheen to read Arnold was no stranger than for her to read Hafez and Sa'adi, which she intended to do, and Noosheen was reading Arnold in the original, after all, which is more than she, Chloe, was going to do of Sa'adi and Hafez. In the long run, the symmetry of the situation was appealing, and it was arranged between them that Noosheen would visit her, or invite her to tea, and they would discuss the poetry of Arnold, Hafez, and Sa'adi. Chloe felt lucky to have a role already, and a chance to get acquainted with an Iranian woman.

Also, she admired Noosheen—thought her beautiful in a way, though she lightened her hair and would have looked better with the heavy, dark hair that most Iranian women had. She had large brown eyes, like the eyes of an icon or one of those charming people painted on tombs, and a dainty figure, smaller even than Chloe, who was not a large woman. And Noosheen was infinitely more graceful, or so it seemed to Chloe, who felt rather clumsy and American and somehow oversized beside her. Noosheen wore stockings and high-heeled shoes. It wouldn't have occurred to Chloe to put on stockings and high-heeled shoes to grocery shop. Noosheen had a baby and a child of two, and her husband, Bahram Ardeshir, was the head of pathology at Azami Hospital.

Heidi Asghari's children were in school, and had to be picked up, so she and Noosheen dropped Chloe and her groceries at Villa Two. Satisfied and encouraged, Chloe climbed the stairs, put her groceries away, and set to work at cleaning the disgusting kitchen. Her anger at whoever it was who ought to take care of this place renewed itself, not that she thought of herself as being above cleaning kitchens. The oven was beyond cleaning, in fact, though she made some headway on the stove. Just at the moment that the steel wool fragmented to rusty bits beneath her hand, she was startled at a voice behind her, from the hallway: "Mrs. Fowler?" A deep Iranian voice, surprising from the small man in white doctor's coat, stethoscope in pocket. Something authoritative in his manner swelled her indignation at the state of the kitchen, as if he were the person who ought to do something.

"I am Dr. Farmani, director of Azami Hospital. In the past, I have received many letters from your husband. I am sorry about his delay. Is everything all right?"

"As you see," Chloe began, in a rush of relief at having found someone at last to help, "the place is a terrible mess, really; it's really very disagreeable finding oneself in such a place, it's certainly not very welcoming or cheerful. I expect you didn't realize . . ."

"The man Hossein comes each day. You must tell him what you want him to do," Dr. Farmani said. He had a mustache and beard like a sultan, and little booted feet. His eyes, Chloe thought, were cold and hard, devoid of sympathy for her labor. She stood before him, steel wool pricking her fingers.

"I wanted particularly to ask you," he said. Chloe squeezed out the wet rag and hung it over the faucet.

"The horrible smell in the hall is in those rugs," she said. "Cats."

"It is said you are acquainted with Dr. Monroe, Hugh Monroe," he said.

"Well—slightly," she said warily, half-afraid he had seen into her heart, or imagining, though it was preposterous, that Jeffrey had written him. Watch and see how my wife gets on with Hugh Monroe.

"Dr. Asghari has heard he is detained in Tehran. Is that right?"

"I only know what Dr. Asghari said," Chloe said. "On account of some problem with his visa? They said it might take several days?"

"Do you by any chance know if—I want to help if I can—do you know if Dr. Monroe travels on a diplomatic passport?"

"No, of course not, he's a physician," Chloe said. "I mean, I would doubt it."

Dr. Farmani seemed to mistrust her. He peered at her eyes. "It is a matter of knowing whom to get in touch with. If I knew . . ."

"I would think just a plain passport, like Jeffrey's or mine."

"Physicians sometimes undertake additional missions, as emissaries or couriers—anyone might. Dr. Monroe travels widely, I understand?"

"Many doctors do. My husband does. They lecture, they are invited . . ."

"Dr. Monroe has been to Moscow, Edinburgh, Geneva."

"Well, I don't know anything about his schedule. Why are you asking me?" Why was he? She was embarrassed by her own cross tone. Then she was struck by another worrying idea. "Are you concerned about him? Is there a problem?"

"No, no, I'm sure he will be along in a few days," said Dr. Farmani, his tone dismissive, unconvincing. "If you have anything for him, I could probably arrange to get it to him." She must have looked puzzled, truly mystified, for now he turned away.

It seemed to him her eyes were wary, her appearance, clutching a dishrag, not convincing; she was wearing what appeared to be a Paris dress, anyway a pretty dress. A woman alone—was it indeed Mrs. Fowler at all? How would one know? Who had met her? Abbas Mowlavi had been in California, and had met Fowler but not the wife. She looked, it was true, like an American doctor's wife—same dyed hair. But of course they would choose someone who looked the part.

He had thought they would send a medical person, someone who would snoop around the hospital, not just someone to hang about in the compound. We will see what she does, he thought, and we will see what happens when Monroe arrives, and when they do I will watch both of them. His stomach crawled anxiously at the thought of Monroe reputedly in Tehran, talking to whom? He had the feeling that forces were being brought down on Azami, he knew not why, and Westerners with falsely smiling faces, people down from Tehran, this woman with her camera lying there unabashedly on the kitchen counter, and, although wearing a wedding ring, no husband.

"Ah, well," he said, "goodbye for the moment. I only thought to stop and ask in case."

"I'm sorry," Chloe said, but could not resist adding, in a rush, "I suppose it's silly, but anyone would be upset, being put in such a dirty place, it's not just me. . . ."

"You Americans are fastidious, it is well known," he said with a smile that stretched his little mustache into a line over his teeth.

Chloe listened to the tap of his boots down the stairs, muffled as he stepped on each horrible rug, ringing against the cement, then the clack of the front door downstairs. After a few moments, she followed him, dragging the horrible rugs down the stairs, across the foyer and out into the yard.

She sat on the steps for a few moments in the twilight, wondering about this strange visit, and about Hugh. He did travel a lot—he spoke of adventures in the Himalayas and so on. He was romantic and went diving in the Caribbean, skied in the Alps. Perhaps he did have diplomatic missions, special charges. Came, she had heard, from a family prominent in Washington. His accent was attractively eastern. She quite liked the idea of Hugh's being some sort of diplomat, not a CIA agent, of course—they were some sort of comedy team who never could get it straight about which thing to blow up. She watched the approach of Hossein, the man who supposedly cleaned and took care around the place, as he kicked at the puppy, which had crept out from its bush. She was horrified but not surprised at this unthinking brutality. Luckily the puppy scuttled out of the way.

He would not kill a dog, Hossein was thinking, now that he had been to Mecca. It was he who used to kill them, without enthusiasm, because he was told and paid to, but now he would not do that work, and no one else had been found to do it, and there were more dogs than ever around the compound, as there were more people in the world—like, even, the number of daughters of his brother—Hossein had no wife of his own—and half-grown curs, as thin as his own arm.

The new woman was sitting on the steps, a gold chain around her wrist. The rugs from the hallway were thrown about in the yard, and so must be dragged in again and put neatly in place. She was watching him, without expression. Did she think he would not take the rugs in again?

Chapter Five
NOT AT HOME

Yon rising Moon that looks for us again—
How oft hereafter will she wax and wane;
How oft hereafter rising look for us
Through this same Garden—and for <u>one</u> in vain!

Outside the western wall of the Azami Compound, the dry bed
of a river, no more really than a broad ditch, bisected the city
of Shiraz. Across the river lay some kind of military base from
which, at intervals during the day, harsh amplified commands
drifted on the air, at times competing with the drone of prayers.
In the mornings, reveille was played on this public address
system—fortunately not too early—and Chloe would lie on her
cot, listening to the notes of the bugle, reviewing, as was her
nature, the satisfactions before the dissatisfactions of her situation.

She was satisfied that, if they could not be with her, the
children at least were safely with Jeffrey—as well as her mother
and the babysitter; and that she still had not received a panicked call or telegram. When she and Jeffrey were traveling
together, she could be shattered at any moment by the mere
thought of calamities at home.

But Jeffrey would be there to deal with things for another
week or so. The dissatisfactions were her ugly room, and that
she was alone here, which was merely strange. She had married
young; she had hardly ever, her whole life long, been alone.

She unwound her ankles from the sheet, which seemed to
shred further each night. Last night she had not heard the dogs
at all. It was rather pleasant to wake alone, she thought, free of
the reproachful groans of another person clinging to sleep. She

had planned a simple daily routine: coffee, hot and strong, and a few pistachio nuts, then an hour with *Teach Yourself Farsi,* which she had begun to study in California. She had not made much progress, but was resolved to be more diligent, and enjoyed tracing the squiggly lines that served as letters. She had already learned the numbers, and the coins—rials and tooman—and after her lesson she would walk to the grocery store, trying to identify numbers and parts of words in signs along the way. She could already write "Coca-Cola," because this sign was everywhere, and at the store had tried saying, "Khoda hafez," which was supposed to mean goodbye but had not produced a response. At the store they gave you your small change in aspirin or gum, your choice. She always chose aspirin. Today she planned to buy some vegetables and some meat, with which to attempt some Iranian dishes when Hugh arrived. If this was only to be an interlude in her life, she wanted it to be an interlude of sweetness and simplicity, walking, cooking, making love with Hugh Monroe, and avoiding the automobile.

Chloe knew that she should soon present herself at the university, to begin her work on Sassanian pottery. She had corresponded with a Mrs. Reza in the department of archaeology, and was expected, but she procrastinated another day. One problem was the telephone, with which to call for an appointment. The phone stood on a stool outside the kitchen and occasionally emitted a shrill white sound when you picked up the receiver; but she had no notion at all how to make it work, or whether, although she had written perfectly in English, Mrs. Reza would be prepared to speak English.

Also, since the university was some distance away, she would probably have to take a taxi. The taxis had been explained to her. You got in with other people, strangers already in the taxi, and paid your share. This was daunting—she was unsure of the fares and of whether the driver would understand her. The taxis themselves were frightening, small, dented Peykans, draped in photos, lurching forward before the lights had turned, trinkets flapping, drivers cursing. Heidi Asghari had explained that the drivers were more used to driving camels than cars, and you had to curse camels to get them to move.

She decided to get a feel for the distances involved by walking first to the bazaar, which was no more than a mile or so away, at the other end of the long main street. Along the way she passed various office buildings and consulates—there was the American consulate, eagle peeling dispiritedly. A department store. A lot of record shops and banks, T-shirts stalls, and shops with soccer balls in the windows. A cinema, a pizza parlor—it might have been Europe but for the exotic spicy smell of the air, and the drifting veils and the quite chaotic upheavals of the pavements, and the strange ditch, called the jube, that ran along the curbings, a menace to wheels and ankles alike. Chloe walked slowly, savoring the rich strangeness. The heroes and heroines of Iranian films stared at her with big dark eyes from posters on walls, the actresses gleaming with gold ornaments.

Most of the shops were shut. Perhaps this was another special day, or a long weekend. Though she had read that Western women could not walk alone in the Middle East, Chloe found that no one here bothered her or looked askance. The men kept their glances strictly to themselves, and the women's bolder stares did not seem unfriendly. It was a relief that an American woman was not regarded with dislike or disapproval. Chloe was used to foreign travel and to the civility of foreigners, but, as an American, was always aware that she might, by her category—she hoped not by her actions—incur incivility. On their travels, she and Jeffrey were always careful not to speak in loud American voices, or wear bright colors, or make scenes. They dreaded being taken for Americans.

She continued to be fascinated at the idea of veils. There seemed to be no rule about them; some women didn't wear them, some wore them tightly pulled around them. She thought it would be awful to have to shroud yourself as if there were something indecent about you, and yet it was exciting too to think that the mere sight of you could stir improper desire, and interesting to wonder if Iranian men were so inflammable they could not look at you. Or else it was all just habit and the libidos of men are the same the world around and these women were not really ashamed of their faces. How do you find out? Though she could see them, even touch them, she regretted that she could never know or understand them, as they moved behind their barrier of Farsi, their minds elsewhere, on the washing or on saffron-scented dishes for their families' suppers. She watched a tiny girl, bouncing a ball with one hand, with her other hand clutching her tiny shroud around her, while her brother climbed along a railing, holding on safely with both hands. Chloe thought of Noosheen, whom she was expecting at Villa Two at two—had Noosheen grown up one-handed?

When Noosheen came, despite the warm day, she was wearing a schoolgirl outfit of skirt and sweater, as if she had costumed herself from Western movies about college life, or perhaps these were her Cleveland clothes. She had brought the collected works of Matthew Arnold for Chloe to brush up on before they began their talks in earnest. Chloe admired her passion for learning. Like Chloe, she had two children, though she was only twenty-four, and had been married four years, two of them spent in Cleveland. It must be hard, with such young children, to keep her English up and continue to study and learn.

Chloe made iced tea and carried it outside. They sat in the garden between her villa and Villa One on two aluminum chairs. "My room is much too ugly to sit in," said Chloe firmly. Today Noosheen was more sympathetic to Chloe's complaints about Villa Two and about the methods of Hossein, who so far had appeared each day at about noon and would push his wide, damp, greasy mop around the floor. Chloe didn't say that she did not like his jagged brown teeth and the feverish sidelong glance of his eyes. But Noosheen was familiar with the general problem of Villa Two, for other American wives had complained. The thing to do, she advised, was to speak to Linda Farmani, wife of Vahid Farmani, the hospital doctor.

"I have already met him," Chloe said. The Farmanis, Noosheen told her, lived in Villa One, and as she and Chloe were now sitting virtually in the garden of Villa One, they could call on her here and now. Noosheen jumped up.

"She is American," she said. "Vahid Farmani met her when he went to Los Angeles. He did a fellowship at UCLA. I think she was an airline stewardess."

Chloe was surprised, hearing this, that a fellow American woman would not have looked in on her before now. She and Noosheen approached Villa One and knocked on the door. They were told by a taciturn servant that Mrs. Farmani was lying down. This seemed odd to Chloe, who never napped. Perhaps she was ill or pregnant, or perhaps it was a colonial affectation of some kind, or the queerly enervating life of a foreign land, the loss of normal American vitality. When Noosheen had left, Chloe herself was nearly overtaken by lassitude, but perhaps, she told herself, this was not owing to the foreignness of Iran, or even to jet lag, so much as to the poetry of Matthew Arnold, which she sat reading in the garden awhile longer, with, as she caught herself from time to time, a wonderful blankness of mind.

Linda Farmani, watching from her upstairs window, was thinking that the new American woman was just the type she didn't like. Visiting Americans believed you had to entertain them just because you were American yourself. Well, she would have her to tea or something, let her see the beautiful house, its tracery screens like the lace curtains of Detroit, where she had grown up, improving by their intricate patterns the features of the crude world. Linda imagined that she of all her friends left behind in Detroit had the finest house, not in a style any of them could have imagined. Her mother still imagined that she lived in a tent—this despite photos and letters, and even a visit, during which she was overcome by fits of sighs whenever she saw a woman in a veil. More wore the veil then. Back in Detroit, Linda's mother had been afraid she would marry a Jew, or a Catholic; a Moslem had never entered her thoughts. This still filled Linda with glee.

Noosheen Ardeshir, arriving home, clapped her hands for Ayah, and felt grateful that she came so promptly and with a pleasant smile, not ugly and lowering like the brows of so many servant girls. You saw the angry ones in other people's houses, looking with straightforward hate at the woman they worked for. Others seemed so modest, eyes downcast, wearing chador, right from the country, then the minute you're out they slap the baby and date soldiers. They all wanted to go to Tehran to train as secretaries. Margaret Yoganadoost's girl had scalded the baby, seemingly an accident.

Noosheen's ayah was Indian, from Lahore, where Noosheen's father, a diplomat, lived, and where Noosheen herself had lived awhile before her marriage. All agreed that an Indian servant girl was much more willing and quick, just the thing while the children were young. And Noosheen's house in Azami Compound was small but even so bigger than most, with Western furniture to dust. Mama and Papa had sent Ayah to her from Lahore on the train. She now slept on the back porch, where if they had one the washing machine would go; then they would have to think of somewhere else to put her. This little porch had seemed to Ayah huge and cozy; her eyes had widened. She had shown all her small dark teeth smiling happily. Noosheen sometimes, having been in the United States, felt a little anxious about the chilly porch, the foam mattress on the floor. An Iranian girl would complain. In America you would have many things, for instance a washer and dryer, to take Ayah's place—gadgets that did not defect or object. All of life was such a puzzle, or, in the words of Matthew Arnold's poem:

And on earth we wander, groping, reeling;
Powers stir in us, stir and disappear.
Ah! And he, who placed our master-feeling,
Failed to place that master-feeling clear.

In the early evening after a solitary supper of pistachio nuts and boiled rice, Chloe ventures outside to the garden again, to sit on a cement bench placed at the intersection of the paths to Villa One and Villa Two. She plans to think about her situation, but the powers of enchantment in the dark Persian garden make it difficult to think deeply or make decisions. She is in any case always more given to idle reflections than to purposive thought. She can hear a fountain. The idea of an early, solitary evening is at once agreeable and dull, but she knows the sensation of dullness will pass. It is more a matter of calming down and learning to lead a life whose natural pace is in harmony with the natural rhythms of the mind, instead of, as in America, life outrunning thought, heedless and rushing.

In America she has her children, her part-time job at the museum, philanthropic activities, wifedom, books piling up to be read, the dog needing to go to the groomer, the toaster to be repaired, the cleaning to be picked up—she has the normal life of an American woman, which she herself does not object to as strongly as some of her friends do. But she agrees that it is too fast-paced.

Especially if you try to have an affair. Nothing trivial or sordid, of course—her model is Colette, or European life in general, so civilized, where people don't divorce, just conduct affairs of the heart discreetly, with the toaster being dropped off at the repairman in an efficient way, not the havoc of American divorce, the chaos of abandoned children and objects and unrepaired toasters. Toasters partake of material life, that is the nature of material life, and Chloe does not disapprove of it, does not despise objects. She thinks of them as having emanations, or animation, or life.

Tonight she feels a little worried about Hugh. This morning

she had felt almost irritated at him, an irritation born of some female insecurity, some doubt, to do with herself, that he was really coming, or that he had allowed himself in some way to be arrested and thrown into an Iranian prison rather than see her, or had cooled off and now looked back on their furtive, charming exchanges as squalid and compromising, or had fallen in love, since she last saw him, with someone more suitable—unmarried, younger.

Then she had told herself she was relieved in a perverse way that he was delayed, felt she deserved to pay some penance for the happiness of being alone in a strange land. To have Jeffrey absent and Hugh there suggested gratification altogether too smoothly arranged, as if by an especially malicious destiny planning ugly surprises. With Hugh not there she could pay in advance for anticipated pleasures, pay by uncertainty, solitude, and serious study, in a land hostile to women, far from her children, in an ugly room. What destiny could then begrudge her just a little fling?

But tonight she worries about Hugh. The Iranians themselves thought him arrested, though of course by mistake. Still you read about mistakes, usually in Turkey or Mexico, an innocent traveler carrying a package for someone, or buying an artifact from an urchin, then, at the border, charges of drugs or theft, and not all the efforts of the U.S. State Department can get you out again, young people wasting their youth, released only years later, staring and white-headed, broken, with rotted teeth.

She is thinking of this now in the darkness, and looking at a quantity of geraniums set out in little terra cotta pots on the terrace of the grand house, just visible in the soft light from a window. It would be nice to have a flower in her room in Villa Two. Villa One had plenty. Villa One had charming windows that were shaped like arches, and instead of shutters it had delicate screens. Far away the barking of the dogs began.

* * *

Chloe wonders where the dogs go in the daytime. Were they all, like the puppy, under bushes someplace? Or does each dog have a respectable daytime life as watchdog to a family? All at once she misses her children with a special intensity, and she misses Jeffrey. She will go inside and write to them. It occurs to her to slip one of the pots of geraniums under her arm and steal it for her room. The Farmanis will never miss it.

Darling kids, So far I have seen people
riding on: goats, donkeys, camels, and horses,
besides cars etc. Love to Dad. See you in a few weeks.
XX Mom

Chapter Six
OLD FRIENDS

And this first Summer month that brings the Rose
Shall take Jamshyd and Kaikobad away.

Well, let it take them! What have we to do
With Kaikobad the Great, or Kaikhosru?
Let Zal and Rustum bluster as they will
Or Hatim call to Supper—heed not you.

Her apprehensions about meeting the archaeologists at Shiraz University were still intensified by her fears of the taxis, so though it was far she finally decided to walk. She had letters of introduction to Mrs. Reza and to a Mr. Farmanpour, letters which, although she was too polite to read them, she imagined described her as a serious person, perhaps even as a real archaeologist, though she was only a conscientious amateur who had read and worked up the subjects, and had majored in art history in college, and volunteered at the museum. She imagined that her lack of real expertise would be only too apparent to the genuine archaeologists, who, however, welcomed her warmly, appeared to look forward to discussing their subject with her, offered her a study cubicle in the library, and invited her to visit the great ongoing work at Persepolis and the fields of shards that lay on the way.

Mrs. Reza took her to the library, a reassuringly familiar structure, with books in English, a Library of Congress catalog, a microfilm reader, and *Time* magazine and the *New York Review of Books* in battered bundles in the periodical room.

"As you see," said Mrs. Reza, "we are quite a modern university. You have the right to use the library at any time. You will find in it your *Atlantic,* your *Good Housekeeping,* your *New York Times.*"

Chloe thanked her. She was watching a student, head demurely scarved, nunlike, gaze vacantly into an English edition of *Middlemarch.* All the books were in English. How odd it was. The oddness was reflected on the knitted brows of the young olive faces. Several of the young women wore those little head scarves, not exactly veils but with their hair neatly invisible. She remarked on this to Mrs. Reza as they walked across the quadrangle toward the archaeology building again. The fortitude with which some women throw aside the veil, the prudence with which others proceed. Is it their families? Do the men in Iran prefer that the women continue or discard the veil?

"The veil? The veil?" cried Mrs. Reza. "There is no veil. The Shah has outlawed it. It is over, the vestige of a bygone day." Chloe, who had been struck by the large numbers of veiled women, wondered at this but did not argue. Perhaps Mrs. Reza was speaking only of the university, where, indeed, no one was veiled.

When she had thanked Mrs. Reza and Mr. Farmanpour

again and left them, Chloe went back to the library and checked out some books, serious works on Persian history, pottery, tombs, and a biographical study of Matthew Arnold, and, though they were heavy, began the long walk home, carrying them in her string grocery bag.

The Azami Compound, as she drew near it, already felt familiar and homelike, and she a part of it, the wife of Jeffrey Fowler, well-known thoracic surgeon soon to arrive, so she wasn't particularly surprised, just startled, to hear a man's voice calling her name. She thought at first of Hugh, but it was not his voice. A taxi full of men had pulled to the side of the street near her, and someone was waving from within.

"Chloe! Chloe Fowler! Dick Rothblatt!"

His head struggled out past that of the man by the window, who also gazed at her behind a drooping mustache. Dick Rothblatt squirmed past the knees of his fellow passenger, fishing change from his pocket for the driver.

"Tooman. Tooman, rials . . . I heard you were coming over. I have trouble with their coins." He stretched his arm to peer at the coins in his palm, plucked out one or two. Dick Rothblatt, familiar, short and rosy. The taxi was paid and drove on. Dick happily took her hand. "Friends in a strange land. I heard that Jeffrey isn't here yet?"

"I didn't know you were here already, Dick," Chloe said, piqued that no one had told her. She was happy to see him, not someone she knew well, just a dermatologist they knew from Princeton, but looking now like an adored old friend. She was surprised at her own pleasure. "How absolutely marvelous," she said twice.

"I've been here a couple of days. How do you like it?"

"I like it, it's lovely. I even love the music. I hate my room, though. We were told an apartment. Have you got an apartment? Jeffrey will die when he sees this place they've put us."

Dick laughed. "Mine is not deluxe. Sort of a duplex; there's an English neurologist and his wife on the other side. It's okay."

Chloe tried to think of the name of Dick's wife. "I'm at Villa Two, is that near you?"

"Villa Fourteen. Next to the ophthalmology building."

"You'll have to come see Villa Two," Chloe said.

Dick had been invited to Shiraz, he said, by Abbas Mowlavi, who was also a dermatologist. They had met during Abbas's fellowship year at Princeton. They talked of the terrible tragedy of his wife and baby.

"Did you ever meet them?"

"No, he married after he came back here. He has a brother in exile, in Paris, a radical. He has to watch his step."

"No one mentions the Shah here, pro or con. No one mentions politics at all."

"Definitely a no-no. Topic interdicted. Or the Savak drags you off in the night."

"There should be interdicted topics in America—jogging, relationships."

Dick took her string bag of books. His arm was strong and well muscled. His glasses were thick. He smelled of cologne. They walked along. Everything in this block was half-constructed, iron rods sticking out of cement-block walls, rusting and crumbling on every hand, abandoned. People squatted on rubble, eating or merely staring.

"They have a lot of good ideas here, then no follow-through. The same at the hospital, from what I've seen. Expensive machines, all broken."

"I'm sure they're much better off without machines," Chloe said.

When she told him that she had not yet seen the hospital, Dick invited her along to see it and have lunch with him in the cafeteria.

"When's Jeff coming?" he added. She understood the association of his ideas.

"It's a little uncertain. But meantime I had this project here—I work at the museum in San Francisco, you know, so I came on ahead. Sassanian pottery." This smoothly oiled statement was sounding more and more reasonable to her, especially now that she knew the names of the Shiraz archaeologists and had a cubby. "They had a vast civilization. There are fields near here where shards just lie on the ground. You don't even have to dig."

"Who were the Sassanians?" he asked. Chloe told him as they walked, a pre-Islamic people who ruled from the third century to the seventh century A.D.

"I'm doing rugs," Dick said. "Now there's a complicated subject. I did a lot of reading. I had no idea. Anyway, I plan to buy a few rugs; there'll never be a better time."

They walked inside the gates of Azami Compound and across the green lawn, past Villa One toward the hospital. Amid beds of petunias and roses, families crouched, unwrapping packets of food—black-shrouded picnickers, men in nylon shirts and serge trousers. They all looked to Chloe too somber; probably they had someone in the hospital, or maybe they were waiting for tests. Here and there she saw the upended backside of someone at prayer, prayer rug spread out on the grass. Chloe had not been able to figure out what precipitated a fit of prayer, since people did not seem all to do it at the same time, despite the calls that could sometimes be heard on loudspeakers from minarets downtown. Chloe and Dick picked their way quietly, politely, unobtrusively.

The hospital was an exotic structure, Moorish and pink, and on the inside much like all hospitals, tiled, smelling of disinfectant. Carts and trundles stood in the halls along the wall. Same apologetic and weary expressions of the faces of people wandering along or waiting by the open clinic doors. Not for nothing were you called a patient.

Then a fierce woman impeded their way, hair streaming like a gypsy in an opera, stepping in front of them from her place along the wall. She thrust a baby girl at Dick. The child was covered with rosy spots. Chicken pox, Chloe thought. Dick pointed her up the stairs. His expression changed as they went on.

Chloe suddenly remembered the name of Dick's wife, "Marlene isn't with you?"

"Marla—Marla and I are getting a divorce," he said. "Nothing rancorous or anything. One of those things. After the kids went to college we just sort of found out who we were, as they say, and we weren't people who need to be married to each other."

"That's common at our stage, isn't it?" Chloe said, noting the marriage-counseled vocabulary.

Dick shrugged. It was only recently he had been prepared to admit, even to himself, that he had contributed to the failure of his marriage by the occasional affair with a nurse or woman medical student. Now that there were so many more of these, it was hard to avoid. Yet he could see Marla's objections and sympathize with them; his own views on marriage were perfectly traditional too. What he couldn't understand was her unwillingness to accept his apologies and repentance, his perfectly sincere intentions to start anew. They would be helped by the fact that Scott, David, and Ellen were off to college and out of the house.

Neither was he very interested in Marla, for they had been married for twenty years, but he had noticed some new quality of vehemence and independence that interested him, and he was generally interested in the subject of women, not just sexually or because he enjoyed their alert and tactful way of listening—the feeling they gave that you could tell them things you couldn't tell a man—but existentially, in their situation, which once you came to think of it had been a difficult one historically and still was.

He was a feminist. He played the violin. His parents had hoped he would be a musician, and he had kept up his skill to the extent of playing in a quartet, but medicine had always been his love. You had to be sensitive to be a dermatologist, and you had to like women—psychology was half the practice of dermatology, as he was always telling his residents. Energetic, likable, and a good psychologist—he was chairman of the department at Princeton, a post high enough and visible enough to please even his mother.

"This is the cafeteria," he told Chloe. "Just get a tray and get in line. Don't be put off by the food—it tastes better than it looks." They lined up behind others, nurses in veils, technicians, some sleekly dark in their white lab costumes, others rosy Westerners whose nasal drawls somehow floated above or through the low Iranian voices.

"So fuck you, I told him," said a voice.

"Tracheostomy," said another.

Chloe hesitated over the white rice, soft and steamy, and the lightly browned rice, so the man with the ladle gave her both. He smiled. "Chelo," he said. He ladled a stew of gravy and peas over her plate, and a man by his side gave her a small plate of iceberg lettuce and pale tomatoes in a small dish. Her heart lifted. She had not yet risen to the difficulties of the vegetable stand, where she would have to gesture and point, so the sight of tomatoes, however sickly, warmed her now. Dick didn't take one. He shook his head at the salad person. They found a table.

"Actually, I wouldn't," he told Chloe when she set her salad at her place. "They have a problem here. We've been seeing a few cases of typhoid."

"Heavens," Chloe said, rather excited at the notion of being imperiled by third-world diseases.

"The little girl in the hall just now, for instance, that could be typhoid, the spots."

"Good grief," said Chloe. She ate a leaf when Dick wasn't noticing; obviously perfectly OK lettuce.

They left the cafeteria and, in the corridor, met Abbas Mowlavi, who was hastening somewhere but stopped with a look of genuine pleasure to see them. His chin was cleft like the chin of a man in a bourbon ad.

"We were having lunch," Dick said. "Have you met Mrs. Fowler?"

"Yes, indeed. Hello, Mrs. Fowler. I meant to ask you over

here to lunch myself one day. I hope you are not too solitary in Villa Two? But you've found Dr. Rothblatt.''

"So surprising," Chloe murmured. "To meet an old friend. Walking along . . ."

"Well," said Abbas to Dick, "are you coming to my clinic this afternoon?" Dick was. "I have promised to take Dick into the countryside tomorrow after work, and perhaps you would like to come too," Abbas suggested to Chloe, perhaps to atone for depriving her of her companion now.

Dick liked Abbas, thought him a forthright and gentlemanly guy and a good doctor, trained at Hammersmith, Princeton, and Johns Hopkins. You couldn't blame them when they got back here for missing the sight of a CAT scanner or a cobalt unit. Hard on them getting all that fancy Western training then nothing to do with it, though to be fair, Tehran did send them very up-to-date equipment. It was just they couldn't get the people to keep it running. People like Abbas must be dedicated patriots, otherwise they'd emigrate. They seemed genuinely to want to improve the health care of their nation. Dick found that exciting too. Here was a chance really to do things, something to be done, a need surpassing the mere acne and drug reactions you got at home in America. Here huge horrible things swelled up on people. Sometimes you had no idea what they could be. There were dire systemic complications of skin conditions which in the West would only be little cutaneous things. Here you could die of impetigo. Or typhoid. He didn't worry about the typhoid, exactly, since medicine was perfectly up to date here and people could be saved, and undoubtedly they had a public health department tracking down the pollution, the well or source. But they seemed strangely unconcerned all the same, Abbas as taciturn as the rest about a disease that in America, where it wouldn't happen anyway, would create a furor. These Iranian doctors had to contend with death more immediately than Americans did, even American doctors. We don't let it in until the last minute; here it might come stealing in any time.

Dick's heart tightened with sympathy for that poor mother

in the hallway, now huddled against the clinic wall, her shawl around her, her brown face sunburnt to paper, her child cuddled in the shawl. The little girl was not going to die, of course; this mother had had the sense to bring her in. Would Marla know what to do if a child got typhoid? All she had ever done, measles, broken arms, was call him up at the hospital and scream hysterically. But she was not a good example of female anything, Marla, just a credulous, silly woman. He tried to pat this peasant mother pleasantly on the shoulder but she shrank from him. Abbas, coming over, smiled at this mistake. He held his arms out for the child, and said something to the nurse, who began to take the child from the woman. The child clung to her mother's shawl, then to the silver ornament around her neck. The nurse pried her little fingers from around it, and handed her to Abbas, who carried her away toward his office.

"Where do these people come from?" Dick asked.

"They come from right here, from the town," Abbas said, and, seeing surprise fleet across Dick's face, added, "From the old part of the city where the plumbing has not been modernized and wells are used."

"Then it shouldn't be hard to find the tainted well," Dick said.

Abbas did not reply so Dick dropped the subject. Dick had been advised not to pursue topics that Iranians seemed to want to drop. You never knew when something was politically sensitive.

Abbas's mind was not on the typhoid, rather on the impression once again that someone was using his laboratory in the night. Certain chemicals disarranged, a beaker rinsed and still drying in the rack, a length of rubber tubing coiled in the sink. Nothing alarming about all this but that it was done in the night—by some insomniac perhaps, perhaps someone doing something dangerous or something that had to be done right away to save a patient in mortal peril. He felt no need to decide which of these things it was, except to resent, if it was something illegal, that it was done in his laboratory, bringing a certain danger to himself. It was the kind of thing you watch—would it happen again? The hastily coiled tubing lay in the bottom of the sink like a poisonous snake ready to strike at the hand that reached for it.

His mind too was on Vahid Farmani, his eyes distracted, barking irrational commands, not listening about the typhoid, his mind on Tehran, animated by fear or ambition—you never knew, any more, whose fear, whose ambition—and he, Abbas, didn't want anything of either but only to treat the sick and be left alone. The Azami Compound was a worthy sort of ivory tower, indispensable to any regime. He considered whether to have the lock changed on his lab, or maybe ask Hossein to stay up and watch some night. Then he decided it was better not to notice anything, and anyway he told himself he didn't care.

Chapter Seven
TEA PARTY

And we, that now make merry in the Room
They left, and summer dresses in new bloom,
Ourselves must we beneath the Couch of Earth
Descend—ourselves to make a Couch—for whom?

As the wife of the chief of Azami Hospital, you of course gave tea, dispensed welcome. Linda Farmani in a few days rose to her duty and invited the new American woman to tea, though she didn't feel gracious toward her, probably because Chloe was here alone and therefore was taking up a disproportionate share of attention being fetched and called on. Linda also asked the other newcomers, who were, she read from the list Vahid had given her, a woman doctor, June Fay, an English couple named Henderson, a Dr. Rothblatt. The name of Dr. Monroe was crossed out. Linda invited, which was to say commanded, Heidi Asghari, Noosheen Ardeshir and Zareeneh Yazdi to come make conversation and help arrange the sweet rice cookies, and put bowls of pistachios around the room.

So far only the women had assembled, and the tea was not yet poured. Chloe was interested in the striking decoration of Linda Farmani's rooms, which were prettier than most of the interiors she had seen so far, all of which had contained rather too much and too large furniture, covered in lurid shades of red or green velvet. Chloe supposed it was just that Linda's rooms were more American, Linda being American, though the strangely large furniture and colors of turquoise and blue seemed Persian enough. There were little tables made of brass trays standing on racks, and white-painted trellises nailed onto the walls, and a coffee table of plate glass supported by wicker elephants, which, though Chloe did not like it at all was nonetheless imposing.

When she commented on the decoration, Heidi Asghari told her that Linda was an interior decorator; she had made a business out of doing Persian-style interiors for the American wives of Grumman and Philco and the other corporations.

"They're afraid to go to the bazaar and they don't know where to find things for themselves. I think that Linda does pretty well out of it."

"Kind of Hollywood Persian," Chloe said. "Well, it isn't so bad," but she was torn between admiration for Linda's enterprise and scorn for someone who would profit from the plight of her dislocated sisters.

Linda Farmani herself was a thin woman, pretty but tense, with dark, sleepless-looking eyes. Her midwestern American accent surprised, for if she hadn't spoken, she might have seemed Iranian herself, dark hair twisted up, earrings of gold. She looked about forty, her husband Vahid about forty-five, and these two had to their surprise just produced a child, which was brought in for the ladies to see. Linda held it as if it were a sack of meat or a log—something inanimate and faintly awful. The baby was called Henry, reminding Chloe of their poor paralyzed friend. Chloe longed to hold Henry properly, and give the poor little thing some human comfort. He did not cry but stared up at his mother, whose glance at him was of panic, or fear.

"What a pity about your husband," Linda said to Chloe, with a grave expression, as if she had heard that Jeffrey was dead.

"Oh, he'll be here soon," Chloe said. "I expect to hear any day."

They were joined by the doctors, who arrived in a gang, faces reddened as if they had raced each other from the hospital. Here were Noosheen's husband Bahram Ardeshir; Heidi's husband Mohammed Asghari, Dick Rothblatt, Dr. Henderson, and some others. Chloe was shocked to think that it was this small brown old Bahram who was husband to the pretty Noosheen; she had not really matched them in her mind at the first meeting. The horrid Dr. Farmani, with no glint of recognition of her, greeted the others as if he hadn't been seeing them all day. People began to talk and pass the tea.

Chloe was brought a cup of tea by a tall, thin man, whose air of aristocratic and elegant cruelty had attracted her notice already. He was slightly balding and wore a dark green silk scarf knotted at his throat. He introduced himself as Dr. Ali Yazdi. His wife was Zareeneh, the tall voluptuous red-haired woman, equally noticeable, who had opened the door for Chloe. Her clothes were imprinted with the names of designers, and she emanated a delicious designer scent. She wore a diamond ring so huge it riveted the eye and compelled the conclusion that it could not possibly be real. But she had seemed rather nice, ushering Chloe upstairs to the party, and clasping her hand with a brisk, mannish, American handshake.

"You have such a bewildered air, like a lovely lost child," said Dr. Yazdi.

"On the contrary I feel most at home, everyone is so agreeable here," said Chloe, smiling her smile, forbearing to add her complaints about Villa Two.

"It's a charming thing in a woman—forgive me if I speak too personally, but I am a connoisseur—I say a lost, bewildered look is charming, but of course we cannot let it remain. That is what I am driving at. Have people shown you around? Have you seen the tombs of our poets Hafez and Sa'adi?" He began an enthusiastic description of these wonders.

"American women are luckier than we," Noosheen was heard to say, in a voice suddenly audible, with a defiant glance to her husband. Chloe had not heard the beginning of the conversation. "They can go where they please, they have passports of their own." Bahram gave a look around at the others, confident of their sympathy for him arising from Noosheen's combative tone. It did not seem polite, at this point, to inquire why Iranian women couldn't travel, though Chloe would have liked to know. Perhaps they had no passports.

"I think the Iranian system is perfectly all right," said Linda Farmani. "It's just a tradition," she explained to Chloe. "If you have a green stamp you may come and go as you please, but if you have a red one, your husband must sign before you can travel."

"You have an American passport," Noosheen said. "Naturally you don't care."

"No, I don't. I have an Iranian passport with a red stamp," Linda said. The topic hung in the silence, no one willing to go on with it.

"Anyway, an American passport is not always such magic. Poor Dr. Monroe," she went on.

"I would guess the visa is the problem there," said Dr. Farmani. Chloe listened more carefully. But no one had any news or specific information about Hugh. A silence again. It often happened, Chloe had noticed, that a thickening, palpable and heavy, swelled over topics here, bringing them to a halt, and people had a habit of looking up or away, not like Americans, who always plunged on with topics, however awkward.

But of course in America no one came and dragged you off in the night. Chloe found she had picked up an uncracked pistachio that she couldn't open, and so rolled it between her fingers, a hard little inedible lump. Passports did not seem an intrinsically dangerous topic so perhaps it was only a sore one.

"Noosheen is a Zoroastrian," Dr. Yazdi said in a whisper to Chloe. "But Bahram isn't. It used to be that Zoroastrians only married other Zoroastrians. Then they changed their views. The rumor is they thought they were getting rather inbred. Rather short and ugly." Dr. Yazdi lowered his voice. "And dark," he said.

"Noosheen is perfectly beautiful," Chloe said.

"Yes, isn't she?" Dr. Yazdi agreed.

Abbas Mowlavi joined the party late, still wearing a white hospital jacket, in which he looked darkly handsome, and it appeared to Chloe that Noosheen was very aware of that too. Noosheen followed Abbas with her large eyes, and smiled flirtatiously at him as she handed him a plate of the repellent gelatinous candy, whose flavor Chloe had not been able quite to identify. She put her piece in her saucer, with the uncracked nut.

It seemed obvious to Chloe that Noosheen and Abbas were attracted to each other, and it seemed natural as well, with her husband so old and thin and Abbas widowed. An unhappy marriage would explain her restlessness and her romantic ideas about American life, freedom and love Hollywood style. Chloe wondered if people had affairs in Iran. Probably not.

Now Chloe found herself standing near Dr. Farmani, who had been listening to the discussion of passports without offering any views himself. Chloe wondered if she dared continue the subject of Hugh. It was the others, after all, who had begun it.

"It's too bad you haven't found Dr. Monroe," she said. "Isn't he a specialist in infectious disease? He could be helpful with this terrible typhoid epidemic."

Dr. Farmani looked at her with an expression she did not

understand. "There is no typhoid epidemic," he said. "We had a case which for a moment appeared to be typhoid. Of course we were concerned. But, after all, it was not."

Chloe had not heard this news. A relief, she said. Why did Dr. Farmani glare at her so?

"It would be most unlikely, typhoid, hardly more likely than in your Omaha, say, or Connecticut." His pride was clearly wounded, and Chloe blushed at her rudeness at seeming to imply that they were behind here or couldn't cope.

"Where are you from, Mrs. Fowler?" asked Linda Farmani, drawing near and fixing Chloe with a smile. Her husband walked away.

"San Francisco, California," Chloe said.

"It is so pretty there," Linda said, though she had seldom been there. San Franciscans were so stuck-up about the supposed beauty of their city, and its supposed good food, but in fact it had always been freezing and foggy when she'd been there, in midsummer at that, and she'd eaten terrible previously frozen fish. You always heard that it was pretty. Linda looked past Chloe and around at her room, the marble floor, the rugs. If she hadn't come out here she might never have discovered this flair she had for decoration, for making something beautiful against all odds. She was proud that their furniture had been chosen, like everyone else's in the compound, from the hospital stores, yet look at the difference.

"Where are you from? Your house is so lovely! It's nice of you to invite me to your party," Chloe recited politely.

"L.A., but I was born in Detroit," Linda said.

"It's awkward about Jeff. I know they were counting on him at the hospital," Chloe said.

"How many children do you have?" Linda asked. It was a question Chloe had been asked so often in her life that she could not later remember the rest of this conversation, during which she reflected on the vulgarity of the wicker elephants.

Her real attention was directed to watching Noosheen and

Abbas. A tea party was a pleasant thing, she thought. Perhaps in Iran flirtations were carried on at tea parties instead of cocktail parties, but life underneath is everywhere similar. There was Dick Rothblatt, wearing a tie, talking to the new young American woman, who was wearing a short skirt and high heels. The skirt too short, it seemed to Chloe, for Iran. She accepted more tea from Linda Farmani with a smile eager and festive.

Abbas, standing behind Noosheen's chair, was looking with new attention at a photograph in a silver frame standing on the glossy table: Linda and Vahid with the Shah and Shabanou. He had seen this photo a hundred times, a ceremonial photograph, taken when the Shah visited the hospital. It implied nothing about the political opinions of the Farmanis, yet it struck Abbas now with a kind of foreboding. Perhaps it was because of Vahid's recent strange behavior, his lack of interest in the typhoid epidemic, his refusal to discuss it, his peremptory commands on a number of issues affecting the hospital, eyes trained, it seemed, toward Tehran, in expectation perhaps of favor or reward. If you took the picture from its frame and looked on the back, what inscription would be written on it? Who was Savak in this room? Who was listening to every word, remembering the words? Someone, without doubt.

These thoughts were prompted by having seen in the street today the mother of Zev Zahdi, a young resident in obstetrics who had been imprisoned three months ago for crimes against the state. Mrs. Zahdi had looked at him and drawn up her veil and looked away, mistrusting him. There had been no point in asking her if she had news of Zev. Zev would turn up again, with scars or fingers broken, or he would never turn up. Abbas had stared at the woman, hoping to convey some unspoken message of sympathy and trustworthiness, hoping to convey the information that he was not afraid to look at her. Could Vahid look at her? But these were the people who would naturally be schooled in long, frank glances, a sympathetic softness of the eye, and they would look at her.

"I don't pretend to approve of everything the Shah does," Linda Farmani was saying, astonishing him, as if she could look into his thoughts. The perfect spy can look into your thoughts. Linda, he saw, was talking to others. When she spoke, she pronounced, impressively. Conversations dropped off elsewhere. She held forth, rather. Perhaps it was her very large bosom that made this seem so. She was unconcerned about the forbidden topic of the Shah. "His methods—well, really. But he's done more good than harm. I think the people realize that."

Though this was not Abbas's view he did not contradict her or pick up the discussion. Neither did anyone else. Abbas could if anyone—he was in a way protected by the outright defection of his brother, who now lived comfortably, safely, defiantly, in the beautiful Parisian suburb of Neuilly. No one would believe in the disloyalty of Abbas because no one would believe that someone with so dangerous a brother would dare be himself dangerous or disloyal. The brothers of renegades must keep to a course of orderly preoccupation with their own affairs. Abbas wondered if he would ever see Paris again. Paris was lost to him, his wife and child lost, brother lost, untroubled mind lost. He could enviously imagine his brother, Emir, eyes blazing with devotion to an old imam, eating a croissant, mind untroubled, while he, Abbas, was condemned to a mind tunneled with thoughts of worms and ashes, caring about nothing.

He thought, suddenly, looking at Noosheen, of how at university he and English fellows, or sometimes with a girl, went on the river, hearts untroubled. Then he thought of the feel of a pole as you sought the bottom and the slow push of the punt, and high English laughter. He had been happy then, and yet he had never liked the soft feel of the mud at the bottom of the river. Had that been the shadow of the future?

"Of course you could argue," Linda Farmani said, laughing, "that teaching them to drive doesn't really improve their lives. Costs them their lives more likely. But it's essential to their feeling of themselves as a modern nation."

"Spoken as a child of Detroit," said her husband.

"We have to have the cars, the TVs, the washing machines."

"It's true, I agree," said Noosheen.

Abbas turned to Noosheen—so small, pretty in her blue dress, it was hard to imagine her a mother. He had known her since childhood. He asked after her children.

"It's that he has bad advisers," Linda said to Chloe. "It's hard for an American to keep quiet about things. I just end up saying whatever I think. If they want to drag me off, let them."

"You Americans are very bent on your inalienable rights," said her husband, looking rather as if he wished she would be quiet. Chloe, sensing a family quarrel on the issue of free speech, asked about the flower-flavored candy.

"Bahram won't give me a green stamp for my passport," Noosheen said to Abbas. "Can you imagine that?"

"We are all Oriental despots at heart." Abbas smiled at her.

Chapter Eight
MORNING CHATS

After a week, despite her horrible room and no word at all from Hugh or Jeffrey, Chloe had begun to feel that colonial life, or whatever this could be called, was peculiarly agreeable. The other Americans, except for Linda Farmani, were friendly and interesting, and so were the golden-earringed Iranian wives, especially Noosheen Ardeshir. The social life was casual and constant; little parties drove out after the work day, with Heidi or Noosheen or Abbas Mowlavi, to view a tomb or monument. Women had servants and were thus free to visit or read. Roses bloomed everywhere. People dropped by—Chloe imagined it was like the life of an eighteenth-century village, say, in England, and quite unlike San Francisco, where you had a calendar and penciled things in.

Although she missed Sara and Max with painful emotion, it was somehow pleasant to be without Jeffrey. She loved him, of course, but he was a strenuous person to be around. He had the normal life of a surgeon—up at five-thirty, late ward rounds— and at dinnertime he was often snappish and preoccupied, and, in truth, a little autocratic—a well-known surgical defect of temperament. She could at least tease him about it. Chloe's absent-mindedness she knew irritated him, but otherwise he was proud of her, and happy to delegate to her the supervision of their family and cultural life—tickets for the ballet, opera, string quartets, and the occasional recital. She had once calculated to herself the amount of time it took to get one ticket: conversations with Jeffrey's secretary, waiting on hold at the various box offices, the inevitability of the need to exchange the night. Here there were no tickets to anything, and it seemed wonderful.

Here was a life that seemed natural, and she felt herself to be growing more inwardly calm when she hadn't even been aware of being tense. She tried to do the same thing each day at the same time, like a nun.

In the mornings Dick Rothblatt always stopped to see her after his jog, on his way to the Dermatology Clinic. They drank their coffee on the broad front steps in a spot where the early rays of sun struck through the light fog of the morning. This picnic out of doors seemed more discreet, as well as more pleasant, than asking Dick in to her terrible room. No doubt they seemed eccentric, two Americans having this public early-morning picnic, or perhaps they did not, for the Iranians themselves were forever spreading cloths or newspaper over any disagreeable section of pavement and sitting down on it to eat.

The women passing by gazed round the corners of their veils to see what it was they ate.

Chloe would bring down toast, and afterward give the crusts to the puppy, with whom she was making some progress. He was waiting each morning, watchfully, within his bushy cave, and darted eagerly out when she tossed the crusts, although he still growled when she extended her hand. She had patted him once or twice as he ate, and once he had wagged his little tail, which ordinarily drooped in a churlish, distrustful way. She had named him Rustum, after the Persian warrior in Matthew Arnold's poem, which she had been reading in preparation for her talks with Noosheen.

As they breakfasted, Dick would confide his marital woes. Chloe saw he was someone who found it easy to confide in women, secure in his expectation of their interest. He had been accused, he said, out of the blue, or at least after intermittent quarrels he hadn't taken too seriously, by an unexpectedly bitter Marla, of neglecting her and particularly their children, by being too wrapped up in his work and hobbies. This was so common a complaint that he hadn't even taken it personally; wives were always accusing their husbands of neglect, in proportion to the success of the husband, or so he gathered from the elliptical remarks made by other husbands in the process of being divorced.

"I've never heard it directly discussed, but they blurt it out, you come upon them at funny hours in the hospital cafeteria. Having dinner at the hospital is a sure sign." He wished men felt more able to talk things over among themselves. Marla used to fill him in on the causes of other people's divorces. She had always figured it out, or even talked it over with the wife, and after she told him—"He's never home at all—he's gained all that weight—they haven't made love in nine years"—whatever it was, he could always sort of see the wife's point.

But not so easily in his own case. He knew he was wrapped up in his hobbies, but not to the neglect of anything else. He was interested in almost everything and had a lot of nervous energy to spend, and was also a perfectionist, was not content with his tennis game, his endurance, his salad dressing, his garden, his cellar, his car, even his stamp collection, which he had officially abandoned at the age of fourteen but still, passing the window of a philatelist, added to. He had other hobbies besides. He jogged, collected, practiced, read, much as he had done as a boy, and had been led to believe it was good to continue doing so. His parents had wanted him to be a well-rounded person with values. And he was.

Each morning Dick and Chloe watched the shrouded Iranian women, ample and slow, in their stately procession to the hospital, as patients or on visits. Chloe remembered Marla Rothblatt—tense and small, with a perfect figure maintained by incessant tennis, skin a little leathery. Did he miss her really?

"It's the story of my life to be at the wrong place at the right time," Dick said. "Here it's a time of my life I could be scoring like crazy and where am I but in a land of modest women." He had not mentioned, in his confessions to Chloe, his occasional infidelities.

"Is Marla seeing anyone?" Chloe asked this morning.

"Not now," Dick said. "I told her she should, I'd pay for it. I think if she got some help, she'd see things differently."

"I meant, does she have a boyfriend?" Chloe said.

"Oh, no," said Dick, looking shocked. "Her energy seems to be mostly into studying." His tone was disappointed, as if he would have preferred a human rival, something more tangible than the intellectual fascination of an M.A. in Social Welfare.

"I suppose, all those years of marriage, I was away a lot— I know it was hard on her. But now I could organize my life to spend more time with her. She could travel with me now that the kids are grown. This should have been the best time, now in our forties."

Chloe shrugged. "Resentments build up—you can't just wish them away."

"I'm not resentful," said Dick. "In Iran, did you know?

They have arranged marriages. You think it only happens in India. But they all say it works as well as anything else. Usually Bahram Ardeshir, the pathologist? His wife is young and flaky. That's one mistake I wouldn't make, a woman under thirty, that's somebody's law." His glance at Chloe was so conspiratorial that Chloe, believing herself to look younger than her thirty-five, was offended. Dick, she supposed, was about forty-five. Did this mean that she counted in his view as someone his own age, or someone too young? He talked to her in any case like someone out of the running—but maybe this was because of his acquaintance with Jeffrey.

But she liked having Dick as a friend. His confidences acknowledged her womanhood, and if he was a man who expected women to be endlessly interested in him, Chloe actually was, had always found the marital problems of new friends more interesting than those of old friends, if only because she hadn't heard them as often.

For her part, she tried slyly to introduce the subject of Hugh Monroe. Should they be worried about him, be trying to find him? One heard of the intransigent bureaucracy here, newly elevated peasants who took the rules seriously, and there were rules about visas, bribes, forms. Perhaps Hugh had failed to bribe or to fill out a form? If they knew where he was, they could send money or whatever he needed. What did Dick think?

Dick had better luck than she with the telephone, and more sense of its ways, and made it work as far as the Hilton in Tehran, whence a faint, distant voice told them Hugh Monroe was not registered. Perhaps the Sheraton? The Intercontinental? But the phone would not work a second time.

"We could call the American Embassy," Dick said, "but I wouldn't worry. If he was in trouble, he would be in touch with them himself."

"I'm not worried," Chloe protested. "After all, what do we know about his travel plans? It's just that if he's in trouble— and that's what they heard—it had better be us who try to help, because no one else will." She had, after ten days, the sense that Iranians did not help each other.

When Dick had gone on to work, Chloe went to her apartment again and watered her plants. She had now stolen one each night, and was pleased with the cheerful and colorful effect on the window sills, though she did not like the slightly unpleasant odor of their leaves. Today she was expecting a visit from Noosheen, but planned to remain firm that they must meet outside in the garden, because of the ugliness of her quarters. And if the geraniums were discovered she planned to say what she thought: why should one villa have all those geraniums and this one none?

Chloe found that she had much more to say about Matthew Arnold than she could have guessed. She talked with authority about the self-disgust of Empedocles, and how he represented the ennui and spiritual desolation of the nineteenth century. "He is a symbol of Western man," she said, thinking to lead up to an interesting discussion of comparative zeitgeists.

"Was Matthew Arnold married?" Noosheen wondered.

"Oh yes. Though not much is known about his life. He hated biographies and destroyed all his papers."

"He was handsome," Noosheen said. "See the picture on the front. Blond. I think blond men are very attractive." She giggled at Chloe's blond hair. "Of course there are no blond Iranians."

"I think Iranian men are very handsome," Chloe politely said. "So dark and handsome." Of course they were also short, and she thought them too thin, and always gasping on cigarettes, and their mustaches were wrong. Some were tall and handsome, to be sure—Heidi's husband, Mohammed Asghari, in a portly sort of way, and Dr. Yazdi, and Abbas Mowlavi, certainly; but Noosheen's husband Bahram, who looked about sixty, was one of the small, attenuated kind, with deep, rabid eyes. Chloe wondered if Noosheen had ever loved him, or whether it was a loveless arranged thing, as Dick had said. Poor pretty Noosheen.

"It is so beautiful," cried Noosheen, reading "Dover Beach." "The man and the woman against all hollow change and worldliness. 'Ah, love, let us be true to one another.' I guess Matthew Arnold never came to Iran. Persian men are not ever like that. They are dreadful compared to American men, they only want you to sleep with them and keep house, you can't say a word. They believe they want you to be liberated, like the Empress—she studied architecture. But they don't, really."

Chloe supposed this would be true of third-world men generally, or perhaps of men generally. It must be hard for a young woman like Noosheen to have glimpsed compatible Western couples, liberated Western romance. To her surprise, tears had appeared in Noosheen's eyes. She fished in her bag and drew out the corner of a cloth, which Chloe realized was the corner of a veil, a chador. Noosheen dabbed at her eyes. It seemed natural to Chloe that Noosheen should be disappointed with husbands, having this older and doubtless conservative husband, and she with her good English, and she had probably read God knows what—Betty Friedan? or she might even have read *The Golden Notebook*.

"I am sorry," Noosheen said. "I know this conversation is not about poetry, but you are so kind. I feel you will understand. It is just that I am not in love with Bahram, my husband. In Cleveland I was, I think, but now that we are here he is like my father, not a very kind man, and he is too old for me."

"Maybe it's just readjustment; it takes some time to get settled," said Chloe, who had learned that to sympathize too strongly made people feel worse. Inwardly she felt herself passionately resent the horrid caresses of old Bahram. "How long have you been back in Iran?"

"My husband does not realize that a woman needs—needs"—she sniffed and mopped again at her eyes. "Excuse me. We were talking about ideals and abstractions. I know real life is not the same thing as literature."

She is intelligent, Chloe thought. Too bad for her. And consider that her whole glimpse of Western life had been in

Cleveland. What would she have concluded from Paris or San Francisco? What sort of life did you glimpse in Cleveland?

Noosheen asked Chloe what her husband was like. Chloe described Jeffrey: light-haired, not really tall but medium. A concerned father, sympathetic doctor—Chloe was conscious that she gave Jeffrey the benefit of the doubt on a few points. Noosheen persisted. Did he mind that she worked outside the home? Did he wish for many children? What was his mother like? Chloe answered these questions as neutrally as possible, but her sympathies were animated.

"Read 'Sohrab and Rustum' for next time," she advised, "since it's a Persian story. I'll be interested to hear what you think."

If Chloe had put a glossy sheen on Jeffrey, making him sound bland, affectionate, American, indulgent, blond into the bargain, she was recalled to a more lively sense of him by receiving a letter from him. Hossein laid it gravely on her pillow when he came at noontime to mop.

"Take this to the American woman," Dr. Farmani had told him, holding meanwhile the foreign letters like a fan before him, or cards, and plucking out the one for the American woman. Carrying it along, Hossein kicked at the cur that lurked outside Villa Two.

As usual, every day, the rugs from the hallway of Villa Two had been thrown by the American woman outside and so must be dragged in again and put neatly in the corridor halfway between this wall and that, the green in front, the red and yellow always in the upper passage.

The odor from the kitchen sickened him—the things she cooked in there, unholy and greasy, reeking of pork. He laid the woman's letter on her pillow and hurried away, dampened his mop at the sink and dragged it along to clean the steps. He could smell the perfume.

Chloe was almost frightened to have a letter already, afraid it bore some scary news, though she knew it could as easily be good news. Perhaps any news would give her this queasy moment of irritation, of reluctance to be reconnected to her own real life. But of course she did wonder when Jeffrey was coming, and longed for news of the children. She tore open the envelope. Jeffrey could not yet predict his arrival. Two weeks more, it would seem, at least, and poor Henry still unable to move a limb but most of the neurologists giving him at least some hope of arm movement. Chloe shuddered, read on. The children: "I took them to the dentist, and Sara had two cavities, Max three, and the dentist said he doubted they were being adequately supervised as regards their brushing. He agreed with me that children that age who have had fluoride treatments shouldn't be getting cavities unless from neglect, or too many sweets. I've asked you so many times to be more watchful about what they eat."

Chloe's despair was immediate. Her own teeth had required endless fillings before she was twelve. Her children had inherited this bad luck, this bad enamel. She did too supervise their brushing, that is, always told them to brush their teeth. It was true she did not stand over them night after night, but neither did Jeffrey; he would always make sure to have something better to do. Anyway they were good children and did brush their teeth; it was bad luck, bad heredity, her fault. She seethed, agonized. And how could she watch, every moment, what they ate? They were school-aged children, they went places without her. Why couldn't *he* watch what they ate? He took no responsibility—her fury rose, and the worrying vision of Sara and Max suffering dental pain.

From the fan of letters Vahid Farmani picked out the other letter from America and threw the rest on his desk. As he read, he was conscious that his throat had somehow sealed itself up with intimations of horror. It was only a letter from Dr. Fowler, University of California at San Francisco, yet his hand shook. He laid it down with the others, picked it up again, might want it for evidence, or maybe should destroy it unread, lest it be used as evidence. So sorry, was all it said, unaccountably, unavoidably delayed. "I do hope Mrs. Fowler can stay till my arrival . . . her project . . . we will appreciate your hospitality to her project undertaken in the same spirit of Iranian-American friendship. . . ." Though Dr. Jeffrey Fowler did not say so, Farmani guessed that this meant that Dr. Fowler was not coming at all. He breathed deeply, got a hold on his emotions, told himself this was lucky, this clarified matters, the better to put him on his guard.

For it was clear to him, obvious, a beacon of clarity, that despite the many letters from him, there was no such person as Dr. Fowler. Or if there was, this letter was not from him. The real Dr. Fowler was perhaps even unaware that he was awaited in Iran, his name being used so that this woman could be planted here. The false Dr. Fowler of the letter obviously a member of the CIA or who knew which faction of what party, the woman their spy. Farmani read the letter several times, to be sure if he had understood it, studying it for clues to its origin, its motives. So sorry, not yet coming, please allow my wife to stay. That was clear, but clumsy. The CIA was always clumsy, that's how you knew they were behind it.

She will be expecting him to say, Oh, Mrs. Fowler, so sorry about your husband, of course you can stay. He will say nothing. Let her wonder if he's got the letter yet. Clumsy of them to put a woman spy in an Islamic country, or fiendishly clever, no, clumsy; you could follow their thinking: "These Muslims think so little of women it won't occur to them to take one seriously." But the CIA had forgotten that he, Dr. Vahid Farmani himself, had an American wife and knew to take them seriously. He resolved to take some measure—something to put the awful woman a little in his power.

The center of social life in the evenings, at least for the Americans, was the Cyrus Hotel on the edge of town, a large structure of cement and plastic turquoise panels, built by the Shah and run by the government to encourage tourism. There was thus a Western-style bar where people hung out like expatriates in a movie, and a restaurant, and a general air of adventure and camaraderie that attracted foreigners, and even the more Europeanized Iranians, like the Yazdis or Abbas. In contrast to an evening at the Cyrus, an evening at Villa Two was unendurably bleak, if only because the light bulbs were so dim, too dim to read by, and when she had asked for others, first of Hossein and then of Dr. Farmani, and was refused, she had bought one herself, and blown out all the lights in Villa Two and Villa Four as well. Chloe's experience with the light bulb was talked of at the Cyrus, and everyone had a story like that about his own quarters.

Beside the foreigners of Azami Hospital, the other people who frequented the Cyrus bar were hotel guests, or Americans or Europeans who lived in Shiraz and worked for Grumman or Procter & Gamble, or Aramco people who came to Shiraz from Saudi Arabia for rest and relaxation. An R and R woman told Chloe that Shiraz was heaven compared to Saudi Arabia, where Saudi youths chase you in pickup trucks right into the American compound.

"Good grief," Chloe had gasped, "trying to kill you?"

"Not really. I don't think they would kill you. But they didn't use to come right into the compound."

"What can you do?"

"Myself, I carry a whip," the woman said.

With such interesting revelations to be had there, Chloe had taken quite unself-consciously to going to the Cyrus each night. Sometimes Dick Rothblatt or Junie Fay would come by for her, some nights she went alone.

One night someone tried to pick her up in the Cyrus bar. She sat drinking alone, too early for the others, feeling convincingly expatriated, and a man in a white suit sat down next to her, his frank American leer rather charming, until she heard the Texas accent. Still, she reserved judgment.

"Loyal Cooley is my name," he said. "Waco."

"Chloe Fowler. I'm from San Francisco."

"Like it here?"

"Yes, I love it," Chloe said, silently excepting her feelings for Villa Two.

"Of course, the poverty," he said.

"Well, yes."

"It isn't quite like it seems, though. These peasant women, they all of them have some gold, gold bracelets or whatever. I heard once how much gold is salted away in these Eyeranian villages."

"That's interesting," Chloe said. "What are you doing here?"

"Consultant," he said. "Consultant and barfly. I get enough of *them* during the day, Eyeranians."

"I'm waiting for some friends," Chloe said. "I'll introduce you."

"Much obliged," he said. "Have you tried to get opium yet?"

"Good grief," said Chloe. "No."

"The Shah runs the show," said Loyal Cooley. This casual mention of the Shah made Chloe's flesh creep. She had already absorbed the local reluctance to pronounce his name. Obviously this Texan is a narcotics peddler, she thought, or maybe he's a narc. She refused his offer to take her home.

Chapter Nine
THE BAZAAR

Some for the Glories of This World; and some
Sigh for the Prophet's Paradise to come;
Ah, take the Cash, and let the Credit go,
Nor heed the rumble of a distant Drum!

"This is my last cigarette," said Dick to Chloe at their morning coffee on her steps. As a dermatologist, Dick had not had to advise people to quit smoking—that was up to their internists. But, with the new evidence about skin wrinkling, it was going to be coming up in his own practice, and he was not the sort of hypocrite who would advise others to quit while still smoking himself. Also, he was persuaded by the evidence of heart attacks, cancer—good God, could there be any doubt? He was especially motivated now by looking at the Iranian men, all of them smoking, it seemed, all of the time. It was pathetic. Victims of U.S. tobacco interests, entrapped by their sad, limited notions of macho. In a way it was embarrassing to be a male smoker. Maybe it was really embarrassment that now stung him powerfully. All the same, quitting wasn't going to be easy.

He had plenty of female support, from Junie Fay, who said, "About time." She had contempt for the whole problem, and her contempt was something of a goad. Of course she didn't smoke, except grass. Chloe Fowler was much nicer and more understanding, even though she was a typical California health nut and didn't smoke either, and ate the typhoid salad.

"This is the cigarette I'll really miss, the first one in the morning with coffee," Dick said. "Luckily there are no bagels."

"You should just give up coffee for a few days," said Chloe in her practical way. "Days or even weeks. The thing is to

break all the associations. The craving is just a matter of con-
ditioned association. We'll switch to tea, like Iranians." How
New York Dick is, she was thinking, or did she mean Jewish?
since the jokes that characterized either of these conditions
were more or less interchangeable, jokes about mothers or psychiatrists, or heartburn or bagels. Of course some people in
California made psychiatrist jokes and mother jokes, but they
were mostly from New York and Jewish. Even Dick had brought
with him a supply of Tums, which he surreptitiously popped
after even the blandest Iranian lunch; and a touch of spice
would provoke him to say something like "I suppose I'll pay for
this later," indigestion forming a conventional part of his discourse, like "hello." Chloe had never had indigestion except
once during pregnancy, and believed you got it from being
made conscious of it by an anxious, obsessed parent. She had
carefully avoided all mention of digestion to her own children.

Dick's digestive lapses, whether regional or ethnic, were
rare, no more than odd touches from time to time. Otherwise he
was funny, courtly, and in an unexpected way attractive, for
someone short with thick glasses—he was even sexy, because of
the vitality with which he bounded around. Vitality was the
secret to sex appeal—she wished she herself did not feel so the
reverse of vital—so languid and growing stupider, it seemed to
her, daily. Sometimes she caught herself thinking nothing at all,
and would hurriedly think of her children, to atone.

"Give up coffee?" Dick said, wondering how he was even
going to get through the day, especially with Abbas smoking in
front of him. He had broached the matter of quitting to Abbas,
who merely shrugged and smiled his beautiful, melancholy
smile, and said he knew he should. Bahram Ardeshir, the pathologist, had shown them the blackest, most horrible pair of
lungs ever seen. They had belonged to a tribesman. "They get
it from building fires inside their tents," the Iranian doctors
had explained, as if cigarettes had nothing to do with it. Dick
fixed his mind on those black, horrible lungs and finished this
last cigarette.

He was dawdling over his coffee, waiting for Junie to join them on an expedition to the bazaar. She was waiting a discreet interval so that it wouldn't seem as if they had spent the night together. In fact he had thought it unwise of her to spend the night—the Hendersons in the adjoining apartment could not help but in time become aware of her, though it probably wouldn't matter to them. But, instead of going back to her own apartment, Junie had fallen sound asleep, exhausted from the horrors she had been discovering on the OB-GYN service.

Dick was tired too, had slept badly after a marathon night. Junie did not really like sex much, it seemed to him, but always wanted to go on and on in case she might. He wondered why it was his fate to love, as opposed merely to sleep with, these tense and nearly inorgasmic women, why condemned to toil to exhaustion for their apparently tepid and infrequent pleasure when it must be just as easy to fall in love with a cheerful, bouncy, normal enthusiast. Slyly he wondered about Chloe Fowler. You simply could never tell. He had slept with a lot of uncomplicatedly sensual women but could never predict in advance. That these were not the ones he fell in love with he supposed was a problem in himself, some unconscious reluctance to find too much sexual competence in his partner. Why this should be so, though, he could not tell, nor did he think it was fair that it was he who tossed and turned, while Junie slept soundly, just as if she had enjoyed it. He had tossed and turned and worried that the Shah had some sort of morals police who came and got you in the night, and about how she was going to leave without being seen in the morning.

Dick believed that Chloe did not realize about him and Junie, with Junie being so much younger and so on, but Chloe had put two and two together, easily, upon learning that Junie had been a student on Dick's service at Princeton. It all followed: Junie and Dick have an affair, it is the last straw for poor Marla—who knows what else she has had to put up with—and she throws Dick out. Probably Dick wants to marry Junie but

Junie isn't interested in commitment. To Chloe's mind Junie, though she seemed perfectly nice, wore her hair too long and wore too-short dresses of rayon acetate printed with flowers. When she realized how it was with Dick and Junie, Chloe felt a little betrayed, though she knew she had no reason to, by Dick's having confided in her, all those complaints about poor Marla and other intimate revelations, and all the while withholding this one vital detail, no doubt because it diminished his right to complain about poor Marla. He didn't want to admit to being an errant husband screwing around, just like all other philandering middle-aged men. Was his heart broken about Marla as he seemed to say, or was he really in love with Junie, or what? It occurred to her that it was perhaps gallantry that prevented him from discussing Junie with her, an instinct, perfectly correct, that women of her age do not like to hear about men's affairs with girls in their twenties, even from men they aren't interested in themselves.

"They are the cruelest people I've ever seen," said Junie as the three of them were walked to the bazaar. "They do everything to women without anesthesia—childbirth, D&Cs, anything. They let them tear themselves up before they'll do an episiotomy. They do *those* without anesthesia. A woman in labor forty-two hours—a terrible breech position—they wouldn't let me do anything to help. Her screams! I might as well not be here, I can't help. I can't stand to see it. Women die in childbirth right here in the hospital. We've had seventeen maternal deaths! Boy, I sure am learning. Chauvinist bastards. They hate women here, the OB men as much as the rest."

"And nobody is doing anything about the typhoid," Dick put in. "Maybe it's the Latin temperament. Que sera sera."

"But this is not a Latin country," Chloe objected, "it's an Islamic country, riddled with inhibitions and taboos, and they believe in kismet."

"It's certainly taboo to mention the typhoid. I've been wondering if they've been instructed, by the Shah or someone, to, you know, *let it happen*. It's happening in the poorer quarters, naturally. There's also a food problem here, and a population problem. These despots . . . Hitler . . ."

"Oh, Dick, really. They probably are doing something, searching out the wells. They don't need to discuss it. Anyway, Hitler *built* hospitals, not that I'm defending Hitler, or the Shah either, they say he pushes drugs, but you shouldn't exaggerate." How impossible that Abbas Mowlavi, or the nice Mohammed Asghari, or anyone she had met here would allow another human being to suffer or die of disease. That's why they stayed, to work for their people; otherwise they could go and practice in Cleveland or Cornwall. She reminded Dick of this.

"Stalin allowed millions of peasants to die of disease and starve," Dick repeated. And, of course, he had. He thought of the boy he had seen that morning, huddled all alone on the bench outside the Dermatology Clinic, reluctant to come in, but then the boy extended his arm, and running along the forearm was a terrible gash of festering black flesh. If you woke up, thought Dick, and found that on your arm you would die of fright; *an American would be dead of fright.* Perhaps the boy had been frightened; there was something in his gaze into the eyes of the doctor that had implored information. Was it a death gash, death flesh? This was a boy of fourteen.

"It's anthrax," Dick had said to Abbas. "I suppose?" He had never seen a case.

"Yes, we see it often. The boy is a handler of goat meat."

Abbas had reassured the boy in Farsi. The boy smiled a little and wiggled on his chair, life returning. Dick had smiled at him. But how many boys are there like this, he had thought, who don't come in?

Dick was in the process of buying a rug, and on an earlier visit had narrowed his choice down to several. As they approached the stall where the first was to be found, the owner scowled, then, recognizing Dick, smiled at them and waved them in. They stood at the edges of the rugs as he unfolded them and stared down into the gardens of flowers and shimmering red. Dick suddenly doubted that he could remember which one it was he had liked. "Meshed? Khorassan? Saruk?" the man intoned. "Sinneh?" A goaty odor of wool and ammonia stuffed their nostrils.

"Sinneh!" cried Dick, remembering the name. It was a beautiful rug of black and red, with tiny flowers and vines. "This one!"

"Oh, lovely," said Chloe politely, thinking how it was like being shown someone else's child—she had seen three she preferred in the pile. Dick, however, beamed down at this rug, and of course it was beautiful.

"This is of the wool of very young animals, that is why the exceptional quality. It is the practice in Sinneh, and note also the very fine knotting. Truly this is an admirable rug, and of course therefore very expensive."

"Obviously very expensive," they agreed. "Too expensive, I'm sure," Dick added, and made a feeble attempt at bargaining, which he had been told was obligatory.

"Don't you think you should get a silk rug? Those are the most valuable?" Junie said.

"Well, I hope to get one silk, one wool."

"There'll never be a better time," Junie agreed.

"Uh—there's one or two more I've seen down the way. I'd like to have another look," said Dick timidly, not looking forward to the prospect of barter and hoping the merchant would just follow him, if he left, lowering the price at each step. Chloe and Junie followed him with, it seemed to him, misplaced confidence in him and developing ideas of their own. The rug merchant shrugged and began to pile his rugs again. Dick and the ladies began to look in the next stall.

"Mikhaham yek qali," Dick had learned to say in all the stalls of the rug merchants of the bazaar. "It's beautiful," Dick said, "but too large. Too big? I've just got a small place. I'm divorcing, so I just have a small bachelor pad. Not that I don't plan to get a bigger place. In general houses and apartments in the U.S. are getting smaller." The next merchant, smiling and nodding with the appearance of great interest, had already begun to pull out another, smaller, from his myriad wares. Dick caught, though, a glance between Junie and Chloe, a nonspecific glance that told him he was embarrassing them or confirming some view they had of him, he didn't know what. "Of course, I know these are heirlooms, you pass them down for generations. I have a daughter and two sons, I suppose I should get three!" He took a deep breath and stopped himself. Why was he going on like this? He wasn't someone who babbled on to shopkeepers. Did he always do this? He remembered long conversations with the checkout girl at his grocery store in Princeton, though he would have said that was because she was pretty. Did Chloe and Junie talk about him, agree between them that he talked too much to shopkeepers? What an irritating idea. But now the man was spreading at his feet the carpet of carpets, unsurpassed. His smile of crooked brown tobacco-stained teeth leered friendship. It was surely a kindly feeling that had made him rifle his pile for the finest, the not-shown-to-everybody.

"That man didn't understand one word you were saying," Junie said, in such an exasperated way that Chloe could not have failed to guess their intimacy.

Now they were carrying a rug, huge and monumentally expensive, between them like a log, with Chloe putting her hands on its underside in a way meant to symbolize helpfulness and walking along sideways with it like a pallbearer. People seeing them coming leapt over the jube ditch and stood in the street to watch. They were silent. Dick liked to think their silence was a form of reverence for a magnificent rug going by.

In the gathering heat of the afternoon the merchants of the bazaar rolled down their metal shutters. Chloe imagined them asleep amid the rugs or sitting in darkness with glasses of tea. She and Dick and Junie took tea in the government tearoom, which remained open for tourists. Minted tea, though Dick glowered suspiciously at the leaves of mint, imagining where they had grown, in typhoid-infected water. Then they wandered to look at the craftsmen making lacquer boxes or wares of brass, condemned by the Shah's forward notions to a nine-to-five life within a restored precinct of the bazaar.

Dick kept admiring his rug, rolled and bound with string, its muted underside hardly disclosing the splendors of the pile side, a wonderful tangle of brambles and rhomboids and birds, admired by both Junie and Chloe Fowler. He thought of how Marla would feel, seeing it in his apartment. Marla would have the good taste to envy it.

It *would* be nice to buy a rug, Chloe was thinking. Judging from the prices, these rugs were not exactly cheap but nothing like at home. She tried to think of ways of getting money, or getting word to Jeffrey to bring extra money. Then she scolded herself; the materiality of her life was just what she wanted for a little time to escape. Austerity was the lesson of Villa Two, which she had thought she was already beginning to learn. But perhaps one for each of the children, as heirlooms?

At dusk, crossing the garden on her way to the Cyrus, she was conscious of the snuffling of the puppy, creeping closer to her dangling hand than he had dared before, his spindly tail twitching with the suspicion of an impulsive wag canceled midway through. He was the wariest puppy she had ever met. Perhaps this was a breed of dog unused to domestication; perhaps these dogs had run wild here for centuries.

In the big house, lights began to come on, rosy behind the wooden lattices. In one way, Chloe rather yearned to be inside Linda Farmani's lovely room, and at the same time she relished her feeling of exclusion, isolation, and anonymity. When Jeffrey came they would have to take their place in the little round of suppers that occupied families in Azami Compound. Really it was good for her to be on her own for a while.

She brought a subject up at the Cyrus that night: Why are we here? Why am *I* here? Dick Rothblatt didn't think in his case there was anything peculiar. The breakup with Marla had nothing to do with it. If they had been together, he would have brought her. She would have enjoyed it. Or maybe he had thought his affair with Junie would be a little less conspicuous in Iran than in Princeton—just till things got settled with Marla. His lawyer had hinted, actually, that if there was anything like that going on, it was well to be discreet. But mostly it seemed to him, as he now said aloud, that he had come to Iran because he wanted to see Persepolis. He was interested in antiquity and also in Islam. And—it just now occurred to him—he was interested to see if the dry desert air of the Middle East would cure the patches of psoriasis from which he suffered from time to time.

"Everybody is here for a reason but me," said Chloe. "I'm here by accident of marriage."

"Not really. There is no such thing as accident," said Dick.

"The Eyeranians aren't bad by and large," said the Texan, Loyal Cooley. "I never mind them." The other Americans exchanged glances. Loyal Cooley seemed to have traveled widely, and to have had a bad experience wherever he traveled. They were always relieved when no Iranians were present to hear Cooley's xenophobic diatribes.

"But where you don't want to mess around," Loyal Cooley said, "is with these crypto-commies, these commie-nazis, like in East Germany. Nazis by nature and commies by training, that is the worst combination, real mean sons of bitches. I'm talking about the time I was driving from Yugoslavia to France. You can drive on the autoroute in East Germany but they warn you to stay on the autoroute; it's just a way through. So okay, but then I see a woman by the side of the road, and a flat, it's just natural to stop, so I stop. We fix the flat, okay, and I'm about to pull out when three carloads of police, soldiers, *federales,* whatever you call them, hem me in, force me back on the shoulder, make me get out, crack my head against the car, accidentally, while they verify who I am, where I'm going. Then they let me go, okay. But the really vindictive thing was they then made me wait nine hours at the border. I show them my papers, they tell me to wait my turn, they throw the papers at the bottom of an inactive pile and I sit there for nine fucking hours. That was my little punishment, see—'you vill do as you are told.' "

The company nodded in genuine sympathy. All the same, they hoped Loyal Cooley wouldn't be around every night. He had been there every night for a week so far. No one knew what he did: "consultant and barfly," he would always repeat. All his stories concerned times his life had been in peril.

"Didn't anything bad ever happen to you in Texas?" Chloe asked mischievously once.

"No, but well, you see, I know a lot of people in Texas."

When Cooley had gone to his room, Dick said, "In London they have *Guide to the Texas Gentry,* put out by the genealogical people, Burke's." The Americans all laughed.

"Someone told me they have more French furniture in Dallas than in France," said Chloe.

"Style *tous les Louis.*"

"You have to admit Tex-Mex food is good," Junie said.

"But it's the Mex that's good," said Dick.

Chloe walked home from the Cyrus with Dick and Junie, and said goodbye to them at her door.

When she went upstairs she noticed at once that someone had been in her room, moved things, left them faintly awry. She didn't at first feel afraid. They could have been that way in the afternoon or at dusk; she might only just now have noticed. It could have been Hossein moving things to clean. Hurriedly she checked for her little wrapped flannel roll of jewelry and her camera, and found them. She had heard people who had been robbed describe their sense of violation and outrage although she didn't quite feel this, no doubt because it wasn't really her room. But she became uneasy all the same and looked carefully in the bathroom and under her cot. She opened the drawers of the bureau and looked in expectantly, looked again more carefully. Everything was there. On the table a sheaf of papers and xeroxes was scrambled and disarranged. It must be secret police looking for documents and disloyalty. It was what you expected in a police state. She told herself not to be shocked, and that there was no danger in having books about Sassanian glazes.

Then suddenly she felt unaccountably faint. She went to the bathroom and washed her face, then lay on her cot. It was fear—the blood rushes to your heart or stomach and leaves you feeling faint. Perhaps it was a routine thing, she told herself, that they come in and search your room. It could have been done this afternoon when she was at the bazaar. It would be the spies of the Shah, Savak; she had heard that they were everywhere and that you would not know which person was the spy. But she had also heard that you could always tell them, that they were perfectly evident, fooling only each other. But that was talking of professional spies. Her mind churned with questions of spies. In Iran, she supposed, you would have amateurs whose real interests lay elsewhere, recruited from necessity or self-interest into part-time informers, observers, assassins, perhaps. Abbas, Mohammed, even Heidi, who knew?

A new chill of fear welled up in her. Her lapis beads. Her favorite lapis beads, the only thing she had worth stealing. They had not been in her jewelry flannel but in the top drawer next to her passport, and, she was sure, would not be there now. Sick with dread, she flung herself at the drawer and tore it open. The beads were there, next to the passport. Elated, grateful, she snatched them up. Chill stone, yet for the moment most precious—valuable, a present from Jeffrey, old and favorite. She would have been literally sick to lose them, desolated, unable to continue. Grateful for this narrow escape, she put them on and warmed them against her throat with her hand, melting under their comforting weight and at the thought of what a close call it had been. Whoever it was might just as easily have tucked them into his pocket along with whatever else he was looking for. She got into bed again, breathing deeply with relief, and fell almost immediately asleep.

Chapter Ten
SHAHPUR'S CAVE

Into this Universe, and <u>Why</u> not knowing
Nor <u>Whence</u>, like Water willy-nilly flowing;
And out of it, as Wind along the Waste;
I know not <u>Whither</u>, willy-nilly blowing.

In the morning it had seemed almost not to have happened. She could imagine having moved things herself, she could almost account for all the disorder. Nothing was gone. With daylight, things are not frightening.

Today was the day of a drive and picnic at Shahpur's Cave at Nam-al-Rush. People had stopped asking Chloe about Jeffrey's arrival, but they still included her in these pleasant hospital outings, and her opinions, owing to her archaeological connections with Shiraz University, were sought when planning sightseeing expeditions. People considerately took her down side roads to stare at ruins. She found it gratifying to have her least exclamation on the beauty of a fragment taken with special force. Luckily she hadn't been asked questions beyond her depth, and she tried to expiate a slight feeling of fraudulence by reading and study. It was her hard luck that she was finding Sassanian pots rather plain and boring, compared to the vivacious masterpieces of China, about which she lectured at the museum. But little by little, *faute de mieux*, her interest was growing.

Besides Jeffrey, people had in the last few days stopped mentioning Hugh Monroe, who had apparently come to seem, like Jeffrey, apocryphal or legendary, just someone who was coming sometime. But Chloe was afraid their silence on the subject of Hugh meant that they had some terrible news of him and were waiting to find out whether it was true.

"Or else they don't care," she had complained to Dick Rothblatt. "Maybe they think that Americans are just capricious and unreliable and don't turn up. Maybe it happens all the time that people don't turn up. And meantime poor Hugh Monroe languishes in some hideous Iranian prison."

The party assembled at Abbas Mowlavi's house. He drove Chloe, Dick Rothblatt, and Heidi and Mohammed Asghari in his BMW, while Ali Yazdi drove his wife Zareeneh, the Hendersons, and Junie Fay in the hospital station wagon. Heidi had confided to Chloe as they walked to Abbas's that she had fears about his driving, and the likelihood that his recent bereavement had made him reckless. "If he won't slow down, we'll insist on getting out," she said. Now, however, they were in the car, and Abbas was driving at a stately pace, playing Mozart tapes. He had a huge tape deck and a horde of tapes stored under the knees of Dick Rothblatt. Squeezed in the back between the Asgharis, Chloe felt cozy and contented. In America, she was thinking, if you had an expensive tape deck like Abbas's in the car it would get stolen.

Abbas, suddenly prey to a feeling for Persian music, had changed the tape. It was no more than a wish for the sweet, energetic wail of a voice like Leila Midias. "My heart has never known such sorrow, when will I again know happiness? Return, oh happiness, to your unfortunate daughter; we will drink together at the well." He was happy enough. Pleasant company. Heidi and Mohammed were his oldest friends in the world—they had been together at Oxford—and the new people were agreeable, and the afternoon warm.

They had to pause at a small bridge to allow a party of people on horses and mules to pass by driving sheep and goats and camels and cows. These were a sort of gypsy people, as nearly as Chloe could tell. The women wore gypsy clothes of spangled nylon and embroidery, and glittered with paillettes of brass. Their brown faces were smiling. Barefooted they pranced alongside the animals, driving scattered children and goats together in a flock, babies and lambs strapped to the backs of pack animals, and the men in ragged pants walking along, looms folded, tents folded, enormous chatter and calling, and a waft of the odor of camels.

"In the days of the Shah—of the old Shah, the father of the present king," said Mohammed, "it was forbidden to take a picture of a camel. He had the idea that it made Iran appear backward."

Chloe took out her Minox. "Would you say they are twenty feet away? Or is it infinity?"

"Those people are an infinity away," Abbas said, laughing.

"In a month," Heidi was explaining, "we won't even be able to cross the road here, it will be so crowded with the tribesmen and their flocks. It's pretty, the migration, it's something to see. I suppose that gypsies originated here. Does anyone know? The same clothes, the beautiful colorful dresses, and the women seem as free as birds. Of course they work very hard."

"I believe that gypsies came from India," said Chloe.

"Yes, you must see the migration," Abbas said. "It's a busy time at the hospital. They drop people off when they go by and plan to stop by at the end of the summer to pick them up if they're still alive. Sometimes all our beds are full all summer with stranded old tribesmen. Often they die while the people are gone, and the families don't find out until they check back in the autumn."

"Oh, how sad," said Chloe.

Abbas liked Rothblatt and Mrs. Fowler, liked their interest in Iran, their questions and smiles of appreciation. Some Americans seemed frightened or offended or critical, sat stiffly; some were reluctant to leave their quarters. Finally, he supposed, he was a traditional man and preferred the modest demeanor and domestic virtues of Iranian women, but there was something attractive about the best sort of American women, their curiosity and poise. The worst ones were all wrong—the terrible voices, the loud laughs. Chloe Fowler's voice was more like that of an Englishwoman's. At Oxford he had had affairs with English girls, who were alike in being stubborn and thick-ankled, but he had liked their high, musical voices, which rocked like little sailboats up and down with their musings. Mrs. Fowler's voice was somewhat lower-pitched. An American woman, he thought, listening to Leila Midias, probably could not sing an Iranian song.

Chloe had imagined that Shahpur's cave would be below ground, under a mountain, but instead it had to be entered at the top of a perpendicular formation of rocks, nearly a thousand meters high, to which it was necessary to ascend along a switchback path on foot or by means of donkeys, which were produced on every hand by a myriad of little boys who lived in a village at the foot and tended coolers of Pepsi-Cola for the occasional traveler. At different times, the caves had been the headquarters of Sassanian chieftains and a hideout for robbers, and a place of worship. Heidi, Zareeneh, and Mrs. Henderson were put up immediately on donkeys. Chloe, who hated riding, wavered between the horrible prospect of clinging for two hours to the bruising back of a donkey and of seeming rather ostentatiously fit, then chose the latter, despite the fearsome incline of the path and the sun, which had begun even now, at eleven, to broil. They were followed at a distance by the little boys on their donkeys, who seemed skeptical of their prowess and determined to be there when the moment came—as it quite soon did for Dr. Henderson—when the hikers would flag and require donkeys. It was really very steep, hot, rocky. Chloe, who had believed that women have more stamina than men, envied crossly the brisk steps of Abbas and Dick Rothblatt and Junie ahead of her. Dr. Yazdi and Mohammed came behind her, more slowly than she. For nearly an hour they toiled along the path, unable to converse and keep the pace at the same time, each more or less satisfied with his performance, the boys riding happily and carrying the picnic.

At the top, the path opened out onto a broad table of rock, like a stage, and at the rear of this stage, forty feet above them, was an overhang of rock. Standing on the stage, stretching up to touch the rock ceiling, stood a colossus of stone, armless but huge, which had been invisible from below because of the angle of the cliffs. They walked amazed around the giant feet, the Iranians patting them fondly as if here was a pleasant, long-lost household god. They debated whether to picnic before or after the descent into the caves.

"In any event," said Chloe, "I'm not going into the caves."

"Do you suffer from claustrophobia?" asked Dr. Yazdi.

"A little," she apologized. It was just that the mouth of the caves, a stairway of wettish rock leading down into invisible blackness, looked appalling to her. This must be claustrophobia. She felt she could not make herself descend those steps, down which the others so blithely gazed in anticipation.

"The boys from the village have flashlights and lead the way," he said.

"Nonetheless," she said.

"Perhaps you are thinking of the Marabar caves, and Miss Quested. Remember Miss Quested?" said Dr. Yazdi.

Chloe, not thinking of books, said that she didn't know a Miss Quested, and Dr. Yazdi laughed with pleasure at catching her lacking in knowledge of her own literature. *"Passage to India,"* he whispered, leaning intimately toward her ear. "When Miss Quested, finding herself alone with Dr. Aziz, imagines she has been molested. Or is molested. It is never quite clear."

"It's been years since I read it," Chloe said. His smile, sympathetic or triumphant—she could not tell which—broadened.

"I'll stay up here with you. I have been down in the caves before," he said. "We can spread out the picnic." While the others filed along out of sight into the interior of the earth, they unfolded a cloth and began to spread the contents of the drinks cooler that had been carried up by the donkeys. She did not quite like the way his hand brushed over hers as they smoothed the cloth on the dusty rock floor. "My idea is to read the great Persian poets while I'm here," she said. "Sa'adi, Hafez. It is a very rich tradition." Her chatter filled the silence.

"Yes," said Dr. Yazdi, "the classical days of Persian poetry were very rich. Both narrative poetry and love poetry, but mostly a distinctive genre of philosophical, meditative love poetry. The manuscripts, which were often illustrated, are great treasures in themselves."

"Yes, I imagine."

"My father was a collector, in a small way. Some are extremely curious," he said.

"I'd love to see them sometime," Chloe said. "Persian miniatures . . . museums . . . so beautiful." She moved away, with a great display of business with her camera, to try to photograph the valley below, leaving Dr. Yazdi to finish putting the paper plates around.

Chloe managed, by earnest photography, to keep conversation with Dr. Yazdi brisk and general. She found something alarming in his intimate manner, insinuating that they shared the same hobbies or beliefs. His manner to others appeared different, even rather aloof. He spoke English like a German in a play. Certainly, she admitted, he was well read. But there was something oily and familiar about him. Perhaps *he* was the Savak agent.

"They have been gone a long time," he remarked, after numberless minutes during which they gazed at the Iranian plain and commented on the birds that darted among the rocks below. "Excuse me, I will walk a little way along the path." Chloe continued to sit, watching him walk to the edge of the chasm and peer into it. She was again thankful she had not gone down. Then it was as if Dr. Yazdi had conjured up spectral music from the bowels of the earth, for she began to hear eerie singing coming forth from the bottom of the cave.

"It is the singing of the cave boys," he called to her. "They guide the party along the path by means of their song. Isn't it pretty?" And it did seem to Chloe the prettiest music she had ever heard, the little boy voices, the strange Persian melody, cadences as in a call to prayer, the words—who knew, but surely words about safety, carefulness, returning to the light.

Now, beneath the sweet voices of the singing boys, they came to hear the rising, agitated sound of adult voices, speaking loudly, an occasional shout. First emerged the little boys with flashlights; then Heidi, Zareeneh, and Mrs. Henderson tottered into the daylight, their terrified faces belying the beauty of the song. The little boys, too, now broke and ran to Dr. Yazdi, shouting and waving their flashlights, and casting frightened glances behind them down the stairs. Chloe's first thought was that something had happened to the stout Dr. Henderson. She could not understand the agitated conversation in Farsi, but Heidi cried, "Quick, hurry, quick," and Yazdi hurried to her. Chloe found herself running too.

"Something really terrible," Heidi was saying. "A wounded man down there, terribly battered. We've come up to get a blanket and Ali Yazdi to help."

The boys danced excitedly at the mouth of the cave, waiting for Dr. Yazdi. Yazdi efficiently negotiated from a donkey boy his sturdy cloak and saddle blanket. Carrying these, he followed the boys.

"What did you see?" Chloe asked Heidi, who swayed in a greenish, faint way.

"I couldn't see much," Heidi said. "One of the little boys caught a glimpse of a foot by the light of his torch, then this arm sticking out at a grotesque angle, and then, as the men investigated, a groan. The person is still alive, a man, and they're going to bring him up. I suppose he fell or something. Horrible. It could happen all too easily, someone going in there alone or in the dark. That's why the little cave boys."

"How awful," said Chloe, although she knew herself to be less horrified than poor Heidi, whose face was very white and moist with shock. So too Zareeneh Yazdi, who sat, shuddering, on a rock.

"They think it's a Westerner by his shoes," Mrs. Henderson said, causing Chloe suddenly to fear that it was Hugh, and that this was why he hadn't called or come. Her stomach crawled; she fought off the idea because it was ridiculous. They were miles from Tehran, and there were thousands of non-Iranians in Iran, and millions of Iranians wearing Western shoes. Dr. Yazdi probably was. Probably they were all, in her party, wearing Western shoes. The chill of terror lodged between her shoulder blades, irrational, immovable. She breathed deeply through it.

"People don't realize how dangerous," said Zareeneh. "These were bandit caves in olden days; this is where they put their victims—murdered them and dropped the bodies down."

"Dragged them all this way up," marveled Heidi.

"Made them walk up, then killed them. Our nurses used to tell us that if we weren't good . . ."

"I thought these were holy caves," Heidi said.

They were surprised after only a few moments to see some activity at the bottom of the steps, but it proved to be Junie Fay, whom Chloe had forgotten. She had stayed below with the other doctors but now approached, wrinkling her nose in disgust.

"Ick," she said. "Trauma is not my thing. It takes a certain type."

"What's happening?" cried the other women.

"Well, they're carrying him out; he's barely alive. We'll be able to tell more when we can look at him in the light."

The song of the cave boys, before so high and sweet, now seemed to the ears of those waiting above to have an operatic dirgelike quality, a little company bringing up their dead from the underworld. Despite themselves, the five women moved toward the top of the path and peered down, soon to see the tiny sparkles of the flashlights, then the faces of the boys, then the doctors, carrying something slung in a blanket, a wrapped shape that swayed unpleasantly. Once at the top they laid it on the ground and unwrapped the bloodied face of a man, barely alive, his tongue sticking horribly out of his mouth, and a hoarse sound rasping from him as he breathed. Dick and Dr. Henderson in English, Abbas and Ali Yazdi in rapid Farsi discussed what steps to take. Heidi had poured water but the doctors waved her away.

"No telling how long he's been down there," said Dick.

Abbas had begun giving directions to the donkey boys, who leapt alertly forward, preparing their animals to carry the man. Dr. Henderson was listening with his ear to the man's chest, his fingers clutching his wrist.

"He's very very weak," he said. "Exposure. There don't look to be any wounds."

"Lacerations," said the doctors. "Superficial? Heart attack? Concussion?" They muttered among themselves as they lifted him onto a donkey, gingerly, draped like a saddlebag, face down over the saddle, and tried to pad his face comfortably against the jiggling ride. His eyes suddenly opened and looked around him in terror. Then they fluttered shut, and he groaned.

"We're going to help you," Dick told him, walking alongside as the donkey lurched away. "Everything is going to be all right." The party set off. Chloe, looking around behind her up at the cliff saw the little cave boys, watching them and drinking the Pepsi they had brought for the picnic and left behind.

"Dear me, what a pity," said Heidi suddenly to her fellow Englishwoman, Mrs. Henderson. "What a sad ending to our outing."

"Yes, dear me," said Mrs. Henderson.

From time to time Chloe looked ahead, with mingled curiosity and dread, to where the moribund figure flopped against the thigh of the donkey. A dying man is an inconvenience on a picnic. Dr. Yazdi pushed by the women and hurried off down the trail, saying he would get the car and be waiting with the engine running at the bottom. They would rush the man to the hospital. It made Chloe somewhat anxious to reflect that though this was a party of six doctors, not one of them appeared to have done anything to help the man. They were doing no more than anyone could do. You preferred to think that doctors could do miracles, but of course they cannot.

At the bottom, with all haste they laid the poor man on the cloak stretched out in the back of the station wagon. Junie and Dick crawled in beside him and crouched over him during the ride. Chloe and Zareeneh sat in front with Dr. Yazdi while Abbas drove the other car. They hastened along the gravelly road. Too energetic speculation was curtailed by ideas of seemliness, in case he was, in his coma, able to hear them. A too-intrepid hiker, they imagined, venturing down there without a flashlight, or with weak batteries. Chloe could not take her eyes off his bloodied hair, of a light brown color, slightly curly, and soft like the hair of a child. Junie stroked the hair off his forehead, and his eyes flickered open.

"I don't like the sound of his breathing," she whispered.

"Pardon!" said the man indistinctly.

"Shhh, shhh," said Junie, holding his wrist.

"He might have been looking for something," Chloe said. "Archaeological, I mean. He could be a scholar or spelunker."

"Oh," cried Junie, "I think this is it." She leaned forward, listening at his lips. She shook him a little. "This is really frustrating. Can't you hurry?"

The car was hurtling along the road at a speed far faster than safe. Zareeneh and Chloe both clutched the dashboard.

"Yeah, I think he's gone," said Dick surprisedly. "Well, the poor bastard." He and Junie began to thump on the chest of the man, who in fact looked the same as he had moments before. But gradually to Chloe's eyes an indefinable deadness seemed to solidify him, even his torn trousers and his socks. Junie pressed her mouth to his dead mouth in a terrible embrace, which Chloe realized was really resuscitation, but Dick shook his head. Whatever had happened could not be reversed. Gradually they sighed and sat up, and arranged the cloths around him. Chloe saw Junie wipe her eyes. Dr. Yazdi drove as fast as before.

Dick wondered if he wanted a cigarette. If he was ever going to backslide, this would be the logical time. He wanted a cigarette, but it was a pallid inclination, not a violent craving, and could be resisted; it was like sex, sometimes, or like looking in a store window at something you thought you wanted. Just a stir. He was pleased. It was no more than looking in the L. L. Bean catalogue, or Orvis at the most.

Presently Junie, who had been staring bitterly at the dead man, crawled toward the front seat, to his feet, and began to pull at his shoestrings. It seemed a bit late.

"Torture," she said. "It's just a hunch. You often find something on the soles of the feet."

It seemed to Chloe that a flicker of dismay crossed Ali Yazdi's features. Perhaps he was offended that torture was the first thing foreigners in Iran would think of, the way Americans are offended when Europeans go on and on about mugging.

Junie had taken off the shoe, a new crepe-soled shoe, and was pulling off the sock, Dick watching with an expression of revulsion exactly reflecting Chloe's feelings. Zareeneh Yazdi, who had never ceased to shudder, buried her face in her hands, but Chloe couldn't help but look. The sole of his foot was pale as alabaster, untouched, untortured. Junie began nevertheless to tear off the other sock. She flung it crossly away. Dick recovered both socks and put them in his pocket. Junie put the shoes back on the dead feet.

"The police. Clues. Don't you watch cop shows?" They laughed, but uncomfortably, wondering if there were police of the regular sort here. You only thought of secret police knocking in the night, but of course there must also be ordinary police to deal with the ordinary matters of murder, traffic accidents, wife beating. The laughter and the thought of television eased the oddness, the sadness, strangeness.

The two autos arrived at Abbas's house, whence they had started. It was now late afternoon. They alighted and stood around irresolutely. It seemed wrong to say goodbye and shuffle off to do something else; all seemed to feel that by mere presence they could somehow dignify this unexpected event, or that they would be needed by the police, or something. Perhaps others were as reluctant as Chloe to return to a solitary apartment to meditate on the unexpected way that death can appear at a picnic and take you away.

Abbas Mowlavi's idea, and Ali Yazdi agreed with him, was to take the body to the Pathology Department, to determine there the cause of death, meantime notifying the police. Ali Yazdi went off to find orderlies to carry the body. But evidently he encountered Vahid Farmani on the way, for he was back in no time, looking exasperated, accompanied by Vahid, who was shouting in great agitation and wringing his hands in violent distress, almost as if he knew the man, though he did not even glance at him. Vahid shouted in Farsi, and Ali and Abbas answered in more reasonable tones, but the others understood none of it. Presently Ali, looking angry, pulled the station wagon into Abbas's carport, with the dead stranger still inside. Vahid Farmani, coming a little to himself, looked at the English speakers and explained, with unconvincing calm, "It has nothing to do with this hospital; the correct thing to do is to take him immediately to the police. Perhaps you could all—not the ladies—go along. Dr. Henderson, Dr. Rothblatt, you, Abbas, of course."

He rushed off. The men piled into the Volvo and drove off to the police station without goodbyes. Zareeneh Yazdi excused herself too. Heidi, Mrs. Henderson, Junie, and Chloe, shaken and eager to talk, decided to go have a drink in the bar of the Hotel Cyrus. Later, writing her postcards in the dim night light of Villa Two, Chloe put only that she had been on a picnic and had a chance to ride a donkey. Could Jeffrey read between the lines her agitated spirit?

Not too much longer before we are all together. Love to Dad and you both.

Mom

Chapter Eleven
THE LOAN

Perplext no more with Human or Divine,
To-morrow's tangle to the winds resign,
And lose your fingers in the tresses of
Thy Cypress-slender Minister of Wine.

The dogs in the night seemed close under her window. She woke with a pang of worry about her family, then Rustum, then Hugh, and then lay awake turning over the strange events of the day with a dawning fearfulness on her own behalf. Until now she had felt safe, even well cared for, in Shiraz, but it was as if she had been injected with some poison of new apprehensiveness, which she could feel proceed through her body like hemlock. At home, after a near miss with the car, after an instant on a swaying stepladder, she had felt fear in a rush and then righted herself, but this fear was systemic, settling over her like a new condition: she was not at home here, but far away where the rules and ideas were not the same and no one was especially designated to look out for her, and people came into your room, and if you died you might be put down in a cave.

The shoes of the dead stranger remained in her memory, clear, especially poignant. Brand new, some kind of Hush Puppies. Why was there something especially poignant about shoes? Shoes are symbols of life and hope. If you knew you were going to die you would not buy yourself a new pair of shoes. When but in choosing new shoes are you ever so legitimately self-absorbed, moving your toes inside them, feeling the stiff, resisting backs, wondering how you will look in them? She thought of the poor little Iranian men she had seen in the bazaar, with their wild, hunted eyes; she imagined them standing at stalls wondering how they would look in new shoes. Every poor person—maybe not in Africa—sometime has a new pair of shoes. When you die your shoes remain; they represent you. You must always have neat, well-tended shoes; her mother had told her this, she had told her children. Even now they had begun to be careful of their shoes. In a foreign land you might die—in a cave, in the river, like the wife and baby of Abbas, or like the women at the hospital when Junie Fay could not save them. Where was Hugh?

Of course she had not really believed Iran would be a foreign land. She saw the deficiency in her imagination, that she had not been able to imagine with sufficient intensity the alien condition. A well-traveled American with no anxieties about hotels, headwaiters, planes—her imagination had provided her with no more than a benign region of camels, and mosques, and well-run hospitals of the American kind.

Even the difficulties—she thought of her outrage at the state of the kitchen, the rugs—had not seemed beyond the power of an indignant woman who was in the right, a woman with standards that no one could seriously question. She had assumed she could put things right, as always. Now she saw that this presumption was naïve, limited, unimaginative, and wrong. She felt her own foolishness. Tears of pity for the poor dead man came to her eyes, and at the same time a feeling of gladness that these correct sensations of fright and humbleness had come to her in time. She was cured of her American presumptions. This was all good for her. What had the man in the cave thought, realizing he was going to die so far away in Iran? This is real, she thought with a shiver. I am not at home here.

Noosheen, in the morning, by the mysterious process that served in the absence of what Chloe considered working telephones, had already heard the news. She had heard it from Heidi. They drank tea in the morning sun in the garden. Geraniums, dry in their pots, bloomed charmingly, and the world recovered something of its normal aspect.

"It must have been horrible for poor Abbas," Noosheen remarked. "I should think such a thing would make him think of the past—you know," talking as usual, Chloe noticed, of "poor Abbas," though when Chloe saw him he always appeared to be smiling and relaxed, addressing himself to some practical matter in the present and not romantically harrowed by his recent tragedy. But Chloe could see how Noosheen might imagine in him some attractive melancholy, especially when compared to the mundane, elderly Bahram. Chloe encouraged Noosheen to talk about Abbas, which she always seemed eager to do, elaborating on his brilliance, the excellence of his education, the bravery with which he had faced sorrow. "He is my true brother. I have always thought of him as my own brother," she said. Chloe thought it must be hard for a young woman like Noosheen, finding herself on the cusp of social change, aware that elsewhere in the world—America, for instance—women had lovers, divorces, married for love, to be herself disposed of in the old-fashioned way. Noosheen told about her marriage. Bahram, a widower, friend of her parents, had paid them a formal visit, almost as if he were another, new person, to ask for her hand. "It was very exciting at the time," Noosheen said. "Ah well. I cannot stay long today. I have a new washing woman, and I cannot bear her, so after I dropped the children and the nurse in the park I came here. The washing woman looks at me with scorn because I am so Westernized, I know, but the pity is I am not so Western I do not mind the stares of certain old women. I suppose they remind me of my grandmother. My mother is a perfectly modern woman in most ways."

"Old women always try to make young ones feel guilty," Chloe said. "We must remember to never do that when we get old."

"If I had a washing machine I think I could control my life much better," Noosheen said. "Another woman to deal with, it's just too much. An ordinary Maytag, like any American woman, it's not much to ask."

They proceeded to talk of "Empedocles on Etna," and Chloe marveled at the shapeless property of poetry: it was like a big sack, to hold whatever it was you were thinking of.

> *The weary man, the banished citizen,*
> *Whose banishment is not his greatest ill,*
> *Whose weariness no energy can reach,*
> *And for whose hurt courage is not the cure—*
> *What should I do with life and living more?*

This made her think of the dead man in the cave, or even of herself, of course, except for not being a man. Noosheen had been caught by other lines, sometimes puzzling ones. When they came upon the lines

> *But the solitude oppresses thy votary!*
> *The jars of men reach him not in thy valley—*

she looked at Chloe with the faintest suggestion of confusion, as if to ask what are the jars of men? When Chloe told her—noises, rude interruptions—it seemed to her that Noosheen pinkened a little. Goodness knew what she had thought men's jars were.

> *And we shall be the strangers of the world,*
> *And they will be our lords, as they are now;*
> *And keep us prisoners of our consciousness,*
> *And never let us clasp and feel the All*
> *But through their forms, and modes, and stifling veils.*
> *And we shall be unsatisfied as now;*
> *And we shall feel the agony of thirst,*
> *The ineffable longing for the life of life*
> *Baffled for ever . . .*

At the mention of veils, Noosheen cried out, "How true, how true!" Earnestly, in the warm sunlight, they discussed pessimism. As she was about to leave Noosheen said pessimistically, "Once you get used to an automatic washer, it's hard to go back."

Noosheen's visit, as welcome as always, today afforded relief from the fears of the night and memories of yesterday, or perhaps it was the poetry that had made Chloe feel better. Here was an ordinary day, an ordinary visit from a woman friend, tea, lawn chairs, problems of love and laundry. When Noosheen had gone, Chloe piled the cups on the steps for Hossein to carry up when he came at noon, and she went along to the shops to buy her groceries. This was always enjoyable; because it involved transactions with real Iranians, she was left with the feeling that she became each day more in touch with the life of Iran.

Chloe was sorry to be cut off from the real Iranians, to whom she could never speak, yet she could peer into their lives—the mother sitting on the ground unwrapping meat and handing it around to the children, the men staring into distance, holding their beads, sitting on the benches in Azami Compound, waiting outside the hospital; or the crisp little nurses in their white half-veils, or the typists coming out of the office buildings at the university, in bright clothes and gold earrings, swaying in high heels. She would have liked to be a friend of one of these families and visit them and see into their house: what phonograph records did they have, what did they talk about; what did the taxi driver say, going home at the end of the day? Or Hossein? Did he talk to his wife? Did he berate her or laugh with her? The women talked and chatted in the bazaar, the men muttered and smoked, glaring out of their stalls, people dozed in the sunny noon hour, or sat unmoving on their haunches at the edge of the road. Some thin, tormented souls were chained to opium.

*   *   *

When she got back to Villa Two, she lingered outside to make sure Hossein had finished her room, then took her milk and eggs up to the refrigerator. It was not so much that she dreaded to meet him as her feeling that he dreaded to meet her. His eyes always slid away from her, burning strangely. Today he had gone, but he had brought the mail and laid it as always on the pillow of her cot, an odd gesture of intimacy from a person who never looked at her directly.

On top a letter bearing an Iranian stamp, in an elegant envelope of thin paper with flowers of blue and gilt surrounding the name of the Hotel Shah Abbas in Isfahan. She knew the writing to be Hugh Monroe's, though she was not sure what he wrote like. Despite her excitement, she opened the envelope with great care, thinking that she could put the beautiful envelope up on her wall.

A note. Her eye went to the signature. Hugh.

Dear Jeff and Chloe:

I plan to be here in Isfahan this weekend, at this hotel. As everyone says you must see Isfahan, that goes for you too. I'll make you a reservation, and hope you can come up after work on Thursday night, or even on Friday, if Allah permits the planes to fly then.

Best, Hugh

That was all. She looked at the envelope with a sense of deep anticlimax. No explanation of his absence, no special clever between-the-lines hint of his fondness for her. Nonetheless, joy and relief welled up in her, and then a start of alarm when she realized that Friday was yesterday, and that Hugh would have given up on them. She prepared to rush to the airline office, then remembered it would be closed until four. She paced in frustration.

"Chloe, are you home?" Dick Rothblatt called outside her

window. She peeked out and waved, and he headed up her stairs. He was coming from the American consulate, he said, where he had been at the insistence of Vahid Farmani, to see about the dead body.

"Because I'm an American—though Abbas came too—Vahid thinks I speak for dead Americans wherever they turn up."

"*Was* he an American? Do they know who it was?"

"They don't know. The police thought he was. They'd have nothing to do with him. Then we went to the Consulate and the American consul took fingerprints, but he said he was quite sure he wasn't American. Who knows? There were no labels in his clothes. And his haircut—what did you think?"

"Have you had lunch? Would you like something?"

"Well—sure. We could go eat at the hospital."

"I have hardboiled eggs. I could make egg salad."

"I'd have a beer?"

"Wine? I like the wine here."

"Fine. The funny thing was Vahid. He was on the phone to the consulate shouting at them—'It has nothing to do with us. Leave Azami out of it. It has nothing to do with Azami'—you got to thinking, Jesus Christ, maybe it does."

"Vahid has a hard life—crazy American doctors, dead bodies," said Chloe, her tone expressing her dislike of Vahid.

"The epidemic is getting worse. Three people have died. In the olden days hundreds of people would have died."

"I must have misunderstood him," Chloe said, thinking that Dr. Farmani had told her there was no typhoid.

"This really is a dump," Dick said, looking around at Chloe's room. The remark surprised her. She had thought she was making some headway, and had sewed a red and green pillowcase out of a flowered fabric from the bazaar, to put over her pillow during the day, and the rest of the piece was draped over the sofa like a slipcover.

"I could give you my rug, you know, loan it to you. I'm getting another one; I've about decided on that Sinneh."

"That would be wonderful," Chloe said, seeing that Dick's rug would add a lot to the room.

"Sure, I'll bring it over later," he said, realizing, though too late, that Junie might be a little irked. He did not feel that Junie was very aesthetic-minded. Her taste was not equal to Marla's, whose keen glance dismissed a hemline, a color, and told him what he needed to know or think about someone's dress, not that she was so damned infallible, but she knew more than Junie, who, after all, had more important matters on her mind. Junie surely wouldn't feel the lack of the rug, temporarily, but she might take offense anyway, as if this were in some way a pass at Chloe Fowler or—he reached nearer the truth of his intuition—as if this were a gesture of affection to Chloe standing in for Marla—Chloe another legal wife, like Marla, whose whims took precedence over those of unmarried women. Dick did not always, he knew, understand women so accurately. Usually they accused him of not understanding, or of being not understanding, which they explained was not the same thing but equally his crime. But he knew he had got to the truth of Junie's probable reaction.

And of course he had got to like Chloe, for her own sake. It was interesting how you seldom got to know the wives of your colleagues. He had always thought of her as a pretty appendage to Jeffrey Fowler, whom he thought a stiffish but pleasant surgeon, more intellectual and less of a fool than most surgeons. Whereas she was really herself, a rather odd woman whose views were often the categorical opposite of Junie's. She was an extremist, vehement like Junie, maybe all women were. He believed that vehemence was sometimes a substitute for sense. Chloe announced once that she was an anti-vivisectionist. That was funny from a woman whose husband did medical research. Once she had remarked that frigidity was a moral defect, a symptom of selfish egotism, and Dick had felt mildly defensive on Junie's behalf.

"I don't know," he said, "haven't you ever just had an inept lover? Sometimes it's just an inept lover."

"I don't think I have," said Chloe, "but maybe I'm just too easily pleased."

Dick had thought that, although this was good news from Chloe's point of view, from a man's point of view you would never know whether you had specially pleased her. You liked to think that you had specially given someone pleasure that another had not, that you were the best lover. He thought of the poem by Browning, read in—my God, high school—where the husband killed the duchess who smiled at everyone.

How could you tell about frigidity anyway? If they scrunched up their eyes and groaned a little how could you tell? Maybe other men could tell. Women told him he was good, except Marla, who only told him when he wasn't good, and Junie, who never bothered to dissemble. How could you tell? It was a subject he had never heard discussed. If only men discussed sex more, the way women do. He had always been shocked at the things Marla told him she had heard from, or told, her women friends, things no man would mention. Anyway, Junie, even if slightly frigid, was not a selfish egotist as Chloe would have it.

What he had liked about Junie, when she was a medical student in dermatology, was her scorn for dermatology, her need for more dynamic afflictions, her restless competence, as if mere boils and rashes couldn't calm her. This was secretly the way Dick sometimes felt himself, although he told himself and her that if she got beyond the prevailing hospital population of drug reactions and mild dermatitises she would see the interest in your lupus, your pemphigus, your jungle rot. But she had gone on to OB-GYN, become a resident there, then chief resident, and he never saw her except in the doctors' dining room, where he remembered her, a cute kid.

Then he had gone down to the OB service to consult about a baby born with thrush so severe it appeared to have been dipped in oatmeal, the very look of it had scared her, and her fright, in turn, had been endearing; her eyes grew large and tearful whenever she looked at the pitiful, itchy little thing or thought of how the mother would feel to see it. After this, they had coffee occasionally, and he began to confide in her. It was at a shaky point in his marriage, he was having a battle over space with the chest service, and was suffering a painful tear of the achilles tendon (tennis).

"My roommate's gone this weekend," she had pointed out one afternoon late, meeting him in the elevator. They exchanged an unmistakable look. "I'll fix you some supper at my place." The roommate, the chief surgical resident, was a man, which he only found out later.

She had grabbed for his cock the minute they were in the door of her apartment, and they'd made it, him wearing his cast, and then gone back to the hospital together later to look at their patients. Quite a large proportion of the residents and interns were women these days, which did have this terrific advantage. Both he and Junie had got to really like, or love, each other besides. He remembered she had actually made the supper too, smoked salmon and cream on pasta, after they had made love and ward rounds.

If Junie complained that the rug was gone, he would point out to her the real source of her objections—jealousy of Marla; meantime he went over to his apartment, rolled the rug, and carried it back to Villa Two, where it did improve Chloe's room a hell of a lot. Dick thought Chloe was being very brave about Jeff's absence; it was now a couple of weeks she had been here alone.

It was only after he had gone that Chloe, looking with satisfaction at the room, which seemed livelier and improved beyond measure by the rug, saw on her pillow another letter, this from Jeffrey.

I just thought you would want to know the results of my conference with Max's summer-school teacher. He is be-hind in math, for one thing, but more alarming to me was her feeling that he is a lonesome little boy, who needs more hugging and physical reassurance. She says she takes him on her lap almost every day, whenever she can. I had strong feeling she thinks of him as virtually a neglected child. Of course I know you don't neglect him, but you can imagine how she received my information that his mother was in Iran!

He was not sure when he could fly out. More later. Love, Jeff. Irked beyond measure, Chloe flung the letter on the bureau and hurried out to try to buy her airline ticket to Isfahan.

Chapter Twelve
DIRTY LAUNDRY

A Hair perhaps divides the False and True;
Yes; and a single Alif were the clue —
Could you but find it — to the Treasure-house,
And peradventure to The Master too.

Getting to Isfahan was perfectly simple, many flights daily, pay with your Amex. Chloe wavered about whether to wait until morning or take a flight that night at seven, knowing it would be more sensible to wait till morning, when if Hugh was not there, or if she was unable to get a hotel room, she could nonetheless look around Isfahan and come back. But it was hard to think of passing a lonely evening in the silence of Villa Two, or even at the Cyrus, when she might be with Hugh; and after all the Shah Abbas was probably a perfectly straightforward hotel, state-owned like the Cyrus, where they spoke English and tourism was encouraged. The mysteries of a taxi in Isfahan were the most she had to fear. Isfahan was after all not a cave. She booked for the night flight and went back to Villa Two to throw her things together. In the taxi to the airport she remembered that she should have put some food out for Rustum. She was not sure he could forage for himself now that she had been providing, and feared that he had been spoiled by civilization.

It was exciting to see Shiraz drop away below, proof that, wherever you are, you needn't stay there. The city looked small and dignified in the twilight, a tiny green patch on the wide brown plain. You could not have said it was Persia or anywhere else, it was just the world. She had the pleasant sense of competence that goes with travel.

Once buckled in, she could reflect upon her situation with Hugh. Arriving without Jeffrey would make it perfectly clear that she meant to go through with something they had only spoken of hypothetically, in the course of some impassioned kissing—an illicit weekend, something so relatively hard to arrange in America, in their respective situations, that it had the glamour of the unattainable. Chloe, and, she trusted, Hugh too, hadn't given up hope of some furtive embraces, maybe at a medical meeting, but unfortunately, because Jeffrey was a surgeon and Hugh an internist, they didn't often go to the same ones. Now the delightful presence of opportunity filled her with happiness and desire, and some misgivings too in case Hugh was not quite ready to have this sprung on him. But what kind of man, in that case, would he be?

Next to her a plump Iranian businessman who said to call him Teddy, and whose necktie was Gucci, told her to look below them, as they approached Isfahan, at the moonscape of brown mounds, like elaborate tunnels, pushing up the earth of the desert.

"Those are the qanats," he said, "tunnels that draw off the moisture of the desert to water the town. They are a mystery that no one has ever understood except the builders of the qanats; it is an age-old secret."

"How wonderful," said Chloe. How wonderful that there are still marvels, strange races of qanat builders. It meant that your own life could become strange.

In Isfahan, with great equanimity, she commanded a taxi and pronounced the name of the hotel. Driving through the streets, she could almost feel she wouldn't mind if Hugh was not there, it was so beautiful, so fabled and fanciful, the cobbled streets, arched porches, mosques. The voices called from minarets. The dusk promised wonders in tomorrow's sunshine of azure and cerulean tile, resplendent domes of shining blue. The shapes of the arches bespoke a confusion of successions, some for the better, some for the worse, of Achaemenians, Sassanians, Macedonians, and Mongols. Over the city, the lights had begun to go on. Chloe exclaimed in pleasure and anticipation. The taxi driver told her in good English that the tallest tower in the huge mosque behind them had once been entirely filled up, by the bloody Tamburlaine, with human skulls.

The Hotel Shah Abbas, built from a palace of the great Shah, was so beautiful, vast, and sumptuous that Chloe at once decided to stay a day or two whether Hugh was there or not. It was funny to imagine Jeffrey getting a huge Amex bill with lots of charges for caviar. She had expected there would be more caviar in Iran than there had been. Well, so far there hadn't been any.

She asked for Dr. Monroe, was given his room number, and motioned toward the house phone. But he was not in his room. She settled, not discontentedly, in the beautiful lobby to wait and watch the other guests, rich-looking tourists with smart luggage, the sight of whom affected her with a sort of pleasurable trance. She tried not to think directly of the happiness of seeing Hugh, but rather let the prospect warm her obliquely. Two women with cameras sat near her speaking French. Within the interior courtyard, visible through the long windows, fountains splashed at either end of a magnificent longwater. A scent of jasmine everywhere.

Hugh came in almost immediately. The Frenchwomen, whom Chloe was watching, saw him, and, following their appreciative glance, Chloe saw him, a handsome man, not in jail or dead, walking in, carrying a plastic bag, looking tall and

Western in his pink oxford-cloth shirt. Her idea of the scale of men's size had altered slightly since she had been in Iran so that he seemed huge. She half rose, gave a little wave, and was seen by him. He approached, smiling the formal, delighted smile of someone who discovers a friend in a hotel lobby.

He kissed her cheek. "You got my letter. I was afraid you wouldn't."

"Yes," Chloe said.

"Where's Jeff?"

Chloe grinned. Hugh was astounded, disbelieving, but looked sincerely jubilant when she told him. Jeffrey somehow in America, Chloe here alone, with him. Chloe watched his expression for signs of discomfort but it was impeccably of happiness.

"I booked a room for you and Jeffrey," Hugh said. "But of course it'd be nicer if we stayed together." He led her toward the elevator, past the desk. Despite her intention of going straight to bed with him, with no priggish demur, she felt herself blush, mind floundering around after a perky remark. Hugh's expression was perfect, not leering or knowing. "Shall I say we won't want it?" he asked.

She heard herself laugh nervously. It was scary going to bed with someone for the first time. The urgency, something clumsy always sure to happen. The possibility of disappointment on either side. She stole a glance at the size of his hands. Strong, manly large hands. She imagined her own body creased with red puckers caused by the elastic in her bra and pantyhose, or wrinkled with cellulite.

"My wife has arrived, but not Dr. Fowler, so he won't be needing his room," said Hugh to the man at the desk. At the elevator he held her back so that another couple could get in and ascend alone. She wished she were perfect, unmarked. Moist sensations of desire. In the elevator Hugh kissed her very ardently. When a couple got in at the mezzanine, they got off and walked the second flight to Hugh's room, so they could clutch each other rapturously in the passages.

He carried her across the threshold of his room.

"This is it, then," he said, smiling at her. She smiled too. Harmless adventure, was her thought. It will make me a better wife. Where has he been these past two weeks?

He began to kiss her and to unbutton her blouse. "Beautiful Chloe," he sighed. Chloe bloomed under his touch. Really, not making love for two weeks, it was bad for you, she wasn't used to it, you needed a man's attention. His chest was hairy and broad. He took off his glasses. It was going to be easy. It was going to go forward smoothly. What was behind it, this wish to have a particular person inside you? It will be terrible if we fall in love, thought Chloe, rapturously clasping him with her knees as he entered her. Her heart overflowed with love and sensation.

Their passion was enhanced by the uncertainty of their situation, by the separation, and by the tracery shadows falling softly through the drawn screen and the musical sound of splashing water in the courtyard below. It was even nice that there was no artificial air-conditioning, thought Chloe, lying contentedly, but warmly sticky, in Hugh's arms. It was the more exotic, the more Persian, the more meriting this unlikely trip. It was the sort of night to look back on, when you were an old woman, as a perfect one, and a perfect evening is more, she imagined, than many people have their whole lives long. She couldn't remember ever, with Jeffrey, having this powerful intimation of the beauty of love-making, and of its connection to the antiquity of the world. Chloe stroked Hugh's large, sunburned back. His hair was fair; he must burn easily. How she loved him. There was also the fun of having got away with something. She realized that she had not really thought of her children all day. I am not happy, I am not lucky, she told herself, lying, for fear that happiness and luck would bring down something bad on them. On the wall a little picture bordered in flowers showed a warrior on a white horse riding toward them waving his sword, and ladies under a tree laughing.

Hugh was Chloe's second-and-a-half affair. She prided herself on being immune to or above matters of erotic fashion, as propounded, for instance, in ladies' magazines, which seemed indeed to affect her friends, who were now becoming lesbians, looking romantically at boys of seventeen, or speaking of the new chastity. She thought of herself as old-fashioned; that is, she had reservations about divorce, and certainly did not believe in open marriage, and did believe in adultery of the old-fashioned scary sneaking-around kind. She saw that it could easily happen to you that you might fall in love with someone or want someone to whom you weren't married, and that this was a well-known pitfall of life, or perhaps a reward for taking seriously the responsibilities of adulthood. So she had been pleased to have this happen to her very pleasantly and so far without consequence. The only problem she foresaw with Hugh was that she could fall seriously in love with him, but she felt protected by the fact of his living in Rochester, New York.

Their natural affinity and sympathy had become gradually apparent during his sabbatical in San Francisco, when they found themselves laughing at the same things, ordering the same things in restaurants, once or twice a glint of sympathy from Hugh when Jeffrey behaved like Jeffrey in some especially boring way, usually by announcing just as others were going off to hear the balalaikas in the square that he and Chloe were tired and going home. Hint of a glance from Hugh, nothing indiscreet, nothing tactlessly critical, for Chloe was a loyal wife, in a way. Just a note of fellow feeling. Then she was seized by terrible gloom when his sabbatical was nearly over, and found herself looking around rooms for him at parties where they both might be. Alone together once or twice on strolls around gardens, they fell into amazed embraces. After her involvement with Hugh, Chloe became, she felt, more beautiful, and much nicer to Jeffrey. But then Hugh had gone back to his usual life as a professor of medicine in Rochester. He had been married twice, she had heard, though he had only mentioned once, and was recently divorced. She didn't really know him very well.

"Now," said Chloe—for they were hungry, were dressing, were going to go down—"Why didn't you call? Everyone in Shiraz thinks you've been arrested. I would say they were frantic, but they seemed rather sanguine, I thought. I was afraid to death. 'Detained,' they said. Dick Rothblatt and I tried calling various hotels. Well—were you arrested?"

"I didn't realize people were worrying," he said blithely. They had found an invitation in their room:

Dear Guest:
 Welcome to Shah Abbas Hotel. You have been one of us since only a few days or a few hours. I will be pleased to meet you tonight between 6pm and 7pm at a business cocktail on your honor. Certainly, you will meet other hotel guests which might be an opportunity for a new deal!
                              Sincerely yours, The Management

"Certainly we should check this out," said Hugh.

At one end of the lobby, in a lounge off the bar, they found a number of foreigners in various groups, sipping very small cocktails presented from trays by circling waiters, and the management, a dark, bowing man, shook their hands. In another mood perhaps they would step forward and speak to the French ladies, or to the businessmen in their ties. As it was, they wanted only to talk to each other. Chloe again brought up the subject of Hugh's absence, feeling, as she complained to him, her resentments rise, as at a found child. She'd been so worried.

"I thought you were in jail; we all did. We called the Hilton—Dick Rothblatt and I—and we spoke to the American consul in Shiraz—he was supposed to be checking." But Hugh only laughed to hear of all this concern. He hadn't sent word because he didn't know they were worrying.

"But it was indeed trouble with my visa. I had to go back to London and wait for one. I'd forgotten to get one. I arrived with no visa, and they wouldn't let me in. I telephoned Guz Mohadim at the Tehran medical school to see if anyone could do anything and no one could. I had to turn around and go back to London—one good thing, Pan Am had to pay—some rule because they had forgotten to ask me if I had a visa. Otherwise I would have been out seven hundred bucks into the bargain."

"It's funny you didn't go to Tel Aviv, or someplace closer than London."

"You had to go back to where you came from."

"You'd been in London?"

"For a few days," Hugh said. "And never once thought of looking to see if I had an Iranian visa."

Hugh was quixotic, Chloe had observed before. Maybe that was why he had been divorced twice, once more than was normal for people their age. Quixotic, mysterious.

Would revelations, intimacies, emerge in the unexpected companionship of days or weeks relatively free of concern about being caught? Chloe felt a little worried about that. An affair might owe its charm to the excitement of agreeable danger. Also, she had so little to reveal, she believed. She felt inwardly ordinary and uncomplicated and was afraid that her plain personality would not support intimacy. Surrounded suddenly by the complicated beauty of the Persian décor, and by the mystery of Hugh, she felt herself to have no reserve of mystery, no temperament sufficient to intrigue others, no self-consciousness or demands. The demands of demanding beauties, she had noticed, were usually met, but she never had any. She could hardly, for example, demand fidelity from Jeffrey, even if he had been inclined to infidelity, which he was not. His vices were his work and his woodshop. Even as a child she had wondered at films where the pregnant woman experiences a craving for pickles and makes the man jump up and go out in the night. During her pregnancies she wouldn't have dreamed of bothering poor Jeffrey, who worked much harder than she did, but what was worse, she had experienced no unusual cravings. She regretted this curse of reasonableness, and longed to be, but knew she could never be, flamboyant.

Hugh's very blitheness was part of his mystery, for two divorces, if that was true, hinted at complications of character, of intriguing difficulties, though in the long run she hoped nothing really sinister, like parsimony or an overwhelming affection for his mother. For the moment it was enough to be in a splendid hotel with this handsome man, to lie, later, in his arms again. The catch of being his wife would be that other women would always be chasing him, maybe just as she had. Had she? She allowed herself, as they stood side by side in the cocktail reception, smiling and greeting others, to enjoy the idea that other people would believe them to be husband and wife.

They had dinner in the hotel dining room. In Hugh's opinion the dinner was not very good, but it was wonderful to Chloe, which showed how her standards had changed in the two weeks she'd been in Iran. They had caviar, which was splendid, but it was brought with thick slices of some American sort of white bread like Wonder bread; Hugh grumbled. Maybe he was a person who fussed at his wives about their cooking?

They had coffee in the garden. The dome of a mosque was reflected in the moonlit long garden pool. Little lanterns bobbed over the heads of the French tourists at other tables. "Très jolie, jolie, jolie," was murmured everywhere. Then they went again to their room, which smelt of sex, like caviar, to enjoy each other again.

When they had sunk into the sleep of the love satisfied, entwined as Persian flowers, they were startled by knocking at their door. They dragged themselves awake. Hugh pulled his trousers on and opened the door. Chloe cowered, indiscriminately fearing a variety of things—morals police, Jeffrey, a fire in the corridor.

An Iranian man in a turtleneck sweater, thuggish-looking but somehow familiar, thrust into the room, with a furtive glance backward down the corridor. Robbery, Savak?

"Hey," said Hugh, backing away. "What do you want?"

"You were in the restaurant tonight," said the man, his tone accusing.

"What of it?" said Hugh, his indignation growing as his head cleared. "Get out of here."

The man pulled a paper out of his inside pocket. "You signed this check?" He confronted Hugh with the dinner check.

"Yes, of course. There."

"Yes, but see, you signed it in red."

"For God's sake," said Hugh. "What of it? My pen was red."

"Red, sir, that is not legal. I think the American Express would not pay."

"Of course they would pay. Give it to me, give me your pen." Irascibly he snatched the check and scribbled his name again. Yes, it was their waiter, Chloe recognized him now. He didn't move.

"Also you did not give a tip," he said.

"Certainly I did," said Hugh, looking at the check again. "There."

"That is the hotel, the hotel keep that," said the man.

"It says 'Waiter.' That's for you. American Express pays that too." Hugh frowned and zipped his fly.

"Yes, but the hotel doesn't give. You pay a cash tip . . ."

Now they could hear that it was desperation in his voice; it was not the voice of a swindler. Hugh snatched bills from the dresser. "Here. Please go," he said. The man was thin and anxious.

He stared at the money in his hand. He seemed to wish to complain of it, then his shoulders lowered, an expression of relief and chagrin crossed his face. He shrugged and stepped backward out the door.

"I never thought we would get to spend a whole night together," murmured Chloe to Hugh when he was back in bed. She wrapped her arms contentedly around him, but Hugh thrashed about, eyes open, disturbed. "The poor bastard. The hotel takes the tip and all. Did you see his clothes?" he said. It crossed Chloe's mind that she must be growing callous; had not noticed the man's poor clothes, his thinness.

* * *

In the morning, hand in hand, Chloe and Hugh wander in the streets. The great Shah Abbas had made the wonders of Isfahan to glorify himself and God in that order. They are stunned by the worldly beauty of the palace, the mosques, the school for holy study now partly converted into their hotel, the polo field where Chloe and Hugh can imagine ancient Persians in rich raiment at their games, and along the edges of the bazaar merchants then as now crouched over wares; calling to one another. Isfahan—so Chloe had read—had been taken by Achaemenids, and Sassanids, and Arabs, and Mongols, Safavids and Greeks, tribes from everywhere, vainglorious leaders, bloody scenes. She and Hugh feel daunted by the evident superiority of this panoply to their own short and skimpy history of sickly pilgrims and a few covered wagons going west. From Omar Khayyam to Sweet Betsy from Pike. In this wall, on that turret, in that grave lie the ornaments of Cyrus and Darius, Alexander the Great, Suleiman the Turk who had eluded the Crusaders, Tamburlaine, Genghis, and numberless other khans. Vainglorious Shah Abbas, to dress his city in such richness of decoration, such intricacy of carving, such fanciful surface, such yellows and blue. The water of the long pools reflects God; flowers bloom untended, as in Paradise.

Hugh Monroe and Chloe, conscientious sightseers, trudge for miles in the dusty streets, ravished by admiration, Chloe clutching her Minox. People stare, friendly enough. "Ciao," call the little boys. A woman says of Hugh "too tall." Chloe photographs, along a wall of the bazaar, a row of plows painted blue. She buys a tile, and plans to put it on the wall of her room. She thinks of painting the wall of her room, or at least the door, this sacred turquoise they use here.

The effects of the beauty—its properties elevating to the spirits and glorifying to God—are somewhat diminished in Chloe's view by the sight of men with machine guns everywhere, and this seems ill-advised too in view of the Shah's expressed wish to encourage tourism.

The Shah probably doesn't realize how this militarism looks. In France, Chloe had never liked the hordes of police around the Place de la Concorde either. Probably it is just that if you were a nice American, you had learned in the sixties—she proposed this to Hugh—to be jittery of police, because you had run up against them on peace marches. This had happened to her, calm and law-abiding though she was, and it had turned her against police.

She had been visiting Alice, her sister, in Los Angeles, and they had gone on a peace march, along with all Alice's friends and the people where she worked. Alice was a lab technician. The idea had been to walk along to the hotel where Lyndon Johnson was staying, chanting, "Hey, hey, LBJ, how many kids did you kill today?" Thousands of people walking from the park near Pico to Century Boulevard chanting, and the day was sunny, so lots of people had begun with a picnic, as they had—Alice and her two kids aged about one and five then. Chloe told Hugh about it.

"In the park Cassius Clay—I suppose he was called Muhammad Ali by then—gave a speech and fired everyone up," she said. A lot of doctors and nurses from the hospital where Alice worked, housewives, kids, hippies, some old people. People sang or carried radios, they carried their picnic baskets, carried toddlers who got grumpy along the way.

"I was carrying Sam, he was about one year old, and my sister was with Dana, who was five," Chloe said. "We noticed that police were lining up along the curb, we thought to keep order and protect the President, whatever, but all at once as we walked these police began pressing in at either side of us. Even then it never occurred to me they would hurt us. I had thought until then that policemen were always there to help you. It's amazing how hard it is to see what's plain. But we never expect this kind of thing. I suppose Americans are kind of innocent.

"The police began to press forward, sort of compressing us, so that you could hardly step without elbowing the person next to you, and I still didn't catch on that this is a technique of crowd control they use when they think a crowd is dangerous. Us! A bunch of lab techs and their sisters and tiny children! But luckily I did feel uncomfortable, and the baby began to cry, I thought from being jostled, so I decided to get out of the march. I looked toward the sidewalk, planning to step out of line, and saw that the policemen now had their arms interlocked, fencing us in, so I said, 'Excuse me, officer, but I want to take this baby over there,' and he looked surprised and dropped his arm—I remember so clearly his expression of surprise, and I stepped out, and looked back to call to Alice that we were over there, and saw them beginning to club the people. They clubbed my sister, my little niece, clubbed all the people as they were walking along singing. And this was America, in California! I stood on the grassy parking strip at the edge of the street and watched people being clubbed, these long batons rising and falling, like the baton of a conductor, and people screaming. I thought I could hear my sister's screams." Chloe could feel the rush of indignation she always felt when she told this story.

"Those were horrible times," Hugh agreed. His expression to her was tender.

"That's when I realized," said Chloe, "that, you know, they can't tell the difference. They can't tell the difference between a peaceful, nice person and a dangerous one. They didn't even try. I've never trusted them since then. A lot of people are cynical now."

"The policeman is our friend," said Hugh with an ambiguous note of mockery in his voice.

Here the great domes of gleaming blue and gold ornamented the Persian sky. Birds swept among the minarets; the walls were a dream of flowered tracery. The modest black wrappings of the women wending their way along seemed to Chloe a proper response to such beauty, the contrition of humble humanity, so transitory and plain. She tried to imagine the happy state of mind of the tile makers who painted the millions of flowers on the tiles, their brushes dipped in the enchanted azure, and of the architects dreaming these shapes and snowy walls and the long pooled gardens mirroring them.

They had a seven-o'clock plane to Shiraz, and so went back to the hotel in the late afternoon to make love and nap and pack. It was Chloe who did the packing, like a wife. Hugh lay on the bed, slightly glazed-looking; like Mars in the Bellini painting, Chloe thought, conscious of her own deficiencies as Venus. She was always lively and invigorated by love-making. She threw her few things into her little duffel bag.

Into Hugh's neat case, open on the luggage rack, she put the things he had carefully arranged in the top drawer of the bureau: black socks, white boxer shorts, three identical silk ties. How tidy he was. Would she do this packing for Jeffrey? Of course. She liked making things fit into suitcases, liked being ready to go, liked to go. Hugh's shirts in their plastic wrap from the laundry. An odd detail struck her. "Royal Hilton Tehran" it said on the little paper strap around their middles. Hugh, sleepily watching her, did not notice her notice this, or did not mind. Hugh had had nine shirts done at the Hilton in Tehran, yet he said he had not been in Tehran.

Chapter Thirteen
AN UNMARKED
GRAVE

*Why, if the Soul can fling the Dust aside
And naked on the Air of Heaven ride,
Were't not a Shame—were't not a Shame for him
In this clay carcass crippled to abide?*

Farmani tried to control his fury, his panic, at the stupidity of
Abbas and Yazdi and Rothblatt to involve Azami Hospital in
this business of the dead man, which was fated, he was sure, to
be a danger to them all: Azami doctors mixed up in the death
of an American, police, inquiries, people down from Tehran,
accusations of muddle, perhaps even some sinister real connection between them—between the dead man and who?

Abbas. No, Yazdi. No, Abbas. It was no coincidence, either, it seemed to him, that Mrs. Fowler had been along when
they found him. He had tried to question Abbas, discreetly:
"How was it you all went to the caves today?"

"I don't know. I try to make sure they get around to see
things."

"Why the caves? Think, Abbas."

"Mrs. Fowler, I think. She has a guidebook."

"Ah," said Vahid Farmani, hardly surprised, but with a
renewed sense of dread and helplessness at his lack of ability to
dislodge or expose Mrs. Fowler from her oh-so-convenient
perch. "Dr. Fowler is taking a long time to arrive, don't you
think?" he remarked.

"Yes, poor woman. It can't be easy for her. But she evidently has a resourceful good nature."

"Evidently," said Vahid. "I don't know, Abbas. These people come here but they're just slumming. They're fascinated to see how sick people can get, it's patronizing, they're just interested in our diseases."

"They are always helpful. Always new techniques, suggestions," said Abbas. "More than that, somebody for us to talk to, professionally. Don't you feel the need of that?"

"No, I think Americans are bad news," said Vahid.

Linda Farmani derided Vahid's fears. He said she could never imagine consequences. She had no imagination, he said. She had no imagination, maybe, she said, but she had an eye for concrete detail. She pronounced Chloe Fowler perfect—perfectly what she was. "Your basic docent."

Vahid had no picture of a basic docent, no understanding of American social types, though he understood something about the doctors. "And a docent can't be a spy?"

"Oh, of course." Linda laughed, liking, in a way, the idea of the conceited Mrs. Fowler a spy. Linda did not believe that they had anything to fear at Azami, from spies or from Tehran either, because there was no problem as long as you weren't political, and they weren't. It was kids, students, who got into trouble, which was very sad and horrible, or once in a while you heard of a woman arrested, but rarely. The danger was not from the Shah, in any case, but from the people around him, and, even more than them, it was the locals—the jailers, the informers, people with private grudges and small ambitions, enacting personal dramas of revenge or policy. Middle-class bureaucrats like Vahid and her were at once too high and too low and too old to be at risk. The other American wives shared her view of the political situation here, and the English wives too. Even so, they did not discuss the beliefs of their husbands, if they knew them. Cloaked in Americanness, Englishness, they voiced only their own opinions, and their right to have them.

"Leendaah," Vahid's mother called her. She always pronounced her name like that, like the name of a harem girl, or the sound of a moan. Vahid's mother had white streaks in her hair that went straight back like the wings of a statue, and her burning brown eyes seemed ringed in white in her muddy skin. She wore only black. Iranians when you met them in Los Angeles were just these dark, attractive men. Someone fixed you up with one, or you met them in a bar or at a party. Real estate had been a good way to meet them, they were already buying houses, that was ten years ago, that's how she met Vahid, he came with a friend who was looking at a house. Dark, attractive, doctors, you didn't exactly picture them against a background of camels and roses and the black shadows under the arches of the sun-painted porches. Certainly you didn't imagine their mothers, the furious brown eyes, gray widow's peak, black veil.

"*I'll* never wear the chador," she had told Vahid.

"Certainly not," he had agreed. "I would not want my wife to take the chador." He had been shocked to think she might wear one. Yet his mother wore chador. She sighed. Eventually you didn't notice them one way or another.

Rejected by the police and the American consul, Dick and Abbas had driven back to Azami with the body still in the station wagon. "Look, let's just put him in the morgue," Dick said. "Vahid won't even know, unless he goes over there. We'll put a sheet over him and tell the attendants something."

Abbas thought about it, then shook his head. "No. It's—how to explain it. These days, around here, if someone asks you not to do something you respect his reasons. You can't always know, he can't always tell you his reasons. It's best to interfere as little as possible."

"What possible difference could it make?"

"Apparently it does make some difference."

"We can't just leave him here. It's—it's hot." He wondered if they had embalmers in Iran, and what they did with bodies. It was obvious they would have to do something quickly. Abbas agreed.

"We may have to bury him," he said. "Then they could dig him up if it was necessary."

Dick shuddered at this repulsive idea, this slightly absurd idea of going somewhere and digging a clandestine grave. For the moment they did nothing, hoping the police would change their minds, the American consul would change his mind, someone would call or come to collect him. They had Dermatology Clinic and rounds. "We could dump him. Downtown. Let someone else find him," said Dick.

"He's already been found, remember. The police know he exists. What would be the use?"

"Oh, I don't know," Dick said crossly; the thing was too idiotic. "Then *they* would have to deal with him."

"I am afraid he is ours," Abbas said.

At nightfall, lacking another idea, Dick and Abbas drove the body out of town, somewhere to the north, sixty kilometers or so, Abbas driving and Dick looking restlessly out the window for places, deserted roads, ruins. In the vast, open landscape, it seemed to him that anyone could see them from anywhere, for miles. Perhaps Abbas had a destination in mind. He turned off on a small road, then onto the sand and toward a large rock formation in the middle distance.

Abbas had brought a shovel from his garden shed. They should have brought two shovels. While Abbas dug, Dick scooped the loosened sand that slid back into the hole. "This is not happening," Dick said. He became preoccupied with the stubborn tendency of sand to erase human effort, rippling down into piles, filling the hole again. He tried not to think of the man, stiff by now, but of a strange consistency. When the hole was nearly waist deep, Dick began to feel funny standing in it. He thought of films of people digging their own graves. Then they shot you as you stood in the hole, or beat you to death with your shovel and pitched the dirt over you. He climbed out.

"Isn't it big enough? We can put rocks over it."

Abbas considered. "Maybe." They stood gazing into the grave.

"But what are we going to say we did with him?" Dick said. "To Yazdi and Chloe and whoever."

"Well, we'll just tell them. We aren't hiding him, we're preserving him," Abbas said. Dick hoped they wouldn't ask, would assume the police had taken him, that he was being buried decently somewhere, had been claimed.

"We should take his watch and things," Dick said, "to identify him, if anyone should turn up."

"Yes, you are right," Abbas said. "There was a ring."

They lifted the blanket. Dick mentally stiffened himself to look. At first glance there was nothing more horrible than before except the blood dried blackly now on the poor devil's face, and one eyelid had fluttered unnervingly up; the whole face was perhaps swollen. At touching him, though, Dick's stomach turned over, and he had to step back to master his nausea, for the hand was soft. He heard himself breathing hard; bitter spit trickled between his teeth. Then he took the watch, a gold watch with an incongruous Indian turquoise band. It was Abbas who took the ring off, cursing in Farsi the swollen fingers. Together they pulled the dead man out of the tailgate like bread out of an oven, nearly dropping the limp and heavy thing, and plopped him into his grave.

"We should have put the blanket down first for him to lie on," Abbas said.

"We can put it over him, to keep the sand out," Dick said. They spread the blanket again over the dead face. Who was he? Had he expected to die in Iran, to be buried alone in the desert, heaped with stones? What were the animals in this desert? What would dig at him? They built the rocks in a cairn-shaped mound.

"People will see it's a grave," Dick said.

Abbas shrugged. "The desert is full of graves."

"The desert is full of graves," he went on, in a moody tone that Dick found scary. "In archaic times, the old Zoroastrians laid the bodies out—up there, for instance—along a shelf of rock, for the birds to pick the bones, and then they put the bones into caves in the rocks. It is not unusual to find a little cave of old bones even now."

"That seems practical," Dick said. "A hell of a lot easier than digging a hole."

"It would have been simpler to sneak him into the morgue," Dick said again, on the way back.

"Vahid was really against it. I suppose he had his reasons. We never ask, as I said, the reasons." After a pause he said, "I think we just say nothing at all, until someone asks, then we explain what we have done."

"I think I should notify the American consul, just to cover our asses. We can tell them he's there when they want him."

"Provided they want him fairly soon."

Dick laughed but shivered, slightly exhilarated by this macabre adventure, hiding a body. As a dermatologist he never saw dead people. Even as an intern he had always left the rooms before the last moments; left the last moments to the relatives. Also, he did not himself like to see that fading light, that cast of blue come over the white of the eye, the drop of saliva at the corner of the sagging mouth. That was why he had gone into dermatology.

"Let's have a beer at the Cyrus," Dick said.

Chapter Fourteen
THE RETURN

Chloe and Hugh took a taxi to the Isfahan airport. The little waiting room was jammed with a crush of enthusiastic French tourists clutching brown-paper-wrapped parcels, who were being boarded on a flight to Abadan. Then it was empty—a bare, deserted room, floored in brown linoleum, with a ticket desk at one end, and the inevitable knot of lingering guards and ancient men swaddled in rags, wearing caps, whose duty it was to clean. A picturesque Saudi swept through, flapping his white robes in a dash toward the tarmac, where a small plane for Tehran was ready. His three wives, glaring through their raccoon masks, watched with, it appeared, a certain detachment about whether the plane would wait for them, and then were herded, clinging, to the waiting plane.

The plane for Shiraz, they were told, would be two hours late. Looking at the handsome Hugh slumped next to her in the plastic chair, Chloe wondered if this feeling of solitude, of individual destiny, that overtakes you in an airport waiting room had not also accounted for her willingness to leave Jeffrey at Heathrow and journey on alone. She had felt herself to be alone already. Now Hugh's very self, of such immediate and intimate interest to her two hours ago, had seemed to recede into the body of an unrelated stranger, well-dressed and well-formed but of no consequence to her, not even an object of erotic curiosity. She was locked into a traveler's capsule, alone. As at Heathrow, Chloe bought postcards. Hugh, after an interval of silence, opened his briefcase and began staring at medical reprints. "Here I am in this historic city," wrote Chloe. "I hope you are brushing your teeth."

Their reverie was interrupted by the American voice of a man they had seen earlier leaning against the ticket counter, and they had remarked his American appearance then—a compact, middle-aged man with short grayish hair and protuberant ears, which gave him a look of good nature. His air was friendly, like a figure on a television screen, his smile confident of the welcome of his fellow countrymen.

"Two hours? And this isn't unusual! Why do I turn up on time every time? Because someday, someday, Air Iran may take off on time." He spoke with a lazy southern drawl.

They smiled. Chloe was surprised at her own welcoming feeling, when ordinarily she would not wish to be talked to by a stranger in an airport. But now to meet another American seemed as nice as a present. This view seemed less marked in

Hugh, who looked up with a start of impatience from his articles. But of course he hadn't been in Iran for two weeks. Or had he? She was not forgetting the shirts. Nine shirts, more than a week, if he changed every day, and most men could get two days out of a shirt.

The man handed them a business card, which Hugh read and handed to Chloe: Benjamin Brigante, U.S.A.F., Brig. Gen. Ret., Technical Consultant, Grumman Corporation. He extended his hand, which Hugh and Chloe in turn shook. Hugh half rose, politely. Chloe noticed with satisfaction that he had better manners than Jeffrey. They said their names.

"Going to Shiraz?"

They nodded.

"Me too. I've got to get back p.d.q. Though haste is relative here. You'll have noticed that. But they've crashed another of my airplanes. My beautiful F-14s. It is such a damn shame. I'm with Grumman—we make the things."

"An airplane crash?"

"This is the second one, and there'll be all kinds of hell to pay. Talking frankly, there's more hell to pay here when one goes down than in the U.S., never mind our so-called sanctity of life. I know, in the U.S., there's the wife, the kids, we get up a collection, somebody gets a medal, everyone feels bad, but basically we have plenty of airplanes. There's not such a lot of high-up paranoid handwringing as here. Here the higher-ups believe that planes shouldn't crash, period. When they do, heads will roll. And of course," his voice lowered, "here heads really do roll, so I guess that keeps things serious."

"Are you a pilot?" asked Chloe.

"Are you kidding? I wouldn't get into one of those things— Iranian maintenance. No way. Of course American-trained, but let me tell you these guys have no mechanical aptitude. None. We've been training them ourselves, back in Texas. We take 'em back there for sometimes four years, and when we send them back they still don't have the concept of preventive maintenance."

Chloe was beginning to feel uneasy about the forthcoming Air Iran journey back to Shiraz.

"The Iranian male, frankly, is not too bright. I don't know if it's the way they're brought up or what. The Iranian female, that's something else, she's alert, she's aggressive."

"Uh—won't you sit down?" said Hugh, hitching his chair to symbolize making room for General Brigante.

"Thanks," he said, sitting down. "And what are you folks doing? Vacation?"

"We're at the Azami Hospital in Shiraz," said Hugh.

"Azami, huh? You have some biochemists there, some hotshots?"

"Why?" asked Hugh. "I suppose."

"Just wondered. This is the second crash in a month. I think privately it's some kind of kamikaze thing. Pilots who think Allah will take them straight to Valhalla if they down a few of Sue's expensive aircraft. There's a lot of opposition to Sue's willful little ways."

"Sue?"

"We call her Sue, just to be on the prudent side. You know who I mean."

"Suicide pilots?" said Chloe, happily intrigued.

"Suicide or sabotage, I think. But, like I say, with Iranian maintenance who can tell the difference? It's a question of intention. The result's the same—either way, the damn things crash."

"But how awful for the pilot," said Chloe.

"Awful for you, too, if the thing falls on your house and, actually, the pilots eject."

After this, with General Brigante telling them horrifying but entertaining stories about the Iranian Air Force, the time passed quickly, though they felt more and more reluctant to get on the Air Iran plane.

Chloe liked the general, despite his having been in the military. When, eventually, they got back to Shiraz, he gave them a ride to the compound in the Grumman car that awaited him.

Chloe wondered if you could get to be an American general without a southern accent.

In the compound, there was a certain unease, for people had noticed that Mrs. Fowler was not in Villa Two and had not been there all weekend, a fact easily ascertainable from the windows of Villa One, and noticed also by Hossein, who confirmed Linda Farmani's observation, which she mentioned to Vahid Farmani.

Vahid thought Chloe might be doing something over at the airbase, might have met someone at the American Wives' Club. It now occurred to him, for the first time, that her object might not be the hospital itself so much as to watch the whole Azami Compound, assessing the loyalties and sympathies of all the people who lived and worked there. At this, he felt a rush of hot dread, not to have seen before that a woman was not an odd choice but was the very perfect choice for a spy, could make herself the confidante of the other wives, be a guest at the parties. It was the perfect situation for a spy, a traitor, an agent, the perfect situation from which to learn things, whatever there was to be learned. There was always something to be learned.

Dick and Junie had thought it was funny when Chloe wasn't around all weekend. Sunday night, after work, they went to the Cyrus for drinks with Abbas Mowlavi, and there fell in with a delightful guy, Richard Dare, an American archaeologist working for the University of Chicago, and an expert on Persepolis, where he was stationed on a dig. This was good luck for Dick and Junie, because Dare offered to show them around when they came down to Persepolis, and they realized it would be a rare inside opportunity to see the great ruins with someone really knowledgeable. The date had not been fixed for the Persepolis expedition because the company had been awaiting Hugh Monroe and Jeffrey Fowler, but they were about to give them up and go without them.

"I plan to come too," said Abbas. "Like most of my countrymen, I'm badly educated in these wonders. It's always strangers and foreigners who must teach us, or who afford an excuse, at least, to learn."

Dare expected to be at Persepolis until the end of August, and said they could find him there any time. Dick hoped the guy would remember—tonight he might be just slightly in the bag. He was a pink-faced blond man wearing whites, a bit self-consciously tropical and colonial-looking, with the wide smile of a host, welcoming and bright, and an eye for Junie. He kept buying her vodkas. Perhaps it had been a while since he had seen an American woman. Dick noticed, rather to his annoyance, that Junie had adopted a rather silly, giggling manner, and said not a word about being a doctor.

Besides Dare, Junie also appeared to like Abbas. So for that matter did Dick, who found him melancholy but compatible, sweet-natured and empathetic with patients, which many Iranian doctors were not, and hard-working. And attractive. Dick had long since stopped being uneasy about his own attraction to good looks in other men. It was—it had been worked out—a wishful process of identification, an almost aesthetic response. Of course he would himself have liked to be a tallish, cleft-chinned dark beauty like Abbas; this was not a mysterious reaction, and Junie's reaction was not mysterious either. But plenty of women had assured Dick that he himself was attractive—they never said short—and praised his engaging smile, his dimples, and, in former days, his sandy hair, slightly grizzled now and thinner but not really thin to the extent that he had to resort, like some pathetic colleagues, to combing it into strange patterns, for instance up from the nape of the neck. In bed, he knew, had been told, he was a good performer.

He wondered if Abbas was getting any and what the Islamic recourse was for an unmarried man. What did you do? But the subject of women never came up. Abbas was friendly in an impersonal, international style; they had no sports team in common, did not read the same paper, had only medicine in which to find perfect collegial rapport, and now, of course, their guilty secret, their bond, the body in the desert.

Most important for Dick was that Abbas was a good doctor. Some Iranians he found boastful, thoughtless, and behind the times, though he also understood the practical difficulties they were up against and sympathized with their wish to use their elaborate Western training on something more serious than dysentery and malaria. Dick was not sympathetic to the wish of Vahid Farmani to have a CAT scanner. There were plenty of things they needed more. But he understood why Vahid wanted a CAT scanner, in order to go on feeling like a real doctor, not just a Peace Corps worker. Basically Dick respected doctors like Vahid and Abbas who wished to improve the health of all Iran.

Junie and Abbas were talking about skiing. "If you're ready to go home, Miss Fay, I'll walk you," Dick interrupted abruptly, and he was a little surprised when she said she was ready to go, as docile as a wife.

As they walked up to the Azami gates they came upon Chloe with, of all people, Hugh Monroe, who was carrying a suitcase.

"Look who I've found," Chloe said.

"Rothblatt! Hey!" said Hugh cheerfully, holding out his hand.

"Well!" said Dick. "At last! When did you get here?"

"Just now," said Hugh. "I don't even know where to go."

"He had no idea people were worried," said Chloe.

"This is June Fay, Hugh Monroe," said Dick. "Junie's in OB-GYN."

"How do you do?" said Hugh. It was a moment, it seemed to Chloe, when the four of them could have abandoned pretenses and gone off home in two pairs, promising never to tell. Instead they began an elaborate business of starting to shuffle off in four separate directions.

"Well, I'm going to roust out the Farmanis and find out where they've put me," Hugh said. "They weren't expecting me tonight."

"Let's go along together," said Dick, taking Junie and Chloe by their elbows. Hugh walked with them toward Villa One.

"What happened about the dead man?" asked Chloe as they walked.

"Well, it wasn't easy," Dick said. "Farmani wouldn't have it at Azami, so we took it to the police. But they wouldn't have it either. They said he wasn't an Iranian, it was a matter for the American consul."

"How amazing! Not a matter for the police!"

"Right. They just came out to the car, looked at the guy, discussed him in their unknown tongue, and shook their heads and went inside. So then we took him to the American consul, of course, a Mr. Collins, and he said it didn't look like an American to him and where would he put it anyway? This was all day Friday, Abbas and I and the body still in the hospital car. Finally I suggested we should just call the American embassy in Tehran and find out what to do, but no one would, Abbas included, and so I did, but they took Collins's line: How do you know he's American?"

"It's like the joke about the grandmother who died in Mexico," Chloe said, "and somebody stole the car as they were smuggling the body back. You must have hoped someone would steal the car."

"Are you sure he was American?" Hugh asked.

"No, not at all. His dying words—you couldn't tell. But he spoke English. 'Pardon' it sounded like."

"His clothes looked like American clothes," Chloe said. "He was wearing sort of Hush Puppies."

"Junie looked at his feet," Dick said to Hugh, "but she didn't look at the brand of shoes."

"You should have looked at them," Chloe said.

"Well, his feet had begun to swell; you couldn't get them off again," Dick said. It was easy enough for others, who were not there, to criticize.

"What did you do?" Hugh asked. "Smuggle him back into the morgue?"

Dick turned his head, and the light from a streetlamp gave him a momentary evasive glitter.

"Well, what else could we do?" Dick said, suddenly deciding not to tell them the rest.

"Where were you this weekend?" he asked Chloe.

"Digging," Chloe said. "Didn't I tell you? Like a real archaeologist." She'd thought of this on the plane.

"That must have been fun," said Dick.

Hugh dropped out at Villa One, to get the key to wherever it was he was supposed to stay. Dick and Junie dropped Chloe at her door. In the darkness they could hear Hugh apologizing to the Farmanis for the lateness of the hour. Then Dick walked Junie over to her place, and, because it was dark and no one was around, it seemed all right to steal inside for the night.

Chloe heard Hugh's careful discreet tap at the street door of Villa Two. How circumspect they all were! She stole along the corridor and down the stairs to admit him.

"Jesus Christ," he shouted in the night. Chloe heard the slap of his feet on the linoleum, the clatter of his cot.

"What's the matter?" she asked.

"What the hell is that?" He moved toward the window.

"Oh, the dogs," said Chloe, laying her head sleepily again on her pillow. "Some kind of wild dogs. They roam around at night."

"What a hellish noise. I don't remember that from before."

"You get used to it."

"You're used to it?" asked Hugh, astonished. After a few moments he came over to Chloe's cot and stroked her hair and drew her covers back. Then he crawled on top of her, for there was no room for two people to lie side by side.

"Just a little quickie, then I'm going to risk stealing out into the night, if I can escape the hell hounds. Now I'm awake," he said. Sleepily, amiably, Chloe parted her thighs.

Dick woke in the night again, thinking as he had last night, after he and Abbas had buried the dead man, that animals would dig at the grave. He wasn't sure what animals lived in the sparse desert, but he imagined wild jackals or cats, starved cats from the city, wandering out across the sand. He had dreamed and the dream was exactly the same as his waking picture of the scene, a dead hand stretching up, a fold of cloth, a voice feebly issuing forth, protesting the hungry slavering of the digging beast. He supposed he must have seen a movie of this scene, its details too predictable to have issued forth from the unconscious, unless the voice—as he suddenly realized— was his own, and the cloth was the hem of his own bathrobe, in which case who were the beasts? Did it have something to do with Marla? It seemed to him it did, and of course guilt feelings about that clandestine burying, and the fear of discovery. He had nothing to feel guilty about, though maybe they could have saved the guy if they had grasped what had happened to him. He always felt guilty if someone died.

But of course the animals were the dogs, the real dogs roaming the compound, now near his own window. He was not fond of animals, especially cats and dogs; that came from not having pets while growing up. He had insisted that his own children have pets—cats and dogs both, over Marla's objection. But he had never overcome a momentary tendency to flinch when the dogs ran up to greet him. He liked horses and cows, and other nice, majestic animals.

In the morning Chloe tied her belt around Rustum's neck and took him for a walk. People stared at her so oddly that she went back inside the compound, woman cruelly dragging small dog, the way people dragged goats and lambs here. He snarled and struggled. He was not going to be an attractive dog, she knew, but she grew fonder each day of his undistinguished color, his expression, perfectly expressive, of growing interest and trust. It was not just for food, either, that he came now when she called, for she was careful not to feed him every time but to vary the routine and assure that he was coming by the direction of his superego not from mere greediness.

When she saw Hugh that evening, he said, "There is no body in the morgue. I went in to look at the guy—in case—you never know. But there was no one there at all. They take away their dead almost immediately, these people, they don't leave them in the hospital morgue, so there were no bodies there at all."

"Ugh," said Chloe, "why would you want to look at him?" It seemed strange to her. Hugh made no answer.

Chapter Fifteen
P I C N I C

Hugh, who had been a popular visitor a few years before, was welcomed back with enthusiasm by the wives as well as the doctors. It was remembered that he liked to play tennis, and Heidi Asghari lost no time in finding the net to the tennis court behind Villa Nine and organizing a picnic supper. Mohammed fixed the net and stamped down the scratched patches on the red clay surface, and Hugh rounded up players. The dead man in Shahpur's Cave was forgotten, or at least not mentioned.

Chloe, who did not play tennis, happily watched a game between Hugh and Abbas, two picturesquely handsome men, the one dark, the other fair, like athletes in a mural depicting international competition. She thought it possible that she loved Hugh because he was handsomer than Jeffrey, though Jeffrey of course was a nice-looking man. But no, it was not strictly looks—was not Hugh also better-natured, more deserving of love? Probably, being beautiful, he had always received love, and it was that which gave him his good disposition. Chloe basked in the sun with her sun hat over her face to prevent wrinkles, legs in tennis shorts outstretched, raising her head from time to time to watch the players.

In tennis whites, she had to admit, Abbas was even better-looking than Hugh, supremely handsome, with Hugh appearing, in comparison, a pinkish-beige color that was not so elegant, and turning pinker with each moment in the burning sun. In a few weeks, Heidi Asghari said, they would have to play in the early mornings; it would be too hot at midday. Naturally Noosheen loved Abbas, thought Chloe admiringly. It was chemistry of an obvious kind.

Hugh was a better tennis player. He had played on his college team. Her heart warmed. She felt as she remembered having felt in high school, thrilled at any evidence of athletic prowess in boys. Those were her first premonitions of sex. Football players with their strong thighs and an aura of liniment clinging to them when you necked in the car after games. Now those boys would look too young to her, their necks too skinny. She watched the strong legs of Hugh and Abbas with a pleasant crawling feeling in her stomach. How strong, how graceful Hugh's forehand drives; a slight expression of pique on the face of Abbas, beneath his smile, at the ease with which Hugh Monroe sent balls spinning by him. She did not feel the tendrils and entails of marriage; her spirit floated free.

Abbas was thinking how off his game he was—he never played now; Americans were always playing. He'd have to make more of an effort, he thought, not to let his game go, though ordinarily there was no one much to play with at Azami. Monroe was as fast as the devil. He was conscious of Chloe Fowler watching them, and of how she leapt up to scurry after balls with the feigned energy of someone who isn't playing but wishes to look as if she might.

The Yazdis came with a net for the second court. Zareeneh Yazdi sat down near Chloe while Ali affixed it to its posts. Chloe was fascinated at the smoothness of her legs. At risk of seeming to stare, she found herself continually darting glances at this miracle of depilation, arms too, smooth as bronze, to go with the bronzed dark hair and sunglasses on which you could read the words Christian Dior along the temple. Chloe had read that men prefer women to be smooth because hair symbolizes masculinity, like Samson. She suddenly felt hairy and Western, though she certainly shaved her legs and underarms in the regular American way. A finger along her shin revealed the slightest prickliness. Abbas, on the court, began to hit the ball too hard much of the time, and she redoubled her efforts at fielding.

Dick Rothblatt and Junie Fay came along, looking rather a couple; Chloe wondered if the Iranians noticed this, and whether it mattered. Dick had still not acknowledged it, not really, to her. They carried their racquets and wore tennis clothes except for Dick's socks, which were black. He looked straight at Chloe, as if reading her mind, and said, "I forgot my tennis socks." Had she been staring snobbishly at his socks?

Something upsetting had happened in his life. He'd just gotten a letter. Chloe wondered if she would find a letter on her pillow when she got back to her room. It seemed as if letters always brought bad news.

"Marla has put the house up for sale."

"Shouldn't she? Isn't it hers?" asked Chloe. Junie rolled her eyes, informing her, by a cool glance, that Dick was irrational on the subject.

"Your kids are away—she probably doesn't want a big house to take care of," Chloe continued nonetheless, thinking that would be how she would feel.

"Well, they have to have someplace to go on their vacations," Dick said. "I didn't agree that she should have it so she could sell it. I was thinking of the kids, a home."

"Maybe—you know—bad memories. People have to start over, change, a fresh start," murmured Chloe.

"She would pick now to do it, with me here."

"I think it's completely logical," said Junie. "A house is a drag, she's busy, maybe she needs the money."

"She's a terrible businesswoman, she's bound to get screwed, she has no sense at all. And she would pick now."

"We're supposed to play," Junie said, waving at the Yazdis, who beckoned from the other side of the court. Hugh blistered a drive past Abbas; it was the end of their match. They shook hands, ceremoniously as at a tournament.

"She must have just been waiting till I was out of the country," Dick went on complaining as he walked with Junie out onto the court.

His game was stronger than Junie's. Though they were the same height, Dick was nimbler, fitter, and Junie was awkward. Marla, fifteen years older than Junie, was trim and a good tennis player. Her face floated before him, small and tanned, the tiniest bit leatherish, her pink lipstick and blue headband—these details were vividly present to his mind as Junie loped around next to him. He could imagine Marla selling the house to the tennis pro or some other gigolo; she had absolutely no idea of the value of money.

He and Junie by some miracle defeated the Yazdis, who were good players nonetheless. Then Hugh Monroe took a couple of games off of Dick while the women spread the picnic, and they all sat under the trees drinking wine or beer and eating lamb sandwiches. Hugh Monroe, Dick noted regretfully, besides being fit and a good tennis player, was abstemious, stuck to beer pretty much, or the occasional glass of wine. Not that he, Dick, was a big boozer, but he found himself thinking about a drink from time to time, and at home he had a good cellar. Had had a good cellar. Left quite a bit of the good stuff for Marla, too. Would she think of moving the bottles from the cellar? He imagined some stranger wandering down behind the furnace, excitedly finding the well-stocked racks. He had in fact taken the 1959 Château Lafite-Rothschild and some other inspired purchases, but the stuff he left behind was by no means bad.

He had begun to keep a list of things like this he wanted to talk to Marla about, remind her about. When they first separated, she had been cooperative about details and telephoned to ask his advice. As she felt her way to independence she had stopped doing this, which was to be expected, but she now often quite irrationally resisted reasonable suggestions. So far he hadn't succeeded in getting through on the telephone, even from the Cyrus. He pictured a ring of real-estate agents in his cellar, turning over the labels, exclaiming, calling for a corkscrew.

Here they were drinking a perfectly pleasant white, grown somewhere around Persepolis. "They have some very nice whites in Egypt," he heard himself saying, even knowing Hugh was not too interested in wine, no more than most American doctors, "and the reds are okay, surprisingly enough. There's one called Pharaon. There's one called Omar Khayyam."

Then Hugh shocked everyone by bringing up politics, calmly observing that, although he had heard that unrest was increasing, things seemed to him on the whole the same, or better, than when he had visited Iran two years before. . . .

"People seem more prosperous, but less cheerful. That's how it seems walking down the street. And as to the peasants, the poor people we see at the hospital, they seem the same."

"They greatly resist change of any kind," said Ali Yazdi.

"Except the automobile," put in Chloe. "Obviously they love cars."

"So I imagine they will resist Marxism too," said Yazdi.

"Little kids eight or nine on motorcycles—it's scary," said Chloe.

"There are more soldiers," Hugh said. "Everywhere on the street, in Isfahan. Machine guns."

"Yes—I think there will be a revolution," Abbas said. The Yazdis, it seemed to Chloe, looked at him with masks concealing surprise.

"But isn't that good? The Shah is a monster. The torture," cried Junie.

"Yes, no one supports the Shah. His people are corrupt and cruel. He has tried to do things too quickly, without understanding, without any understanding—and yet . . ." He hesitated. How dark, how tragic, his eyes, thought Chloe. He could be a sheik in a movie.

"Well, then," Junie said.

"There will be terrible bloodshed, one can't want that. If the people could wait, if they would understand what prosperity can bring them. You've seen the air force, you've seen the police, the machine guns. The rebellion will not be a well-armed, well-organized fight, and so, of course, the Shah will be successful, and afterward more cruel, more watchful than ever." His voice became low and urgent.

"Uprisings succeed because of the will of the people. History is full of examples, the collective will, people without guns overpowering armed might, eventually," said Dick. He had the regular American view.

Abbas shrugged, imagining the short run, the shouting, wounded people, confusion. "People are very ignorant here still, very superstitious. I'd rather the Shah would change. There is more hope of making him change than of throwing him out."

"The world is always ruled by uniformed people and the rich, why expect Iran to be different?" agreed Ali Yazdi.

A company in tennis whites, at leisure amid the tangled thicket at the edge of the courts, bare legs in view, easy and laughing, while the peasants in question trudged by in their somber draperies. Chloe wondered if, when they uprose, these poor would fall upon Zareeneh Yazdi as well as upon an American woman.

"Of course," said Abbas, "it's always the middle class who suffer in the end."

Chloe wasn't so sure about that.

"And the intellectuals," said Yazdi. "Tell me, where do intellectuals rule?"

When the revolution comes, Abbas thought, and then interrupted his thought with the realization that he had not before fully, out loud, as it were, formulated this certainty: there would be a revolution. His next thought was to wonder—the idea just thrust itself in upon the larger preoccupation—if he should sell his BMW now or hold on to it. He believed, though not as strongly as Emir, his brother, that things must change here, so probably he should sell now. After a brief period of upheaval, then things would get better and you would still after all need a car, but in the meantime a BMW was kind of a conspicuous, capitalist car.

Chloe noticed now that Zareeneh Yazdi was wearing panty hose with her tennis dress; this accounted for the supernatural smoothness of her legs.

Chapter Sixteen
DAILY LIFE

Whether at Naishapur or Babylon,
Whether the Cup with sweet or bitter run,
The Wine of Life keeps oozing drop by drop
The Leaves of Life keep falling one by one.

Now that she belonged, however secretly, to Hugh, was part of a couple again, Chloe felt more than ever a part of Azami Hospital too. Being the appendage, even the secret one, of some man, was more natural to her than being an expert on Sassanian pottery. She supposed that anyone could see through her pretension of expertise on Sassanian pottery, but she continued to be taken seriously and to take it seriously herself, studying industriously, and appearing at the workshop at the university, where she was allowed to turn over cases full of shards, and had learned to delight in a trace of green glaze or the impress of a forked stick so charmingly evoking some disappeared potter now himself clay. Indeed, she had begun to love Sassanian pots.

She had surprised herself by having a gift for the painstaking work of fitting shards together. From a heap of fragments she could find matching bits with a facility that amazed the real archaeologists. She would find a bit, then the next bit; under her tweezer would grow the pattern, the form of the curve of a vessel lip. Perhaps it was practice, from childhood jigsaw puzzles. To her it was no harder than that. Yet the Iranian archaeologists marveled, assuring her it was an unusual talent. Chloe sat for hours with shards spread on the restoring table under a lamp, arranging them in piles. When an important restorer arrived, expected shortly from Tehran, she was to learn the technique of gluing them.

Sometimes, absorbed in her work, she would realize with a quick start of surprise that she hadn't thought about her children as she used to do, perhaps not all day. She had a sense, new to her, of being separate from them, not "Sara's mother," "Max's mother," so much as an expert on pots. At such moments she would imagine that they had forgotten her too, and thought of her as a dim abstraction, far away, originator of postcards and fond sentiments from afar, that was all.

She recognized that her pottery did not sound interesting to doctors, involved as they were in dramas of life and death more dire than those they were used to in America. They passed the evenings in the Cyrus bar in shocked recital, if no Iranians were present whose feelings might be hurt, of the preventable medical horrors, the suffering, and the undoctorly treatment their patients sometimes received. If an Iranian doctor joined them, they became polite and emphasized the great strides. All acknowledged that the good doctors—Abbas, Mohammed, Vahid Farmani, and even Ali Yazdi—were models of dedication and compassion.

Chloe, being discreet, most often went to the Cyrus bar with Junie, or with Junie and Dick, but never with Hugh, who would come along alone, or, some evenings, go without her, for a few beers and medical talk. In his specialty of infectious diseases, he found much to occupy, interest, and distress him. He was especially critical of the reluctance he sensed on the part of Vahid Farmani to implement simple public-health measures to control contagion.

"I've been talking to Vahid about a polio project during the tribal migrations," he said. "You could administer the vaccine as the people come through Shiraz. You could virtually stamp it out. But he could care less."

"Prevention," said Dick Rothblatt. "You can't talk to them about prevention. They think it's hopeless, I guess, and that you'll never get people to take pills, or follow through, or watch where their drinking water comes from. They could clean up the water. The typhoid. But prevention doesn't interest them at all."

"Ab-e-inja bad ast," said Chloe, using one of the phrases, unusable until now, from *Teach Yourself Farsi*: "The water is bad." She was delighted whenever she found a word that was the same in English and Farsi: *bad*, for example.

"One thing that bugs me," Dick Rothblatt said, "among the many things, I mean, is the way they treat the poor patient. They talk right in front of him, in English, which he can't understand, and they never talk *to* him. They never tell him what's the matter with him or what's going on. When I make rounds, I make the resident stop and explain to the patient what we've just said, not that I can tell if that's what he's doing; sometimes the patients look more petrified after the resident talks to them."

"You can die of fright," Chloe said.

"Yes, you can, absolutely," Dick agreed. "It's their attitude. These are just peasants to them, or representatives of a disease. 'This is a liver,' they say. It's the attitude here I don't like."

"Frankly, a lot of American doctors are like that too," Chloe said.

"I know it, but they're worse here," Dick said. "The people are scared to death to go to the hospital."

"American doctors are very bad that way," persisted Chloe. She felt that Dick and Hugh were themselves sometimes insensitive, if not to patients, then to the problems of Iranian doctors. Once they had been joined by a Dr. Gomez, young, fat, puffing with anxiousness, in the hospital cafeteria.

"Dr. Monroe, would you have a minute?"

"Of course," Hugh had said affably, though without rising. Dr. Gomez glanced at the chair next to him and nervously sat in it. Then he leaned so close to Hugh that Hugh instinctively leaned backward and scooted his chair an inch or two.

"I have a research project," said Dr. Gomez. "Naturally it is not what I could hope if in the U.S., but I wonder if you can advise me regarding publication, and how I can get some funds maybe from the U.S. to continue. I can publish my preliminary results very soon, you see, and then perhaps attract some other funds."

"What is the project?" Hugh had asked politely, but Chloe had heard in his voice his lack of interest, and, days later, when she had asked him if he had looked in on Dr. Gomez, Hugh admitted he had forgotten.

"I have a hard time remembering their names," Dick confided. "It's really embarrassing. It's just that I never heard names like that before, so I have no associations with them."

"I try to think of a similar English word," Chloe said. "Noosheen, for instance, moonshine."

"But after you get used to the name it's just a name like Dick," Dick said. "Abbas, Mohammed, those are easy."

"Have you noticed that they get to looking more American, too? I mean, it's in one's head," said Hugh, laughing.

"Only the ones you know, though," Dick said.

Abbas Mowlavi joined them, as he often did in the evenings. Was it he, then, Chloe occasionally wondered, who was the agent for Savak? It seemed to Chloe that she was half in love with the entire company—Heidi, even Junie, though she was prickly and superior and looked down on ordinary housewives, not without reason. Even the English Hendersons, so pink-faced and owlish in their identical National Health spectacles, their clothes, in spite of their rather strong body odor, always so clean, freshly ironed it seemed by Mrs. Henderson. Chloe even liked General Ben, who was not someone who would ever come her way in America. Chloe liked the comical way he said things he must know perfectly well to be what people would expect of a wicked American general, though at times he spoke of gooks and Nam so unself-consciously she wondered if the proper view of matters was known to him. Chloe believed he had never met anyone who had been against the war, and that if he had he would have become something more sympathetic than a military officer.

The only one she didn't like was Loyal Cooley, the Texan, who hung around and bragged or complained. They all found his voice too loud, his stories too tall—the endless perils he had encountered on his travels outside of America, or for that matter outside of Texas, for bad things had befallen him in New York and San Diego, too. He was both a hawk and a racist, and told racist jokes.

"Black guy comes in for a vasectomy, all dressed up, white hat, fancy duds. 'Rastus, why you all dressed up?'—'If I's gonna be impo'tant, I's gonna look impo'tant!' " Chloe's ears had burned but the Iranian doctors had all laughed heartily. "What do you call a white guy with two blacks? 'Victim.' "

Once General Ben and Loyal Cooley had been going on embarrassingly about Nam and hound dogs, and football, and, as Chloe was withdrawing to talk to the Asgharis, she had heard Hugh join the conversation, under her very eyes transformed into an unrecognizable creature of another, inarticulate race, whose discourse was conducted in loud monosyllables concerning trout, and who knew what else if she and the other women hadn't been there.

"They had a linebacker then who was just a little guy, no more'n five ten," said General Ben, "could run forty yards in five seconds."

"That was Ernie Beatty," said Loyal Cooley, "only white guy on the team."

"Tennessee State," said Hugh.

"Heisman," said the general.

"Fractured ankle," said Loyal Cooley.

"Three suspensions that year," said Hugh.

"What do you call a white guy with five blacks?" said Loyal Cooley. "Five? A coach. Eight? Quarterback."

Poor Dick Rothblatt too seemed baffled by this unintelligible conversation, of a sort Chloe had been hearing all her life but which they perhaps did not have in New York, and certainly not in Iran. Chloe thought Hugh and the others rude to talk in sports shorthand in front of Iranians, gracious people who were making an effort to speak another language on topics of general interest. She was embarrassed. People would think Americans weren't capable of elaborate discourse on complicated subjects. In fact, in front of Iranians, she felt ashamed of her friends, seeing them as the braggart, the war-crazed general, and the dumb doctors with endless discourse on diseases but never books or cultivated subjects.

"Two thousand? Warden. Ten thousand? Postmaster general." The Americans laughed, ashamed of their laughter.

Tonight General Ben Brigante said to Dick, who was standing with Chloe and Junie at the bar, "Come sit down with me. I've been standing around all day," and he seized his glass of white wine and carried it to a table.

"I want to recruit you," he said. "As a spy, you could say."

"Me?"

"Yes, a spy should be someone like you, intelligent, watchful. You keep your eyes open. I've told you about the airplane crashes. We're quite sure it's somebody at Azami who is poisoning the fuel. We've found hospital chemicals, other things."

"If I were a saboteur," said Dick, uncertain how seriously

to take this, "I wouldn't leave my chemicals around." He felt suddenly defensive of Azami Hospital.

"You wouldn't, I wouldn't, but these are Iranians. Or it could be the chemicals were left behind in a hurry."

Perhaps he was serious. He was often seen with Americans in uniform, or with Iranian officers. "Who wants them to crash?" Dick asked.

The general shrugged. "You could say anybody and you'd have a perfectly good chance of being right. There's Sue. If there's an uprising, Sue doesn't want her planes to fall into the hands of the rebels."

"You work for—Sue—don't you? Why can't you call him by his name?"

"Then there's the rebels themselves," the general went on. "When the moment comes, they want to have taken the planes out beforehand. Then there's the CIA. If there's a rebellion and Sue doesn't make it, then they don't want these planes falling into the hands of the Russians."

"Russians?" said Dick, who had not even thought of Russians.

"They're in the game. They always are. About the only people around here I'd say who want the F-14s in the air, besides me, because I don't like to see all that scrap metal out of what was once a beautiful airplane, are the Russians, because that's obviously who's going to wind up with them if there's a successful revolution."

"Complicated to understand," said Dick, confused but pleasantly excited at such strategic talk. "There are Russian spies here, then?"

The general looked meaningfully around the room.

"And the rebels," Dick went on. "Do they have spies? One knows about the Shah's spies, of course. Who *are* the rebels, actually?"

"The leader is in Paris, an old mullah, but backed by the Russians, or that's what everybody says. Me, I'm not political. If you ask me, these people here have plenty to complain of. But

I'm just doing my job, as Eichmann used to say, and that's to keep the airplanes flying, despite Iranian pilots and Iranian maintenance and all the other despites. I would really like to know who is getting chemicals from Azami."

"Why don't you just put guards around the planes?"

The general turned gloomy and stirred the ice cubes in his glass with the tip of his finger.

"I'm not sure whose side I'm on," said Dick. "I mean, I know I'm not on Sue's. I haven't given it any thought."

"Thoughtfulness is not required in a spy. Watchfulness, but not thoughtfulness."

"I'd hate to give myself airs, airs of thoughtfulness," Dick said. "All the same . . ."

"Keep your eyes open all the same," said General Ben, "though we may have seen the last of it for a while. Now that they know they can do it, they may decide to sit back and await the day."

"The day," said Dick. "Will it be soon?" He had suddenly thought of the strange disorder he had encountered in Abbas's laboratory some mornings.

"I doubt it," the general said.

"As far as I'm concerned," Loyal Cooley could be heard saying nearby, "French food is just caca. Not the food so much as the pretentious bull-caca that goes with it. The maître d'. The wine list. It used to be in Waco you went out to dinner, you ate, but now they tell you all the stuff they do to it—the sauce, the descriptions are as bad as the food, you can't tell what the food is anyway, they just pour cream and all that shit on it and put it under the broiler. It's that they want to impress you instead of feed you. Goddamnit, I go out to eat—to eat."

Chloe thought he overdid the simple-rube act. Probably CIA. He must think they were really stupid. She could not tell from General Ben's expression what he thought of Loyal Cooley.

It sometimes seemed to Dick that beneath Loyal's antic façade lay a sentient being. At such times it was possible to imagine glints of watchful attention in his watery blue eyes.

"They mostly have English doctors here," he had remarked to Dick earlier. "Right? Like Dr. Henderson?"

"Henderson and a few others. Mostly Americans," Dick had said.

"Ever have Belgians or Frenchmen? It used to be that your educated Iranian spoke French, know that? Still that way in Egypt, your upper class didn't want anything to do with the English, which you certainly can't blame them."

"There was a Dutch radiologist when I came," Dick said.

"No French doctors?"

"I haven't met any," Dick said, stomach tightening. The man in the cave could have been a French doctor. Was Cooley looking for the man in the cave?

"Your Texans," said Ali Yazdi when Loyal Cooley had gone lurching drunkenly off toward his room, "are not as sympathetic as other Americans."

"The size of their belt buckles is inversely related to the size of their pricks," said General Ben. "Back east we have a joke: 'How do you find Texas?' Answer: 'You walk west until you smell it, then you walk south until you step in it.' " All the Americans laughed but not the Iranians.

"Florida," said Chloe scornfully when General Ben had left, "is entirely populated by senior citizens and dope pushers. And have you ever seen a picture of the Fontainebleau Hotel?"

Chapter Seventeen

FAMILIAR EVENINGS

Ah, my Beloved, fill the Cup that clears
To-day of Past Regrets and Future Fears:
To-morrow! — Why, To-morrow I may be
Myself with Yesterday's Sev'n Thousand Years.

At dusk, waiting for Junie after a long day, Dick falls asleep sitting in the hard bentwood chair in his apartment, and has the dream he has begun to have in the nights. In this dream, the dead man, a doctor, is walking toward him holding a leafy branch, which he sweeps before him like a broom. When he is near, the man looks at him and says, "You should have waited. I was getting better. I would have been all right if you had waited."

"We couldn't wait any longer," Dick says to him. "It's your own fault." Then the man thrusts the branch at Dick's eyes but a bird swoops down and wrests it from him. Then Dick sees that he himself is wearing a yellow butcher's apron, and that is the end of the dream.

After work, in the evenings, Abbas drives his car to a poor quarter of the city and walks the streets there, hoping to spy a well, in a courtyard or set into a wall, where the pollution might arise. He does not really expect to find it, but the exercise is calming. He thinks of the lines of the Koran: "He may bring forth those who believe and do righteous deeds from the shadows into the light." The doing of righteous deeds in shadow, that was all anybody could do now. Not that he was righteous or a believer.

Others may connive, hope—let them. It is one thing to flutter leaflets down from the sky and a lesser thing just to walk along the street hoping to spy something in the tilt of a drain, in the direction of a ditch, that could explain disease. It was bold in others to want to change hearts, inspirit hearts. He did not mistrust it—admired, even, the increasingly desperate and often horrible acts of the *mujahedin*.

Most of the time Abbas, because he has no wife, and various Americans have supper at the hospital, where the food is free, or sometimes the Americans eat at a restaurant Chloe thinks of as the Pepsi-Cola, because that is a sign she can read in Farsi. In the impossible kitchen at Villa Two she has tried her hand at some Persian dishes, but she couldn't manage the rice right, and was too shy to discuss with the butcher which cut of meat was which, though he spoke a little English. The cuts were unfamiliar, and they were all lamb, which she believed to be unhealthy, like all red meat.

"Persian food would be better for a little seasoning," she had confided her opinion to Heidi. "If it were more like Indian food, don't you think?"

"You're asking an Englishwoman about seasoning?" Heidi had laughed.

"Their buildings are so fancy but their food is so plain. What does it mean?"

"Poor people anywhere—do they have spices?" Heidi said. "In America? What spices do poor people use in America?"

"Well, I don't know. The same as anywhere. It depends on what kind of poor people you mean, black or Puerto Rican or what. In America, we don't really think of poor people as a single category with single habits," she said, wondering if this was true. "Garlic would be hardest to give up," she added.

"Persians don't use much garlic," said Heidi. "But they use rose water. I've never quite liked it."

"That must be it," said Chloe, tasting something funny in the rice.

They were eating at the Pepsi-Cola at tables of Formica, chrome chairs, linoleum of green and paste color, which she had grown accustomed to. Here you got a pretty good chelo kebab and fresh fish flown in from the gulf; it was ten times cheaper than the Cyrus, and everybody agreed that the food was as good. No wine. You drank tea or Pepsi-Cola. Chloe drank regular Pepsi now because they didn't have diet Pepsi. She could remember a time when she would have thought drinking regular would lead to death. The tea in Iran was strong as tonic. The doctors called it battery fluid. It was delicious, but if you drank too much of it you couldn't sleep, and she had passed a few sleepless nights staring at the mound of Hugh in the other cot.

Hugh chose most nights to stay with her on this second cot, rather than return to his own quarters, where he had at present a roommate, a snoring surgeon from North Carolina, to whom he had given, he said, no explanation for his absences. He would stay the night but then would steal out at dawn, with the first moan of prayer, when, fortunately, there seemed to be few faithful up to observe. He crept in at night, when the coast was clear, usually about ten. They were at a loss as to how to get him another key. Chloe had pretended to be afraid of losing hers, and asked for another from Dr. Farmani and been refused, and she had not found a locksmith, so for now Hugh was obliged to cough in the shrubbery beneath her window, she to steal down the steps to the front door. Hugh would scuttle inside at a moment when no one was passing by, which was easy enough after the front gates of the compound were shut for the night, an arrangement at once connubial and excitingly clandestine.

Hugh had adapted to connubial comfort without question and without analysis—a cheerful companion and ardent lover with no thought, it seemed, for the future. Perhaps he took domestic harmony for granted, was accustomed to find everywhere some nice woman in his life, arms extended, dinner ready, legs spread later. Chloe saw that she was just the nice woman of the moment; then they would go back to America and someone else would be the nice woman. And sometimes the nice woman would insist on marriage. Then he would marry her, because he was so cheerful and obliging, and then when she found out she was just a functionary, she would leave him; that must be the explanation for his two divorces.

She didn't mind being the nice woman, she told herself. For one thing, there was so much love-making. She had always kept secret her reverence for sex, which she believed she felt more keenly than other people but that it would, if expressed, be too easily mistaken for sexual boasting or sentimentality. What she felt was something akin to deep rapturous happiness and amazement that there were inexpressible forces that caused waves and atoms and emanations in her toward Hugh, or if not just him toward another handsome man. It was all very well to say "nature," of course, but what is nature? Whatever it was, she felt herself deeply, darkly, a part of it.

After a near disaster on Hugh's teetery cot, they had taken to love-making on the sofa, struggling awkwardly around the wooden arms or in a semi-sitting position, which Chloe secretly feared revealed the tops of their heads, to be seen by anybody walking by, head tops bobbing up and disappearing below the sill. And, when she thought about it, she found herself irritated that Hugh had not asked about contraception, simply taking for granted that she was doing what was necessary, just as she did at home, though that was not among the things she held against Jeffrey, whose offer of a vasectomy had horrified her, thinking as she had been that this would have the effect of controlling her life. As it was she wore an IUD.

She did not complain to Hugh about her life in California, or about Jeffrey, to whom she felt loyal in a way. Also, she was not able to formulate to herself just what it was about Jeffrey, or about Jeffrey and her, that wasn't perfectly harmonious, nothing you could say in a divorce court. But Jeffrey's crossness, his bad temper, contrasted so clearly with Hugh's cheerfulness and good humor that she found herself remembering more often than she liked certain passages with Jeffrey: once when he had turned the car around and driven them home, although they were all dressed for their outing, because the children had wrestled in the back seat. Once when he had been cutting salami and had brandished a butcher knife at her, and once when making love, during which the door had creaked and he had lifted his head and said harshly to her, "You didn't lock the goddamned door."

At the time she had laughed. To speak in such an angry tone to someone you are making love to! But it came back to her often. You wouldn't speak that way to a new lover, or to anyone you really loved. She felt that Hugh would not speak that way to anyone ever.

On the other hand there was something a trifle opaque about Hugh's radiant sweetness. If he had inner depths or torment they were not apparent. Vigorous, handsome, and intelligent. Lucky for him. Fortune had also favored him with an expensive watch, an elegant wallet of some lizard skin—these seemed to be his only possessions. Back home in his regular life he might for all she knew be a voracious collector of things, but she doubted it. He seemed indifferent to objects. When he took his shoes off at night he put them neatly against the wall, the toes pointing toward the wall, and hung his pants over the back of a chair. The socks in the shoes, the coat in the closet. When did he shine his shiny shoes, which did not seem to gather as hers did the dust of the Iranian streets?

There was no hint of an explanation for the nine shirts. She could never discuss his lie with him because she would seem demanding and proprietary. She was afraid to seem like that kind of woman, like a wife who would say, "Where have you been?"

She had tried once or twice to talk to Hugh about what they would do when they got back. She didn't have any ideas of her own—didn't want to break off their affair, but of course Jeffrey mustn't find out; would they go back to quick glimpses of each other at medical meetings, the occasional trip to San Francisco by Hugh to lecture? What would she do if Hugh suggested she divorce Jeffrey and marry him? This he did not seem likely to do at the moment, but who knew whether he would miss her when they got back to the U.S. again, immured in their lonely daily lives. His happiness now, his affectionate manner, his protestations of love, even, for he whispered "I love you" sometimes: were all these to end?

Chloe despised herself when she thought like this. She was going to go back to Jeffrey as had been planned all along, and would think of this as a lovely interlude and great good luck, but that was all. Would she really want to move to Rochester, New York? Hugh being fatherly to the children, taking them to Marineland—impossible to imagine, but then it was all impossible to imagine—America itself, representing itself to her imagination as a mélange of freeways and muggers—this must be the way foreigners think about it too—and her unweeded back garden and a stack of mail and unpaid bills and an appointment at the gynecologist and the dog for rabies booster, cats for feline distemper, children for tetanus and polio boosters, Pap smear, new transmission, rear brake linings, porcelain crowns. Such thoughts as these stimulated a rush of anxious maternity, and Chloe would write a long letter to the children full of lively description, injunction to goodness and cooperativeness; urgent desire to hug and kiss them and the happiness of seeing them and Grandma soon.

Chloe had come to understand Noosheen's passion for washing machines when the old machine in Villa Two gave out and she was obliged to wash things by hand in the laundry tub and drag them, pounds of sodden cotton, leaking up the stairs to the roof. She hadn't before appreciated the weight of wet clothes and could see why you would have to learn to carry them in a basket on your head. She had also come to enjoy hanging out the clothes. She had begun by flinging things haphazardly over the line, but now was putting things in neat groups, bras at one end, wind-filled breasts all pointing the same way, panties next to them. Now in the hot weather she never wore stockings. She had never accepted wash-and-wear clothing, but she had discovered that by stretching the skirts of her cotton dresses and smoothing the wet hems with her fingers, she didn't have to iron them. She pulled at the collars and plackets. She had not at first done Hugh's wash but really it seemed very little trouble to throw his socks and underwear into the water along with hers.

In other ways too her life with Hugh was like marriage. Some nights Hugh brought the *Herald Tribune* or London *Times*, and they sat reading, squinting under the dim bulb as the dogs gathered in the shrubbery and the last call to prayer went forth over the cricket sounds. Sometimes Hugh told her about being a boy in New England, making maple syrup. She was charmed at any individuating glimpse into his past. The evenings grew hotter, the nights hotter, the sounds blown about on a new wind from the desert. Like married people they exchanged hospital gossip. When Chloe told Hugh about Noosheen's unhappiness and aspirations, her studies, her dislike of her washing woman, her crush on Abbas, Hugh grew unaccountably impatient.

"Jesus Christ, Chloe, you encourage that silly young woman," he said.

"No, I don't encourage her, but I am sympathetic. She has no one else to talk to. Her family is away, she's very unhappy. . . ."

When you are overwrought, a calming mental exercise is to imagine yourself throwing away junk mail. You read the envelopes one by one and throw away unopened each thing that is addressed by means of a label stuck on. Father Henry's Boys' Village, the Christmas Pledge Drive, Save the Delta, Poets' Collective, Sea Gull Fund, kidneys, blood, lungs, heart, cancer, muscles, cysts, birth defects, brain damage. Some you save:

unwanted children, starving children, baby seals. Envelopes for the starving stack up.

To think of the envelopes stacking up almost destroys the happiness of being far away, hanging up clothes on an Iranian rooftop, with nothing much to do, with a lover. It occurs to her that she is tasting some of the fun and power of being a man, being far away, on her own, working at something, sleeping with someone she won't mention to the person at home.

"Really," said Jeffrey in his next letter, "when you think how you'll be home in three weeks, it doesn't make sense for me to pack up and come now." At first surprised, Chloe found herself more or less indifferent to this news except for the disappointment to the children, who must have been looking forward to traveling to Iran and Rome, especially Sara, whom they had thought old enough to get something out of it. What had Jeffrey promised her instead?

Only three more weeks was the thing that struck at her heart. A period to happiness. But perhaps happiness does not exist without a sense of its limits. As they say too of life. Three weeks. It caught in her throat.

Jeffrey also wrote to Vahid Farmani that he wasn't coming after all. Vahid just showed the letter to Linda with a smirk. He was unsurprised. He knew it wasn't from the real Fowler anyway and was just a manifestation of the plan ticking away outside his control.

Hossein lies nights in the doorway of the Farmanis' kitchen, cool against the marble stoop, listening to the dogs, to the little tunes of radios flickering on the ear, thinking, though he is old, of having a woman, or thinking with disgust of women, of the American woman's washing, or of a house he knew where girls came in from the country. He no longer thinks of returning to his family in the country, in a village near Suse.

Chapter Eighteen
LOCAL COLOR

Ah, make the most of what we yet may spend,
Before we too into the Dust descend;
Dust into Dust, and under Dust, to lie,
Sans Wine, sans Song, sans Singer, and, —sans End!

The days passed. One Monday Abbas Mowlavi took Chloe, Junie, and Mrs. Henderson to a mosque. "Persons not conveniently dressed, not admitted," read the sign. "Any transgression will be denounced to the police." "*That* gives you pause," said Chloe.

Abbas had brought veils for them to wear. "You can rent them for a few tooman, outside the mosque, but I think it's not perhaps too nice," he explained. Chloe's veil was sprigged pink, those of Junie and Mrs. Henderson black. Chloe's veil held the faint scent of powder or perfume. She wondered if it had belonged to Abbas's wife, and whether he remembered her by this scent. If someone you loved died, you could keep the things that smelled of them. She'd never thought of this. But now the veils would smell of her and Mrs. Henderson.

In her veil she felt clumsy and kept dropping the ends. Abbas showed them how to wrap themselves, but he was no expert either. "You clamp it under your arm to start with, I think," he said. "Sometimes the other end they hold in their teeth." Chloe wondered how she looked. Mrs. Henderson's white hair and pink cheeks were all wrong. She looked like a rosy nun or elderly madonna wearing earrings of turquoise plastic. Junie was too tall and awkward. "In America this would be objected to, making the women cover themselves but not the men; there would be a class-action suit," Junie said as they took off their shoes.

The inside of the mosque was entirely covered in mirror, a cathedral-size room in mirror mosaic. It seemed a worldly idea, for everywhere she looked she saw not Allah but a fragmented Chloe, pink-sprigged and manifold, amid the shimmering glass. In one corner stood the bier of a sacred person. Abbas explained he was the brother of an imam, and people kissed the mirrored bars of the cage that enclosed his coffin. Chloe saw a small woman in black, kissing the golden cage, her eyes tightly closed in passionate devotion. Chloe thought it was Noosheen, until she remembered that Noosheen was not a Muslim but a Zoroastrian. She wondered what sort of church the Zoroastrians had, and whether they wore veils. A heavy musky scent of incense, dusty rugs, and perhaps of bare feet, hung in the thick air. The effect on Chloe was oddly erotic. Chloe knew this place ought to be sacred, but when she breathed deeply the profane richness of the screens, the sultry burning of the lamps overhead, the sighs of prayer, she thought of harems. She thought of lounging here on cushions, with pistachio nuts and wine, voluptuous and indolent, waiting for Abbas. She the always-chosen, the nightly chosen, whispers, pleasure. The milk and wine of her breasts. The man would be Abbas—someone like Abbas—but in robes, in turban. The handsome men of the desert; to think that beneath their womanly skirts they were all equipped like men.

A wizened holy man, squinting and sour, glared at their clumsily draped faces. He knew them for Western women. Chloe shrank reverently over the tomb of a nephew of a prophet, absorbed in her imaginings.

Each day Chloe read a little of the Koran, a chapter a day, feeling no more interest in it than in the Bible, which it seemed to resemble, and which she had never read all the way through, just the Old Testament up to Leviticus, and the famous parts, studied in the Episcopalian Sunday school long ago. She knew she was illiterate in an essential cultural subject, but by toiling in the Koran, she told herself, she was in a way making up for her previous deficiency. In the Koran, the world was created by God in six days, and woman out of man, with this original pair being driven out of a garden; and there were characters named Lot or Abraham or Moses, so Mohammed had evidently read the Old Testament, and even, probably, the New.

Chloe did not know why she was not spiritual. She believed in a general way that people should be spiritual, it was just that she was not. She hoped she might have natural piety. She would not scoff at God, or nature, or at the Koran, either. Indeed, while reading, she would fall into a mood of humble chagrin at her own spiritual failings, and feel the wish that something would seize her soul with faith or even with violent and emphatic skepticism. Instead she felt only the charm of the Day of Judgment:

> *Surely among delights*
> *Shall the righteous dwell,*
> *Seated on bridal couches they will gaze around;*
> *Thou shalt mark in their faces the brightness of delight;*
> *Choice sealed wine shall be given them to quaff. . . .*

A shiver of regret would seize her that she herself would undoubtedly be a victim of "The Inevitable."

"I suppose you are a Muslim," Chloe said to Abbas as they left the mosque.

"By birth. I am afraid I'm not very religious," Abbas said, apologetically and after a moment of pensiveness, like a fallen-away Catholic.

"I believe there are many similarities with Christianity," said Mrs. Henderson.

Abbas smiled. "Unlike Jesus, Mohammed was human. He was subject to human vulgarities, like desire and jealousy."

"I wish I could read Arabic. I would so like to read the Koran in the original," said Chloe politely.

"I believe there are some good translations," Abbas said. "How are you coming with your Farsi?"

"Not very well," she admitted. In fact it had been nearly a week since she had looked at the textbook, though she had learned to say *"Che qadr"* in the market.

"I think I need a teacher. The book isn't very satisfactory. I often have questions."

"For instance?"

"For instance, is there no word for 'please' or 'thank you'?"

Abbas laughed. "Probably you have got some old colonial book," he said.

Another day he took them to see the tomb of Cyrus, king of the Achaemenians. This king once had lain in a sepulcher atop the rather desolate stone cairn they now beheld. Chloe, who had been put in charge of the guidebook, read out to the others: "According to Strabo this was inscribed 'Oh man, I am Cyrus who founded the Empire of the Persians and was king of Asia. Grudge me not therefore this monument.' "

Once, said the book, the funerary mausoleum had been decked with rich hangings, the body reposed in a sarcophagus of gold, the sarcophagus lay on a gold couch, and near it were arrayed various treasures of gold. Magi guarded the tomb, and lived nearby in fragrant gardens. The Americans viewed with satisfaction the desolation of the spot, the simple splendor of the enduring stone. Two Iranian men, their eyes leering out wildly from faces dark with dust, squatted in the shade afforded by the monument. Guards or perhaps just loungers, they motioned to the travelers that it was all right to climb the giant steps of the ziggurat and peer into the empty treasure chamber. Dutifully the Americans boosted each other up and stared into the stone cavity, empty except for a bit of plastic wrapper blown into one corner.

When they climbed down, the guards leapt up to lift the ladies down the last high step. With expressionless faces, their hands skimmed over Chloe's breasts, pressing furtively. Chloe glanced at Junie, whose pinkness suggested that this had happened to her too. Chloe pretended not to notice; she thought of laughing at the men, if only she could convey how she despised their little triumph over Christian women—women entirely indifferent to skinny little brown men who smelt of camel and tobacco and wore rags. As it was she said nothing, but she felt irritated and looked away, smiling her bright smile at her friends, as if she did not even see these functionaries. It now struck her that the Iranian women—Noosheen and Zareeneh Yazdi—had not climbed the monument. How stupid she felt herself, to mind what these poor men did, she who was so incalculably more fortunate.

Noosheen's husband Bahram had come along, though he rarely joined these sightseeing expeditions. Chloe was struck by how Noosheen walked before or behind him, and looked away when he looked at her. Perhaps they were having a quarrel. Bahram was the picture of a concerned husband, handing her in and out of cars and providing other attentions, like an old cuckold from Boccaccio or Chaucer, and Noosheen had just the same expression, under her expression of sweetness, of willfulness, a classical young wife. Chloe found these analogies comforting evidence of the consistency of human nature, any nation, any age. The Iranians are like us, she thought. Seeing Bahram, Chloe could better understand one of Noosheen's confidences: "I do not really like the act of love," she had said. "But I feel that I might if he were . . . different."

"Do you have an M.A.?" Noosheen asked Chloe now, as they walked back to the cars.

"No," Chloe admitted. Most of her friends did. She had always planned to get an M.A. but could never think in what.

"I hope to get mine," said Noosheen.

"In what?"

"Well—in English literature," Noosheen said, widening her eyes, a tremor of surprise in her voice that it was necessary to ask something so obvious. "English literature of the nineteenth century!" she added.

"Oh, of course," said Chloe, who had been thinking of being felt up by the horrid Iranians.

"Do you think I should?"

"Well, sure," said Chloe easily. "Victorian literature is wonderful."

"My husband doesn't want me to. It means a long period of study. First I must finish my B.A., that's another year to begin with. Then—it could be years. Also, would my degree be any good? I don't know if the teachers at Shiraz University are very qualified. I wanted to go to Wayne State. It was all fixed. But with perseverance it is possible to study here. Do you think I should?"

Chloe hoped this was only a rhetorical question, and that Noosheen was not seriously depending on her answer, for she had no idea what Noosheen should do. It seemed rather a useless specialty, Victorian literature, for someone living in Iran, although it would no doubt be a consolation in itself. And, after all, a twentieth-century American was as remote as an Iranian from people in a Dickens novel, neither having ever seen a winkle or a verger or a dust heap. An M.A. in English literature—why not?

"You can always teach," she said.

"Yes," Noosheen agreed, sounding dubious. Suddenly she stopped and pointed toward the river bank ahead of them. Her eyes had widened with, it seemed, a sudden rage. "Look, look at that, look there!"

She was pointing to a spot among the stones where tribal women, their wrappings tied back, strong brown arms wet, or wading with skirts hitched up, wrestled wet cloths and beat them on rocks. Doing the washing. Boxes of Tide near them in baskets on the shore. It was picturesque and pretty.

"That, that is the real Iran," cried Noosheen, her voice informed with a curious passion, her glance at her husband full of irritable triumph.

They planned to return to their automobiles by a different route, in order to see a little village that lay beyond the monument. Dick strolled slowly behind the others, looking for potsherds, mind idly dwelling on the dead man, on Marla and the house, on whether things had been misplaced in the laboratory yesterday. It was the house, for some reason, that was uppermost in his mind this afternoon. He was remembering how happy they had been when they moved in. After months of looking, it had struck them both immediately as inevitably theirs. Marla had called, with the realtor standing there, for him to rush over. A big, lovely house, something the kids could bring their kids back to, practically a mansion, and now she wanted a condo.

He had fallen into the habit of keeping an eye out for potsherds, at first intending to give them to Chloe, but now he had got interested in them. It occurred to him that he had some other little bits of pottery, picked up here and there—Mesa Verde, Yellowstone—which with these might make a nice collection; he could get them mounted.

This long road took them through a village of mud hovels, roofed in straw. Women squatted before the hovels; goats roamed in the dung and mud of the street. A trickle of water wetted the dust. People looked at them without curiosity or interest. A child smiled at them. Chloe liked, somehow, the acrid smell of meat cooking over a dung fire.

"*This* is the real Iran," said Abbas. "Most of the people still live like this. The tribal people, who move their flocks, live better than these villagers."

The children were thin; the little girls had ragged black shawls over their heads. Heaps of broken pots and rusting tubs of oil stood outside the doorways. Behind the houses, from somewhere they heard keening and wailing.

"Where are the men?" asked Hugh.

"In the fields. There is some agriculture here. Or they have gone to Tehran, hoping for work. The people don't want to work in the fields any more."

"What is the wailing?"

"Oh, a death or a funeral."

As the party stood, observing the life of the villagers as if it were a pageant, a play being shown to them by their Iranian guide, Dick's notice fell on a child propped against a rubble wall, a girl of eleven or twelve, whose arms had the appalling stick-like thinness of the starving, the wrists thicker than the bony limbs, wrists like bracelets of bone. Her eyes, staring and dull, saw Dick. The child's desiccation and lassitude were shocking. He had only seen starvation in photographs or films. Yet the villagers were cooking something, there was a smell of charred lamb. Illness, it must be. She was crouching silently, the head swaying slightly, as if she lacked the strength to hold it up. A dirty rag was wrapped around her shoulders, a child's veil. Women of the village walked by without noticing her. The Iranian doctors must notice. The dull eyes watched them.

"That child is sick," Dick Rothblatt said to Vahid.

"Yes," Vahid agreed. "She has the look of hepatitis."

"We should take her back with us," Chloe said, frightened that the child would die right now before them.

"In general the health of the peasants is very good," said Vahid Farmani.

"They suffer from easily preventable infections," Hugh disagreed.

"It's very discouraging. They must be educated first. Otherwise they don't take their medicines, they don't come back for follow-up care," said Farmani. They had begun to walk slowly along the rutted path between the hovels.

"The little girl!" Chloe cried.

"I could perhaps ask someone where her mother is," Abbas said, and called out to a woman near him. The woman answered him.

"Yes, they have given her up," Abbas said.

"At a certain point there is nothing one can do," Farmani explained. They were walking rapidly on.

"There are always incentives," Hugh said. "In every culture, even the most resistant, a way can be found to make people come in. And the people here are relatively advanced. You work with the tribal leader, or whomever it takes and you could stamp out these things."

"Yes, we have much to do," said Vahid, walking more quickly toward the road where they had left their cars. They were leaving the child; not even Dick or Junie looked back at her.

"But couldn't we help?" Chloe asked, her face white with indignation. This was the third-world lesson, of course she knew that, that you see some evidence of hopelessness, you confront the passive acceptance of death, you did what you could but it wasn't much, you had to get used to the whole bleak apparatus of reality. It was what was supposed to happen. She felt faint with anxiety.

"I'm trying to think of something to do," Dick assured her, but could not think what.

That night he had a dream that he was standing with a stick in his hand, a part of a tree, the leaves still on it, leafy and full, but with the stub end gnarled and bloody as if it had been wrested from its socket. He beat the man in the cave to death with it.

"Who was it that spoke," said Chloe to Hugh on the sofa that night, "of the deep, deep peace of the double bed, after the hurly-burly of the chaise longue?"

"It's true," Hugh agreed, "it'd be nice to have a double bed. A queen-size, while we're at it."

"Of course she was really talking about marriage," said Chloe, wishing suddenly to be married to Hugh.

Chapter Nineteen
NEWCOMERS

O Thou, who didst with Pitfall and with Gin
Beset the Road I was to wander in,
Thou wilt not with Predestined Evil round
Enmesh, and then impute my Fall to Sin!

The little dying girl haunted Chloe with feelings of shame and fear. There's little you can do, after all, to ward off evil and bring yourself some luck, even for her, a privileged woman; what chance for the little girl? Chloe always wore her lapis beads now, afraid to leave them in her drawer and comforted each morning by the tiny chill stones against her throat, then by the warmth her throat gave them, and the warmth of her fingers as she touched them. Lapis lazuli was supposed to bring out your character. If you were bad it made you worse, if good better, it intensified your qualities. But she could not see that any of her qualities were intensified. Was she worse or sillier than usual? It seemed to her that in some ways she was better— calmer and more agreeable to others, better unless you counted sleeping with Hugh Monroe as being bad.

She should have given the little girl something. Did anyone know whether inanimate objects might not really bring luck? Was there something about atoms? There was a theory: some blandishing and promising atoms collected together create a field, a force, and an object made of those atoms when worn had an effect. Chloe was pretty sure her lapis beads were lucky. She thought of the little girl in the village, with a brass disk on a chain around her neck. In documentaries about primitive tribes you saw the puny children decked in amulets put there by the frightened mothers. In Iran the poorest woman, in black shrouds, seemed to have a golden chain or charm, so there must be something in it. Down the centuries people believing in luck—could they all be wrong?

In the bazaar she bought a pair of tiny silver charms, old, set with glass and silver paper, clumsy and simple, but powerful-looking, and she planned to make her children wear them even though they would object.

She knew she'd gained weight. It was something in favor of the chador that you could be fat inside it and no one would see you. She knew she shouldn't care what people think. She was too vain to be happy fat in California but here it didn't matter. Hugh didn't seem to mind or notice a slight dimpling of her thighs, was never deterred in his always rather single-minded object by the increase of an inch around her waist. She wished you could wear veils in San Francisco.

Her friend Heidi wore head scarves when walking in the street. Chloe, tying a scarf over her own bright hair, saw it was true that one felt more comfortable. And she had strangely begun to feel uncomfortable with her upper arms bare. It was not that people stared, or that there was any objection to upper arms. The feeling, she recognized, came from within herself, presenting itself as a crawling sensation, as if you were in a draft above the elbows. It was really simpler, when you were just running out to the store, to evade the issue of being a Western woman, pale and fair, by putting on something long-sleeved, and a scarf. Chloe thought it was foolish of young women like Noosheen to want to lighten their fine, dark hair.

Her beads she always wore, and her wedding ring, of course, and the head scarf, and rather wished for a cloak or veil. If she wore her beads, that left only her camera worth stealing, so she had taken to leaving the door open for Hugh, or leaving the key under the mat where anyone would think to look. She had given up taking photographs. Sights found at first so ravishing, so voluptuously lacking in perpendiculars, so lavishly floral, vined, entwined, mirrored, filigreed, carved, inlaid, cushioned, screened, now appeared to her if not normal at least not so compellingly in need of being photographed. They seemed to be aspects of an enduring material world whose existence did not need to be confirmed in inept photos by American ladies. Indeed, it was a material world in process of amelioration, since everywhere the government had set people to refurbishing and polishing the lovely crumbling palaces and pavilions, and decayed corners of mosques.

The sociable and regular rhythm of Azami life was continuing despite disquieting rumors and disruptions. News of strikes in other towns reached them, and Chloe realized that the soldiers with machine guns she had seen in Isfahan had been there in expectation of some riot or insurgence. They had been, it appeared, prepared to kill their countrymen.

She, like the other Americans, though regretting these intimations of bloodshed, viewed them with equanimity, even approval. They had the regular American belief that tyrants must and will eventually fall. They didn't even mind the occasional manifestation of anti-Americanism. They didn't take it personally, and they were all leaving anyway. Chloe hated the thought that she had only three weeks left. Meantime, she did have something anti-American happen to her, startling her, if only for a moment.

The American Wives' Club met the third Thursday of the month, the English Wives' Club had a tea each Wednesday. On Wednesday nights the Iranian doctors had dinner in the Reza Café and went to the English-language films, as a way of keeping up their English and having a good time. On weekends the inevitable dinner party, sightseeing, tennis. Chloe liked the dinner parties best. Persian dinners were so pretty. At first they had surprised her. You are led into the other room, or a table is brought to the room where you are, all laid, a glorious buffet, with none of this shuffling dishes in and out from the kitchen that Chloe was used to and preferred until she came to see that the Arabian Nights fantasy way of presenting a meal was really better, as if a genie had waved it onto the table, though you knew, of course, that women had toiled over it. Chloe was not always invited to the dinner parties, though people always invited the attractive Dr. Monroe. Sometimes, for form's sake, he went. Chloe tried not to mind.

She knew that without Jeffrey she didn't really belong. As at summer camp, she was conscious of having to earn her place here. People, except for Linda Farmani, seemed to like her, but she was accustomed to being liked; a sympathetic listener, ready with toast and coffee, she made them comfortable. Listening to people and cooking for them were second nature to her, a reasonable price for the attention of others. Still, she was feeling slightly embarrassed, with all the hospitality she had received, not to have done more for others, and resolved to have something, perhaps a drinks party, or a little supper of her own. This inspired her to continue the refurbishment of her room, whose ugliness she had partly got used to, and she was grateful for the activity too to support her spirits, which, when she sat quietly, oppressed her with thoughts of the little village girl, and of all lame people and starving people, and of her own children, so unaccountably separated from her and far away.

She thinks Dick's rug looks wonderful in her room. She has put it in the center, where it can be seen from her chair or when she lies in her camp bed, and where it covered a worn spot on the linoleum. Any plain cell or tent can be thus transformed; you can carry your rug with you like a bedouin so that wherever you go will be beautiful. She sits on it amid the flowers and birds, protected, surrounded by the rich borders, and envies Dick his rug, and thinks how nice he is to forgo the pleasure and protection of his rug. She thinks of young women sitting by the rug loom, their eyes wet with strain, and being put out on the sand when their fingers grow too clumsy. Could that be true? Probably. Women are always expendable when they can no longer perform their duties. In America her life is safe because she can take the toaster and pick up the children from school. Here it is useless, without function. How strange, then, that it should be here that she feels full of purpose and calm.

She has a color in mind for her room, blue, something like lapis, but with more green in it, not a color you would paint anything in California except the bottom of a swimming pool, but the strong color they use here for window sashes and doors and porches. This color wards off evil. She buys the paint. She thinks it looks reassuring. She can see why it wards off evil. She paints the grayish plaster of the hallway, and then the door to her apartment, and then, encouraged, rather giddy with the success of this powerful measure, the outside door of Villa Two, let the Azami people remonstrate if they will. She loves this bright, uncanny color. She paints the window sills in the kitchen. Then she invites people to tea for the following day, and goes to the bazaar to buy pistachio cakes and tea.

It is here that she has the unsettling experience. Just walking along, not seeing, really, the women so invisible in their shrouds, when all at once one of them steps in front of her, impeding her passage along the sawdust hallway, and as rapidly as an executioner with a sword, the woman lays a finger along Chloe's throat. As delicate as a blade, as swift, then is gone. Chloe thinks for an instant that it has been an affectionate touch, a sisterly gesture of some kind, then that the woman had reached impulsively for her beads. Guiltily she realizes that she shouldn't wear them showing. Ostentation, so many women here with nothing, she ought to have realized that here was a gesture of hate or warning. It is disconcerting to be hated by another woman. Chloe did not think this had happened to her before. What had they seen in her heart? She tucks her beads inside her blouse.

Nearly everyone accepted her invitation. At first, the Iranians regarded General Ben with a certain reserve. He regaled the gathering with terrible anecdotes about Vietnam, embarrassing

Chloe beyond speech. Why remind them that Americans had been the bullies of the world? How could General Ben not see that? Instead he said what Chloe had never actually heard anyone say, though of course she knew there were people who thought this: "We should have just gone in there with the nukes and got it over with." Of course, she reminded herself, it was not surprising that a general should be committed to military success. What was more surprising was that she continued to like General Ben, and even still more surprising that the Iranians also seemed, as he rattled on, to come to like him too, leaving Chloe alone in her dismay at his views. Noosheen sat next to him on Chloe's cot, sipping her tea and listening with unmoving eyes as he criticized Iranian customs.

"Of course women can escape," he was saying, "if they have money. They can get a forged exit visa or they can get themselves smuggled out through Afghanistan or Russia. A friend of mine helped a woman get out. An American woman married to an Iranian, no passport. The husband didn't want her to go. They put her in some rugs, like Cleopatra." He laughed. Noosheen clutched her cup. Chloe thought of the terrible situation of not being able to leave if you wanted to leave, a man, a marriage, a country. In America, what could stop you—if you had the money?

"They think of women as property," he said, "all these Arabs do. No offense, as the kids say."

"I'm not offended," Noosheen said. "I agree completely. Although, you know, we in Iran are not Arabs."

Nor did she seem offended when the talk ran on to the general subject of the modesty of Iranian women, and the conservatism of Iranian men on this point.

"I used to think that all the fuss that people make, in America, about how advertising exploits women and so on, I always thought people would do better to press for more important reforms, like reforming the child-support laws," Chloe was saying. "But now I've come to feel that there's something reassuring and nice about not always being greeted by huge billboard-sized breasts and so on.''

"Actually they're all sex-mad here," Junie said sourly, "despite the purity of the billboards. The repression and mystery turn them into sex maniacs. It would be better to have dirty billboards." She put her cup on Chloe's tray, an inlaid tray of ivory and wood, of which the ivory was probably plastic, bought in the bazaar.

"Actually Iran is not an Arab country," Noosheen said.

"Actually I find them sexy, in a way," Dick said. "The veil is kind of erotic—the legs flashing by under the robes. They wear sexy stockings, some of them, have you noticed? Black mesh. High heels. Like a porn film."

"You hear that the whores in Tehran don't wear anything at all under the chador. Then they flash as the man comes by," said Chloe.

"Who told you that?" asked Linda Farmani.

"I heard it at the English Wives' Club," said Chloe, wondering if Linda had ever been invited to the English Wives' Club and whether she wanted to be.

"I didn't think they had whores in Iran," Dick said. "I never heard of any."

Chloe had invited Linda Farmani, who surprised her by coming, sitting with aplomb on the edge of Hugh's cot and seeming not to notice the wretchedness of the place, notwithstanding the improvements of which Chloe was so proud, and the considerable asset of Dick's rug.

"Foreigners often don't take things really seriously here, our laws, our customs," said Linda. "They think our rules don't apply. For instance, I'm sure that in California Mrs. Fowler would never snitch her neighbor's plants."

This was said with so affable a smile at General Ben, that Chloe almost for a moment didn't take offense; a shock only set in after a moment, when the talk had gone on to something else and no rejoinder was possible. Chloe resolved to explain herself to Linda later: I didn't think you'd miss them, she would say. Of course—wasn't that what thieves always did say? Her ears heated up. It came to her that no one had ever criticized her in public before. Moreover, she would not in California have stolen a neighbor's plants. What was becoming of her? Looking at the others, their smiles affectionate, the conversation turned to something else, she saw the moment had passed and that she was the only sufferer. What was becoming of her?

After the guests left, as Chloe stood at the kitchen sink, washing the cups, she observed an arrival. The apartment next to hers, whose occupants would share the kitchen, had been empty since she got there, but it now appeared that someone was coming to live in it. Chloe watched from the window, even pushing aside the screen to fold her arms along the warm window sill and lean out a little, the better to see. It was a taxi; a driver was carrying suitcases to the front steps. Vahid Farmani stood on the sidewalk and watched the luggage, and a man was helping a stout woman out of the back seat. Americans, by the look of their clothes. Following a wave of Farmani's hand, the two looked up at Villa Two. Chloe stared back at them with interest. The American woman was keeping both hands on the handle of her purse; probably she had carried a load of jewelry in her purse.

The three approached Villa Two and entered. Chloe reflected with satisfaction that the foyer was no longer the smelly place it had been when she had come, and enjoyed a pleasant sensation of philanthropic virtue. Footsteps on the stairs and the sound of the key in the lock across the hall, the door shutting after them, voices. Then Vahid telling them he would see them later. Chloe sighed. It was a nuisance to think of that fat woman in the kitchen wanting the coffeepot, and strange food in the fridge, and it would be harder for Hugh to slip in unseen. But did she even care who saw him?

* * *

It was nearly six o'clock. She thought she might walk over to the Cyrus. From the bathroom as she combed her hair she became aware of voices rising, drifting through the wall, indistinct but vehement. The woman was shouting.

She returned to her living room to wait. The knocking, as she half-expected, followed in a moment. Perhaps she was becoming psychic. The man's face was red and tired; he wore a tie clip.

"Excuse me. Harold Erdman. Is there a hotel in Shiraz, do you happen to know?"

"Oh, yes, it's called the Cyrus." She pronounced it as it was pronounced: Kurush, let them figure it out. Then she relented and said it the regular way. " 'Kurush,' we would say 'Cyrus.' "

"Thanks," he said, and went back inside his door again. Before long Chloe heard them bumping and carrying bags down the stairs again.

"I'm just going there now," she said as she passed them on the stairs. "Maybe you should come with me, and then send for your bags."

"You stay with the bags, I'll go fix the hotel," said Dr. Erdman to his wife. At this unlucky moment, Dr. Farmani himself strolled up with the Erdmans' key. Dr. Erdman stood rooted, embarrassed to be caught in flight, bags packed.

"Tell him we're not staying, Harold," said the voice of Mrs. Erdman from the upstairs window. Dr. Erdman glanced up toward the window in lieu of explanation. Dr. Farmani followed his gaze. The fat eyes of Mrs. Erdman glared at him, but she did not address him. The eyes of Dr. Farmani exchanged, for one instant, with Chloe, an enigmatic glance.

"Tell him filthy. What do they think we are?" shouted Mrs. Erdman.

Does Farmani think I've put them up to this? Chloe wondered. How good, how docile and polite she had been compared to Mrs. Erdman.

"More comfortable, perhaps, in a hotel," said Dr. Erdman to Dr. Farmani.

"They promised explicitly," shouted Mrs. Erdman. "Harold, somebody's lining his pockets out of this, put the Americans in here and pocket the hotel money, something like that."

Dr. Farmani glared at Chloe, as if she were the author of this scandalous rumor. "I don't know these people," she felt herself wanting to say, wishing to defend herself even to the horrid Dr. Farmani. "I don't even know these people"; her emotions a tangle of sympathy for Farmani, dislike of the Erdmans, embarrassment at their bad manners, and anger at them for not toughing it out as some other, more virtuous, people had. Dr. Farmani would not be thinking of this.

"If, of course, the hotel, more comfortable," he was saying.

"Since it's just a few days," Dr. Erdman was saying.

"Unhappily we have no financial arrangements for that," Dr. Farmani said.

"Oh, understood," said Dr. Erdman. "We'll take care of it ourselves. It'd be a help if you'd phone them."

"They speak English perfectly well," said Dr. Farmani haughtily. In spite of her dislike of him, Chloe applauded his hardness of heart toward the Erdmans.

Then, later at the Cyrus, there they were in the bar, bathed and cheerful, talking expansively about their sufferings in Villa Two. He was an otorhinolaryngologist from Johns Hopkins. They complained that the Cyrus was expensive, but they were only staying a week, had been in Egypt, and were going to the Philippines with this stopover in Iran.

"We thought it would be a good chance to buy some rugs," Dr. Erdman said. "I mentioned it to Farmani. He's going to write down for me the names of the good shops."

The Erdmans were further convinced that the Cyrus was worth the extra expense when they heard Loyal Cooley's nightly discourse, tonight about a perilous trip he'd taken to some caves in Tunisia.

"Dysentery. Oh, hell, everybody had it, right from the first day. We got over worrying about it. We got expert. You only have one pair of jeans, you have to abandon shame. You got used to seeing someone just squat like a jackrabbit, same expression, sort of frantic fear, vulnerable, whip down the jeans. No rocks you can hide behind, remember this is the desert, you can see for miles. It makes a group close. In the silence, not a cricket, not an animal. Oh, they do have pit vipers. We killed two of them in camp. The bite of the pit viper's uniformly fatal. I had snake-venom antidote but no one else did. They all stuck close to me after they found out I had it.

"We walked fifteen hours a day. And this trip cost me thousands, besides. Out of eighteen people, only ten made it. It went from thirty-five, forty degrees in the morning to ninety in about two hours. Some people were really mad, paying all that money. Couldn't blame them. We made it, so it was worth it—wonderful caves. They hadn't realized how tough it would be, the tour leaders; this was their first time too."

Chloe looked around her, as usual, for a show of sly condemnatory glances from her friends but found in their countenances a certain opacity, a certain regional inscrutability, Dick looking, suddenly, very New York, the Erdmans Indianian—well, they were all Americans, including Loyal Cooley, including herself, and all were strangers.

"When I saw that base camp I knew that some of us were not gonna make it. Adversity says a lot about human nature. Right away I began saving my water. The second day I poured out my alcohol. I'd started out with a little alcohol, you know, thinking it would be nice at night. A pint of vodka poured out on the sand and it didn't even make a mark on the sand. If you had a granola bar it would have been worth two hundred dollars. We had eight people drop out in the first two days. One guy had a heart attack, one guy they thought had a stroke, one lady, really fat, had some problem with her leg. The others, heat exhaustion. Well, they should have screened these people. How could she climb on those huge fat legs?"

"Who was sponsoring this?" asked Mrs. Erdman.

"The Houston Art Museum."

"Did you see any cave paintings?" asked Chloe.

"Oh, sure, wonderful paintings, more beautiful than Lascaux, fifteen million years old. Or maybe fifteen thousand, anyway really great.

"Not a living creature except us, and the pit viper, and scorpions. If you heard something at night it was either a pit viper or somebody getting up with diarrhea. I was the most important guy in camp because I had the opium. I got it from my doctor, in case. Every night, you should have seen them line up, I put two drops of opium on their tongues. Even so there was diarrhea.

"Survival, that's the only thing on your mind. It's uplifting, in a way, just the simple thing of wondering where to put your foot next, when would you get some water. My wife didn't pour out her vodka. I could hear her in the dark, sneaking sips. One woman—somebody smelled chocolate on her breath—there was nearly a riot. But some people shared. That's human nature." All the travelers deeply sighed.

Never mind, my darlings, you wouldn't like it here much and it's getting awfully hot. When I get home (soon!) we will start *diving lessons,* and what else you would like to do this summer, much more fun really.

She got a letter from Sara, which said,

Dear Mom, Max broke my doll's dishes, he stepped on them.

Chapter Twenty
B L U E

The Ball no question makes of Ayes and Noes,
But Here or There as strikes the Player goes;
And He that tossed you down into the Field,
He knows about it all—HE knows—HE knows!

Dick one morning notices as he walks past Villa One on his way to the hospital an open door, a door that is usually closed. At the bottom of the house, and inside the doorway, he can see a wooden bench. This would not have attracted his eye or made an impression, except that during the split second of his perception, Hossein steps into his field of vision and squats on his haunches in the doorway, and Dick realizes with horror that this is where Hossein lives, in a dark, barely furnished room at the bottom of Villa One. Comes forth each morning and makes his ineffectual rounds in the various kitchens and bathrooms of the compound, maybe sleeps in there on the mud floor.

Does he have a family in there, does someone wash his shabby gray clothes? All the men he sees in Iran look somehow untended, shirts ironed as though by themselves; no female presence or care seems to attach to them. Not the doctors of course; their wives are as busy as American wives with children and parties and self-improvement. But the taxi driver, the man in the wagon—is this the price of female docility and seclusion that women revenge themselves by failing to nourish and tend? No wifely fingers on collar, at the knot of tie, a brush of shoulder, a pat. His heart taps more loudly for an instant at the thought of the pleasant but lost ministrations of American wives.

He is shaken anyway this morning by another harrowing night of dreams, ghastly guilt dreams of the staring body, hands stretching out of the grave to get him, exactly as if he had murdered the man. He supposes he feels guilty not to have saved him, or not to have made him a deathbed promise, or guilty to have let him go like that so uncomforted. He feels that these bad dreams do him credit, in a way, but he hates them. Last night he had brushed away the dust from the face of the corpse and it was the face of the little village girl.

On Wednesday, Chloe went with Heidi to the English Wives' Club tea. In the presence of her countrywomen, Heidi, usually natural and responsive, became reserved and polite, exclaiming over the tea in a high, official voice. Tea included "crisps," imported from England, which seemed to Chloe merely a form of inferior potato chip; and cucumber sandwiches, strangely spiced, and there were Iranian biscuits manufactured at a factory owned by the husband of Margaret, the oldest and most prosperous and therefore the dominant lady of this group. All the women smoked continuously, and were voracious for news of the outside world.

At her first visit they had asked Chloe all about California and also about Women's Lib, a subject remote from Iran, and also from England.

"Well," Chloe had said, "there've been great strides. Equal pay for equal work, and making sure women can advance in the job market, that kind of thing. I think they've accomplished a lot, even if they've put some people off with their methods. But the old bra-burning days are gone. I don't know—I can see that compared to here some of their goals might seem kind of frivolous."

"And what about the impotency problem?"

"The what?"

"Impotency? You read that Women's Lib has caused American men to be impotent."

"No, I never heard of that," Chloe said loyally.

"That's what they think in England," said Tina, laughing. They all laughed. English wives of sexy dark foreigners.

"Anyway," said Tina, "it's a man's problem."

"Impotency is not *our* problem," agreed the other ladies. Their accents varied by region and class. Chloe wondered if they would know each other if they were all back in England. And today there were two newcomers, one in fact Irish, called Nora, and the other Australian, Betts: these two women declared themselves resolved to keep their children speaking English, ideas that were met with a kind of defeated scorn by the real Englishwomen, mothers of little Farsi speakers. Chloe privately believed that the Englishwomen would not have been friends with Nora and Betts were they not all English-speakers isolated here together. Nora was a bit religious-looking, Betts peroxided and brisk, like an American but with the dreadful Australian accent. Maybe they wouldn't have been friends with Chloe either, a peroxided American. But here, now, they were all sisters.

The talk today was of a terrible event in Abadan, the oil-refining city to the south.

"But what has happened?" asked Chloe.

"This thing of the theatre in Abadan," they said. "Of the people being burnt up in the theatre in Abadan."

Set afire, it was said, by religious fanatics who objected to movies, and inside more than three hundred men were trapped and died.

"If that's who really did it," said Heidi, with a significant expression.

"Of course," said Tina, "they'd like nothing better than to blame the fundamentalists. The government, I mean."

"Why not the fundamentalists? They don't care if you die, you go to heaven. They are really bloodthirsty. Islam is bloodthirsty, I mean, and these are fanatics."

"Yes," said Margaret, "you go right to Allah, so what does it matter?"

"Whoever did it, they're all Iranians," Tina pointed out, and this received nods of unsurprised assent. Chloe pressed for details. She never saw a newspaper, had no radio. The newspapers were in Farsi, after all, though you could walk down to the Cyrus and get the *Herald Tribune;* it was just that she had enjoyed not having a newspaper, and quite right, too, if this was the horror it contained. The fumes, the flames, and the doors had been locked. It was intended by the killers that the poor men die—poor little thin men in rags watching a movie. Her heart swelled. They had trimmed their mustaches and gone to die.

"I suppose things will really shut down now," said Margaret.

"They've sent troops to Abadan," Tina said.

"My God, how horrible," said Betts, lighting a cigarette. "Was it the mullahs or the Shah then?"

"It doesn't matter," Margaret snapped, "they're all Iranians."

"What does Mohammed say?" Chloe asked Heidi, as they drove back to the compound, and Heidi just shrugged. "What can anyone say?"

The English wives were gloomy about the future of Iran. The difference in mood among the American wives proved, Chloe supposed, a difference in American temperament—naturally more optimistic or naturally more self-centered—for the subject of Abadan did not come up on Thursday when she went to the American lunch. This was held in the garden of a Grumman wife and was an altogether larger and somewhat impersonal party. Rows of bridge chairs had been set up under the shade of the garden portico, and a projection screen suggested that there would be entertainment. Food was buffet style, with iced tea and lemonade; and a whole table of American PTA-style desserts—mainly chocolate cake and apple pie. Chloe looked around for Linda Farmani, who was not there, and was overjoyed to see Heidi and her English friend Tina, Englishwomen though they were. Chloe, relaxed by familiar faces, and then by the familiarity of the occasion, began to enjoy it and to hate it, the way she hated these things in California too.

"Linda Farmani did us," a woman told Chloe, speaking of her décor. "Well, you know, we have to do so much entertaining. It's practically like an embassy, so the company said we should go ahead. She has a wonderful feel for an Iranian look— well, adapted to what an American would like."

"Her own house is certainly pretty," said Chloe.

"I would never use a decorator at home. I think the décor should express the person. But here I wouldn't have known where to start, you know, where to get things, but she just barges into the bazaar, she hasn't an ounce of fear."

"I guess she speaks the language," Chloe said.

"Absolutely like a native. She gave us a rather wonderful raw-silk wall covering, then a lot of brass."

"It sounds lovely," said Chloe, politely.

First came announcements, then dues. The forthcoming meeting. Thanks to the program and refreshment committees. Announcements: "The only way to be sure the mail gets there is to send it in the pouch. Remember, everything goes in the pouch," a woman reminded them. Everyone nodded. The woman speaking, thin and tan, with white earrings, wearing a smart golf dress, was somehow familiar. Heidi and Tina watched it all with the appearance of interest and had come, they said, though they usually did not, because there would be an interesting speaker, someone who had begun life as a tribesman, riding the plains on a donkey, and was now Minister of Education of all Iran.

This interested Chloe also. You never met government officials in the U.S. because they were so far away. This man was accessible and nice, by the look of him—a portly, curly-haired man, dark-skinned and authoritative, being talked to in the doorway by the hostess and another woman. He carried a cassette of slides. He smiled beautifully and walked over to the lectern.

"I began here, in this village [slide]," said Mr. Khatem, "a son of a tribal man. My father had seven donkeys and a camel, and many goats. Therefore we were rich, yet I could not read, nor could my parents. Now families like mine can read. We have not tried, you see, to catch the children and put them into schools. No, the schools go along, along with the tribe, on trucks like these [slide]. They go to where the tribes rest in winter [slide] or here in summer, grazing [slide]. This is me with the Empress, that other woman is a friend of hers, also interested in education, and they have come, this is at Kaswin near Tehran."

Chloe saw a slide of two beautiful but artificial-looking women in white fox jackets shivering on a cold plain, surrounded by grinning children in colorful but ragged clothes, holding up slates.

Flocks of snowy sheep swarmed along a green hillside, mountains behind. A child with a shepherd crook.

A blackboard, with lovely lines of Persian writing across it, children sitting in front of it on stones, Mr. Khatem himself holding a pointer.

"Tribespeople dancing, made happy by literacy. This is my own tribe where I began, yet here I am today a respected and prosperous public servant, in a land where people can rise and prosper according to the wise provisions of our king."

The American ladies applauded with great enthusiasm and asked intelligent questions.

Heidi gave Chloe a lift home. They were driving in Heidi's Peykan, a nice little car; it seemed to Chloe more sensible than the huge American cars driven by the Grumman wives, or the Bell Helicopter wives, which you saw parked along the wide suburban streets of new villas out beyond the university.

First they dropped off Tina, then drove into the compound and into the driveway of Heidi's bungalow to the row of garages behind, where they were surprised to find Noosheen, sitting in her car outside her garage, huddled over the front seat as if in pain, the door open, but she immobile. Heidi and Chloe, astonished, saw that she was crying blue tears. Heidi rushed to her and embraced her, leaning clumsily in at the door of the car, and came away blue herself.

"What is it? What is it?" they cried. Noosheen, sobbing, extended her streaked blue arms.

"Good God, she's been inked," Heidi said. Chloe had heard of that—it happened occasionally that some religious fanatic would throw ink on an immodest woman or a foreign woman, or just someone without her head covered. They had heard of it happening at Abadan and in Tehran. It had not happened here, and why, anyway, should it happen to Noosheen? Chloe thought of the American wives with their Texan accents and their powder-blue golf dresses, uninked. Blots of black-blue dye stained Noosheen's simple cotton shirtwaist; her arm was blue where she had held it against her face. Heidi gathered her out of the car.

"I can't go home," Noosheen said. "I can't go in there. What if Bahram is home, or the washing woman?"

"Where did this happen?"

"In the bazaar."

She had come from her class in Victorian Poetry, and as she still had an hour before the ayah expected her home, she drove to the bazaar intending to buy some cases of Pepsi while she had her car nearby to carry it home in. She intended to patronize as usual the soft-drink vendor who kept a stall just inside the gates of the bazaar. When it happened, she herself was carrying a case of heavy tins, and the bazaar boy was following with three more on a cart, and they had reached the sidewalk outside the bazaar, walking to where she had parked near the main post office. They walked past the poor stalls arranged along the plastered wall outside the bazaar, the vendors of plastic shoes and T-shirts. The T-shirts said "Stanford University," she remembered, because the thought had just struck her that at Stanford University probably the study of Victorian poetry would be very advanced. Mounds of pistachio nuts, and scarves of magenta net, the strong smell of straw and dung—everything as usual. Two old women in black chador lurched along the sidewalk toward her in their overrun sandals, and a young man with narrow, burning eyes.

It was he who, stepping quickly forward, with a motion of his arm threw something at her. She had no moment to realize it was she whom he was attacking until she felt her face wet, the wetness on her dress, on her arm where she had flung it up. The cry was hers, and the pain in her ankle where the cans fell against it. Her eyes stung so that for a second she had feared acid. The old women tugged their veils and passed by. The man hurried away ahead of them, without looking back at Noosheen.

Stupefied, she blotted her face with her skirt. Her tears washed away the stinging. She limped toward her car, leaving the cans in the jube. The boy followed with the rest, avoiding her gaze. She rushed to get in her car, out of sight. There seemed to her to be a loudness all around her, the voices of people seeing her, speaking of her, but no one spoke to her. What could anyone say?

In the car, in her book bag, was a length of veil, to wear at the mosque or when visiting her aunts or for certain times when it was agreeable to wrap up in it. "The Iranian security blanket," she had called it, laughing with her friends. With her veil she now blotted her dress and wiped her face and arm. The blue dye, or ink, or whatever it was, trickled down her leg and into her shoe. It seemed viscous and horrible, like blood of a dying person; it puddled in the instep of her shoe. Her heart raced with the shock.

But why had this happened to her? This was something done to immodest women in provincial cities—in Abadan or Qum, perhaps—but not here in the university city of Shiraz, and she was not an immodest woman but a virtuous wife. The injustice only struck her now. But for an instant—was this true?—she had accepted that it had been intended for her, had known it was she who deserved it. This guilty feeling was now replaced by indignation, like a seed swelling in her belly.

A modest woman yet when ink stains you you think you

deserve it, you think the punisher has looked into your heart. People looking at you think that too, that the thrower of ink has a secret way of knowing, that his hand is guided by the hand of Allah to the flighty, short-tempered mother, or to her who looks at men in a certain way, with certain thoughts. Bahram—she now realized—would think this. He would wonder what the punishers, avengers, fanatics knew. Bahram would not embrace a woman with blue limbs, perhaps would not even speak to her. The new fear, of Bahram's disapproval, animated her; she would have to get home and wash. Trembling, she started the car and drove to the compound, and as she parked, shaken, in the garage port, here were the comforting Heidi Asghari and Chloe Fowler, angels of sympathy and indignation. Heidi took her into her house to scrub her there.

Heidi had English towels, which were not American towels, she apologized, but better than Iranian towels, and she went to get them. Noosheen undressed, not worried by Chloe standing there, just in a hurry to get the inky clothes off. Out of her bra straps came her blue arms; the stuff had soaked through her dress onto her thighs. She had no pubic hair. Chloe tried not to stare but it did make a person look strange, statuelike. She could not tell if Noosheen was naturally this way or if she shaved herself. Chloe was not so conscious on herself of that little fat pad of flesh over the pubic bone.

Heidi called out that the bath was ready. They hoped the ink would wash off, but it was indelible, resistant, something invented by people who hate women enough to mark them, maybe to hurt them. Maybe in a slow way it burned into the flesh and could never be removed, or caused a toxic reaction from which later you died?

"Lemon, pumice," Heidi said.

"Peroxide," Chloe suggested.

Strangely enough, luckily, it came right out of clothes. Heidi reported this. Noosheen soaked, then got out and sat in her towel while Heidi ironed the dress dry. Noosheen's misery was mitigated by the kindness of Chloe and Heidi; she was not sure she could expect such kindness from any Iranian woman she knew here, certainly not Zareeneh or Soraya, though of course her old friends would be kind, and her mother, if only she were here. No men would be kind.

There had been women with the man who threw the ink. Were they with him or merely in front of him? Did they know what he was going to do, approve, cook up the stuff in their fireplaces to give to him to throw on her? There were mad people about. More and more mad people about, even people who had before been calm might drive their cars at you, or break your windows. Bodies lay in the jube, it was said, and were collected very early in the morning by the men who shoot the dogs. No one knew where they were taken; their families never knew. This stain didn't come off the skin. This American woman, this Englishwoman were, she knew, unaware of many things that were happening here in unhappy Iran.

Chapter Twenty-one
FALSE FRIENDS

But helpless Pieces of the Game He plays
Upon this Chequer-board of Nights and Days;
Hither and thither moves, and checks, and slays,
And one by one back in the Closet lays.

Whom Allah leads astray, no guide has he. In the days that followed, this text oppressed Noosheen, arriving unbidden in her consciousness from some childhood reading of the Koran. The shadow of blue was still visible on her skin. Although he had said nothing, Bahram must have seen it. Obviously she was in the category of people led astray, or this wouldn't have happened to her. She tried to calm herself, to think through the logic of the words: for if it was Allah leading you astray, you all the more had to think for yourself; it was no good looking to Him.

Then there were those who believed that your husband is His representative. If that was so, then it would be your husband leading you astray and you had better not follow him. No guide has she. On the other hand, if your husband was a loyal guide with your best interests at heart, it was he who went against the will of Allah, assuming it was Allah's wish to lead you astray. It was insoluble. Why would Allah wish to lead someone astray anyway? You would think that people went astray by themselves, to the dismay of Allah. But that was not what the text said. Her heart swelled with distaste for Allah, as well as for her husband, and father, and other old men.

And, if you are astray, how do you get back on the right path? Some sign alerts you, perhaps the ink. Then, is it up to you, or to your husband, or to Allah, to decide what to do next?

And can it be that things are true now, in the modern world, that have not always been true, for instance about the spirit of women? Maybe women were subject, abject, deservedly low in the time of the Prophet, but perhaps emerging along the line of some divine plan so that now they were more free than in the days of the Koran, more deserving of freedom, more the equal of men than they had been back then. How else to explain the denigrating tone of the Koran but that women had been unworthy creatures back then? She thought of Empedocles, alive before the time of the Koran and at a time when women were highly regarded. Even so he had foreseen the hard times that were coming for humankind.

The stain of blue must be to Bahram a sure indication of her spiritual condition. It must pain him. He was in so many ways a kind man, kind to her and the babies. She could imagine the shock, the chill to his soul, a wife stained blue. Bahram always too busy for badness, studying and helping the sick. She felt his goodness to be as much a burden to her as badness would be, if he were bad.

Sometimes, looking at her hands, her spirit would fire up with indignation at the unfair stain, and then at other times it would seem deserved.

On Sunday night, at the Cyrus, Dick sent a cable to Marla:

DELAY SELLING UNTIL RETURN MARKET CONSIDERATIONS UNWISE IMPORTANT TO DISCUSS. LETTER FOLLOWS. DO NOT SELL UNDER-LINE. LOVE DICK.

In the late afternoon Wednesday, Dick borrowed the hospital station wagon and drove northward out of Shiraz, hoping to find the grave site. He half believed that the promptings of his dreaming self should be attended to, that he would make some discovery, or somehow at least allay this dreadful curse of troubled sleep. Anyway he enjoyed driving, could think, away from Junie, Abbas, Chloe, the rest, about things—about his life. About how he had had no reply from Marla, though he really preferred not to think about that, or he could think about where his life was going, not a subject you ever wanted to zero in on but could hope an inspired change of direction might waft across your mind, some intimation of a future course he hadn't thought of before.

As soon as he was well beyond the outskirts of town, though, he knew he wouldn't be able to find the grave. The landscape was too strange, to his eye all undifferentiated rocks and plains. But he drove on in the hope that as he neared the allotted kilometers—they had traveled sixty-three or four—he would find something familiar, an outcropping of cliff like a stone visage stuck somewhere in his memory suddenly appearing to him. And it was true that as he neared the place they had turned off, the landscape assumed a kind of familiarity, born, he guessed, of his concentrating fears the other day. It, the dead man's grave, was somewhere around here. He drew off the road and into the field at the foot of one of the steep escarpments and parked. He got out of the car and circled round it, gazing up. He believed he remembered looking with Abbas at the same rock ledge above him though in fact the strata were all horizontal here, tilted in another direction. There was no sign of the grave.

There was something looming, forbidding, about the steepness. It was like finding yourself suddenly next to a very much taller person in a dark place; he had a sense of being looked down upon, perhaps watched. He saw no one. If the ancients had dragged the bodies of their dead to ledges like that, how had they got them up there, anyway? He studied the conjunctions of the rock, and, thinking that he could see a painful route, felt an impulse to climb it, with the idea too that from its height he might be able to spy the fresh grave below. The element of risk was appealing; if you fell, he thought as he grappled rock outcroppings and scrambled along, you would not be found. Only a couple of hundred feet, but of a daunting steepness.

Once he had gained the ledge he felt better, then unhappy looking down, and worse looking out to see the absolute, barren, wide landscape. Something about these open landscapes had always filled him with dread. He had first felt it in New Mexico, which he had always heard of as beautiful but found horrible in its scale and impersonality. New Mexicans doubtless felt daunted by the tall canyons of cities, the gloomy shadows of buildings.

He wondered if Zoroastrian bones had really been laid up here. This would be a place, all right, for vultures to help themselves, high enough so that humans could not disturb them, nor be disturbed by the disgusting spectacle. He studied the rubble of pebbles and roots—there were things that might be bones, might centuries ago have been bones, or might be the whitened roots of the gnarled shrubs that sprang from the rocks. He stood here for a quarter of an hour, mind empty of thoughts, a start of reluctance when he viewed the route of descent. Then he began to scramble down. There had been no grave. Perhaps this was the wrong place altogether. Without losing the sense that he had been sent, been intended to find the place, he headed toward Shiraz again. Like returning to the scene of the crime. Some inner prompting remained, but he drove back, and went directly to the Cyrus.

There he had a drink with Richard Dare, the archaeologist, who had reappeared in the Cyrus bar after a few days of absence; he had been at Persepolis at the dig. Dick, Junie, and the others had at last set the date for their great expedition to the famous ruin. Perhaps Dare would be there?

"Quite possible," Dare said. "If so, you must let me show you *my* Persepolis. I feel very proprietary about it by now." There were still depths, layers, boxcars of antiquities there, he said, awaiting the shovel, awaiting the expert from London or New York, awaiting the whim or dictate of the Shah.

"Though the Shah doesn't have any real feeling for the antiquities," Dare said. "He's interested in restoration, but it's the Islamic period that interests him. The tribesmen find things from the classical period and sell them to us. They know they're worth something." He lowered his voice. "Between us, I've managed to pick up some very nice things for myself. Some jewelry, several little heads. A necklace that's very very good."

This excited Dick's imagination. He liked the idea of owning a Persian antiquity, the jewels from a mummy—had they had mummies? He thought of the Queen of Sheba—where was Sheba? And of beautiful slave girls, and of how one's ability to imagine antiquity was entirely blighted by the movies you had seen as a child. But Richard Dare seemed to see the days of antiquity before him, and when he spoke of the beautiful carving of the friezes, his voice trembled.

He and Dare joined Chloe Fowler, Hugh Monroe, General Brigante, and the Texan, Loyal Cooley, in the dining room.

"When she heard what she'd been eating, she got mortally ill," Cooley was saying. "I didn't feel so hot myself, but hell, I figured I'd kept it down thus far. But it shows you the power of suggestion. They had to get a doctor."

"Mr. and Mrs. Cooley ate bats in China," Chloe told Dick, with a pleased expression.

"Well, I wish this were a, what, a hamburger," said Hugh of his plate of lamb and rice.

"A taco. A taco. I think about tacos all the time," Chloe said. "I don't even eat them that much at home."

"An egg cream," Dick said. "An egg cream is something I would never dream of drinking in America. I haven't had one since I was twelve. But it's true—the other day I found myself thinking about egg cream."

"What exactly is an egg cream?" Chloe asked.

It turned out that none of them knew what an egg cream was. Dick was astonished. An egg cream! A regular everyday thing. As he explained it, the others agreed it sounded more disgusting than it would taste.

"Your little friend Noosheen came to see me the other day," General Ben said to Chloe.

"Really?" Chloe was surprised. She wouldn't have known how to find General Ben, how had Noosheen known? "When? What about?"

"She wanted me to smuggle her into Afghanistan," said General Ben. "Remember our conversation? I guess she remembered every word."

"Poor Noosheen. But what did you say?" Inwardly Chloe was chagrined that she had not realized Noosheen was as desperate as that.

"I've heard of it done, as I said," said the general, "but I'm not myself personally in touch with the people—it would be tribesmen or merchants. I said I was afraid I wasn't her man."

"Oh, indeed," said Chloe. "I hope you didn't tell her husband, in some misguided impulse of male solidarity." She spoke vivaciously, wishing to protect Noosheen from being talked about, and to protect her own surprise. She began to prattle in a way that Dick thought of as her dumb blonde act. She wasn't dumb but could genuinely seem so. That was very Californian. Their eyes glaze over, and they are thinking of exercise or drugs—Chloe not drugs, of course, yet she did take quantities of salad, despite his warnings. She had begun leaf by leaf but had now built up to huge platefuls of deadly lettuce and the rather pallid poison tomatoes, which Dick would rather die than risk. She had reported no difficulties, though it was possible she wouldn't report them. She was probably full of waspy prudery about digestion. Once he had brought a girl home to dinner who was shocked when they passed out Tums after dinner. "It's not very complimentary to your Mom's cooking," she'd said. He'd never thought of it like that. They—that girl and probably Chloe—would rather die, probably, than hear stomachs mentioned.

"Which loyalty comes first?" Chloe asked. "Whom would you *betray* first—the fellow male, the fellow family member, or the fellow American?"

"Or the fellow doctor?" added Dick. "Or the personal friend?"

"Patriotic people turned their families in, in Nazi Germany," said General Ben. "Country comes before family."

"The mistress or the wife?" wondered Chloe.

"It would just depend on the circumstances," insisted Dick. "There are no fixed principles."

"I don't think I would betray anyone," said Hugh, with a manly seriousness that corrected any impression of self-satisfaction such a remark might have been thought to contain. "But it would be according to how well you knew them. The less well you knew them, the easier it would be."

"Are we talking about loyalty on principle or self-interest?" Dick asked.

"Men would usually betray people before abstractions," Chloe said. "It's a difference between them and women, or so people say," though she wasn't sure of it.

"Who would you trust more, your foreign mistress or a fellow American doctor?" asked Dick.

"The fellow American doctor," Hugh said, again very seriously.

The slight obtuseness of the usually intelligent Hugh on this subject served to focus in Chloe an emotion of anger at him that had been simmering. She was angry that he didn't realize she was angry, that he never spoke of the future or of Them. Hugh was mysterious. When she tried to imagine what he was thinking, he was opaque as a stone. Usually she liked that in someone else. She could always look into Jeffrey if she wanted to, but she did not want to. She had looked in once or twice and found only crossness and clutter—it had been like looking into someone else's purse at an apparatus of anxiety—toothpicks, scalp remedy, bus tickets, a letter from his mother.

But what maddened her now about Hugh was his incuriosity about her. She wished to be opened, inspected. Didn't he think it was odd that she was still here and Jeffrey wasn't? That she loved him and risked her marriage and stayed on in this strange land to sleep with him? Didn't he wonder how she and Jeffrey were getting along? What marital advice might he give her? But he accepted her like a beautiful present, and she had begun to see that he was used to getting wonderful presents. He must assume his needs were taken care of by right, so that his splendid altruism wouldn't be damaged.

Free of entanglements himself, did he imagine she was free of them? Did he imagine she just existed in what she stood up in, alone, like a statue or a sprite? Had he no sense of the dentists, parent-teachers associations, dog kennels, real-estate agents, aunts all standing in a circle around her, hemming her in and propping her up? Did he imagine she could just pop out and over, in some thrilling trajectory, all quotidian reality? He seemed to have no sense of her as a hemmed-in person, but perhaps, to be fair, that was a tribute to her free spirit, or a condition of this idyll. Or, more likely, he had no interest in her actual circumstances. Perhaps—the idea had occurred to her before—his wives had divorced him because he was so blithe, so uninvolved. Her face thinking of all this, in the dim restaurant light, had flushed a color she knew was becoming.

Dick Rothblatt's often mordant absorption in mundane materiality was more to her taste. She was sorry to see him so tormented about his house. It was hard for men, the way they lost their houses after they had put up all the shelves and painted—not that Jeffrey ever painted—but Dick had, she felt, and had paneled his study, and worked a long time on the kitchen and made a studio for Marla, in her painting phase.

Something linked Dick and Hugh in her mind, though the nature of their complicity eluded her—doctors together or men together? Men believe each other before they believe women, even women they love, as Hugh had just admitted. But Dick? She had thought of telling him about Hugh's shirts, not with any idea of disloyalty to Hugh but because Dick would be sure to explain that there was an emergency laundry service at the Tehran airport, or that she, Chloe, was blind; somehow he would explain Hugh's lie.

But then she had had a feeling, just like the feeling of standing outside her parents' shut bedroom door, or looking at the covers of certain books that would turn out to have horrifying pictures or stories of death, the feeling of an important shimmer, almost a hum, off the cover that told her she ought not to press on with this inquiry. Perhaps Hugh and Dick were up to something? Perhaps the CIA was involved? Good-natured Hugh would never suspect that he was being used; and he would do things for patriotic reasons, Dick doubtless too. How surprising it was when people lied. It was the last thing you expected.

After all, the mystery of the otherness of another is charming. Chloe is not someone who wishes to possess all knowledge of others. She considers that rude. But who can blame her if she wishes just a little that someone would want to know all about her; she would not tell, but it would be evidence that she was interesting or desirable. On the other hand, she has friends with jealous husbands who say, Tell me what you did, where you went, what you are thinking. She would not really want that attention. Is it not better to be alone, attentive, smiling, full of love of an outwardly directed, disinterested, sort?

Hugh never does ask about her. She wonders whether he knows her maiden name. She sees it is quite possible that he might want to marry her and would not have inquired about her maiden name. He thinks of her as Chloe Fowler, which she is really not, she is Chloe Linden. She, on the other hand, has many times thought, but has never been able to say, "What about your shirts?" How beautiful, she thinks, Hugh's cufflinks, his exquisite watch with its alligator band—a Must of Cartier?

Dick is thinking of Junie's odd behavior that morning over the dead man's watch. She had spent the night—the Hendersons had gone to Isfahan. Getting up in the early dawn, she had taken the dead man's watch from the bureau and waved it at him. "Mind if I take this?"

"Why?" He wasn't sure she knew it belonged to the dead man. She might think it was his own—quite an elegant watch, Patek Philippe, with an incongruous band.

"Because I broke my band. How'm I going to get that fixed in Shiraz, Iran? Still, Iranian watchbands must break, there must be someone. I'll wear it just for today. Hmmm—nice watch!" She had gone off without coffee; there was a woman in labor she was anxious about. Dick, whose first clinic was not until nine, had lain in bed awhile longer, wondering whether there was any chance of Abbas seeing it on Junie's wrist. But she herself must have seen it on the dead man. Had there been other funny things about Junie's behavior? He remembered, slightly revolted and with new apprehension, the way she had stripped the shoes off the dead man. Maybe she'd been looking for some mark of identification she knew about. You heard that the CIA recruited young women from the Seven Sisters; that had been one of their main bases of recruitment. True, that had been in Marla's day; young women Junie's age were more leery of the CIA and the government generally. Junie's grandfather, though, had graduated from West Point, probably the whole family had a pro-military bias the CIA could prey on, something like that. How little he knew about Junie, really, beyond her fierce views, so apparently left-wing, so ardently feminist.

What if, now that they were in it together, he couldn't trust Abbas? Different rules obtain in a country where people are dragged off to be tortured and murdered. You couldn't blame them if they lied or evaded—but could you trust them? Someone like Abbas especially, with a tragedy in his life—that made for a certain burnt-out quality. If it came to an official inquiry, it would be every man for himself; he couldn't expect Abbas to stick his neck out. He could imagine Abbas saying to the authorities, "I think you'll find that Dr. Rothblatt knows something about the whereabouts of the body."

All at once Dick realized that Vahid Farmani didn't want the body there *because* he knew something about it. His hysteria was not owing to a mere antipathy to dead strangers, was not mere intransigence but *informed alarm*. There were funny goings-on, bodies, things moved, occasionally, in the laboratory overnight. Things known to Abbas, and Vahid Farmani. Vahid and Abbas in league, or else opposed to one another, making moves like chess players, without speaking of their deadly game. He himself, innocent Dick Rothblatt, drawn into it. His feeling was a mixture of fear and importance. Deadly games dignify life, even if you sensibly wish to avoid them. Chloe, he thought, looking at her, so pretty, so animated, came to life strangely in the evenings and often left the Cyrus precipitately, as if she had meetings to go to, strange doings in the darkness. She had not gone down in the cave, almost as if she had known what they'd find.

General Ben, who always had his car, drove them back to the compound. Chloe alit at Villa Two, called goodnight again to her companions, and climbed the steps to her apartment, where she hurried to wash and brush her teeth before Hugh came in. It was romantic to imagine him chivalrously hovering at the dark end of the path that ran between his bungalow and the Infertility Clinic. Tonight, having had perhaps a bit too much wine, she dozed a few moments under her lamp, waking only at the sound of his voice beneath her window. She started awake in the dim room. The low bulb of her lamp gathered insects through the riddled screen.

There was something strained and urgent in his voice. She hurried out into the hall and down the stairs. He tottered in. His face was gashed and swollen; blood drooled from a cut at the hairline and spilled onto his shirt. He smelt oddly of blood.

"My God!" cried Chloe. Had he fallen? Been hit by a car?

He said nothing but followed her up the stairs and swayed toward her armchair. Blood dripped off his fingers onto the linoleum floor. She thought of Noosheen and the ink. She rushed for one of the thin dishtowels Hossein left each day, and Hugh mopped at his face with it.

"My dear, what is it?"

"Somebody was in my apartment, going through my stuff." His voice, in contrast to his damaged face, was perfectly calm, normal. "He tried to run, I chased him—he got away easily in the dark. But then somebody grabbed me from behind. It had to have been a different person, waiting outside all along."

"Is it bad?" asked Chloe, mastering her stomach, for she was queasy about blood. It didn't appear to be too bad. Hugh got up and studied himself in the bathroom mirror. "Not too bad. It hurts."

"What did they want?"

"Evidently some medical records I was keeping, about a patient I saw. At least that's what's gone." He sat down again, seeming dazed and weakened.

"Do you think you should tell someone? Farmani? Abbas? Is it an Iranian patient? Were they Iranians?"

"No. I don't know." He was grim. "I only know I'm going to Tehran tomorrow and get this straightened out."

Ah, thought Chloe, Tehran. It obviously bore upon his absence, his being in Tehran when he said he wasn't. She wondered if she should mention that she had noticed his shirts.

"Ah—is it anything you can tell me about?" she asked.

"No. I'd tell you about it if I could," Hugh said, "but I promised I wouldn't tell anyone," and Chloe understood from her knowledge of Hugh's character that he would therefore not tell her. This was an irritating goody-goody side of him. You didn't tell anyone except your mistress, that was the way to look at it. You had to tell someone. An Eastern prep-school goody-goody, valuing secrecy and other male foolishness, without a doubt a CIA agent.

Chapter Twenty-two
DIVIDED LOYALTIES

The Moving Finger writes, and, having writ,
Moves on: nor all your Piety nor Wit
Shall lure it back to cancel half a Line,
Nor all your Tears wash out a Word of it.

The battered Hugh sleeps fitfully at her side. Chloe hardly sleeps, turning over certain matters in her mind about Hugh. Does he travel on a diplomatic passport, as Dr. Farmani had asked? He has been to Geneva, Moscow, Rangoon. Why? Nine shirts laundered at the Tehran Hilton when he said he was in London, and now someone has bashed his head in. Does someone do that out of the blue, except in America? Chloe tries to imagine reasons for the shirts, for the travels, but can't think of any except that Hugh is some kind of spy or emissary, mixed up in something, or maybe an international criminal mixed up with dope or diamonds or guns. Which would it be? What sort of criminal would the admirable and attractive Hugh be? Or what sort of patriot, for he had been to the best schools, the sort that prepare you for the CIA, or maybe he was a Russian spy, though that was more common in England. She hadn't heard of a person from a good American school being a Russian spy. In America, treason was more a proletarian thing.

But Hugh? So handsome and selfless, working long hours in Azami Hospital, full of genuine concern for Iranians, so cheerful and uncomplicated by nature, though cheerfulness could be a pose—all those divorces?

Should a woman stay with a spy? With a murderer or swindler? What is the cutoff point for loyalty? Her previous views had been categorical: a woman should not stay with a criminal. She disapproved of women who stayed with bad men, saying, "My man right or wrong," and she thought it insulting to women to hold that they had no higher duty than the simple one of loyalty to some appointed master, like dogs, and were not supposed to make moral judgments or think. There were women who interested her, like ones who conceive babies on visits to prison. The idea overwhelmed Chloe with disgust.

Eva Braun! If you loved a bad man and stayed with him, you were just as bad, so she both wishes and does not wish to know what Hugh is up to. But she is sure he must be up to something or people wouldn't jump him in the night, and she is sure she isn't going to mention the nine shirts. She is conscious that she might have found these thoughts exciting a few weeks ago; now she is troubled. Perhaps it is her more active sense of Iran as a real place, her more careful way of seeing that the people are thin and frightened, their lives not to be tampered with by Americans but running along according to principles of individual destiny quite apart from hers, or Hugh's.

Hugh, his bruises livid by morning, took a cab for the airport, bent on Tehran, saying grimly that he would be back in the evening or the following morning. His mood, understandably, was angry. Chloe went early to the university to avoid the heat, which was daily becoming worse, too hot to walk in the midday. At the gates of the university, she was astonished to see soldiers silently putting students into trucks. Other students stood watching on the sidewalk, shaking their fists and muttering, but the scene was curiously listless, as if this were somehow between the acts of a play. "What does it mean?" Chloe asked of Mrs. Reza.

"Nothing," Mrs. Reza said. "When the weather is hot, the students are always like that. The police keep order; that is their job, after all."

In the evening she went, more from habit than from inclination, to the Cyrus. She, Abbas, Dick, and Junie had gone to the garden to avoid Loyal Cooley, who had been holding forth on international currency:

"The rial isn't too bad, as foreign money goes. At least you can spend it here and there in the Middle East. Try the zloty anyplace but Poland. I got stuck with about five hundred dollars' worth of zlotys once. You used to be able to spend them in East Germany; now even the East Germans won't take them. That's because of the Polish brassières."

"Polish brassières?" they murmured politely.

"The East Germans used to accept the zloty. Polish women used to come over into East Germany to get underwear, the East German bra was a lot better, you can imagine what the Polish is like and they would just take off their Polish bras and try to flush them away. That way they jammed up the plumbing, till the Germans had to stop letting them come over. Also shoes, they'd leave them in big piles in the street."

The company sat hushed with wonder.

"Poles are incredibly anti-Semitic," said Dick after a time.

In the garden you could take a glass of tea after supper and enjoy the fragrant night, the lights strung over the long reflecting pool. Music drifted, barely heard, and crickets sang.

"What do you think—what is thought—of Beethoven here?"

said Chloe, as they listened to the notes of the Emperor Concerto on the public-address system.

"We revere Beethoven. I would give all our Iranian composers for him. We have poets, but we have no great composers." Abbas's voice oddly passionate.

"That can't be true," objected Chloe.

"Nonetheless." He smiled.

"What will become of the students?" Chloe asked, talking of what she had seen that afternoon.

"Nothing." Abbas laughed. "The jails are full, after all. Though I have noticed they are enlarging the garrison."

When he had gone, Dick said to Chloe, "He's attracted to you." He was interested in Chloe's reaction, whether she would seem pleased. He wondered if she was lonesome. He wondered if she would sleep with Abbas if he made a pass at her. "He wouldn't do anything—he knows Jeffrey and so on—but just from the way he mentions you, always bringing you up."

He watched her, but she didn't seem anything but politely complimented.

Chloe did wonder how Muslim men were in bed. Maybe they were terrific, intense, insatiable; you heard of men with harems who had to do it ten times a day. So many experiences are cut off from the life of a middle-class American housewife.

"You always think people are attracted to people," Junie said to Dick, crossly. "You seem to relate everything to sex. I think it's stupid."

Chloe supposed this would initiate a quarrel. Dick and Junie often quarreled, albeit on impersonal subjects, but in a personal way that made Chloe sure that everyone must know they were lovers.

"It's a view of life, all right," Dick said, pleasantly, not disposed to quarrel. He paid for their tea and they drifted off together into the street.

"It's the Islamic view of life, so prurient, so disgusting," Junie went on. "We had a girl—fourteen years old, beaten horribly by her bridegroom, because she hadn't done the thing with the sheep's blood. The whole concept of virginity is prurient and disgusting."

"Oh, I don't know," Chloe said, for the sake of argument. "Maybe it's more charming to lose your virginity with a lot of pomp and ceremony and sheep's blood and fear and general acknowledgment of your altered state, better than in the back of a car, I mean."

"I would think," Dick said.

"Or maybe men function better if they're a little bit pepped up by these lurid rituals of possession and virility," said Chloe.

"Now wait a minute," objected Dick.

"In Philadelphia—these were Saudis, not Iranians, but still—a guy killed his sister because she was sleeping with her boyfriend. And he got off. The jury just said, Well, it's their religion," said Junie.

Dick didn't want to be drawn into an argument with Junie, because Junie was contentious and inflexible. You could never win an argument because she would never yield a point, even when proven wrong. Sometimes bystanders were drawn in to adjudicate, as now, walking home from the Cyrus, when the discussion changed somehow, from whether most things were related to sex, to Freud and penis envy. Dick understood this quarrel to be symptomatic of a strain in his relationship with Junie, brought on to some extent by her increasing involvement with Iran. She stayed most nights now in her own quarters exhausted. Each day brought some obstetrical crisis, some opposition of her opinion to that of a benighted Iranian chauvinist, clashes, heartbreaking errors, maternal deaths. She had lost weight. Dick tried to comfort and cheer her, but she often fell asleep while he was making love to her.

When they had arrived, agreed to have this fling in Iran and avoiding talk of the future, a slight apprehension had existed on either part that the other would not be able to support the mood of light tenderness and professional camaraderie they hoped for. Dick, especially, feared that Junie would want to marry and have babies. He believed—he knew—that young professional women wanted as much as other women to marry, have babies, and, of course, why shouldn't they? He, however, was not ready to start up another family, for sure.

Junie feared that Dick would want to marry. That was Chloe's impression too. He was not a convincing bachelor. The regularity of his morning visits to her, for instance, his evident pleasure in the little domestic routine, his confident reliance on intelligent female companionship meant, Chloe supposed, that he would remarry momentarily, whether Junie or not was hard to guess. Their quarrels on trivial subjects seemed to contain a note of impatience.

"But there is no such thing as penis envy," Junie was saying. "Freud just thought there was because he thought his prick was such a fine thing everyone must want one. But everyone doesn't."

"It *is* hard to imagine having—you know—nothing down there," Dick pointed out, in defense of the fatherly fellow physician whose edicts had never seemed personally to impinge upon his life.

"Women don't have nothing," screamed Junie furiously. "They have something. Phenomenologically, something. They experience it as *something*, therefore do not feel the lack of the other thing."

"That's ridiculous," Dick said, teasing her along. "It's a well-established observation, penis envy."

"It is *something* there, just as much as your hand or your ear. Nothing would be if there were *nothing* there," Junie persisted.

"Look," said Dick, "my analyst was a Jungian, I don't even believe in Freud, it's just that it's so obvious."

"The trouble with doctors is that they never read anything," Chloe snapped.

Chloe dropped back a few steps, taken with sudden melancholy, and a recollection of the visage of the paralyzed little girl and her own strangeness. It was always at night, walking along a street or across a compound that she most felt her strangeness. Inside the walled gardens people murmured, out of view, belonging here. A lightbulb strung on a cord hung over the black flowers. Chloe could imagine the moon on the long pools, but she couldn't see the pools or the dusty grass or the roses. The ditchlike jubes seemed to yawn and widen under the curbings. She crossed carefully at corners, clutching a male elbow. The few automobiles proceeded slowly, as if blinded, as if sleepy after dinner. The mad cacophony of the day was gone. No one lurked in the shadows, just some men coming out of the film, a young couple, the young woman wearing the tightly tucked scarf, students. Voices coming from the upstairs windows of a restaurant. No one was old.

She and the others were shut out from Iran by the thick walls, by the murmur of Persian words opaque to the ear. But it was peaceful to be shut out and to slip along the walls and through the windows going nowhere, going off to make love. It was nicer, Chloe thought, to be outside than in, for if you were inside your walled garden, it would be your garden and you'd have to weed it.

Gardenless, childless, husbandless, how strangely happy she was these days. If something happened to Jeffrey, and she was tempted to remarry instantly, assuming someone would have her, she hoped she would remember this happy, unencumbered feeling and think twice.

By thinking of Jeffrey, it is as if she has conjured up the letter she finds waiting on her pillow:

Dear Chloe,

I'm sorry not to have written for a week or so. I've been mulling this letter over in my mind. I've written Farmani, by the way, so he knows I'm not coming, but I suggested he let you stay on to finish your work at the university, since it's only a few more weeks.

Well, to get to the point, the situation between you and me. I guess we both know it hasn't been wonderful. I haven't known what to do about it, and I'm sure you haven't either, and when we try to talk about it, we never quite get to the point. I for one believe you can't really talk about these things. I mean, you can say I should be home more, and I can say clean up the house, and we can try to do whatever, but it isn't really getting at the problem. I know there are these routes—shrinks, counselors, therapists—but I don't think either of us has a lot of faith in that kind of thing. God knows we know enough people who've gone those routes.

The kids are fine, by the way, I should have said, and Henry is coming along—at least he's not a vegetable.

I guess I should come right out and say that I think we should get a divorce. I realize we've been in this holding pattern in part because I was unwilling to take the responsibility. I was unwilling to be the bad person, the one at fault. I kept hoping that you'd do something so I could blame it on you. But now I see that even though you aren't perfect, that's not the point, the point is not blaming the other person but facing up to your own behavior, not trying to maneuver the other person into a position of guilt. Now I'm able to do that. So: it's my fault, I accept the responsibility, everyone will say what a shit Jeffrey Fowler is, and that's okay with me. Of course I want to do what's fair for you and the kids in every way. Don't worry about the financial end of things.

I suppose it's obvious that there is somebody who has helped me understand all this—I don't mean a shrink. I mean that I'm in love with someone, and her support and love have made me see things much more clearly. I suppose you guessed that when I went so willingly back to California—I practically shoved you aboard that plane to Tehran. You must have been puzzled and scared, and I think you are a brave lady. I know that after these weeks there in Shiraz you will recognize that you are able to stand on your own two feet and maybe you even prefer it. We'll talk about details when you get back. I guess it's a little bit chicken to write you like this, but it seemed worse to hit you with it when you got home.

Chloe looks at the letter, first at its physical characteristics, as if to see whether it is genuine. Then she reads it once more, with a growing amazement that begins to swell into fury, as though at a trick by which she is going to lose her neck. Stunned and amused; amazed and angry. Enraged. She cannot describe the pale, swooning sensation that seizes her. It is in a way the letter she has hoped for, that she could never herself write, and now can't bear.

She sits down on her cot and reads it again. Yes, he had almost shoved her onto the plane. She feels her throat constricting, as if she were being choked. Duped. Tricked. What a fool she is. Now she can see that he had plotted; now she can see that he has been having an affair all along. With whom, for heaven's sake? He'd be happy she had taken up with Hugh. Maybe he'd even planned it—maybe Henry hadn't had an accident at all, and it was all a pack of lies so that Jeffrey could go home. Maybe Jeffrey and Hugh are in collusion somehow. Take her, she's yours. Perhaps Jeffrey wants her to have a little professional success—Sassanian pottery—so that he won't have to support them. My wife the archaeologist, he will say in court. Now she sees his plan. How she hates the ignominy of her thoughts, but cannot change the wild, vengeful embarrassed emotions that tumble over each other across her mind. What is the name of her principal emotion? She seeks it—vainly—and then finds it: chagrin, chagrin, chagrin, chagrin. She reads the letter over and over.

Chapter Twenty-three
TRAVELING LIGHT

Waste not your Hour, nor in the vain pursuit
Of This and That endeavour and dispute;
Better be jocund with the fruitful Grape
Than sadden after none, or bitter, Fruit.

When Chloe awoke in the morning, she lay enjoying as she did each morning the distant cries and military music, the dappled sun in the leaves outside the window, Rustum's little barks below the window—for he was now impatient to see her each morning when she came down to have coffee on the steps with Dick. Then the confusion of memories rushed in on her, of the battered Hugh, the students yesterday, and then Jeffrey's letter. Her emotions, as she crawled from her cot, were still those of astonishment and indignation. It seemed too treacherous a letter for even Jeffrey to have sent. You just didn't send such a letter to someone far away in isolated Iran, beyond discussions, beyond reproaches, beyond repentance. She searched her memory for signs of Jeffrey's having taken up with someone else and found none at all. It had seemed to her he was always home, except a little late for dinner a few nights, or gone for an hour on Sunday morning to check his research rats. She was almost admiring of Jeffrey, now, so cleverly had he got himself into whatever it was without her knowing it.

This morning it seemed to her that it was just that Jeffrey should leave her, or, if not just, inevitable, because of her affair with Hugh; female transgression was being paid for as usual. Down the centuries nothing had changed, and by some cosmic process, which operated evidently at great distances as easily as in San Francisco, as if by satellite, transgression in Iran affected the atomic structure, or would it be the chemical structure of Jeffrey's heart? So this freedom and happiness in Iran were not, after all, to come free of cost. She wasn't really surprised. She lay in her cot a few moments longer than usual, savoring these reflections with a kind of bitter interest. Perhaps she hadn't noticed what Jeffrey was up to because she hadn't cared. This thought was dismissed. Of course she loved Jeffrey, difficult as he was, and had no wish to change her orderly and secure life, which seemed, in the abstract and at this great distance, precious to her. And anyway Jeffrey would have changed his mind by the time she got back. Think of the children.

At this she was seized by the most violent fear: that Jeffrey meant to keep the children. His letter said nothing about them; he was with them while she was far away. She could imagine what he might say to a judge, about maternal desertion, maternal uncaring. She could imagine the satisfaction of his mother, who had never really liked her, it was borne upon her now—and would have suggested the strategy by which they meant to prevent Chloe from ever seeing them. . . . Thus her thoughts raved, out of control, and regained perspective only when she reminded herself that neither Jeffrey nor his mother would like to be in full-time charge of two young children.

But what about the new woman? Maybe she was intensely maternal? "The real mother off in Iran"—she could hear the things that could be said against her. This precipitated a fit of anxiety so intense she had to sit down and breathe deeply. Jeffrey, somebody who resisted taking the children to the park or the movies—was he now seized by proprietary paternal emotions he had never felt before? Was it an aspect of his anger at her? She remembered all the newspaper dramas she had ever read, about desperately warring parents stealing their children back and forth, hiding in motels, having to go and live under assumed names in Florida.

Chloe got a hold on herself. The reality would be that Jeffrey would take the children on weekends, if that. The reality would be that by the time she got home he would have thought twice, or forty times, about all this, and changed his mind.

She fortified herself with such rationalizations as she got up and made a pot of tea, battling a knot of fury and panic that seemed to have struck her painfully in the middle, like a fast tennis ball. She tried to will it or think it away. She didn't want to know anything about Jeffrey's sordid affair; she would never ask. She had no right to ask. Jeffrey was just acting this way because he was missing her. She was humiliated. She would say nothing of it, she decided, to Hugh or anyone else. She would say nothing and it would, as life problems often do, go away. She had never thought of herself as someone whose husband leaves her.

She took her tea and went out into the garden. It was too early for Dick, but the sun was already hot. Rustum rushed to her and licked her hand. The garden furniture had been moved around to the other side of Villa One, she had heard, for a reception there for some grand people down from Tehran—the Minister of Health, she had heard, and a party of courtiers who would stay in the summer palace. Without chairs, Chloe emulated the Iranian villagers and old men in the square. She had wondered how they bore it, such an odd posture, hunkered down on their haunches, arms resting on knees, chin resting on arms, but now she tried it and found it was perfectly comfortable. Probably also it correctly aligned your intestines or female organs to a more healthy position. This was the healthy position to give birth in, she had heard.

Crouching, she watched the early-morning activity along the road, women walking to the clinics, nurses in white, an ancient ambulance creeping among the people walking on the road. She was startled at the approach of one of the black-shrouded women; she often saw them glancing at her sunglasses, but none had ever approached her. It had always seemed to Chloe, when she came close enough to them in the bazaar to see the wrinkled eyes, the set squints, that they could prevent these signs of early aging if they would wear sunglasses themselves.

Now Chloe was startled to realize that the woman was Noosheen. She squatted down next to Chloe, drew the veil from her face, and gathered it around her shoulders.

"You see I am a chastened spirit now," she said. "I wear this now. I don't want it to happen again."

"Oh, it couldn't, could it?" Chloe said. "It wasn't you, it just happened to be you."

"It doesn't come off. Look." Noosheen extended an arm. The blue stain turned her olive skin faintly green, like the arm of a mermaid.

"Bahram doesn't say anything. I don't know if he sees it— he doesn't really see *me*," she said. "But of course he must see. I don't know how to speak of it to him. I know what he must think."

"Well, he must be very angry at whoever would do such a thing," Chloe said soothingly. "Perhaps he thinks it's you who can't bear to speak of it."

"He is right, I can't bear to speak of it. But I know what he must think."

Chloe could not believe that the mild-looking Bahram could conceal excesses of brutality or mistrust. "I think you should discuss it. That's always the best thing, to bring things right out in the open." Oh, the irony of this advice. But she was sure it was good advice, and that things should be brought out in the open, except for things that mere politeness dictated you conceal. She would never reproach Jeffrey, for instance, for his rather puny physique, since he couldn't help it, though she had always believed he could improve it by working out and not smoking.

"I want to leave. I want to go to my parents," Noosheen said, and only now did Chloe detect the quaver of desperation that accounted for the rather deceptive calm in her voice. "I have been wanting to leave Bahram for a long time, but the only problem is my parents are in New Delhi, India."

"There must be something we could do to get the stain off. Salt and lemon juice," said Chloe.

"You must help me," Noosheen went on, in the same urgent voice, her eyes not meeting Chloe's but staring in a frightened way off into the middle distance.

"I know what you will say, but I have thought of all. My children, what will happen, what my life will be. Such thoughts are not easily arrived at. I have been tormented in the night four nights now, but I think many nights before that since we have come back to Iran. I want to leave my husband. I think that in time my parents will help me to have my children with me, because my father is an influential man, but now first I must leave Bahram, so that it will be done and none can dissuade me. Otherwise they will expend the same energy trying to dissuade me, naturally."

Chloe would not pretend to try to dissuade her. Anyone would want to leave a dry old cross husband she had been forced to marry. The situation of arranged marriage, so romantically dreadful in fiction, appeared, in life, merely intolerable. Millions of women down the ages forced to sleep with old men they didn't love or desire. The situation had never really interested or affronted her before, but now it seemed intolerable. A young woman, so like herself but for the accident of being Iranian, should be able to marry the man she loved.

Or was this a stupid American notion, as so often claimed? She shuddered to think of the embraces of the desiccated Bahram, could almost imagine his tiny, dry cock between her own thighs, poking her. She thought of the affectionate glances between Abbas and Noosheen and could imagine Noosheen's beautiful body, blue like the body of a goddess in a miniature painting, entwined with Abbas in the act of love, his the heavy penis of a sultan, the two as one, emblem of sultry sexuality, in an arched pavilion cooled by the waving fans of servants who had been blinded so as not to behold this inspired copulation.

"Of course, I would help," she said impulsively, "but I

don't see how I can." And these words rang in her own ears mockingly, so typical of complacent American detachment, of superiority, of all the people who hadn't helped the Jews or been able really to believe in evil and death, political evil and death. Not that Noosheen was in danger of dying, but when a rational person comes to you and says they need help, when it is they themselves who have decided to overturn their lives, ought not a rich and comfortable American listen?

"I mean," Chloe said, "tell me what to do."

This appeared to stop Noosheen for a moment. Probably she had been expecting Chloe to know what to do. "I need to go to India; that is where my father is. The problem is the passport. I do not have a green stamp for my passport. I have thought I could ask Bahram to sign my passport, say I am going on a visit to my mother and father, but he would suspect me, because it is not the season for visits, and the children are in school. Ordinarily I join my parents in Beirut or Athens for our holiday in September, when it is hottest here and also in India. I weighed whether to say perhaps that I was feeling ill and wished to see my mother, but that is the last time Bahram would send me to India, since the health care is better here, and he is a doctor, obviously. I also thought of saying it is my parents who are sick, or one of them, not both, but in that case it is Bahram they would call, and I cannot ask them to summon me, because they will not be in sympathy with this intention of mine to leave. So you see I have to leave first, then all will fall into place."

"You could take my passport," Chloe said. The moment she said it, she saw the plausibility of the suggestion. They were nearly the same height. The only difference was the color of Noosheen's hair. Chloe had read in a spy novel that women can easily pass for one another. To the eye of a guard, women are interchangeable. "Then I can go to the American consul and say my passport is lost or stolen. They will give me another," she went on.

Noosheen gaped at this bold and simple idea. "How can you be sure they will give you another?"

"Well, it happens all the time. People are always losing their passports and having them stolen." She paused a moment for the notion to take hold. Yes, as she reviewed it: simple, bold, practicable.

"Let's go inside; let's look in a mirror," Noosheen said. They looked at their two faces in the mirror, looking nothing alike, yet who would see it? A further lightening of the hair . . . Chloe dropped the passport into Noosheen's purse.

"You can mail it back to me, in case I can't get another. What could be simpler? But you must act at once, because I'm supposed to go back myself, in two weeks."

"I will, then, if you believe you can get another without difficulty," said Noosheen, with the firmness of the resolved and desperate. She embraced Chloe and rushed off to see about tickets and peroxide. She would come back in the afternoon to practice an American demeanor. Chloe's own heart raced with excitement.

She drank the rest of the tea in the pot, right down to the hot grounds, and stared out between the geraniums at the light shimmer of leaves in a rising breeze. It portended, perhaps, a change of weather, though it was only August, and the heat would endure for weeks yet. She did not know when the weather broke and changed here. It would be nice to see a storm.

She thought of her dresser drawer, now empty of passport. She sought a chill of terror, a sense of having done an irrevocable action, a *frisson* of importance or drama. But she was unable to produce any of these sensations, for she knew that for an American doctor's wife the loss of a passport is not the end. She had a not-unpleasant, abandoned feeling, the feeling of fatedness, kismet. Yes, this was the feeling she wanted, of pleasure to be rid of her passport, symbol of her earthly situation. Passportless and free, and unable to return to the United States.

This enabled her to see her gesture as a childish response to Jeffrey's intention to dump her. So what, I can't come home anyway, she was trying to say. The reality of Jeffrey's letter came back upon her.

It was important, she saw, to be the leaver, not the left. She must decide in her own mind to leave Jeffrey. You seldom get to do anything you believe in, for something you believe in, she thought. Life requires no decisions and no actions from a person like her. She thought of people in lifeboats, deciding which one to eat; she thought of polar expeditions, of herself rolled in a rug, crossing over into Afghanistan. If it came to that, it was reassuring to think that General Ben would undoubtedly find a rug merchant quickly enough for an American woman.

Regarding Jeffrey, it soon occurred to her that it was not reasonable to resent and fear the same action by another that one had been planning to take oneself. She was sure she had been planning, unconsciously, to leave Jeffrey. Of course it is more disagreeable to be rejected than to reject, but she saw that she ought to be grateful that both of them were of the same mind. It was lucky, really, that Jeffrey had someone else.

She did wonder, though, who it was, and she minded that although Jeffrey had someone she herself did not, not really, for she could not imagine herself proceeding directly to marry Hugh, however agreeable this interlude. Nor was she sure that Hugh would suggest it. This meant, she guessed, that she was not in love with Hugh; if she were she would now be delighted, whereas she was not exactly delighted, only relieved, now that the pique had worn off, and concerned for the children, though that was a little abstract and in her heart she didn't think they would be worse off without Jeffrey. They would be better off, she told herself. There would be plenty of time to worry about the house, the division of the furniture, and all the other distresses of divorce her friends had reported.

She did not seem to be able to summon, from some reserve of feeling, much emotion at all about this. How odd, in a crisis of life, this rather flat and apathetic uninterest. She wondered if she ever felt things enough. Too much? What *was* the appropriate amount of self-concern? She watched the old women in black, or the bright-skirted tribal women carrying water, and wondered if they ruled secretly in their houses and analyzed

their emotions, or perhaps emotions came to them as head-
aches, or as death.

"For its own works lieth every soul in pledge," she read in
the Koran. She wished it would rain. She liked to see wind
come up and the sky darken, and the quickening of things, of
laundry on the line. You never saw that in America, but here
the things hung on washlines, and would twist and flap in a
wind, and all the dogs cowering under bushes again, and the
jubes would flood; she'd like to see that, with shoes and tin cans
and paper and the tops of carrots all floating along in the
rushing water of the jube. It would be disgusting.

"It's knocked the props out from under you," her mother
would say, or she would say, "You have to have the props
knocked out from under you before you can fly." How conventional I am, thought Chloe, filled with scorn for herself. I can
live alone, and have affairs, and travel to foreign lands as long
as I know I have a husband, but if I didn't I'd be scared. After
all, wasn't it really Jeffrey's fault she did these things—ran off
to Iran, slept with other men? If he were nicer or easier to be
with . . . Chloe had always felt sorry for men. They seemed so
forlorn and unprotected. But now she saw she was in Jeffrey's
power, as Noosheen was in Bahram's power, and now, in the
power of men, she felt afraid.

Later, at the Cyrus, she heard Loyal Cooley talk about the
importance of passports. Her pulse quickened fearfully.

"I carry my passport and traveler's checks around my neck,"
he said. "I have a bag around my neck, I just put them in there,
then I don't worry—you know me, I get drunk and wander
around—this way I don't have to worry. Without a passport
you've had it."

Dick had in his pocket a small box containing a necklace. He
had bought it from Richard Dare, whose name, it had not
escaped him, seemed entirely appropriate for an alter ego of
himself—an adventurer, on digs, in foreign bars, perhaps not

entirely trustworthy? Dick hadn't much liked the dealings. He loved the necklace. The necklace was not visibly valuable, contained no jewels or stones, was made of beads of clay, rather drab, in fact, in colors of cinder and brown, with eyes painted strangely on the sides, glaring up at the wearer. She would not have been a queen, said Richard Dare, but a serving woman, although beloved, valued of somebody. Mourned.

At times, at the hospital, when there was no one in his office, he could not resist taking it out to look at, though Dare had warned him against this, for it would be illegal for a foreigner to have an antiquity. No one saw.

"I think I'm going to leave Jeffrey," she said to Dick over white wine. "And Jeffrey thinks we should."

"Really?" exclaimed Dick, taken by surprise by this sudden confidence, this sign of restlessness in the restfully stable Chloe. "You've decided?" She nodded.

"Well, it's usually for the good," Dick said. "I was all for it when we did it. Though now sometimes I think it was a lot of trouble. We should have just been a little more tolerant."

He means Marla should have been more tolerant, thought Chloe.

"Yes, I've had some time to think," Chloe said. Looking her most radiant. "It helps to be away, to think. I'm very relieved," she said. "I know it's for the best," as if the whole thing had been her own idea. One has, after all, one's pride.

Chapter Twenty-four
CINQ À SEPT

You know, my Friends, with what a brave Carouse
I made a Second Marriage in my house;
Divorced old barren Reason from my Bed
And took the Daughter of the Vine to Spouse.

Chloe didn't go immediately to report the supposed loss of her passport; it was a day or two before she could bring herself to think seriously about her impulsive transaction with Noosheen, and when she did it was with misgiving and satisfaction both, imperfectly sorted. She was in a way happy without her passport, and she congratulated herself that women were free of the temperamental constraints that confine men to the rules and regulations of their own devising. Women did therefore dare things with passports that men would never have done. On the other hand, her misgivings grew. "I'm Chloe Fowler," she told the American consul, in the seedy consulate full of filing cases of wood-grained Formica. He had a middle-western accent, but wore Iranian clothes. "I left my passport in my room, I think. Anyway, it's gone. Or it could have been in my purse, though I wasn't conscious of anything else being missing, either from my room or from the purse." Her recollection of the time her room had been searched gave her now, she felt, an injured, convincing tone.

"You're saying that you've lost your passport?"

"Yes, I've looked everywhere, naturally, and it simply isn't there."

"Oh, Jesus," said the consul. "It's getting rough, you know. You heard what happened to your colleagues the Erdmans?" Chloe had heard that the Erdmans, though there so briefly, had bought sixteen rugs. "Some for their sons and daughters-in-law," Heidi had said, "ten for themselves."

"No."

"They overstayed their visa by four days, so they put him in jail for four days. Took him right off Pan Am in Tehran." Despite herself, Chloe giggled. "And what happened to her?"

"They sent her off without him. They take these things seriously here nowadays. They don't like us here, you know. Oh, the Shah likes us, your Iranian doctors, they like you, but the guy that stamps the passport, the guy that issues the visa, they don't like us, they drag their feet. Things take weeks, things get lost. If somebody flouts the law, they can lock them up or confiscate things."

"I'm supposed to go September 10. I have my ticket," Chloe said.

"I hope it isn't an excursion ticket," he said. "You might have to change it. It won't be anything getting the passport. I just telephone our embassy in Tehran. But then you have to get a duplicate residency visa from the Iranians. That's what could take some time."

Chloe composed herself and determined not to be rattled or frightened by this. She filled out the forms he gave her.

"Suppose it was stolen—can someone else use it?" she asked as she was leaving.

"Sure, if they look like you," he said.

Life so seldom requires action that Chloe was quite unused to the feeling that came over her now, at last, of having taken a rash action. It went to her head like drink; she was woozy with anxious qualms on Noosheen's behalf. Perhaps she was recklessly sending Noosheen into danger, apprehension, arrest. Perhaps she should have counseled her firmly to stay. I'm out of my depth, was her thought, directing the lives of others. At twilight, when she thought he would be home, she went to Abbas's to ask his advice, for he was bound, she felt, to have from his long acquaintance with the Ardeshirs a more balanced view of Noosheen's real situation and perhaps would advise her to ask for her passport back and counsel Noosheen in patience.

She was surprised, she could not have said why, to find him cutting roses at the side of his garage. "Come in," he said. "How nice to see you."

Rather formally, they sat in his living room, which had the sort of wood and upholstered furniture of hospital issue you saw here, and pretty oil paintings of flowers and cups on tables. She explained her mission. She admitted that she had encouraged Noosheen to leave, but, intent on confession although she was, something at the last second prevented her from admitting that she had given away her passport, literally empowering Noosheen to flee. This was what she had intended to confess, but now it sounded too desperate, too silly, too dangerously meddlesome. This realization impeded her account. She faltered.

"Would you like some tea? Some sherry?"

"Not really," she said. She had nonetheless the feeling that there was something she wanted. The moment was slightly bleak, inhospitable because something was withheld. Perhaps he was angry or disapproving of the way she had busied herself with Noosheen's life. "I am so sure that Noosheen loves you," she said.

He laughed. "Oh, Noosheen. It's true Bahram is not perfect for her. I've known her since she was a child. However, she's not in love with me. I know her parents. She was a reckless, obstinate little girl who was famous for riding a bicycle off a bridge. You must ask her to tell you the story."

He had poured two glasses of sherry.

"You could help her," said Chloe, wishing more than ever to pass along the responsibility for a reckless child who dashed off bridges. His beautiful smile was princely in its indifference.

"But it's you I want," he said, handing her the little glass. This impulsive remark seemed to affect her.

Her eyes widened. She took the glass. She felt heat flash her face. How unexpected men are. How plausible an idea.

"You are mysterious to me," he went on. "It's partly that."

She was beautiful; he liked her pale translucence and the increasing voluptuousness of her body. "If I made love to you I would solve you a little. But perhaps it's simpler than that."

"I guess it's always rather simple," Chloe said, laughing, feeling herself attracted to this proposition. It would be, in fact, perfectly simple. They could go in the bedroom this minute and take off their clothes.

And indeed why not? They simultaneously recognized that they were staring. Each shifted. Abbas half rose. His the dark beauty of the warlike Turks in paintings, the Ottomans, painted with their daggers, their brocades. He leaned across the table to kiss her. She, in leaning toward him, laid her hand on the thorned stems of the roses and gave a cry of pain. As in the fairy tale, a drop of blood sprang to her palm. They rushed to Abbas's bedroom.

Her generally anxious state of mind caused brief apprehensions to flit into her thoughts—the worry of getting undressed with someone for the first time—what he will see, and, almost worse, what you will see, for though you know what he will see, what you see may surprise or disappoint or throw you off stride, intimations beforehand notwithstanding, and then what if he reacted to the clear difference between the color of the hair on her head and her pubic hair, or that she had it at all—here she thought of Noosheen, but no, he had been to school in England, after all, it was just that she had never slept with a person from the Middle East, or, indeed, anywhere but America, though these kisses were quite recognizable, causing her to think she would devote her life to pleasure, to giving and receiving pleasure, like this.

As they moved toward the bed—neatly made, India Madras bedspread—she saw him see that she had noticed the picture on the bureau of a woman and baby. But he said nothing, and she was spared the awkwardness of "I'm sorry." She couldn't tell if the woman was beautiful. Of course she must have been. A year is not long, only a year. She wondered if he had slept with anyone since, and who. His embraces were not of the starved but of the bountiful, bestowing kind, even leisurely, a lot of foreplay, so that Chloe, who had always been bored by foreplay, hastened things along. Not too much, just until she was reassured that things were going to go forward, and that Abbas wasn't going to cry, "This is madness," and get to his feet.

Abbas whispered Persian words, delightfully unintelligible. She knew she ought to wriggle vivaciously in his embrace, but was captured by a sort of ecstatic languor, a heaviness previously unknown to her in this situation, so that she could barely lift her arms to stroke his back. Her arms and legs seemed not to belong to her; she was only a center. When, after the climax, he lay against her, she saw that she had pleased Abbas too.

"I suppose I meant for this to happen—hoped, I mean, unconsciously," she sighed later as they sorted themselves out from the jumble of shoes and clothing on Abbas's bedroom floor.

"I'm glad," said Abbas. "I naturally had not dared to hope—or hoped, perhaps, but scarcely dared to plan." They smiled at each other, and Chloe, who had thought herself in charge of the situation, being the American, now had intimations, unfathomable but reassuring, of centuries of dark gardens, Persian poems.

There were not going to be any odd Islamic consequences, whatever those would be. Abbas, a sophisticated man, more handsome than Hugh, really, in a way, she thought, and as good, but now a stranger again, making tea. How odd sexual passion is, coming on like a fit. Her head now clearer, her body calm and light again, she felt that her life was not over.

She returned to the subject of Noosheen, her unhappiness, her love. "I even wonder if I should have encouraged her in her academic ambitions. She asks my advice. I wondered what you think. . . ." This glowing olive color of Abbas more attractive than paler skin, his shaving lotion some regular Western brand she couldn't name. Rich people here tall, like Abbas, only the poor ones small, except Bahram, beautiful rugs here, a lot of electronic equipment, that BMW, Abbas must be rich and choose to live here and devote his life to the poor. He had pounced on her as smoothly as a leopard. He had seduced people before. Something purred in Chloe. She knew there is no such thing as seduction. Of course Noosheen loved him, how could she not?

"Oh. I have to go! I'm having dinner at the Asgharis'," she said. What would happen now? Nothing. She would leave, though the paths outside were now encumbered by nurses coming for the evening shift, workers leaving the hospital, in the air the call to prayer; she would be seen by all the industrious and righteous. Sensing her hesitation Abbas brought her a black veil. On it the soft scent of powder, perhaps that of Mrs. Henderson, worn at the mosque. Chloe wrapped herself in it, clumsily as before, pulling the front down over her hair. Romantic subterfuge. They laughed as she glided out unseen onto the path among the others.

In a veil no one sees you. You may speak to them, they to you, yet you remain unseen. Invisible even though the man in the donkey cart has to rein up as she steps distractedly in front of him; it is not she who impeded his course, just someone, a woman, unknown. Eyes do not look at her; she is impressed by the difference. Now she remembers that in America when you walk along the eyes of the people approaching you assess you. You see them look at your shoes, and you think, Is something the matter with my shoes? My stockings?

"Well, it was just fucking, it didn't mean a thing," she plans to say, like a man, if reproached. But who could reproach her? She is cheered and fortified in her renewed sense that she is her own woman to do with as she pleases. She would have liked to tell Junie Fay. Junie she is sure would be approving of such liberated behavior. But of course she won't tell anyone. Neither will Abbas. Will they do it again? Why not? Chloe's cheeks so glow with daring and happiness, walking home, that she is sure anyone could tell she is not a modest Iranian woman.

Some interesting gossip at dinner: Noosheen Ardeshir has disappeared. Her husband confided it to Mohammed; he has no idea where she is; he has telephoned her brother in Tehran. She could not have flown home to her parents because she has no passport. He is certain, he says, that it was because she was so unhappy to be back in Iran; he understands her perfectly. But he is worried—where can she be staying? He doesn't know the names of her friends. She might have met millions of people in her Victorian Poetry class. The nurse seems stupid with the baby, which cries constantly. Reported second hand, thus, stripped of the anxious tones of the husband, the account does not suggest what emotions underlie it. If a young woman disappears in America, you imagine a car accident, or murder. Noosheen lying in a coma in a strange hospital, or abduction, body buried in a shallow grave dug up by dogs. Chloe feels it is a credit to Iran that no one seems worried that Noosheen has met with foul play.

The Yazdis walk home with Chloe and the others. "You must come some evening and see my collection, I spoke of it, I believe. The collection begun by my father of Persian miniatures," says Dr. Ali Yazdi to Chloe, taking her arm to help her across the jube. She feels the silk of his sleeve against her upper arm. His cologne. His wife is far behind them.

"I should like to very much," Chloe said. "I've seen some in the bazaar. And the little pictures painted on ivory. I am going to buy one of those."

"Mine of course are very rare. From only special dealers. Many ordinary ones have been bought by Western dealers, but the very special ones have remained in Iran. Some are very curious, you know."

"Really?" says Chloe politely, not understanding the significance of this word. Curious.

"Cunnilingus," says Dr. Yazdi, leaning toward her. The startled Chloe withdraws her elbow. She is not sure she has heard correctly.

"Fellatio," says Dr. Yazdi. "These distinctive contributions by Persia to the arts of love."

Astonished, Chloe says nothing.

"You know what I'm talking about, I suppose," says Dr. Yazdi intimately. She feels her cheeks burn like a Victorian's. "The arts, the refinements of love are discussed in the earliest Persian texts; some of the earliest of history," Dr. Yazdi said.

"Um," says Chloe, heart beating with surprise. He knows what she did in the afternoon, or it is because she is a woman alone. Dr. Yazdi would not speak to a woman with a husband of things like this. She sees how he, they, must see her, loose and free, alone. But of course in a Middle Eastern country so conventional about the status of women, of course she must seem fast and free. She thinks of Zareeneh Yazdi, soignée, smooth-legged, flying to London for shopping, what might she not do there in hotels with Englishmen? Or perhaps this is just the way Iranians talk about love?

Or perhaps it is known what she is up to with Hugh? With Abbas? Perhaps they think all American women are whores? This is the way you talk to a whore in Iran? Or else there are no whores in Iran. What do I care what Dr. Yazdi thinks? They know about me. Perhaps they will write to Jeffrey. Her heart races. The minute you are unprotected, the minute you are light, men can tell. Not just Islamic men, all men can tell, she thinks.

"Thank you, Dr. Yazdi," she says at the door of Villa Two. "You are all so kind. Goodnight. Goodnight."

Chapter Twenty-five
REMORSE

A Book of Verses underneath the Bough,
A Jug of Wine, a Loaf of Bread—and Thou
Beside me singing in the Wilderness—
Oh, Wilderness were Paradise enow!

She awoke with a feeling of remorse, like a stone. Usually her depressions were two days before her period, like everyone else's; now she woke with an Empedoclean weight upon her of dismay and embarrassment, head aching, faintly sick at her stomach. She groped along to the kitchen to make coffee, hoping Dick Rothblatt wouldn't come too early, and that only he, not Junie or Hugh, would turn up. She could somehow talk to Dick, even if she couldn't tell him the truth about this, and he always made her laugh. She was a silly, promiscuous woman, but he seemed to like her.

Her bleak mood did not escape the notice of anyone she saw throughout the day. She half-heard the monotone of her voice, its flatness. "I'm tired, I didn't sleep," she explained to those who asked. Even Mr. Farmanpour asked. It was curious, but her trance of remorse enhanced her ability to concentrate on the assemblage of shards, which she could ordinarily do only for an hour or two before her restless energy ("short attention span," a teacher had once said censoriously) drove her to something else. Now she sat four hours in the afternoon, in the hot light, despite the growing heat, picking at the bits with tiny tweezers, achieving another inch along the side of the huge terra cotta beaker she had been given to work on. At moments her thoughts drifted to what she had done. Defensive phrases tumbled one after another through her brain: a pleasant occasion, a handsome man, curiosity, pleasure, all very natural, following the natural instincts without hurting others, people do odd things on vacation. I was only trying to help Noosheen.

In the evening, Hugh returned from Tehran. She was glad to see him. She loved him. Making love later would be pleasant. But he hadn't found out anything in Tehran, he said. The people he went to see wouldn't see him. He was grim when he spoke of it, his mood as heavy as she had seen in him. He looked like a wartime President, except that his eye and ear were still horrible vegetables, cabbages or plums. He planned to complain of his security to Vahid Farmani. "I don't like this feeling of being in a risky game I have no stakes in," he said. She didn't press for details, didn't care. Her curiosity was subdued, or in abeyance, or she had perhaps given in, when she had failed to mention the shirts way back then, to her own emotional and erotic needs; she had surrendered her right to ask. Perhaps she even liked the idea that Hugh was complicit in some large operation of power and interest. This was perhaps the secret of the allegiance of criminals' wives—whom she still despised in principle—this feeling of being connected to influence.

Hugh suggested dinner at the Reza Café. It was Wednesday night, so the Iranian doctors came in for pizza before the English-language film at Cinema Pars. Chloe was surprised that anyone could bear to go to the films, now that the men had been burned in Abadan. This theatre could be set on fire, too, the doors locked, as in Abadan, locked by fanatic killers so that the patrons would be sure to die.

Abbas was with the others. They came laughing up the stairs. His expression at seeing her was for a moment astonished, and she realized that this was the first time she had been seen alone with Hugh. Or perhaps he was astonished at Hugh's bruises. Then he joined in the greetings. His words to her communicated, but most discreetly, their bond. Chloe's heart pounded like a schoolgirl's. She felt her face warm. It occurred to her that given a few weeks—less—you could sleep with every man in this room, a small room like this, if you were a free woman on your own. Some, though, were not attractive.

She and Hugh went to the movie with the others. Chloe watched the exits, breathing deeply, fearing to catch a warm burst of air or smoke. If the theatre was set on fire, she and the others, sitting in a small balcony, which cost more, could rush outside to the fire exit. Chloe longed for someone to try the door, to make sure it was unlocked, but no one did. She did not give in to her hysterical wish that someone try the door.

The film was *All the President's Men*, about Watergate. She would have thought it would not be allowed, but here was a whole theatre full of Iranians watching a film about the fall of a powerful leader. The audience was completely silent. Chloe thought their mood was fascination. Hugh thought it was on account of the complicated English and relatively slow action.

"It says something that they would allow a movie like that," Chloe remarked to Dr. Ali Yazdi afterward, as the Iranian doctors stood on the sidewalk, deciding where to go for coffee. Ali looked surprised at such a direct remark, its implied criticism of the Iranian political climate. Chloe saw that it sounded more critical than she had intended it to sound, and to just the wrong person, Dr. Yazdi, who, it seemed from his jewelry, would have good connections in Tehran.

"I mean you wouldn't think there would be much interest in American politics here," she said.

"Robert Redford is very popular here," he said.

Abbas gave a short laugh and walked away ahead of them. He was thinking that it had been a fascinating movie, two men able to accomplish so much within a framework of laws and immutable regulations and constitutions. To do something in Iran, you would have to be a lone assassin or a guerrilla. Though it was not his style of thing, he rather more admired the youngsters hiding in the mountains, or the little newspapers printed in secret by people who risked their lives. Woodward and Bernstein had not risked anything, certainly not their lives.

Luckily it was not necessary to risk your life, if you were a doctor, to do good; you could do it under any regime.

"It will be hard, going back," Chloe said to Hugh, the lightness of her tone concealing her emotion, its nature unknown, like something hot swallowed, waiting for his word to dissolve it, some medical balm of a word from Hugh, though she didn't know what it could be. What would he say? What could he say but yes that it would be hard going back; this he said. But that was not what she had meant. Hard going back to separate lives, he in Rochester, New York, she in San Francisco. "Never seeing you," she explained, careful in her tone, though, to show she wasn't nagging or making an ultimatum. Just an observation. "I've got so used to you."

His look at her seemed prolonged, seemed more astute than she might have given him credit for. Perhaps he did think of her, have, that is, a theory about her character, or an understanding of her—perhaps she was more a subject than she had thought. But her glint of comprehension was only momentary and was perhaps imagined, the way sometimes the pictures in a gallery could seem to look at her with friendliness and understanding, if she wanted them to, "Pinky" or Mrs. Siddons seeming to say that you and she have a lot in common.

"I know," Hugh said. "I've been trying not to think of it."

"Should we think of it? Hugh?" cried Chloe.

"When we get back we will think of it, whether we ought to or not. Then we'll see. That's the real world, after all."

"Oh, I know," said Chloe, with a light, uncaring laugh, thinking that the world around women were hanging on the words of men, right as they spoke; how she despised it.

"I love your dynamite big cock," Chloe says later in bed, and a whole lot of other things like this not her usual way of talking but men seemed to like it, compliments to their cocks and generally a loose way of speaking in women in hot moments, if the woman didn't talk that way usually. She herself thought it odd that they didn't think it was odd that a prim ladylike woman such as she should come out with these things, but that was the point. Predictably, Hugh grinned. Perhaps he wondered what had heated Chloe up these nights; she wondered herself.

One night thereafter Hugh confided that he had once seen a book called *The Arab Art of Love*, which extolled the external genitalia of women in terms that were unfamiliar to a Western man.

"Cucumbers, or melons," Hugh said. "Different shapes of fruit. Just bend over slightly," said Hugh to Chloe, who was standing with her back to him in her thin nightdress. Chloe obeyed, rather apprehensively. "Yes," said Hugh, "there is a kind of outline. Very exciting to Arabs," seeming, after a moment, rather excited himself.

"You are a pear, Chloe," said Hugh, which disappointed Chloe, rather, though pears were a perfectly nice fruit. It was not a part of yourself you ever saw.

In the days that followed, though no one spoke of Noosheen, she preyed horribly on Chloe's mind. She thought of Noosheen in flight; imagined her wrapped in chador, veil flowing behind her as she sped along a dirt road, or carrying a few belongings tied up in a cloth, or wearing smart Western clothes on a flight to London, using Chloe's passport, pulling her gold earrings, fidgeting anxiously in her seat, or hidden in a wagon, swaying along behind donkeys over the mountains, wherever the mountains were. Perhaps the silence of other people was out of consideration for Bahram, who continued to come to work, his manner subdued, and otherwise to behave as if no domestic crisis had entered his life. They heard that he was making inquiries and contacting people in Tehran. Heidi and Chloe discussed Noosheen, though Chloe did not confide her knowledge or her part. The two women were sympathetic. "She hasn't been happy since she got back here," Heidi said, and "You never know how Bahram is in private, I suppose. But Mohammed thinks the world of him. It's just a sad situation."

"It was the ink, I imagine," Chloe said. "It changed her. Made her feel blue." She began to laugh at her silly joke, then broke off in case Heidi should think she was cruel.

"At least no one thinks she's dead," Chloe observed. "In America, you would assume she was dead."

Regarding Abbas, the torments Chloe was experiencing on her own behalf were familiar to her from high school: the fear that she had made a fool of herself and would not be respected; adoration and desire in a provisional form, which could be switched to distaste and fury depending on developments; an attitude of wary waiting and a mood of heightened interest in the world itself, the noise of bees sounding loudly in her ears, the hibiscus and jasmine stronger, sensation, sensation. When she did see Abbas, each day usually, by lingering outside the hospital on her way back from the university, or when eating lunch with Dick and Junie, she analyzed her emotions afterward and found them to be affection and fascination. His demeanor was perfect, communicating affection and regard to her, and nothing to any bystander. They did not, however, find themselves again alone.

She had somehow exasperated Junie, who was never admiring of other women but now seemed especially impatient with Chloe, who couldn't think what she might have done in particular, though generally, Junie gave her to understand, she symbolized lightweight self-indulgence and indolence. Words erupted during one of their lunches, always before so friendly, in the Azami cafeteria.

Chloe had brought up Noosheen. "She should have some counseling," Dick said. "Someone to help her adjust to her reality situation. When they find her."

"Really, how can you say such a thing?" Chloe disagreed. "One thing good here at least is that they aren't ridden by psychiatrists. Not that I don't think people need someone to talk to, but she had people to talk to. Me for one. And she has poetry. That is what art is for, isn't it, to help people bear reality? They get on very well here without Freud."

"And without Jesus," Dick said. "At least they're spared Marx."

Chloe disagreed. "Maybe they could use Marx."

"That's ridiculous," said Dick. "Show me a Marxist society where the people are any better off than before."

"China," said Chloe.

"Do I want to go back?" said Dick suddenly. "Back to all that acne, all those medical students, all those little proto-right-wing, guaranteed-rich kids. Endless boils and liver spots. I don't know. Not really." Psychiatrists were another thing, though. He had continued to have his recurrent dream about the body in the desert. He supposed it really referred to his burying his father, but he would just like to have talked to Edelstein about it, about the idea that he was feeling so repaired in spirit these days because he had in some sense really buried his father.

"I know," Chloe said. "Here a person can really do something." Junie gave a sharp laugh. Her face had grown thinner—like a fox's face, Chloe thought.

"That's a laugh, Chloe. What do *you* do anyway?" she said. Chloe had no reply. Junie's remark, unexpectedly cruel, was nonetheless true. What does Chloe do? The others talked of other things in hasty voices.

Junie was right, she agreed, thinking about it later back in Villa Two. She doesn't blame Jeffrey for loving someone else. She is unworthy, unsatisfactory, a terrible wife, an absent mother, indifferent, untidy, indolent, unfaithful—who could blame him? She dreads his going around San Francisco telling the story of his marriage. Please let him not testify or confide in people. If she marries again she promises to undertake it more knowingly, more sincerely, to be better. Her mood is one of pity and sympathy for Jeffrey.

How would it be to marry Abbas and stay in Iran, of course sending for her children, who would benefit from an international upbringing and learn to speak Farsi? Funny to think of Sara wrapped in a little shawl, wearing little earrings; in California all she wanted to do was go to swimming practice. Max would have to go to school in England like Abbas; that would be better than the schools in California. They would have another baby. A letter to Jeffrey saying, "I'm not coming back; put the kids on the plane." What a relief to follow this line of thinking. Max and Sara arrive with little suitcases, a court order. Rice diet better for the teeth. What a relief to follow the line of thinking that began with Abbas's serious smile and intent expression of passion and understanding. She could make him happy.

Noosheen halfway across India by now. It was mysterious; no one spoke of it, because of Bahram. No police out searching. Private inquiries? Was he doing nothing to find her, to get her back? If he had appeared distressed, frantic, if there had been an outcry, Chloe would have confessed something to him, had prepared a half-confession in which she unwittingly might be able to reassure him, she without realizing . . . Chloe hopes Noosheen, who seemed so confused among the barriers and thickets of Arnold's verses, can manage trains and the lie at the border. Western clothes, sunglasses, a hat, it should be easy, if only she hadn't got sentimental and tried to take too many things with her. Iranian jewelry, photos, books in Farsi. Probably they search your bags.

"It's true, it'll be hard to think of you going back to be Jeffrey's wife," Hugh said suddenly from his cot in the darkness. "You are my wife."

"I'm an archaeologist in far-off Iran. I'm nobody's wife," said Chloe, distantly.

In the middle of the night she wondered if Abbas would try to see her again, and whether she wished it or not. In his sleep Hugh sighed. He slept in his T-shirt, nothing on the bottom. She got into his cot with him and crept close to his hairy, warm thighs. One of these days she would suck his cock. She had selfishly ignored his wistful hints. She would try to be a better person soon.

Chapter Twenty-six
O U T C A S T

Indeed the Idols I have loved so long
Have done my credit in this World much wrong,
Have drown'd my Glory in a shallow Cup,
And sold my Reputation for a Song.

In the following days, Chloe continued in a preoccupied state of misery and happiness she recognized from her adolescence; how strange it seemed that the decades do not diminish the symptoms: slyly looking or hoping to get a glimpse of someone, practicing a bright, intimate, but perfectly respectable expression to wear when happening upon him. Chloe despised herself as she grimaced in the mirror, or turned her head to try to see more of herself. She would just like to try it with Abbas once or twice again, she told herself. Desire is irrational, transitory. Otherwise Hugh suited her perfectly, and her fondness for him grew. When she tried to recall herself to a sense of her real life, need for her children, impressions of the future, she could not.

Perhaps, she thought, her voluptuous languor was owing to the heat, which increasing by slow degrees each day had now become stifling at midday. The doctors and the students went about their ways, but Chloe found that she lay on her cot after lunch, aimlessly staring at the circling flies, watching for a stir of branches, hoping for a breeze so she could bring herself to go to the university. Villa Two, like other Iranian houses, it was explained to her, was constructed so that if a breeze arrived it would be drawn right into the apartments by means of the stairwell and a tower that came out on the roof. The trouble was that no breeze arrived. At noon, the stillness, the airlessness which descended, coincided with a mood of menace, the report of terrible events. Soldiers had shot some students in Qom.

If she woke at dawn when Hugh left, she would get up and walk with Rustum in the garden. This was the perfect time of day. Thus it was that she saw the arrest of Vahid Farmani by a party of soldiers or police.

The police saw her watching but paid no attention. Perhaps they did not think she understood what they were doing. The police were young, and wore starched, short-sleeved shirts, and they had big shoes that flopped like clown shoes. But their faces were frantic and grim. They were pulling the reluctant Vahid out of his door, punching him brutally in the back, as she watched, and kicking gratuitously at his shins, like angry children. He uttered a thin cry and twisted his body around to look at Linda, who watched from the doorway in an old nightgown. Vahid Farmani was shouting at the soldiers and calling out to Linda in Farsi, so that the words "Linda, Linda" were all that Chloe's ears could discern.

At the end of the garden by the gate of the compound a black Peykan waited with two taxis. Vahid was thrust into a taxi, and all three cars backed rapidly out of the gates. As he turned in the back seat of the car, for a glimpse of his wife, his eyes met Chloe's. His had a resigned, mute, doglike look. Chloe stood, watching from the flowerbeds, and Linda in her doorway broke now into loud sobs. Chloe hesitated. It would seem unsisterly and cold to ignore the terror and misery of another American woman. Chloe crossed the garden and timidly approached Linda.

"What's happened?" she asked. "Can I help?"

Linda looked at her, astonished. "You!" she cried. Her hair was down over her bare shoulders, showing a strand or two of gray, and her eyes stared like the eyes of a madwoman.

"But what's happened?" Chloe persisted. "Why are they taking him?"

"I don't know why they are taking him. He is arrested. They never say why." She abandoned herself to a frenzy of weeping, head bent against the panels of her front door. "He is dead," she said again and again. "They'll kill him. I'll never see him again. That's how it is here. Don't you know anything?"

Suddenly she was calmer and looking searchingly at Chloe: "Who did you tell?"

Tell? "About what?" Chloe asked, thinking back, trying to think, whether she had in fact told, or said, something, whatever it could be, to someone, to endanger poor Dr. Farmani. Perhaps she had said something. Perhaps to Loyal Cooley, the Texan CIA agent, or to General Ben, who worked, after all, for the Shah. Misery assailed her. She could indeed have said something terrible about Dr. Farmani, about his cruelty in the matter of an extra key, or his unsympathetic attitude about the cleaning of Villa Two.

About the typhoid. It came to her. "I have certainly criticized his handling of the typhoid. But to whom, who am I?"

"Maybe that's it. Oh, who knows? I don't know everything," cried Linda, breaking again into tears. "Things go on."

Chloe, wildly examining her recollections, was moved to embrace Linda comfortingly. It was strange how she had not felt authorized to embrace the wretched Noosheen at a similar moment and yet could enfold Linda, who didn't even like her.

"I'm sure he'll be all right," she tried to say. "Perhaps it's just for questioning?"

This suggestion brought further wails from Linda. The torture, the broken limbs. "Go to hell, go to hell," she sobbed, and rushed into her house.

That evening the Americans who had heard the news congregated anxiously at the Cyrus, which seemed safe and neutral, like an airport lounge, international territory where police wouldn't come, and Chloe was made to recount in detail what she had seen befall Vahid and what Linda had said. It was already apparent that Ali Yazdi had taken over as head of the hospital.

"But what do you suppose he did?" Dick Rothblatt said.

"The typhoid," Chloe said, "probably."

"I always thought he was a Shah person," said Junie Fay. "He's really gone up in my estimation."

Dick hated to mention the body. The others appeared to have forgotten about it. To him it seemed clear it was Vahid's handling of the body that had brought on his doom. Either that, or by his refusal to have anything to do with the body he had been unable to prevent what he feared, that association with it would bring him or the hospital down. "It had nothing to do with Azami Hospital," he had cried of the body, but perhaps the authorities in Tehran had thought it did all the same.

Perhaps even now they were beating him, torturing him, putting electrodes on his penis, on the soles of his feet, saying, "What do you know about the disappearance of Mr. X.? Where is he?" And Vahid didn't know, only he, Dick, knew, and Abbas Mowlavi, unless Abbas had told Vahid. Perhaps they were in league. You had no way of knowing for sure. Perhaps he and Abbas had merely been doing Vahid's dirty work in disposing of the body. So Vahid either did or didn't know about where the body was. This was or it wasn't the question the torturers were asking him right now. His head spun.

"Farmani was trying to cover up the typhoid, and Yazdi let it out," Junie speculated.

"It could have something to do with the airplanes," Dick said. "General Brigante thinks someone gets chemicals from Azami to sabotage the airplanes."

"Vahid trusted Yazdi. They were close. He might have told him any of his fears, and then Yazdi turned him in," said Junie.

"Perhaps political crimes we know nothing about," said Mrs. Henderson. "I rather think that's more likely."

"Maybe he's been a member of the resistance for a long time. How would we know?" agreed Junie.

Dick felt terrible and responsible. It was surely something to do with the clumsy handling of the body situation. Vahid had been petrified with fear over it, and now, for that matter, since he and Abbas were implicated, they should all feel afraid.

"Maybe he's been embezzling, something like that," someone said.

"*I* think Dr. Yazdi denounced him to the authorities so he would get to be head of the hospital," said Chloe, motivated more by her dislike of Yazdi than from any intuition of this.

This interpretation struck the others. It comported with what they knew of Yazdi, of the authorities, of the social aspirations of both men, of human nature—all the bits of assent from everybody present, collected themselves into the official explanation. It became, in everybody's mind, the explanation—even Chloe's, for it sounded plausible to her too. She thought of his folded silk scarves, Pierre Cardin.

Altogether there was nothing to be done. Like a blind chorus the Americans commented, then they had drinks. Luckily, they remarked, things did not really affect them because they were all to leave soon anyway. But they had been noticing a new insolence, a *lenteur*, in the service at the Cyrus—they all had instances of it—and there were various stories about the student uprising at the university, and Dr. Henderson, out driving in the hospital station wagon, had seen heavy artillery on the highway to Pasargadae.

Nonetheless they were surprised to hear from General Ben later that night that he had advised Mrs. Brigante not to return from Fort Lauderdale. They had not realized things had gone so far. And the next day they heard that the Mitsubishi wives, charming little creatures who took tiny steps and paused at the jubes as at great ditches—they were all leaving, someone worrying about their welfare back in Japan. Procter & Gamble had its dependents on alert. Chloe thought of all the substantial cement-block houses and pretty gardens in the American section by the Shah's summer palace, with the long American cars parked in front. She imagined the American wives rolling down their metal shutters and fastening the grills. But she could not imagine herself leaving. These alarms seemed excessive. Life went on the same. The following day Dr. Ali Yazdi instituted some organizational reforms at the hospital and ordered a cobalt unit from West Germany.

The abrupt deposition and arrest of Vahid Farmani left a void, a pall felt at the hospital immediately. The Americans were indignant at the seeming calm of the Iranians, though they understood that this Iranian appearance of uninterest, as if Farmani had never existed, might be reticence rather than callousness. Each had expected, however, that the Iranian person closest to him would confide an attitude, a theory at least. What had Farmani really done? Dick tried to bring the matter up to Abbas, who would only say, "That's how it goes here. It's deplorable, of course."

Abbas didn't know what Vahid had done. He'd been surprised by the arrest. He thought—something told him—he would try to sell his BMW after all, and he spoke to Jahlal Hakemi, a resident known to have money, and Hakemi was interested.

Linda Farmani abandoned herself to stormy weeping only for the remainder of the first day. She told herself she had to keep her wits about her; there were the hospital, baby Henry, things to do for Vahid. She asked herself whether she really believed she could outwit Vahid's enemies. She had lived in Iran for seven years; did she fear Iranians more or less than at first? Life is cheap to them, someone had said that; they are so cruel to each other. Yes, someone had said that, at the American Wives' Club, or in a book. A book by Pearl Buck, maybe, talking about the Chinese? Life is cheap and now they had Vahid's life, or maybe it was just a minor affair, maybe he'd be back soon. If she went back to America, all her years here, her pretty rooms, her speaking Farsi, none of this would matter; it would be as if she hadn't lived at all.

She thought it was she herself who had brought this down on Vahid because she was American. That made him more vulnerable; they hated an American wife here, even more than they hated an English wife, though she had never put herself forward or pushed. But she had made some mistake. What? Maybe only that she should have been nicer to Chloe Fowler. She herself was in no danger. American wives were not thrown into prison. But how horrible that she had odd thoughts, for instance to wonder if Vahid's salary would be paid if he didn't come back.

She dressed in somber navy blue, and tied a scarf on her hair, and went to the garrison where only a few months ago she had taken some American visitors named Nelson, to see the ancient structure. Back then she had thought nothing of the busy reconstructions they had seen. Now she wondered if they were building these new cells for prisoners. Maybe someone would tell her if Vahid was there, but no one did.

She went to the hospital. Here, in the familiar dining room, she openly wrung her hands and urged people to write letters to the Shah. Her large, purple-lidded brown eyes were ringed with dark, tragic shadows; her lips were swollen with her anxious way of catching them between her teeth.

Walking home, she came upon Chloe Fowler in the garden. She ground her teeth. Policy, policy, she told herself, and smiled at Chloe. The Yazdis had still not returned the garden furniture, so she squatted beside Chloe amid the remaining potted geraniums while Hossein resentfully swept and puttered at his garden duties, glaring at this unseemly commerce between Farmani's wife and the troublemaking foreign lady. Chloe was humbled to see Linda, humbled to think of the triviality of her own problems, mere matters of erotic choice, mere marital problems.

"I'm sure you didn't mean any harm," Linda said. "Try to

think. Who have you talked to? What have you said?" Her voice was sweetly smooth.

"No one, honestly," said Chloe, defensively. "Except the people around the Cyrus—General Brigante? I did mention the typhoid. And conditions at Villa Two."

"I know, you were out to get him from the first," Linda suddenly cried, jumping to her feet. "That's what he said. But you were mistaken. My husband is not political. He never has been. Does it make you feel good to do something like this to an innocent person? Do you like to think of the sufferings of an innocent person, you meddlesome bitch—has it ever occurred to you you might be wrong?" She walked swiftly into her house, leaving Chloe amid the shards of a flowerpot that she toppled in her flight.

Chloe was shocked and stung to be accused, so unreasonably, of something as serious and alarming as bringing on the arrest of Vahid. She felt her face flame. There was something exciting, too, to think you could be imagined so wicked, mischievous, and powerful. Only another American woman would pay you that compliment. But she didn't really believe that a remark about Vahid's handling of the typhoid could cause him to be dragged off, or that Linda could really believe so either. Linda was evidently speaking in passion and terror, casting about for someone to blame. If it weren't so serious she would have thought it was silly.

She went for her groceries in the late afternoon, when the shadows made things cooler. As she walked home, she saw Heidi Asghari coming toward her from the compound. Suddenly, Heidi turned and went into a shop. It was strange. Had Heidi not seen her? Chloe, passing the shop, saw that it was a toy shop. Heidi was inside gazing at the shelves. Chloe hesitated but did not go in.

At dusk, as she was dressing, the phone rang in the hall. This was such an infrequent event that it frightened her. The feeble ring seemed, at first, to be a pained cry from under the floor or a hallucination. The caller was Heidi. "I'm so sorry," she was saying, in a rushed voice, "it's a bother, but I'm afraid my dinner party's off, something's come up for Mohammed."

"Oh, that's too bad," Chloe said.

"Well, I'll do it again soon," Heidi said. "I'm sorry."

"Oh, me too," said Chloe, thinking that she had nothing to fix Hugh for supper.

"But I'm planning to go to Heidi's!" Hugh said later. "No one has told me not to. I left Mohammed just now and he said he would see me at eight."

Chloe could hardly realize what had happened. Heidi had uninvited only her. Could they all believe she had somehow been behind Vahid's arrest? She was astonished. As far as she knew, she had never in her life been unwelcome. She was at first too shocked to feel hurt, then she felt hurt and indignant.

"Ah," she said. "She means that the dinner party's off for me, then." She told Hugh about Linda's accusations.

"Shall I stay home with you?" asked Hugh solicitously. "I'll make some excuse."

"No, no," said Chloe at once. "Then they'll know we've talked. No."

But she waited up for him, asking eagerly as he tiptoed up the stairs, "Did anyone speak of me?"

"Of course not. I mean, no one speaks of anything. No one even spoke of Farmani."

"But they think I somehow put him away." Chloe couldn't help but laugh, though she knew it wasn't funny. The thought that her friend Heidi, or worse, Abbas, could think such a thing of her was nearly unbearable.

"Chloe," said Hugh, unlacing his shoes, "you *don't* always think before you speak. You don't take them seriously here. You don't realize that their lives are at risk, their families. You just say whatever you think—I've heard you talk about the body, the epidemic, God knows what else. People here are good people, trying to do the best they can for Iran. They are in danger all the time."

His tone was that of a man addressing a child. Tears of indignation shot to her eyes. As she was about to retort, she thought of Noosheen. She had had nothing to do with the arrest of Farmani, but she had certainly meddled in the life of Noosheen, who now, fleeing across unknown spaces, hiding in airport toilets, or landed penniless and desperate in India, or murdered by unscrupulous wife smugglers and her husband left grief-stricken, her babies deserted—this certainly was owing to Chloe's meddling. Chloe felt at this moment that she would sell herself to bring back Noosheen and get her own passport back, so she could leave this wretched country.

Still, just though Hugh's accusation of meddling might be, it was disloyal of him to rebuke her. He ought to stand behind her, she thought; he ought to believe in her. All at once her tears blinded her. She went into the bathroom.

"I'm glad it was a nice party," she said, in her bright, normal voice through the door. When she came out, Hugh went in. Chloe hurried to her cot and crawled in, and closed her eyes so that she would seem definitively asleep. But her heart was pounding with wakeful rage, and with an unfamiliar but unmistakable emotion—self-reproach. And fear. But with luck Hugh wouldn't find out about her part in the flight of Noosheen.

No Iranian now saw or spoke to her. Chloe tried not to think about it or to mind. It was unjust but just. She only hoped that Abbas did not believe with the others that she was a spy or informer. She would be leaving, she knew, in ten days, if her passport came. No doubt it would come. She would leave in ten days but this seemed a meaningless unit of time, neither long nor short. She did not intensify her activities and do the things she had been meaning to do. Hugh had offered to lend her money for a rug. She could go to the bazaar and look at rugs.

She wanted to finish her large beaker, a late Elamite beaker from the second millennium, and see the nearby city of Pasargadae. But her energy, her will, seemed already departed.

Darling kids. To think I will see you soon! The hot weather here is really hot. You wouldn't like it. Love, Mom.

She worked at the university in the mornings, as if she had all the time in the world, and in the afternoons drifted or slept. She took to sitting on a bench near the hospital entrance, near the flowerbeds where people could be seen walking in and out or squatting amid the roses to picnic or whisper, sometimes to weep. Chloe had been married to a doctor for a dozen years, but was still frightened by hospitals, emblems of the menace and arbitrariness of fate. Try to think of them as places of healing, Jeffrey would say, but how can you, with this woman swaddled in blue sitting on the ground pressing her cloth against her wet eyes, swaying in her grief like a wind-shaken dahlia.

Chloe would think about that woman, would try to imagine her at home, what her cooking pots were like, whether she had a radio, a line of children eating soup of peas and rice. A husband with a thin mustache. Did they kiss? Did anyone kiss the old dried faces, kiss the old men with thin shoulders? It appeared not. People appeared to shiver. Chloe watched them unwrapping their sandwiches. Who kisses the old?

Now, when she imagined the life of others, it was their pain she imagined, their suffering, their fragility, never their happiness. Why? It was safer to be herself, a person formerly happy, usually happy. She tried to imagine the happiness of women, wiping the hands of her little boy, that one, the other wearing a gold bracelet. Sometimes women would buy beautiful things in the bazaar, or a new broom, and feel pleased. A new broom was what she needed in Villa Two.

She wished she could see inside the woman's house, see her kitchen, see her shoes, plastic shoes walked over at the heels, think her thoughts as she looked at her shoes. What if all her thoughts, every minute, were of misery and sorrow? Chloe thought of all the women she had seen in photos, trudging with water jars and burdens. What if their every thought was sorrowful, miserable? Was this even possible? Surely the most unhappy mind is distracted at times by mere perception; by the beautiful tree in bloom, of the grayish fuzz of moss along the bark and the radiant light through the petals.

She never took off her beads. She understood the men who stood staring on street corners, heads wrapped in dirty rags, fingering their strings of beads. A sensation of permanence—hard, significant objects, with poems and rules to go with each one, and the interest of Allah invested in each one, in each bead as in each sparrow.

One night Hugh frightened her a little, making love, kissing and sucking at her breast. It suddenly seemed to her when his teeth had closed around her nipple, that he would bite her. She stiffened and pushed him away, and he turned the attention of his fingers to other parts of her, his kisses gently to her throat. She did not tell him what she had for a moment felt afraid of.

One afternoon there was a knock on the door. Chloe opened it, and was surprised to see a woman standing there in a nylon peignoir, blue, trimmed with ribbons. She was sixtyish, blond and well preserved, face made up and powdered, pink lipstick, smiling.

"Yes?"

"Hello," said the woman. "I'm Sugar Dunham, from Chapel Hill. My husband Homer Dunham and I have just got here, and I was just changing, and I went out in the hall to go to the kitchen for a drink of water, and I'm afraid I've locked myself out. Do you by any chance have a key?"

"I'm sorry," Chloe said. "There's only one key. That's how it is here, only one key. Come in, I'm sorry." Sugar Dunham stepped inside and Chloe closed the door. Sugar looked around, noticing apparently with approval, or even envy, the rug, the geraniums, the cheerful turquoise border around the window. Chloe felt gratified at the surprise on this new woman's face.

"My husband will be back. They're showing him around. We're supposed to stay a month but I'm already having my doubts. This is really terrible, isn't it? How long have you been here?"

"Nearly seven weeks," said Chloe.

"*Seven weeks,*" said Sugar Dunham, as if she couldn't believe it, "Oh, honey," she said.

"It isn't so terrible when you get used to it," Chloe said. She wished to explain how much worse it had been before, but this seemed like too much trouble. "Won't you sit down?"

Sugar Dunham sat on the sofa. She seemed to shudder as she looked at the cushion. Chloe had forgotten that Rustum was underneath the sofa. Unused to strangers, he snarled near Sugar Dunham's ankle. She looked around her in wild fear.

Chloe made her a cup of tea and talked to her about what sights to see: the garrison, the tombs of Hafez and Sa'adi. Dr. Dunham was brought back to Villa Two presently, by Ali Yazdi, who was able obligingly to send for a duplicate key to the Dunhams' room, as if nothing were simpler than a duplicate key.

Somewhat later, someone knocked again at her door, and it was again Sugar Dunham, now coiffed and wearing an expensive Pucci knit of chartreuse and turquoise.

"We're going to dinner with the Yazdis," she said. "But I have some time, and was wondering . . . "

"Come in," said Chloe.

Sugar was carrying a bottle. "I was wondering, honey— would you like some vodka?"

"Well, maybe," said Chloe. "Yes. Thank you. Sit down."

Sugar Dunham handed her the bottle and a plastic lime. "I always bring a little something when we travel," she said, sitting on Chloe's sofa, looking carefully first. "You'd be amazed how often it comes in handy. And now, I really want to know . . . "

"Sure," said Chloe.

"Tell me honestly . . . "

"Of course," said Chloe.

"Tell me honestly, honey, are you all right here?" Sugar Dunham's voice dropped confidentially. Chloe suddenly saw herself through Sugar's eyes—a fat, disheveled primitive, imprisoned two months in this dismal room, perhaps afraid to talk about it. Sugar's face was bright with concern. Chloe would have liked to say: No, I'm not all right. For some reason not. It's Hugh, Abbas, my husband, Jeffrey. I must go back. My life is no longer in my hands. I can't make it out. Also I don't care. Where are my children? Why should I be ostracized and criticized and enveloped in a mantle of gloom? Where is my passport? What have I done?

But the ingrained habit of reticence, or her imperfect understanding of her feelings, or simple lassitude, prevented her from speaking. She managed no more than a warm smile of thanks, appreciating the solicitude. But the kindness of the woman's tone brought her close, for the second time in recent days, to tears. She who never wept. Then her tears overflowed, like the tears of Linda Farmani, and became huge sobs, which Sugar Dunham regarded with attentive solicitude, proffering Kleenex.

"I don't know what's the matter with me," Chloe said. "I feel so confused."

"Well, my God, look around, who wouldn't," said Sugar Dunham. "Or it could be pre-menstrual syndrome."

Chapter Twenty-seven
PERSEPOLIS

The expedition to Persepolis, which they had all looked forward to as the summit of their enjoyment of Iran, was arranged for the weekend after the end of Ramadan, but it was shadowed by the growing mood of rumor and fear. One heard of further ugly incidents in the South—new riots; an American man killed by the side of the highway, apparently by robbers; two students beaten by an angry mob in Abadan. In Tehran the prime minister was changed. There was no word of the imprisoned Vahid Farmani, or of the vanished Noosheen.

As the day of the journey approached, they had word that in Tehran one hundred thousand people had demonstrated against the Shah. The confusion and anxiety that settled over the spirits of the Iranians further lowered the spirits of the Americans, though nothing was openly discussed between them. Neither did Hugh discuss his bruises, nor did he mention his trip to Tehran. Chloe wondered how he had explained his bruises to people.

The Hendersons had argued for postponing the Persepolis trip on account of the danger, but for the others, whose visits were soon to end, this would be the last weekend to see the great ruin—Chloe's airplane ticket was for the tenth of September, and Hugh and Dick were to leave the twelfth. So they went ahead with their plans. Rooms were booked in the Darius Hotel in Persepolis—one for Junie and Chloe, one for Dick and Hugh, one for Abbas and a newcomer, a Dr. Ames. The Hendersons nervously elected a day trip, declaring themselves willing to drive back to Shiraz after *son et lumière*. The Americans believed this to be because of the expense. The Dunhams said they preferred to go along with the Hendersons, and with them it appeared to be a case of the known evil, Villa Two, over the unknown evil of an Iranian country hotel, of which they had depressing expectations even though they were assured it was deluxe. For a time it appeared that the Yazdis would come along. The Yazdis continued to socialize as usual. Chloe had been amazed at the docility with which the compound had accepted the ascendancy of Ali Yazdi, whom she believed to be a usurper and informer, and now, judging from his continual presence with one or another of the many foreign visitors, obviously the Savak agent. Though, when you came to think of it, Abbas was always with foreign visitors too. . . . She did not think about this too carefully. At the last minute, in any event, the Yazdis decided not to go.

Of course it didn't matter who was Savak and who wasn't, or what she thought, for soon she would leave. She foresaw clearly the form of her return to San Francisco: Jeffrey would pick her up at the airport. An ugly scene or two. He would have moved out already or be poised to do so—no emotion stirred when she thought like this—poised to move out as soon as she got there to be with the children. In the kitchen; exactly the same disorder in the knife drawer, exactly the same uncurtained window, and the blind that had fallen down still rolled in the corner waiting for someone to go buy new hooks to hang it by. The same thin sheets, cotton and polyester, the cotton after ten years mostly washed away, leaving them essentially polyester, nearly transparent in the center—pale vestiges of floral sprigs, designer sprigs, nearly washed away. Pillow cases unmatching, differently sprigged, different designer. You can never get the same kind when you go back to get more; the designs have changed. She hadn't known that or she would have stuck with white.

Had Jeffrey talked to the children, explained, prepared them? Or was he leaving that to her? Were they upset or calm?

Now she didn't care. When she thought of anything she thought of being in the movie theatre in Shiraz. What if the fire had started in Shiraz? She could imagine it licking round the curtains, smoldering in the chairs, could imagine the bodies of the thin desperate men stacked up like sticks by the doors. In this vision she and the others were in the balcony, in their reserved seats, from which they could escape, but they stood horrified, inhaling the smoke, watching the flare of stick bodies, which crackled as they burned like paper.

She did not know why this vision came again and again to her, not a dream, but a notion that came vividly into her head like a daydream, pictured, insistent.

They assembled early in the morning. "I'll get in back," Chloe told the others. As she was always the smallest, her seat was always in the back seat in the middle. June and Dick got in on either side. Hugh rode in front with Abbas, and the new doctor rode in the hospital station wagon with the Hendersons and Dunhams. On the way, they stopped to look at a wayside shrine that had been there, said a sign in French and English, since six hundred years before Christ. The shrine was devoted to Ahura Mazda, God of the Zoroastrians, who taught kindness and wisdom.

"Thank you, O Ahura-Mazda, for beautiful Iran," said Chloe, and said, silently, as was her habit when visiting religious sites, a prayer for the long life and happiness of all those she loved. She excluded herself.

"Thank you, O Ahura-Mazda, for my backhand," said Hugh aloud, whatever he said silently.

Chloe also wanted to stop on the way in the great fields where Mrs. Reza had told her shards lay on the surface, a museum of the history of simple daily lives of people who lived centuries ago on the desert near the city of Persepolis. Sure enough, bits of pottery lay on the ground beneath the low grassy clumps and weedy flowers. The short-sighted Chloe was obliged to crawl on hands and knees, peering intently at the roots. The others strolled, stopping occasionally to bring something up and show it to her. To them broken bits of pottery, to Chloe— for her studies had not been in vain—a matter of joy to find an example of early green glaze, or the even earlier unglazed, stick-incised conventional border, or the all-over-incised, glazed interior—it amused the others to see her face light up over a particularly good bit.

But they had to leave off at the approach of a soldier across the field, waving his arms censoriously. They put down their shards, but Chloe furtively thrust several of hers into her bra and pockets. Abbas called something reassuring to the man in Farsi and they returned to the car. The Hendersons, driving up just then, asked what they had been looking at but didn't get out of their car.

"Some broken bits of pottery for Chloe," Hugh said.

Dick had pocketed some shards too. He looked at Chloe. There was no question but that she was a little subdued these days. She was so pretty. He thought of giving her his necklace, when they got back. He himself would run the risk of smuggling it through Iranian customs; then in the airplane he would bring it out, or he would go to see her sometime in San Francisco and give it to her there. He had been thinking of giving it to Junie, but the truth was that Junie didn't care for jewelry, though she went on wearing the dead man's watch. He had even thought of giving it to Marla, or of keeping it for when Ellen graduated from college. But then he would think of how unreasonable Marla had been about the house, and of how Ellen always lost things. Chloe liked jewelry, and always wore a string of blue beads.

Further along the highway they stopped to relish their first glimpse of the magnificent ancient city, Persepolis at last, set high on an escarpment of sheer rock, a citadel of immense grandeur, lofty columns, and broad staircases visible even from here. They were stirred, as they had expected to be.

"Somehow, no matter how often I see it," Abbas said, "it is the most beautiful and moving sight."

"Magnificent," said the others. "Magnificent."

"Alexander the Great," said Sugar Dunham. "The horses, the panoply."

"This was Darius and Cyrus," her husband reminded her.
"Oh, sweetie, I know, it was Alexander who *burned it down.*
It's just that I have more of an image of him," she apologized.

As they drew nearer, the company could see bright tents on
the plain at the foot of the walls of the tower in the city. These,
erected for the Shah's millennial celebration, were surrounded
by trees planted in orderly rows and were thriving on careful
irrigation. In this encampment the rich and powerful and famous and curious had assembled for a lavish festivity organized
a few years before to celebrate the thousandth year of the reign
of the Pahlavi family. Abbas explained with a touch of irony
that the festival had not been popular. Hungry people protested
the vast expense. And the family of the Shah had not in fact
ruled for a thousand years. Now, harmlessly deserted, the tent
city looked pretty, and did not seem to symbolize the wicked-
ness of monarchy or the poverty of the people so much as the
transitory nature of all temporal power. The inevitable seedy
cats strolled in and out of the deserted lanes and walks. Up
close, the tents seemed to be of plastic laminate. Several dirty
children crouched to watch, and their old grandmother, near
them, adjusted her veil. Except for these people, the site was
deserted. Above them, on the walls of the ruin, tourists could be
seen, tiny as fleas.

The city of Persepolis itself also suggested transitory grandeur. They parked their cars on a strip of tarmac at the foot of
the ancient wall, which, lower on this side, rose on the other to
a height of forty feet. Near the parking lot, at the foot of a broad
stone staircase, were a gate and tiny kiosk where tickets were
sold, and old men hung around to volunteer as guides. Above
them towered vast columns and strange plinths and capitals,
and the stone heads of bulls. They hurried excitedly up the
steps, steps wide enough for ceremonial visitors, for the entrance of princes, and the stones were worn low and smooth by
the wheels of chariots and hooves of horses.

At the top, looking ahead, they saw acres of ruins, vast,
deserted, elaborate, a surreal landscape of columns holding

nothing, stairs leading nowhere, broken figures, blocks of stone. Sometimes these had been organized and numbered by archaeologists, whose neat notations could be seen. New paving stones here and there completed an antique design. Otherwise, they could imagine, Persepolis must look much as it had when people fled and the embers had cooled, two thousand years ago. Chloe had a *Guide Bleu*, in French, and Junie had Fodor. They stood at the top of the steps, turning their books round and round, trying to face the direction of the maps.

"À gauche, la porte de Xerxes; au centre, la plate-forme supportant les colonnes de l'Apadana," began Chloe.

"Oh, thanks a lot," said Junie, who had continued to be strangely brusque with Chloe. She strolled off in the opposite direction, followed after some hesitation by Hugh and Dick. Abbas walked back down the great staircase to look more closely at the friezes, and Chloe, wishing to follow the recommended route of her book and to take photographs, strolled off in her own direction, disappointed that Abbas had not come with her.

Alone, her melancholy mood prevailed. The mighty ruin dictated a certain historical perspective from which the troubles of modern Iran, to say nothing of one's personal fortune, lost immediacy, lost pang. But she still regretted that she would soon fit into the category, divorced woman, that she had always felt to be so disadvantageous, associated with poverty, quarrelsomeness, yearning, hard-up sexuality, general lack of dignity—modern pretenses notwithstanding—compared to married women and widows. She had always hated the idea of being divorced, but now, as it occurred to her, gazing at the Apadana, she didn't care.

Chloe guessed she was getting her period; she felt some discomfort. She hoped she wasn't getting a bladder infection. It wouldn't be surprising, all that love-making, and Hugh had wanted a few times recently to take her from behind, her on all fours, wasn't there a joke about that, psychiatrist telling you to change your marriage? But she couldn't remember what the joke was. From behind, so that he enters more deeply, making her have to pee right after, and now that familiar burning beginning, but anyway, all these doctors, she can easily get some sulfa. Not a good time for it to come on, in Persepolis, but endurable. Little infections, prospective troubles, had no interest.

They had only an hour or so to wander now, after which they would go to the check-in at the Hotel Darius, and then come back for the *son et lumière*. They would visit the city again in the morning, which, according to all authorities, was the best time to photograph the bas reliefs. Chloe was happy to be alone, to wander among the stones, to enjoy her mood of philosophical gloom, her meditations upon transience, and to seek an imaginative transportation into dusty history, where Persepolis in all its splendor would somehow become actual to her. She found, though, that a truly elevated state did not develop. Perhaps she was too permanently dead, too flat, numbed by Villa Two or something. Nothing stirred, as she looked at the stones, except objective admiration, distant and practical. What fine immense columns, how handsome the vast stone steeds and guardian bulls, how delicate the carving of the coiffures of the immortals pictured upon the stairs. She thinks of Omar's lines,

> *How Sultan after Sultan with his Pomp*
> *Abode his destined Hour, and went his way.*

That these streets had been full of living people, walking along, hearts full, hearts pounding, should have struck her with its poignance, she knew, but she felt indifference. The pity of all this destruction should have struck her, rubble where magnificence had been. But it didn't make any difference, she thought, rebelliously, and it probably didn't make any difference if a bomb fell on, say, New York, beyond the immediate tragedy of death. What would be left anyhow in ten centuries? To lose

Paris or San Francisco might be a pity, but even those—for she must sternly adhere to this line of thought, no sentimental reservations—even Paris and San Francisco, made no difference to the universe, to history, to the bare ground that went on being. Even the bomb—what difference did it make?

What, anyway, does anything matter? What does anything mean? For it was all gone. These are the appropriate thoughts to have in such a place, she thought, with a touch of satisfaction at the proper cast of her thinking, at her emotions, which swelled and rose, unnamable, at the mute stones, the dumb faces in the carving, processions of ancients, each snail-like curl of beard as fresh as then, strong legs protruding from their little tunics, oxen with long horns, men carrying fish, figures marching in profile, their eyes looking straight out at Chloe.

Strolling up and down the staircases, craning her neck up at the immensely tall columns, inspecting the carvings was absorbing work and pleasure. In the distance Chloe could see the Hendersons wandering around. She was surprised to encounter Hugh, and to realize he'd been hanging back, tactfully, not liking to disturb her reverie. When she caught his eye, he stepped forward briskly with a "now that you've seen me" expression.

"Really something," he said.

"Amazing," she said.

"Does it make you sad?" he asked.

"I guess. Does it you? The idea is supposed to make us sad," said Chloe.

"Maybe us especially," said Hugh.

Chloe felt her eyes sting but could think of nothing to answer. Hugh put his arm around her shoulder and hugged her, and patted her bottom in the time-honored proprietary affectionate way.

This was seen by Dick Rothblatt from a distance, around a wall.

"Chloe and Hugh!" Dick said to Junie. The thought just

struck him. Remembered scenes peeled backward across his mind, rewinding Chloe talking to Hugh, Hugh lingering on the dark path. Smiles. "Do you think they're making it?"

"Of course, obviously," said Junie.

"I didn't realize that," Dick said, baffled. Why should Marla or Junie—even Junie—find these things so obvious. Yet it was obvious, once you thought of it at all. He felt—what? Hurt, or strangely taken aback. Did he expect Chloe to have confided this? Well, yes, in a way, after some of the stuff he had told her. Or was it that he had thought there was something pure about Chloe—not that he respected purity, of course, that sexist, old-fashioned concept. Yet some women did seem to be . . . above sex, or to have it hidden away somewhere in their lives out of the prying view, like a lovely sachet in their stocking drawer.

He felt rather angry with Chloe.

"What makes you think so?" he said.

"Well, I don't know, no one thing," said Junie. "It's just so totally obvious."

"It's some female talent, noticing things," said Dick.

"She could be fucking everyone in the compound before you'd notice," Junie said.

Chapter Twenty-eight
SON ET LUMIÈRE

We are no other than a moving row
Of Magic Shadow-shapes that come and go
Round with the Sun-illumined Lantern held
In Midnight by the Master of the Show.

The party checked into the Darius. Their cases were taken to their rooms. Junie and Chloe, in theirs, took out their sweaters, in case it would grow cool at the *son et lumière,* and unpacked their toilet articles. To Chloe there was something restful about having a female roommate, and maybe Junie felt this too, for her manner, lately so hostile, seemed for a moment to melt. Looking together into the mirror, they combed their hair, and joined the others in the garden for a glass of tea. All at once a waiter told them to rise and hurry off, so as not to miss the vaunted spectacle of the sun setting over the columns, and over the tombs and distant hills. Obediently they left, their tea unfinished, and drove in their two cars to the parking lot by the gate of the city, and rushed toward the steps, alarmed by the growing redness of the sky. Junie clattered a tripod with her, and bore a heavy camera on her shoulder.

At the gate it appeared that a problem had arisen. They found the guards in the process of shuttering the ticket booth and locking the gates above. Abbas had a long conversation with them in Farsi, then returned to the others. "A difficulty," he said, "though perhaps not an insurmountable difficulty. They say they are planning to close, that they have had an order that there will be no performance tonight. My own opinion is that they just feel like closing, but I think this can be solved in the usual way." The Americans stared resentfully at the knot of guards, who stared back, it seemed with a trace of satisfaction at this power they had to thwart rich tourists. Abbas returned to talk to them. Moments passed. From the tone of the voices, the quarrel was bitter, even violent. Abbas shouted with the rest. Then, all at once, arms waved, smiles spread among the parties. Abbas smiled. Like a chorus, the Americans smiled too, bowed toward the guards, stirred.

"He's crossed the palms," Hugh said.

"He's getting them to open just for us; that can't be cheap," said Dick.

"The show will go on," Abbas said, smiling, as the guards neatly restored the "Open" sign and propped up in its wicket the notice of times of performances, prices, languages, and waved them in.

"Lazy fellows," said Abbas. "That's the trouble here, they have no interest in whether things work or not. They are thinking it is for them to decide whether to open or not. All is caprice and bribery in this country."

They were to view the spectacle from a wooden grandstand that had been erected in the courtyard of the great central palace, which they had learned from the guidebooks was called the Tripylon. There they settled themselves, with growing enjoyment, to wait for the dark. Chloe had forgotten her sweater in the car; Dick borrowed Abbas's keys and gallantly went back to get it.

They were awed by the splendid sense of having nearly to themselves this ancient and remarkable place, though in fact a few Iranian tourists had also profited from Abbas's negotiation and were scattered here and there in the grandstand. After the last pink, darkness fell as rapidly as a shutter. All at once the lights were extinguished, and a deep, amplified voice boomed in the darkness, in a rather British accent, "I am Cambyses, son of Cyrus the Great. It was I who chose this spot on which to build, to the glory of the Achaemenians, a sacred city of Pars." Drums boomed in the loudspeaker, and then the triumphal march from *Aida*.

Then a light illumined the door of a tomb in the hill above them, and from there another voice returned: "I am Darius the Great, son of Cambyses, and it was I who built the sacred city of Pars, to the glory of the King of Kings." Now, nearer to them, another door was lighted in the hillside.

"I, Xerxes, here built in my day, too, much that is beautiful, to the glory of the King of Kings, Ahura-Mazda, to whom I prayed that the sun eternally shine on these palaces and on this kingdom," intoned a third voice.

Now they were again for an instant in blackness, and when the spotlights picked out the ruined columns nearer them, the great voices had taken on a tone of lament. "Oh, what, O Ahura-Mazda," began Cambyses again, "have been our crimes that you have shaken down these walls which we erected to your glory?"

Chloe sighed contentedly to think of the desolation of history and the crimes of antiquity. Xerxes had, it seemed, destroyed the Acropolis in Greece, and it was this that brought down Alexander upon them, to destroy Persepolis in revenge. Living and dying by the sword. From the dark plain came the voice of Alexander, a brash tenor, boasting of his power, and of the beauty of his mistresses, and of his vengeful plan. "Give up, O Persepolis, your treasures. I have brought ten thousand mules and five thousand camels to carry them away," he crowed. The *William Tell* Overture swelled up.

Chloe, who had always scoffed at *son et lumière*s and thought them a silly genre of entertainment, thoroughly enjoyed the majesty of the lights and shadows on the great ruins, and the evocation of the kings who had built it, and the sense, momentarily reassuring, that this long and mighty history included her, and her friends, and the one or two Iranian tourists, and, somewhere, the projectionist and someone playing the tape. Her pleasure was a little diminished, though, by the discomfort in her middle, a menstrual feeling of urgency and pain.

"I, Darius, King of Kings, expect, O men of Asia, your

tribute. Bring me, Kushia, your ivory; Putaya, your chariots; Zranka, your cattle; Arabians, your dromedaries, Skudians, your lances; Sagartians, your horses; Hindush, your vases; and Parthians, your camels.

"Bring me, Gandara, the great humped bull, Bactrians and Egyptians, cloth and animals, and, pointed-hat Scythians, bring me bracelets and trousers. You Ionians must bring bees and woolen skeins, and the Harauvatish the skins of lions. Cicilians, I will have from you your fine rams.

"Katpatuka, Haraiva, Babylonians, all, your tributes. Syrians, your cups and jewels, Susians, Armenians, Medes."

It occurred to Chloe that if Persepolis had been burned by the drunken soldiers of Alexander in 330 B.C. then it had been ruins ever since, ruins for two thousand years; and that all the Sassanians and khans and shahs and glorious kings thereafter had seen it as she was seeing it now, these cautionary and reproachful ruins, and Alexander himself was the last, before days of *son et lumière,* to see it ablaze with light.

At last, as the words seemed to retreat into the tomb, in the black hill beyond the illumined movements, the bare lightbulbs above them went on, signifying the end of the performance. They stood, murmured, gathered their cameras and coats, and Chloe excused herself to go to the ladies' toilet at the foot of the stairs, saying to the others as she raced down the steps that she'd catch up to them.

The toilet was not as squalid as she had feared, though it was of the hole-in-the-ground variety. She'd gotten used to these. They always stank. As she squatted over the pit, the lights in the toilet went out, making it a bit complicated and precarious moving her feet. In the darkness the splash of her urine seemed very far below, down into archaeological strata where Achaemenians had peed. She thought she had gotten her period. She felt in her bag for a tampon.

She expected the lights to go back on, but they didn't. The place was relentlessly closing for the night. She expected the others to be waiting outside the lavatory door, but they were not. She could not even hear them. She stayed by the doorway until her eyes grew accustomed to the darkness.

For a moment she could see the amphitheatre steps but no farther. To the right was a path leading toward the entrance, or was the entrance the other way? She paused, knowing her own propensity for turning in the wrong direction. She was irritated that neither Hugh nor Dick had thought to wait for her.

She retraced her way up the steps again, to where they had been sitting, hoping to be able to see from the high seats the direction of the entrance. The silence was strange; it was the silence of the desert, with no mechanical sounds, no horns or calls, only small insects and somewhere an animal cry. She held tightly to the chain handrail, fearing to lose her footing in the dark and miss a step. She stopped at the row they had been sitting in, and from there, seeing nothing, she climbed to the top row of the bleachers, where she could get the best view. Where was the moon?

From here she could see that the entrance was below and to the left a few hundred yards. There was the top of the ticket kiosk, and a small light from within it illumined a few feet around it. She decided that the others had forgotten about her and were walking toward this entrance, or had gained it and left. They would in a moment remember her. If she kept her gaze fastened on the ticket kiosk, there was the gate through which they would pass. Or she could hurry after them, sure, now, of the direction. But the silence made her hesitate. Something new had happened but the darkness gave no clue at all about what it was.

She could call out. In the silence she would be heard for miles. She feared, oddly, to hear her own voice echo among the tremendous stones, like the deep fake voice of Darius over the loudspeaker. "I am the Queen," she could call. "You have forgotten me. Beware the curse of Alexander's Queen."

Now she could hear an alarming chorus of angry voices, shouts and muttering, male and female, in the direction of the entrance.

And now she did see people moving at the entrance. She put her bag on her shoulder and began to descend the steps. Then the after-image of what she had seen made her look again, straining her near-sighted eyes. She felt in her bag for her distance glasses. Bringing things into focus, she could see that the figures at the gate were guards, not her companions, and the lights came from headlights, shining from the darkness outside the walls. An impression of activity, different from the lethargic keepers and lounging guides who had clustered around the entrance when they had arrived. Where there had been dozing old men, now people strode briskly.

More men walked into the light. With surprise she saw that they carried guns, what looked like little machine guns. Four men stood a few feet apart in front of the stairs, like a net waiting to catch anyone who wanted to descend on them, and two more men, thumbing the shoulder straps of their guns, pushed into the darkness of the deserted city. These were not the guards, then, but police or soldiers. She heard her own gasp in the hushed air. The blackness was suddenly intimate and warm, as if she had been stuffed into a closet.

Now she hears voices again, mutterings, amplified by the stones, harsh commands, protests, nothing you could make out to be English or Farsi but a familiarity about the rhythm of objection, complaint, maybe the voices of Hugh or Dick, or the voluble Sugar Dunham, or the high voice of Mrs. Henderson. Then a woman's scream, sudden, like the false scream in a funhouse, but terrifying and sudden out of the blackness—Junie, if you could tell by a person's scream. Chloe feels herself grow more still, concentrating; she has to think now, and not do the wrong thing. Something is going on here.

It could be a turned ankle, a sudden fright, yet this is no time to seek simple obvious explanations, for there are people with guns down there, and sneaking, and screams. The best thing is not to move. If they had flashlights, they might see her up here, or maybe not even with flashlights, for she is high up. If this is nothing, the others will come and find her, and if it is something . . . But what can it be? Some people are born knowing about danger, others have to infer it imperfectly from second-hand data, TV, guns in films. This has a filmic aura of stealth and darkness. Her heart beats loudly. She doesn't know what is going on here but will wait and see. Her eyes are growing used to the dark.

Dick remembered Chloe had gone to the ladies' room and began walking back toward it to get her when the lights went out, so he instinctively turned back toward the safety and reassurance of the others, seeing, in an instant, before the scene was dispelled, a man pointing a gun at Abbas and Hugh, all of a sudden, by the gate. A man in bluejeans carrying a machine gun, Hugh throwing up his hands. Dick's eye and mind took this in, then it was gone. Hugh and Abbas dived off in opposite directions, ducking behind stones, Hugh with a curse. The man then indifferently waved the gun at Dick instead, motioning him closer. Dick stepped obediently closer, astounded. How had they dared defy a man with a machine gun? He supposed it was instinct, you do it without thinking, impulsively, and sometimes get shot, you leap at the throat of the intruder, you throw yourself into the water after the drowning person, and you drown.

What was happening? Why? The man pointed him along a dark stone aisle. Behind him he heard cries, shouts, a curse, Dr. Henderson, Mrs. Henderson, maybe Junie's voice among the others. Someone behind him had a flashlight, whose narrow beam illumined a frieze, conjuring a horde of staring stone Achaemenians watching Dick. Dick shuffled along, aware that someone else shuffled along behind him, another man, Iranian probably, wearing a suit. Probably he was the father of a family that had been at the *son et lumière*.

They found themselves being shoved into a wooden shed

filled with picks and other excavation tools and various boxes, an assortment of objects momentarily visible in the light of the flashlight, before the door was slammed on them, and bolted. Dick's companion began irascible shouting in Farsi, and by the sound was feeling along the walls, tripping on things. Dick tried the door, which was fast. He threw his shoulder against it a few times. In the complete darkness, the frenzied activity of his companion was irritating. They needed thoughtful silence. "Ssshhh," he hissed at the man, "quiet, shhh." The man stopped.

Then from somewhere distant, Chloe or Junie screamed, or it could be Mrs. Henderson, anyway a woman, a fully articulated scream, a lunch whistle. This triggered a rush of frantic associations, soldiers, rape, Junie, attired in comic-book dress, ripped off the shoulder, skirt short almost to cunt, shrinking in a corner with horrified face as animal soldiers advance—why Junie not Chloe? But somehow Junie was more the type to get raped.

No further screams. Dick stumbled over a box of something, sat on it instead, settled straining to listen. His companion sighed rhythmically as if trying to control fear or weeping.

"Do you speak English?" Dick asked. Only sighs in answer. The darkness was solid. Now that he wasn't smoking he didn't carry matches.

He thought again of the way Hugh and Abbas had neatly jumped aside, as if without fear of getting shot, losing themselves instantly in the night and not being pursued. The gun was pointing at him alone, and at this man, but not at Hugh or Abbas. Perhaps at Junie or Chloe; just noticeably not at Hugh or Abbas, who had vanished as if at some signal. He sat silently, resenting his own docility, but what could he do but wait a little, see what developed? Each moment passed with excruciating deliberation, almost ticking, moments became hours, in the phrase.

He could hear no one nearby, but in the distance shouts from time to time, and engine noises, as if vehicles were drawing up below the ruins on the plain. Because of the strange acoustics of the place, he could not tell in what direction the people might be, how nearby, how many. Their captor had been Western, sandy-haired. He heard no women's voices.

His companion lit a match, lit a cigarette. Dick saw his face illumined, a middle-aged man with graying hair, mustache. His eyes had been looking at Dick, trying to see him in the dark. It showed a hell of a bad judgment to light up in here; who knew if there was dynamite or whatever. Dick shook his head, frowned, but the match had gone out. The glow of the man's cigarette grew and diminished with each breath.

"What time is it?" Dick asked. "Time? Watch?" Understood, evidently, for the man lit another match and leaned toward Dick. Dick thrust his wrist toward the man, and the man was showing Dick his own watch. Somewhere near eleven, it appeared, before he shook the match out. Then another match, held higher, revealed the space a foot or two around them. Plenty of tools with which to escape when they could, though the moment was clearly not yet propitious.

Chloe safe probably in the women's john, if she'd had the sense to stay in there, or else—had she too absented herself according to some plan? In the same way she had in fact absented herself from the cave when the body of the man was found there? The array of coincidences was troubling but his suspicions lacked the crucial ingredients of explanation and hypothesis. There was no plausible game for them all to be in. It was all very well to say CIA, that catchall, you still had to have a hypothesis, and anyway it was ridiculous, since she was Jeffrey Fowler's wife, from San Francisco, which he knew for a fact, he'd known them for years, Hugh Monroe too, though her involvement with Hugh was new to him. There always had been something a little elaborately romantic about Hugh; you heard of him studying viruses in Borneo, or skiing glaciers somewhere in July. He suddenly thought of Marla reading about all this in the paper, a massacre at Persepolis, American doctors die in dangerous drama—she would wonder what he had been up to, what had been his game, and she would believe he had had one.

His thoughts raced fitfully; it was like having insomnia, night thoughts, waking ravings. He tried to slow them down, tried to feel his way calmly toward an explanation.

They've put me in here separate from the others, Dick thought. What do they want? It's something to do with the man in the grave. Intimations of torture tightened his throat. Who had betrayed them, he wondered. Abbas? or Hugh? The dreadful explanation, further elaborated, presented itself. It was no accident but by design that he found himself alone in this hut, except for this unexplained fellow. The others marched off together, he himself singled out in this isolation. Their captors would be coming back to get him, to make him confess his part in the murder of the man in the grave, or in the cover-up of the murder. Dick struggled with this unreasonable paranoia. He had not killed the man. A party of men would hardly need to invade Persepolis in order to seize Dick Rothblatt. He knew it was just his tendency to feel guilty. He told himself to stop it. He wished the man would decide to smoke another cigarette, but probably, with crafty prudence, the fellow had decided to cut down, in case they were in for a long imprisonment.

The invaders had not been Iranian, could have been American or anything else Western—he had not heard them speak— so they were not the Shah's secret police, say, or a troop of rebels. They had to be here looking for someone or something— Hugh? Abbas? But it would have been simpler to find either of those two back at the Azami Compound. The guns bespoke a belligerent or illicit intent. The only other tourists were this man and his family; except for them and a few guards and guides there had been no one here.

Now the man, sitting in the dark, tugged at Dick's coat, pressed the pack of cigarettes into Dick's hand. Dick hesitated, desire and fear contending, expanding his trachea. Fear of his own nature. If ever he was going to relapse this would be the time, wouldn't it? The smell in the shed was of dirt and stone.

"Thanks," he heard himself say, and grabbed one urgently.

Chloe tries to figure this out, tries to review in an orderly way the possibilities, as if it were a secret that would yield itself up to reason, if you started at A, like Mr. Ramsay. Junie had screamed. The others had vanished silently, either captured by or in league with the armed men. It made no sense to imagine that armed men pursuing them would have to besiege all Persepolis to catch them, when they could wait until later and catch them in their hotel, or on the road tomorrow. They were therefore in league. But with whom? Abbas? Dick and Hugh? One of these but not the others? What had Persepolis to do with it?

She thinks of once, when she was a child of what—three? four?—and wandered off at the fair, at the Indian show, and was lost in the fairground. She had sat right down where she was, and waited, knowing they would find her, and didn't budge, even when she heard her name over the loudspeaker. Chloe Linden, Chloe Linden, said the immense amplified voice. She had huddled under a picnic table and waited and sure enough they came and found her, and that is what she would do now, just stay put until rescued.

Now, minutes or hours—stretched long meaningless rubber-band units of time—however long later the sound of a shot. The idea of gunfire there all the time was now actual, but startling all the same to Chloe huddled on the grandstand seat, tucked away up above, thinking she could see the prowling figures stalking through the ruins, see their lights at least, hear the heavy rumblings of their purpose, whatever it was. One shot, then silence afterward, a deepening and serious silence, filled with new ideas of menace, retaliation. Who had they shot at? At Hugh or who? Why?

Chloe, frightened by the gunshot, sits stiffly by her post high up above, able to track the little lights wending in and out among the stones. She is cold, though it is a hot night. She is forgotten about, no one is looking for her, the thing is to sit still and unseen. She wonders if Junie has been captured. Who are they? She can imagine that perhaps since this afternoon America is at war with Iran and these people have come to capture them, but it makes no sense to imagine, as she fleetingly had, that Abbas has led them into a trap here, since they all could have been arrested quite easily in the Azami Compound, as Vahid Farmani had been; there was no need to pursue them crazily through the night. She thinks with guilty alarm of the contraband potsherds in her purse.

The invaders are busy. Flashlights, ropes, muttered consultations, shouts. Once she hears two men drawing near the bleachers, never looking up, say in plain English, "It'll take a winch, whatever he thinks." When they move on, she takes from her purse her black veil, brought to wear in case of going to see a holy sight, and wraps herself, to be warmer and more invisible during the night. If they come near, she will ditch the potsherds behind the bleacher seat. Despite her willed intention not to think terrifying or sad thoughts, her imagination develops the scene in which her children are told of her death, and fears come about their motherless adolescence. Her longing for her children is an idea, almost, that it is they who could rescue her, were they only here; had she not so wickedly left them.

Chapter Twenty-nine
PLUNDERERS

Although it must be warm, it seemed cold. This was fear, she guessed, compared to which she hadn't ever been afraid before, not like this. It was a matter of trying to calm yourself down, trying to think what to do, trying to breathe. What would she do when it got light in the morning and they could see her? She'd better have a plan, better line up a place to hide in out of sight when it got light, in case they would shoot her because she was up here watching, even though she couldn't see anything.

She was sure there had been gunfire. Had there been enough to shoot all the others? Surely not, she thought, only a shot or two, not enough to execute her friends by, so they must be all right. As she thought lurid thoughts of execution, she was aware of a kind of hum produced by her own body, the toxins of fear producing a chemical hum, and her throat was dry so that she could hardly swallow, and she had an ache in the places at either side of the base of her throat, just where a killer would put his hands. She might be overlooked by accident, like the Filipino nurse who hid under the sofa. Killers with their adrenaline, their toxins surging, they too make mistakes and overlook people hiding.

If anyone came, or when it grew morning, she could lie right here in a kind of trough formed between the topmost seat of the bleachers and the supporting wall behind it by some cement buttresses. Or maybe she should crawl in it now so as not to risk attracting any attention if it were to grow light. For how long had she sat here, anyway hours, mesmerized by the silence and by fear? Half expecting a bullet to split her skull as she moved, she eased herself over the backrest of the seats and lay on her side full-length behind the seat, half in the trough, her arms pinned oddly to her sides by the narrowness of the space. She lay, shivering in the hot night.

Then she was unable to keep lying there, pinned in like that where if they came she couldn't run; she could imagine them suddenly standing over her pointing guns down at her head, and now she was no longer cold but wet with hot sweat, her steamy panic building till she had to move. This was how it happened—you sat still until you couldn't bear it then bolted like a rabbit right into the sights of the police rifles, snipers waiting for you, knowing when you can't bear it a moment longer, and they were right she couldn't lie still, not in this position on her side looking up where she would see their faces as they pointed their guns.

She thought of the photographs of the men standing in a ring around the little boy in Warsaw, pointing their guns at him. She thought of the photograph of the man being shot by the Vietnamese general, of the expression on his face, of pain and disgust.

She had to climb out of this tight place. She was sweating, that was why she was cold, and she thought she could feel blood trickle down her leg. She moved slowly along the row and crouched at the top of the stairs, keeping low, but she could bolt down the stairs if someone should approach through the open space in front of the grandstand, or she could run along the top row if someone came up the stairs.

Anyway, the thought came to her, you have to save yourself; no one is going to come and save you.

With the first light coming in through an aperture between the roof and walls of the shed, Dick could see that this was a flimsy structure with no actual windows and no bolt on the inside, so that although they couldn't get out, anyone could come in unless they could concoct some sort of barricade from the kegs and timbers stacked along the wall. Dick listened alertly for clues about what was going on outside. He heard no voices, no gunshots. Then the silence was broken by the noise of an airplane close overhead, a drone as loud as doomsday, then sputtering to silence somewhere close by. He tried to see out the crack between the eaves, and when he couldn't, he was boosted by the Iranian, whom he could now see was a man in his forties, graying, in a neat business suit, with nothing about him otherwise to provide a clue to his condition. This man had subsided passively onto what looked like a keg of plaster, disconsolate head drooping toward his knees, one hand clutching worry beads, but now he jumped alertly up when it appeared he could help Dick look out. He did not himself seem to wish to see, though he could have by standing on his keg, but instead hung back and watched Dick for signs of understanding or plan. Outside, there was nothing to be seen except an empty vista of stones.

Dick threw his shoulder a few times heavily against the door, as he had done at first, and found it as solid as before, but not so solid they couldn't ram it open with one of the boards stacked in the corner. Then he realized it would be simple and quieter to pry the door off its rather loose hinges, and looked around for an implement.

At the same moment, almost as if it had yielded to his shoulder, the bolt slid and the door opened a crack, then decisively, and Hugh Monroe peered in. Dick felt a moment of alarm, as if Hugh were the captor.

"Quick," said Hugh. "Quiet." He stepped inside, and pulled the door shut behind him. He spoke in a whisper.

"What's going on?" cried Dick.

Hugh glared around the dark shed. Except for the bruises on the side of his face, the ones that had been there already, he appeared unhurt, normal, even rested. Dick stared, trying to quell his odd suspicions.

"Where were you?" asked Dick.

"There are some people, they could be Americans, an airplane, and a lot of Iranians with uniforms. But they aren't the army. It's hard to see. It looks like something being unloaded.

I think they rounded everybody up last night and they must have put them in the museum; that's the only structure except this, and there's a guard outside it. Some of their people are walking around, but I think we can keep out of sight. I don't think they've hurt anyone."

"How did they miss you?" Dick asked.

"Well, I was looking around for Chloe. They never saw me."

"Did you see Chloe?" Dick asked.

"No."

Dick remembered the sudden way Chloe had grabbed her purse and streaked down the stairs.

"They didn't expect anyone to be here last night." This suddenly came to him. "The place was closed. Abbas got them to open it."

"Well, that's right," Hugh said. "A bunch of American tourists weren't in the plan. Let's get out of here." Dick found himself following Hugh cautiously out the shed door, half wondering if Hugh would deliver him into the hands of the captors. The Iranian man stepped out behind them, then stepped back in again, and stood in the doorway peering after them as they crept along the path that led to the main staircase, he hoped not into a trap.

It became clearer to him, as he thought of it, that Hugh must be involved here; it would explain his bruised face, his confident demeanor on the path ahead, his accurate knowledge of Dick's place of imprisonment. The Iranian man had had the sense to see that he was safer inside. But Dick felt quick-witted, equal to this, whatever it was. From the path he could see their cars parked below on the desert, amid other vehicles brought there in the night, a rabble of old trucks and a van, men loading boxes into the trucks.

Distant, in the other direction, was the airplane Dick had heard, some kind of light cargo plane with the belly open, and people running up and down ladders. He and Hugh hid behind the monumental protoma of a horse's head and watched. Boxes were being unloaded; men carried them to the trucks, passing things out of the hold, wobbling on the ladder, and handing and hoisting things in. Now they could see that a huge stone head, massively heavy, was being dragged along the sand, festooned with ropes. Near the trucks, the Iranians were opening one of the boxes and taking out guns.

They'll never get that head in there, thought Dick, feeling an abstract interest in the effort; but the plane had some sort of winch, and inhaled the giant artifact in moments. They could now see that the pile of rubble near the plane was entirely heads and limbs of giant rams and sphinx-like gods, stone figures entire or broken bits of cornice or column, all to be carried away, and more objects were being lowered from the walls of Persepolis by ropes to the sand below.

Chloe with the arrival of the dawn could dimly see her watch, and calculate an end to this terror, estimate the distance from here to there, figure out what was going on. She could gaze out. She could see. It appeared that a party of men had sealed off Persepolis and now with the dawn could be seen making their way among the ruins. Some were wearing ordinary clothes, carrying guns, and some were in military outfits—dark men, apparently Iranians. They did not seem bent on rape and vengeance and they were carrying archaeological artifacts. It grew lighter. She reasoned that if she could get from here into an enclosed space—say the museum, where the others must be, or the women's bathroom again, or the little plywood projectionist's booth suspended at the other side of the courtyard—she would be safer. Slowly, recklessly, she climbed down the bleacher steps.

At the foot of the steps she paused, mesmerized by the sound of voices approaching—American voices. At first she thought it must be Dick and Hugh. All the same she shrank into a shadow. Then—it was with a kind of horrified calm—she saw that the American walking toward her, with others, briskly striding across the Queen's courtyard, was Richard Dare. Richard Dare, the shifty archaeologist; she had never liked him. She stood frozen in an attitude of female passivity, sculptural and invisible. Dare turned around and looked in her direction, as if remembering that he had seen someone there, but she stood motionless, and, although she was full in his view, he did not see her. What came to her mind was a comedy movie, where Jerry Lewis or someone like that wearing women's clothes walks through carrying a mop or bucket and no one sees him. That must have become part of her unconscious knowledge, that if you cling to a bucket, or wear a veil or widow black, no one sees you.

All at once her elbow was gripped firmly from behind. She gasped and turned. Abbas pulled her further into the doorway behind them. He shook his head for silence; they waited till Dare's steps disappeared. Then Abbas led her around the periphery of the courtyard, apparently thinking, as she had, of the projectionist's shack on the other side, where one could unseen watch events. Chloe's mind warmed with relief and apprehension at the same time. Was she saved or captured? They hastened up the ladder and inside.

On the plywood wall of the projection booth, Chloe saw a plan of Persepolis with the toilets and gates indicated, and the exits. She saw where they were, where she had been. From this vantage, Abbas looked out the peephole beside the spotlight lens.

"What do you see?" she whispered.

"I'm not sure. Iranians, Americans. I think guns—it seems the Americans are gun runners. The Iranians, therefore, would be . . ."

He turned, and smiled his melancholy smile, as if it did not matter. "Rebels, perhaps."

"Will they hurt us?" Chloe asked.

"We'll stay out of the way."

She shivered, as if thawing out. "It was frightening, last night. Through the long night."

"Yes," he said. Presently he added, "Have you ever passed a night like that, in danger, in the dark?"

"No."

"No. An unusual experience. There are better ways to spend the night."

Not an arch or flirtatious remark, just a statement of fact.

"Yes," Chloe felt her blood speed up with inappropriate longing. Could they not discuss this? When but in danger did one need comforting embraces. He was looking out the peephole again.

"I can see Monroe and Rothblatt," he said. He drew back so Chloe could see Dick and Hugh, lying on their bellies behind a mound. Hugh was crawling up it to peer over the top.

Chloe could now see what she could not before, and what Hugh would see when he got to the top of the mound: statues and artifacts being loaded into the airplane she had heard, now taxied up under the walls of the city, open at the underside, surrounded by men loading and carrying, intent upon the difficulties of managing huge objects of stone.

Abbas pushed her rather abruptly away from the peephole and looked again, as if the significance of what he had seen before had just struck him.

"My God," he said. "Look. They're loading the statues."

It looked that way to Chloe too.

"It makes sense! That's why the guards were bribed to close last night, so these people could come in and loot the treasures of Persepolis!" His voice trembled.

"It's Richard Dare," she said. "I saw him."

"A harmless archaeologist, bringing guns."

"I don't see the guns," said Chloe.

"Over there. Those crates of guns, loading on the trucks."

"Oh, yes."

"My God, my God," said Abbas, "I wonder what I can do? This can't be permitted. They don't understand, they are ignorant peasant boys, the stones mean nothing to them, they have given them away!"

His dismay intensified, along with a feeling of moral correctness that verified it; he was right to feel this patriotic, this admirable dismay. Foremothers shrouded in veils murmured from the sky, a sort of spectacle of ancients with jugs on their heads approving his indignation, ancients on their horses, with long white beards, tents stretching out into the desert, camels all around, and dancing people, joyous in his release from some self-preoccupation, some tense and Western inwardness. Here was something he could do something about. It would be just a very small act at that, to notify the authorities, or the resistance, or anyone who could come in here and stop this. It was not so very much to do.

Shahs, imams, all were as transient as himself, but the stones of Persepolis were Persia, and that Persia was something to him after all. Mere people, mere factions—he would have preferred to stay in London but he'd come back to Iran, for the sick people, or maybe he had come back to save these stones. He felt the exhilaration of righteous action. He would alert the military post behind the Darius. A pleasant feeling of desperation and justification swept over him, seized his being, transported him. Chloe Fowler's eyes watched him, dark with fear.

"Perhaps I can talk to them," Abbas explained. "They don't understand. They are young, they know nothing."

"The soldiers?" asked Chloe, to whom it did not seem possible that he could imagine stopping this elaborate spectacle below, for which all these trucks, airplane, guns, ropes, and dozens of men had been marshalled. How could he?

"Or I could telephone somewhere. The police—the army . . ." his voice grew excited, distracted, his accent grew strongly Iranian.

Below them, as they watched Hugh achieve the crest of the mound, they saw Richard Dare materialize from the opposite, invisible side.

"In it, all together!" Abbas shouted.

"Oh, shhh," cried Chloe, "they'll find us here. Abbas!"

"Chloe. I'm going to do something."

"No, please stay," she said.

"Stay here, this is safe. I'll come back." He touched her shoulder, and then was climbing down the ladder. She watched him run along the edge of the courtyard, off toward the staircase of Apadana. She wanted to scream after him but did not.

Abbas ran through the ruins toward his countrymen loading guns. Indignation and loyalty rocketed through his blood. Whatever happened, it must not happen that these treasures be stolen. "For whatever good works ye send on before you for your own behalf, ye shall find with God."

Richard Dare pointed his gun at Dick and Hugh. They stood, aghast, Dare as astonished as they. Richard Dare! What was he doing here and why had he raised his gun? Perhaps they could for an instant have grabbed him, but had not. Now it appeared that he would shoot them, but he did not. He, like Dick and Hugh, was all at once distracted by a fleet of off-track vehicles approaching directly across the sand from the direction of the Darius. These could be seen to be four military-type vehicles, which parked at some distance from the airplane. Soldiers leapt out, carrying machine guns, and rushed, firing, toward the plane; rescue, perhaps, or reinforcement. Other men rushed, like warriors of antiquity, toward the high platform of Persepolis itself. Dick saw the distant figure of Abbas Mowlavi running toward them, waving his arms. Dick and Hugh exchanged a fraction of a glance, expressive of their shared moment's impulse to run after Abbas, to rescue, to help, like good Americans. The moment passed.

"Believe me, if we don't get this stuff out of here, these crazy spicks will blow it up themselves," said Richard Dare, in an apologetic tone, turning back. He turned again and was waving his gun at the advancing men. He fired aimlessly at them, and turned again to Dick and Hugh.

Dick saw him bring the gun up again. It was shocking to see someone you know transformed with greed and purpose, not even recognizing you, or recognizing you and determining to shoot you, having passed ordinary limits of compunction, civility, conscience, raising his gun right at someone he used to drink in the Cyrus with. Panic electrified Dick's spine; he suddenly broke and ran. He spun around the corner and ran on weak legs, stumbling down the ceremonial staircase, expecting a bullet between his shoulders, but not waiting for it. The noise of his feet clattering, stumbling, plastic heel taps economically nailed to his shoes now ringing through all Persepolis.

Chapter Thirty
THE WHISPER

Oh threats of Hell and Hopes of Paradise!
One thing at least is certain — this Life flies;
One thing is certain and the rest is Lies;
The Flower that once has blown for ever dies.

Dick flattened himself against the wall of the Apadana stairway. The sun poised above him between the columns like the flame on a candle, and a bird flew across the sky. The sky was deepening blue, as if he were down in a well, and the sound of shooting, far off, echoed. No one had followed; Hugh was not with him. He crouched, wondering what to do, analyzing with growing acumen the sounds, direction, changes, chances. He could hear men calling to each other, the crack of rock falling— a rope broken, a stone leg lost—all this in the distance. He was relatively calm. It was better to be under the open sky than in the prison hut. Dare and his people would be off and he was not sure what he had to fear from the Iranians, the recipients of the guns. He tried to find a comfortable position, squatting like this, but his quads ached however he bent.

Now to the sounds in the distance were added the sounds of other trucks, or cars maybe, shouts, wilder cries, wails winding up, and now bursts of gunfire from automatic weapons. Sweat trickled down his sides from under his arms. If you were out long in this sun, you would die. He retreated farther down the stairs, into the shadow where the sand stank of urine or damp.

The implications of the new situation frightened him again, fighters coming into the ruins, not just down on the desert by the plane, people perhaps attempting to hide, as he himself was hiding, from the machine guns. Whose machine guns? His fear was growing customary to him, an alternate state from which he could retreat for a moment and re-enter with wits sharpened. He had changed his shoes for dinner last night. He wished he had kept his Nikes on.

Shooting, wild cries in Farsi, a shout repeated over and over. The clear probability that the fighting was coming closer. He wondered where the construction shack was and whether he could get back there. Still he stayed motionless, his mind reviewing like crossword clues the possible explanations, without caring which fitted. The military could rescue them if they could avoid being shot first. Maybe someone at the Darius had seen the plane, or maybe the Darius was seized, maybe it was a war starting up. He shifted, half stood to give his knees a change. He had been in college during the Korean War, then he had gone to medical school, and by then was too old for Vietnam. He had missed all the wars and battles. He was surprised at how prepared, adroit, clear-minded he felt. On the wall of stone a carved warrior dragged two prisoners along by their hair, their eyes glaring backward at him, their expression after all these centuries still alive with baleful disappointment. Probably their actual bones lay somewhere here, out on the plain amid the shards or deeply buried now after how many centuries, twenty-two centuries, two eons or rather millennia.

*   *   *

Unfolding below Chloe, as if she were meant to film it from her projection booth, a drama of battle, men scurrying over and around the stones and troughs, retreating from the ramparts of the ruin, leaping, crouching, standing up behind a fallen stone to fire at other soldiers below on the plain, whose numbers, in a little trail, like ants, streamed toward the ceremonial staircase. There are more shouts than bursts of gunfire, strange long wails and yelps. The men call to each other harshly, and those who have no guns wave their arms. All are Iranians, looking small and dark in the distance. The man at the museum door has disappeared. From the desert, the immense belches of the airplane engine starting up nearly drown the nearer noises and pale the shots to little pops of harmless sound. On the plain, near the trucks, a few fallen men, as tiny as sticks, lie on the ground. Near her, quite near now, at the circumference of the courtyard of the Tripylon, new men are hiding or creeping along. They are approaching the museum, meaning perhaps to go in and shoot the people inside. Chloe stares, unmoving, at their progress.

She cannot tell the ones from the others; who is shooting whom? All are dressed in khaki pants or jeans, they wear short-sleeved shirts of white or khaki, but it is not the white shirts against the khaki shirts; sometimes these are huddled together, and shout at another man climbing a wall. The men arriving in an ant stream are soldiers but some have taken off their military coats. She sees a man take aim with a gun and fire, and another man falls. Each wears a white shirt. They are so cruel to each other. She is seeing death before her eyes and she can believe it. It is clear.

Her heart beats faster. Can they see her? What would they do to her if they could? Pull her out? Horrible gang rapes, your insides get torn up then they have to kill you to hide you from Amnesty International, make you disappear, make you drink some kind of acid, she'd read about that, but that had been the Philippines, or was it Argentina? Latin America worse than Islam, what was it about Latin America? Was it the Spanish? Was it Catholicism? Was there something in Islam, some mediating tenet of the Koran that kept them from being as cruel as Latin Americans, or were they just differently cruel, the cruelest people always Spanish-speaking, or maybe Portuguese, but why? Speaking English doesn't save you from being cruel either, though, look at Ireland. There you couldn't help thinking worse of them because they spoke English, hence could help being cruel and stupid, were they worse than the Latins whose heritage cruelty was? Islam too a heritage of cruelty, cutting off limbs, plucking out eyes, towers filled with the skulls of the slaughtered. Try to think of a country not brutal and horrible, some islands somewhere maybe, or Egypt, or she'd thought America, until Vietnam, American soldiers raped women there and murdered them, you read about it, how could you admire America after that? Hire a veteran? What a joke, how could you hire a veteran after that? American soldiers speaking English, too.

Suddenly, just below her, from somewhere, a young man in military dress scuttles along the perimeter of the amphitheatre, his eyes rolling to see each way, like lighthouse eyes under the brim of his military hat. If she had a gun she could shoot him from here, only she doesn't, doesn't know how to shoot, doesn't know if he is an enemy or Persepolis guard. He has a rifle, which he drags behind him so that it makes a trail in the dust. He is clutching it by the barrel; even she sees he's going to shoot himself in the side. He could pull it to his shoulder in seconds and shoot her if she moved a muscle to alert him. His eyes rove the stones, looking for the tops of heads, or round mouths of guns. Chloe can see that he is very young, a teenager, eyes boggling at danger all around, afraid, hand stiffly clamping the muzzle of his gun. Suddenly as she watches, his knees buckle and in slow motion he sags to his knees and flops backward, head clattering against a column of stone. Chloe stares, expecting blood to run from his split head. He lies in the dust, still clutching the gun.

She stares, heart pounding at a new level to see death so close up. Terror pumps blood and other chemicals and strange substances into her body like coffee drunk all night. Frightened people have been known to move cars—little puny people.

Is he really dead? She leans forward closer to the aperture of the booth, fixing him with her eyes, trying to reanimate him with her eyes. She cannot remember having heard a bullet. She draws her veil more tightly around her. Perhaps he is breathing. Something about him seems to stir or live, though he lies inert. He is in some way different from the dead man they pulled from the cave.

As the hot sun rises rapidly in the sky, the shadows grow deeper, mistily blue; cool, long columnar shadows stripe the atrium of the ancient palace. Once it had a roof and walls and was cool, but for centuries it had baked under this sun. She watches the Iranian youth. The flies begin to gather on his face, too horrible for words. Then one hand flutters but cannot move to his face. Not dead. She thinks of the man of the cave. If the boy is alive perhaps he can be helped. She will have somehow to help him. But she sits without moving.

She will have to use her judgment. She isn't sure she has been called on before to use her judgment. Certainly not in a matter concerning her death. But whether she now stays here or moves, in which direction moves, how clearly understands the temper of the men out there, will affect whether she dies or survives. Her heart speeds up smoothly, into a stronger mode; her mind is clear. She clearly sees that she knows nothing about the men out there, has been too idle to learn.

Flies. She thinks of films and photos, Africa, flies on the eyes of children there, India too, the camera shaking with disgust, the little starved children too weak to lift thin arms and brush the flies away. India, the flies, they must be worse there, the cow dung, the heat, but she has never been to India, has only seen photos, has only seen photos of dark little Middle

Eastern fighters, why not find homes for them, who cares, it's all desert.

The flies still crawling slowly over the face of the boy lying there. She cares. She cannot bear it. She is not free of self-congratulation, to have found the unbearable, but still.

She figures she can creep down there, wrapped in black, and brush away the flies. She hears no shots for the moment, and anyway the shots are not meant for her. Not meant for women.

Who would shoot her? They don't even know her. Mankind: why visited with flies? Is he dead? But he stirs, hand too weak to brush away the flies clustered blackly on one spot over the eye, as if drinking his tears, and now crawling on his lips.

Chloe feels faint, the heat, the horror of these flies. It is her duty to prevent them. She has the notion, brief and incomplete, that this is as much as she ever could do, and that she will not have another chance, ever, to be heroic, never to be in an open lifeboat, never lost leading others to safety, never to be called up in any way except now. Doubled over as if in pain, without thinking further of the shooting, she creeps down the ladder.

She could somehow, perhaps, drag him into the ladies' toilet. She tries to repudiate a sense of virtue as she wraps herself closely and approaches him. Is he a soldier of the Shah? A member of the marauding party, a defender of Persepolis, or a despoiler? Anyway, she is going to save him from death from heat and flies. Looking upward and all round in case the guns are pointing, she takes him by the foot and drags him a foot or two into the shade. She has been expecting him to be as heavy as a marble god. Instead he is as light as a starved person. She moves him without difficulty and without consequence. She kicks at the gun and it falls away from his hand and lies in the dust.

Getting him through the ladies' room door is harder, as he begins to waken, and tries to impede his progress by clutching at the bare ground. Once inside he lies back, perhaps unconscious again. She remembers how she had felt once, falling out of a swing. She had had the wind knocked out of her. This was not the same.

Inside, she wets her veil and dabs it at his forehead. The eternal duty of women. He stirs. She thinks of the man of the cave, and of the blood on Hugh. The eyes of this boy flutter open for a moment, then he swoons again. Perhaps he has just fainted in the sun, for there is no mark, no blood, except where he must have struck the column. She has not heard a shot. He struggles to sit up, and leans against the wall, eyes rolling back in a scary, mortal way, mouth open. He looks at her without alarm or understanding. On his sleeve he wears a packet of pink velvet, held on with elastic, a prayer or talisman. She puts her hand to her lapis beads.

Then she realizes someone is knocking at the door. She stops breathing, hand lifted in mid-air. She listens. They knock again. "Chloe," someone whispers. "Chloe, are you in there?"

She doesn't answer. Who is it? Who knows her name? The sound of her name frightens her even more than a nameless summons. Now someone is looking not just for people but for her. Her mind races, realizations jammed together in a half second.

"Chloe, help," says the whisper. Yes, appeal to her womanly helpfulness. Chloe, help. She doesn't move. Is it an American voice? Is it Abbas come back? From a whisper you cannot tell. The soldier is looking at her, wondering if she will answer and betray him. He wears an expression of dread. She shakes her head. Why isn't she answering, screaming, flinging herself gratefully toward the door imagining rescue, imagining the welcoming arms? Not so fast, she is thinking, and then hears footsteps, more confusion outside, and no one whispers after that.

Now outside were harmless-sounding soft spats of gunfire, absorbed by the immortal stones. What had the sounds been of Alexander's men, what was the sound of Macedonian fury, Sassanian fury? We perish each alone, thinks Chloe; she feels she had seen the point, and that was the point and she wouldn't forget it. Sassanians, Achaemenians, Americans, what was the difference?

The soldier looks at her with great surprise, and then he looks around the ladies' toilet, with evident dismay, causing Chloe to wonder if she had brought him in here in violation of some severe Islamic stricture, thereby jeopardizing his soul. He gets to his hands and knees, shaking his head like a dazed horse, then stands. Chloe covers her face and turns away.

"Do you speak English?" she says. She watches him over her shoulder.

She feels his anxious stare, feels him move toward the door, hears the door open and him steal fearfully out. From outside she hears another shot or two, and the noise of the airplane taking off rises above them.

Chapter Thirty-one
FOUND AND LOST

For some we loved, the loveliest and the best
That from his Vintage rolling Time hath prest,
Have drunk their Cup a Round or two before,
And one by one crept silently to rest.

With the shadow and the sound of the plane in the sky, things changed in Persepolis. As after a play, people stepped out into the open spaces, walking normally. Where Dick had imagined there was no one at all, he now saw many people—Iranian women in shawls, workmen, men wearing the vaguely military clothes worn just now by people who had been shooting each other. It was still not clear whether these were newly arrived soldiers of the Shah or rebels, whether they had found a truce or had never been opposed, or whether one faction had been driven off entirely. No one seemed to have cleared off except the Americans in the airplane. People emerged from ditches and looked up into the sky, watching after the plane, letting the sun fall on them. A woman stretched aside her veil and squinted up into the sun. Like cave dwellers after a long siege, they communicated an air of relief and deep breathing. Here and there a man had fallen. Quite near him in the court of the Apadana sat a dead man, his arms flung loosely around a column.

In the ladies' toilet, Chloe was encouraged by the matter-of-fact sound of activities in the courtyard. She opened the door and peered around, less worried about her friends than she had been a moment ago. Things seemed calm. How one clings to the appearance of things and wants to believe, she thought. But surely it is all right now, even if you can't tell why it is all right or what has changed.

Moving outside, she heard her name being shouted in chorus; it sounded like Dick and Sugar Dunham. Chloe! Chloe Fowler! Ned Henderson! for they were calling for him too.

To be safe, she thought, she should return to her vantage point in the projection booth and look down again. She crept carefully up the ladder. From here, where she had felt immune, safe, removed, like a battle commander, she could see a panorama of soldiers and vehicles, and their own forlorn cars still parked where they had trustfully left them yesterday evening—the hospital station wagon and Abbas's BMW. In the firing, people had fallen. Soldiers were gathering someone up from quite near their car. In the shade of one of their trucks lay a row of men, and a woman was giving them water. This battle was only minutes over and already a woman was out there giving water. The soldiers laid the person they had just moved alongside the others. He was wrapped, was the face wrapped? She felt especially uneasy about this figure, lying so close to their car, in case it was Hugh who might have rashly run out there, or Abbas or Dick, or even fat Dr. Dunham in a panic, unused to Iran. The distant woman waved the edges of her veil over them, like a black flag of death, though no doubt she meant only to fan them. It was already eleven o'clock. The thought sprang unbidden to Chloe that if you didn't eat for twenty-four hours you would lose half a pound.

Now she saw Dick and Hugh with Sugar Dunham.

"Where were you, Chloe?" they cried as she came up, and she explained how she had huddled through the night, had hidden, had watched.

"I was locked in a tool shed," Dick said.

Hugh said nothing.

"Where were you?" Chloe asked.

"I hid in a drain," he said.

"When we saw the guys with the guns, everybody scattered except me," said Dick. "I just stood there like a shmuck."

"I think the others were in the museum," Chloe said. "I think they had them locked in there."

Sugar Dunham gathered Chloe in a motherly embrace. "Honey, you sure you're all right?" she said.

"Where's Junie?" Dick asked.

"She was in the museum with us," Sugar assured him. "She was just the most amazingly brave."

"Junie! Fred Dunham! Ned Henderson!" they called, as they walked through the ruins toward the ceremonial steps, making their way quickly, trying not to look at a dead man or at the clusters of Iranian fighters who stood about, or sat on fallen columns and paid no attention to them. Dick saw the man he had been locked in the shed with, now walking with his stout wife, her head in a devout veil. The man raised his thumb to Dick. Dick wished he would offer him a cigarette.

"Are you all right, Chloe?" Hugh asked.

"Of course," she said.

They descended the staircase. The eyes of the Assyrian immortals under their curled coiffures seemed indifferent to the modern disruption. Clasping their spears they marched along unchanged. At the ticket booth an old man was setting out piles of currency and postcards, while, slumped in the booth, a boy sobbed. There was the important sound of new trucks approaching, and, in the air, the distant sound of planes.

Ahead of them, near Abbas's car, they suddenly saw a small lavender figure, lying or crawling.

"It's Junie!" cried Dick. Yes it was. Chloe remembered the lavender dress.

Hugh and Dick rushed forward. Sugar Dunham clung to Chloe, and they crept forward more timidly. Now they could hear, from somewhere, a terrible wail. It came from the huddle that was Junie. Dick and Hugh were lifting her to her feet. Junie screaming, screaming, a sickening sound to Chloe, for she had an idea what it must mean.

Junie's screams, they could see as they came closer, had been drawn by a bloodstain on the ground. Chloe hadn't realized blood would be so thick, a gelatinous film embedded with fine pebbles and dust, not yet dried in the sun.

"They shot him, they shot him," Junie was saying, her voice breaking with hiccuping sobs. She had dropped to her knees again, kneeling beside the stain while Dick and Hugh clung helplessly to her elbows. When Dick picked her up again, her knees were engraved with gravel. Her hand was sticky red, where she had put it in the puddle of blood.

Chloe looked away—away from the stain and across the vacant desert, feeling sickness stir in the pit of her stomach.

"Just get in the car, honey," Dick was saying. "Come on, Junie, let's sit in the car." Junie's hysterical grief rather silenced the rest of them. Chloe was not sure why Junie was claiming all the grief. She gave Junie a Kleenex and told herself that one bloodstain did not mean, necessarily, anyone they knew.

Great dramas, your perspective on life, your life altered for all time and at the end you have to get into a car and drive home, Chloe thought as they climbed into Abbas's BMW.

"Well, I don't have the keys," Dick Rothblatt said. "Abbas has the keys."

Hugh got out again and stood by the car, looking around.

The Hendersons were waddling toward them, waving a scarf. "You could go with the Hendersons," said Hugh, leaning in the car, looking at Junie, whose distress seemed the most palpable, outside control, though it had subsided to sobs and murmurs in the throat. Maybe she had been raped, maybe terrible things had happened to her in the night. She, Chloe, had merely seen, but she had seen—she enumerated the horrors in her mind— the flies clinging to the eyes of a wounded person, seen men shot and fall. Seen the thick puddle of blood.

The thick puddle of blood seemed to have nothing to do with Abbas, was perhaps not his, perhaps life did not seep out along with it. You bled, you cut your finger and bled and still you lived. You got your period and lived.

But the bleeding had begun. Emblematic, shaped like a continent, the spreading stain through the pebbles along the hard earth. The Hendersons, approaching, stepped around it.

"A nasty few hours," said Dr. Henderson. "Is your car all right?"

"We don't have the keys," Hugh said. "Dr. Mowlavi had the keys, and we don't know where he is. We'll wait for him here for a while."

"Dr. Ames, we brought him, we should take him back. But where is he?" said Mrs. Henderson.

"We'll keep an eye out for him. He must be somewhere. You go on," Hugh said. Dr. Henderson's face brightened. He unlocked the doors of the hospital station wagon and motioned the ladies to get in. "There will be a locksmith or someone at the hotel; we'll ask there." But he made no move to start the car.

"Hotwire," said Dick. "I don't know how to do it," turning back to the BMW.

"No," said Hugh, "neither do I. Look, I'll have a look around for Abbas, and meet you at the Darius. You have to go there anyway to collect the bags." Hugh and Dick exchanged glances. It was, it struck Dick, a glance newly communicative, informed by a shared awareness, an unspoken agreement to silence, something they both knew and nobody else knew, whatever. It was a look he had exchanged with Abbas, too, when mention was made of the body in the desert. It struck him that he had not had this sort of relation with Hugh before. They were friendly colleagues, but they had not been in collusion. Now they were in collusion. They had seen Abbas run toward the shooting, toward the men, and they, American men, had not run.

If they had dashed out after Abbas to save the relics of Persepolis, then they would all have been shot, Dick told himself. But they could have helped, could have taken on Richard Dare, could have thought of something. Impulsive Abbas, running out into the path of men with guns. Dick felt uneasy. All those movies you saw as a kid, you knew it was supposed to be you running in a zigzag pattern through the line of fire to save something. Dick could see that Hugh knew—something in his glance showed a shade of rue, that it was supposed to be him.

No need to tell Chloe or Junie about this notion, since there was nothing to tell, strictly speaking, about that moment of hesitation more agonizing in retrospect than at the time. In memory it stretched out, emblematic of all betrayals and treachery. Hugh, Dick felt sure, would also not tell.

Hugh would not tell Chloe, his lips against her breast, murmurs against her throat, telling her other things. Chloe lying under him, he could imagine them—quite involuntarily, no voyeur he, why did the scene present itself to him in this voyeuristic form? The others were still talking excitedly.

"We found ourselves face to face with Dare," Hugh said. "Abbas ran out at that point. He was excited, he saw they were stealing things. We sort of stood there."

"There is blood on the door handle. Somebody's bloody hand," Junie sobbed. Dick thought there was something accusing in her tone. That was unfair.

"Were you trying to find me?" Chloe asked. "Was it you who called me, in the bathroom?" For it had struck her.

"No, we were near the stairs."

"Well, he must be alive, or he would be here lying dead, isn't that right?" said Junie suddenly, straightening up. No one said that people could have carried him away. Chloe did not say she had seen some people carry someone away, for, after all, who knew whom they carried?

"Maybe he's here; why are we assuming the worst?" said Dick.

Why had she told them about the whisper at the door? It might not have been Abbas. It might even have been Richard Dare, trying to trick her to come out. Help, Chloe, the voice had said, and of course she had not helped. Helped do what? It had frightened her to hear her name. But it was all so vague, so strange, there was nothing to tell, really.

They sat fitting the little pieces together. Except she did not tell them it could have been Abbas at the bathroom door. Richard Dare, stealing artifacts, bringing guns! It became a story; they wove it together sitting in the hot car waiting for Abbas to come walking up with the keys. "Look here," said Dr. Henderson from the station wagon, "the rest of you get in. I don't think you should sit here in this heat."

"I agree," said Hugh. "Let's get out of here."

"Abbas . . ." cried Junie.

"If he's okay he'll come out here and here's his car, and he has the keys. I don't see that there's any way of knowing where he is," said Hugh. "I think we'd just better leave."

"Jesus, a BMW," said Dick. "I hope it's okay."

"I know he's dead," said Junie. "We can't just leave."

"My dear, the sooner we talk to the authorities," said Dr. Henderson.

They crowded eight in the station wagon. Chloe and Junie, being smallest, had to sit on the flat shelf in back, where the body of the man had lain. The carpet seemed invisibly stained. Junie, no longer crying, now took off her glasses and wiped them. Dr. Henderson still did not start the car.

"Where were you? Where was the Iranian family?" asked Chloe.

"Where were you?"

"In the museum. They just rounded up everyone and locked us in the museum," said Dr. Dunham.

"We were in love," said Junie, beginning again her hysterical weeping. "I loved him." The others looked at her in shocked amazement. Hers was not ordinary grief; she seemed to be saying she and Abbas were in love.

Chapter Thirty-two
PEBBLES

YESTERDAY *This Day's Madness* did prepare;
TO-MORROW's *Silence, Triumph, or Despair:*
Drink! for you know not whence you came, nor why;
Drink, for you know not why you go, nor where.

Maybe he's not dead, thought Chloe. People we know aren't dead, not until they're old, why assume the worst? She felt tired, that was all, and unable to assess the possibilities or the meanings of things. Mrs. Henderson began in the front seat to hum. The wish to tell her to shut up began to give Chloe a headache. Dr. Ames came up, excited, and began to go over it all again: "The men at the entrance with guns, we were all herded into the museum, I tried to get out through the window, we probably won't really know what was going on till we read it in the newspapers. . . ." Hugh, Dick, and Dr. Henderson stood in front of the car muttering; she couldn't hear them. It was hot in the station wagon. They sat a long time and unaccountably she dozed off. When she woke, it could only have been a moment, her head jerking up as though someone had pulled a string, they were in front of the Darius Hotel. Hugh told them to get out and go in to get their bags. His the voice of an exasperated tour director. Maybe he had directed the whole thing? Why was he now hurrying them away? All at once she felt ready to die of thirst.

Military vehicles were parked in the parking lot next to a French tour bus with people piling out of it. In the lobby a confusion of soldiers and tourists stood in subdued groups while a voluble man negotiated something at the desk. Hugh, consulting with another clerk, reported that they, Chloe and the others, were expected to check out as if nothing had happened, as if they had slept in their beds, made love on fresh sheets, paid for drinks beside the orange-scented pool. Chloe had an Ancient Mariner's impulse to tell the new people what had just happened to them but they were all speaking French.

"But it was Persepolis we came to see," the tour guide was screaming.

When they had finished at the desk, Chloe bought a Pepsi in the gift shop, and Hugh bought two bottles of water. He carried them back to the car, but he didn't get in with the others as they climbed in.

"Somebody—I'd better stay, find out what's happened. You go on. I'll do something about Abbas's car," he said. He did not say, I will find the body of Abbas, but that was what Dick knew he meant. For an instant he was inclined to volunteer to stay and help but he was unable to overcome his reluctance. His stomach crawled to think it could be true that Abbas lay dead out there someplace. Abbas had gone for help, was all; he would turn up. Anyway Junie needed him, poor girl, she looked near collapse, an odd bruised blueness under the surface of her pale skin, as if she had been beaten, or fallen against something. Eyes red-rimmed like a mouse's. It struck him that today her eyelashes were white. Ordinarily they were black. Despite her disdain for makeup, she must put mascara on them; she must even sleep in it. That touched him.

"You had nine shirts done at the Tehran Hilton and you

said you weren't there," cried Chloe all at once to Hugh. He looked surprised at this sudden accusation.

"Well, that's true," he said, after a pause. "I was there. I wasn't supposed to tell anyone."

"You just thought no one would notice the shirts, not notice that you didn't turn up for ten days!"

"Well, I didn't think I had to account to all of Shiraz for my whereabouts," Hugh snapped, an unaccustomed note of asperity in his voice. He stepped away from the car window.

"Me in Shiraz by myself, the Iranians totally paranoid about where you were," Chloe was going on, unable to stop herself. Dick thought it was an inopportune time for this. Should he slap her? Why did he have this impulse lately to slap women?

"Maybe I should stay here with you," he said to Hugh but Hugh's expression seemed to indicate that he would do better going back to manage these hysterical women.

Chloe's head under the low station-wagon roof grows hot with the heat of the metal; the ruts in the road jar. She tries to fix her mind on the tragedies she has witnessed, especially on the gory corpse she saw from far away. But she can only see it in the way she sees the future of her life, from far away through the wrong end of a telescope, the figures tiny and bright, like the brightness of the blood across a light-blue shirt—short-sleeved, ironed—who ironed for him?

Her mind does not grip tragedy firmly from both sides as if it had ears or handles, tragedy too insubstantial and it turns the minute she thinks about it into a thought about some inferior thing, some material circumstance, the hot trickle of sweat between her shoulder blades, her dress sticking to her back. Dead, she says to herself, and grows as still as she can within herself to try to hear the reverberations, the terrible resonance of this horrendous word, to try to experience its effect on her, on anyone, inside her, but it slips down inside as neatly as a small pill, doesn't choke, slips down without impediment, not a hot burning pill or anything. Just "dead." Dead, dead, dead, just echoing like mere words in any empty tunnel, echo chamber, like inside a barrel at the funhouse. How strange to think of that, of stepping into the spinning barrel of the funhouse, remembering herself as a child, not dreaming of death or of anything. But had that been the moment, long ago and forgotten, when, stepping into the spinning barrel, she had first had an intimation of death? And was death a spinning and a stumbling? *Abbas* is dead she says, and still gets not enough effect, not the effect she knows there should be; maybe it's she who is dead.

In the landscape, in the very air, a sense of menace and animation. Trucks full of soldiers roll along the highway. Soldiers stand at the crossroads, milling around. Up from the horizon two military jets bolt straight into the sky, making twin tracks behind themselves, like rails; the shriek of the engines seems upon them.

"Those must be from Shiraz," somebody says.

"Something else is going on," Dick says. "Something general. It must be."

"War, or civil war," Chloe says. "Or revolution."

Viewed from that perspective, things seem too calm. There are only two trucks of soldiers, two airplanes in the sky.

As they watch, the airplanes, before their astonished eyes, drop like stones out of the sky and disappear. They must have crashed, but miles away, so that there is no sound and no flames show. Then, as the party heads toward Shiraz, two plumes of smoke rise in the northern sky.

Planes falling on villages. Dick's stomach crawls to think of the molten metal, the bodies. He is thinking of General Ben and his ideas of saboteurs—someone, perhaps, from the hospital. Or it is just Iranian maintenance. How could you know? He thinks of the poor men in the planes, or would they have ejected?

Was there something that he, Dick Rothblatt, could have or should have done?

News of the fighting at Persepolis had not reached the Azami Compound, and, thinking them all safe at the Darius, no one was concerned for them—but all in the compound were, in fact, in a flurry of departure and change. Yesterday there had been a significant riot near the university, with hundreds of students arrested, and another in Tehran, where thousands in the streets had been fired on by soldiers, and more than four hundred people were dead. These events were described by people dashing down the hospital corridors or across the grounds. Dr. Ali Yazdi was pacing in the garden of Villa One, waiting for the tourist party to come home. He believed that the Americans should all leave without further delay. Probably, he explained, at this moment there would be no difficulty getting planes to Tehran and thence out of the country. Even if their tickets were for some other day, he was sure the airlines would make every effort to get them on planes. It seemed to Dick and Chloe that he feared to be compromised by their presence as much as he feared for their safety.

"No danger—not, I think, to you—but it will be better until the political situation calms if all foreigners leave—all the foreigners are leaving from town—the American consul I think is advising it to all."

They stood in the garden. No one had mentioned Abbas, but Dr. Yazdi, or someone, would have to be told. Told what? Chloe looked up at her windows in Villa Two and thought it was strange that they were open, the turquoise sash so pretty and inviting in the sunshine. Dick began the account of the marauders. Chloe did not think she could bear to hear it, and so wandered toward her own apartment.

"Hugh stayed behind to try to find him," Dick was saying. Or his body, he was thinking.

"This is an extraordinary story," cried Dr. Yazdi. "The treasures of Persepolis, you tell me! And Abbas swept away! We will telephone the Darius. But he'll turn up, of course. Abbas is a 'survivor,' as you say."

"Do you have someone who could help us with the plane reservations?" Dick asked. "Who all am I talking about?"

"You and Dr. Monroe, Mrs. Fowler of course, the Dunhams, Dr. Ames, let me see—the Hendersons. The others I have already been on to, the Schwartzes, the Freys. Oh, and not forgetting Dr. Fay, you want to make her reservations too. She was not with you in Persepolis?"

"She's gone to her apartment," Dick said. "She is very upset by the whole thing."

"Who would imagine, her seeming so strong. And little fragile, flowerlike Mrs. Fowler, though she did look pale, came through brilliantly. What an experience!"

"Maybe I'll gather up the plane tickets, then I'll know what I'm talking about," said Dick. "I'll get everybody's tickets and come to your office."

"Hurry, my dear fellow, and then we'll go down to the ticket office in person, for I doubt that we'll get through by phone."

Chloe was thinking she'd better go to the American consulate and ask about her passport. Failing that, maybe they'd let her on the plane anyway. They wouldn't want American women stranded in Iran; they'd just say go ahead. Then, once away, she could chance the consequences of arriving in the United States. Passport lost, had already applied, danger in staying. It sounded all right. The worst that could happen was Ellis Island for a few days. She climbed the stairs to her apartment, and was surprised to find Linda Farmani coming out of it. Evidently she possessed a second key. Her heavy hair was down like a charwoman's; her mouth was colorless in her pale face.

"I'm moving in here. After you leave, of course—I've been

bringing in my things," she said. Her face wore the same jittery expression it had worn when Vahid was taken away, and she bit fitfully at the corner of her lips. If this were America, you'd think she was on speed, Chloe thought.

"But you're leaving Villa One? Have the Yazdis put you out?" Chloe asked, not at all surprised that the Yazdis would do such a thing.

"The Yazdis? No, no, but I can't stay there. Villa One is for the head of the hospital." Chloe saw that Linda had piled her things on the bureau.

"Americans are being advised to leave at once, doesn't that apply to you?" she asked Linda.

"I suppose," Linda said, absently moving toward the door. Chloe walked downstairs with her, to go to the consulate.

In the street things were much the same as before. People idled along, cars screeched, animals brayed. Was it her imagination that people drew back from her as she came toward them, or turned to look at her? She adjusted her veil more carefully to cover her hair.

The consulate was shut. A penciled note on the door announced it would be open after lunch, but it was now after two. She dawdled outside for a while, but was too excited to sit there and felt too strange to bear sitting still. She'd come back, she could telephone. She wished she had bought a rug. *Abbas* is dead, she kept telling herself; without effect.

Gathered in her shawl, she crouched on the steps of the consulate and waited. People passed by. As she watched more closely she saw that their steps were quicker than before, and their eyes were looking far ahead. An intangible aura of change was palpable in the dusty, scented air, as on the day it becomes autumn, and people are heard to say that the weather has changed. One day it is suddenly autumn. Their quickened steps had the animation of squirrels preparing for winter. Or was she imagining this? A rich Iranian woman in a kelly-green gabardine suit stepped smartly by in her high-heeled snakeskin shoes. Two little boys racing by on small bicycles, suddenly wheeled and tossed a small stone into Chloe's lap.

She heard them giggling wildly as they peddled away, around the corner out of sight. Did they know she was American? She nestled her face in the folds of black cloth. She was thinking, all at once, of caves collapsing, as by a shudder of the earth, or bombardment, little stones like this pouring down into laps, onto heads, and finally the earth itself shuddering down and filling up the cave rooms, burying the idols and pillars, and blocking all the tunnels and escapes.

Chapter Thirty-three
THE LOVED ONES

Alike for those who for TO-DAY prepare,
And those that after some TO-MORROW stare,
A Muezzin from the Tower of Darkness cries,
"Fools, your Reward is neither Here nor There."

In his apartment, Dick packed, not at first noticing the letter from Marla, rather a fat envelope, which distressed him when he saw it; he knew it meant papers to sign, probably house papers. He flung his socks into his bag and snatched up the letter.

It's a wonderful young couple with a darling baby. I'm just happy it's someone I can feel glad is in our house and loves it the way we did. They're just starting out, so they had some difficulty with a bank loan, so they're going to pay me directly, as I don't need the whole cash sum right now. They'll pay $350 a month and more later when they can. He's a talented artist, and she is a potter.

Dick read the papers over again, heart pounding. Sold. And there was nothing about interest or the term of the mortgage. He couldn't believe that anyone would let her sell without taking interest, but it didn't say. He couldn't believe that his house—huge, magnificent—could be sold to some flaky young artist with no money and no collateral; there must be more to it, and she was being vague this way to torture him. She was as clear to his mind as if she had been present, small lines at the upper lip, hair lighter than when she was younger, anxious eyes full of a kind of abashed reverence for art, which she was always too tense to try, didn't take painting classes like other women. Also didn't bake for the bake sales at the children's schools when they were little; something about the idea of it seemed to frighten her.

One thing about Junie, she was not afraid to try things. It was strange that he couldn't remember him and Marla being happy; he couldn't remember them being passionate. All their love-making—years and years—had coalesced into the routine and automatic practice that continued, practically to the day of their divorce. But they must have once been happy and passionate. You get this amnesia, he thought, to insulate yourself from the poignancy of the end, the disappointment, the metaphysical lesson. A picture came to his mind of Junie, grabbing for Abbas's cock and saying, "My roommate's away." How and when could she and Abbas have fallen in love—that serious, that solemnized emotion requiring endless dreamy talk?

Then he thought for some reason of Chloe Fowler: what he admired in her was her independence of mind, and yet this quality, shared by both Marla and Junie too, had not caused Chloe to turn away from normal female pastimes, like Junie, or to become, like Marla, belatedly assertive. It was Chloe's independence of mind that seemed to enable her to support the nominal confines of a traditional role. She didn't appear confined. Once she had told him that when she thought of working in an office, or as a doctor like Junie, visions of misery and desiccation swam before her eyes, like the roots of an uprooted plant. Dick loved the idea of Chloe cheerfully planted and blooming. She would be a pot of marigolds, or something slightly more tender, a trail of lobelia. Marla would be something like a zinnia.

Abruptly, he gathered up his ticket and passport and walked over to Junie's apartment to collect hers. He found her sitting, tear-stained, on the lumpy sofa in her apartment, staring at her hands. "Hi," she said, with a pitiful quaver. Her two front teeth, he noticed, were really rather large, like a chipmunk's.

"Dick, tell me, no shit, are you mad at me?" Mad that she loved Abbas?

"No, honestly not, Junie. No shit," he said, smiling as reassuringly as he could. He wondered if they had actually made love and if so whether she had been more responsive with Abbas. But did not ask. He remembered Dave Weigandt, the surgical resident she'd been living with before him, and imagined her saying, "You're not mad, Dave, no shit?"

"You could stay here, Junie. Linda Farmani is staying, others are. Abbas is going to show up. You should wait for him." Just to show he was forgiving.

She sighed. There was about her the faint odor of fever, that sweet, tired smell.

"I hate Iran. I can't wait to get out of here," she said.

"Get me your ticket and passport. I'm getting us on the first plane possible out of Shiraz, then in Tehran we'll take it from there."

She sighed and stood up, and aimlessly rifled her top bureau drawer. "He's dead, I know. I touched his blood."

The stone had not hurt Chloe. She got to her feet and began to walk back to the compound. Just inside the gate she heard the familiar barking. In the confusion of their return, she had forgotten about Rustum. Here he was looking apprehensively at her, as if he believed himself responsible for her dereliction these two days. What had he done? His tail beat frantically. It curved around in an unpleasant arc so that the tip really touched his back. It should have been bobbed—he looked like the sort of dog whose tail would normally be bobbed at home. He watched her intently. He must be hungry. She saw from his eyes that he was now a perfectly socialized young dog, had learned all the dog lessons of adoration and dependence, and had none of the acumen of the wild.

"I can't leave Rustum," she said to Dick as he came up.

"Oh, don't be silly," said Dick vehemently.

She was going to be silly. She felt suddenly certain of that. She knew all the things there were to be said against transporting an ugly mongrel dog to America in a time of crisis, but she didn't care.

"I've ruined him. He doesn't know how to live in the wild." Jeffrey hates dogs, was her thought, and then her thought: but of course it doesn't matter!

"He'll learn quick enough," Dick said.

"The other dogs wouldn't accept him. Probably they'd kill him." Though in fact she knew nothing of dog society.

"They don't let dogs into the U.S. You can't just bring them in from anywhere."

"I'll get a certificate. They can put him in quarantine. You get a vet, a certificate." Without Jeffrey, she could have a dog. The children should have a dog.

"I'm not going to help you with this, Chloe," said Dick curtly. Like other men, he must despise women, Chloe supposed, despise their odd obsessions, their inconvenient whims, lack of business sense, and lack of propriety. All the same, she wasn't going to leave this poor Rustum, and she had a lovely sense of rising on a tide of irrational determination, afloat. Not going to leave Rustum.

"Just get me your airplane ticket and passport. I'm going

now to see about the reservations," said Dick. He could not forbear adding, "I was surprised about you and Hugh. I hadn't realized."

"What about it?" said Chloe, with an edge to her voice, a warning tone. They climbed her stairs. Could it be, she was thinking, or was it imaginary, that the thick stench of cat piss she smelled now had been here all the time? Could it be she had got used to it?

"Well," he said, "it's none of my business. I only said I was surprised. I mean, felt made a fool of, a little, all that walking you home et cetera, guarding your virtue."

"And now you don't think of me as virtuous?" Chloe said, meaning to take a light tone, to turn this conversation aside. She had never doubted that she was virtuous—not bad, at least. Her parents had never made her feel herself to be bad.

"Virtue is a funny thing to call it," Dick said, with a laugh that Chloe found suddenly infuriating; she felt an ire worthy of Junie rising in her cheeks and earlobes.

"Oh, Dick, I cannot believe you believe that chastity and virtue are the same thing," she snapped. "Anyway, your life is one of candor and aboveboard, right?"

"My relationship with Junie was perfectly obvious."

"At least Hugh is approximately my own age," Chloe continued. "Anyway, you were trying to conceal your relationship with Junie. Deceit, subterfuge. All that business of coffee with me in the mornings, then she'd happen to stroll by."

"Keeping up appearances is not the same thing as deceit," Dick said.

"Isn't it?"

"Not at all. You keep up appearances to spare the feelings of others. We're in a modest Islamic country. Junie's conduct would be disapproved of. To say nothing of yours, I might add."

"My conduct!" screamed Chloe. "Oh! How can we even speak of this, with Abbas dead, and . . ."

Tears came to her eyes, the first tears she had shed. It was as if her tears had dried up in the hot desert air. "How can we bicker about sexual propriety when our friend is dead?" she said.

"Did Jeff find out about Hugh? Is that the problem?" Dick asked.

"Jeffrey does not know about Hugh, there's no connection. And I have not discussed my relationship with Jeffrey with Hugh," said Chloe.

"I think Abbas will turn up," Dick said. "There are a thousand explanations."

In Chloe's apartment she found her airplane ticket. Dick stood by, his heart crowded with random urgent subjects, things he wanted to talk to Chloe about. It was as if the plane were on its way, winging toward them, about to sunder them. "Junie and Abbas really were in love," he said. "I had no idea. It took me completely by surprise."

Chloe felt, unmistakably, the twist of the knife. Why was Dick being so unkind? Did Abbas love Junie?

"I never knew it," Dick went on. She forced a sympathetic smile. He did not seem to mean to wound.

"Well," she said, "do you mind very much?"

"Not really, I guess," Dick said. "But nobody likes to be taken by surprise. She could have told me, we're friends, after all. Or Abbas could have told me. I feel like a fool, hanging around to claim my—my rights—from time to time. I thought I was being supportive. Instead I was acting like a pig. They were in love and she was planning to stay with him in Iran, together to reform Iranian medicine. Sweet, no?"

"Oh," cried Chloe, tears flooding down her face. To think of it, hopes and life destroyed. "Poor Abbas, all that tragedy in his life and just when happiness had begun again." How like life that was, she thought. "The bloom is gone and with the bloom go I," said the Koran.

"Poor Junie too. She's completely collapsed. I had to give her Valium."

"It's just terrible," cried Chloe, the thought popping into

her reluctant mind that it was deceitful of Abbas to sleep with her when he was in love with Junie. Of course she was prettier than Junie? But not nearly so young. How she detested herself for these frivolous thoughts. Why was she cursed with a nature that could not grasp the tragic and went on with egotism and vanity in spite of her conscious wishes?

"Well," Dick said, getting up and crossing to his rug, which he began to roll up. "Well, shit." She could not tell, really, what he was feeling. He made it into a tidy roll, and tied it with string.

"Abbas was so nice," Chloe said, hearing her ordinary voice, feeling the inadequacy of her emotions and power to explain them. "Junie can—can take comfort that he died for Iran, in a way." How could she be saying such fatuous things?

"Oh, shit," said Dick. "She's not his widow."

They were interrupted by a thumping and shuffling on the stairs outside Chloe's room. Dick went to the door and looked out, then stepped outside.

"Oh, here, let me help," Chloe heard him say. He reappeared carrying a large playpen. Linda Farmani came in with a shopping bag and baby Henry.

"I don't mean to be pushing you out," she said.

"You'd better fly out with us," Chloe said. "We don't have tickets—I don't even have a passport. The idea is that if we go to Tehran somebody will get us out."

How can two people be in love who are never even together? she was thinking. Had they ever made love? Well, undoubtedly, who knew when or where, it doesn't require special equipment or a lot of time. She could understand how Junie might not tell Dick, she wouldn't want to wound him, him going through the thing with Marla, female treachery on every hand, he'd even seemed upset to realize about her and Hugh.

"Don't be silly, I'm going to stay," Linda said. "Vahid will be released. Now with the changes, they'll release him. And anyway, where would I go? Back to L.A.? Back to Detroit?"

"I think she was basically attracted to the idea of service to

Iran," said Dick, coming in with boxes. "Of course, Abbas is an attractive guy, too."

"Have you ever been to Detroit?" Linda's voice carried an unfamiliar note of hysteria.

"No, no," said Chloe.

"It's the murder capital of America, after Atlanta. Or rape. The black girls especially, they'd be missing from gym one day, or come back with a bandage on their heads, oh she got raped, people'd say. It was usually their fathers. There are good neighborhoods around Detroit, though. Grosse Pointe. Beautiful houses with weeping willows. When I was little it was the weeping willows I envied, I wanted a large lawn and weeping willows, I don't even know what the houses were like inside. Vulgar, I guess. Auto executives. But now it's the murder capital too. We don't have that here. I almost got raped once in Los Angeles; I never told Vahid about it."

"Everyone almost gets raped," said Chloe.

"Did I hear you say you don't have a passport?" Dick said. "Is that possible?"

"That kind of thing doesn't happen in Iran. They respect women. And there aren't any blacks. I know it sounds prejudiced, but I like it better without them."

"It's not only possible," said Chloe. "I don't have one."

"You'd be prejudiced too if you grew up in Detroit."

"What happened to your passport?" Dick shouted.

Chloe sighed and could not reply.

"I'm just plain afraid of them," said Linda. "Plenty of things that happened."

"Let me take my stuff out of the bureau, so you can get settled," Chloe said, thinking what a bigot Linda was.

"I like the turquoise color," said Linda, touching the painted window sill. "I wasn't sure when I first saw it. Or I could go back to L.A.? Maybe I could set up a business decorating for Iranians, there's enough of them there. I could do real estate, that's what I did before. I've thought about L.A., but of course I can't do anything until Vahid comes home. I had a condo in

L.A., before Vahid and I got married. I sold it, like a fool. They say you can't touch anything in L.A. now."

"God knows why," said Chloe.

"Well, it's got the climate. And things are happening there, that's where it's at," Linda said. She gazed tragically out the window toward Villa One, and rearranged the interval between two of the pots of geranium.

At the thought of Los Angeles palm trees and restaurants that look like drive-ins with Rollses parked in front, Chloe felt her misery, diffuse except where it involved Abbas, focus on at least one of its components, her reluctance to return to certain things, especially automobiles and streets with no one walking on them. America in general. Of course no one *had* to live in L.A.—people could move. At least she could live in San Francisco. People more or less got what they wanted. But why was there an L.A.?

"But I don't know anyone in L.A. now," Linda said.

"I didn't turn your husband in," cried Chloe. "Really, how could I? I don't know why people thought so. I'm only me. And I think it's rotten of them to put you out of Villa One, that's your home, after all, Dr. Yazdi is a terrible person, he . . ."

"The Yazdis? No. It's Bahram and Noosheen. Bahram is the new head. He's well known to be a moderate—I suppose they think he will placate the dissidents. There are new ministers, changes, every day. He's trying to get some moderates in there, but of course it's too late now."

"Noosheen!" cried Chloe. "Is it possible? She's here?"

"Yes, she came home yesterday. She was at her brother's in Tehran."

"Well, *she* has my passport," said Chloe, too relieved to wonder why Noosheen had not used it. "I better go find her. Does she know we're back?"

"I don't know," said Linda.

"Does she know about Abbas?"

"I don't know."

Chapter Thirty-four
UNHAPPY COUCH

What! out of senseless Nothing to provoke
As conscious Something to resent the yoke
Of unpermitted Pleasure, under pain
Of Everlasting Penalties, if broke!

Chloe rushing to Villa One found Noosheen supervising the unpacking of her boxes. She was wearing chador, which, when she flung her arms out to embrace Chloe, swept over Chloe like a Dracula cape, and she wore some sort of familiar scent, American—Charlie, maybe. Her face was bright with a new animation.

"Oh, Chloe, thank heaven you are safe. News has come about the horror at Persepolis. Terror is everywhere. In Tehran, even here. But you are safe!"

Chloe's relief at seeing Noosheen safe soured a little into anger, but her heart was thankful. She took it as a personal sign of forgiveness that she was not to be tortured with something terrible happening to Noosheen for which she would be at fault; this time she was not to be punished for her meddling in the lives of innocent, vulnerable, desperate people. But she felt cross, angry at Noosheen for having caused her this fear.

"Thank heaven I am able to see you," said Noosheen. "It makes me heartbroken to think that you are leaving, my dear friend and mentor."

"But I thought you were in India," cried Chloe. "How come you're here?"

"There are still no chairs, let us sit out here in the garden," Noosheen said. They sat in the bushes, among the geranium pots. "Well, as you see—I am not. It didn't work out. How grateful I will be forever for your help, as a true friend. That I will never forget."

"Did you try? Didn't you try?"

"Oh, yes, I tried," she said. "I dressed in Western clothes and went to the airport. Sunglasses, careful makeup, everything. But then there was a problem in your passport. You had no resident visa."

"Of course I did," Chloe said. "Stamped in. I got it in San Francisco."

"No, it was not there. And so without it I could not leave. I was not properly in so I could not get out. They said I would have to go to the American Embassy and get them to help me get a resident visa, I don't know what, but I knew I could not go on fooling them. It is one thing to slip out at the airport, another to sit in the embassies. No one would believe me for long."

"That's impossible. All my stuff was in order," Chloe said.

"If I was a man they'd put me in jail, that's what they told me," said Noosheen. "Ah, well! 'No mischance chanceth but by God's permission.' "

"May I see?"

Noosheen handed her the passport, and Chloe leafed through it. It was perfectly true, there was no visa. On second glance she could see that a page had been cut out; the pages jumped from 4 to 7. Had Noosheen done this herself? Or who? Her passport had been lying right in her bureau drawer, unused except when she took it to the bank to cash traveler's checks. But of course someone had come in and rifled her bureau drawers. Hossein could have done it any time. Now how was she going to get out? She threw it down, no worse off than before, no better off, but then she picked it up again and put it in her purse.

"What did you do then?" she asked.

"My brother and sister-in-law had brought me to the airport. They took me home again. I was not quite truthful to them: I told them Bahram had done many bad things to me."

"So they were helping you?"

"Yes, but now I think it was all for the best, because in Tehran things are changing very fast, and it helped me to understand some things I had not understood before."

"Like what?" asked Chloe.

" 'Empedocles on Etna.' I could understand it completely. It applies to our modern world, it applies to Iran; that is the test of great poetry, that there is always meaning, at any era, don't you agree? Where Empedocles says we are becoming slaves, 'And we shall feel our powers of effort flag, And rally them for one last fight—and fail; And we shall sink in the impossible strife, And be astray for ever.' The Koran says this too. That is Iran. The way we are going we might as well jump into the crater."

"What will happen?"

" 'We shall fly for refuge to past times, Their soul of unworn youth, their breath of greatness.' Arnold. We are on the eve of a great spiritual renaissance here, I believe it. I could see the signs—in Tehran they are everywhere. There is a leader at hand. The common people believe he is the Twelfth Imam. I don't believe that, of course, but what if it were true?"

Now Chloe was feeling, she realized, besides relief to see Noosheen, that it was rather mercurial and unreliable of Noosheen to have come back so contentedly and quickly. She, Chloe, might have been condemned forever to a troubled conscience and a life of concern for someone who like the wind changed directions or lost interest, like a child. She should have seen that Noosheen was a restless child.

"What will you do?" Chloe asked.

"Well, there isn't much I can do, of course. What can a woman do? But there are things at the hospital, and the children, and there is something—I am translating poetry. There are certain poems of Matthew Arnold that I think will be an inspiration to others in the cause, only I am not putting his name on. Oh, I am not putting my name, no fear, it's just that I am afraid a Western poet would not be well received, so I am putting 'Ancient Persian Manuscript.' I am sorry you cannot judge the translation. I would like your opinion."

"What is the text?" asked Chloe.

"Well, it is from 'Rugby Chapel.' I will copy it out, with my translation, so that when your Farsi gets better . . ."

"Oh, I'll never learn it now," said Chloe. Now she would never learn Farsi. She was, she knew, herself the restless child.

"The Twelfth Imam is

> *'Not like the men of the crowd*
> *Who all round me to-day*
> *Bluster or cringe, and make life*
> *Hideous, and arid, and vile;*
> *But souls temper'd with fire,*
> *Fervent, heroic, and good,*
> *Helpers and friends of mankind,'*

quoted Noosheen.

"You heard the bad news about Abbas?" Chloe asked, scarcely daring to ask for fear she had not, for fear she would have to tell Noosheen herself.

"Yes, oh, yes. I am so full of sorrow. My brother Abbas."

"If he is dead, it was some kind of guerrillas who killed him. It was the people who believe in the Twelfth Imam. Not exactly helpers and friends of mankind."

"It was Americans, that's what I heard," said Noosheen. "My poor Abbas, he was a martyr. His memory will live always, a martyr who died to save the treasures of our heritage. But one other terrible thing I have to tell you. They found the body of that old man, Hossein."

"Really? What happened?"

"It is so horrible. It is a thing that has happened before. He was attacked by a pack of dogs in the street, late at night. He had been stealing things from the laboratories at the hospital! Think of it. To sell, I imagine, poor man. They found him this very morning, half eaten up. And the wild dogs also attacked a guest from Texas who was staying at the Cyrus. They fell upon him, but he was able to fight them off. He is in the hospital."

Chloe heard herself utter a horrible giggle; despite tears flooding to her eyes again.

In the evening she ate with Junie and Dick in the hospital cafeteria, the usual chelo kebab and canned peas. Hugh came in. His face was sunburned and strained. They had no need to ask him what he had found.

"There were a number of men killed. Boys. They had taken the bodies to the village. For their mothers to come and get them, I don't know. I brought him back. I've seen Ali Yazdi."

They guarded their faces from signs of weeping. Junie's face seemed less her own than the face of a tragic woman in a poster against war or starvation. In her grief, Junie was all women, but Chloe felt, uneasily, that her own face was unchanged. There was some lack of connection between her face (given to smiles, even radiance) and her heart. Hugh and Dick passed the cruet of salad dressing, estimated the chances of getting a plane out of Shiraz in the morning; their faces were tired but manly and unchanged, hearts inscrutable. Around them, nurses in their little veiled caps and thin men, off duty, in argyle pullovers, a normal mutter of Iranian speech, no edge of panic or sadness. They hadn't heard.

Alone in her room, Chloe packed her other bag. The first, packed before dinner, stood at the door. Matched bags of French nylon from La Bagagerie. She was sorry to leave her books, especially *Sassanian Pottery*, the standard work by Professor H. Raban. She hesitated over it. A heavy, rare work printed in 1937. If there was going to be more trouble in Iran, there would be students involved, and they might burn the library, or the Shah might shut the university down. She put the book in her suitcase, thinking that this might preserve it for civilization, and of course she would return it later, at the right time, for she had complete reverence for the sanctity of the library book.

Dead. How awful that she couldn't keep from thinking of her own situation when someone was dead and she ought to keep thinking of that. But how? It was not enough to recite, "How sad." She couldn't find sufficient thoughts to capture in words the hard, pincerlike feeling, deep down inside her windpipe. Someone dead whom she had loved—had she? Whom did she love? Everyone? Anyone? How to keep from thinking of herself, the real object of such questions. It was of love, large, universal, she ought to think, and of large, universal death.

She hears a tap below her window, and, thinking it would be Hugh, calls down that the door is open. She hears footsteps, is surprised when Dick, not Hugh, comes in.

"I couldn't sleep," he says. "Anyway, tomorrow will be—I wanted to say goodbye, in case tomorrow, in the confusion . . ."

Chloe sighs. "It's hard to know what to say. It's a sad way to leave. Is Junie very sad?"

"Very," Dick says. "Of course." He pauses, stifling the little tone of querulousness he can hear piercing the solemn tone he is attempting. "How could they have been in love? They—Junie was always with me. When were they ever together?"

Chloe feels, deplores in herself, an unreasonable interest in the same question. What does it matter? Yet if one is to understand anything, you have to try to understand it all. Dick reconsiders. There were endless hours, whole nights, Junie had not been with him.

"Do you care about that part?" Chloe asks.

"As I said, I feel like an idiot. That said, I guess not. I feel so bad about what happened, that doesn't leave much room. Anyway, Junie and I aren't in love exactly."

"I understand," Chloe says. She smiles her smile. "Would you like some tea? Or there's some beer. We should drink it up."

"Beer, thanks," he says. She crosses the hall to the kitchen. The Dunhams can be heard striding around, talking, in their quarters. Their three suitcases stand in the hall, as if they expected porters and limousines.

"Chloe," says Dick when she comes back. "I hope it works out with you and Jeff." He won't, he thinks, mention Hugh. Covertly he examines the room for signs of Hugh, but there aren't any.

"Well, it won't," says Chloe firmly, though she doesn't plan to admit that Jeff has found Another. A certain righteousness in her expression suggests that Dick is being callous to talk of trivialities like marital discord and the future. Yet when but in the atmosphere of death is one more inclined to think of the future? He wishes they would fall into each other's arms in a comforting way.

"I'll come see you," he says. "I come to San Francisco a lot. I have two former fellows who work at Moffitt Hospital; they often invite me."

"Yes, be sure to," Chloe says. "It's sort of like the end of camp, isn't it? Everyone says they'll keep in touch." But there had been death. They sought for a more dignified comparison than camp. He takes off his glasses and puts them in his shirt pocket. Chloe bustles fitfully around the room. When men take off their glasses they mean to kiss you. Yet she doesn't move forward. When Dick has gone, she notices the Koran lying on the table, a repository of gnomic revelation and gnostic wisdom, like the I Ching. She'd asked the I Ching things before. She opens the Koran and sticks her finger on a verse:

> *But for the offenders we have got ready the fire whose smoke shall enwrap them.*
> *And if they implore help, helped shall they be with water like molten brass*
> *Which shall scald their faces. Wretched the drink! and an unhappy couch!*

Chapter Thirty-five
NINE SHIRTS

Chloe stayed awake as long as she could, waiting for Hugh, who did not come. In the night she dreamt of a rug. Waking later she could not remember whether the rug in her dreams was a real rug she had seen somewhere or an ideal rug, concocted of the imagination, born of a rich dinner, or of a belief in beauty. Paisleyed shapes in deep, bitter colors glowed on a forest field. The shapes were confused in the dream with the tastes of fruit whose peelings had been boiled to obtain the colors; and with the cries of snails or sea creatures similarly sacrificed, and the sacrificed fingers of little children tying the knots. As you walked on it, this cacophony of life cried up. It was the rug of life.

When she woke, the bareness of her room without Dick's rug struck her with sadness. The room had recovered its cell-like ugliness, yet she was attached to it now. She was glad to think it would remain in Linda Farmani's hands and that Linda liked the arrangement of flower pots. It is a charming room, really, she thought.

It remained to find a kennel or box for Rustum. Ordinarily she would have asked Hossein. Only with this thought did she remember what she had heard about the poor old man's fate. She tried to imagine it. She tried to imagine the last thoughts of the sad old creature, but she couldn't. She wondered if he had had a family, and whether anyone would miss him. She had planned to put out all her rials, to leave them lying on the table for him to find.

She set out looking for boxes, first at the back of the hospital, then at the vegetable market, where she found a serviceable wooden crate full of the leaves broken off cauliflowers, and managed to indicate that she would like to buy it. Had Rustum been with the dogs who killed Hossein, she wondered? If he had tasted human blood, would he now crave it, as leopards and tigers were said to do? Would he be a safe pet with children? She pulled the crate after her along the road.

The plane was to leave at noon. Ali Yazdi arrived in the road inside the gates with the hospital station wagon and two taxis. The foreigners began to assemble. Little outposts of baggage were established on porches. People stood in the road. Chloe came out on her doorstep with nails to fasten up the crate, once she got Rustum inside it. On the top she had painted her name and address with turquoise paint.

He came when she called him, his gait happy, and trustfully allowed her to lift him inside. He had barely enough space to turn in. She put some scraps of food inside, but he ignored them, and whimpered when she nailed down the lid. She was thinking of coffins, comforted that the flight to Tehran was only a short one, and she would probably be able there to get a proper cage from the airline.

She was obliged to ask Ali Yazdi if he would take Rustum in the station wagon. She was obliged to smile at him.

"Of course, dear lady, since you choose to rid us of one of our canine pests," and he bowed in his suave way. "We will be sorry to see you all go," he said as they drove along the flowered corridor to the airport. His insinuating manner was gone now, and in its place an expression of scowling purposiveness, as if he wouldn't wait for them to go. Chloe looked back at her window, its bright turquoise color, its geraniums, all symbolic of solitude, industry, and peace.

The airport was crowded with Western dependents, and had a certain cheerful, far from panicked air, with dozens of blond tots, materialized out of the secret back gardens of the American district, chasing around the dirty waiting room. The mothers stood in clusters, chattering excitedly, festooned with travel bags, backpacks, and huge shoulder purses. Iran Air had put on a special extra flight, with special open seating, so all had relaxed, and no one pushed or shrieked.

Noosheen came to see Chloe off. "I will send you a copy of my thesis," she said. "When I write it. 'Say not thou of a thing, "I will surely do it tomorrow" without "If God will." ' " She giggled. "The Koran. This is not goodbye. When you come back, perhaps I will still be living exquisitely in Villa One!" She hugged Chloe.

"Oh, I'm sorry to be going," cried Chloe, greatly surprising herself by this utterance. What about her children? What about real life?

"At home they will be so happy to see you," Noosheen reminded her.

"Oh, yes," Chloe agreed.

Hugh Monroe had not arrived, and Chloe began to feel worried, though no doubt he was attending to last-minute things. She began to see significance in the fact that he had spent the night in his own apartment. Was he sulking because of Rustum? But that would be more like Jeffrey. When Hugh did arrive, as the people began to surge toward the check-in counter, he explained that he had gone to see whether Loyal Cooley was well enough to travel.

"But he really isn't," Hugh said. "In another few days, perhaps. It's too bad to leave him, but he's a pretty sick man."

In his cage, Rustum began to whine and snarl, so that nearby people drew their children to them.

"This is Chloe trying to expiate her imperialist guilt," said Hugh. "Are we going to travel the whole way with that noise?"

"Dick gave me some phenobarbital for him," said Chloe, resolved not to be drawn into bickering about Rustum.

"I doubt they'll let you check in with him," Dick said, though he did see a few other animal cages among the assembled luggage. "They will," said Chloe, for some reason much surer that Iran Air would agree to take Rustum than that it would take them, at last, or that the plane, when it came, would fly. Dick's rugs, wrapped in sheets and tied with rope, looked like bodies. Junie had bought a small rug and three enormous round brass trays. Amid this welter of desperately assembled possessions stood Hugh's neat suitcase and expensive briefcase, discreetly black.

"Well, back to Tehran," she said, when they had got on the plane, and she was sitting in between Junie and Hugh, uncomfortably consigned again by her smallness to the middle seat. Hugh's long legs stretched into the aisle. Junie pressed her face against the cold glass of the porthole window and sighed. The plane rose high above the desert. Chloe thought of the jet airplane crashes but did not torment the others with her horrid imaginings.

"What were you doing at the Royal Tehran Hilton?" she reminded Hugh when they were airborne. "You said you weren't even there." It seemed to her that Junie's closed lids stirred with a flutter of interest, and Dick, behind them, leaned forward to hear.

"Well," said Hugh, "it was supposed to be secret. A few days before I was scheduled to leave Rochester, I got a call from the dean asking me to go a few days early to Tehran, to see an important patient. 'Important patient' was exactly how he put it, with no extra significance, no reverently lowered voice, just an important patient, so that it could have been a rich Iranian businessman, anything, but then I also got a call from the State Department, giving me a contact number. So it was pretty obvious.

"His own doctors thought he might have malaria, that's all I was told, and to go to the Hilton and somebody would be in touch. So I left London—I'd been lecturing at Hammersmith Hospital—a few days early, and when I arrived in Tehran, someone was in touch, a Dr. Moshir, who met me at the airport and drove me to the hotel. He explained that someone else would be in touch. There was still no indication of the identity of the patient and from this guy no discussion of the case, but he was a doctor, and I had guessed."

"The Shah?" said Dick.

Hugh nodded. "I got to Tehran I guess eight at night, had dinner, and went to bed. In the morning I got a phone call: someone was coming for me. It was all a little cryptic, a little solemn, but not per se mysterious. Around noon someone rang up from the lobby. I went down. Three people, including this same Dr. Moshir. One drove, the other guy sat in front, I sat in the back of an old Peykan with the doctor, and he explained that the patient was the Shah, that they were a bit puzzled by certain things about his case, they appreciated my having a look, there were reasons for secrecy. If people thought his health was frail there would be panic, etc. So—of course I thought it would be interesting to meet the Shah. We went to the medical school, the Shah came there, through the back way, and I was given an examining room and instruments, and was told that the lab facilities were at my disposal."

"What was he like?" Chloe said, gratified that her lover was as important as this.

"The Shah? A regal character, not tall but erect, smiling, affable but remote. Extremely courteous in his replies when I took the history. He appeared ill—jaundiced and anemic, and had fever, but I didn't think he had malaria. He, his doctors and other attendants, emphasized that there must be no discussion whatever of his case. I had to promise not to mention that I had seen him and to keep the whole thing confidential. To emphasize this, they took my passport, saying they'd fix it so that my arrival dates coincided with my original travel plans. In fact they hadn't stamped my passport at the airport, though they'd looked at it; the authorities must have been watching for me.

"Anyhow, I was told to return to the Hilton, and wait to be contacted by a French doctor presently in Iran, who had also seen the Shah and wanted to discuss the case. The examination and lab work took two days, during which I saw the Shah twice—I saw her, too, the Czarina, whatever she's called. A nice woman, rather overdressed.

"Anyway, the next day, this Frenchman, Dr. Juneau, called,

said he was in Shiraz but was coming to Tehran. We would meet, was that all right? By now I was overdue in Shiraz, and sworn not to admit that I was in Iran at all, so I said yes, please by all means hasten to Tehran, or I could come to Shiraz, which I was planning to do anyway, and we could talk there. He said he'd check into that possibility and call me back. But he didn't. Several days went by."

"You were just stuck there?"

"I began to hassle Dr. Moshir. He said they didn't know what had happened to Dr. Juneau, and, finally, that I might as well go along to Shiraz but to remember the extreme secrecy of my mission. This was all conducted with an air of urgent concern, not only about the health of the Shah, which indeed was a matter of concern—he clearly seemed to me to be a very sick man—but for the political consequences if it became known he was sick. They didn't spell out the consequences, I suppose they didn't know them, but no one was to have even the faintest suspicion. When the Shah left the clinic he left the back way, collar turned up, in a little car. It was interesting, all right. And now they appeared to be greatly concerned about the whereabouts of the French doctor. They seemed to have fears for his safety. That was not too reassuring to me, as you can imagine. I got the idea that there might be people out to get Dr. Juneau, why not me too? But why? Then the business of the guy jumping me in the compound and going through my stuff; obviously they were looking for the history. That's when I went again to Tehran. There I found that Dr. Moshir had disappeared and no one would talk to me. I couldn't get through anywhere. I went to the medical school where I'd been, and it was more or less just people rushing around. They seemed too disorganized to worry that I might now talk and spill the beans somehow or not cooperate. No one seemed to know anything."

Oh, really, thought Chloe, this all seems preposterous. I don't believe him.

"Who called for me?" It occurred to her again. "At the bathroom door? At Persepolis?"

"Not I," said Hugh.

"It must have been Abbas. Or Richard Dare." It occurred to her again that if she had let him in perhaps he would not have been killed. What had he wanted? Still, it could have been Richard Dare.

"What was your diagnosis?" Dick asked Hugh.

"I didn't make a diagnosis. Some sort of neoplasm, I guessed. All I did was rule out malaria."

"What was she wearing?" asked Chloe.

"Who?"

"The Empress!"

Chapter Thirty-six
BAD NEWS

There was the Door to which I found no Key;
There was the Veil through which I might not see:
Some little talk awhile of ME and THEE
There was—and then no more of THEE and ME.

The plane landed shortly at Mehrabad Airport and taxied toward the giant passenger building. The passengers stood in the aisles and pushed each other, and lifted down their packages; they broke from the plane and swarmed across the tarmac, ignoring the little buses that stood to receive them. Inside the terminal, at the Iran Air counters, extra clerks, with unusual efficiency, handled the long, agitated line of foreigners and Iranians who were buying tickets, and uniformed officials traveled along it assuring people that extra flights were being added so that all might depart. Even so, the waiting rooms were a pandemonium of weeping and shrieking, and the floors were strewn as thickly as a stadium with paper cups, cigarette packages, and plastic sacks.

There were no flights directly to San Francisco, but Chloe was able to book a flight to Los Angeles via Rome. The ticket clerk did not ask to see her passport. Rustum would cost two hundred dollars extra, and was transferred to an Air Iran metal cage. Sensing freedom, when his box was opened he tried to bolt, but was captured by a glaring Hugh. Hugh, Dick, and Junie were able to get on a flight together to New York via London. Now Chloe for the first time felt the reality of their parting, felt keenly her own reluctance to tell them goodbye and make her way alone. What would she and Hugh say to each other? What did she want to say?

She did not feel as worried about the irregularity in her travel documents as Hugh and Dick did. Surely the Iranians wanted them to leave? But Hugh insisted that he go with Chloe in a taxi to the American Embassy in downtown Tehran to get some sort of paper that would ensure that she could leave the country. "Probably they can give you some special diplomatic status, or a duplicate passport, something like that."

"If not, I could just stay here. I could stay at the Hilton. I'd be all right, while I waited for clearance," Chloe said.

"You could, and I'm sure it's perfectly safe. Or we could try bribing someone at the airport. I'm sure it'll be all right," he said.

Taxis were abundant outside the airport terminal, the drivers milling and calling out. Carefully, as they had learned, they chose one and agreed on the price to downtown Tehran and back. The driver, a dark, round-shouldered man, wore a vivid knitted cap of red and green. "The American embassy! Of course I know it," he cried, grinning vivaciously. "We will try! We will go as close as we can!" The car lurched into an ominously heavy stream of traffic, portending a slow trip into town. Chloe saw for the first time the ugliness of Tehran, all rectangles of cement block, cement, treeless. She thought of beautiful Shiraz.

"Alone at last." She smiled at Hugh, leaning against his strong shoulder, suffused, all at once, with the pangs of sadness that had been deferred by the business of packing and flying here. "It's over, or almost over. That feels strange. I feel awfully sad."

"You'll feel better when you're safely on the airplane," Hugh said. "Safely airborne with a gin martini. You have a resilient nature."

"Gin? I never drink gin," Chloe said. "Anyway, I won't. I don't really want to leave. I don't know. Going back. Missing you. And I feel disappointed, in a way, I don't know why. Oh, Hugh." She sighed. She understood her fear of going back. The future seemed so unpatterned, so like a vast dance floor, flat, immense, and she a wallflower in an ugly dress, visited with depressed longings, restless self-depreciations, desire, desires for events unspecified. She tried to imagine being married to Hugh, with new rooms to paint. It was just possible to feel an interest in that, and to imagine painting the door sills and lattices of Hugh's charming Cape Cod house, or so she imagined it would be, with the turquoise blue of safety and haven. But of course he hadn't asked her, and anyway she knew she ought to try to imagine something more independent and resourceful, like digging potsherds in Egypt or Jordan.

"Well," said Hugh abruptly, in a tone of unfamiliar petulance, "what about me?"

Caught by surprise, Chloe's attention shifted, stirred, focused on Hugh. "What do you mean, what about you?"

"You'll pick up life as if nothing happened, you've never once said you're sorry to leave me. After all I have to go home alone, just when, just when . . . I'm in love with you, Chloe, it's hard to just pack it all in."

His expression was puzzled, as if he were not quite getting at what he meant. Chloe's heart jolted out of its track of contemplation of herself in the little Cape Cod kitchen, which she could easily picture, teak, with Mexican tiles and built-in ovens, and a kitchen clock, and herself glancing at the clock, Hugh late. He is speaking of love!

"I know you've been married twice," she said. Hugh's glance was puzzled at this non sequitur.

"Where did you get that idea?"

"Everybody says so," she said.

"Tha-that's r-r-ridiculous," Hugh said, an uncharacteristic stammer making her suppose he was lying.

"Oh, Prophet! Speak to thy wives, and to thy daughters, and to the wives of the Faithful, that they let their veils fall low," said the taxi driver suddenly to the stalled traffic.

"It's more than even love," said Hugh. He stared out the window, averting his face, the nature of his emotion completely unclear to Chloe, but rippling the muscles in front of his handsome ears. It appeared from his silence that he could not explain. "It's okay for you, you'll go home as if nothing has happened, you'll pick up your life. But you haven't even asked me how I feel. In fact no one ever does ask. *You* never ask. I'm just useful. I do everything, not that I mind, but it's I who make reservations, arrangements, it's I who have to hunt for Abbas and, you know, see him and drive him back, and I get beaten up and lied to and stranded in Iranian hotels or sneaking around in the dark all the time to visit you, and getting up at five in the morning, did you think I liked that? Okay, okay, I did like staying with you, it was worth it, but still . . ." She saw to her surprise that a tear stood in his eye, at his pitiable lot.

She was stricken. His accusations were perfectly true: she let him do everything and didn't try to understand him. Was it because he was so tall? She was struck speechless with the remorseful conviction of her own callousness. She had no notion of his real nature and in fact had been rather suspicious of it. And he had no notion of her real nature, and if he had he wouldn't like her. He didn't realize that she was meddling, deceitful, and useless; wasn't aware of her unnatural lack of probity, deficient maternal feeling, her repellent pragmatism and moral indolence. Didn't know how she had meddled in the life of Noosheen, or slept with Abbas. If she were to confess her deeds, his disappointment didn't bear thinking of. It would be kindest, since they were to part, to leave him with some illusions, some kindly feelings. And now, it seemed to her, she did not want to leave him at all, for she saw that in comparison to her own frivolity and superficiality he had depths she had not discerned before. All this self-reproach flashed before her, as if she were drowning, and, being unfamiliar to her, had a toxic effect of silencing her.

Hugh was wiping his glasses. Chloe's remorse grew. For an instant she could imagine Hugh transparent, like one of those demonstration mannequins, all the organs and structures seen inside—Hugh, usually so opaque, now revealing the complexity of his innards, emotions of various colors running up and down little pipettes and coiled tubes. She had made no effort to understand. What on earth did Hugh mean by love, anyway?

"Bad women for bad men and bad men for bad women; but virtuous women for virtuous men!" said the driver suddenly.

I must be a bad person, she was thinking. It had never before occurred to her as plainly as this that she was perhaps a bad person. An unfaithful wife, a neglectful mother, making no contribution, making no one happy. Whereas Hugh was good. Her panic and misery made her speechless. It had never before in her life occurred to her she might be bad. And yet in time he would leave her, she thought. As with Jeffrey, did this matter? Does she love him?

Her mind whirled. Was it necessary to decide on your own character? No. Yes! It was necessary to take herself seriously as a moral agent. It mattered, in the fabric of the world, whether a person was good or bad. How terrible! She saw the answer and she was bad.

"But I do love you," she said. "I would have thought it was obvious." Despite herself, a quarrelsome note sounded in her voice.

"Well, I'm sorry I'm so obtuse," said Hugh.

"Oh, I'm sorry. Of course I love you," said Chloe apologetically.

"Of course I understand that Jeffrey—that you have your life . . ." said Hugh, in his normal, courteous tone.

"When we get home," said Chloe, "do you think that things will be different? Or the same? I guess I mean that we won't know till we get home."

"I suppose," said Hugh, not sounding convinced.

No, that's not right, she wanted to say. Let's decide the future right now, and abolish all uncertainty. The world has neither joy nor certitude nor light.

"I know I'm not a fascinating person," Hugh began again. "But if . . ."

So intent upon herself—how would she know? Perhaps he was. How she had failed him.

"Chloe, when we get home can we talk about the future? What will happen?"

"Oh, Hugh, of course."

All at once they realized the car had stopped. They were in the mouth of a narrow street, stucco balconies overhead, clothing draped from the balconies. Hugh opened the car window and stuck his head out, looking apprehensively around.

"Is blocked off," the driver said. "They got many streets blocked off." He began to back the car. Hugh and Chloe looked around them. An odor of saffron. At the end of the street, a man waved his arms. It appeared that they would have to do something here, were being menaced and impeded.

On the main street, at each of the four corners stood the familiar trucks of the army, stuffed with soldiers squatting on the flat beds. Chloe felt Hugh's body grow tense. She drew away from him. The driver began again to back his car, this time around one of the trucks, turned around and started forward in a direction exactly opposite to the one they had been going. Around the next corner people came into view, walking in large parties in the street. The driver stopped to let some of them pass, then drove a short distance on the curb. Something loud clattered against their car.

"What's going on?" Hugh asked the driver.

"There will be another protest today," he said. He stopped again, the car obstructed by another crowd. Women in black veils, their faces uncovered, glared at them. Some boys carried a sign. All were walking in one direction, rapidly. People had seized the streets from automobiles. Other cars were stopped; their drivers shouted from the windows.

The din and murmur of collective anger began to beset the ear at first distantly, as one approaches the sea through calm banks of whispering grass, drawn by the growing roar. They were drawn to the roar. The driver seemed to point the nose of his taxi at it. The sound excited, it warmed the blood. Flocks of people in black or white, little boys and girls.

"What do they say?" Chloe asked the driver.

"They are saying, 'Death to the Shah,' " he said. "They are going to the Jaleh Square. The square is near the embassy. I'm not sure we can get there."

"Are we far?" asked Hugh.

"Not far. You can walk there. I think it is better."

"But how will we get back?" Hugh asked.

"Oh, I will wait for you, of course." He leaned out the car window and spoke to someone in the street. He laughed. "Yes! There will be a million people in Jaleh Square!" he said.

"Yes! Let's walk, let's see!" said Chloe.

"I don't know," said Hugh. The car had stopped. People walked toward them down the street. They seemed like those ants in Africa that would walk right over the car, unstoppable. The noise grew, people working themselves up; little boys, skipping and dancing, cried, "Death to the Shah!"

"I will stay right here," said the driver. "You must walk to the end of this street, then across the square, then you will see the building on your right. That is the embassy of America."

"He won't wait for us, will he?" Chloe said, clinging to

Hugh's arm as they alighted. He stepped along swiftly, here and there pushing someone.

"No," he said. "We have to make this fast. We'll just size up the situation."

They took a few more steps, clinging, people pushing past them. Someone took Chloe's shoulder and squeezed it in a cruel pinch, then walked on without looking. People did not look at them. The faces were angry. Chloe thought of the Los Angeles peace march and saw that this was different. These faces were sullen, as the faces of the police had been. In Los Angeles the marchers were happy but the police were full of rage. Here, too, angry soldiers, up ahead, waving the people by. She grew afraid, but it was thrilling. What can happen to you as your feet tread along the ground, the ground is the ground, others are simply others, there were no guns or knives, they would not be pushed. There were women, wearing white, in numbers, like beehives of nurses, arms linked like chums. Old mullahs in black robes, white-bearded, wandered along. When Chloe stumbled on the broken pavement, Hugh clutched her. They were swept along in the torrent of people who erupted from every doorway, every alley, every car stuck on the street as surely as if in thick mud.

"I didn't feel it, before, did you, in Azami Compound? Not even on the streets," cried Chloe. "This anger—I never felt this; no one ever said." Her body sang in response to the hum and din of the rising voices.

"Yes, of course, each time I took someone's hand, someone sick. Their thin, dry hands, something in their silence. I've felt it all along," said Hugh.

"It's funny that you never mentioned it," said Chloe.

"They're rising up," said Hugh. "I didn't think they would."

"And the Shah will just shoot them. That's the difference. Lyndon Johnson couldn't shoot us—in the sixties, that was different, but here . . ."

"Yes, this is different," said Hugh.

"But it's the same, too," said Chloe. "People by marching can bring a tyrant down."

"They haven't brought him down," said Hugh.

"They will! Don't you feel that?" cried Chloe, joyful to think that people had power over their lives and the course of things. Power after all, palpable here.

"They are cruel, they are still a cruel people," said Hugh. "Chloe, I think we should turn back. We aren't going to get through. The embassy won't be open in all this."

"Just to the edge of the square, then," said Chloe, knowing Hugh was right. The throng, the shouting multitude would prevent them from crossing the square. But she wanted to see the whole sea, the whole black and white sea to the horizon of signs and shouting people, and the fists, for the fists went by them, pounding in the air, people chanted, and above them they saw cameras, television films being made. Would they be on television, on NBC, say? Chloe Fowler and Hugh Monroe, arms embraced, marching against the Shah? She laughed aloud. It did not seem that she could ever go back to San Francisco. Here you were a part of history.

"How lucky we are to see this," cried Chloe. "Let's just go to the edge of the square!" They pushed ahead until it was impossible to go further; the people ahead of them had stopped, and people crowded up behind them, so no one else could fit into the square. At the feeling of people pressing from behind, Chloe began to grow afraid. She could imagine being trampled. She could not see over the heads of the tallest. It was as if an eclipse had occurred. People jostled her, she felt their elbows, felt a gentle but insistent pushing from behind.

"Hurry," said Hugh, "turn back!" But to turn back was to struggle against a beating surf. Thrusting their arms before them, they turned to push through the crowd. Sometimes people stepped aside. Others, like inanimate objects, had to be pushed, rocked back on bare heels, on their plastic sandals, straight-armed. Hugh, bigger than the Iranians, went first, pushing along. "Excuse me, excuse me," he said.

"Pardon me," Chloe said, "excuse us, we have to get back." With difficulty, from among the maze of alleys, they found the little street where they had left the taxi. To their surprise, it was still there, its driver standing on its hood to watch developments along the street. He greeted them with a vigor that surprised them, that surprised perhaps the man himself. He was invigorated by the exciting marching, singing, shouting. He leapt from the hood to the ground. "Back to the airport!" he cried. "Yes?"

"Is that possible?" Hugh asked.

"Get in, get in," he said, starting his engine already, and speaking to people outside the car. People hammered on the top of the car and leaned in to grin, but they did not seem unfriendly.

"How thrilling," said Chloe to the driver. "Thousands of people."

"Yes," he said.

"The Shah will have to pay attention," she said.

"Yes," said the driver. "It is not so good for foreigners, I think. But I will get you safely to the airport and peace be on you. 'Let him then who will, believe, and let him who will, be an infidel.' The words of Mohammed."

"Thank you, brother," said Hugh, which Chloe greatly admired. She would not have thought to call the man brother.

Women thrust leaflets at them. Some were in Farsi. One, in English, said:

A Verse for Our New Leader Beloved Ayatollah Khomeini:

> *Then, in such hour of need*
> *Of your fainting, dispirited race*
> *Ye, like angels appear,*
> *Radiant with ardour divine!*
> *Beacons of hope, ye appear*
> *Languor is not in your heart,*
> *Weakness is not in your word,*
> *Weariness not on your brow.*

It seemed to Chloe that these were the words of Matthew Arnold.

As they drove into the airport, Hugh began to take Chloe in his arms, but was constrained by the muttering of the driver, by some sense that his political or religious zeal would be inflamed or offended by any emotional desperation or erotic display. They clung furtively. Would this be their last embrace, Chloe wondered? Except for a polite, perfunctory kiss as they took their respective planes? He to London–New York; she to Rome–Los Angeles? "Oh, Chloe," he murmured into her ear.

"Oh, Hugh," she said, thinking of the rushing and desperate winds of change.

Chapter Thirty-seven
DEPARTURE LOUNGE

Ah, Love! could you and I with Him conspire
To grasp this sorry Scheme of Things entire,
Would not we shatter it to bits — and then
Remould it nearer to the Heart's Desire!

Dick Rothblatt was waiting on the pavement by the taxi stand, anxiously scanning the flood of arriving cabs, looking for Chloe and Hugh. "Thank God," he said. "We heard a rumor they were going to close the highway between here and Tehran."

They told him of what they had seen there. "Crazy Chloe of course wanted to plunge into the throng," said Hugh in a way that Chloe saw meant that he was concerned about her. One danger, that without a correct visa she could not get out, was unresolved. She was still in danger of being kept in Iran.

How can I imagine being in danger? I've had no experience of that, she thought, resentfully, although she had had fear enough in the past few days to learn in. But it had not really stuck. It was still hard to imagine a country keeping you in when it wanted you to go. Surely Iran would say to her, Go.

Inside the terminal waiting room, Junie and Dick were encamped with Dr. Ames in a corner section of plastic chairs, with coats and bags thrown over empty chairs to reserve them for Chloe and Hugh. The drugged Rustum lay apathetically in his new metal cage, as if knowing he stood no chance against it, but he stirred feebly when he heard Chloe's voice.

The loudspeaker called the arrival of another plane from Shiraz. They watched the passengers straggle in, loaded with baskets and sacks, wearing layers of clothes—people none of them had ever seen before, residents of Shiraz—businessmen and schoolgirls, people with money. Conspicuous among them was Zareeneh Yazdi, wearing a sumptuous dark calf-length mink, despite the sweltering weather, and enough gold chains to coin a statue. She waited at the end of the gangway for her daughter, a plump, dark-haired, sallow little girl of eight, who tottered down the steps clutching a teddy bear and two rag dolls. The beaming Hendersons were right behind. Zareeneh waved at Chloe and the others, and rushed over to them.

"Thank heavens I am here on time," she said. "I have this for you." She opened her bag and thrust a paper at Chloe. It was the torn page of her passport, with the exit visa stamped on it. Chloe stared at it and at Zareeneh. Various explanations rushed to mind to explain this. Had Dr. Yazdi taken it? Why was Zareeneh returning it? They had parted? Political differences?—Why was it being delivered in this way?

"Ali found it. It was in Vahid Farmani's desk." She smiled. Now she took the teddy bear and dolls from her little girl and put them carefully in an opaque plastic bag. She put the plastic bag on a chair of its own, threw her coat over it, and settled herself on the chair next to it.

"Are you leaving, Zareeneh?" asked Dick.

"Oh, it is so sad. I cannot believe it is really necessary but Ali says we must not be foolish. He is foolishly staying another moment, there is so much to do at the hospital, and to help Bahram settle in."

"Where are you going?" asked Chloe.

"I? Oh, I am going to Geneva," she said.

Now, two hours before the time of departure, with no problems indicated on the manifest of departing flights, other concerns began to preoccupy each traveler. Dick began to think of the necklace in his pocket. Chloe at the sight of Rustum lying drugged in his cage began to worry about him, that someone would protest that the space he would take might be taken by a person, though surely animals traveled with the luggage, and a person couldn't travel in there. Zareeneh Yazdi began to rustle nervously among her hand luggage, with sudden fears, it appeared, that she had left things behind. Her face would be transfixed an instant with panic, she would dive into a bag, hands groping inside, find or not find what she sought, highly anxious, all the time smiling. Her little girl indifferently read a book.

"They can see that it goes there, Chloe, the numbering matches, the paper matches," said Hugh, fitting the pages of her passport together. Perhaps it's illegal to use a torn passport, she thought.

"They're so legalistic. Think of the Erdmans. They look for reasons to put you in jail," she said. They looked without success at the newsstand for some glue to stick it with.

"Maybe something like toothpaste?" suggested Dick. "Zareeneh, do you have any glue?"

"No, I'm sorry," she said.

"And what is this?" Dick can imagine them saying when they see his necklace. "A national treasure. Do you know what the penalty for that is, sir?"

"I have some Scotch tape," says Zareeneh.

"That's probably okay, we'll just be up front about it, and tape it in," says Hugh.

"It all boils down to whether they want you to go. They can always find a reason to keep you," Zareeneh says.

"If for some reason they don't let me go," Chloe says, "promise me you'll take Rustum. Promise." She says it to any-one, but no one volunteers to believe this request has been to him. "It would only be, you know, a few days. I would have to wait here and get it straightened out. Then I'd come and get him."

They look at Rustum. Asleep he looks more attractive than when awake, but he is still a nondescript dog, and when awake rather rambunctious, and they cannot imagine him being wel-come in America, either officially, by the American customs, or by Jeffrey, when she gets him home.

It was delicate. There would be something proprietary, something official, about agreeing to take Rustum; it contained some implication for the future, some implied obligation, con-nection, continuity. Dick watched Hugh with close attention. Hugh was just shaking his head over Chloe's silliness, and made no commitment.

"They'll let you take him back to the Hilton while you make your arrangements," he said, laughing. "You have to deal with this yourself, Chloe."

Chloe fell silent, wearing, Dick saw, a sulky expression.

"We could take him," Dick said, "as far as New York, but you'd have to collect him there."

"My plane goes to Rome–Los Angeles," said Chloe wretch-edly. "But thank you, dear Dick." She was surprised and touched by the difference between a true friend and a so-called lover like Hugh, when it came to hard sacrifices.

"Jeff will be crazy about him," Hugh went on, in the same disagreeable tone he had been using to Chloe, and which Dick resented, though she appeared not to notice it. Dick was also struck by Hugh's reference to Jeffrey, as if he didn't realize that

Jeff and Chloe were splitting up. Perhaps there was some new development, or perhaps—it struck him that she had said as much—Chloe hadn't confided in Hugh her marital problems? He was somehow rather pleased at this notion, that Chloe had confided in him but not in Hugh. Well, she could have all kinds of reasons for not wanting to involve Hugh—not wanting to put him on the spot, maybe, or not wanting to get further involved.

Chloe put her mended passport in her purse. Rather dazed at this unexpected delivery from the presumably last hurdle, except for the arrival of the aircraft itself, she sat down and wrote postcards to the children. But her thoughts brimmed and flooded. I'm escaping, Chloe thought, but the idea came without the swell of relief and gratitude she had expected. She felt, instead, illicit and unfinished. She thought of her Sassanian beaker, her work table. She had finished nothing, left nothing behind, and was returning to nothing, or so it seemed, over the weeks, over the oceans. Men could start over in the Yukon. She should have been a man like that, leaving lives and people behind, going off on dog sleds into wild places. She could do that now; she could go anywhere, Los Angeles, Detroit. But she knew she wouldn't, because of her prudence and indolence. She'd go back to San Francisco and put up an undignified fight for the house, or Jeffrey would have changed his mind and she would just accept that things were as before. And Hugh . . . In his pocket airplane tickets: Tehran–London, London–New York. What were they going to say about the future?

How do you profit from experience, anyhow? Can you bank it, get interest, watch it grow? You grow sadder and wiser or older and wiser, but the corollary to wiser is always something undesirable.

She must contemplate, commit herself in some way, take some action worthy of all this, but what? When she took actions, they were usually wrong. It had never been too bad, drifting along, but it was, she now felt, no longer possible. She'd changed, even if she didn't know how. What on earth did she feel, what should she do, about Hugh?

* * *

Dick thinks of smoking. They all sit, subdued and anxious, in the encampment of plastic chairs in the corner, away from the cloud of cigarette smoke that dominates with its fatal miasma the center of the great waiting room. Near them, abject, exhausted women slump in the chairs, cradling limp babies, their knees surrounded by bundles. Men smoke in little groups and pace together from window to wall, uttering little barks in their strange language.

Dick, checking in his pocket for the antique necklace, finds Marla's letter, and for lack of anything else to read, pulls it out and continues reading.

. . . one thing about you being all that way is, it really helps me to think things out on my own. You've always been such an influence on me, not always for the best if I let my temper get the better of the situation! But you have always made me stand on my own two feet for better or worse, and that was something as I see now I needed to get through. Now that I've been . . .

Dick casts his eye over the rest of the page to see if it switches to the subject of real estate. Apparently not. Relaxed, he skims along; more in the same vein, Marla's usual vein—no mention of the kids. She's gotten a dog. As he reads, inattentively, a sudden chill strikes him. He backtracks a paragraph.

I wonder if in some ways it wasn't the house that caused the trouble between us, and now that I'm settled in the apartment I feel so much freer to think. I've been thinking about all you said before you left about reconciliation. I know people never change, but maybe I've been wrong in thinking it was you (or me) who ought to change when it's just dramatic how not having the house and all those memories and responsibilities . . .

He can see her, alone in her apartment, writing this. Dick shivers. What is he reading here? He reads hurriedly but carefully on. His hand begins to shake like an old drunk's. Reconciliation? What is the emotion that accelerates his heart? Fright, he realizes. He is appalled. All that he had wanted, had thought, is now being offered and he is appalled.

All at once, with a clattering of numbers in the board above them, their flights are posted and they are being advised to check in. Airline clerks and customs officials come in, in military throng, and array themselves behind counters between this room and the international departure lounge behind them. All round, people line up to pile their luggage on the counters, pushing it slowly along toward the dark little men with mustaches, carrying guns.

Chloe and the others assemble their suitcases. Chloe feels the creep of apprehensiveness, Dick feels himself sweat. Will the customs people be instructed to look for artifacts? The necklace burns in his pocket. He has never been searched bodily except once in Israel. Up ahead at the customs counter people are emptying their pockets in front of expressionless soldiers; men paw around in the satchels and string-wrapped cardboard boxes. Dick thinks maybe he'd better put the necklace in the suitcase after all. He unzips the suitcase and plunges the necklace into the center of dirty clothes and things thrust in unfolded. How horrible if they open the bag and all this dirty laundry comes springing out.

Chloe is indifferent, has nothing to hide but her shards, and doesn't think they will care about those. When her turn comes, the men seem to see her indifference and to feel, therefore, indifferent to her, contenting themselves with a cursory glance at her ticket and her passport, loose leaf and all, and wave her on. She is only a woman. Her feeling is not entirely of relief.

They wave Junie on in. They take a moment with Dick. They look in the suitcase with the necklace, look at the necklace and wave him on in. He doesn't know whether to be relieved or disappointed that they didn't think it valuable or genuine. It is

Hugh they stop; they look over his papers and call a superior, a soldier from the sidelines. Chloe and the others watch anxiously from the safe, the international, side of the departure lounge, with Hugh technically in Iran.

"It must be the stamp; it didn't get stamped when I came in," he says across to them. "Because of . . ." He looks grim—indeed, frightened, Chloe thinks, and very reasonably. Officials confer. Hugh glares helplessly at them, and over at Chloe and Dick. At another counter, men are opening Zareeneh's bags one by one, and shaking out the beautiful clothes, and feeling in the linings.

If they don't let Hugh out, I'll stay with him, Chloe thinks. But would they let her back in to Iran?

Anyway she isn't really worried. They are Americans, aren't they? Leaving where no one wanted them to stay. Poor Zareeneh, she thinks; even if you didn't like Zareeneh, her bras being lifted out, shaken out, by soldiers. Anyone can see the good things are in the teddy bear, that was so obvious. But the guards don't see it. The daughter hugs the teddy bear and the two rag dolls. At last they wave her in. Zareeneh is compelled to repack in view of everyone. At other counters, other Iranians repack in view of everyone.

At last Hugh comes through, like a cork popping out, stuffing his passport away, sighing. His face is shiny. "That had me worried," he says.

"Did they just say 'go ahead'?"

"They called someone."

"Thank God," says Junie in a shrill, rapid voice. "Thank God we're getting out of this awful place. I never thought we would. I really never thought we would. Did you? Did you really, in your heart, Dick?" Dick imagines Junie becoming hysterical, slapping her. Maybe he just wants to slap her.

"In Persepolis I didn't think we'd get out. After that I did," Dick says.

"It's going to get very interesting here," says Hugh, "but I'm just as glad we won't be in on it."

I don't know, thinks Chloe. "I don't know."

"You don't seem happy, Chloe," says Dick.

"No, I'm not. I feel—I feel—it didn't turn out very well, did it? This visit to Iran."

"I don't know. It turned out," Dick says, "as well as could be expected. Except for Persepolis."

"Which wouldn't have happened if it hadn't been for us. But that isn't what I mean. It's more—I don't know. I just feel that now I know how to be good. But I'll never have another chance. We're just going back to America, where I'll never have another chance to be good."

Now they sink lethargically into new chairs, subdued by the growing weight of private reflections, the corrosive sadness of parting and change. Yes, thinks Chloe, her thoughts turning to home, it was wrong of me to stay with Jeffrey. I didn't love him enough. Marriage is an ancient contract with universal rules, rules always the same despite local differences—fidelity and cooperation and affection—all those things I never gave. She feels ashamed to have imagined she was specially exempt from the ancient marriage rules.

She realizes that she has thought of her children, in the past few days, hardly at all. Now, all at once, she is able to picture them again, staring at her gravely as out of a photograph—Max's rather large ears, Sara's golden braids. She is overcome with her sudden sense of them as separate from herself, and of how it is impossible, just by knowing things herself, to spare them the pain of having large ears or of knowing the things they know, or of having horrible thoughts—thought by them already, no doubt—which she doesn't know, and doesn't want to know, their brains deep as the universe with atoms of thoughts not hers. Maybe everything is electricity, she thinks. Braces, she thinks of, and of their touching little clothes and of how sweet they were as babies.

It's true you don't give your children enough time, enough thought, she thinks; they are there for you to feel tender toward but do you knit for them or paint murals on their walls, or play games, even if you don't like games?

How wrong of her it has been to judge Junie, poor Junie, who worked so hard and made a contribution, even if her mind isn't subtle; she is young, for one thing. People shouldn't judge Junie until they can make a contribution themselves. She will make a contribution. She will try to make a contribution. Does she want or deserve Hugh?

What's he going to say to Marla? Dick wonders, mind leached to perfect blank idiocy. How can it be that he can't begin to imagine the idea of going back to Marla? Maybe it has always been the house he loved, the house as surely as any beloved child keeping them together with its needs of paint and cleaned-out gutters and a kind of cornmeal compound to be spread in the garage to soak up the oil that dripped from Marla's Civic.

Maybe Abbas was really in the Savak, thinks Chloe. It's true that he was always around. She wonders if he had told Junie what had happened between them. Such inconsiderate indiscretion seemed hardly imaginable, but it would explain Junie's hostility.

It's wise of Chloe not to jump into anything with Hugh, thinks Dick. One thing at a time. He thinks she is being rather brave, considering her situation, a woman facing divorce, approaching middle age, no job skills. He can't imagine Chloe doing social work, sitting behind a desk with a little sign MARLA ROTHBLATT on it, in that greenish painted room, papers all around, sullen Hispanics outside the door. Couldn't imagine her acquiring that certain tarnished, exasperated look that

Marla had developed since doing social work; it wouldn't work for Chloe. But she'd have to do something.

How pretty Chloe is, tired and flushed, little dry creases beginning at the corners of her eyes, delicate dry skin, will wrinkle early probably. She would like the necklace. He will give it to her. Had they seen it was an ancient artifact and yet let him take it? Or seen that it wasn't an ancient artifact and he'd been swindled. Try not to mind whichever way it turns out. It doesn't matter, better if it's fake, in a way, then you can take it out and give it to Chloe, a souvenir, even if not valuable. Who else would appreciate it?

Like survivors of summer camp, ardors endured together, tender camaraderie—will they vanish like the friends from summer camp? Will they endure like survivors of a massacre? Chloe wonders, looking at Dick, at Hugh, soon to return to Rochester, New York, at the powder-white Junie, her face pinched and cocktail-waitressy; she wasn't pretty really, just had bloom on her side, had had bloom, but it would come back, but she was too thin, like one of those West Virginia women, a miner's wife maybe, it's an Anglo-Saxon type, thin and pitiful.

But Junie is a doctor, Chloe reminds herself; she's lucky to have something like that.

Hugh just nodding off, a handsome man in his early forties, thinking of what? drowsy in an airport, rumpled.

Dick paces, passes near the jostling caviar queue. Chloe notices again his jouncing walk, off the balls of his feet, like a fighter; he must have practiced it sometime when he was young, walking around his bedroom; now he just walked that way.

Even if I am bad, thinks Chloe, it isn't too late to be better. Or is it? And in what does better consist?

She should have been nicer to Jeffrey. Probably all he needed was kindness to have been a nice person. Probably he *was* nicer, perfectly nice with his new love. It was all her fault, she has never loved him enough. She sees that Hugh, immersed in the *Herald Tribune*, steals glances her way, of an uncertain character.

She has, for a moment, a sensation of perfect indifference to her personal fate; she will marry or not, will divorce, will suffer illness and die; she is for an instant serene in knowing that it will all happen as it will happen. Her mind, as usual, takes another turn on this. It is the Eastern lesson. She has learned something after all. Kismet, and after all could the universal will have anything so very bad in store for her? Anything worse than for other people?

It is hard to believe so.

Chapter Thirty-eight
BELUGA

Indeed, indeed, Repentance oft before
I swore — but was I sober when I swore?
And then and then came Spring, and Rose-in-hand
My thread-bare Penitence apieces tore.

Junie appeared to sleep. It seemed to Chloe that she was not asleep, but didn't want to talk. Whenever anyone came near her eyelids screwed down tighter. Thus she did not see, though Chloe and Hugh saw, a man who kept gazing strangely at her and making little movements toward her, only to retreat each time as if he were being jerked on a line. Finally he came decisively forward. Junie opened her eyes alertly, as if he had come to hurt her, and indeed his expression was hostile and wary.

"Excuse me," he said, speaking in a strongly French accent. "Excuse me, but I think, is it possible? that you are wearing my watch?"

Junie stared at him, looked down at her wrist.

"I don't know," she said, "am I?"

"May I?" He took her wrist and peered closely at the watch. "Oui, bien sûr," he said. "Could there be another, see the Navaho band, a Patek Philippe, même modèle. But this is very strange. Perhaps you would give the explanation to the officials of Iran, for I am going to call them."

Dick and Hugh tensed and drew closer, protectively. "What's the problem?" Hugh said. "Maybe you could explain?"

"Certainly. This is my watch, stolen from me in Shiraz and under circumstances which I have been protesting."

"Dr. Juneau?" said Hugh, after a moment. "Are you by any chance Émile Juneau?"

The Frenchman looked startled at this mention of what was evidently his name.

"I'm Hugh Monroe," said Hugh. "We were to meet."

"Monroe? Mon dieu. I have been telephoning to you at Shiraz."

"The watch came from a dead man in Shahpur's Cave."

Dr. Juneau looked pained at the grisly history of his watch. "Ah, yes, the cave," he said, indignation swelling his eyes.

"Won't you sit down?" Hugh asked.

This is too much, thought Chloe. We're supposed to believe anything. Junie happening to sit there, happening to wear a watch. "Some coincidence," she remarked, with asperity, to Hugh.

"Not really," he said, "when you consider every Western person in Iran must be in this airport today."

She hadn't thought Junie was connected to Hugh's game. That was a surprise.

The doctor sat with formal bearing on the edge of the waiting-room chair. "I was, as you know, on a particular mission," he said, hesitating delicately and glancing at the others, seeking to know from Hugh whether he should continue.

"I've told them all about it," he said. "Plenty of things have been happening to me, too."

Dr. Juneau leaned forward and spoke in a low voice. "Understood. Alors—the Shah has been our patient since 1974, when we saw him in Paris. He was diagnosed at that time as having lymphoma. He was treated with cyclophosphamide and did very well. In our view he had an excellent response and we attended a long-term remission, if not a cure."

"Oh, I see, a lymphoma," said Hugh. "This wasn't mentioned in the history. I suspected something—perhaps cancer of the pancreas, but in fact there was very little evidence of that. In fact, he had no lymphadenopathy."

"That is interesting," said Dr. Juneau. "He originally presented with mild anemia and hepatosplenomegaly. What was the blood count now?"

Hugh hitched his chair nearer the doctor and they began to converse in numbers. "The chest x-ray showed no abnormalities," said Hugh.

"Anyway, now he falls ill again, and we are called. I fly from Paris with the old medical records, and proceed to Shiraz, where the Shah is staying, I am told, in his summer palace. I descend at the Cyrus, that hotel there. The very night of my arrival, and I am half dead with jet lag, is that not what you call it?"

"Yes," they said.

"I telephone you, we speak. Suddenly some men appear in my hotel room. They have guns. They search my room, evidently looking for the medical records. But here is the amazing true intervention of fate, for in fact I have left my briefcase on the plane."

"What if someone had found it?" Hugh asked.

"I was not worried about that, for in fact there is another name, of course, on the dossier. We always referred to him as Louis."

"Who were these people?"

"My belief was that they were Iranians connected with the Iranians in Paris and that there had somehow been a leak in Paris about my mission. The Iranians in Paris oppose the Shah."

"And these were their colleagues?"

"I suppose. But in any case they fall into a fury when they find no dossier in my room, and now turn their guns on me. They oblige me to dress and leave the hotel with them. I am blindfolded and treated cruelly.

"We drive some distance out of town—at least, I could not any longer hear the sounds of Shiraz—and I am put in a hut. Other men come, and I am brutally tortured." He drew his breath at the memory. He appeared quite recovered, bore no marks or bruises.

"They want to know about the Shah's health?"

"Exactly. Naturally I tell them. I do not feel it is information so vital it is worth losing an eye or an ear for. Would you?"

"Of course not," Hugh agreed. "He is probably suffering a recurrence of the lymphoma—it would explain the fever and jaundice. But I didn't make that diagnosis." He seemed quite disappointed with himself.

"And as I did not see him, I cannot be sure, but that is my presumption too. They hoped, of course, malaria."

"But what did they do then?" asked Chloe.

"I am left in this place, with a guard, for an unknown length of time, perhaps several days. Then new men come, apparently Russians. After a great deal of most alarming consultation among them I am put into a car and driven still further into the countryside. It is late evening, not yet entirely dark. With one man I am made to climb a path appallingly slanted?"

"Steep," said Chloe.

"Yes. We walked I noticed more than one hour. And that in fact is when this man, this Russian, took my watch. Believe me, I understood what that portended. Although I am very weak— the torture—I had very little to eat—I am on my guard. We go together into the cave, and here I am planning to break away and run, or else to push him, when by good fortune he slips himself and crashes down the rocks." He paused, dramatically. "I threw rocks at him. Then I ran up out of the cave, then down the steep path—I am half dead myself before I get to the bottom, and fall in a faint, am found by some villagers, and taken to a hospital. That is all.''

The others murmured, stirred. Junie had taken off the watch and handed it to him.

"We found the man still alive, it must have been the next day. But he died soon after,'' Dick explained. "We never found out who he was.''

"And we never found out what happened to him,'' Hugh said. "He was put into the morgue at the hospital, and then when I looked, he wasn't there.''

"No,'' Dick said, "he never was in the morgue, Abbas and I buried him. Vahid Farmani told us not to put him in the morgue. He said to take him to the American embassy, to the police—we did all this, no one would take him. So we had to bury him—it was hot . . .''

How puny men are, frail and mortal, their bodies have to be hurried into the ground, thought Chloe crossly. She thought this a disappointing story but Hugh was laughing. "How neat and tidy,'' he said. "What if we hadn't met? We'd never have known.''

"Well, I would have written to you at Rochester. I know who you are,'' said Dr. Juneau.

Only men like secrets and intrigue, thought Chloe. Why is it women are always blamed for it? She, it seemed to her, only wanted things to be simple. She had almost got hold of simplicity. It was like a dream that you forget. It slips away. In the noise of the loudspeakers, under the flashing lights of the notice board, she felt some vestige of understanding trickle and slip away, increasing her panicked sense of loss and dread.

As they had been speaking, an animated line had formed near a customs window whose purpose they could not quite discern, and Dick got up to draw nearer and find out, in case it was something they needed to get stamped or cleared.

"It's caviar,'' he reported. "You buy government-produced caviar right there. That's what all the fuss is about.''

"We must get in line," cried Dr. Juneau, leaping to his feet. "It is excellent, the Iranian caviar. Me, I always take some back. Do not neglect to do so!"

"Will my things be all right here?" asked Zareeneh Yazdi at the same moment. "I am going to get my caviar. Will you keep an eye?"

"Sure," they said.

"I always like to take it to people; they're always so glad to get it. Our Iranian caviar is better than Russian," she said.

I have to think what I'm going to do, Chloe thought. She could picture her plane landing in San Francisco, Jeffrey—no, she'd go home unannounced in a cab—no, what if the woman friend was there; anyway she didn't have a key, she'd have to call him. But what time of day was it going to be? She had to decide what course of action to take next. She could not go drifting along as she always had done, she had to make decisions, had to take herself seriously. It mattered what she did. Her insides felt like the sawdust of this floor. Did she have any American money to pay for the taxi?

"Do you by any chance have a cigarette?" asked Dick of Zareeneh, walking along with her to the caviar line, out of earshot of the others. He didn't want to buy a whole pack, then he'd just smoke the whole thing. He didn't want to smoke in front of Junie or Chloe. Guilt and self-contempt made the first drag seem better.

A conga line of caviar seekers had developed, each person clinging paranoiacally to the person in front. Dick was several people behind Zareeneh, and she was twelfth. Dr. Juneau was just behind her. Dick counted the line twice. Each transaction seemed to take an inexplicable length of time. The person at the head of the line came away with a stack of small paper-wrapped packages. It must have been five hundred dollars' worth of caviar. Dick looked in his wallet.

"Iranian currency only, no credit cards," Zareeneh called back to him.

"Could you save my place?" Dick asked the well-dressed

man ahead of him in line. He thought he would go back and ask the others if they wanted any caviar and suggest, if they had Iranian money, that this was a good way to spend the last of it. The man did not say yes, but he smiled in a friendly way.

"It's two hundred touman a package, two thousand rials. A package is two hundred fifty grams," he told the others. "The line is long but we could take turns standing there."

Caviar, thought Chloe. So emblematic of all luxury, all desire. She didn't want any.

"It would just spoil by the time I got it back to California," she said.

"No thanks," said Hugh, "but you can have my touman."

"Come and spell me on line, will you, if I don't come back in twenty minutes?"

"On line," thought Chloe. So New York, such a silly expression.

Luxury, desire. She imagined she would never feel the need of these. She felt permanently flat, going home. It was like heaping caviar on flat, stale crackers, what a waste of the rich mystery of flavor. Iran, Persia. The rebels would have horses, guns, they would rise up, you could see from the faces, the thrilling faces, the fists, that they would rise up.

Even women. They would rise up. The Shah would kill them, but he couldn't kill them all. Some would have risen who could not be killed. She herself would be in California. Junie—Junie, staring at the *New England Journal of Medicine* in her lap—was she feeling this flatness too? Let Jeffrey go to the divorce court, Chloe thought; she was not going to bother.

Why did they not post the departure for their plane?

"I'll feel better when we get on the plane," said Hugh, pacing. Has he forgotten that they are getting on separate planes? Is he eager to leave her?

"Why would they keep us? They don't want us here," said Chloe.

"Not us," said Junie. "Not us, we're harmless enough."

* * *

"Jesus, I hope they don't run out," thinks Dick, watching the line, worried at the size of the plastic sacks full of packages of caviar that people carry off. The stacks in reserve, piled high behind the woman at the counter, are shrinking. Again he counts the people ahead of him. Zareeneh is nearly the next up; she would tell him if there was a problem, or anything special you had to do. Did you have to show your passport or your ticket? "I don't want to get caught up in this," he thinks, but he is, he can tell, from the crawling unease of his stomach each time the woman turns and takes from behind her off the dwindling stack one, two, six, nine tins of caviar.

Now a man is screaming, he is ahead of Zareeneh, and she looks round at Dick, her large black eyes rolling in fright. The man is screaming, "But my plane is leaving, don't you understand? I don't have time to change the money. Look, French francs, if you don't want dollars, francs."

"I can spell you now if you want," Chloe says to Dick, coming up behind him. But he'd got interested in this altercation up ahead.

"Thanks, I'm okay. Are you going to get some?"

"No," Chloe says.

"Deutschemarks, then? Look, take this." The man tears off his watch. "Take this, Rolex, look."

"Is that an American?" asks Chloe.

"I don't think so," Dick says. "He has some kind of accent."

"Thank God," says Chloe.

"Can you come here, please," the man is shouting at someone sitting near their own encampment among the chairs.

"Please, sir, there are others waiting," they hear Zareeneh saying.

"Look, have you got rials?" says Dick to Chloe. "If I could borrow some? Could you go ask Junie how much she has?"

"I left mine," Chloe says. "I'll go ask Junie." Hugh comes

back in a minute with Junie's rials, and is fishing in his wallet for his. He hands his money to Dick.

"How's it going?" he asks.

"It's useless; if this guy gets the money, he's going to take it all," says Dick miserably. "And if he doesn't take it, Zareeneh will." The man is piling banknotes on the counter in front of him, counting them. Three other men standing to one side are handing him banknotes. A tremendous pile of reddish bills grows on the counter.

"Do you want me to help you stand in line for a while?" asks Hugh.

"No, it's okay," says Dick, unhappily aware of the cigarette burning between his fingers. Hugh doesn't seem to notice it. Dick looks around for an ashtray. The floor is a sea of cigarette butts.

"Unhappy Iran," says Hugh, in a melancholy tone.

Without looking down, Dick drops the cigarette and steps on it, "Yeah, we're getting out just in time."

"They're going to be boiling Americans in oil pretty soon. I feel kind of bad about Cooley."

"This son of a burned father," hisses Zareeneh, "wants all the caviar in Iran."

"It's been kind of fun, in a way, hasn't it? Though it doesn't seem very appropriate to say so. If you could have seen them in the streets . . ."

Dick reflects, without saying so, that he too would have thought it fun to have Chloe Fowler for a lover.

"Chloe finds riots exciting and fun. Her everyday life must be kind of boring. Jeff . . ." Hugh pauses, sighs. "Jeff's okay, but he's never been a particular friend of mine. He's very much a surgeon."

Dick perfectly agrees with this term of opprobrium.

"Of course she's devoted to her children," Hugh says, his tone increasingly morose. Dick understands that Hugh is trying to confide in him, or bring it all out in the open, but he finds himself unwilling to respond. If Chloe hadn't told Hugh that she was leaving Jeffrey, then it wasn't up to him to betray her confidences. How did things stand between them? It was impossible to tell. It looked as if they planned to go their separate ways. But always, in the affairs of heart of one's friends, it's best to say nothing, he knew that much.

"That's a thousand, count it," says the man ahead of him.

"Dust on his head!" says Zareeneh, bitterly.

The caviar clerk begins slowly to count the leaves of money. It seems to all the other people in line as if she counts with particular deliberation, even hate. Is there no limit per customer? Could this heap of money compel all that caviar? Zareeneh is sending them dark, flashing looks, as if enjoining them to kill the man.

"Maybe there's a limit per customer," says Dick.

Behind them people begin to mutter and push. Dick feels a hard elbow in his back. Just as well that Junie and Chloe aren't here, if things get rough, he thinks.

"We'll miss Chloe too. It's unusual to get to know a woman without her husband. Some of them are quite nice." He means a joke, a touch of innuendo, but Hugh doesn't smile.

"For Christ's sake hurry," screams the caviar customer. "My plane's leaving." His friends have deserted his side and are sprinting toward a departure gate.

"We don't have much time either," Hugh says. They watch the methodical clumsiness of the woman's fingers. Does she hate this man only, or does she hate all of them? Will she treat Zareeneh with gracious celerity?

"Oh, for God's sake," moans the man, in agony, his head swiveling first to look at his bolting friends, then at the way the money seems to stick to her fingers. Now she turns, lifts down some packages from the shelf behind her, and begins to put them into a big plastic sack. Dick finds that he is holding his breath. He turns and irritably pushes back at the man behind him so rudely shoving.

Now, with a terrible animal moan, the customer snatches up the plastic sack and dashes across the waiting room, leaving the huge wad of money and another dozen tins waiting to be packaged. The implacable woman begins again to count the money. Zareeneh steps briskly up to the counter and raps on it with her jeweled fist. She smiles and opens her purse, speaking in rapid Farsi. The woman begins to assemble packages.

"Sixteen! She's taking sixteen!" whispers Dick to Hugh.

"Maybe I'll buy some for Chloe," Hugh says. "She'll be sorry she doesn't get some." He hands Dick some touman notes. Behind them, actual shouting has begun, and the pushing intensifies. Dick now notices with surprise that the line extends clear to the restrooms. Are these all passengers for the London plane?

"Hurry," says Zareeneh to Dick. "The plane will be leaving."

"Stupid bitch," thinks Dick bitterly, as if we can hurry. As if we can help this. He tries not to watch the next transaction; it is too stressful.

"Would you watch my things?" Chloe says to Junie. "I'll go see what's taking them so long. They've called the London plane." She just wants to walk, is made restless by a stirring of desire, for Iran, for Hugh, for something. Maybe they could find a hiding place to make love in? But there isn't time. Zareeneh Yazdi, her face moist in the hot room, smiles as she comes toward Chloe with an immense plastic sack that says Mehrabad Airport Caviar Shop. Triumph, relief, every last obstacle overcome, says her expression. Chloe wanders up to Hugh and Dick.

"Look at all these people, they're all Westerners, it's disgusting," said Chloe, of the hysterical line.

"Some are Iranians," objects Hugh. "Zareeneh bought sixteen packages."

"I've got three hundred dollars' worth of rials here," said Dick. "Shall I just spend it all?"

"I always save enough for a gin martini on the plane," says Hugh.

"I don't mind the danger. I would rather stay," said Chloe, her stomach turning over with reluctance to hear them speak of the plane, and gin and ordinary life.

"On airplanes is the only time I drink them," says Hugh.

She doesn't mind the danger; she thinks she had almost got hold of something. But what? Why did she feel this inappropriate feeling of desire, this wish to be in Hugh's arms, or someone's arms? She thinks of nymphomania. Maybe, like a ghoul, like a vampire, once you see blood and hear guns that changes you, that interests you. Can it be interest, not desire, that quickens the blood, quickens the breath?

Lucky Noosheen, thinks Chloe. I could stay with Noosheen and help her. But of course this is not a place you would want to stay, where people are shot before your eyes, and blood rolls out across the gravel, and the guns are being distributed to everyone, and little girls in villages are left to die.

"My life has been a flower, what do I know?" she says. Dick and Hugh look at her, not following her.

"What would you have, a terrible life?" asks Dick.

"No, of course not. Of course not," she says.

"It's okay," said Hugh, meaning to reassure her. "We'll soon be on the plane."

"Attention. All passengers to Rome, now boarding at gate seven," said the loudspeaker. Dick discovers that although there is now no danger of not getting up to the caviar window before they have to go, he is trembling. The man ahead of him is served. "Aha," says Dick happily, slapping his banknotes down on the counter in front of the caviar clerk. Her eyes, catching his for one instant, have the opaque glint of copper pennies. He will open a tin on the plane, he decides. Does Junie like caviar?

"One always feels so sad at the end of a trip," Chloe says.

"Do you?" asks Dick. "I don't. I'm always glad to get home." The woman is putting his packages in a large plastic sack. He recognizes the numbers as she counts in Farsi, "Panj, haft . . ."

"That's three thousand grams, that's three kilos," Dick says. "We can have a hell of a party with three kilos of caviar."

"No, I always feel sad," Chloe says. "Sometimes I begin to cry. I always have. Tears, sobs, as we land. Often. I thought that was the normal thing."

"You have it all wrong," said Hugh.

"Attention, all passengers to London on Iran Air flight 154, to London, Heathrow, all passengers should be on board, all on board please, gate six."

Chloe races along with Dick and Hugh, back to the luggage. Junie is standing, her coat over her arm. Dick fishes in his plastic sack and hands two packages of caviar to Hugh. Behind them, people in the caviar line have begun to scream.

I will try to be better, thinks Chloe. I'll try to be good.

"Hurry up, for God's sake," says Junie. "The plane's ready." They load themselves with bags and stagger toward the gates. Hugh puts Chloe's two cases under his arms. A row of airplanes stretches across the airfield, poised for escape. Eagerly hundreds of passengers throng toward the various gates of departure, men pushing wagons heaped with bags. I always have it all wrong, thinks Chloe. But how can I get it right? It had seemed that she was getting closer, but there is no time to think about it now, as she struggles along behind Hugh and Dick and Junie. They walk her to her gate and set her bags down.

"Call, Chloe, as soon as you get home," Hugh says. He gives her a kiss as fervent as is consonant with propriety. Dick kisses her. Junie kisses her.

"Yes, let us know that you're home safely," Dick says.

"Yes, yes, I will," she says, emotions sealing her throat against more words. Emotions, unnamable, tears starting. Going home alone.

Hugh hands Chloe the two tins of caviar. "One for you, one for Jeffrey," he says.

"Thank you," she says. "Thank you." Without looking back

at them, she girds herself with her carry-ons and stumbles out across the hot concrete. The odor of Iran is gone, clove and straw; now it is of jet fuel. She crowds herself in among the people climbing up the metal steps.

She will eat both the tins of caviar herself, is her thought, settling in her seat. At least, she certainly won't give one to Jeffrey. This idea makes her feel a little better, though she is still as wretched as ever she has been in her life. All airplanes, all steps and bags and seats in the world are alike and she is home already. She fastens her seatbelt. Tears wet her cheeks. People will think they are tears of joy and relief.

A Note on the Type

This book was set in a digitized version of a type face called Baskerville. The face itself is a facsimile reproduction of types cast from molds made for John Baskerville (1706–1775) from his designs. Baskerville's original face was one of the forerunners of the type style known to printers as "modern face"—a "modern" of the period A.D. 1800.

Composed by American–Stratford Graphic Services, Inc., Brattleboro, Vermont. Printed and bound by The Haddon Craftsmen, Scranton, Pennsylvania.

Designed by Virginia Tan.